TURBULENT
WATERS

TURBULENT WATERS

Cross-Border Finance and International Governance

RALPH C. BRYANT

BROOKINGS INSTITUTION PRESS
Washington, D.C.

Copyright © 2003
THE BROOKINGS INSTITUTION
1775 Massachusetts Avenue, N.W., Washington, D.C. 20036
www.brookings.edu

Library of Congress Cataloging-in-Publication data

Bryant, Ralph C., 1938–
    Turbulent waters : cross-border finance and international governance /
Ralph C. Bryant.
        p.   cm.
Includes bibliographical references and index.
    ISBN 0-8157-0072-5 (cloth : alk. paper) —
    ISBN 0-8157-0071-7 (pbk. : alk. paper)
    1. Capital movements.   2. International finance.   3. International
Monetary Fund.   I. Title.
HG3891 .B793 2003
332'.042—dc21   2002151830

9 8 7 6 5 4 3 2 1

The paper used in this publication meets minimum requirements of the
American National Standard for Information Sciences—Permanence of Paper for
Printed Library Materials: ANSI Z39.48-1992.

Typeset in Adobe Garamond

Composition by R. Lynn Rivenbark
Macon, Georgia

Printed by R. R. Donnelley
Harrisonburg, Virginia

Contents

Figures

Tables

Box

Foreword

Societies develop institutions for fostering actions taken jointly on behalf of their members. Such institutions and actions constitute collective governance. Public forms of collective governance are exercised through governmental institutions.

Today's world is organized politically into nation states with sovereign national governments. Within national borders, public governance is exercised through each nation's various levels of government. For the world as a whole, however, institutions fostering cross-border collective governance are nascent or altogether absent. This nation-dominated political structure of the world will continue for the foreseeable future.

The economic structure of the world has evolved in ways increasingly mismatched with its political structure. The economic links among nations have grown more rapidly than economic activity itself. As rapid economic integration has proceeded, borders have become less important, and many differences among national economies have eroded. The policy autonomy of national governments has accordingly been undermined. Yet collective-governance problems with dimensions spilling across national borders have grown in importance relative to problems of domestic governance. This growth of problems with cross-border dimensions, and hence an evolving need for international collective governance, is certain to continue in future decades.

Increasing integration in the world economy, often termed "globalization," has been especially dramatic for financial activity. Just as within nations, financial transactions that cross national borders facilitate saving and investment and thereby advance the well-being of individuals. Financial markets and institutions, however, especially those engaged in cross-border finance, can produce turbulence and generate instability. Most individuals are unsure what to believe about the increasingly close links among national financial systems, for example, whether globalization promotes or instead threatens prosperity for the majority of the world's citizens.

International collective governance and cross-border finance are the two core themes analyzed in this important new book by Ralph Bryant. The book explains basic concepts about financial activity and collective governance, focuses attention on their international dimensions, and then leads general readers to an enhanced understanding of key policy issues and how national governments should try to resolve them. Ralph's analysis provides fresh insights about what is often termed the international financial architecture, though his book casts its net far wider and deeper than the domain of specialized issues preoccupying financial policymakers and financial-market participants. The book's ambitious goal is nothing less than to provide a pragmatically sound vision for the evolution of international governance for the world economy and financial system.

Ralph Bryant's study exemplifies a new emphasis in Brookings research, embodied in our recently renamed Governance Studies program. That program is preserving its traditional core strengths of analyzing the performance of American political institutions. But it is also undertaking new and broader analyses in areas that transcend national borders and academic disciplines, in particular the role of nongovernmental actors in domestic and international policy debates and the diverse challenges of managing an increasingly integrating world economy.

Ralph Bryant is a senior fellow and the Edward M. Bernstein Scholar in the Economic Studies program at Brookings. Financial support for this project area has been provided by the Bernstein Scholar Fund, established by the Bernstein family after Eddie Bernstein himself had been a scholar in residence at Brookings. As Ralph mentions in his concluding chapter, Eddie Bernstein was a key American architect of the international economic institutions created at the end of World War II. Brookings is grateful that the Bernstein Fund has permitted continued analysis of the international issues that were central in Edward Bernstein's distinguished career as an economist and public servant.

On a personal note, I want to add that a draft of Ralph's book was the first manuscript I was asked to read on becoming president of Brookings in the summer of 2002. At the time I found the draft a terrific introduction to that part of my new job. I learned a lot from the manuscript, admired the clarity with which it was written, and found the subject and prescriptions close to my own preoccupations. I am pleased to launch this first-rate piece of work into the vital public debate about collective international governance.

STROBE TALBOTT
President, Brookings Institution

Washington, D.C.
April 2003

Acknowledgments

I began thinking about the issues analyzed in this book many years ago when serving on the staff of the Board of Governors of the Federal Reserve System. After joining the Economic Studies program at Brookings in the second half of the 1970s, I continued to focus on international economic and financial issues. Some of the material incorporated in the book is a revision of writing done in the 1980s. The financial crises of the late 1990s were a new impetus for refining my views on the issues. The main part of the drafting began between 1999 and 2000. The first draft of the book was restructured and rewritten between 2001 and 2002.

Throughout my years of research and writing on these issues, I have benefited greatly from interactions with numerous colleagues and friends. For the ideas in this book, major contributions in catalyzing insights, refining thinking, or improving exposition were made by Barry Bosworth, Coralie Bryant, John Helliwell, Dale Henderson, Bob Litan, Paul Masson, Larry Promisel, and Alice Rivlin. Among the many who provided insightful and helpful comments on various versions of the manuscript, I would especially like to thank Juliet Bryant, Susan Collins, Max Corden, Barry Eichengreen, Morris Goldstein, Carol Graham, Peter Isard, Ed Kane, Warwick McKibbin, Louis Pauly, Jacques Polak, Dani Rodrik, Jan Aart Scholte, Bob Solomon, Peter Sturm, George Tavlas, Ted Truman, Delia Velculescu, Shang-Jin Wei, and Louise White.

I am indebted for skillful research assistance to Elif Arbatli, Pablo Montagnes, Rachel Rubinfeld, and Jungyon Shin. Martha Gottron did an excellent job of copyediting the manuscript. Other valuable editing help came from Larry Converse, Tanjam Jacobson, Brenda Szittya, and Janet Walker. Gloria Paniagua ably verified the manuscript, and Julia Petrakis prepared the indexes. I am grateful to Jen Derstine, Linda Gianessi, Theo Merkle, and Evelyn Taylor for their thoughtful administrative support of my research at Brookings.

My wife and children, in addition to making helpful substantive and prodding suggestions, were gracious in putting up with the inevitable pressures that surround writing and publication. The book is dedicated to my parents, who have been inspiring role models for how to lead a life combining intellectual rigor, caring service to others, and sensitive nurturing of the heart and soul.

1

Introduction: Financial Turbulence and Financial Governance

The world economy in the final years of the twentieth century was afflicted with financial turbulence. Millions of people in emerging-market nations lost their jobs, endured severe recessions, and suffered sharp declines in wealth. Life for them turned topsy-turvy as their nations' financial systems were thrown into crisis. Many residents of wealthy nations also experienced losses. U.S. citizens were less affected than residents of other nations. But they, too, were buffeted by the turmoil.

Journalists and other observers attributed the financial turbulence to large, disruptive flows of money spilling across national borders, spreading financial instability from one part of the world to others. There exists an "enormous, several trillion-dollar pool of money," wrote one commentator, "that sloshes around in what is effectively a supranational cyberspace, moving by computer in and out of off-shore banks and chasing profits in 24-hour markets, all largely beyond the reach of governments' control."[1] Colorful metaphors abound. The owners initiating these capital flows have been likened to legionnaires without commanders roaming the globe. They have been described as an "Electronic Herd" and "a new class of voters—

1. Jessica Mathews, "We Live in a Dangerous Neighborhood," *Washington Post*, April 24, 1995, p. A19.

1

stateless citizens of the world . . . casting votes for and against economic policies of the 200 or so nation-states."[2]

Cross-border finance was indeed often at the heart of the financial turbulence. Many developing nations could not or did not fully service their external debts in the 1980s. The resulting crises severely shook their economies. The Tequila crises pummeled Latin America in 1995 after the devaluation of the Mexican peso. The epidemic of Asian financial flu that began in Thailand in July 1997 spread contagiously to many other Asian nations, including Indonesia, Korea, Malaysia, the Philippines, Hong Kong, Singapore, and Taiwan. In August 1998 the debt default in Russia and the devaluation of its currency triggered a reevaluation of credit risks throughout the world's financial markets. Even domestically within the United States, most investors ran for cover in the fall of 1998. Brazil suffered a financial crisis in January 1999 and again in the summer of 2002, Turkey in late 2000 and early 2001, Argentina in much of 2001 and 2002.

Financial activity and financial markets were not invariably unsettled in the last several decades. Even during the less turbulent periods, however, journalists and analysts became increasingly preoccupied with issues of cross-border finance. Sweeping generalizations about "globalization," applied to most aspects of the world economy but especially to financial markets, are now commonplace among popular analysts and throughout the news media.

What should the average citizen believe about globalization, in particular the increasing linkages among national financial markets? Is the more rapid and pervasive movement of money across national borders helpful, promoting greater prosperity for all the world's citizens? Or is the periodic turbulence associated with cross-border finance hazardous, placing prosperity at risk for many of the world's citizens? Does the balance of benefits and risks vary significantly from one nation to another? Within any given nation, who gains and who loses among the different types of individuals and institutions? Does globalization entail poverty and injustice for some? Does it favor financial capital at the expense of labor?

Throughout most of the twentieth century, government officials and academic experts debated questions such as these about the financial and trade transactions crossing nations' borders. But the debates about globalization intensified, and the disagreements became even more polarized as the century drew to a close. Larger numbers of individuals and groups not

---

2. Friedman (1999); Jordan (1999).

hitherto engaged in the debates, dissatisfied with their experiences or perceptions of globalization, began to express strong views. The large street demonstrations in Seattle at the time of the Third Ministerial Conference of the World Trade Organization in the fall of 1999, in Washington and Prague during the spring and fall 2000 meetings of the International Monetary Fund and the World Bank, and at subsequent international meetings in numerous other cities are prominent illustrations of the increasing intensity and polarization of views.

It is a safe prediction that the debates and disagreements will continue in full force during the first several decades of the twenty-first century. Even more than before, average individuals will come to understand that the forces of cross-border finance and trade are having significant effects on their own welfare and the welfare of neighbors and fellow citizens. Thus average individuals will increasingly seek guidelines for assessing the controversies about globalization and for forming judgments about the policy decisions that are made in response.

Financial Activity

A first requirement for understanding cross-border finance is to have a sound understanding of the benefits and risks of financial activity *within* individual nations. To be sure, new and difficult issues arise with cross-border finance that are not present in domestic financial activity. Yet those insights about financial activity and financial markets that are truly fundamental apply to both the domestic and the cross-border aspects.

As explained in the initial chapters of this book, the financial system of a nation can be likened to a reservoir that collects the savings generated in the national economy. Savers place their funds in the reservoir. Investors draw funds out of it. Saving and investment decisions can be, and are, taken independently. The level of the reservoir rises and falls in response to changes in the economy. The existence of the reservoir greatly facilitates the operation of the economy, thereby enhancing the welfare of the nation's citizens.

Although the reservoir benefits the economy, it can also be buffeted by large waves and strong winds. The waves and winds can sometimes evolve into storms. The storms can in turn badly damage the economy and adversely affect welfare. To some degree, financial storms are inevitable. Financial activity is fundamentally fragile, potentially vulnerable to instability. These risks are also explained in the chapters that follow.

Cross-border financial flows are tantamount to a ladling of saving funds from one national reservoir to another. As the second half of the twentieth century progressed, individual nations' reservoirs became progressively better connected. The levels of the savings fluid in most national reservoirs are thus much more closely linked now than they were at the middle of the twentieth century.

The much higher degree of integration among national reservoirs today misleads some commentators into describing the world financial system as though it were fully unified, with a nearly uniform level of savings funds throughout a single global reservoir. The actual situation of the evolving world financial system, however, is intermediate. It is farther away from the case of completely separated national reservoirs than from the opposite case of a fully unified global reservoir. Nonetheless, the actual situation is an untidy, intermediate state well removed from either of the polar extremes.

The existence of an increasingly integrated world financial system greatly facilitates a vigorous and prosperous evolution of the world economy, thereby enhancing the welfare of many of the world's residents. Unfortunately, the increasing integration of national financial systems also enhances the risks associated with financial activity. Because financial activity is fundamentally fragile and potentially vulnerable to instability, cross-border finance exacerbates the potential instability. The growing pervasiveness of cross-border finance raises the probability that financial storms will occur and, if they do, can become more virulent and spill across national borders more contagiously than those arising in former times within domestic reservoirs. That financial storms on a worldwide scale are now possible was made vividly manifest by the events of August–October 1998.

Intermediate, Messy Globalization

The extent of integration among national financial reservoirs is, as just noted, partial rather than complete. The "intermediate-ness" in financial systems is just one of many manifestations of the same phenomenon in other aspects of the world at the beginning of the twenty-first century. The economies and the polities of individual nations, and hence their agglomeration in a global economy and a global polity, are at highly awkward stages of evolution. Chapter 4 explains this generalization and highlights its implications.

The complexity in the global economy and global polity has many dimensions and imposes numerous constraints on feasible evolutions for behavior and institutions. Throughout the following chapters, this book grapples with the world's hybrid, intermediate messiness.

Nothing better illustrates what I mean by messy and intermediate than the economic significance of national borders. National borders declined in *relative* importance over the second half of the twentieth century, as stressed in subsequent chapters. Yet national borders are still extremely important, economically as well as politically.

Journalism and popular discussions often repeat superficial generalizations about globalization and the diminished significance of national borders. Globalization is interpreted not merely as a widening, deepening, and speeding up of worldwide interconnectedness in all aspects of contemporary social life.[3] Many generalizations go much further. For example, the world at the beginning of the twenty-first century is often asserted to be a "global village," with the nation state "withering away."

Some observers view the trends approvingly. Examples include Kenichi Ohmae's *The End of the Nation State* (1995) and Thomas Friedman's *The Lexus and the Olive Tree* (1999).[4] Other observers perceive the trends as alarming. Examples include books whose titles warn the reader: *One World, Ready or Not: The Manic Logic of Global Capitalism* (William Greider, 1997); *False Dawn: The Delusions of Global Capitalism* (John Gray, 1999); *Global Village or Global Pillage* (Jeremy Brecher and Tim Costello, 1994); *Your Money or Your Life!: The Tyranny of Global Finance* (Eric Toussaint, 1999); and *World on Fire: How Exporting Free Market Democracy Breeds Ethnic Hatred and Global Instability* (Amy Chua, 2003).[5]

Much popular commentary about globalization is unhelpful in understanding the intermediate messiness of today's actual world. Sometimes the commentary amounts to nothing more than globaloney. The commentary correctly observes that the degree of economic integration across national borders, especially in financial terms, has increased greatly and will continue to increase. But it then often leaps, altogether unjustifiably, to such thoughts as full globalization has already arrived or will soon do

---

3. The phrase in the text is the definition of globalization offered by Held and others (1999, p. 2).

4. Friedman discusses both the favorable and problematic aspects but puts much more weight on the former.

5. Several colleagues at Brookings, concerned that anti-globalization views frequently overlook basic economic points, contribute constructively to this debate; see Burtless and others (1998).

so; identifiably different national economies are a thing of the past; national borders have virtually dissolved and no longer matter; nation states are unnatural units in a global economy and will soon be relegated to an unimportant status.

The awkward truth is that national borders, though less significant than in the past, still have enormous salience. A thoughtful approach to public policy choices for individual nations, and for the world as a whole, must eschew sweeping, superficial generalizations about globalization and focus instead on the status of the world as it actually exists.

International Collective Governance

Some situations in social groups or particular regions require collective action to supplement individual actions. Social and regional groups, or entire societies, thus choose to establish and maintain institutions to catalyze that collective action.

Collective governance is a rough synonym for collective action. *Governance* is in principle a broader concept than *government* because governance can subsume the activities of nongovernmental groups as well as government institutions.

Collective governance exercised through government institutions is likely to be required in numerous territorial jurisdictions, at a variety of levels. Local governments exist even for small municipalities. They are prominent features of social life at the level of provinces or states. National governments catalyze collective actions for nation states as a whole. The activities of international institutions established by national governments can be understood as nascent collective governance above the level of nations themselves.

In the messy, intermediate world of recent decades, collective-governance problems with dimensions spilling across national borders have grown in importance relative to problems of domestic governance. This growth of problems with cross-border dimensions is certain to continue well into the twenty-first century.

National governments will thus inevitably be forced in the future to interact more with each other. If they are wise and farsighted, the interactions will result in more cooperation. As part of that cooperation, the governments will ask international institutions to carry out a wider range of functional responsibilities and hence will delegate greater authority to them. This class of issues, at the broadest level, falls under the rubric of *the evolution of international collective governance.*

Collective governance is difficult and contentious even within a single nation with a relatively homogeneous population. In a heterogeneous, multination world of progressively increasing economic and financial interdependence, collective-governance problems are several orders of magnitude more difficult still. Much of this book analyzes the possibilities for, and difficult constraints impeding, the evolution of international collective governance.

The primary focus is on issues of collective governance for financial activity. Financial activity can be enormously beneficial in promoting growth and efficient resource allocation when it functions smoothly. Completely unconstrained financial activity, however, may not be able to deliver these benefits. As already indicated, the financial system reservoir is prone to storms. Problems to be discussed in the chapters that follow—for example, informational asymmetries, adverse selection and moral hazard, informational cascades, herding behavior and contagion, excessive volatility in asset prices—cause financial activity to be inherently vulnerable to instability. Corruption and crime can contaminate or be conducted through financial institutions.

The appropriate societal response to the dangers associated with financial activity is to establish and maintain a collective-governance "utilities infrastructure" for the financial system. Within an individual nation, the critical features of this infrastructure include standards for accounting, auditing, and information disclosure; legal procedures for enforcing contracts and adjudicating disputes; prudential supervision and regulation of private financial institutions; an effective but limited potential for crisis management and crisis lending ("lender-of-last-resort" provisions); and, not least, sound and predictable macroeconomic policies that shape the general environment within which the financial system and the wider economy operate. Although a few details of the collective-governance financial infrastructure within nations remain controversial, the general need for such an infrastructure is universally accepted.

If a well-functioning collective-governance infrastructure is a precondition for a domestic financial system to operate smoothly, why isn't an analogous infrastructure needed *on a world scale* for the smooth operation of the conglomeration of all national financial systems? One's intuition wants to respond that the same logic does apply at the world level. And the *economic* aspects of the logic are, indeed, persuasive. *If* there could exist, above the level of nation states, analogues to the functions carried out within domestic financial systems by nations' central banks and supervisors of financial institutions, the global economy and financial system could evolve in a smoother and more stable manner.

If cabbages were horses, all could ride like kings. But cabbages are not horses. And because the *political* preconditions are not satisfied in our messy intermediate world, the logic cannot be fully applied to the global financial system. Collective-governance institutions that can effectively carry out the functions of a supranational financial infrastructure do not yet exist.

To be sure, international institutions already exist with limited responsibilities in the areas of finance and trade. The International Monetary Fund (IMF) and the World Bank, created after World War II, are two important global financial institutions with universal (worldwide) membership. The Bank for International Settlements (BIS), originally created in 1930 to manage reparations and debts resulting from World War I, has evolved in recent decades into a bank and meeting place for the central banks of large, wealthy nations. The Organization for Economic Cooperation and Development (OECD), established in 1960–61 with membership originally only for the more advanced industrialized nations, was the successor institution to the Organization for European Economic Cooperation (OEEC), a post–World War II European institution. The General Agreement on Tariffs and Trade (GATT) was another creation of intergovernmental negotiations at the end of World War II. The GATT agreements are now folded into the successor World Trade Organization (WTO), created in 1995 after the 1986–94 Uruguay Round of trade negotiations.

These international financial and economic organizations are nascent venues for international collective governance. In the chapters that follow I will have much to say about intergovernmental cooperation and these international organizations that function as loci for it.

Controversies about the international organizations are frequently linked to the fierce debates about the merits and demerits of globalization. Joseph Stiglitz, a former chief economist at the World Bank, recently added fuel to the fire of globalization critics with his strident condemnations of the IMF. Stiglitz's polemic in turn induced vigorous, even strident, refutations, including the widely discussed response from Kenneth Rogoff, economic counselor at the IMF.[6] My book addresses the same issues about globalization and the international organizations. But I pay more attention to the challenges of collective governance and try to speak in a balanced, dispassionate voice.

A key fact is missing from the harsh criticisms that anti-globalization activists level at the international financial and economic organizations: these organizations are only new seedlings in the gardens of collective governance. When viewed against the long sweep of history, they have tentative mandates and highly limited authorities. Fragile plants may eventually grow into mature trees. Every mighty oak was once an acorn. But when appraising institutions for collective governance, it is essential not to confuse acorns or saplings with the venerable, deep-rooted trees that may eventually cast broad shadows on all their surroundings.

Pragmatic Incrementalism

This book argues that a clear need exists for the further evolution of international collective governance, not least for the building of an internationally agreed infrastructure for the world financial system. Once one recognizes the hybrid, intermediate status of the world polity, however, one has to be practical about how to make progress.

In the later chapters of the book, I encourage a stretching of intergovernmental cooperation in key economic and financial areas. And I strongly endorse a further strengthening of international financial organizations. I argue, in particular, for substantial evolutionary reform and a restructuring of objectives for the IMF.

My evolutionary approach, *pragmatic incrementalism*, does not shrink from strongly supporting a gradual strengthening of international governance. But neither does it unrealistically demand too much, too soon. Positioned in the middle of the road, pragmatic incrementalism is distanced

6. Stiglitz's criticisms are in *Globalization and Its Discontents* (2002); see also Stiglitz (2000). Rogoff's response circulated as "Open Letter to Joseph Stiglitz" (2002). Stiglitz cannot be accurately characterized either as an adversary of globalization or an enthusiast for it; his book addresses globalization issues from several perspectives. His often overstated and sometimes unfounded criticisms of the IMF, however, have played into the hands of those who assert sweepingly that the international financial institutions have exacerbated the evils of globalization. Stiglitz was the chief economist and a senior vice president at the World Bank during three years from 1997 to 2000; his criticisms of the World Bank are mild or absent altogether even on numerous topics where the analytical and policy views of the IMF and the World Bank are quite similar.

from the ditch on the right-hand side that is the extreme *untrammeled markets view* and removed from the extreme in the other direction, the left-hand ditch of the *sweeping institutionalist reform view*.

The untrammeled markets view sees government failures as pervasive, at both the national level and the nascent international level. In that view, efforts to mount governmental action are more likely to be "the problem" than a "solution." That view thus seeks to sharply limit collective governance. It trusts, or at least hopes, that markets and individual nations themselves will cope resiliently with any difficulties that materialize.

In sharp contrast, the sweeping institutionalist reform view sees market failures as pervasive, internationally as well as domestically. It believes that financial markets periodically go out of control, especially with cross-border transactions, and thus wants either to rebuild separation fences at national borders or else to delegate greatly enhanced authority to international institutions.

Neither the untrammeled markets view nor the sweeping institutionalist reform view is based on compelling analysis. Both views, furthermore, are politically unrealistic. Market failures and financial turbulence put great pressure on governments to "do something." The untrammeled markets advice to "Don't do something! Just stand there!" invariably buckles under crisis-generated political pressure (usually, appropriately so). The sweeping institutionalist reform view errs in the opposite direction by badly misjudging the relevant political constraints. Over the next decade or two, political considerations are unlikely to permit a radical increase in the authority of existing international institutions. Creation of additional international institutions, de novo, will be at least as constrained by political difficulties. The cosmopolitan dream of establishing global federalist governmental institutions—the beginnings of a world government to exercise collective governance formally at the world level—stands no chance of fulfillment for many decades into the future, at the earliest.

In today's world, political leaders and their citizens retain many illusions about the effective degree of their nation's sovereignty. They often fail to appreciate the significant differences between de jure sovereignty and de facto autonomy (to be emphasized in chapter 4). National governments therefore encourage each other and the international institutions only to tiptoe, timidly, towards the establishment of a nascent collective-governance infrastructure for the world financial system.

My stance of pragmatic incrementalism argues for moving more briskly. Timid steps on tiptoe will not keep pace with the rapid evolution of collective-governance problems. Pragmatism invariably requires caution. But it also often requires that decisions be expeditious and ambitious rather than protracted and timid.

Yet the only feasible approach is incremental. A series of continuing, small steps for strengthening international governance is the most that can be hoped for. Progress is an evolutionary path, not the playing out of an endgame that can be specified now for many decades into the future. For most of the economic and political areas where cross-border spillovers are growing in importance, simplified policy nostrums abound. But the nostrums—silver bullets in American cowboy parlance—either cannot magically resolve the problems or else have no prayer of being adopted.

H. L. Mencken observed that, for every human problem, there is a solution that is neat, simple—and wrong. Mencken's warning will serve well as the subsequent chapters dig deeper into the evolution of international collective governance for cross-border finance.

The Policy Dilemma for Individual Nations

Because of the cross-border and supranational nature of the problems on which I focus, this book necessarily concentrates on collective governance for groups of nations or for the world as a whole. The governmental decisions about finance and economics discussed here require cooperation across national borders. But the bulk of governmental decisionmaking in the world inevitably takes place within individual nations. For the most part, national governments steer courses that they themselves set independently.

For any individual nation, the government confronts a trade-off between national autonomy and openness to the global economy. Many dimensions of a nation's openness are of course attributes that cannot be changed and about which the nation's residents and their government cannot exercise any choice. No choices can be made, for example, about the size and location of the nation's geographical territory, its endowment of natural resources, and its past history of economic and cultural links with the rest of the world. But in some degree, varying considerably from nation to nation, a limited range of choice about openness does exist.

Some decisions of a nation's government, for example, require choosing how much relative weight to give to values, norms, and institutions that are indigenous to the nation. Some collective measures can help to shield the indigenous values and institutions from being overwhelmed by foreign values and institutions. Some national economic policies are better than others for promoting economic conditions within the nation that are identifiably, if only marginally, different from economic conditions abroad.

Extreme openness to the world economy, with no effort to nurture local conditions and to buffer them from foreign influences, threatens to undermine any separate national identity. Openness creates pressures for the acceptance of foreign values, foreign culture, foreign economic practices and conditions. Openness requires subjecting the national economy to the stringent, and sometimes fickle, discipline of foreign financial markets. Openness can generate political and social backlashes in domestic politics.

Yet openness can also bring very sizable potential benefits (discussed extensively in subsequent chapters). The scope for moderating openness to sustain indigenous values and institutions, furthermore, may be sharply limited in practice. No matter how much a nation's residents may wish to resist foreign pressures to become homogenous with the outside world, it must be asked whether the nation has cost-effective means at its disposal to achieve some degree of insulation and divergence from the rest of the world.

The difficult trade-off between autonomy and openness surfaces in a variety of ways and is important for all nations. But the trade-off is especially problematic for emerging-market nations that have advanced beyond early stages of economic and financial development and have begun to use modern technology intensively but have not yet evolved the increasing specialization and governance infrastructures of the most advanced nations.

Predictably, issues about the trade-off arise in an acute form for financial activity. The government of a small, open nation, for example, may even question whether the nation can feasibly sustain its own free-standing financial system with indigenously controlled financial institutions and indigenous supervision and regulation of those institutions.

Goals for the Book

When a legal case comes before a court, the plaintiff and defendant initially mobilize detectives or research lawyers to marshal and interpret facts. Later, on the foundation of the previous analyses, a prosecuting attorney and the defendant's lawyer will argue the case in court, acting as advocates. Ultimately, after listening to the arguments from all sides, a judge renders a decision.

My primary purpose in writing this book and its companion volumes has been to fulfill the functions of the detectives and research lawyers (what economists often describe as *positive* analysis). In the second half of the book, I also have a second, *normative* purpose, analogous to the advocacy functions of the lawyers arguing in court. Throughout, as detective and then advocate, my aspiration is to represent not just one side, but all sides, of the issues. I have therefore taken pains to identify places where there exist serious disagreements in analyses, interpretations, or advocacy positions. You, the reader, I perceive as the ultimate judge not only of the advocacy positions but also of the detective analysis that undergirds them.

As detective, my goal is to provide, in effect, a map and guidebook. Both citizens and policymakers need a set of basic concepts and analytical ideas that can enhance understanding of the problems of cross-border finance and international governance. Considerable background and some lateral vision are required before the issues can be placed in appropriate perspective. Hence the early chapters of the book are frankly pedagogical.

As the book was being written, I was prevented from going to my office one April day by street demonstrations and police barricades at the spring meetings of the IMF and World Bank. The demonstrators had gathered in Washington to protest poverty, inequality, injustice, and instability in the world economy. Those evils result, in their view, from globalization and inattention to the problems of poorer people and workers, both in the United States and in the developing nations of the world. The demonstrators appeared to believe, in one fashion or another, that international organizations such as the IMF, the World Bank, and the WTO are culpable in fostering those evils.

My reactions that day were troubled with cognitive dissonance. Like the demonstrators, I deplore the inequality, poverty, injustice, and instability that are widespread in the world. Like them, I believe that economic and financial globalization comes with serious costs, with a dark downside. And I believe that nascent international governance has at times been ineffective, even occasionally failing altogether to achieve its limited goals.

Having for much of my professional life studied the trends of increasing interdependence and their implications, however, I know that globalization has also generated substantial benefits. I believe that the majority of developing nations, not least their poorest citizens, would have fared even less well in recent decades if their economies had not become more open to the world economy. The fragile seedlings of the international organizations are merely ancillary extensions of the national governments who planted them. In the instances when the international organizations have failed in collective governance—have failed to improve welfare within individual nations and in the world economy as a whole—it is essentially because the governments of the major nations have failed to demand and support the appropriate policies. Assertions that the IMF, the World Bank, and the WTO are powerful, independent entities that on balance have systematically *worsened* the evils of inequality and instability are based on extremely shaky, typically insupportable arguments.

To genuinely understand the world's economic and financial problems, to propose coherent remedies for the costs of globalization and the failures of international governance, one must first identify the deeper causes. As concerned citizens, we should complain that poverty and injustice are widespread. We must try sensibly to attack their root causes. But in no valid sense can the international organizations be labeled the root causes of poverty or injustice. Beating up on the international organizations is about as effective as dragging the ministers of local churches into the courtroom, complaining that they are culpable because sinners' ways prosper.

My fondest hope for this book is that its analysis of fundamentals will constructively advance the understanding of the proverbial man or woman in the street. I have tried to explain the root causes of financial issues, the basic benefits and costs, in clear and simple language. The initial chapters in the book are my best shot at explaining, if you will, why sinners' ways can prosper in the realm of finance, yet why men and women of good conscience may agree that financial activity is, and should be, a prominent feature of economic life.

Perhaps my detective writing may even be useful to economist colleagues? Portions of the exposition, to be sure, will be old hat to specialists. But it cannot be helped if in places I bore my fellow economists. My chief aspiration is, again, educational—to facilitate a balanced understanding of these important issues for a wider audience of noneconomists, many of whom may hitherto have regarded the issues as too arcane or inaccessible to merit attention.

My subsidiary purpose in the book, like the prosecuting and defending attorneys in court, is to advocate practical policy recommendations. The second half of the book therefore summarizes broad guidelines for national policies and for intergovernmental cooperation. Whereas the early parts of the book look carefully in the rear view mirror at where the world was in the twentieth century, the final parts look ahead at where it is, and should be, headed over the first several decades of the twenty-first century.

Much of the recent policy concern with cross-border finance, and quite possibly your own interest in reading this book, is driven by anxieties generated by recent financial crises. Accordingly, much of what follows is about financial turbulence and how to mitigate its consequences when it does occur. When considering policy reforms, however, whether for an individual nation's government or for the world financial system as a whole, I eschew a preoccupation with crises. I am most concerned with the broader issues of how the world polity, and the world economy and financial system, should evolve in *noncrisis* periods. In effect, I primarily emphasize the *prevention* of economic and financial crises. The true preoccupation should be the encouragement of healthy growth and financial stability— *prosperity management* rather than crisis management.

Companion Volumes

I began the project that produced this book aspiring to write a single, integrated treatment of both the fundamentals of cross-border finance and specialized policy recommendations for enhancing international financial governance. I wanted the book to help a general audience develop understanding and to form views about the merits of the specialized recommendations beginning to be debated publicly. Simultaneously, I hoped the analysis would prove useful to policymakers and to fellow specialists, or at least constructively provoke them.

I succeeded in completing a draft of a single, integrated manuscript. But several friends and colleagues argued that that first manuscript was in places too technical for general readers, yet in other places too general for professional colleagues. My fondest hope, again, is to reach general readers, not merely fellow policy wonks. With the comfort of general readers uppermost in mind, I thus accepted the advice of my colleagues and rewrote the manuscript. The book as it now exists maintains a relatively even level of discourse and suppresses specialized, technical material that could deflect attention from top-level concerns.

Because the specialized analyses have been deleted, the normative recommendations in the second half of the book necessarily are summarized. Restructured and rewritten versions of the original specialized material may be found in three companion volumes, comprising the series *Pragmatic*

Choices for International Financial Governance, likewise published by the Brookings Institution. The companion volumes, titled *Crisis Prevention and Prosperity Management for the World Economy*, *Prudential Oversight and Standards for the World Financial System*, and *Crisis Management for the World Financial System*, are described further at the beginning of chapter 9. Policy specialists, as well as general readers who wish for more supporting argument, amplified descriptions of alternative points of view, or more extensive background than can be found in the second half of the book are urged to consult the companion volumes.

A Road Map and How to Read the Book

After this introduction, chapter 2 plunges into analytical fundamentals. It begins by reviewing basic ideas about financial intermediation, its substantial benefits, and its associated risks and costs. To clarify the essential ideas, chapter 2 suppresses the cross-border dimensions of financial activity and treats financial transactions as though they were entirely domestic.

Chapter 3 introduces the concepts of collective governance and applies them to the nonprivate institutions and procedures constituting the infrastructure of the financial system. It explains why such an infrastructure is essential for a healthy, stable evolution of financial activity. For clarity, it continues to suppress the international dimensions of financial activity, thereby highlighting the purely domestic aspects of collective governance.

Chapter 4 opens up the analysis to the actual world economy. The chapter emphasizes that the globe is divided into many diverse nations, each with a geographical territory defined by national borders and each with its own national government. The chapter sets out the dominant political and economic themes—often termed *political economy*—that are required background for coherently analyzing this multination world polity.

Chapter 5 begins the process of adapting the fundamental ideas in chapters 2 and 3 about financial activity and its collective governance to chapter 4's messy, intermediate world of heterogeneous nation states but increasingly integrated national economies. Chapter 5 contains some historical background and an empirical overview of recent decades. It also explains how and why the cross-border dimensions of financial activity are today so much more important than in the past.

Chapter 6 completes the adaptation of the fundamentals in chapters 2 and 3 to a context of many nations and multiple currencies. It discusses the potential gains from cross-border financial intermediation and introduces additional uncertainties and analytical issues that afflict capital flows in a multination, multiple-currency world. It also carefully analyzes the mishaps and instabilities that can characterize cross-border finance.

Chapter 7 begins by raising in more detail the question already identified above: whether, and if so, along what dimensions the multination world financial system may require some form of international utilities infrastructure for collective governance. It then steps back to address analytical issues about international collective governance at a general level. The discussion presumes that pressures will grow for the strengthening of various forms of intergovernmental cooperation and hence also for the strengthening of international institutions. Chapter 7 distinguishes between governance and government, reviews alternative forms and venues for intergovernmental cooperation, and then discusses the range of nascent governmental functions that might conceivably be exercised at international or supranational levels. It defines the range of conceivable functions for intergovernmental cooperation on financial issues and then concludes with an overview of the international financial institutions (intergovernmental consultative groups and actual international organizations) operating at the beginning of the twenty-first century. For readers not familiar with the institutions' origins and operations, the appendix to the book provides more detail about the IMF and other international financial institutions.

Chapter 8 provides background analysis for all the conceivable functions of intergovernmental financial cooperation—what has come to be called the *international financial architecture.* Not all the conceivable functions could or should be exercised in the short or medium runs. But sound analysis requires comprehension of a blueprint for the architecture as a whole, not merely for modifications that may be added in the near future. Chapter 8 emphasizes issues that have so far been relatively neglected in journalistic and academic debate. It highlights supranational collective surveillance of cross-border traffic regulations and of national exchange rate and macroeconomic policies. Because IMF lending intermediation among national governments in noncrisis conditions is much less understood than emergency financial assistance as part of crisis management, chapter 8 provides analytical background about that function for intergovernmental financial cooperation. The chapter concludes by examining parts of the blueprint that, though currently not regarded as important, are likely to become salient over the longer run.

Given the background in earlier chapters, chapters 9 and 10 shift into a forward-looking mode and turn to international governance issues that deserve high priority in the first decades of the twenty-first century. Both chapters summarize recommendations for strengthening collective governance, within nations and at international or supranational levels. Both explore *architectural reform*—how to nurture the evolution of key dimensions of a financial utilities infrastructure for the world financial system.

Desirable enhancements in the nascent world utilities infrastructure fall into three groups. Chapter 9 covers the first group, *supranational surveillance and lending intermediation*. National governments and international organizations should upgrade their collective monitoring of cross-border traffic regulations and of nations' macroeconomic, exchange rate, and balance-of-payments policies. Concurrently, they should streamline and strengthen intergovernmental lending intermediation for the liability financing of payments deficits in noncrisis periods.

Chapter 10 summarizes reform recommendations for the other two groups, *prudential financial oversight* and *crisis management*. Strengthened prudential oversight requires governments and international organizations to make further improvements in the surveillance, supervision, and regulation of financial activity and in the associated design and monitoring of financial standards. Improved capabilities for crisis management require greater intergovernmental cooperation for collective responses to financial turbulence, both domestic and cross-border; the needed procedures and capacities include the contingent provision of emergency lending during financial crises, the handling of moral hazard difficulties, and the involvement of private financial institutions in concerted lending.

The International Monetary Fund is the international institution most centrally involved in architectural reforms for supranational surveillance and lending intermediation and for crisis management. The IMF also has a prominent role in reforms for prudential financial oversight. Chapter 10 thus concludes with analysis of alternative views about the IMF's institutional mandate and recommendations for how it should be defined.

The recommendations summarized in chapters 9 and 10 are discussed and justified in detail in the three backstopping volumes in the companion series *Pragmatic Choices for International Financial Governance*.

The final chapters in the book provide concluding overviews, taking stock of the conclusions and complexities of the earlier analyses. Chapter 11 focuses initially on issues of cross-border finance as they arise for key policymakers in a single individual nation. The chapter subsequently reverts to the cosmopolitan perspective of chapters 8 through 10 where policy choices are analyzed as collective choices for the global community, not as choices for a single nation.

Chapter 12 summarizes an appropriate perspective for thinking about financial activity and financial turbulence. It provides the average citizen a balanced answer to the issues of financial globalization and what to believe about the progressively stronger linkages among national financial markets.

The stocktaking in chapter 13 focuses on the evolution of international collective governance for the world economy and financial system. It reviews main themes and broad principles and selectively highlights key political issues. An underlying objective for the concluding chapter is to sketch an interim vision of how the world polity and financial system might evolve for the first several decades of the twenty-first century.

Inevitably, some readers will not be able to take the time to read every chapter in the book. In recognition of that fact, this introduction and the final chapters are designed so that they may be read as a partial overview of main themes and conclusions. In the last movement of his final string quartet, Beethoven posed the question *Muss es sein?* (Must it be?).[7] If you should fall into the group of busy individuals with severe time constraints and hence feel forced to jump to a "bottom line"—Muss es sein?—your best recourse is to turn directly to chapters 11 through 13. That partial reading will at least permit you to sample the flavor of the book's analysis and its recommendations.

An inquiring reader, and certainly a reader not inclined readily to accept my analytical summaries, will not be satisfied merely by reading this introduction and the concluding chapters. The issues raised in the book are complex and controversial. A deep understanding requires an investment in the analytical framework that underpins the main themes and conclusions. Much the most informative way to read this book, therefore, is to follow the King of Heart's advice to the White Rabbit in *Alice's Adventures in Wonderland*: "begin at the beginning and go on till you come to the end: then stop."

Some readers dislike footnotes. Others find them useful, even indispensable. I follow a middle course about them in the chapters that follow.

7. Beethoven also supplied his own answer: *Es muss sein!*—Yes, it must be.

A majority of the footnotes identify the source of a quotation or additional sources in the literature. Those notes are intended to help intrepid readers who may want to know where to look to have the point at issue amplified, or to learn more about the perspective that other authors have taken. A few of the footnotes explain in a more detailed way, occasionally in a more technical way, the point at issue. Footnotes of this latter type are infrequent. General readers who prefer not to be diverted can ignore all the footnotes without any significant loss of the main argument.

2 Saving, Investment, and Financial Activity in a Single Closed Economy

Financial institutions and financial markets are essential features of an advanced, smoothly functioning economy. Financial activity is helpful and yet also hazardous. It generates many benefits. But it entails risks and costs.

To clarify fundamental concepts, it is revealing at first to suppress the international dimensions of financial activity. Temporarily, therefore, suppose there is only one single economy in the world so that financial activity is entirely "domestic." This initial suppression of the complications stemming from multiple nations, different currencies, exchange rates among currencies, and cross-border transactions will throw the cross-border complications into clearer focus when they are highlighted in later chapters. To really understand cross-border finance, one must first comprehend what financial activity would be like if cross-border finance did not exist.

Basic Concepts: Investment, Saving, and Financial Activity

The primary goal of economic activity is the consumption of goods and services. In a modern complex economy, the production of those goods and services requires the use of durable assets, for which economists use the term *real capital*. Some real capital assets are *nonreproducible* natural resources, such as land and mineral deposits. But most—for example, factory buildings, machinery equipment, and transportation vehicles—are man-made and *reproducible*. Without the investments in real capital made in the past, the production of goods and services in the economy today—and hence consumption today—would be much lower than it is. New investments in reproducible real capital, as well as replacement investments for assets that depreciate and are scrapped, are essential ingredients for vitality and growth of the economy.

If an economy is to invest in real capital, it must refrain from consuming all its income today, saving the amounts that are invested. In financially complex economies, most decisions to save are made independently of decisions to invest. The *ultimate savers* are primarily households. They set aside a fraction of current income, rather than spending it on current consumption, to increase future consumption possibilities either by themselves or their heirs. The *ultimate investors* are primarily business enterprises. They purchase and employ the real capital goods to facilitate the production of goods and services. Business enterprises borrow—that is, they issue financial claims against themselves—to be able to purchase and employ more capital than would otherwise be possible.

The savings generated in the economy are like a pervasive fluid. And the financial system can be likened to a reservoir for these funds. When the current-period consumption of households and other economic agents falls short of their income, the resulting savings flow into the reservoir. Businesses and others whose current-period spending exceeds their income draw funds out of the reservoir as they borrow to finance their excess spending. The existence of the reservoir permits the saving and investment decisions of individual economic agents to be taken independently, even though, when measured after the decisions have been made and inconsistencies among them have been eliminated, the flows of aggregate saving and aggregate investment are necessarily equal for the economy as a whole.

Many economic and noneconomic forces affect saving and investment decisions and thus influence the level of savings in the reservoir and associated interest rates for lending and borrowing. In particular, the reservoir's level rises and falls with the pace of activity in the real sectors of the economy.

Imagine a hypothetical economy without financial instruments of any kind and without the financial system reservoir. The behavior of spending units in such a world would be severely restricted. Each unit would have to invest in real capital assets whatever part of its current income was not consumed. No unit could invest more in real capital than its current saving because there would be no way to finance the excess expenditures. In the absence of financial instruments and the reservoir, therefore, no unit would be able to satisfy its needs and preferences for an intertemporal pattern of spending that differed from the time profile of its income. Resources would be allocated inefficiently. The economywide levels of saving and investment, and hence the growth of the economy, would be substantially less than they are under institutional arrangements where ultimate investors can borrow through the issuance of financial instruments.

Basic Concepts:
Financial Intermediation and Financial Institutions

Financial intermediation, broadly conceived, is the entire complex process through which the myriad independent decisions of individual ultimate savers and individual ultimate investors are reconciled. The reconciliation is facilitated by *financial intermediaries*—institutions such as banks, savings and loan companies, finance companies, and insurance companies—and by *financial markets*, such as stock exchanges and the interbank overnight-funds market.

The assets of a financial intermediary are liabilities issued by ultimate investors and, in an increasingly complex financial system, by other intermediaries as well. The liabilities of a financial intermediary are assets of the ultimate savers and, in a complex financial system, of other intermediaries. Unlike the ultimate investors, whose principal assets are real capital goods, the financial intermediaries have both their assets (for example, loans) and their liabilities (for example, various types of deposits) predominantly in the form of financial instruments.

The financial instruments issued directly by ultimate investors are termed *primary securities*. Some of the primary securities issued by ultimate-investor businesses take the form of *equity claims* (also referred to as stock shares)—evidences of fractional ownership of the net worths of the businesses. The holders of equity claims assume all the risks and participate in all the gains accruing to the business in proportion to the degree of their fractional ownership. The remainder of primary securities issued by ultimate-investor businesses are *debt* instruments, such as loans from financial intermediaries or bonds traded in financial markets. When a household acts as an ultimate investor by purchasing a house with borrowed funds, it issues a primary debt security known as a mortgage. A debt instrument is a contractual obligation by the borrower to repay the borrowed funds, together with interest, at a specified future date. *Indirect securities* are debt or equity instruments issued by financial intermediaries rather than by ultimate investors.[1]

Financial markets facilitate the trading of financial instruments that have standardized features and are readily negotiable (hence "marketable"). Such financial instruments, often termed *marketable securities,* are legally binding contracts representing evidence of a debt or equity claim on an ultimate investor or a financial intermediary. Financial markets entail a variety of supporting services, often provided by specialized institutions such as brokers and dealers that execute market transactions and rating firms that evaluate the riskiness of particular debt or equity instruments.

Financial activity is a synonym for financial intermediation. *Financial institutions* include both financial intermediaries and financial markets. *Financial system* and *financial sector* refer loosely to the multiple activities of financial institutions engaged in the promotion of financial intermediation.

One can think of financial intermediaries and financial markets as a *utilities infrastructure* that facilitates the movement of saving in and out of the financial system reservoir. The utilities act like a network of pipes, pumping stations, grid transmission lines, and temporary storage warehouses. In effect, they attract the funds of ultimate savers, funnel the savings into the reservoir, and make it easier for ultimate investors to withdraw savings from it. Without the utilities infrastructure, the fluid in the reservoir could not move easily from ultimate savers to ultimate investors. Transaction costs would be too high. Risks would not be borne by those best suited to bear them. Saving and investment decisions could not be made separately. In effect, the economy's saving and investment transactions would be fragmented into numerous local puddles partially or wholly disconnected from each other, rather than collected into one single reservoir.

The utilities infrastructure is the core of the financial system. Ultimate savers and ultimate investors must have confidence in the reservoir and its ancillary utilities if they are to rely on this infrastructure for their financial transactions. Privately owned and operated financial institutions are the dominant components of the financial infrastructure. As is emphasized in chapter 3, however, some dimensions of the infrastructure also entail *collective governance.* Most notably, smooth operation of the financial system

---

1. The terms primary securities and indirect securities were developed by Gurley and Shaw (1960).

requires a legal system backed by governmentally organized courts; accounting standards, audit procedures, and data collection and dissemination ensuring an adequate disclosure of financial information; a governmental monetary authority responsible for economywide monetary policy; and government institutions responsible for the supervision and regulation of the private financial institutions.

Characteristics and Advantages of Financial Activity

A hypothetical economy without financial instruments and without the financial system reservoir would be severely restricted in its possibilities for growth and efficient resource allocation. A hypothetical economy in which ultimate investors could borrow through the issuance of primary securities but in which the only financial instruments were money and primary securities would likewise be constricted, although to a lesser degree. In actual economies, in which financial intermediaries and financial markets—the utilities infrastructure—are pervasive, ultimate savers and ultimate investors have numerous choices and enjoy important efficiencies that otherwise could not exist.

Maturity Transformation, Risk Pooling, Risk Evaluation, Liquidity

By issuing claims against themselves, financial intermediaries offer ultimate savers a much wider menu of combinations of risk, return, maturity, and liquidity than would be available if the savers had to lend directly to the ultimate investors. Many intermediaries engage in *maturity transformation* so that most or all of their liabilities have shorter maturities than their assets. And the liabilities of intermediaries tend to have smaller default risk and greater predictability of value than their assets. Ultimate savers can therefore hold financial assets of greater liquidity than the relatively illiquid primary securities issued by the ultimate investors.

Financial intermediaries facilitate the transformation between primary securities and the financial assets held by the ultimate savers because they can, for example, reduce the risk per dollar of lending through the *pooling of independent risks*. Financial intermediaries develop specialized expertise in the collection and evaluation of information about the creditworthiness of ultimate investors. And financial intermediaries can further reduce the costs associated with maturity transformation through their greater efficiency in negotiating, accounting, and collecting. Financial intermediaries thus make it possible for ultimate investors to finance their purchases of real capital assets at lower interest rates and easier terms than if they were forced to borrow directly from the ultimate savers. Similarly, financial intermediaries provide ultimate savers much greater flexibility to adopt intertemporal paths for their consumption that differ from the intertemporal paths of their income.[2]

The markets that trade financial instruments are quintessentially *auction markets*. Trading tends to be centralized and conducted by numerous participants. Transaction costs are relatively low. Prices are quoted continuously and adjust immediately in response to changes, actual or expected, in market supplies and demands. In contrast, real capital assets and many types of goods and services are traded in *customer markets*. Trading is less centralized. Products are more differentiated. Transaction costs are higher. Because products have "price tags" that are not changed continuously, market clearing in the first instance occurs through quantity changes rather than price adjustments.[3]

The auction characteristics of financial markets allow individual savers a flexibility in the holding of securities analogous to the flexibility associated with their direct claims on financial intermediaries. For an individual holder, a negotiable security is liquid if she can sell it in the market, at her discretion, without substantially affecting the market price. Similarly, an ultimate-investor business enterprise may be able to borrow funds more cheaply and easily than would otherwise be possible if it can issue negotiable securities that are traded in an actively functioning financial market. The de facto liquidity provided by financial markets thus complements the maturity transformation of financial intermediaries in reconciling the differing needs of ultimate savers and ultimate investors.[4]

Financial markets provide liquidity not merely for ultimate savers and investors but also for financial intermediaries themselves. Individual intermediaries as asset holders enjoy liquidity advantages analogous to those of ultimate savers when the intermediaries have the option (in effect, backup

---

2. The classic analyses of financial intermediaries include Gurley and Shaw (1956, 1960); Goldsmith (1958); and Tobin and Brainard (1963).

3. The differing behaviors of auction markets and customer markets are analyzed in Okun (1981).

4. A few financial economists define the liquidity of assets very broadly as a service yield provided by assets according to how easily they can be turned into cash, either by sale or by serving as collateral for external financing. Some even go so far as to argue that unimproved land provides liquidity services because a sizable fraction of its value can be used as collateral to borrow external funds. Those definitions of the liquidity of an asset inclusive of its ability to serve as collateral are too broad and potentially confusing. The concept summarized in the text is the usual definition.

insurance) of buying or selling marketable securities. And a significant fraction of the instruments traded in financial markets, instead of primary securities, are the debt or equity obligations of financial intermediaries themselves (indirect securities). Intermediaries can thus raise additional funds through the securities markets.

Direct versus Securitized Intermediation

Analysis distinguishes between direct and securitized intermediation. *Direct intermediation* occurs when a financial intermediary is interposed as a separate asset-holding entity in the chain of financial links between ultimate savers and ultimate investors. It is a straightforward case of direct intermediation, for example, when a commercial bank extends a multiyear loan to a nonfinancial firm and carries the face value of the loan on its own balance sheet until the date of maturity. Similarly, direct intermediation occurs when a household borrows funds under a mortgage contract from a thrift financial institution (such as a savings and loan association in the United States) and the thrift intermediary holds the face value of the mortgage on its books until maturity.

In contrast, *securitized intermediation* occurs when financial institutions play an essential role in placing primary securities in the asset portfolios of ultimate savers or other intermediaries but without acquiring and holding those securities on their own balance sheets. For example, a merchant bank underwriting a new issue of bonds for a nonfinancial firm but retaining none of the new bonds in its own asset portfolio is engaging in securitized intermediation.

Securitized intermediation combined with the operation of financial markets not only complements, but can substitute for, lending by financial intermediaries for their own accounts. Instead of obtaining a new loan from a commercial bank, for example, a business enterprise can raise additional external finance by issuing marketable securities. Instead of holding relatively liquid assets in the form of deposit claims on intermediaries, an ultimate saver can purchase marketable securities.

The *securitization* of liabilities of ultimate investors leads to a different sharing of risks among savers, financial institutions, and the ultimate investors than would otherwise prevail. The explicit maturity transformation characteristic of direct intermediation entails extensive risk bearing by financial intermediaries themselves. With securitized intermediation, financial institutions shift some or all of the risks to the purchasers and issuers of the securities.

The distinction between direct and securitized intermediation can be blurred in practice. For example, suppose commercial banks initiate loans to nonfinancial firms, hold the loans on their balance sheets for a transitional period, and then "pool" the loans together, issuing a standardized security, representing a pro rata claim on the pool of loans, to be traded on a financial market. A similar blurring occurs when intermediaries initiate mortgage claims, carry them on their own books for a transitional period, but then get the mortgages off their balance sheets by creating and selling mortgage-backed negotiable securities to be traded in financial markets.

Still more complex are note-issuance facilities or commercial-paper facilities organized for nonfinancial firms by financial intermediaries. Suppose a bank legally binds itself to assist a firm in periodically issuing commercial paper (short-term, negotiable debt obligations of the firm tradable in a secondary market), but with a commitment to purchase any residual amounts of the issues that cannot be sold to others (or alternatively to provide the borrower with a guaranteed standby direct loan). In normal times the underwriting bank plans not to hold any of the paper itself; that credit risk is assumed by the purchasers of the paper (who could lose if the borrower were to fail before the paper matures). Over a longer term, however, the underwriting bank does bear credit risk, since if things go badly it may have to lend to a borrower in whom other lenders have lost confidence.

The cases just described are examples where direct and securitized intermediation are subtly combined. They may also be described as an "unbundling" of several intermediation functions. The bank performs the initial risk evaluation and prepares the legal documents, for example, but shifts part of the risks of actually holding the primary securities to other lenders.

As a financial system's institutions and markets become more advanced, the unbundling of intermediation functions tends to become more prominent. Greater complexity in securitized intermediation permits greater differentiation and unbundling of risk bearing. In principle, virtually any existing type of financial contract can be securitized. And most have been. Securities backed by pools of bank loans or mortgages are now common. Even credit card debts and automobile loans have been securitized.

The potential complexity of security instruments, and hence securitized intermediation, is endless. Innovative bankers and brokers are continually inventing *derivative securities*, new financial instruments whose value is somehow linked to, or derived from, preexisting securities. Such derivatives are, in effect, complex combinations of financial contracts called *futures* and *options*. The principal value of derivative securities is often a function of complex formulas, the arguments of which are the prices or values of the preexisting securities. Some derivatives are traded in open financial markets. Others are bought and sold through so-called private placements or "over-the-counter" markets.[5]

The more numerous and complex the securitized financial instruments in a financial system, the greater are the possibilities for individuals to tailor their financial activities to their own idiosyncratic needs and preferences. The counterparties in financial transactions can choose combinations of features and risks that will facilitate their own activities. They can also better eschew combinations that do not. The benefits to individuals and society as a whole from such differentiation and unbundling of intermediation functions may be substantial.

But securitization can be a double-edged sword. The greater the degree of securitization and market trading of securities in a financial system, the higher the proportion of financial activity that can be significantly affected by large short-term variations in security prices, driven possibly by volatile shifts in expectations. Later sections of the chapter address the possible costs to individuals and society of high-frequency variation in financial prices.

Financial Contracts: Uncertainty, Information Asymmetries, Principal-Agent Complexities

In a world characterized by uncertainty and risk, will borrowers be able to repay lenders what they owe on the agreed schedule? Even if they can pay, will they do so? If payments are not made on schedule, will they be made with delays, or may the lenders lose their funds permanently? These questions permeate every dimension of financial intermediation. Lenders and borrowers are aware of the uncertainties and risks, and accordingly most financial contracts are complex. The legal aspects of financial instruments are especially preoccupied with whether the contracts will be honored as written, and if not, what consequences will otherwise ensue.

---

5. A futures contract is an obligation to purchase or sell something at a specified future date at a specified price. An options contract is a time-dated right to purchase or sell something in the future at a prevailing market price. The buyer of a put option has a right (but not an obligation) to sell; the buyer of a call option has a right (but not an obligation) to purchase. The writer of an option is obliged to purchase or sell if the buyer of the option chooses to exercise the option. For technical details, see, for example, Hull (1997, 2002).

When a bank considers lending to a business, for example, it first evaluates whether the business seems creditworthy. It then sets the maturity, terms, and conditions of the loan to try to ensure that it will receive its funds back with an appropriate return. Purchasers of a business's bonds evaluate the riskiness of the business and the probability that the bonds will be serviced as promised. Owners of deposits in a bank must have confidence that they can withdraw their money at any time (demand deposits) or that the bank will definitely redeem the funds upon maturity (time deposits). Whether the borrower will repay is a central preoccupation even for equity claims on ultimate investors. The purchaser of an equity claim expects, when he might later want to sell the claim to someone else, to have the principal amount of his investment recouped; to compensate him for the greater risk, he also hopes to earn an even higher return than is typically paid on a debt instrument.

Suppose, fancifully, that uncertainty and risk could be banished from the economy, that all individuals could have the same access to perfect information, and that every financial contract could reasonably be expected to be honored as written. In such a world, interest rates for all types of financial debt instruments would be identical, equal to a basic interest rate on short-term, riskless assets. The subject of financial intermediation would be hopelessly boring. In sharp contrast with that fanciful world, the pervasive issues of uncertainty, risk, and the differing amounts of information available to different participants in the financial system make life exciting—even turbulent.[6]

Many aspects of financial instrument contracts and financial intermediation can be analyzed as *principal-agent problems* characterized by *information asymmetries*. Consider an example in which a bank (the *principal*) makes a loan to a business borrower (the *agent*). This transaction typically entails two types of information problem, known as hidden-knowledge and hidden-action situations. The borrower-agent has better information than the lender-principal about aspects of the environment that will influence the profitability of the investment to be made with the loan, and

6. Some of the fundamental uncertainty and risk issues at stake are suggested by the following query about the lending of books out of a personal library: Who is more foolish, he who lends a prized volume, or he who returns it? Economic theorists often ignore the uncertainty and information issues inherent in appraisals of creditworthiness by analyzing hypothetical financial systems in which information is "perfect" and equally available to all participants. Such hypothetical analyses are of little interest for the purposes of this book.

hence the probability that the borrower will be able to repay the loan. The borrower may have the superior information even before signing the loan contract or may acquire it subsequently. In either case, the information asymmetry between the borrower and the lender gives rise to issues of *adverse selection*. When setting the terms of the loan, the lender is at a disadvantage relative to the borrower unless the borrower can somehow be induced through appropriate incentives to signal the nature of the superior information through his actions. The essence of a hidden-action situation is likewise an asymmetry in information. The borrower can take actions, unobservable by the lender, that may damage the soundness of the lender's loan without the lender being able to monitor and adjust to the borrower's behavior. Hidden-action situations are often referred to as problems of *moral hazard*.

Information asymmetries, adverse selection, and moral hazard often occur outside as well as within the financial system. In the used-car market, for example, sellers have lived with the car for some time and know whether it is a "lemon" or a "peach." Buyers, however, often cannot discern whether a used car on offer is a lemon, which leads to adverse selection and problematic functioning of the used-car market.[7] With fire insurance, the insuree may or may not be careful about storing flammable materials in the basement; regardless, the insurance company typically cannot monitor the insuree's behavior. More generally, the provision of any insurance typically gives rise to moral hazard. The insured, because of the insurance, has a diminished incentive to avoid the insured-against event.

Information asymmetries and the uneven distribution of information among borrowers and lenders are endemic characteristics of the financial system. Borrowers will always know more than those who lend to them what their intentions and expectations are about investment projects and about their willingness and ability to repay. All financial activity is riddled with problems of adverse selection (hidden knowledge) and moral hazard (hidden action).[8]

---

7. Akerlof (1970).

8. Economic theorists in recent decades have devoted increasing attention to the lending and borrowing decisions of economic agents in conditions where information is imperfect and unevenly distributed. Early examples include Stiglitz (1975, 1985); Leland and Pyle (1977); and Stiglitz and Weiss (1981, 1990). More generally, in all of what has come to be termed the economics of information, the dominating consideration is the lack of information on the part of some market participants about what others are doing, what others know, or where the best trading opportunities may be found.

The existence of financial intermediaries stems in part from their comparative advantage in coping with the information asymmetries and principal-agent dilemmas associated with financial instruments. Relative to most individual ultimate savers, a financial intermediary can perform more efficiently as an appraiser of creditworthiness and as a "delegated monitor." Ultimate savers can therefore shift to intermediaries the burden of coping with the information asymmetries. But financial intermediaries cannot overcome the problems completely.[9]

Lenders, especially financial intermediaries, try to mitigate the consequences of information asymmetries and principal-agent issues by designing financial contracts that address these issues. Requiring that a borrower offer secure collateral for a loan is one of the simplest, most straightforward examples; the collateral works to offset the adverse selection and moral hazard difficulties otherwise confronting the lender. In general, the goal of contract design is to incorporate features in the contract that, despite information asymmetries, induce behavior by borrowers that will improve the probability of lenders being repaid.[10]

In principle, one can imagine "complete contracts" in which all contingencies faced by the contracting parties are foreseeable and spelled out. In such contracts, the borrowers have appropriate incentives that ensure they will not abuse their relative information advantage. Complete contracts would also specify all relevant decisions given the range of contingencies. And the decisions would be legally verifiable in the sense of being measurable and enforceable by a court.

For one reason or another, however, virtually all financial contracts are doomed to be "incomplete." Some contingencies that the borrower and lender may face are not foreseeable at the contracting date. Even if all contingencies could be foreseen, too many exist to write into a practical contract. Monitoring the contract—observing that the contracting parties abide by its terms—may be excessively costly. Enforcing the contract may entail prohibitively high legal costs.

---

9. Diamond (1984, 1991) analyzes why financial intermediaries have cost advantages relative to individuals and nonfinancial firms in collecting information about the creditworthiness of borrowers and monitoring loan contracts with the borrowers.

10. As noted by Kreps (1990, p. 577), "the problem of moral hazard [is one in which] one party to a transaction may undertake certain actions that affect the other party's valuation of the transaction but that the second party cannot monitor/enforce properly. The 'solution' to a problem of moral hazard is the use of 'incentives'—structuring the transaction so that the party who undertakes the hidden actions will, in his own best interests, take actions that the second party would (relatively) prefer."

Consider the case of a collateral requirement in a financial contract. Although the posting of collateral by a potential borrower would reduce adverse selection and moral hazard difficulties confronting a lender, in many cases the borrower may not have suitable collateral to offer. Even when collateral is posted, the lender knows that in a future period, if the borrower should choose or be forced to default and the contract's collateral clauses should have to be invoked, the valuation of that collateral will be uncertain. Future valuation of the collateral may depend on the interim behavior of the borrower.

The issues in designing financial contracts are complex. No details need preoccupy us here. The critical point is that it is usually impossible to write financial contracts that altogether overcome the information asymmetries and principal-agent dilemmas. Adverse selection and moral hazard problems, and thus lender risk and uncertainty, and efforts to determine appropriate pricing for this risk and uncertainty, are the very essence of financial activity.

Risk Premiums and Market Valuations of Financial Instruments

An economic agent comparing the relative merits of two assets will be willing to hold the asset with the greater risk and uncertainty only if, other things equal, she expects to receive a higher return on that asset. The expected return on a financial instrument includes a component typically referred to as the *risk premium*. To simplify, the risk premium on an asset is the excess of its expected return over a riskless rate of interest. Assets widely perceived as carrying relatively higher risk earn higher expected returns, reflecting the presence of a relatively larger risk premium.[11]

If expectations change about the risk and uncertainty associated with particular assets, participants in the financial system will require an adjustment in their expected returns. In effect, relative risk premiums will change. If the financial instruments are traded on markets, the markets will speedily impose a price change reflecting the changed perceptions of the risks. If the financial instruments are not readily traded on markets, the contracting parties will have more difficulty in adjusting the effective prices. In many cases, the *existing* financial contracts for nonmarketable assets may not be adjusted at all. But at the least, the pricing for *new* contracts of that type of

---

11. The notion of a completely riskless rate of interest is straightforward in theory but possibly problematic in practice. At a minimum, an interest rate thought to be riskless will be associated with an assumed probability of zero that the payor of the interest will default or go into bankruptcy.

instrument (their interest rates and the other terms) will be altered to reflect the changed risk perceptions.

In discussions about risk premiums and financial contracts, a distinction is sometimes made between credit risk and market risk. The *credit risk* associated with a financial instrument refers to the probability that the borrower will not repay the lender in accordance with the financial contract as written. Credit risk is a function of the perceived *creditworthiness* of a borrower and reflects, among other things, the perceived probability of default or bankruptcy of the borrower and the perceived probability of recovering funds if the borrower should default or enter bankruptcy. *Market risk*, typically used to refer only to negotiable assets traded in active markets, stems from possible changes in the prices of assets because of changes in market conditions or uncertainties not immediately associated with changes in the creditworthiness of particular borrowers.

A fundamental point about risk premiums remains to be made: if the expected returns associated with two assets are relatively uncorrelated, an investor may wisely choose to hold some amounts of both assets even when their expected returns are equal and one entails more risk than the other. Holding some amount of each asset permits the investor to lower the total risk of her asset portfolio through *diversification*. The kernel of truth in the recommendation that asset portfolios should be diversified is captured in the aphorism that risk-averse investors should refrain from putting all their eggs in one basket.[12]

In analytical models of risk evaluation that depend on extreme simplifying assumptions, it can be shown that the relevant uncertainty for any particular asset is not the total variance on its return but only an *undiversifiable* component.[13] This undiversifiable component reflects the covariation of the asset's return with an overall market index of rates of return in which assets are weighted by their relative importance in the overall market. The risk premium on an asset depends, in effect, on the amount of its undiversifiable risk and on a marketwide *price of risk*. When extreme simplifying assumptions underlying models of risk evaluation are somewhat relaxed, the analytics become more complicated. Limitations on the number of assets held in a portfolio make the estimation of undiversifiable risk

12. The classic discussions of portfolio diversification are Markowitz (1952, 1959) and Tobin (1958).

13. The exposition in this paragraph draws on Tobin and Brainard (1977), who in turn summarize the analysis in, among others, Lintner (1965) and Sharpe (1964).

difficult and increase the importance of own variance. But it is still analytically possible to describe asset returns in the market in terms of a riskless rate and a single price of risk. Relaxing still other assumptions (such as the existence of a riskless asset and the homogeneity of expectations), however, makes the analytics much more complicated. As Tobin and Brainard put it, "These complications not only make it difficult, both conceptually and empirically, to measure the relevant risks on particular assets. They also make it impossible to speak of, let alone estimate, a single price of risk."[14]

The basic points to keep in mind about risk valuation are that the relative sizes of risk premiums on different types of assets are the main factor explaining observed differences in rates of return, can vary sharply with changes in expectations, and to some extent depend on the correlations or lack of correlations among the perceived risks.

Geographical Variations in Financial Activity

Imagine a hypothetical, super-efficient financial system having no market imperfections and very low communications and transportation costs. The savings fluid in the reservoir for that economy would behave like water. Following a change in underlying circumstances somewhere in the economy, the fluid in all parts of the reservoir would adjust almost instantaneously to reestablish a single uniform level. Savers would move funds so adeptly from lower-return to higher-return locations, and borrowers would shift so promptly from higher-cost to lower-cost sources of financing, that market interest rates and yields on investments, adjusted for risk premiums, would speedily become equalized throughout the reservoir.

More realistically, however, now consider an economy and financial system characterized by asymmetries in the distribution of information, by differential access to financial institutions, and by significant communications and transportation costs. For this economy, the savings fluid in the reservoir must now be described as viscous—more like molasses than water. Given sufficient time for adjustment to changes in underlying circumstances, a uniform level of the viscous fluid would prevail. Nonetheless, if in one region of the reservoir the "taking out" activity during any particular short run substantially exceeds or falls short of the "putting in" activity, the level in that region can be temporarily lower or higher than elsewhere in the reservoir.

---

14. Tobin and Brainard (1977, p. 240).

Suppose investment opportunities become more favorable in a particular region of the economy. This situation might occur because (for example) a technological innovation differentially benefits the region or because new, commercially exploitable supplies of natural resources are discovered in the region. Before the new information has become widely available and all plans have become correspondingly adjusted, the region will have an excess demand for savings. Desired withdrawals from the reservoir by the residents of, or owners of assets in, the favored region will be temporarily larger than planned inflows. The region will pull savings from other parts of the reservoir as investors in the projects with higher than average expected returns successfully bid funds away from investors whose projects in other regions are less promising. Investment within the favored region will not be limited by the current flow of regional savings. Indeed, during the transitional adjustment period there need be little relation between the investment and saving of that region's residents. If one could calculate balance-of-payments accounts for the favored region, one would observe a net savings inflow (a current account deficit). Eventually, rates of return on investment, adjusted for risk premiums, will converge throughout all regions of the economy. But as long as perceived rates of return are unusually high in the favored region, the reservoir will not have a uniform level, and funds will flow from the rest of the reservoir to the favored region.

The greater the geographical, social, and cultural heterogeneities across regions in the economy and the greater the extent to which access to financial institutions differs across regions—more generally, the more viscous is the flow of savings from one part of the reservoir to another—the more important will be geographical variations in the intensity of financial activity. Regional variations in financial activity tend to be closely associated with regional variations in real economic activity.

These elementary points about geographical differences will be highly consequential in subsequent chapters focusing on financial transactions that cross national borders.

Differences among Financial Contracts

Ultimate savers (lenders), ultimate investors (borrowers), and financial intermediaries have differing needs and preferences when coping with uncertainties and risks. The financial system, in the process of reconciling these differing requirements, generates a variety of financial instruments, with very different characteristics. Popular discussions of financial matters often fail to appreciate the importance of these differences.

Although it is not necessary here to dwell on the specific differences among financial instruments, a few distinctions are central. These distinctions become especially important in the actual world of multiple nations, multiple currencies, and cross-border financial transactions.

Money, Debts, Equity Claims

First, recall the distinction between primary securities and indirect securities (the liabilities of ultimate investors versus the liabilities of financial intermediaries). Indirect securities—the financial debts of and equity claims on the financial intermediaries—are sometimes referred to as intermediate, or *inside,* financial instruments. For the closed economy as a whole, inside assets are offset by matching inside liabilities. When accountants "consolidate" the financial system as a whole, the inside assets and liabilities wash out. What remains in the consolidation are the assets of the ultimate savers who hold claims on the financial reservoir and the liabilities of the ultimate investors who have borrowed from it.

Next, consider several fundamental points about *money.* For efficient transactions, the economy requires an agreed unit of account and an asset that can be used as a means of payment (sometimes referred to as a *medium of exchange* or a *transactions medium*). An asset usable as a means of payment may also be regarded by some actors in the economy as a store of value. No advanced economy and its financial system have functioned without an agreed unit of account and some asset, or assets, readily and widely usable as a means of payment. Assets readily and widely usable as a means of payment are typically referred to as money.

The money assets typically held by households and businesses are deposits in commercial banks and other privately owned financial intermediaries, plus a modest amount of currency notes and coins. In so-called narrower statistical definitions of money, the deposits may be only demand deposits. Broader statistical definitions may include time and savings deposits as well, and possibly even still other types of short-term claims on private financial intermediaries. Vast amounts of ink have been spilled on the subject of which definition of money is the most appropriate for macroeconomic analysis. Fortunately, that issue is not relevant here.[15]

---

15. My own contributions to the sea of ink about the definition of money include Bryant (1980b, 1983).

It is necessary, however, to distinguish between reserve money and inside money. *Reserve money* assets are means-of-payment liabilities of the monetary authority, typically the *central bank*. Currency notes and coins are reserve money. So are the *reserves* held at the central bank by the private financial intermediaries. (The term *high-powered money* is a frequently encountered synonym for reserve money.) In contrast, *inside money* assets are claims on the private financial intermediaries (such as demand deposits, time deposits, and savings deposits in commercial banks and thrift institutions). Reserve money is potentially under the close control of the central bank. Inside money is not; it is determined at any given time not only by the central bank, but also by the behaviors of the financial intermediaries and the nonfinancial general public. It is this difference between reserve money and inside money that requires analyses of the financial system and the economy to differentiate clearly between the two.

I have likened the financial system to a reservoir. Another revealing metaphor is to envisage the financial system as an inverted pyramid balanced on a small apex, the balance sheet of the economy's central bank. The aggregate liabilities of the central bank—reserve money—are roughly equal to the size of its balance sheet.[16] The relationships between the reserve money tip of the financial system pyramid and all the upper layers of the structure (the balance sheets of the numerous private sector financial institutions) are complex and elastic. The inverted pyramid is a flexible, rather than rigid, structure. Especially over longer periods, it is capable of dramatic changes in size and shape that are independent of changes in the small tip of reserve money controlled by the central bank.

The flexibility of the pyramid does not mean that the central bank is unable to influence the size and growth of the financial system. Other things being equal, an incremental expansion of reserve money will stimulate an expansion of the pyramid as a whole; an incremental contraction will have the opposite effect. Nonetheless, the central bank can control the financial pyramid only within some range of tolerance. In particular, the central bank cannot closely control the supply of *broad money* (inside money plus currency notes and coins), whereas it does have the power to closely determine the supply of reserve money.[17]

Owners of *liquid assets* can readily redeem them, or sell them in markets, at a fairly predictable nominal value. Reserve money, inside money, and

16. This sentence abstracts from the (typically) small amount of the central bank's net worth.
17. The monetary policy decisions of the central bank are discussed in chapter 3.

readily marketable assets with short maturities are prime examples of liquid assets. Most other financial assets are relatively *illiquid*; they cannot be readily redeemed or sold in markets without significant risks of discounts from their nominal value. Long-maturity bank loans are relatively illiquid debt instruments. Negotiable securities traded in actively functioning financial markets, even those such as twenty-year bonds or equity claims, are less illiquid than nontradable debt instruments such as loans, yet not, of course, as liquid as money or securities with very short maturities.

Now recall one further distinction among types of financial instruments. *Equity claims* are different in an essential way from *debt instruments*. An equity claim represents fractional ownership in an enterprise and the profits it earns. In sharp contrast, a debt instrument is a promise to pay a fixed amount of money at a contractual interest rate on or before a specific future date. This difference makes the two types of instruments highly imperfect substitutes for each other (even for debt instruments that have a very long specified maturity). Correspondingly, equity claims and debt instruments entail very different types of uncertainties and risks. The most important risks in holding debt instruments, such as a company's bond or its loan from a bank, arise from uncertainties about future rates of interest and inflation and the possibility that the borrower will default on the obligation. In contrast, the most important risks in holding equity claims arise from faulty business judgments by companies' managements and from uncertainties and risks in the real economy, such as unforeseen changes in the relative scarcities of raw materials, surprise disruptions in labor markets, and unanticipated changes in technology.

The salience of the distinctions and the relative importance of the magnitudes—direct versus securitized intermediation, liquid versus nonliquid assets, and debt versus equity—vary with the degree of development of the real economy and the financial system. I return to these themes in chapter 6.

Control versus Liquidity: Direct Owner-Investors and Portfolio Creditors

Because the needs and preferences of ultimate borrowers and ultimate lenders are fundamentally in conflict, each of the contracts characteristic of the financial system reservoir reflects a trade-off among the conflicting requirements. The details of the balancing of borrower and lender interests differ greatly from one type of contract to another.

Consider the perspective of ultimate borrowers, such as the case of a profitable business enterprise engaged primarily in the production of goods and services. Suppose the current owner-investors—the holders of the existing equity claims on the enterprise—wish to make additional investments to expand the scope or nature of its activities. Consider the extreme case in which the firm has not previously borrowed directly in the form of loans from banks or other intermediaries, has not issued any securitized debt-instrument obligations such as bonds, and has 100 percent of the existing equity owned by a small homogeneous group of individuals. Should the current-owner group be willing to borrow significant amounts from outsiders for the new investments, to supplement whatever savings may be internally generated within the firm? Or should it eschew external savings?

The advantage of relying on intrafirm saving is that the current owners can thereby retain full control over the firm's decisions. If the owners borrow external funds or issue additional equity claims against the firm, the new creditors or shareowners will wish to institute some form of monitoring of the firm's future decisions. The new creditors may even insist on some degree of influence or control over future decisions. Because of the perceived risk of giving their savings to the borrower, the new creditors will require the borrower to pay an *external finance premium* (in effect, an incrementally higher cost above the implicit interest rate that the borrower must pay to use its own internal funds). This external finance premium may reflect all of the following: the creditors' expected costs of evaluation, monitoring, and collection; a "lemons" premium resulting from the fact that the borrower inevitably has better information about its prospects than do the creditors; and the costs of distortions in the borrower's behavior that stem from moral hazard or from restrictions in the lending contract designed to contain moral hazard (such as collateral requirements or restricted covenants).[18] The borrowing of external funds thus comes with significant costs. The obvious disadvantage of relying only on internal funds, however, is that the pace of the enterprise's growth will be restricted to the pace of its own accumulation of savings.

From the perspective of the current owners, a "perfect" use of external savings would entail liberal lending by outside funders, at a low rate of interest for a long maturity with no provision for early termination or selling of the loan contract, coupled with no surveillance or influence over the current owners' decisions. The maturity date far in the future and prohibi-

---

18. Bernanke and Gertler (1995) develop the concept of the external finance premium and emphasize how variations in its size can be important for understanding financial activity.

tion against the lenders liquidating or selling their assets before that date would assure the current owners of uninterrupted use of the external funds over a long horizon. An absence of any interference in the enterprise's decisions would ensure continued autonomous control by the existing owners.

To state these perfect conditions is to emphasize their implausibility. Lenders will not agree to financial contracts that keep them inextricably stuck to an enterprise on terms and conditions that might undermine the lenders' own interests. They will demand that the enterprise pay a sizable external finance premium. Existing owners contemplating the borrowing of external savings thus face an inescapable trade-off. An incremental use of external savings will entail some diminution of control, yet choosing not to use external savings will constrain growth.

Prospective lender-savers confront a trade-off analogous to, but the reverse of, that facing prospective borrowers. The "perfect" claim on the ultimate borrower from the lender's perspective will have a high expected rate of return, a short maturity date, provisions for readily liquidating or selling the claim if the lender should for any reason wish to do so, and at least a potential for exercising surveillance or control over the borrower's future decisions. Such a contract would achieve maximum liquidity and flexibility for the lender, and, should the lender choose to exercise it, an influence over the borrower's actions, thereby reducing the lender's risk and the probability of loss of the lender's funds.

Again, however, the perfect conditions from the lender's perspective would be unacceptable to the owner-borrower. The borrower, hesitant in any event to surrender some degree of control or influence to a lender, will certainly be unwilling both to surrender some control and simultaneously provide the lender with an easy option of withdrawing his funds at the lender's whim. The greater the degree of control to be relinquished by an owner-borrower, the more the borrower will insist on the lender sticking with the enterprise in foul weather as well as fair. Thus the lender, too, inevitably faces a trade-off. The lender cannot expect to exert significant control over the borrower's activities without sacrificing liquidity and shortness of maturity (more generally, relinquishing the easy redeemability of the lending).

Different financial contracts embody dissimilar treatments of the trade-offs among liquidity, maturity, and control. The most salient of these differences are those between debt-instrument contracts on the one hand and equity claims on the other. Debt instruments can entail some degree of influence from a lender (loans to an enterprise from its lead commercial bank are an example). By and large, however, a creditor must own equity shares in an enterprise to exert substantial amounts of influence or control.

One should also distinguish, for any given enterprise, between holders of equity claims that own a significant fraction of the total equity versus holders that own only a small fraction. An owner of a tiny fraction of an enterprise's equity shares will be exposed to the potential gains and losses of the enterprise (in proportion to the fraction of his ownership). But with only a tiny fraction of the equity shares, that owner will not be able to exert a significant influence on the enterprise's decisions. If the owner's shares are marketable because they are publicly traded on a stock exchange, however, the marginal shareholder may have at least the illusion of a somewhat liquid investment, since his tiny fraction of the enterprise's shares may be promptly offloaded by selling the shares on the stock exchange (albeit at a price that is uncertain before the sale is actually made).

Analysis should likewise distinguish between two broad classes of creditor-lenders to a borrowing enterprise. A group of *direct owner-investors*, often small in number, are the key decisionmakers that really control the business enterprise. They are differentiable from other creditors because they own or effectively control a sizable fraction of the total equity claims on the enterprise. Everybody else other than the direct owner-investors—that is, all other individuals or institutions lending to the enterprise, whether through loans in the form of debt contracts or through holdings of bonds or equity claims—may be labeled *portfolio creditors*.

Direct owner-investors have dominant control, but they tend to be committed to the enterprise irrevocably, come good times or bad. The portfolio creditors are not committed as tightly, if at all, to the borrowing enterprise. Though without significant decisionmaking influence, portfolio creditors enjoy the partially offsetting advantage of a greater ability to escape from their financial contracts, reversing their extension of credit to the enterprise, if times turn bad.[19]

What minimum fraction of the total equity claims on an enterprise must be held before analysis identifies that group of holders as direct owner-investors exerting effective control? This question is murky even if attention is restricted to the purely domestic aspects. It becomes murkier still once the cross-border and cross-currency dimensions are considered

19. Direct owner-investors are typically individual ultimate savers or other enterprises that in turn are owned primarily by individual ultimate savers. Portfolio creditors can be either financial intermediaries or individual ultimate savers.

(chapter 6). For now, a rough-and-ready, if arbitrary, benchmark can serve as a rule of thumb. One may suppose that direct owner-investors hold at least 10 percent of the total equity claims, perhaps as much as 25 percent. A figure of 50 percent or more would comfortably qualify as constituting effective control in all but atypical circumstances.[20]

Sticky Capital and Skittish Capital; Voice versus Exit

The distinction between direct owner-investors and portfolio creditors leads to further important distinctions. Particular lenders and creditors in the financial reservoir can be arrayed along a spectrum according to the degree to which their financial claims represent *sticky capital* or, at the other extreme, *skittish capital*. The behavior of sticky capital is dominated by *voice*. Skittish capital is prone to exercise the option of *exit*.

Direct owner-investors are the archetypal holders of *sticky capital*. Because they own a sizable fraction of the equity claims on an enterprise and thereby exert the dominant influence on its decisions, the stakes for them are much higher than for any of the portfolio creditors. In key respects, direct owner-investors are stuck to the enterprise in either fair weather or foul. Because their ownership stake is high, their investment—their lending of savings—cannot be readily reversed. Even if conditions confronting the enterprise turn markedly adverse, they have little choice but to remain engaged and make the best of the unfavorable change in conditions.

Portfolio creditors are much less likely to perceive their commitments as irreversible. For most or all of them, credits to the enterprise are perceived as *nonsticky capital*, contingent on whether the enterprise's fortunes are working out as satisfactorily as when the lender's original commitment was made. The degree of nonstickiness, moreover, can change on short notice.

---

20. It is possible to imagine circumstances in which direct owner-investors in practice exert effective control of an enterprise with ownership of only a small fraction of the total equity (conceivably, with even less than 10 percent). In opposite extreme situations, direct owner-investors might conceivably hold a large fraction of the total equity (say, 35–55 percent), yet still not exert effective control. Such cases, however, are atypical. The discussion in the text ignores some issues about the effective control of enterprises that are important in real life. These include the relative powers exercised by professional managers (who may or may not be owners of sizable fractions of the corporation's equity shares) and whether there is a close or only loose correlation between the "control" of an enterprise and the "ownership" of its shares. Berle and Means (1932) was an early influential contribution to the literature on corporate control. For a textbook treatment, see Tirole (1992). Other references on corporate control and governance include Blair (1995); Blair and Stout (1999); and Tirole (1999, 2001).

The behavior of portfolio creditors may suddenly turn volatile, their commitments switching from firm to footloose with perhaps only minor alterations in information or expectations. Portfolio creditors can be preoccupied solely with their own expected return over a short horizon. They may be little concerned with the enterprise's long-run profitability and stability. Footloose extensions of credit to an enterprise with a time horizon limited to the short run—or, similarly, footloose market purchases of its equity shares—represent *skittish capital*.

The distinction between sticky capital and skittish capital is a distinction between two ends of a spectrum. Many intermediate points exist along the spectrum, characterized by varying combinations of stickiness and skittishness. The sticky-skittish spectrum in turn is correlated with the spectrum running from voice to exit.

Exit options and *voice options* in political and economic life were originally identified by Albert Hirschman.[21] From the perspective of an individual lender to an enterprise, the possibility of selling or otherwise terminating his credit, thus transferring his wealth to a different asset, is an *exit option*. Rather than remaining engaged in the activities of the enterprise and exercising *the option of voice*—trying favorably to influence the behavior of the enterprise—a skittish capitalist may choose to withdraw his wealth altogether. Such disengagement entails walking away, in effect an easy exit, rather than loyally staying involved to try to exert a constructive influence. Sticky capital exerts voice, remaining loyal. Skittish capital has little compunction about heading for the exit on slight provocation.

Stickiness versus skittishness and voice versus exit are themes that surface prominently in discussions of cross-border finance. The basic concepts, however, apply to financial activity purely within the confines of a domestic financial reservoir.

Different Financial Institutions at Different Stages of Development

The process of economic growth is closely associated with the expansion and increasing diversification of financial intermediation. Economists and historians agree, furthermore, that the financial system plays a critical role in the entire process of economic development. The causation between

21. Hirschman (1970).

growth and financial intermediation is complex and probably bidirectional. Growth in the production of goods and services and the accumulation of real capital have stimulated expansion and adaptation of the activities of financial institutions. No less important, innovations in financial intermediation have catalyzed real growth.[22]

As economic development proceeds, the financial infrastructure of an economy tends to expand relative to the real infrastructure. In other words, the network of financial interrelations among decisionmaking agents in the economy acquires greater density at an even more rapid rate than the network of goods and services transactions. This phenomenon has been evaluated with the "financial interrelations ratio," the ratio of the aggregate market value of all financial instruments to the value of tangible net national wealth (the value of all real capital). Increases in the financial interrelations ratio, however, may not continue without limit. Once a relatively advanced stage of development is attained, the financial infrastructure may grow only proportionately with the real infrastructure. A related conclusion is that the ratio of a capitalist economy's outstanding primary securities to its income rises sharply in the early stages of financial development but then eventually reaches a plateau.

Financial institutions tend to become relatively more important as economic growth proceeds. In particular, the share of financial intermediaries in the issuance and ownership of financial assets tends to rise over time. This trend reflects the growing separation and institutionalization of the functions of saving and investing. In the advanced industrial economies, the proportion of total financial assets accounted for by financial intermediaries has continued to increase even after the rise in the financial interrelations ratio has ceased.

A further manifestation of the links between financial and economic development is an increasing diversity in the types of financial institutions and in the types of instruments in which they specialize. At an early stage of development, banks with narrowly defined functions tend to emerge and dominate the financial system. As economic and financial growth proceeds, there is a gradual decline in the banking system's share of the assets of all financial institutions and a corresponding rise in the share of new types of institutions, such as thrift intermediaries, insurance companies,

---

22. The pioneering literature on the financial aspects of the growth process is dominated by the work of Goldsmith (1955, 1958, 1966, 1969, 1985) and Gurley and Shaw (1956, 1957, 1960). The generalizations in the text are drawn from this literature, in particular Goldsmith (1969).

government and private retirement funds, investment companies, finance companies, and securities brokers and dealers. Commensurate with the increasing specialization of the financial system, the relative share of direct intermediation in total financial activity may decline, while financial markets and securitized intermediation become more important. At any rate, the declining relative importance of the banking system entails a smaller role for direct intermediation through commercial banks.[23]

Evidence about the relative importance and catalytic role of securities markets in financial systems is inconclusive. More research needs to be done before economywide generalizations about securitized intermediation can rest on solid ground. In principle, the extent of securitization of the liabilities of ultimate investor-borrowers can be strongly influenced by factors other than the stage of development of the financial system or variations across geographical regions in real and financial activity.

Consider, for example, the information available to economic agents. Information of all sorts—in particular the information necessary to assess the creditworthiness of borrowers—is unevenly distributed in societies. Because information is differentially available, different agents have widely differing abilities to assess the risk of investments. The expertise of financial intermediaries in collecting and evaluating information about risks and creditworthiness is, as already emphasized, one major reason why intermediaries play a vital role in the process of economic growth.

Societies differ, however, in the social conventions and legal requirements that govern the availability of information. Such differences influence the structure of the financial system. Imagine two societies, one with and the other without laws and customs requiring ultimate borrowers to disclose extensive information about their income statements and balance sheets. The society without such laws and customs may emphasize personal connections and loyalties in assessing creditworthiness rather than extensive disclosure and wide dissemination of information; that society may even regard extensive disclosure as potentially destabilizing. The society with extensive disclosure requirements, because of its less uneven distribution of information, would have less skewness in differential ability to assess and monitor the creditworthiness of individual borrowers. Other things being equal, financial markets and securitized intermediation would be more developed in the society with extensive disclosure. The valuations

---

23. Important illustrations of this point occur in developing, emerging-market countries today, where banks are considerably more important (in relative terms) than in the industrial countries.

of securities in that society's markets could better incorporate information about creditworthiness. In the society with restricted disclosure, in contrast, access to information about the creditworthiness of individual ultimate borrowers would be highly skewed. To an even greater degree than in the extensive disclosure society, financial intermediaries would have a comparative advantage relative to the general public in evaluating investment proposals. Other things being equal, a smaller proportion of financial intermediation in the restricted information society would be channeled through financial markets.[24]

Potential Problems within the Financial System

Thus far I have reviewed basic concepts and described how financial activity can benefit the economy. Now I consider problems that financial activity can cause.

Mishaps: Mistakes and Accidents

Even in a well-functioning financial system, mistakes and accidents occur. Particular investments in real capital can turn out to be disappointments. Financial transactions associated with those investments, and with other individual financial claims, can go sour. Mistakes and accidents are inevitable in an economy in which the actors are fallible human beings, uncertainty and risk are rife, and asymmetric-information and principal-agent complexities abound.

By *mistake*, I mean a financial transaction for which, given information widely available at the time the contract is written, the lender or the borrower, perhaps both, make judgments that are demonstrably faulty by objective standards. Judgments depend in part on expectations about the future. The force of "faulty" is that a large majority of other decisionmakers, confronted with the same circumstances and with the widely available information, would form different expectations about the future and would recommend against the parties entering into the contract. For example, if an ultimate borrower takes out a bank loan for investment in capital goods whose production technology is widely known to be high cost and inefficient relative to available alternatives, or for investment in capital goods to

---

24. Whether a society should prefer extensive or restricted disclosure of information about creditworthiness is a complex issue. Advantages and disadvantages have been claimed for each approach, and examples of each are readily found in different parts of the world economy.

produce and market a new widget that has already been shown in many consumer surveys to be a dud, the investor and the bank, or both, are probably making a mistake.[25] A lender may do a demonstrably sloppy job of assessing the creditworthiness of a borrower. A borrower may flagrantly conceal relevant information about his creditworthiness. A borrower may even fraudulently misrepresent his circumstances and deliberately plan not to honor the contractual obligations into which he is entering.

With the passage of time, faulty judgments and transparently incorrect expectations tend to come to light. It then becomes clear to the contracting parties and others that the financial transaction was a mistake. Typically, the financial contract cannot be honored as written, and the consequences of the mistake must somehow be dealt with.

Accidents are even more common. Lenders and borrowers may form expectations and reach judgments that seem plausible given the circumstances and the best information widely available at the time they commit to their financial contract. But unexpected changes in the economy can alter the viability of financial transactions, making it difficult or impossible for borrowers to honor the terms of their contracts. What is plausible ex ante turns out not to be so ex post.

It is convenient to use the single term *mishaps* to refer generally to financial transactions plagued by mistakes, accidents, or both.

What happens when, because of a mishap, a financial contract cannot be, or is not, fulfilled? Sometimes the lender and borrower can agree to rewrite their contract. Alternatively, the allocation of losses from a defaulted contract and the resolution of disputes may be submitted to arbitration. In still other cases, defaults may trigger recourse to litigation. If the mishap has been severe enough to render a borrower insolvent (that is, causing the value of assets to fall below the value of all liabilities), bankruptcy proceedings of some sort will be inevitable.

Defaults, insolvencies, bankruptcies, arbitration mechanisms for dispute resolution—all are inescapable features of capitalist economies with complex financial systems. Such situations are unfortunate. They generate losses for individuals and costs for the economy. However, given pervasive uncertainty and risk, coupled with innovation in the economy, they also have a beneficial silver lining. Mistakes typically *should* lead to losses, in

---

25. Of course, the particular investor, the particular bank, or both probably do not possess (or correctly interpret) the information that is widely available to others. Were they to have it, they would most likely avoid the mistake.

part to create incentives that will reduce the chances of future mistakes in similar financial contracts. Accidents are often associated with fundamental changes in the economy, reducing the profitability of some types of economic and financial activity and increasing the profitability of others. Obsolescent products and industries *should* be phased out to sustain the long-run health of the economy.

Accounting, Audit, Data, and Legal Systems

Because of inevitable mishaps, a smoothly functioning financial system must be supported by procedures for the monitoring and enforcement of contracts and for working out the consequences when particular financial contracts are not honored. Standardized and widely accepted procedures for accounting and auditing are necessary accompaniments for successful monitoring and enforcement. The collection, aggregation, and widespread dissemination of data about the activities of financial institutions are also basic requirements. And the legal system must provide a foundation of laws and rules that facilitate the resolution of disputes about contracts and the handling of defaults and insolvencies.

A utilities infrastructure, acting like a network of pipes, pumping stations, and storage warehouses, is the essential core of the financial system reservoir. Privately owned financial intermediaries and privately operated financial markets are prominent parts of that core. Other key components, reflecting collective action by the society's residents, are not private, but governmental, or a mixture of private and governmental. The legal system is a vital nonprivate part of the utilities infrastructure. Institutions and procedures for accounting, auditing, and collecting and disseminating data typically have nonprivate as well as private components. Chapter 3 discusses other essential nonprivate components, such as the central bank and governmental institutions for supervising and regulating private financial intermediaries.

Why are sound accounting standards, audit practices, and data dissemination important? The short answer is that the economy and financial system cannot allocate resources efficiently if the information available about businesses and financial institutions is seriously incomplete or grossly misleading. Full, timely, and accurate disclosure of financial results and other information material to investment decisions is a necessary—albeit not sufficient—condition for the appropriate identification and pricing of risk. Standardized norms and rules for presenting information, applied consistently over time, mitigate the difficulties of comparing the financial performances of different business and financial institutions. Standardized audit procedures, providing for periodic reviews by outside, independent auditors of internal control mechanisms and financial statements, ensure accurate, timely disclosure and facilitate the legal verification of contracts. Data for individual financial institutions and aggregated data for the various parts of the financial system, compiled and disseminated by statistical agencies, provide a foundation for all participants in the financial system to evaluate trends and risks for the system as a whole.

The legal system is a foundation for all aspects of the economy, not least the financial system. The legal system identifies property rights and their status relative to other rights; establishes procedures for resolving disputes about how financial contracts are written and interpreted (including rules for how and when disputes can be brought into courts of law); governs what practices are appropriate in the monitoring, enforcement, and legal verification of contracts; and sets out rules to condition arbitration procedures as an alternative to court proceedings.

The default and bankruptcy provisions of the legal system are critical for the financial system. Bankruptcy can take a variety of forms, such as liquidation of the defaulting borrower's assets or business, court-overseen reorganization, receivership (a third party selected to run the business and work out the consequences), structured bargaining supervised by a third party, or administration of the assets or business by a judge or other court-appointed official.[26] *Liquidation* is a harsher course of action from the perspective of the defaulting borrower than is *reorganization*. In U.S. law, liquidation occurs under Chapter 7 of the bankruptcy statutes; the defaulting borrower's operations are shut down, the existing assets are liquidated, and the proceeds of the liquidation are distributed among creditors according to some priority rule. Reorganization bankruptcy, occurring under Chapter 11 of the statutes, typically entails a court-approved stay of all litigation in which the borrower is a defendant; during the period of reorganization, the defaulting borrower is allowed to continue operating and to repay creditors from future earnings, rather than shutting down and repaying the creditors from the proceeds of asset liquidation.

Why have bankruptcy procedures at all? The basic rationales are, again, to promote efficient resource allocation and a stable evolution of the economy in the face of inevitable mishaps. A good bankruptcy procedure

---

26. See, for example, White (2002) and Brierley and Vlieghe (1999).

should, as much as possible, preserve the ex post value of a debtor in default. By providing the debtor with temporary protection from creditors and possibly with access to interim finance with some form of de facto seniority, bankruptcy reorganization procedures enable an enterprise whose value as a going concern exceeds its breakup value to continue to operate.[27] To this end, it may be necessary to protect the debtor enterprise from creditors who wish to invoke remedies available to them individually as a result of the nonperformance of the debt contract. But a good bankruptcy procedure should also penalize the debtor (in the case of a business enterprise, its management) to provide adequate ex ante incentives for the debtor to manage its assets well while undergoing bankruptcy. By specifying ex ante rules for the distribution of partial or delayed payments on impaired debt claims among different creditors—and more broadly for an appropriate distribution of the debtor's ex post value across its creditors (one that respects the priority of claims among the various classes of creditors)—bankruptcy procedures reduce uncertainty and make it easier for markets to price risk.

The legal provisions governing bankruptcy are necessarily complex: they require a subtle balancing of the rights and obligations of debtors and creditors. Hence the objectives of bankruptcy are partly in conflict. The bankruptcy laws must encourage adherence to the ex ante provisions of financial contracts. If debtors were not substantially penalized in bankruptcy, future debtors would be tempted to escape from their financial contracts by resorting to bankruptcy. At the same time, the bankruptcy laws seek to prevent an uncoordinated, costly "grab race" among creditors that could lead to a fire-sale dismantlement of the debtor's assets and a collective loss to all parties that is much larger than the losses that would otherwise occur through a cooperative bargaining process. The great difficulty in the design of bankruptcy laws is to strike the best possible balance between the competing objectives.[28]

Financial Storms: Herding Behavior and Contagion

Ideally, the financial system should be highly resilient. Particular mishaps should not cause systemwide difficulties. Though mishaps cannot be prevented altogether, they should have merely local significance.

---

27. De facto seniority for interim finance means that the claims of new interim creditors are given precedence over those of previous, prebankruptcy creditors.

28. Subsequent chapters comment further on standards for accounting, auditing, and data dissemination and on the legal provisions incorporated in financial contracts.

In practice, such ideal resilience is unattainable. Even when sound legal, accounting, and auditing systems are in place and even when financial contracts are carefully designed, mishaps have the potential to set off waves in the reservoir that can spread well beyond the locality in which they originate.

Small mishaps usually have small consequences. If a mistake or an accident affects only the original borrower and lender and a few others closely associated with them, the consequences may well be contained locally. Only a few ripples may disturb the reservoir. The more sizable the original borrower and lender, and the more extensive their interrelationships with other economic agents, however, the more widespread may be the spillovers. In effect, sizable waves rather than ripples may be set in motion. Large enough waves have the potential to generate stormy conditions throughout the entire financial system reservoir.

Storms can spread and become virulent because the financial system is prone to herding behavior, contagion, and excessive volatility in asset prices. The result of such behaviors can lead to overreactions, even to panic, occasionally turning a storm into a hurricane.

The features of the financial system that permit storms to spread are, paradoxically, the same features that generate the benefits of financial activity. The maturity transformation provided by financial intermediaries permits ultimate savers to hold their savings in the form of short-term, liquid assets while ultimate investors simultaneously issue long-term, illiquid liabilities. The negotiability of securities traded in financial markets provides liquidity to the individual saver while facilitating the access of ultimate investors to long-term financing. Yet maturity transformation and negotiable securities come symbiotically linked with the problems of information asymmetries and risk evaluation. Seen through negative lenses, the financial system provides excessive opportunities for liquidity and is excessively quick in transmitting asymmetric (and sometimes misleading) information.

The incompleteness and uneven distribution of uncertain information about risk is again crucial for understanding why herding behavior occurs. It is costly for any individual lender (ultimate saver or financial intermediary) to acquire additional information. So imperfectly informed lenders often resort to shortcuts in assessing risks and new developments. Incomplete, sometimes incorrect, information is passed along, not only about actual mishaps, but even rumors of mishaps. Furthermore, financial system participants may merely examine each other's behavior to make inferences about how expectations of the future are changing. Observing the decisions of others who have already acted, for example, a participant may merely imitate those decisions, reasoning that the information signaled by others' actions is more consequential than any further information available to him. The end result of such "informational cascades" is that participants in the financial system may herd together rather than act as heterogeneous individuals forming independent, diverse expectations. In crisis conditions, informational cascades may turn into informational hurricanes.[29]

Herding behavior may even exhibit features of crowd psychology. As Bernard Baruch argued during the 1930s Depression, "anyone taken as an individual is tolerably sensible and reasonable—[but] as a member of a crowd, he at once becomes a blockhead."[30] The behavior is like that of blackbirds on a telephone line: if one or two fly off, they all fly off; when one or two come back, they all come back.

Still another twist on crowd psychology is captured by Charles Dickens in an exchange in chapter 13 of *Pickwick Papers*. When Pickwick and his traveling companions are observing a local election campaign, Snodgrass asks Pickwick whether he should emulate the crowd's enthusiastic shouts. Pickwick advises that "It's always best on [these] occasions to do what the mob do." Snodgrass follows with the question: "But suppose there are two mobs?" Pickwick amplifies: "Shout with the largest."

Episodes of turbulence, during which financial agents exhibit herding or panicky behavior, are common in financial history. Exuberant trading in tulip bulbs in Holland in the 1630s and the South Sea Bubble in 1720 are notorious examples from the distant past. More recent examples are the stock market crashes in 1929 and 1987, and the 1997–98 events in stock and exchange markets after the Asian and Russian financial crises.[31]

Information skewness and herding behavior can give rise to contagion effects, which in turn increase the potential for a storm in the financial system to intensify. For financial instruments bought and sold in auction

---

29. Informational cascades are defined and the resulting behavior analyzed in Bikhchandani, Hirshleifer, and Welch (1992, 1998). Lee (1998) examines "informational avalanches" that lead to market crashes.

30. See Baruch's foreword to the reprint of MacKay (1841).

31. For more on the history, see for example Kindleberger (1978); Kindleberger and Laffargue (1982); and MacKay (1841). For summaries of the financial events of 1997–98, see among many others Kristof and co-authors (1999); Agenor and others (1999); and Kenen (2001).

markets, prices can change quickly and by large amounts. Contagion thus can spread rapidly in securities markets. It tends to spread less rapidly among claimants on financial intermediaries. There, too, however, a decline in confidence in one financial intermediary can lead to a sudden decline in confidence in its creditors. With herding behavior and contagion, even otherwise healthy financial intermediaries may come under suspicion. Though the contagion may spread less quickly among financial intermediaries than directly in financial markets, the consequences for financial intermediaries can be even more virulent.

When confidence declines in securities markets, the damage can often be contained better because of the immediate change in prices. In contrast, when a decline in confidence buffets banks and other financial intermediaries, the immediate consequences of contagion are on balance-sheet quantities rather than on prices. Intermediaries may experience runs on their relatively liquid deposit liabilities. And most of their assets are typically illiquid. Because an intermediary is assumed to have better information about its own assets than prospective purchasers, it will be able to sell its assets only by sharply driving down their effective prices. Just at the time when an intermediary may need access to other intermediaries to obtain an infusion of liquidity, moreover, its potential sources of liquidity may dry up. If an intermediary does sell its assets at fire sale prices, it damages its own balance sheet and prospective solvency. Those owning claims on the intermediary will thus have still more of an incentive to run.

A hallmark characteristic of contagion is that turbulence occurs in different parts of the financial reservoir almost contemporaneously. The initial causes of the contagion may be clearly traceable to fundamental shifts in economic conditions. For example, several parts of the financial system may all be subject to a common large shock (late spring blizzards that destroy crops over a wide geographical area). Or turbulence may spread rapidly because of extensive interdependencies among parts of the financial reservoir (bankruptcy of one large financial institution undermining the soundness of the balance sheets of numerous others). In instances of contagion due to such common shocks and within-system spillovers, the shifts in fundamentals should and typically do give rise to prompt readjustments of risk assessments and financial prices.

But there is also another type of contagion—*pure contagion*—in which turbulence is traceable not to alterations in economic fundamentals but rather to sudden shifts in the interpretation of existing information. Economists have tried to understand pure-contagion effects as a situation in which financial activity is subject to multiple equilibriums and self-fulfilling expectations (discussed in more detail later).[32]

At first blush, herding behavior and contagion in the financial system might appear to be "irrational." But what may appear irrational at the system level may be entirely rational for individuals.[33] When individuals all race for the exits in a burning theater, their behavior can be fully strategic, yet at the same time collectively damaging. Analyses of economic and social behavior have identified numerous instances in which noncooperative competition and unconstrained maximization by individual agents, while rational for each individual, can be irrational for all individuals together. In the financial system, an unchecked crisis is a situation in which each financial institution and customer can behave rationally and strategically and yet, through herding behavior, still produce a collective outcome that is highly undesirable for society as a whole.[34]

Storms in the financial system are not necessarily traceable to mishaps that originate within the financial system itself. Mishaps that originate outside the financial system, in the production and consumption of goods and services, have just as much potential to trigger waves and storms in the financial system. The viability of financial contracts depends on the entire range of actual and expected events in the economy, both real as well as financial.

Excessive Volatility in Asset Prices?

The markets in the financial system in which negotiable financial instruments are traded provide sensitive valuations, promptly reflecting new information. The liquidity in the markets facilitates the easy transfer of existing debts and equity claims from one owner to another.

---

32. Masson (1999a, 1999b) distinguishes between these different forms of contagion.

33. For discussion, see, for example, Bator (1958); Olson (1971); Kahn (1966); Schelling (1974); and Hirsch (1976).

34. Technical analyses of herding behavior and related phenomena are found in, for example, Diamond and Dybvig (1983); DeLong and others (1990a, 1990b); Scharfstein and Stein (1990); Banerjee (1992); Lakonishok, Shleifer, and Vishny (1992); Avery and Zemsky (1998); Allen and Gale (2000a, 2000b); and Bikhchandani and Sharma (2001). The concluding sentence of Bulow and Klemperer (1994, p. 22) emphasizes that "it is precisely because bidders are rational and strategic that they are so sensitive to market information and adopt behavior that leads to frenzies and crashes."

Remember, however, that the markets for primary securities—the negotiable liabilities of ultimate investor-borrowers—are also valuing the economy's past investments, its real capital goods. Today's market valuations of these existing assets ("old investments" in reproducible real capital goods) may diverge from the costs of similar assets produced today ("new investments" in those reproducible real capital goods). When discrepancies arise between the market valuations of old investments and the replacement costs of newly produced counterparts, the incentives to undertake new investments are altered. The expansion of existing businesses and the formation of new ones is stimulated when the market valuations of old investments significantly exceed the current replacement costs of the same assets, and vice versa when market valuations fall well below current replacement costs.

The sensitivity of market valuations, especially in stormy weather if herding behavior and contagion magnify the consequences of triggering mishaps, can entail sudden, sharp changes in market prices. Such changes in market prices may unhitch asset valuations from the long-term profit and risk calculations that are the fundamental determinants of whether investments in reproducible real capital goods will be advantageous for the economy. Sensitive market valuations and easy liquidity, therefore, can turn out to be a mixed blessing.

Criticisms of "inappropriate" valuations and "excessive" variability in the prices of financial instruments were voiced clearly by John Maynard Keynes in the 1930s. The liquidity provided in financial markets is useful, Keynes stressed, because investments that are "fixed" for the society as a whole are thus made "liquid" for individuals. Yet an element of precariousness is thereby introduced into investment decisions:

> The Stock Exchange revalues many investments every day and the revaluations give a frequent opportunity to the individual (though not to the community as a whole) to revise his commitments. It is as though a farmer, having tapped his barometer after breakfast, could decide to remove his capital from the farming business between 10 and 11 in the morning and reconsider whether he should return to it later in the week. But the daily revaluations of the Stock Exchange, though they are primarily made to facilitate transfers of old investments between one individual and another, inevitably exert a decisive influence on the rate of current investment. . . . Certain classes of investment are governed by the average expectations of those who

deal on the Stock Exchange as revealed in the price of shares, rather than by the genuine expectations of the professional entrepreneur.[35]

One might suppose, wrote Keynes, that expert professionals, because they possess knowledge and judgment beyond that of the average private investor, could correct any vagaries introduced into financial market prices by ignorance or crowd psychology. But Keynes argued that the energies and skill of the professional investor and speculator are mainly occupied with foreseeing changes in market valuations a short time ahead of the general public rather than with making superior long-term forecasts of the probable yield of an investment over its whole life. In a famous passage, he likened financial market security selections to

> those newspaper competitions in which the competitors have to pick out the six prettiest faces from a hundred photographs, the prize being awarded to the competitor whose choice most nearly corresponds to the average preferences of the competitors as a whole; so that each competitor has to pick, not those faces which he himself finds prettiest, but those which he thinks likeliest to catch the fancy of the other competitors, all of whom are looking at the problem from the same point of view. It is not a case of choosing those which, to the best of one's judgment, are really the prettiest, nor even those which average opinion genuinely thinks the prettiest. We have reached the third degree where we devote our intelligences to anticipating what average opinion expects the average opinion to be. And there are some, I believe, who practice the fourth, fifth, and higher degrees.[36]

The assertion that financial markets can generate excessive volatility in asset prices, resulting in prices that significantly deviate from underlying fundamental valuations, has been subjected to intensive technical study in recent decades. Researchers have focused, for example, on the contention that the prices of equity claims vary by a multiple of the underlying variability in dividends and earnings. Another hypothesis is that the prices of long-term bonds fluctuate more than can be explained by the variability of short-term interest rates. Evidence has been marshaled to show that the

35. Keynes (1936, p. 151).
36. Keynes (1936, p. 156).

valuation of businesses in financial markets has sometimes drifted far away, for extended periods, from estimated valuations based on the replacement costs of the businesses' actual assets and the present values of the future returns those assets could be expected to earn.[37]

Related avenues of technical research have investigated the possibilities that financial markets can be afflicted by multiple equilibriums or disrupted by bubbles sparked by transient speculation. The idea that financial markets could settle either on a bad equilibrium driven by pessimistic expectations or, alternatively, on a good equilibrium where optimistic participants generate a favorable outcome is closely related to the phenomena of herding behavior and informational cascades already discussed. Loosely defined, a bubble occurs when the actual price of an asset deviates from its fundamental valuation because of *self-fulfilling expectations* of changes in price. Multiple equilibriums and bubbles involve situations in which self-fulfilling expectations of financial market participants change in ways that are not identifiably related to changes in economic fundamentals. Rapid shifts in expectations with corresponding shifts from one equilibrium to another are a likely explanation for why financial markets can exert lax discipline in buoyant boom periods but then reverse themselves to impose excessive discipline in conditions of financial crisis.[38]

Technical research on the volatility of financial market prices and analytical models generating multiple equilibriums is ongoing. As yet no clear consensus has formed about how to interpret the empirical evidence. Nonetheless, a large number of economists, probably a majority, subscribe to at least a weak form of the hypothesis that financial markets can at times generate "excessive" volatility in asset prices. At the least, it is widely acknowledged that the financial system has a proclivity to be buffeted by

37. Relevant studies include LeRoy and Porter (1981); Shiller (1979, 1981, 1984, 1989); Modigliani and Cohn (1979); Brainard, Shoven, and Weiss (1980); Flavin (1983); and De Bondt and Thaler (1985).

38. Contributions to the technical literature on analysis of multiple equilibriums, speculative bubbles, and related expectational phenomena include (in addition to the references on herding behavior and contagion cited in previous footnotes) Diamond and Dybvig (1983); Salant and Henderson (1978); Flood and Garber (1982); Blanchard and Watson (1982); and Caplin and Leahy (1994). Masson (1999a) provides a recent survey; see also Obstfeld (1998). In the literature about international financial crises, considered in chapter 6, analytical efforts to study multiple-equilibrium situations are known as "second-generation" models (to distinguish them from earlier models that emphasize economic fundamentals but ignore the possibility of self-fulfilling expectations). Research that stresses so-called conformity and "neighborhood" (or "network") effects is another related literature; see, for example, Brock and Durlauf (1995, 2002); H. P. Young (1996, 1998, 1999); and Durlauf and Young (2001).

occasional storms. It is noncontroversial that the market valuations of old investments in real capital goods are much more volatile than the replacement costs of newly produced counterparts.

The issue of volatility in the market valuations of assets brings the exposition back, full circle, to where this chapter began. The most basic function of financial activity is to reconcile the needs and preferences of ultimate savers to the very different—frequently conflicting—needs and preferences of ultimate investors. Several reasons have already been given for believing that this reconciliation may not proceed smoothly. Indeed, the financial system may at times even produce "reconciliation failures." Given the phenomena of financial storms—mishaps magnified by herding behavior and contagion and by the extreme sensitivity of market valuations of financial instruments—the financial system is an imperfect, and periodically even a faulty, reconciliation mechanism.

When stormy weather arises, no matter whether it initially originates inside or outside the financial reservoir, it not only buffets the reservoir. It can also disrupt the broader real economy. To extend the analogy, the financial turbulence may itself become an important determinant of "droughts" or "floods" in investment in reproducible real capital goods (and the corresponding real aggregate saving behavior).

The droughts or floods in investment, moreover, are not just a consequence of financial turbulence. The very notion of reconciliation failure is a reminder that the causal links between the financial system and the real economy are bidirectional and complex. If ultimate savers and ultimate investors really are to make decentralized, independent decisions, the benefits of which are great, there must inevitably be a precariousness about the process through which the (ex ante) individual saving decisions and the (ex ante) individual investment decisions are adjusted so as to be consistent in the aggregate. (The aggregated saving and investment decisions, when aggregate saving and investment are measured ex post, must of course be identical for the economy as a whole.)

The reconciliation dilemma confronting society as a whole is expressed in another memorable passage from Keynes:

> An act of individual saving means—so to speak—a decision not to have dinner today. But it does *not* necessitate a decision to have dinner or to buy a pair of boots a week hence or a year hence or to consume any specified thing at any specified date. Thus it depresses the business of preparing today's dinner without stimulating the business

of making ready for some future act of consumption. It is not a sub-stitution of future consumption-demand for present consumption-demand—it is a net diminution of such demand. Moreover, the expectation of future consumption is so largely based on current experience of present consumption that a reduction in the latter is likely to depress the former. . . . If saving consisted not merely in abstaining from present consumption but in placing simultaneously a specific order for future consumption, the effect might indeed be different. For in that case the expectation of some future yield from investment would be improved, and the resources released from preparing for present consumption could be turned over to preparing for the future consumption. . . . The trouble arises, therefore, because the act of saving implies, not a substitution for present con-sumption of some specific additional consumption which requires for its preparation just as much immediate economic activity as would have been required by present consumption equal in value to the sum saved, but a desire for "wealth" as such, that is for a poten-tiality of consuming an unspecified article at an unspecified time.[39]

The problematic coordination of the plans of savers and investors is thus still another reason why financial activity can generate volatile valuations of assets. Tobin has identified the "highly imperfect" coordination of saving and investment through the financial system as "a fundamental source of macroeconomic instability and of the opportunity for macroeconomic policies for stabilization."[40]

The preceding discussion can be condensed into a summary generaliza-tion: The financial system is inherently fragile, inherently vulnerable to instability. Financial activity cannot be free of risk or problems. Deep-seated, innate features of financial activity expose the reservoir—the col-lection of savings and their allocation to investments—to episodes of stormy weather, even to an occasional hurricane-level crisis.

39. Keynes (1936, pp. 210–11). The passage is quoted in Tobin's Nobel Prize Lecture (1981).
40. Tobin (1981, p. 16); see also Tobin (1984).

3 Collective Governance for Financial Activity

S ocieties develop institutions for fostering actions taken jointly by or on behalf of their residents. Such institutions and actions constitute *collective governance.*

The utilities infrastructure of the financial system requires collectively organized institutions as well as privately owned financial intermediaries and privately operated financial markets. This chapter summarizes fundamental points about those nonprivate institutions and their vital roles in supporting a healthy, stable evolution of financial activity. To understand the basic ideas, it is again helpful to suppress the international dimensions of financial activity, thereby highlighting the purely domestic aspects of collective governance.

Collective Governance and Government

Collective action requires purposive, cooperative behavior by one or more groups. Virtually by definition, collective action entails group consultation and group decisionmaking. Institutions for collective governance grow out of consultation and decisionmaking by groups. For practical purposes, collective governance is a synonym for collective action.

Imagine a spectrum to represent the ways that individual agents formulate and implement decisions. At one extreme of the spectrum, decisions by individuals are atomistic and completely decentralized, made without consultation with other agents and without any cooperative efforts to share information. Collective activities and thus collective governance entails moving away—in some degree, in some form or another—from that extreme of decentralized decisionmaking.

Groups can form in a multitude of ways. At one extreme, they can be narrowly exclusive. At the other, some groups are sufficiently comprehensive to include most or all individuals in society. Even loosely organized groups can be construed as engaged in some type of collective governance, if only informal. Many groups go further, establishing and maintaining institutions to facilitate their collective activities.

Strictly speaking, *governance* should not be used as a synonym for *government*. Actions taken by or through governmental institutions are one very important form of collective governance, but not the only form. Government entities are an important subset of institutions fostering collective action, but only a subset. The concept of governance is much broader than the concept of government. Governance can encompass collective action channeled not only through government institutions but through many other groups or institutions that are not part of government at any level.

As societies increase in complexity, new forms of collective action continue to evolve. The types and numbers of nongovernmental institutions proliferate. Even more than in the past, therefore, "governance is no longer the preserve of governments."[1]

The broad concept of governance and the narrower concept of government both entail purposive behavior underpinned by a presumptive sharing of goals. But government is typically backed by formal authority, by powers to ensure implementation and compliance with collectively decided policies. For the types of governance not taking the form of government, the shared goals may or may not derive from legal and formally prescribed responsibilities. Many nongovernmental groups may have weak powers to ensure compliance.

Another difference between governance and government stems from the comprehensiveness of the groups through which collective action is fostered. The broader concept of governance embraces the activities of closely limited as well as widely inclusive groups. Hence governance subsumes all

---

1. Chapter 7 emphasizes the particular importance of this theme for collective actions across national borders. The quotation is from Rosenau (1997, p. 444). A similar theme is emphasized in Rosenau and Czempiel (1992).

of "civil society," the numerous groups and associations that are neither commercial (corporations, for example) nor governmental. A government institution, in contrast, typically derives its authority from—at least in principle, if not always effectively in practice—the entirety of individuals in the territorial jurisdiction where the governmental collective action is exercised.

Market Failures and Government Failures

Capitalist, free-enterprise economies rely heavily on decentralized decisionmaking. Markets generate consistency among those decisions. The essence of the explanation for the emphasis on decentralized decisions and market institutions is straightforward. Individual needs and preferences are heterogeneous. Economic life is complex. Highly decentralized decisionmaking expressed through markets is the least inefficient way to cope with this diversity and complexity.

At the same time, valid reasons exist for avoiding exclusive reliance on markets. The most fundamental rationale for collective governance is to foster cooperative action in contexts in which individual decentralized decisionmaking would otherwise produce an inferior outcome. Analysts use terms such as externalities, market failures, and public goods to refine understanding of this rationale and to evaluate types of collective governance.

An *externality* arises when an activity by one agent affects, favorably or unfavorably, the well-being of other agents who are not decisionmaking participants in (who are "external" to) the activity. Economic inefficiency often results from externalities, because private costs (benefits) differ from social, collective costs (benefits). Polluting smoke from a factory that causes discomfort to neighborhood residents, for example, creates a negative externality. A favorable externality occurs when a homeowner beautifies the landscaping on his lot, thereby raising property values and improving the attractiveness of living in the neighborhood for other residents.[2]

Market failures arise when decentralized private decisions do not result in efficient allocations of scarce resources. Externalities of some sort are

2. More precise definitions of externalities require that the utility or production relationships for, say, agents B and C be affected by variables chosen by agent A when A does not pay attention to the effects on the welfares of B and C. If A were to receive or pay compensation for the activity that gives rise to costs or benefits for B and C, the situation would not qualify as an externality that creates inefficiency and resource misallocation. The technical literature also makes other distinctions, such as that between pecuniary and technological externalities.

usually involved in market failures. Because of market failures, collective remedial action that "internalizes the externalities" may be desirable. Such remedial action typically involves the supply of *public goods* (or amelioration of public "bads"). In the absence of a collective catalyst, public goods tend to be provided inadequately, if provided at all (public bads tend to be inadequately ameliorated). Public goods have one or both of two distinctive properties: if a public good is provided, all who value it tend to benefit whether or not they contribute to the cost of providing it; and if a public good is provided to any individual, it is or can be provided at little or no additional cost to others.

Externalities may not cause a misallocation of resources if transactions costs are negligible and if property rights are well defined and enforceable. In many practical situations, however, property rights are not well defined. Transactions costs are often nonnegligible. Thus there will exist, in particular circumstances, a potential role for collective action—some form of centralization of decisions—to try to correct market failures by supplying public goods (or increasing the incentives for others to do so).[3]

Just as in the particular case of herding behavior in financial markets, market failures more generally are deeply rooted in decentralized decisionmaking. Business cycles, for example, are a prominent feature of the way decentralized market economies function. Booms and then busts may be more prevalent in the financial system than in the broader economy as a whole. But booms and busts are endemic even in production and employment.

The existence of numerous market failures is not a sufficient reason for concluding that the society should dispense with markets and decentralized decisionmaking. Not at all! Collective governance that aspires to correct market failures can itself be costly or misguided. Even collective governance organized through smaller, nongovernmental groups can be ill advised and counterproductive. Interventions by government institutions have still higher probabilities of going awry.

Government failures can be just as damaging as market failures. A supposed government remedy for a negative externality can be even worse than

---

3. For discussion of the general analytical issues raised by externalities, market failures, and public goods, see, for example, Bator (1958); Coase (1960); Kahn (1966); Olson (1971); Baumol and Oates (1975); Schelling (1974, 1978); the contributions in Barry and Hardin (1982); and Greenwald and Stiglitz (1986). The growing importance of externalities and public goods in modern industrial societies is a major theme in Hirsch (1976). The literatures on herding behavior, multiple equilibriums, and network and neighborhood effects identified in the footnotes to chapter 2 are also highly relevant.

the disease. Government bureaucracies, like any large private organizations, can sometimes be rigid and inefficient in implementing their objectives. Government institutions can be captured by special interests or even undermined by explicit corruption, thereby creating negative externalities themselves.

In virtually every political jurisdiction, even in small localities but especially in larger geographical areas, the interests of residents tend to be heterogeneous and partly in conflict. Unambiguously preferred methods of resolving conflict seldom exist. The greater the heterogeneity, the larger the likely difficulties. Most consequentially, the interests of the individuals who exercise government power in the jurisdiction may differ significantly from the interests of some or all of the rest of the population. The extent of such differences depends on the scope that exists for government officials to advance personal goals by abusing public responsibilities.

Effective collective governance requires accountability and transparency. Their absence makes government failures probable. Without accountability of government institutions, the conflicting interests of the jurisdiction's residents are unlikely to be resolved with everyone's interests being taken into account. Thus public goods are much less likely to be supplied efficiently. Achieving accountability depends on government actions having substantial transparency. A jurisdiction's government cannot possibly be held accountable if the jurisdiction's residents have inadequate information about the government's goals and activities.

It is not possible to specify in advance and in a contractually binding manner exactly what decisions may have to be taken by government officials in all the conceivable circumstances that may arise. Given this uncertainty, it is practical to grant government officials general authority to formulate and implement a wide variety of decisions. Yet the jurisdiction's residents need to retain a residual right—for example, through periodic elections—to deprive the officials of their authority if the officials are no longer thought to be exercising the authority appropriately. (The situation is partly analogous to that in a large, privately owned corporation, in which the shareholders grant general rights of control to managers but retain the possibility of replacing the managers if the rights are exercised inappropriately.)

Just as society does not repudiate markets merely because of market failures, society does not eschew government institutions merely because government failures are widespread. The market failures and issues of collective governance that are the rationale for government activities do not obligingly become unimportant just because government entities can and do make mistakes.

A pragmatic, balanced view of political economy recognizes that government institutions and markets are typically complements rather than substitutes. Each provides a constraint on, and facilitates the functioning of, the other.

Essential Elements of Collective Governance for Financial Activity

Government institutions may catalyze, or undertake themselves, many types of collective actions. The primary concern here is with the functions of government especially pertinent to financial activity. The focus here is thus on the provision of those collective goods (or mitigation of collective bads) that are essential underpinnings for the smooth functioning of the financial system.[4]

One essential element of collective governance for financial activity is a *reliable legal system* backed by governmentally organized courts. Equally essential are *sound accounting standards*, *effective audit procedures*, and the *collection and widespread dissemination of information about the financial system*.

Accounting, auditing, and adequate disclosure of information require collective monitoring. To be effective, monitoring requires the possibility of collective enforcement actions. Monitoring and enforcement are the essence of the supervision and regulation of financial institutions. The functions of government thus include the *prudential oversight of financial activity* as an important special case of collective surveillance.

A further essential characteristic of a sound financial system is the exercise of *collective leadership in times of financial crisis*. As part of this leadership, a lender-of-last-resort institution may provide emergency assistance to temporarily illiquid and troubled financial institutions. Such collective action is a specific example of the more general government function of crisis management.

The *macroeconomic policies* of a national government critically influence the general climate within which a nation's financial system and the wider economy operate. Both the monetary policy of the nation's central bank and the fiscal policies of the different layers of government jurisdictions are

---

4. To provide background and establish context for government functions dealing with financial activity, the full range of possible governmental functions is sketched in chapter 7.

critical components of the general macroeconomic environment. Thus macroeconomic policies are no less a collective good, and no less vital, than many other collective goods supplied by government.

The preceding dimensions of collective governance for financial activity are examined further in the remaining sections of this chapter.

One other possible collective good for financial activity merits brief identification. A local or national government may establish a financial intermediary operated as a government (or quasi-government) institution. If a government intermediary exists, its financial transactions will promote different matches among borrowers and lenders in the financial system than would otherwise prevail if financial activity were left entirely to private sector financial institutions.

Why might members of a society wish its government to be directly involved in financial activity, channeling savings to particular ultimate investors? Three possible motives, all controversial, can be identified. First, explicit imperfections—market failures and externalities as discussed above—may be thought to exist in some parts of the nation's financial reservoir. Government lending, it could then be argued, might beneficially offset such imperfections and thereby enhance the efficiency of the financial system. Second, government lending might seek to reallocate financial resources to achieve social goals. Certain investment projects might be deemed to have social returns that exceed the market returns available to private lenders and investors. Rather than undertaking the projects itself, financed directly with government investment expenditures, the government might provide loan guarantees to private investors or lend to them at below-market interest rates, thereby inducing private investors to undertake the projects they would not have otherwise favored. Third, a straightforward redistribution goal might be the driving force behind the establishment and operations of the government intermediary. The intermediary's lending in that case would aim at a transfer of income to a particular category of borrower (for example, less-informed or less-advantaged individuals). The redistribution would be achieved by subsidizing the borrowers' access to credit (through mechanisms such as loan guarantees or below-market interest rates).

Management of Financial Storms

The tension between potential market failures and potential government failures is nowhere more intense than in the financial system. Financial storms magnified by informational cascades, the herding behavior of private decisionmakers, and systemic contagion can cause bad floods or droughts. No one but ideological extremists, however, would favor the centralization of lending and borrowing decisions in government-operated financial institutions. The inflexibilities and inefficiencies associated with centralized financial decisions would probably be much worse than the private herding behavior and market overreactions they were intended to avert.

Rather than centralization, financial system participants and policy-makers, from at least the beginning of the nineteenth century, have advocated a middle ground. Because the financial system is prone to panicky behavior in times of distressed conditions, most analysts have agreed that society requires some sort of central financial institution, a lender of last resort, that can catalyze cooperative action and provide temporary liquidity assistance during crises. Yet most analysts have also agreed that this provision of collective leadership and temporary assistance must be carefully circumscribed to prevent abuse and government failure.[5]

The lender-of-last-resort institution, as a key part of the utilities infrastructure of the financial system, has a fundamental rationale. Society should, and does, want to mobilize collective action that tries to mitigate the damaging consequences of stormy financial weather. The desired function is partly analogous to the coordination of emergency assistance for the worst-hit victims of real-life floods, droughts, hurricanes, and earthquakes. A central task of the lender of last resort is to calm unwarranted panic and hasten the return of more normal financial conditions. A closely related task is to lend to financial institutions during crisis episodes when private financial market participants are not able, or at least not willing, to lend. The lender of last resort must be prepared, on behalf of the society as a whole, to accept lending risks that are temporarily unacceptable to all other lenders.[6]

The first of these collective-governance tasks has been labeled *crisis management,* the second *crisis lending.* A common presumption is that both

5. According to Kindleberger (1978, p. 161), the phrase *lender of last resort* came into financial English from the French legal term *dernier ressort,* the legal jurisdiction beyond which it is impossible to take an appeal.

6. Some types of distressed financial conditions, as noted earlier, can be usefully analyzed as a problem of multiple equilibriums. As Fischer (1999, p. 6) observed, "a panic is the realization of a bad equilibrium when a good equilibrium is possible, and there is a need in such situations for some agency or group of institutions to take the lead in trying to steer the economy to the good equilibrium."

tasks should be performed by the same government institution, a central bank. In principle, the two tasks could be separated. For example, a government institution could be given the responsibility for coordinating the collective management of financial crises but not be given authority itself for crisis lending.

It has long been recognized that a lender of last resort might err in its crisis management and crisis lending. To try to avert such government failure, analysts have suggested principles for circumscribing the behavior of a lender of last resort. For example, it is argued that in a financial crisis the lender of last resort should distinguish between solvent and insolvent institutions, extending loans freely to the former (because they may be temporarily illiquid) but avoiding any loans to the latter (because they are not merely illiquid but also will be unviable after the crisis has passed). Such principles are discussed later in the chapter.

Prudential Oversight and Supporting Governance Systems for Financial Activity

Emergency action in financial crises by a lender of last resort, if taken, even if merely anticipated in noncrisis periods, creates a moral hazard dilemma. If private financial institutions can confidently count on a lender of last resort extending assistance on a stormy day, on sunny days they may have insufficient incentives to behave prudently in their own lending decisions. Financial activity necessarily entails the assumption of risks. Some level of risk taking by financial system participants is thus essential and highly desirable. But financial institutions will be tempted to take risks that are excessive from society's point of view if they believe that emergency funding will always be readily available, at little cost to themselves, to bail them out of trouble.[7]

This moral hazard dilemma, coupled with the objectives of trying to prevent stormy financial weather and mitigating its damaging consequences if it should occur, leads policymakers and analysts to advocate some form of collective governmental oversight for financial activity. Broad agreement exists that the government (in particular the lender-of-

---

7. Kindleberger (1978, p. 161) states the basic dilemma as follows: "If the market knows it is to be supported by a lender of last resort, it will feel less (little? no?) responsibility for the effective functioning of money and capital markets during the next boom. The public good of the lender of last resort weakens the private responsibility of 'sound' banking."

last-resort institution) cannot accept a residual responsibility for the stability of the financial system unless the government also engages in supervision and regulation of financial institutions to ensure sound practices and prevent excessive risk taking. I use the term *prudential oversight* for these supervision and regulation functions. Prudential oversight is a critical collective-governance component of the utilities infrastructure for the financial system.

Prudential oversight is analogous to the establishment of minimum-standard building codes that help to minimize the damage from earthquakes and hurricanes. It has similarities to land-use zoning policies that discourage people from living in exposed flood plains, in low-lying coastal areas exposed to hurricanes, or on top of geological faults where earthquake risk is unusually high. Prudential oversight of the financial system is also strongly conditioned by the potential demands for crisis lending and crisis management. If the lender of last resort is expected to provide assistance in emergencies, it will wish to encourage potential recipients to behave in a way that reduces, or at the least does not increase, the probability that emergencies will occur, and if emergencies should occur and assistance has to be extended, that reduces the private and social losses incurred.[8]

An advanced economy is unimaginable without at least one financial instrument—money—that serves as a widely accepted means of payment and generalized store of value. As checkable demand deposits in financial intermediaries became the predominant means of payment in modern economies, procedures for facilitating transactions through and among the intermediaries correspondingly assumed an increasingly vital role in the financial system. More recently, electronic arrangements for making transactions are accounting for a progressively larger fraction of all payments and receipts. As electronic payments grow in relative importance, the role of financial intermediaries in operating the society's payments mechanism is likely to become still more important.

Smooth operation of the payments mechanism is widely agreed to be especially important for the stability of the financial system. Most policymakers and analysts thus believe that the government, as part of its functions as overseer of the soundness of the financial system, should regulate, and thereby protect the integrity of, the society's payments mechanism. If

---

8. Stiglitz (1994) provides an overview of the prudential oversight roles of the government in financial markets.

pressed to state this view more formally, such individuals would describe the payments mechanism as a collective good that would not be supplied in an optimal way for society as a whole in the absence of governmental regulation and supervision.

Deposit insurance for deposits held in financial intermediaries is yet another dimension of prudential oversight. Such insurance plays a helpful role in reducing the likelihood of stormy weather runs on the intermediaries, thereby helping to dampen the spread and intensity of financial distress. If some agency of government provides deposit insurance, however, moral hazard issues again rear their head. The classic case against a guarantee of deposits is precisely the other side of the coin: by mitigating the threat of withdrawal of deposits, deposit insurance removes a check on imprudent risk taking by the management of the intermediaries. Insured depositors have no incentive to monitor risks taken by the bank. Banks with insured deposits can raise funds for projects at interest costs not commensurate with the projects' risks. If the government does decide to provide deposit insurance, it will thus also be driven to concomitant supervision and regulation of the intermediaries to reduce the moral hazard problems that would otherwise exist.[9]

The preceding rationales for prudential oversight are macroprudential, driven by a concern for systemic stability of the financial reservoir. Many analysts and policymakers would also identify a microprudential rationale, driven by concerns with the stability of individual financial institutions and the protection of individual consumers. The goal of microprudential oversight is to avert inappropriate conduct or the failure of particular institutions, thereby protecting individuals with deposits or other claims on the institutions and the local communities who depend on the lending activities of the institutions.

A prudential protection rationale for the supervision and regulation of financial institutions does not raise issues or problems peculiar purely to financial institutions. Some defenders of the microprudential rationale, however, believe it to be peculiarly applicable to financial intermediaries. The balance between microprudential and macroprudential rationales also depends on which types of intermediaries are the focus of the supervision and regulation. The macroprudential motives are particularly important

---

9. The moral hazard issue arises in its most acute form with "level-premium" deposit insurance. Proposals for the reform of deposit insurance that recommend relating the premium paid by a financial intermediary to the riskiness of its asset portfolio are intended to reduce the moral hazard incentives.

for banks and the payments system. Microprudential motives carry relatively greater weight as a justification for the regulation of brokerage firms and institutional investment funds.[10]

Yet another family of arguments, a concentration-competition rationale, can be advanced to justify the supervision and regulation of financial institutions. The contention is that collective prudential oversight is required to obviate an undue concentration of economic power.[11] Unlike the macroprudential and even the microprudential rationales for oversight, the concentration-competition rationale is not distinctively applicable to financial institutions. Financial intermediaries and financial markets do pose some special regulatory issues because the nature of their business differs from that of nonfinancial organizations. But the same general issues of concentration and competition arise in connection with virtually all types of economic activity in the private sectors of mixed capitalist economies.

For prudential oversight of financial institutions to be successful and efficient, supervision and regulation must be backstopped by a well-functioning legal system and by adequate procedures for accounting, auditing, information disclosure, and data collection and dissemination. Reliable legal institutions and robust collective-governance arrangements for accounting, auditing, and data provision are, as observed in chapter 2, fundamental supports for a financial reservoir.

The essential points about these institutions and arrangements merit emphasis again. Because of inevitable mishaps, a financial system must be supported by procedures for the monitoring and enforcement of contracts. It must incorporate procedures for working out the consequences when particular financial contracts are not honored. Widespread acceptance of standardized procedures for accounting and auditing underpins the successful monitoring and enforcement of contracts. The collection, aggregation, and widespread dissemination of data about the activities of financial

---

10. Edwards (1999, p. 191) writes that "the overriding goal of public policy underlying the regulation of institutional investment vehicles ... is 'investor protection'." Clark (1976) stresses the microprudential rationale for the supervision and regulation of financial intermediaries, even for banks.

11. Such a situation could develop, it is feared, unless governmental restraints prevent a few financial institutions from becoming very large and thereby acquiring an excessively dominant position in the financial system. A related line of reasoning asserts that supervision and regulation can promote or manage competition among financial institutions, thus improving the allocation of the economy's financial and real resources. Still another strand of thought, related but not identical, suggests that supervision and regulation can be helpful in ensuring competitive equity among financial institutions.

institutions are necessary supports for evaluation of risks and trends for individual financial institutions and for the financial system as a whole. The legal system must provide a foundation of laws and rules that facilitate the resolution of disputes about contracts and the handling of defaults and insolvencies.

Macroeconomic Policies

The lender-of-last-resort and the prudential oversight functions, underpinned by the legal system and arrangements for accounting, auditing, and data provision, are the central collective-governance components of the utilities infrastructure for the financial reservoir. But another component is also essential. The macroeconomic policies of the government help to shape the general climate within which the financial system and the wider economy operate.

Fiscal policies—the budget revenues and expenditures of the varying layers of government jurisdictions, and the balance among the revenues and expenditures—are a critical part of the general macroeconomic environment. The monetary policy of the central bank is the other critical part.

When budget policies and monetary policies are appropriate for the current circumstances of the economy and are sustainable, the financial system can more easily carry out its essential functions. Stable and predictable macroeconomic policies act like a calming influence on the reservoir. At the least, stable and predictable macroeconomic policies do not themselves contribute—and are correctly understood not to contribute—to turbulent waves or brewing storms.

Conversely, if budget policies or monetary policies, or both, should themselves be a destabilizing force for the rest of the economy, the perceptions and behaviors of participants in the financial reservoir will inevitably reflect such instability. Inappropriate macroeconomic policies will make the planning and operation of private firms and institutions, nonfinancial as well as financial, much more uncertain and difficult. With its potential for herding behavior and overreaction, the financial system may even exaggerate the expected consequences of the inappropriate macroeconomic policies.

Poorly conducted monetary policy can be especially disruptive. Recall the metaphor of the financial system as an inverted pyramid balanced on a small apex, the reserve money liabilities of the central bank. The conduct of monetary policy entails wise management of this reserve money base of the financial pyramid. In normal times, reserve money should grow incrementally and reasonably smoothly in accordance with overall real growth in the economy. If the incremental growth is too rapid and too erratic, inflation in goods prices will be excessive and variable, adding to the uncertainties afflicting private decisions. If reserve money should contract precipitously and erratically, the broader economy is likely to fall into recession. During times of financial distress caused by factors other than government macroeconomic policies, the central bank acting in its lender-of-last-resort function may need adroitly to generate sudden sharp increases in reserve money, followed later by sharp decreases. If the central bank is itself a source of instability, it will have low credibility and a much diminished capacity to counter the stormy financial weather.

The essential point here is the interdependence among the collective-governance aspects of the utilities infrastructure. General macroeconomic policies, prudential oversight, and responsibilities for crisis management all tend mutually to interact with each other—for good or for ill.

Implementing Prudential Oversight

What more precisely does the prudential oversight of financial activity entail? Prudential oversight can be justified on several different grounds: systemic and macroprudential, microprudential, concentration and competition. Because there are multiple rationales, prudential oversight has multiple dimensions. The government officials responsible for supervising and regulating financial institutions—*the supervisors,* for short—typically formulate and implement a wide range of policies.[12]

The supervisors can set licensing and authorization procedures for the establishment of new financial institutions. The supervisors probably have authority not only to review proposals for transferring ownership interests in a financial institution to other parties, but also to deny the transfer if appropriate criteria are not met. The supervisors may set minimum requirements for a financial institution's capital adequacy (net worth) and monitor whether financial institutions satisfy the requirements.

---

12. The terms *supervisor* and *supervision* are most often applied to government oversight of banking and insurance companies, whereas *regulator* and *regulation* are more frequently applied to oversight of securities firms and securities markets. My use of the word supervisors should be understood to include both supervisory and regulatory activities.

Supervisors establish guidelines to proscribe activities by the financial institutions deemed undesirable and hence illegal.[13] Illegal activities include fraud, the use of an institution for criminal purposes, trading abuses in securities markets, and insider misconduct and self-dealing. So-called connected-lending abuses—when the officers of a financial institution make low-interest loans to themselves, relatives, or other officers—are an illustration of insider self-dealing.

The supervisors may monitor the procedures that financial institutions use to assess the creditworthiness of borrowers and the quality and riskiness of individual assets. They may evaluate the techniques used for management of the overall riskiness of the institutions' balance sheets. The supervisors may set guidelines or evaluate an institution's own guidelines designed to prevent an undue concentration of assets or excessive exposure to single borrowers or groups of borrowers.

Perhaps most important, the supervisors try to ensure that a financial institution maintains adequate and transparent accounts, that it has in force adequate procedures for external audits, and that it publicly discloses information, including audited financial statements, correctly reflecting its condition.

As they exercise their prudential oversight responsibilities, the supervisors confront numerous difficult issues. One of the most general is the relative degree of reliance to be placed on market-based incentives versus direct, explicit regulations. Where incentive-based regulations that operate indirectly rather than directly are possible, they usually prove less costly and preferable. Requirements that financial institutions disclose timely and accurate information about their financial condition are a key example. Periodic disclosures of an institution's financial condition permit market forces to do a substantial part of the needed enforcing and monitoring. A deterioration in the institution's condition, if transparent to the wider community, will be punished by increases in its borrowing costs and declines in the market price of its stock. Such declines will in turn put pressure on the institution's management to take corrective action. The pressures also work in reverse: disclosures of information about a safe and well-managed institution's condition will enable it to obtain more favorable terms and conditions in its relations with its creditors than those available to institutions perceived as more risky.

---

13. Alternatively, supervisors have the authority to evaluate guidelines for proscribed activities developed by the institutions themselves.

Market-based regulations align the incentives of the supervisors and the regulated institution's owners and managers. Requirements that an institution maintain adequate capital (net worth) are an important example of such regulations. A capital adequacy requirement gives managers and owners a strong incentive to be prudent. If an institution with large net worth acts imprudently and goes bankrupt, the owners will experience large losses. Conversely, if an institution's net worth falls below some low threshold, managers and owners will be tempted to take excessive risks rather than avoid them.

Consider a badly managed bank that gets into trouble. If the bank's managers and owners have only a small equity stake in the bank because the capital-adequacy requirement is set very low, they might be tempted to "go for broke," taking on new, highly risky loans such as the financing of an expensive new sports stadium in a distant suburb. If the stadium does not catch on, too bad, but the supervisors were probably going to close the bank anyway. If the big bet on the stadium does pay off, however, the bank will look golden. The owners and managers will enjoy any upside gains that accrue; the downside risks to them are small because so little of their own money is at stake. In effect, the downside risks are borne mainly by the society's taxpayers, who will have to foot the bill if the bank does fail. With low net worth, the bank's management is inappropriately tempted to act like an American football team that is behind late in the fourth quarter. Ordinarily, throwing a "Hail Mary" pass would be too risky a gamble; in a go-for-broke context, however, such a pass might win the game.

The setting of standards for capital adequacy is far from straightforward. A financial institution's net worth is measured with uncertainty and error. Its portfolio of assets continuously fluctuates in value, but many of the assets may not have a current market price. Net worth is calculated only at periodic dates. If net worth could be monitored accurately and consistently, the supervisors could set a relatively low standard for minimum net worth and promptly close down an institution whose net worth fell below the required minimum. But with substantial lags and uncertainties in measurement, the supervisors are forced to set a higher minimum standard to be sure that the true value of the institution's capital is above a target minimum level. A high minimum standard raises the probability that the supervisors will not have to deal with an actually negative net worth if they must eventually close an institution. The other side of the coin, however, is that supervisors may inappropriately constrain growth of the financial sector if they set the minimum standard excessively high. Broad agreement exists that capital adequacy requirements are socially desirable. Yet the details of the requirements entail messy and controversial choices.[14]

Some types of prudential regulation inevitably take the form of direct restrictions rather than market-based incentives. Restraints on insider misconduct and on excessive lending to a single entity are examples. The purpose of regulations prohibiting insider misconduct and self-dealing is in part to prevent owners or better-informed investors from taking unfair advantage of less-informed individuals. Such situations are further examples of information asymmetries that lead to market imperfections.

Although the supervisors cannot ignore such problems, direct regulations to deal with them are difficult to formulate. Direct regulations may also lend themselves to government failure. Consensus exists that rigged markets have thin trading, do not function well, and are therefore socially undesirable. Because asymmetric information is a core characteristic of financial activity, however, trading in securities is necessarily based on differences in information. How much and what sorts of information supervisors should require to be disclosed is thus inevitably controversial. Some analysts would argue that detailed government regulations can make matters worse rather than better; in that view, caveat emptor should be the primary guiding principle.

The design of regulations and standards for prudential oversight is a key part of the supervisors' responsibilities, but monitoring and enforcement are equally essential. Without sufficient monitoring, and enforcement if necessary, the best-designed regulations can prove to be merely hortatory rather than actually binding. Issues of market-based incentives versus direct supervision are relevant for monitoring as well as for design. Extensive disclosure requirements facilitate indirect monitoring by private sector investors. Private agencies that assess creditworthiness and that rate securities can complement the monitoring activities of the supervisors. Private

---

14. In principle, the supervisors would like to take into account variability in value of the institution's assets when setting a target minimum standard for capital adequacy. Hence supervisors might define the relative riskiness of broadly defined categories of assets and then set an appropriate minimum standard for the ratio of eligible capital to total assets weighted by their risks. Still more complex approaches entail the supervisors' monitoring the overall risk of the institution's entire portfolio of assets, thus defining capital adequacy in terms of "credit risk modeling" of all assets with complex mathematical models (perhaps undertaken by the supervised institution itself rather than by the supervisors themselves).

rating agencies and other complementary private sector organizations, however, cannot deal with all potential externalities or abuses and thus cannot be a complete substitute for direct monitoring by the supervisors.

Who monitors the government monitors? What if the supervisors themselves fail to execute their responsibilities appropriately? Supervisors may succumb to what is known as *regulatory capture*, that is, excessive affinity between the regulators and the regulated. Bribery and corruption are extreme forms of regulatory capture, and hence government failure. Lesser varieties, such as regulatory forbearance, are more subtle but potentially just as serious. *Regulatory forbearance* occurs when the supervisors postpone corrective action against a financial institution that is failing to comply with supervisory requirements (for example, permitting an institution to continue to operate when its capital appears to have fallen below the minimum standard). It is human nature to hope that currently perceived problems will correct themselves with the passage of time. Politicians and government officials may have an added incentive to rely on such hopes since any costs of postponed action may be borne, not by themselves, but by their successors in office.[15]

One proposed solution to the problem of regulatory forbearance is to require that supervisors follow strict guidelines for their intervention, established in advance, rather than relying on discretionary judgment. But strict rules are not a magic solution ensuring beneficial results. Invariably, there is a trade-off between rules and discretion. Simple rules, rigidly enforced, could lead to closures of healthy institutions that should not be shut down or to continued operation of unhealthy institutions that really ought to be closed. Less rigid enforcement of rules, permitting greater discretion to the supervisors, reduces the likelihood of such mistakes but raises the probability of mistakes from regulatory forbearance.

Moral Hazard: A Fundamental Observation

Moral hazard difficulties inevitably arise from the collective-governance provision of collective management and emergency lending during a finan-

---

15. Regulatory forbearance is a concept that can have a variety of meanings. Toward one extreme, forbearance occurs when supervisors permit an individual financial institution to operate without meeting all of the existing prudential standards and regulations for a limited period of time while remedial actions are being taken to reduce risk exposure and correct other weaknesses. Toward the other extreme, regulatory forbearance may permit numerous insolvent or marginally solvent institutions to operate as open institutions for lengthy periods, with the true status of the institutions shielded from the general public.

cial crisis by a lender of last resort. Similar difficulties are created by providing insurance for the deposit liabilities of financial intermediaries. Should society therefore forswear the provision of lender-of-last-resort support to the financial system? Should it forswear deposit insurance? Occasionally one encounters individuals tempted to answer these questions yes. But the appropriate answer is, unambiguously, no.

Private insurance companies do not accept the pervasiveness of moral hazard as a valid reason for failing to provide any insurance. Rather, the optimal behavior is typically to supply the insurance, but combine it with incentives that seek to limit moral hazard. Homeowner insurance against fire, for example, typically insures only a fraction of the value of the home so that the owner has a clear financial stake in preventing a fire. City governments establish fire departments to respond to emergencies. The existence of a local station with firefighting equipment does create moral hazard: homeowners may be less preoccupied with fire prevention (for example, may smoke in bed) than they would be in the absence of the local station. But no support exists, as it should not, for prohibiting the writing of fire insurance and the establishment of local fire stations.

With moral hazard as with so many other aspects of life where difficult trade-offs have to be made, society must find a balanced position. In the case of local fire stations, a community should not support too small a station with personnel and equipment obviously inadequate to prospective fires. Yet the community ought not err in the opposite direction either, supporting a station a great deal too large and expensive for the local context.[16] Emergency lender-of-last-resort assistance for financial crises entails an analogous trade-off. Severe financial crises are imaginable. Some observers may therefore always conclude that the collective good of backup emergency financial assistance should be still larger than it is. Yet excessive expansion of the committed size or scope of lender-of-last-resort assistance would reduce rather than increase welfare by inducing private agents to take less cognizance of risk and less care in the evaluation of their lending and borrowing decisions. Just as it is possible to have too large a fire department, a collective-governance policy for financial crises could encourage too little caution in private behavior.

As with the writing of fire insurance and the maintenance of local fire stations, prudential oversight measures and policies for lender-of-last-resort behavior in the financial system seek to limit the moral hazard associated

16. Orszag and Stiglitz (2002).

with the provision of deposit insurance and emergency crisis lending. Supervisors and lenders of last resort recognize that the proper goal is *containment* of the moral hazard, not its complete *elimination*. The only way to eliminate the moral hazard altogether would be to abandon the contingent provision of collective action in financial crises. Such a course would certainly be worse than tolerating some degree of moral hazard while designing measures to contain it within acceptable limits. At the same time, vigilance is needed to ensure that moral hazard incentives are kept within reasonable bounds.

If properly understood, moral hazard issues are only one aspect of societal decisions about whether the government should provide deposit insurance or lender-of-last-resort support for financial crises. If government-sponsored activities can reduce the total economic losses associated with crises (taking appropriate account of any costs or risks arising from the provision of government assistance), the true economic risks associated with financial crises can be correspondingly reduced. A reduction of true risks encourages greater ex ante risk taking by private actors than would occur without expectations of government actions in a crisis. Provided that the additional risks undertaken are adequately compensated by expected benefits, the resulting outcome will be economically efficient and socially desirable. Moral hazard becomes a serious issue only to the extent that the expectations of government support in a crisis encourage private actors to assume risks beyond levels that are economically appropriate.[17]

The proposition that sound public policy should seek to contain, but not to eliminate, moral hazard is fundamental. It undergirds everything said in the remainder of this book.

Storm Management: Further Issues

Suppose a bad storm begins to be observed in the financial reservoir. The triggering event for the widespread general distress might be, for example,

---

17. Mussa and others (2000, p. 98) illustrate the point cogently: "People may choose to live in more expensive houses because (fairly priced) fire insurance allows the risks of losses from fire to be diversified and borne (for a fee) by those willing to accept such risks. Although risks of losses from fires are larger because people choose more expensive houses, economic efficiency is actually improved relative to a situation where fire insurance is not available. In contrast, if fire insurance induces home owners to undertake actions (like smoking or overloading electrical circuits) which increase fire risks and which (unlike house value) cannot be monitored and fairly priced in insurance policies, then there is a moral hazard distortion."

the threatened or actual insolvencies of several important nonfinancial firms. Such insolvencies, expected to lead to bankruptcy proceedings, might in turn generate a deterioration in confidence in individual banks lending to the insolvent firms, with contagion then spreading the distress still further in the financial system. Such conditions have an element of *systemic risk*. Systemic risk is present when disruptions at particular locations in the financial system—at particular financial intermediaries, in particular market segments, in a particular payments or settlement system—cause, or have a strong likelihood of causing, widespread difficulties at other intermediaries, in other market segments, or in the financial system as a whole.[18]

In conditions of systemic risk, what should be the paramount responsibility of the central bank?[19] Which actions should it consider first? The overriding priority should be prompt adjustments in the overall conduct of monetary policy designed to ensure an adequate liquefaction of the financial system as a whole. In generalized conditions of financial distress, private economic agents outside the financial reservoir and, even more so, the financial institutions inside it are likely to scramble to protect themselves by acquiring additional liquid assets. The demand for liquid assets, and even for high-powered money itself, may quickly exceed the available supply at existing interest rates, thereby placing strong upward pressure on interest rates. In such circumstances, the central bank may need to carry out open-market purchases of securities, thus temporarily providing more reserve money to support the scramble for additional liquidity. The central bank, furthermore, should probably not delay an accommodation of the increased demands for liquidity by waiting until financial institutions come to its discount window. The central bank may need to act promptly, even in anticipation of further private demands. In addition to large, open-market purchases of securities, reductions in reserve requirements may also seem desirable.

No less important, after the storm has subsided, the central bank must be equally skillful to adjust monetary policy in the opposite direction.

18. This definition of systemic risk appears in the "Promisel Report" (Bank for International Settlements 1992).

19. Recall that the functions of crisis management and crisis lending could be exercised together or separately. For simplicity of exposition, I suppress that issue here and merely assume that both crisis management and crisis lending are carried out by a single institution, referred to for short as the lender of last resort or the central bank.

When increments of liquidity injected into the financial system during a crisis are no longer demanded and needed, they must be withdrawn.

The argument just summarized is a cardinal proposition in the theory of central banking for a single economy. When a generalized financial crisis threatens, lender-of-last-resort policy should be first and foremost a matter of the overall conduct of monetary policy implemented through general open-market operations.

Second—still important, but nonetheless secondary—the central bank may need to counter the conditions of financial distress by *direct* loans to individual private financial institutions. This second proposition is controversial with a minority of analysts. That minority reasons that indirect support to the financial system, through open-market purchases of securities that supply incremental liquidity to the market generally, is sufficient. The advantage of indirect support is that market decisions can then sort out which troubled borrowers will benefit from the incremental liquidity rather than the central bank itself having to make such decisions.

The view that general liquefaction of the financial system through open-market operations is sufficient by itself to mitigate crisis conditions is, however, not convincing. Despite the obvious problems involved, the central bank may find it necessary or desirable to lend directly to private financial institutions. The basic activity of financial intermediation depends on the intermediaries maintaining both their depositors' confidence and their own ability to initiate borrowings to meet temporary deposit drains. If grave suspicions have arisen about an individual intermediary, depositors may precipitously withdraw large amounts of funds; market borrowings to finance the deposit loss may not be possible. Such a temporary squeezing out of the market can occur for an intermediary even when suspicions about its solvency are unjustified.

The difficulty with relying solely on general monetary policy is that financial activity is inevitably saddled with asymmetric information and uncertainty. Even in untroubled times, information about the probable solvency of a financial intermediary is difficult to obtain and frequently out of date. Uncertainty rises sharply when a financial crisis threatens. Creditors of financial intermediaries, especially in a crisis atmosphere, are acutely aware of the information asymmetry and moral hazard involved in reaching judgments about a troubled intermediary's solvency. If an intermediary that has come under suspicion and about which information is thought to be unreliable should decide to offer higher interest rates to its depositors or creditors, that action by itself can be interpreted by the depositors and creditors as a confirmation of the intermediary's troubled status. In practice, therefore, an intermediary that is basically solvent yet illiquid may not in crisis conditions be able to borrow incremental liquidity from other private participants in the financial system.

The central bank and the prudential supervisors of financial institutions may be able in crisis conditions to appraise the balance sheet of an individual financial institution more dispassionately than market participants possibly subject to panic psychology. The central bank and the supervisors are likely to have, or be able to acquire, more accurate and complete information. They may also be in a stronger position than private market participants to impose conditions on a borrowing institution in order to ensure its continued solvency. The central bank and the supervisors are in any case better placed to estimate the broader social costs of the failure of multiple financial institutions. Such a collective perspective may make them willing to take risks of lending in crisis conditions that private lenders are not willing to take.

These various arguments lead to the conclusion that even if the central bank has correctly gauged its general provision of incremental liquidity to the financial system as a whole, in principle it may still be necessary or desirable in crisis conditions to consider direct lending to individual private financial institutions.

In the nineteenth century Walter Bagehot suggested guidelines to be followed by a lender of last resort when it lends to individual private financial intermediaries. Many others have since reiterated and refined his suggestions.[20] The lender of last resort, Bagehot suggested, should be guided by three principles in a crisis. First, distinguish between solvent and insolvent institutions, extending loans freely to the former but avoiding any loans to the latter. Second, require the solvent institutions to put up sound collateral against the emergency loans extended to them. And third, charge a penalty (above-market) rate of interest on the emergency loans.

The principle that lender-of-last-resort assistance should be given only to solvent banks is merely an extension of a widely accepted tenet of capitalism. Few citizens of democratic societies wish to keep badly managed, unprofitable nonfinancial businesses alive through government support (the interested owners themselves being obvious exceptions). For the same

---

20. The main nineteenth-century reference is Bagehot (1873); see also Thornton (1802). For more recent references, see, for example, Hirsch (1977); Kindleberger (1978); Kindleberger and Laffargue (1982); Meltzer (1986); and Fischer (1999).

reasons, a financial intermediary should typically be allowed to fail if it has been poorly managed and taken foolish risks. An admiral in the British Navy, John Byng, was executed in 1756 for his failure to relieve British forces on Minorca. Voltaire, commenting on the incident, suggested that it was a good thing to dispatch an admiral from time to time *"pour encourager les autres."* It seems unnecessarily harsh to argue that financial intermediaries should fail from time to time just to encourage the others. But it would surely also be a mistake, even in conditions of financial distress, to use general taxpayer funds to keep a financial intermediary alive that has consistently been badly managed.

Though the Bagehot principles may at first seem straightforward, major difficulties become evident as soon as they are examined closely. Acting on the first principle requires the lender of last resort to be able to differentiate unambiguously between solvent and insolvent institutions. That distinction is moderately complicated even in ordinary, noncrisis periods. In conditions of generalized distress and systemic risk, the distinction becomes especially murky. The most notable difficulty stems from a complex interaction between the status of troubled institutions and the behavior of the lender of last resort itself. Whether an individual institution should be judged merely illiquid rather than insolvent turns of course on how the financial crisis will be resolved. That judgment in turn depends on how successfully the central bank fulfills its responsibilities. If the lender of last resort is too timid in its lending and crisis management, erring on the side of not lending to institutions that are at risk of being insolvent after the crisis subsides, the probability rises that the outcome of the crisis may be a bad equilibrium in which otherwise solvent institutions fall into insolvency. But if the lender of last resort lends aggressively to a large number of institutions, including even those whose precrisis and postcrisis solvency is seriously at risk, it can raise the probability of a better general outcome for the crisis, but also find that after the crisis it has become a creditor to insolvent institutions. In a crisis decisions must be taken speedily. Yet the quality of information about the financial conditions of particular institutions becomes more uncertain. The guideline to lend exclusively to solvent institutions is therefore very much easier to state than it is to implement.[21]

---

21. The infamous cases of the Franklin National Bank in 1974 (Spero 1980) and Continental Illinois Bank in 1984 (FDIC 1997) reveal just how difficult it is to make the distinction between illiquidity and insolvency. Those cases also illustrate the pressures on the lender of last resort to extend emergency lending to a troubled institution if it is believed that a failure to lend to the institution will greatly increase systemic risk.

The guideline requiring institutions borrowing from the lender of last resort to post sound collateral mitigates partially, but only partially, the difficulties in judging between illiquid versus insolvent institutions. If an institution suffering illiquidity is able to offer secure, marketable collateral against an emergency loan, the lender of last resort may interpret this offer as a positive indication of the likely postcrisis solvency of the institution. Accordingly, the lender of last resort may feel less uncomfortable with a speedy mid-crisis decision to extend an emergency loan.

But the mitigation is at best partial. The only sensible ex ante interpretation of the requirement for "sound" collateral is that the collateral should be secure and marketable *in the absence of the crisis conditions.* In the midst of a crisis itself, of course, many otherwise sound assets are not readily marketable; that is why illiquid institutions need to obtain emergency loans from the lender of last resort in the first place. An unambiguous verdict on the soundness of collateral is possible only after the crisis has blown over. Again, however, the ex post outcome may depend critically on whether or not the lender of last resort chooses actually to lend. The lender of last resort will thus be forced to make judgments about whether specific collateral instruments are sound under more normal, noncrisis conditions. Those judgments may not be that much easier than judgments about whether a borrowing institution will be solvent once the crisis subsides.

Collateral requirements for emergency lending can be problematic in still other ways. A solvent financial intermediary with large immediate needs for liquidity may find it difficult to promptly provide sufficient collateral that is acceptable to the lender of last resort; a decision not to lend to such an intermediary could result in the failure of an otherwise viable institution. In some cases, the lender of last resort and the prudential supervisors might have enough information about the soundness of the illiquid institution to render the collateral requirement redundant. An opposite type of risk also exists. An intermediary that is insolvent or only marginally solvent may possess some collateral acceptable to the lender of last resort and hence obtain an emergency loan; the troubled institution may thereby be able to continue excessively risky, go-for-broke behavior. The lender of last resort's loan is protected because of its claim on the collateral, but the interests of other creditors and society at large are not.[22]

22. The collateral required for the Federal Reserve's discount window lending to the Franklin National Bank in 1974 and the associated problems raised during the workout arrangements following Franklin's failure provide a fascinating example of the difficulties in implementing the guideline that emergency loans must be backed by sound collateral. See Spero (1980, chaps. 4–6).

The guideline to lend at a penalty (above-market) interest rate is similarly complicated. The rationales for the penalty rate include its constraint on the demand for emergency loans by institutions that do not really need them, the incentive it provides for borrowing institutions to exhaust all their other potential sources of liquidity before turning to the lender of last resort, and assurance of quick reversals of the emergency lending once the crisis has passed. More generally, the penalty interest rate helps to limit the moral hazard problem that the very existence of a lender of last resort creates. Again, however, the only sensible interpretation of the guideline is that the penalty rate should be higher than the market interest rate that would prevail in the absence of crisis conditions. If the lender of last resort were to charge a penalty rate relative to the interest rate at which financial institutions would lend to each other in the midst of a market panic, that rate could be very high indeed and could well result in very little, if any, emergency lending. In an actual crisis, the best that the lender of last resort can do is to make a difficult judgment about what the market interest rate would be in the absence of the crisis and apply any penalty to that estimated rate.

Given the severe uncertainties and difficulties of making crisis judgments about the future solvency of troubled borrowers, the lender of last resort may sometimes act on judgments that, with the wisdom of hindsight after the storm is past, prove to be wrong. What principles should the lender of last resort and the prudential supervisors then follow if they have in fact made emergency loans to an individual financial institution that turns out to be insolvent and has to be declared bankrupt? Broad guidelines can be easily summarized: moral hazard precedents should be contained by imposing costs—"punishment"—on those responsible for the decisions that led to the troubled institution's insolvency. Thus losses should be born by shareholders and managers in the first instance, with remaining losses allocated in reverse order of legal precedence. Use of general taxpayers' funds to cover losses should occur only after every feasible alternative has been exhausted. Yet as much as possible, the ex post value of the bankrupt institution should be preserved. A failed institution should promptly either be sold, with its assets valued as much as possible at market prices, or else be liquidated.

Like the Bagehot principles themselves, those broad recommendations for coping with a failed institution are easily stated but often extremely difficult to implement. Moreover, the various principles are partly in conflict with one another. The objective of imposing costs to contain moral hazard can be inconsistent with preserving the ex post value of the failed institution. The particular circumstances of the crisis and failure will strongly condition how the supervisors and lender of last resort try to strike a balance between the conflicting objectives.[23]

If the central bank extends emergency loans to troubled institutions, some observers will invariably criticize the loans as a bailout and an encouragement for future moral hazard. The term *bailout* can refer to the troubled institution itself. It can also be argued that the central bank's direct lending to the troubled institution "bails out" that institution's private sector creditors. In a worst case, the central bank's emergency loans facilitate the withdrawal of an equal amount of credit by the private creditors, facilitating a transfer of credit risk away from the private creditors to the central bank.

Suppose the private creditors have previously been negligent in monitoring the behavior of the troubled institution. It may then be especially inappropriate for the private creditors to escape with their funds intact, not paying a price for their negligence. Charges and countercharges about "bailouts" are virtually certain if some of the troubled institutions receiving emergency loans from the central bank turn out to fail despite the emergency assistance.

Because of the information asymmetries and moral hazard inherent in all financial activity, the notion of bailout is intrinsically ambiguous. To appreciate the difficulties, consider first the simpler case of private creditors who lend funds to a borrowing enterprise or financial institution. Suppose that problems surface with the business of the individual borrower (but not, at least as yet, a situation of generalized financial problems and systemic risk). Incremental lending by the creditors in these circumstances may be sensible and desirable. Or it may merely be throwing good money after bad. The interpretation of the situation depends on the details of the circumstances, which condition the creditors' judgments about the future solvency of the borrower. Any judgment about future solvency is always somewhat uncertain. Loans always embody a risk premium.[24]

---

23. Recall that a similar conflict in objectives bedevils bankruptcy procedures (chapter 2).

24. A rise in the risk premium charged the borrower may seem a desirable condition for incremental lending by private creditors, the more so if information asymmetries have worsened and doubts are rising about the borrower's future insolvency. But charging the borrower a higher interest rate may also have the signaling effect of calling the attention of other financial system participants to the borrower's troubled status. The creditors' judgment in effect requires an estimate that the borrower has an x percent probability of future solvency if they decide to make incremental loans, which is higher than the y percent probability of solvency without the new loans. The creditors have no definitive basis for setting a threshold value above which x (or y) must fall. The higher they set the threshold, the greater the probability that the borrower will not be able to sustain solvency. The lower the threshold, the greater the risk to the creditors that they will suffer losses because the borrower will turn out to be insolvent despite their incremental loans.

Suppose the private creditors decide in favor of some incremental lending. Critical observers could term the creditors' actions a bailout of the troubled borrower. Alternatively, suppose the creditors fail to reach a consensus judgment, with some loyal creditors deciding to grant incremental loans but other skittish creditors insisting on redemption of their existing lending. The loyal creditors could then be characterized as permitting the skittish creditors to be bailed out. Yet the language of bailout does not fully illumine the decisions made in these examples. Nor could any outside observer confidently claim that the private sector decisions were inappropriate (certainly not without considerably more information about the details).

Creditors' judgments about the solvency of troubled borrowers become even more difficult if the judgments have to be made against a background of generalized financial distress and systemic risk. And of course the moral hazard issues intensify. If the lender of last resort rather than private sector creditors lends directly to troubled borrowers, the solvency judgments and moral hazard repercussions are still another order of magnitude more difficult. Not only will observers then speak of a bailout of the troubled financial institutions receiving emergency loans from the central bank. They will assert that the central bank has bailed out private sector creditors of the troubled institutions, permitting private lenders "unfairly" to transfer part or all of their credit risk to the public sector. Actions by the central bank criticized as bailouts, furthermore, raise the possibility that society as a whole—general taxpayers—will have to foot the bill if emergency lending during the crisis proves to have been to troubled borrowers that cannot survive after the crisis.

Even for the most difficult crisis cases where a government lender of last resort lends directly to troubled institutions, the language of bailouts should be used more cautiously than it typically is. The term carries primarily negative nuances: presumptively, a bailout is a bad thing that probably should not have occurred. In contrast, as the brief discussion here suggests, decisions about direct lending by the central bank in a financial crisis are highly complex. Normative assessments of them are seldom straightforward, even with the wisdom of hindsight.

Because of the moral hazard difficulties associated with lender-of-last-resort support in financial crises, the suggestion is often made that private financial institutions should be induced to share in crisis lending and crisis management. In particular, the recommendation is that private sector creditors to troubled institutions experiencing a liquidity drain should somehow be "bailed in" rather than "bailed out" (induced to refrain from withdrawing their funds instead of being permitted to withdraw while the lender of last resort is injecting its emergency assistance).

Concerted lending is a term for one mechanism for bailing in private creditors. Concerted lending entails a core group of private institutions cooperating with the lender of last resort to extend liquidity assistance to intermediaries experiencing a drain. The central bank acts as the crisis manager and the lead lender but persuades a small group of other financial institutions, typically large banks with venerable traditions and high market shares, to pony up funds as well. Concerted lending thus helps to redistribute liquidity in the system, reducing the need for the central bank to create new gross liquidity. The collective action involved in concerted lending puts direct pressure on members of the consortium to continue lending to illiquid institutions under attack, and sends indirect signals to other financial institutions that they too should avoid participation in the panic.

Concerted lending and bailing in, if it can be successfully arranged in a crisis, is usually desirable. But severe obstacles must be overcome. In recent decades, many significant changes have taken place in financial systems, such as the declining relative importance of banks, the proliferation of nonbank financial institutions, and the increasing prevalence of securitization of lending. Because of these changes, concerted emergency lending tends to be even more complex to organize than in earlier decades. A fundamental complication stems from the fact that cooperative decisionmaking in large groups is more difficult than in small groups.[25]

The awkward truth is that exhortations to avoid "bailouts" and to encourage "bailing in" are at best murky guidelines. Just as the lender of last resort can never be sure ex ante whether a troubled borrower's situation is one of illiquidity or insolvency, it can never ex ante make definitive judgments about whether its emergency lending will, with the wisdom of hindsight, be seen as an unjustified bailout of the borrower or of the private creditors that lent to the borrower before the crisis.

Crisis management—the exercise of collective leadership during and immediately following a crisis—need not always involve emergency direct lending. Indeed, for the cases of private institutions that have already become insolvent, the only appropriate role for collective governance is to facilitate orderly, expedited *workouts* of the situations. A workout may

---

25. The analytical foundation for this conclusion is developed rigorously in the technical literature on game theory.

entail a rescheduling of debt, its restructuring, or both. A *rescheduling*, defined as an extension of the debt's maturity and hence the time horizon for its servicing, may be possible if the troubled borrowers are only marginally insolvent. A *restructuring* typically entails writing down some portion of the present value of the existing debt and rewriting new contracts for the remaining portion. Restructurings thus usually result in partial losses for creditors. In the most severe cases, as a necessary condition of restoring general confidence and promoting recovery from the crisis, workouts may require reorganizations of failed institutions or even liquidations that efficiently sell off their residual assets. These more severe workouts necessitate creditors acknowledging large losses.

The requisite workouts entail negotiated agreements between troubled borrowers and their private sector creditors. The lender of last resort does not have a direct vested interest in these workout agreements (unless it extended emergency loans and thus has claim on the collateral assets). Even so, it may nonetheless be able to catalyze the agreements and assert the general public interest in a speedy resolution. In many crises, this facilitation function may be just as important as the readiness to lend to temporarily illiquid institutions.

How in normal times should the lender of last resort describe its prospective behavior if a crisis should threaten? Decisions about what to say and what not to say, in advance of any crisis, raise subtle issues and illustrate again a difficult trade-off between rules and discretion. Principles and rules for crisis management and crisis lending, if articulated clearly ex ante, might reduce the frequency of crises by reducing uncertainty about how the lender of last resort will act. They could help to induce stabilizing private behavior, for example, by encouraging the holding of less risky assets known to be usable as collateral for emergency lending in a crisis. By spelling out rules in advance, the lender of last resort and prudential supervisors could partially tie their own hands (limit their postcrisis options), thereby rendering them less vulnerable to inappropriate political influence or the temptations of regulatory forbearance.

But the other side of the trade-off is also compelling. It is impossible to spell out detailed rules in advance of every imaginable crisis contingency. Overly simplified rules might have to be abandoned in the complex heat or aftermath of a crisis, thus damaging the credibility of the lender of last resort and the supervisors. More important still, deliberate vagueness—*constructive ambiguity* has become the favored phrase—can have favorable effects. Constructive ambiguity may help to contain moral hazard. If it is uncertain whether emergency lending will be forthcoming in a future crisis, and if forthcoming on what terms and conditions, risk-averse participants in the financial system may be more cautious than if they felt confident that they would be rescued at low cost. Another advantage of some ambiguity is that it permits greater flexibility of response in crisis environments where information is especially highly skewed and uncertain. Policies announced in advance about concerted lending raise analogous issues.[26]

Because of such incentive complications, the lender of last resort again confronts a subtle trade-off between reducing moral hazard and promoting financial stability. If it emphasizes before a crisis the desirability of bailing in creditors through concerted lending, it may thereby mitigate the moral hazard created by its contingent willingness to engage in emergency lending. But that same emphasis may work to reduce resilience and inertia in the financial system if crises should occur, thus raising the probability that the lender of last resort may actually have to engage in emergency lending.

No perfect resolution exists for these trade-off conundrums. Any announced posture of the lender of last resort in advance of crises, ranging from the extreme of detailed articulation of procedures to the other extreme of a virtual absence of any announced principles, can be problematic. Some amount of ambiguity is inevitable and desirable. Probably the worst stance of all is to permit private financial institutions to expect that crisis management and crisis lending will somehow be mounted in distressed conditions but then to decide during an actual crisis that the functions cannot or should not be performed.

A final issue merits identification. The central bank's conduct of general monetary policy entails, in essence, the management of the reserve money base of the inverted financial pyramid of the financial system. If collective leadership for financial crises is to be successful, must the lender of last resort have the capacity to create reserve money, that is, to change the size of the small tip that supports the whole pyramid?

---

26. Suppose the lender of last resort were to emphasize that it will not grant emergency loans to prospective illiquid borrowers during a crisis unless major private creditors of the troubled institutions simultaneously agree to concerted lending. Such a policy, aiming to enforce a bailing in of private creditors, could exacerbate skittish behavior and financial market turbulence if stormy weather threatens. If the lender of last resort is expected to insist that the private creditors of institution A continue to lend to A if A experiences trouble in a crisis, the creditors may be especially alert to pull the plug on their A lending at the slightest hint of a crisis, getting out *before* the central bank twists their arms to participate in concerted lending. Moreover, the creditors might have enhanced incentives to promptly pull the plug on their lending to institutions B and C as a way of forestalling potential exposure during a crisis.

If one reasons from first principles, the ability to create reserve money is neither necessary nor sufficient for the exercise of collective leadership in crisis management. Nor is it strictly necessary as a support for all forms of crisis lending. Concerted lending by private sector creditors, for example, can be organized without any backstop ability to create reserve money. Indeed, financial systems throughout most of history have *not* been supported by an institutionalized lender of last resort. Until recent decades, if collective leadership was provided at all in a crisis, it was usually organized at the last minute in an ad hoc, explicitly temporary form. The leadership of J. Pierpoint Morgan in arranging concerted lending in the 1907 financial crisis in the United States dramatically illustrates this point.[27]

Financial crises typically involve a run from the deposits of private financial intermediaries perceived to be weak to deposits in other intermediaries perceived as strong, with the process exacerbated by informational cascades and contagion. The result of such runs by themselves is a movement of reserve money from weaker to stronger intermediaries but not a large net increase in the demand for reserve money as a whole. If private institutions could accurately distinguish between insolvent and merely illiquid intermediaries, financial markets themselves could react to such runs by recirculating reserve money back to the illiquid but solvent intermediaries losing it.

Because of the preceding points, some degree of constructive crisis management is possible through concerted lending even when the capacity to create reserve money is not present. But other features of financial crises, especially problematic when systemic risk is great, lead to the conclusion that the potential to create reserve money is essential.

In a severe financial panic, deposits are withdrawn not only from the financial intermediaries perceived to be weakest, but to some degree from all financial intermediaries together. Ultimate savers flee to those assets deemed to be safest of all. One such asset is currency itself.[28] Worse still, a financial crisis in an individual national economy open to the rest of the world typically triggers shifts out of domestic currency assets held in the

---

27. Morgan was the preeminent banker of his day but of course a private citizen. Neither federal nor state government institutions were influential in the resolution of the 1907 crisis. See, for example, Chernow (1990, chap. 7). The Federal Reserve System did not exist in 1907. In fact, the Federal Reserve was created largely in response to the financial crises of the late nineteenth and early twentieth centuries, in particular the crisis of 1907.

28. Before its effective dethronement as a monetary asset late in the twentieth century, gold was another.

national financial system into assets held abroad or denominated in foreign currencies. A common feature of these other asset shifts is that they cause either an *increase in demand* for, or an actual *decline* in, the reserve money base of the national financial pyramid.

All things considered, an ability to increase the supply of reserve money—and, even more so, to offset private actions that would otherwise cause a decline—is thus a critical component of successful crisis management. In contemporary national economies, the central bank as lender of last resort is typically the sole institution with the requisite authority to make incremental changes in the reserve money base. The capacity for creating new reserve money, although not strictly necessary for all dimensions of crisis management, is essential for exercising the paramount responsibility of adjusting overall monetary policy through general open-market operations.

Which Institutions for Collective Governance?

Which government institutions should perform the collective-governance functions of the financial system's utilities infrastructure? At one imaginable extreme, every identified function—crisis lending, crisis management, prudential oversight, monetary policy, budgetary policies, custody of the legal system, accounting, auditing, and data collection—could be lodged in a single institution, say, a conglomerate ministry of finance-justice plus central bank. The other extreme would be to parcel out each of the different functions to a different government institution.

It is not feasible to discuss here the issues of which government institutions should have custody of the legal system and which should establish and monitor standards for accounting, auditing, and data dissemination. Analysis of those institutional issues, though important, would take the exposition too far afield.

Similarly, it would not be appropriate here to analyze carefully the thorny issues about political independence of the central bank from the rest of the government. Advocates of complete independence want the central bank to pursue, or at least to be free to pursue, fundamentally different objectives from those pursued by the rest of the government. For example, they assert that a central bank should focus exclusively on the goal of price stability. Opponents of full independence object to the idea of the central bank pursuing different objectives, or objectives that have not been specified by democratically elected officials.

I take the compromise view that the central bank should have some measure of political independence in its day-to-day implementation of monetary policy but that it should pursue objectives that have been set by democratically elected political leaders. (This view has been summarized as the central bank having *instrument* independence, but not *goal* independence.) A corollary of this view is that monetary policy and government budget policies should be administratively lodged in separate institutions, even though the two institutions should conduct extensive consultations to ensure a sufficient coordination of the two sets of policies.

Apart from macroeconomic policies, the remaining collective-governance aspects of the utilities infrastructure for the financial system are crisis lending, crisis management, and the prudential oversight of financial institutions. Should these functions, together with monetary policy, be handled all in the same institution, the central bank?

The most important aspect of this institutional question is whether general monetary policy and crisis lending should be conducted together with, or separately from, the prudential supervision and regulation of financial institutions. In the former case, the functions would all be lodged in a single government institution; in the latter, the functions would be parceled out among different government agencies. Neither normative arguments nor practical experience have been sufficient to generate a consensus on this matter.

Advocates for separating prudential oversight from general monetary policy tend to be concerned about a possible conflict of interest between the two functions. In times of troubled conditions, it can be argued, a central bank with supervisory responsibilities may be tempted to maintain interest rates at a lower level than would be warranted by general monetary policy because of a concern about the adverse effects of higher rates on the profitability and solvency of financial institutions under its supervision. (Such behavior would be a subtle form of regulatory forbearance.) Some tension seems inevitable between the objectives of monetary policy and maintaining systemic stability on the one hand and the microprudential objectives of regulation on the other.

Yet separating the two sets of functions would not necessarily make the resolution of this tension easier. If supervisory and regulatory responsibilities were lodged in a separate agency outside the central bank, occasions might arise in which the officials in charge of monetary policy, fearful of systemic stability, would want to provide emergency lending to particular financial institutions, whereas the supervisory officials, fearful of moral hazard precedents and possible losses from insolvencies, would instead recommend no emergency lending and liquidation of the institutions. Such conflicts between objectives have to be resolved in any case, whether the prudential oversight functions have been given to a separate government agency or whether all the functions are lodged together in the central bank. Advocates of keeping the monetary policy and prudential oversight functions together also observe that the central bank would have to be deeply involved in crisis lending to particular institutions even if the formal authority for supervision were given to a separate agency. According to this view, decisionmaking would be less balanced and less efficient with a separation.

The institutional allocation of the prudential oversight functions also depends on how the residual costs of liquidating insolvent institutions are borne. If substantial amounts of taxpayer money have been and will in the future be used to cover such costs, closure decisions will have an especially high political content. In such circumstances, it may seem politically more natural to lodge the authority in a part of the government other than the central bank. Central banks themselves may even feel relieved, and feel their reputations may be less subject to tarnish, if prudential oversight is formally located elsewhere.

Thus it is not clear whether prudential oversight and the monitoring of standards are likely to be better handled when under their own roof, or in combination with monetary policy under the roof of the central bank. Nor is it clear whether general monetary policy and crisis lending are better conducted together with, or separated from, prudential oversight. The most careful study of the question observes that the arguments for combination and for separation are both inconclusive. About half of the nations examined in that study separate the functions, and the other half combine them.[29]

One further institutional issue warrants mention. Analysts and policymakers tend to agree that crisis lending and general monetary policy are so closely intertwined that they must be conducted together by a single

---

29. Goodhart and Schoenmaker (1993, 1995). A wide range of institutional arrangements prevail among nations regarding which entity of government bears exclusive or primary responsibility for the supervision, regulation, and oversight of financial activity. A few nations have designated a single agency to supervise and regulate a wide range of financial institutions (such as banks, securities firms, and insurance companies) and financial markets (such as securities exchanges, derivatives, and commodity exchanges). For most nations, however, the oversight responsibilities for financial activity are shared among several government agencies.

institution, the central bank. But some have noted that crisis management can in principle be separated from crisis lending. For example, the dominant responsibility for crisis management could be lodged outside the central bank, somewhere else in the government. Some separation, or at least sharing, of the roles of crisis lending and crisis management is likely to occur if the functions of supervision and regulation of financial institutions are separated from the central bank.

4 Political Economy in a Multination, Intermediate World

The planet Earth is, it might be said, a single closed system like the economy hypothesized in chapters 2 and 3. After all, no one on the globe has transactions with other planets or stars. When any one borrower has a liability on its balance sheet, there exists somewhere else on the globe a matching asset on the balance sheet of a lender. The financial system in the world as a whole may thus be likened to a global reservoir.

But the globe is very far from a homogeneous economic entity. It is divided into many highly diverse nations, each with a geographical territory defined by national borders. Each nation has its own national government. Most nations have their own national currencies. Most have institutions, social norms, and histories with distinctive cultural and ethnic characteristics.

Yes, transactions crossing the borders of nations—financial even more so than economic—have become much more important in recent decades. Some individuals and groups, not merely in their financial and economic transactions, but sometimes even in their social, cultural, and political activities, are to a limited degree "transcending" national borders in the sense that their activities are less firmly rooted in a single geographically defined nation. Nonetheless, the globe remains highly fragmented, especially when viewed from a political and social perspective.

Beginning with chapter 5, the analysis focuses on the cross-border aspects of financial activity in this complex, multination world. As essential background, however, it is first necessary to turn to some fundamentals of global political economy.

Basic Structural Features of the World Polity

The dominant building blocks of the world polity, the political structure of the globe, are nation states. The national governments of these states are the dominant locus of governmental decisions.

The citizens of each nation state, and hence the leaders and civil servants of its government, are predominantly concerned with the welfare of the nation's own residents. Only citizens can vote in national elections. Domestic politics within nations thus have much greater salience for a nation's residents than cross-border politics.

Most nations have "mixed" economic systems. Dominant reliance is placed on decentralized decisions by private sector agents and institutions coordinated through price signals in markets. The economic systems, however, also accord major roles to government interventions and to other, nongovernmental forms of cooperative decisionmaking (collective governance in the sense of chapter 3).

Individual nations typically have different layers of subnational political jurisdictions—regions, provinces, counties, municipalities, and so on. Subnational government institutions are influential in these regional and local jurisdictions. Domestic politics within individual nations reflect complex interactions among local, regional, and national institutions.

Outside rather than within the nation states, a few international organizations play catalytic political roles. Government institutions at the level of the nation state, however, are the most influential political entities for relationships among nations.

Many types of nongovernmental institutions exert political leverage within nations. Increasingly, such institutions also play critical roles in political interactions among nations. Large multinational corporations and multinational banks receive the most attention; they probably are the most influential. Yet not-for-profit NGOs (nongovernmental organizations) have grown in numbers and influence. Still other cross-border institutions and groups of cosmopolitan individuals—for example, scientific, academic, and research associations—have likewise become politically significant. The latter have even become salient enough to attract the attention of international relations theorists and to earn a new label, "epistemic communities."[1]

In recent years, the term *civil society* has also entered the discourse of political and international relations analysts. Civil society typically refers to the wide variety of groups and associations that are neither commercial (such as corporations) nor governmental. In a global political context, international civil society includes transnational NGOs and epistemic communities (those with extensive cross-border relationships).[2]

The political structure of the world is therefore highly complex. This book emphasizes primarily economic and financial activity, not that political complexity. The analysis thus focuses on private financial institutions, private nonfinancial corporations, and key government institutions. The key government institutions are national-level governments and a few international organizations. Those governmental institutions are by far the most important political entities for collective governance of cross-border finance.

Increasing Pluralism and Diffusion of Power in the World Polity

The second half of the 1900s was characterized by increasing political pluralism—a marked expansion in the number of governmental decision-making units, and a greater diffusion of power among them. Increasing political pluralism was in turn accompanied by rising nationalism.

A great enlargement in the number of independent nation states has been a highly visible aspect of this trend. In the early years after World War II, the increase in nation states reflected primarily the dissolution of colonial empires. In other cases, however, it stemmed from the fragmentation of existing states. Dramatic examples of this fragmentation occurred toward the end of the century. For example, the Soviet Union broke up into fifteen states, and Yugoslavia disintegrated into five states in the early 1990s.

---

1. P. Haas (1992a and 1992b); Sebenius (1992); and Keck and Sikkink (1998).

2. The concept of civil society may have first been emphasized by the philosopher Hegel. Often-cited contributions to the literature about civil society include Almond and Verba (1963); Cohen and Arato (1992); Hann and Dunn (1996); Putnam (1993, 1995, 2000); and Seligman (1992). Wapner (1995, 1996), Lipschutz (1996), Smith and others (1997), Keck and Sikkink (1998), Scholte (1997a, 1997b, 1999, 2000a), Cutler and others (1999), O. Young (1999), O'Brien and others (2000), Warkentin and Mingst (2000), and Scholte and Schnabel (2002) discuss the applicability of the concept at the global level.

Consider the number of member nations in the International Monetary Fund. In July 1944 only 44 nations participated in the Bretton Woods conference, accepting the original IMF Articles of Agreement. By the end of 1960 the number of members had grown to 69, by 1970 to 118, by 1980 to 142, and by 1990 to 155. In 2000 the number of member nations had reached 182, more than four times the number at the establishment of the organization.[3]

Another manifestation of the trend has been the declining political and economic hegemony of the United States, which was at its height at the end of World War II. Concurrently, the political and economic influence of the colonial powers continued to wane. By the 1990s the other dominant military power at the end of World War II, the Soviet Union, had crumbled politically, with many parts of it falling into economic disarray. Most fundamentally, increasing pluralism has led to a global political situation in which one or a few nations no longer effectively dominate all aspects of international decisionmaking.

Power is an elusive concept in political and social theory, with several different dimensions. Nationalism and hegemony are similarly problematic concepts. Entire books will continue to be written on those subjects. I restrict the comments here to a few suggestive indications of the greater diffusion of economic and political power among the world's nations.

The distribution of the world's population is one indicator. The number of people on the globe increased by roughly 140 percent in the second half of the twentieth century, from 2.52 billion in 1950 to 6.06 billion in 2000.[4] Population growth rates were typically much higher in the developing nations than in the developed ones (the annual averages over the entire fifty years were 2.12 percent and 0.77 percent, respectively).[5] The

3. By August 2002 the IMF had 184 member nations. The data for IMF membership are taken from International Monetary Fund, *Annual Report* (various years) and *International Financial Statistics* (various monthly issues and *Yearbooks*). Member countries in the United Nations grew from 51 in 1945 to 185 in 1998 and rose to 190 after Switzerland became a member in the autumn of 2002 (www. un.org/Overview/growth.htm). The General Agreement on Tariffs and Trade had only 37 contracting parties in 1960. By January 1, 2002, there were 144 members of the World Trade Organization; some thirty additional nations were at various stages in the process of applying to become WTO members. Data for GATT and WTO membership are from the WTO website (www.wto.org).

4. Population data used in this paragraph are taken from the United Nations, Population Division of the Department of Economic and Social Affairs, *World Population Prospects: The 2000 Revision.*

5. These growth rates use the UN Population Division's definitions of "less developed" and "more developed" regions. The UN grouping of "more developed" countries, which includes some countries in Europe not usually classified as industrialized, comprises all regions of Europe (including Eastern Europe) plus Northern America, Australia, New Zealand, and Japan.

relative size of developed-nations populations thus declined continuously over the half century. For example, the share of more developed nations fell from 32.3 percent of the world population in 1950 to only 19.7 percent in 2000. The share of the United States in world population was 6.3 percent in 1950 and only 4.7 percent in 2000.

The economic and probably also the political power of a nation, relative to other nations, is influenced by the size of its population. But the volumes of its production and consumption, its stocks of real capital assets and natural resources, and the extent of its international trade are presumably at least as important. Comparable data for these economic magnitudes are not available for every nation. The available data contain significant inaccuracies. Conversion of national currency values into values expressed in a common currency unit, a necessary step for comparison of nations, introduces well-known difficulties.

Nonetheless, all the available data for national income and product accounts broadly support the generalization that economic activity has become more widely diffused across nations since World War II. The decline in the relative dominance of the United States is especially striking. From one-third or more of the world's total production in the years immediately after World War II, the U.S. share has fallen to about one-fifth. Some of the decline in the U.S. share of world output in the early decades after the war coincided with a rebounding share for Western industrial nations such as Germany, France, and Italy. Japan experienced a faster-than-average growth after World War II that lasted until its slowdown and recession in the 1990s. The vigorous growth of newly industrializing nations, especially in Asia, and the boost in the fortunes of oil-exporting nations after the oil price increases of 1973–74 and 1979–80 were two important factors contributing to a falling share of the industrial developed nations in total world production in the closing decades of the century.

The greater diffusion of economic activity across nations in the world may not have reduced and might even have worsened skewness in the distribution of global income and wealth between the world's poorest and richest individuals. The seven industrial nations in the Group of Seven (United States, Japan, Germany, France, United Kingdom, Italy, and Canada) have only about 11.5 percent of the world's population but produce and consume nearly half or more of the world's output. The United States alone enjoys some one-fifth to one-fourth of global production but has only 4.5 percent of the world's population. Seen from the opposite perspective, the four nations India, Pakistan, Bangladesh, and mainland

China together contain more than two-fifths (about 42 percent) of the globe's people, yet account for only one-sixth or less of world output.[6] If analysis takes into account the distributions of income and wealth *within* as well as *between* nations, the skewness is still more dramatic. For example, the incomes of the highest quintile of the world's population (the richest fifth) are well over 100 times greater than the incomes of the lowest quintile (the poorest fifth). Some evidence exists that across-nation differences between middle-income and relatively wealthy nations may have narrowed somewhat in the final decades of the twentieth century. Child mortality has been reduced and average life expectancy has increased throughout most parts of the world, even in the poorest nations (the main exception being southern Africa, where the HIV/AIDS epidemic has been particularly devastating).[7]

In response to the increased geographical diffusion of economic and political power, political influence has shifted somewhat in international organizations. The increase in the number of independent nations has caused especially marked changes in the organizations that do not have weighted voting, such as the General Assembly of the United Nations. Even where the statutes of international organizations mandate weighted influence, however, the effects of increasing political pluralism are evident.

6. The share figures in this and the preceding sentences pertain to the year 2001 (the latest year for which worldwide output estimates were readily available at the time of publication). Underlying data are from the World Bank's *World Development Indicators 2002* report published in August 2002. I use an approximate range of figures for output shares rather than precise percentages because of the large differences between gross national products (and gross national incomes) calculated at current versus purchasing-power-parity (PPP) exchange rates. Cross-nation comparisons that convert nominal output and income data to a common currency using current exchange rates are well known to understate the outputs of poor nations; conversions using PPP exchange rates are an attempt to correct for this bias. Large differences exist between the two types of estimates. For example, the U.S. share of world income and output is 30.7 percent calculated at current exchange rates, but 21.6 percent at PPP exchange rates. The combined share of India, Pakistan, Bangladesh, and mainland China is only 5.2 percent at current exchange rates, but 17.5 percent at PPP exchange rates.

7. Substantial controversy surrounds estimates of recent trends in economic inequality within nations, across nations, and for the world as a whole. Note that trends across nations need not be the same as those within nations (for example, inequality could have declined among some set of nations, while it increased within many of those nations). Comparisons of averages across nations can be very different from comparisons across individuals. Recent examples of the debate in the literature about the measurement of inequality include World Bank (2002), Milanovic (2002), Burtless (2002), and Bhalla (2002). Baker and Noordin (1999), using World Bank data on income shares by quintile groups within countries, estimate the ratio of the highest world quintile to the lowest as 135 in 1998; an update of their figures for 2000 data shows a ratio of 120.

Table 4-1 summarizes data for the quotas of member nations in the International Monetary Fund to illustrate the point. The United States alone had well over 30 percent of the total quotas in the initial years of IMF operations. By 1984 this share had fallen to 20 percent. By 2002 it had declined to only 17.5 percent. The two nations that instituted and dominated the negotiations establishing the IMF, the United States and the United Kingdom, together commanded more than half of the total quotas and votes at the outset; that proportion had fallen to only 22.5 percent by 2002. The falling shares of the United States and the United Kingdom were offset to some degree by upward adjustments in the shares of other industrial nations, especially Germany and Japan. After the 1960s, however, the largest reallocation of shares was in favor of developing nations, first the oil exporters and then the rapidly industrializing "emerging-market" nations.[8]

The preceding paragraphs say nothing about tanks, missiles, and aircraft carriers. Examination of the military dimensions of power could weaken, or even overturn, inferences drawn from economic and political variables. Military considerations would certainly justify more of a disproportionate emphasis on the United States than seems appropriate in an economic or political analysis. The same could be said for a very few European nations, China, and perhaps one or two other nations. (Before the 1990s, however, the Soviet Union would also have received disproportionate emphasis as a military power, a reminder that power in any of its dimensions is sometimes transient.)

Two further caveats are appropriate. First, even if one ignores military considerations, there is some risk of exaggerating the trend of increasing pluralism. The economic and political dominance of the United States has

---

8. A country joining the IMF is assigned a numerical quota (originally in U.S. dollars, now in special drawing rights, or SDRs) that determines, among other things, the size of its potential access to IMF resources. A nation's quota relative to the quotas of other member nations is the most basic determinant of the nation's rights and obligations in the IMF relative to those of other nations. A nation's voting power in the IMF is closely correlated with, but not exactly proportional to, the size of its quota. Each member nation has 250 votes plus one additional vote for each part of its quota equivalent to 100,000 SDRs. Large nations therefore have a slightly smaller share of total votes than of total quotas; small nations have a slightly larger share of total votes than of total quotas. Formal votes are seldom taken in the executive board of the IMF; this tradition of decision by consensus tends to give the smallest nations somewhat less of a voice in decisions than they might have with strict application of formal voting. IMF quotas are discussed in more detail in the companion volume *Crisis Prevention and Prosperity Management for the World Economy*.

Table 4-1a. *Number of Members in the International Monetary Fund*

Members	1948	1959	1972	1984	1992	2001
Industrial nations	15	20	22	22	24	24
Western Hemisphere	2	2	2	2	2	2
Europe	12	16	17	17	19	19
Asia and Oceania	1	2	3	3	3	3
Developing nations	31	49	103	126	148	160
Western Hemisphere	18	20	23	32	32	32
Europe	3	2	5	6	23	30
Asia and Oceania	3	12	19	24	28	31
Middle East	5	9	16	16	15	15
Africa	2	6	40	48	50	51
Total	46	69	125	148	172	183

Sources: IMF, *International Financial Statistics* and *Annual Reports,* various years. Data refer to end of calendar year.

waned since World War II, but it has not disappeared. The United States is still the single most influential nation in world economic and political affairs. It no longer seems a hegemon, in the sense that it is sufficiently powerful to establish and maintain the essential rules governing interstate relations. Yet the United States is still strong enough to retain a de facto veto in many areas of international relations.[9]

Second, Europe in recent decades has exhibited a complex evolution that, in part, runs counter to the trend of increasing pluralism. As the twenty-first century began, the European Union and its associated institutions such as the European Commission and the European Court of Justice embodied the results of incremental but cumulatively decisive steps toward political integration within Europe. The European Union was formerly termed the European Community and before that the European Economic Community (often referred to as the Common Market). Those changes in name are significant. To be sure, still other forces within Europe are more centrifugal rather than centripetal. The Lombards in Italy, the Catalans and Basques in Spain, the Scots and Welsh in the United Kingdom—even

9. For definitions and discussions of hegemony, see, for example, Keohane and Nye (2000) and Keohane (1980, 1984).

Table 4-1b. *Quotas in the International Monetary Fund*
Percent of total, except as indicated

Quotas	1948	1959	1972	1984	1992	2001
Total (millions of SDRs)	7,909.0	13,957.5	29,168.6	89,301.8	141,404.3	212,414.9
Industrial nations	76.01	77.01	69.31	63.68	62.53	61.47
Western Hemisphere	38.56	33.49	26.74	23.36	21.81	20.49
Canada	3.79	3.94	3.77	3.29	3.06	3.00
United States	34.77	29.55	22.97	20.06	18.76	17.49
Europe	34.92	37.78	35.48	33.26	32.78	32.77
Belgium	2.84	2.42	2.23	2.33	2.19	2.17
France	6.64	5.64	5.14	5.02	5.24	5.06
Germany		5.64	5.49	6.05	5.83	6.12
Italy	2.28	1.93	3.43	3.26	3.25	3.32
Netherlands	3.48	2.96	2.40	2.54	2.44	2.43
Spain		0.72	1.35	1.44	1.37	1.44
Sweden		1.07	1.11	1.19	1.14	1.13
Switzerland					1.75	1.63
United Kingdom	16.44	13.97	9.60	6.94	5.24	5.06
Asia and Oceania	2.53	5.73	7.09	7.06	7.94	8.21
Australia	2.53	2.15	2.28	1.81	1.65	1.52
Japan		3.58	4.11	4.73	5.83	6.27
Developing nations	23.99	22.99	30.69	36.32	37.47	38.53
Western Hemisphere	6.12	7.10	8.84	8.91	7.97	7.49
Argentina		2.01	1.51	1.25	1.09	1.00
Brazil	1.90	1.07	1.51	1.64	1.54	1.43
Mexico	1.14	1.29	1.27	1.31	1.24	1.22
Venezuela	0.19	0.11	1.13	1.54	1.38	1.25
Europe	2.88	1.09	2.02	2.48	7.93	8.13
Russian Federation					3.05	2.80
Asia and Oceania	12.20	11.71	10.37	10.32	9.47	10.32
China, P. R.				2.68	2.39	3.00
China—Taiwan	6.95	3.94	1.89			
India	5.06	4.30	3.22	2.47	2.16	0.98
Indonesia		1.18	0.89	1.13	1.06	0.77
Middle East	1.44	1.14	3.48	8.14	6.26	7.29
Iran	0.44	0.25	0.66	0.74	0.76	0.70
Saudi Arabia		0.07	0.46	3.59	2.26	3.29
Africa	1.34	1.95	5.99	6.47	5.84	5.30
Nigeria			0.46	0.95	0.91	0.83
South Africa	1.26	1.07	1.10	1.03	0.97	0.88

Sources: See table 4-1a.

the French in the Rhones-Alpes region and the Germans in Bavaria—seek to augment their subnational political power at the expense of the national governments in Rome, Madrid, London, Paris, and Bonn/Berlin. Such intra-European forces of fragmentation undermine the national governments even as the national governments themselves struggle with ceding some sovereignty to the Brussels institutions of the European Union. As events in the former Yugoslavia remind, moreover, the forces of fragmentation and ethnic nationalism are not absent even in Europe.

The broad trend of increasing political pluralism and the diffusion of political and economic power will presumably not continue in the twenty-first century as strongly as it was observed in the second half of the twentieth century. But the United States and some other industrial nations might well experience a further marginal decline in their weight in the decisionmaking of international organizations. The forces of nationalism will surely continue, possibly grow even stronger in some parts of the world. Beyond doubt, the problems of marshaling collective decisions among multiple, none-of-them-dominant national governments will persist throughout the initial decades of the twenty-first century.

Increasing Integration in the World Economy

Increasing economic interdependence among nations—economic transactions across national borders growing faster than transactions among domestic residents—has been a second pervasive trend in the past half century. In fact, a gradual trend toward increasing openness of national economies has probably been operative since the Napoleonic Wars in the early 1800s. From 1914 through the 1940s, to be sure, this trend was interrupted by two destructive world wars and the intervening years of turbulence and economic depression. The pervasiveness of the trend since the late 1940s, however, is a well-established fact.

The most familiar manifestations of the increasing openness of national economies involve cross-border trade in goods and services. Most nations' exports and imports have been growing more rapidly than their national outputs. Correspondingly, the aggregate flow of trade across borders for the world as a whole has been expanding faster than total world production.

The cross-border debtor-creditor relationships of national economies have become progressively more "internationalized" at a pace even faster than for cross-border trade in goods and services. International lending and borrowing, with assets and liabilities denominated in several different national currencies as well as domestic currency, have risen at a faster pace than aggregate financial activity itself and have caused an increasing degree of integration in nations' financial markets. Relative to conditions at the end of World War II, there is now significantly less scope for individual nations to maintain financial conditions within their borders different from those prevailing abroad.

The increasing relative importance of transactions across borders is abundantly illustrated in national statistics.[10] Anecdotes and examples frequently appear in the news media. Here are two revealing examples. The head of the Levi Strauss company was quoted as saying that "our company buys denim in North Carolina, ships it to France where it is sewn into jeans, launders these jeans in Belgium, and markets them in Germany using TV commercials developed in England." Of the largest 500 companies based in the United States in the mid-1990s, 100 were using software services based in India.[11]

For a provocative example of financial interconnectedness, consider Mary Jo Paoni, a secretary in the Midwest town of Cantrall, Illinois. Paoni's state pension fund in the mid-1990s bought shares in the Brinson Emerging Markets Fund, Germany's Dresdner Bank, the Thai International Fund, and the Thai Euro Fund. The pension fund's investments made Paoni a roundabout (and unwitting) small owner of the GUM department store on Red Square in Moscow (through loans to GUM of the Dresdner Bank and share purchases of GUM by Brinson). It also made her a roundabout owner of the Bangkok Land Company, and hence of Muang Thong Thani, a large urban development project outside Bangkok. In the financial turbulence of 1998, Muang Thong Thani and the Bangkok Land Company failed, and the GUM department store fell into deep trouble. The Illinois state pension fund, and Paoni, shared in these losses.[12]

Two underlying sets of causes have led national economies to become more closely intertwined. First, technological, social, and cultural changes have sharply reduced the effective economic and psychic distances between

---

10. I provide some summary statistics of the pervasive trend toward economic openness in chapter 5, with emphasis on the increasing relative importance of cross-border financial activity.

11. The example of software services in India comes from a *Financial Times* article, "India Emerges as World Center for Software," on July 3, 1996. Both examples are quoted in Scholte (1997a, p.435).

12. See Kristof and others (1999).

nations. Second, many of the government policies that traditionally inhibited cross-border transactions have been relaxed or even dismantled.[13]

The same improvements in transportation and communication technology that make it easier and cheaper for companies in New York to ship goods to California, for residents of Strasbourg to visit relatives in Marseilles, and for investors in Hokkaido to buy and sell shares on the Tokyo Stock Exchange also facilitate trade, migration, and capital movements spanning nations and continents. The sharply reduced costs of moving goods, money, people, and information underlie the profound economic truth that technology has made the world markedly smaller. New communications technology has been especially significant for financial activity (see chapter 5).

Such technological innovations have increased knowledge of potentially profitable international exchanges and of economic opportunities abroad. Those developments, in turn, have changed the tastes of consumers and producers. Foreign goods, foreign vacations, foreign financial investments—virtually any goods and services from other nations—have lost much of their exotic character. Hence not only have the effective economic distances between nations significantly dwindled, but so too have the psychic and social distances.

More than twenty-five years ago, Daniel Bell wrote about the "eclipse of distance." He had in mind not merely geographical distances and the shrinking of time required to travel across them, but also the foreshortening of economic, social, and psychic distances.[14] In the "globalizing" world at the beginning of the twenty-first century, have the shrinking forces identified by Bell progressed so far that one must now speak of the "eclipse of territoriality" and identify "supraterritoriality" as the distinguishing feature of globalization?[15]

It is true that some types of economic and social interactions have such a global nature that it is tempting to describe them as "transcending" national borders. Thomas Friedman reports that his mother, Margaret, was playing bridge on the Internet with three Frenchmen in the summer of 1998 and complained that "they keep speaking French to each other and I can't understand them." When Friedman chuckled, his mother took

---

13. The next few paragraphs are adapted from the general preface to the Brookings-sponsored series of books on *Integrating National Economies*, published in 1994–96.

14. Bell (1999, pp. 313–14).

15. Scholte (1997b, 1999, 2000a, 2002).

umbrage and said, "Don't laugh. I was playing bridge with someone in Siberia the other day."[16] The National Basketball Association (NBA) in the United States has marketing-television offices in Paris, Barcelona, London, Taiwan, Tokyo, Hong Kong, Melbourne, Toronto, New Jersey, and Mexico City. By 1998 NBA games were broadcast to an estimated 600 million households in 190 nations. Fans from more than 50 nations regularly log on to the NBA's Internet website.[17] Examples such as these demonstrate that some information exchanges and some transactions facilitated by electronic technology really do occur as if borders are nonexistent.

Although technological innovations and social and cultural changes have created enhanced incentives for increased contact among residents of different nations, they would not have produced such dramatic effects if they had been countermanded by policies of national governments. National governments have traditionally taxed or restricted goods moving across national borders and tried to limit the cross-border movement of financial funds. Those policies erected "separation fences" at the borders of nations. From the perspective of private sector agents, the separation fences imposed extra costs on cross-border transactions. They reduced trade and international capital movements and in some cases even eliminated them.

After World War II most national governments began, sometimes unilaterally, more often collaboratively, to lower their separation fences, to make them more permeable, or sometimes even to jettison parts of them altogether. The multilateral negotiations under the auspices of the General Agreement on Tariffs and Trade—for example, the Kennedy Round in the 1960s, the Tokyo Round in the 1970s, and the protracted negotiations of the Uruguay Round in the 1990s—stand out as the most prominent examples of fence lowering for trade in goods. Although contentious and marked by many compromises, the GATT negotiations are responsible for sharp reductions in at-the-border restrictions on trade in goods and services. After the mid-1980s a large number of developing nations moved unilaterally to reduce border barriers and to pursue outwardly oriented policies.

The lowering of fences for financial transactions began later and was less dramatic. Nonetheless, by the 1990s government restrictions on cross-border capital flows, especially among the industrial nations, were much

---

16. Friedman (1999, p. xviii).
17. Friedman (1999, pp. 251–52).

less important and spread more widely than at the end of World War II and in the 1950s.[18]

By shrinking the economic and psychic distances among nations, changes in technology would have progressively knitted national economies more closely together even in the absence of reductions in governments' separation fences. Reductions in separation fences would have enhanced interdependence even without the technological innovations. Together, these two sets of evolutionary changes reinforced each other and strikingly transformed the world economy.[19]

The Economic Significance of National Borders

The growing diffusion of power among more political jurisdictions has intensified issues about "sovereignty" for nation states (see below). The formal juridical independence of nations has progressively come into conflict with the increasing integration of economic activity across their borders. In effect, the globe has witnessed a growing mismatch between its political and economic structures. The effective domains of economic markets have corresponded less and less well with governmental jurisdictions. Economic interdependence has been gradually undermining the policy autonomy of national governments and the controllability of national economies.

The world polity and economy are thus at highly awkward, intermediate stages of evolution. The political structure is multilayered, overlapping, so heterogeneous as to seem bewildering. Economic structure is neither fish nor fowl. Markets and governmental interventions coexist. Decentralized decisionmaking is dominant but is frequently supplemented by doses of collective-action governance.

The many dimensions of intermediate complexity can be described, without exaggeration, as messy. Thoughtful observers must grapple with this hybrid, intermediate messiness.

---

18. Chapter 5 returns to this question. The companion volumes *Prudential Oversight and Standards for the World Financial System* and *Crisis Prevention and Prosperity Management for the World Economy* provide details and historical perspective on the lowering of separation fences for cross-border financial transactions.

19. Economic historians are still actively debating among themselves whether there was just as much economic integration across national borders in the late 1800s as there is today. In any event, since the first half of the twentieth century was afflicted with two world wars and a global depression, all of which greatly reduced cross-border transactions, there is an important sense in which the increasing integration of national economies in the second half of the twentieth century should be labeled *re-globalization* rather than simply *globalization*.

The complexity is vividly illustrated by the economic significance of national borders. Although national borders have declined in *relative* importance during the last fifty years, they are still extremely important economically as well as politically. Casual journalism and popular discussions of "globalization" typically fail to understand the intermediate messiness. As flagged already in chapter 1, such commentary advances extreme conclusions. Either today's world has beneficially become a global village, or, conversely, the manic logic of global capitalism is destroying valued social behavior and institutions indigenous to nation states.

Popular commentary correctly perceives that financial and economic integration across national borders has increased greatly and will continue to increase. But it then often leaps to extravagant claims that full globalization has already arrived or will soon do so; that national borders have virtually dissolved and no longer matter; that nation states are unnatural units in a global economy and will soon wither away.

The economic significance of national borders is addressed in the book *How Much Do National Borders Matter?* by the Canadian economist John Helliwell. The book marshals a variety of evidence from the research of many economists. This evidence strongly refutes the generalization that cross-border economic linkages have intensified to the point that they are as tight as those within national economies, after taking due account of the costs of distance (such as transportation and communication costs).[20]

Without doubt, national borders are less important than they once were. They can be, and increasingly are, transcended for certain types of electronic transactions and information exchanges. An increasingly large number of individuals and groups have loosened their identifications and affiliations with locally or nationally defined geographical territories as they have identified more strongly with epistemic or even global communities. But it is a wild exaggeration to assert that national borders are dissolving and that geographical distance and territoriality will soon be superceded. For a minority of individuals, a few dimensions of economic and social life can be accurately described as "supraterritorial" or "truly global." Yes, those dimensions are becoming gradually more salient and affecting larger numbers of individuals. For most people in most parts of their lives, however, such labels mislead more than they inform.

---

20. Helliwell's book was published in 1998 by the Brookings Institution as a sequel to its *Integrating National Economies* series. For an update on the empirical evidence, see Helliwell (2000).

Why do national borders continue to have such great salience? The separation fences at national borders created by past actions of national governments are one part of the explanation. The separation fences have not been completely disassembled. Nor have they become so porous as to be irrelevant.

But other factors, no less important and at least as fundamental, are also at work. Many nationwide institutions and even the nation states themselves reflect, to some degree, an efficient specialization of economic, social, and cultural networks.[21]

Such specializations are analogous to those through which more narrowly based institutions establish the identities of their participants and thereby promote economic relationships. Institutions arising from social groups, whether at the level of the family, the firm, the local community, or even the nation, help to define the rights, values, expectations, and responsibilities of group members in their relations with one another and to foster the credibility of the groups in their dealings with others. The institutions thus reduce uncertainties and lower transaction costs that would otherwise dampen the internal economic relations among group members and the external relations with others. A social grouping as large as a nation has much more loosely defined rights, values, expectations, and responsibilities among its residents than the analogous values and obligations among, say, a family unit, a firm, or a local community organization. But even at the level of the nation there may be a significant reduction in uncertainties and transaction costs that would otherwise prevail. Given the greater ease of operating within known indigenous institutions, cultures, and information networks, for example, and given the shared standards and norms to which they give rise, firms may perceive less uncertainty associated with domestic than with cross-border transactions and thus manifest greater trust in dealing with domestic than with foreign firms. Because national institutions and cultures and the social capital to which they give rise differ so greatly, transactions costs thus tend to remain much lower within than among national economies even in the absence of at-the-border separation fences created by government taxes, regulations, or restrictions.

The fundamental economic and social forces identified in the preceding paragraph are not yet well understood. Further analysis is required before

---

21. See Helliwell (1998, chap. 7), which in turn draws on, among others, Ben-Porath (1980), O. Williamson (1989), Hart (1995), Putnam (1993), Knack and Keefer (1997), and Platteau (1994). Helliwell (2000) updates the main conclusions emphasized in his 1998 study.

policymakers can confidently make normative judgments about whether the current levels of border effects are appropriate, "too high," or "too low." What is clear, however, is that national borders have economic influences, in size and extent, that are large, pervasive, and durable. To quote Helliwell (1998, p. 129):

> Would the global economy serve the world's people better if it were to become a seamless web in which national borders no longer matter much for the distribution and nature of economic activity? There is a widespread belief that this tight global economy already exists, but the evidence shows that such a perception is dramatically mistaken. This makes it even more important to ask why the border effects are there, and why they remain so large even where there are few if any formal border barriers to support them.

Collective-Governance Problems with Cross-Border Dimensions

The fact that national borders are less important than they once were, yet still matter greatly, is one illustration of the messy, hybrid nature of today's world. Another key illustration is the complex mixture of private markets and government interventions that, in one way or another, characterizes every national economy. Nations could not possibly function well without decentralized market-based decisions. Nor could they function well without some forms of cooperative, centralized decisionmaking (chapter 3). Yet both market failures and government failures are pervasive. How should society strike a balance between the risks, both of them severe, of the two types of failure?

Collective governance would be difficult and contentious even in a single closed and homogeneous nation. In our multination heterogeneous world of progressively increasing economic interdependence, collective-governance problems are several orders of magnitude still more difficult.

To understand why this is so, one must first recognize that the increasing openness of national economies has caused collective-action problems with cross-border dimensions to become more numerous and conspicuous over time. Collective-action problems are the externalities, market failures, and hence public goods challenges (chapter 3) that lead to consideration of possible collective intervention, most notably by government institutions. Collective-action problems with cross-border dimensions have become gradually more important in three broad ways.

First, economic activities in one nation have increasingly produced consequences that spill across borders and affect other nations. Illustrations of such spillovers abound. Given the rapid diffusion of knowledge, science and technology policies in one nation have generated knowledge that other nations can use without full payment. Labor market policies have become matters of concern to other nations because workers migrate in search of work; policies in one nation can trigger migration that floods or starves labor markets elsewhere. Given the impact of modern technology in creating international networks among financial institutions, lax supervision and regulation of financial institutions in one nation have eroded the ability of other nations to enforce banking and securities rules and to deal with fraudulent transactions. When one nation dumps pollutants into the air or water that other nations breathe or drink, concern about the pollution extends well beyond the polluting nation, and the actions become a matter for international negotiation. Indeed, greenhouse gases such as carbon dioxide that are emitted into the atmosphere when individual nations burn hydrocarbons for generating electricity contribute to global warming and are thereby a matter of concern for the entire world.

Second, as cross-border economic integration has intensified, national governments have experienced diminishing autonomy for their policies. The *autonomy* of a nation's policies is best defined in terms of the effectiveness of its collective-governance structures in achieving national objectives. In the case of macroeconomic policies, for example, the degree of autonomy depends on the effectiveness with which national policymakers can vary monetary and fiscal instruments to influence national target variables such as the national inflation rate and employment within the nation's borders.

Increases in cross-border economic and financial integration make it more difficult to use national policies to control events within the nation's borders. The typical increase in interdependence reduces the effects of national policy instruments on national variables relative to their effects on variables in other nations. It also means that policy actions taken by foreign governments and nonpolicy disturbances originating abroad spill over into the home nation to a relatively greater extent. To an uncertain degree, and frequently in an undesired direction, such externally generated forces buffet the domestic target variables of the home government. Increases in the openness of a national economy thus typically diminish the degree of control that a nation's policymakers can exert over national target variables.

The economies of smaller and highly open nations have always been buffeted; their policies have typically been constrained, sometimes severely, by foreign economic events and policies. Increasingly, however, all nations have been constrained. As national economies have become more closely intertwined, policy decisions in any single nation have thus become more difficult to make, and more uncertain in their consequences. In particular, central banks are less able to maintain financial conditions within their domestic reservoirs that diverge greatly from financial conditions elsewhere in the world.[22]

Cross-border spillovers and individual nations' diminished autonomy for their own policies have raised, more insistently than in the past, the issue of whether nations may be better able to achieve their economic goals if they work together collaboratively in adjusting their policies. Of course, such forces can sometimes be allowed to persist without explicit international cooperation. States in the United States adopt their own tax systems and set policies for assistance to poor people with little formal cooperation or limitation. Market pressures operate to force a degree of de facto cooperation. If one state taxes corporations too heavily, it knows business will move elsewhere. Analogously, differences among nations in regulations, standards, policies, institutions, and even social and cultural preferences create economic incentives for a kind of arbitrage that erodes or eliminates the differences. Such pressures involve not only the conventional arbitrage that exploits price differentials (buying at one point in geographic space or time and selling at another) but also shifts in the location of production facilities and in the residence of factors of production.

In many other cases, however, cross-border spillovers, arbitrage pressures, and diminished effectiveness of national policies can produce unwanted consequences. For many types of externalities, national governments may need to cooperate to promote mutual interests. For example, population growth, continued urbanization, and the more intensive exploitation of natural resources generate adverse externalities not only within but across national boundaries. Favorable externalities generated when benefits spill across national jurisdictions probably also increase in importance (for instance, the gains from basic research and from control of communicable diseases).

---

22. For a more detailed and technical discussion of the autonomy of national economic policies and the controllability of national economies, see Bryant (1980b, chaps. 10–13).

Some collective-action problems with cross-border dimensions have existed for many decades. But technological change and the reduction of separation fences at national borders have heightened their importance. When one nation produces "goods" (such as scientific research) or "bads" (such as pollution) that significantly affect other nations, individual governments acting sequentially and noncooperatively can deal less effectively with the resulting issues. In the absence of explicit cooperation and political leadership, that is, of *international collective governance,* too few collective goods and too many collective bads are supplied.

The third way in which collective-action problems with cross-border dimensions have become more important is that they have increasingly generated challenges to the principles of sovereignty for individual nations.

In its international legal connotations, *sovereignty* entails mutual recognition among territorial entities that have formal juridical independence. In broader connotations, sovereignty applied to nations presumes that each nation has, within its geographical territory, indigenous political and authority structures and that these structures are free from interference by outside actors. Sovereignty presumes, in other words, a norm of nonintervention in domestic affairs. Domestic political authorities are, in principle, the sole arbiters of legitimate behavior within the nation's geographical territory.[23]

The residents of a sovereign nation are presumed to be free to shape their behavior to their own values and to select their own political arrangements without interference from other nations. Similarly, property rights, inherently territorial for most types of assets, are allocated by nation. The so-called global commons, such as outer space and the seabed outside national territorial waters, are the sole exceptions. Each nation is presumed to have sovereign rights for its residents to exploit their property in accordance with the nation's own preferences and policies. The presumption of political sovereignty for nations is analogous to the concept of consumer sovereignty for individuals (the presumption that the individual consumer best knows his or her own interests and should be able to exercise them freely).

---

23. The connotations of sovereignty emphasized in the text are termed "international legal sovereignty" and "Westphalian sovereignty" in the international relations literature. Krasner (1999) distinguishes among these two and two other connotations ("domestic sovereignty" and "interdependence sovereignty"), reviews the intellectual history of the concept, and provides numerous references to the international relations literature. See also Rosenau (1997, chap. 11).

To be sure, sovereignty is a complex, slippery concept. One recent analysis goes so far as to assert that the principles of sovereignty have been violated throughout history and that the sovereignty of nation states in practice is best understood as organized hypocrisy.[24]

It is essential to distinguish between *de jure sovereignty* and *de facto autonomy*. The constitutional, de jure independence of a nation in no sense guarantees that it will be able, de facto, to prevent external influences from shaping decisions taken within its borders. The political processes, institutions, and leaders of individual nations are constrained, often severely, by the actions of other nations' governments and by other aspects of the external environment. Moreover, increasing cross-border economic integration is, as emphasized above, gradually eroding the autonomy of national policies. More will be said below about the contrast between de jure sovereignty and de facto autonomy.

Notwithstanding the preceding complexities, the existing world system of nation states continues to be based largely on the presumption of de jure sovereignty. The member nations of the system continue to endorse—virtually always in rhetoric, although not invariably in practice—the norm of nonintervention by external actors in domestic affairs.

With the pronounced increases in economic integration across national borders in recent decades, challenges to the presumption of sovereignty have increased and have been based, more often than in the past, on a cosmopolitan global perspective. Historical violations of sovereignty typically involved stronger nations intervening in the domestic affairs of weaker nations, abrogating the norm of nonintervention through coercion or even imposing their will through military force. In earlier eras, few individuals or groups challenged the premises of sovereignty by claiming that universal, nonnational values should take precedence within a particular nation over the preferences or policies of that nation as expressed through its political processes. In the final decades of the twentieth century, however, progressively larger numbers of individuals and groups, and occasionally even their national governments, have identified circumstances in which, it is claimed, nonnational values should trump local, national values.

Some groups have increasingly seized on human rights issues, for example, or what they deem to be egregiously inappropriate political arrangements in other nations. An especially prominent case occurred when citizens

24. Krasner (1999).

in many nations labeled the former apartheid policies of South Africa an affront to universal values and emphasized that the South African government was not legitimately representing the interests of a majority of South Africa's residents. Such views caused many national governments to apply economic sanctions against South Africa. Member nations of the North Atlantic Treaty Organization advanced an analogous rationale for their intervention in Kosovo in 1999.[25]

Examples of value conflicts are not restricted to human rights issues. Groups focusing on labor market issues are troubled by the fact that many developing nations have, relative to the most advanced industrial nations, weaker rights for workers to form unions and bargain collectively, less stringent safety regulations, insufficient bans on child labor and forced labor, few or no guarantees against discrimination, and few or no provisions encouraging equal pay for women and men. Such views often lead to recommendations for applying trade restrictions or other sanctions on nations whose labor market policies are deemed to fall below acceptable world standards.

Groups focusing on environmental issues have characterized tropical rain forests as the lungs of the world and the genetic repository for numerous species of plants and animals that are the heritage of all humankind. Such views have caused Europeans, North Americans, and Japanese to challenge the timber-cutting policies of Brazilians and Indonesians. A controversy over tuna fishing with long drift nets that kill porpoises is yet another revealing example. Environmentalists in the United States whose sensibilities were offended by the drowning of porpoises required U.S. boats at some additional expense to amend their fishing practices. The U.S. fishermen, complaining about imported tuna caught in a manner that kills more porpoises than they are allowed to kill, then succeeded in persuading the U.S. government to ban such tuna imports (both direct imports from the countries in which the tuna is caught and indirect imports shipped through third countries). Mexico and Venezuela were the main nations affected by this ban. A GATT dispute panel sided with Mexico against the United States in the controversy, which further upset the U.S. environmental community.[26]

---

25. Real or alleged human rights abuses have always been the most common motivation for external intervention in the domestic affairs of a nation. In the past, however, interventions often took the form of a strong nation applying political pressure or military force in a weaker host nation where the human or property rights of citizens of the strong nation were deemed to be inadequately protected.

26. A similar but even more complex dispute between the United States and four Asian countries, concerning shrimp imports and endangered sea turtles, was brought to the WTO in the 1990s.

A common feature of the preceding examples is the existence, real or alleged, of governance failures within other nations or of what have been termed "psychological externalities." Those criticizing governance failures in foreign nations or claiming the presence of psychological externalities typically assert what they believe to be higher-level, universal values and thus reject untrammeled political sovereignty for nation states. They argue that the sovereignty norm of nonintervention in internal affairs should be modified in the circumstances that they identify. They wish to constrain the exercise of sovereign authority by individual nations through international negotiations or, if necessary, by even stronger forms of international collective governance.[27]

Levels of Governance, Subsidiarity, and National Sovereignty

When collective governance is judged necessary to respond to market failures, should the collective action be centralized or decentralized? In particular, where there are several layers of government jurisdictions, what principles should guide the allocation of powers among the layers?

When one reasons from theoretical principles, strong arguments can be advanced for centralization. Centralization may be required when actions in one jurisdiction spill over into others, thus affecting (favorably or unfavorably) the welfare of other populations. Centralization may be appropriate if the supply of public goods is of higher quality or lower cost when provided through a single rather than multiple jurisdictions. A central governmental authority for a large region may be better able to facilitate redistribution within component local jurisdictions, or especially among component jurisdictions, thereby promoting equity for the region as a whole.

But theoretical principles can also generate strong arguments for decentralization. Local governments may be better informed than central authorities about the preferences of local residents or about conditions affecting the local implementation of policies. Even if a central authority had equally

---

Environmental and protectionist issues were deeply entangled. In 1989 the United States had required its shrimp boats to use turtle excluder devices and also banned shrimp imports from countries whose shrimpers did not use the devices. The WTO's dispute settlement process in 1998 resulted in a controversial ruling that pleased neither the environmentalist nor trade community. The controversy was still alive in 2000. Numerous WTO documents deal with the dispute; see also Stewart (1998) and Appleton (1999).

27. Kaul, Grunberg, and Stern (1999) is a general survey of the literature on global public goods and the issues that global public goods are increasingly raising for international collective governance.

good information, centrally decided policies could be less responsive to local conditions. The central authority might administratively prefer simple, uniform policies across localities or might feel obliged to implement policies of equal treatment for all its component jurisdictions. Decentralization might also better facilitate the expression of local dissatisfaction with governance and therefore be preferable for encouraging accountability. The residents of a local jurisdiction can manifest dissatisfaction by voting against an incumbent government or even by moving into another jurisdiction.

Abstract theoretical arguments cannot resolve this issue in a general way. The appropriate allocation of collective-governance powers depends on the context and the governmental function. Within most modern-day nation states, political authority is and probably ought to be dispersed across several different layers of government. The responsibilities of each layer need to be shaped by a subtle balancing of the advantages and disadvantages of decentralization.[28]

Of all the general arguments in favor of decentralization, perhaps the weightiest are those pertaining to accountability. When political authority is concentrated and centralized, the risks rise sharply that accountability will be diminished. The effects of centralization on transparency are more ambiguous, but it seems plausible to argue that transparency too could often be diminished because of the centralization of authority.

Because of the risks from lesser accountability, a general presumption exists in favor of *subsidiarity*. This term, whose origins lie in Catholic theology and governance practices for the Catholic church, has been widely used in Europe in recent years to discuss alternative allocations of powers within the European Union. The European debate has canvassed different models of federation (regionally) and different visions of how a federal Europe might eventually be organized. The continental concepts of subsidiarity and confederation have been contrasted with Anglo-Saxon concepts of federalism (for example, as manifested in the United States).[29]

28. For examples of the technical literature on these issues, see Cooper (1974, 1986); Olson (1969), Oates (1972, 1977); McGuire (1974); Rubinfeld (1987); and Begg and others (1993, chap. 3).

29. For detailed discussion, see Peters (1992), Sbragia (1992), and Begg and others (1993). The Begg and others study distinguishes between federation and confederation as follows: "For our purposes, the critical distinction lies in the degree of sovereignty of the members. In a confederation, the central authority cannot impose decisions on any of its members, since each member has veto power. Indeed, in an important sense there *is* no central authority, merely a mechanism for coordinating the decisions of independent members. In a federation, by contrast, central decisions do not need to be

Subsidiarity is the presumptive principle that decentralized allocations and exercises of political authority are to be preferred in the absence of compelling reasons for centralization. In other words, lower-level, local jurisdictions should make decisions unless convincing reasons exist for assigning them to higher-level, more central authorities, with the burden of proof always resting on the proponents of centralization.

Could the world polity eventually contain global federalist governmental institutions? That question is virtually irrelevant today. Worse still, the notion of global federalist government is an unhelpful fantasy when making collective-governance decisions in today's intermediate polity.

The beginning of wisdom when thinking about the evolution of international collective governance in today's world is, as suggested in chapter 1, to reject extreme stances such as the untrammeled markets view and the sweeping institutionalist reform view and instead adopt the approach of pragmatic incrementalism. A pragmatic incrementalist must also avoid confusion about national sovereignty and have a keen awareness of the distinction between de jure sovereignty and de facto autonomy.

Abrogations of the principles of national sovereignty, as observed earlier, have been commonplace in history. From the perspective of an individual nation for whom the principles are violated, it is essential to distinguish two classes of abrogation. The first class includes external interventions that disregard the nation's sovereignty and that are harmful to the nation's welfare. The second class includes reductions in national sovereignty that are welcomed by the nation's rulers and that enhance its welfare.

Power is distributed very asymmetrically across nations. A strong nation may violate the sovereignty of a weaker nation through coercion, by threatening sanctions, for example, unless the weaker nation modifies some aspect of its policies that the strong nation wants changed. Or strong nations may simply impose their will, by force in a war. Such violations of the norm of nonintervention typically worsen the welfare of the weaker nation's residents (at a minimum, of the nation's political leaders). Reductions in sovereignty for nations suffering coercion or the imposition of force are understandably viewed by those nations as adverse. Throughout modern history, therefore, weaker nations have always been the strongest

---

unanimous. If an appropriate majority of members votes in favour of a measure, this becomes binding on all" (pp. 23–24). Møller (1995) outlines a vision of the European Union as a decentralized confederation rather than a "United States of Europe." Peterson (1995) analyzes "functional" and "legislative" concepts of federalism for the United States.

proponents of the sovereignty norm of nonintervention. The nations with greatest political and military power have found it easiest to develop justi-fications for overriding the principles and norms of sovereignty in particu-lar circumstances where they desire outcomes that conflict with those prin-ciples and norms.

Reductions in sovereignty that improve welfare for a nation or several nations simultaneously are an entirely different matter. If the rulers of a nation willingly enter into welfare-enhancing arrangements that in some way supercede the principles or norms of sovereignty, the departures from the status quo are not well described as "violations." The sovereignty-reducing arrangements are invited; they are voluntary accords. Were the arrangements not expected to improve welfare, the nation's rulers would not agree to them. Refraining from the arrangements is an option. Often, the nation may effectively retain the ability to terminate its consent to the arrangements if they do not work out as anticipated. Examples of such arrangements include contractual commitments with other nations and participation in international treaties or conventions. By virtually any cri-terion for judging the actions of a nation's political leadership, it can be sensible to override the principles and norms of sovereignty by voluntarily entering into such arrangements.[30]

The preceding observations apply to an individual nation's approach to its sovereignty. Now focus on some points about the autonomy of its national policies. A farsighted national government, aware of the gradually diminishing autonomy of its policies, will not only eschew an excessive preoccupation with loss of its formal sovereignty. It will actively seek vol-untary, cooperative agreements with external actors that can enhance the nation's welfare in the face of the diminishing autonomy of its policies. Cooperation with other nations'governments, directly or through interna-tional institutions, may generate international collective-governance poli-cies capable of offsetting some of the adverse effects associated with the eroding autonomy of its own policies.

---

30. Krasner (1999) distinguishes between voluntary agreements that are *contracts* and those that are *conventions.* In an international convention, a nation's rulers agree to abide by certain standards regard-less of what others do. In a contract, the nation's rulers agree to specific policies in return for explicit expected benefits. Krasner points out that conventions and contracts override the principles and norms of "Westphalian sovereignty" but *not* the principles of "international legal sovereignty." In fact, he stresses, "all contracts and conventions are facilitated by and are a confirmation of international legal sovereignty. What is critical for international legal sovereignty is that the [nation's] ruler retains the right to terminate the contract and that the contract or convention is voluntary" (pp. 26–27).

What does it really mean to yield sovereignty and try to offset declines in autonomy by voluntarily entering into cooperative arrangements with other national governments? What is meant by *cooperation*? Cooperation among national governments, as I envisage it, has a limited and precise meaning. Cooperation occurs when several governments take into account the interactions between their nations' economies and polities and as a result mutually adjust their national policies or collectively undertake an international policy. The essential ingredient in cooperation is an agreement among the governments to behave differently in certain circumstances than they would have behaved without the agreement. To be durable, agreements need to be binding and enforceable. In contrast, noncooperative decisions are characterized by an unwillingness to enter into binding commitments. Each government adapts its independent decisions to what it observes or expects others to do. But in the absence of cooperation, no constraints exist on its own independence of action, and no assurances exist that the actions of other governments will be constrained.

This concept of cooperation is not a synonym for amity, harmony, or altruism. The essence of cooperation is a self-interested mutual adjustment of behavior. Such cooperation may—and often does—undermine the formal sovereignty of nations. But it is "Pareto-improving," that is, it makes participants to the agreement at least as well off as they would have been in the absence of the agreement.

What will the world polity do about international collective governance in the shorter run? For at least the next several decades, national governments will almost surely insist on retaining the formal principles and norms of de jure sovereignty. By itself, that insistence need not be of great consequence. What is more important is whether national political leaders will better understand, and publicly acknowledge that they understand, the continuing trends causing gradual erosion of the de facto autonomy of their national policies.

Confusion in the wider public about both sovereignty and autonomy may well persist even if political leadership turns out to be farsighted. Rhetoric about "losing sovereignty" will surely persist, especially among individuals and groups that want to slow, or even to try to reverse, the increasing economic integration across national borders.

Some already established firms or sectors in national economies will continue to have frankly protectionist motives for reversing the increasing cross-border integration. If they are shortsighted, domestic firms may try to maintain their established positions merely by excluding foreign-produced imports instead of continuing to compete and innovate in open markets. Such firms or sectors are likely to continue trumpeting the rhetoric of sovereignty losses, deliberately trying to obfuscate the true, rent-seeking explanation for their opposition to the cross-border integration.[31]

Many other parts of society may be fearful of globalization but honestly confused about how public policies should react to it. For those individuals and groups, the constructive focus of concern should be declines in autonomy and particular harmful effects, but not losses of sovereignty.

All things considered, national governments will continue to be reluctant to delegate significantly greater authority to international institutions. Confusions about sovereignty and illusions about autonomy will continue to inhibit nations from acting collectively to foster their mutual interests.

The principle of subsidiarity can help to guide national governments through the morass of collective-action problems with cross-border dimensions. But subsidiarity will not be a sufficient guide. Moreover, as cross-border spillovers requiring intergovernmental cooperation become still more salient and as popular awareness gradually spreads that de facto national autonomy has in fact been lost in large measure, nations eventually will be forced to consider enhanced supranational collective governance of one sort or another. In particular, pressures will almost surely grow for the energizing of various forms of intergovernmental cooperation and for the strengthening of consultative forums and international institutions to serve as the loci of that cooperation. Chapter 7 returns to this theme.

National Autonomy versus Openness to the Global Economy

An individual nation confronts a difficult trade-off between reaping the benefits of openness to the global economy on the one hand and trying to

---

31. Identification of firms or sectors acting from protectionist motives is frequently difficult because the human rights and environmental impacts of a product or an industry (more generally, "psychological externalities" like those discussed earlier in the chapter) can mask protectionist lobbying. The subtle mixing of protectionist pressures and public interest concerns in the design of product norms and technical standards is well illustrated by a debate in the European Union about regulation of the paper box industry. Sweden and Finland produce paper mainly from new trees, whereas German and French producers employ significant amounts of recycled paper and rags. The EU in the early 1990s considered a regulation requiring paper boxes sold in the EU to contain a minimum fraction of recycled paper. As discussed in Baldwin (2000), the proposal sounded like an environmentally friendly,

preserve some degree of national autonomy on the other. Openness undermines the ability to sustain local economic conditions that differ from conditions outside the nation. Attaining the maximum benefits of openness may require the nation to accept a substantial erosion of indigenous values and institutions. Yet efforts to shield local economic conditions and indigenous values and institutions from unwanted foreign influences may require the sacrifice of gains in economic efficiency and hence of improvements in economic well-being.

The smaller and more open the national economy, the steeper the trade-off is likely to be. Toward the extremes of smallness and openness—say, an Estonia or Vanuatu or Swaziland—the ability through national policies to nurture indigenous culture, institutions, and identifiably different national economic conditions may be so limited as to seem negligible. When national economies are large and less open, such as in Japan or Brazil, the trade-off may still be relatively steep, but at least less than with extreme openness.

Some authors have taken the strong position that even for larger nations, the trade-off between autonomy and openness does not, for practical purposes, exist at all. Thomas Friedman, for example, has espoused that view. Writing about the choices facing an individual nation, he asserts:

> The historical debate is over. The answer is free-market capitalism [in a global economy]. . . . Ideologically, there is no more mint chocolate chip, there is no more strawberry swirl, and there is no more lemon-lime. Today there is only free-market vanilla and North Korea. . . . In the end, if you want higher standards of living in a world without walls, the free market is the only ideological alternative left. One road. Different speeds. But one road. When a country recognizes this fact, when it recognizes the rules of the free market in today's global economy, and decides to abide by them, it puts on what I call 'the Golden Straitjacket.' The Golden Straitjacket is the defining political-economic garment of this globalization era. The Cold War had the Mao suit, the Nehru jacket, the Russian fur. Globalization has

---

"public interest" regulation, but it would also have effectively undermined the resource-based advantage of Swedish and Finnish firms, much to the joy of the French and German industries. (Finland and Sweden subsequently joined the European Union in 1995 and the regulation was not adopted.)

only the Golden Straitjacket. If your country has not been fitted for one, it will be soon.[32]

The view that all nations should welcome a Golden Straitjacket, the ideology of unadulterated free-market capitalism, is a first cousin to the untrammeled market view about possible reforms for cross-border finance. Like the untrammeled market view, the Golden Straitjacket and its enthusiasm for market fundamentalism is an extreme position that denies the possibilities of a middle ground.

To wear Friedman's Golden Straitjacket is to give primacy, exclusively, to the goal of economic efficiency. Yet a nation's residents may value other goals as well, including the preservation of indigenous norms and institutions and the retention of "local" decisionmaking. Recognizing the powerful forces of economic interdependence and the associated benefits for a national economy need not be tantamount to entirely forswearing efforts to shape the way that external forces influence the economy. For most nations, a limited range of policies does exist that can introduce some degree of differentiation from—at least a marginal amount of friction with—the outside world.

This limited range of policies was referred to earlier as the "separation fence" at the nation's borders. To repeat, few nations have completely disassembled their separation fences. Nor have the fences become so porous as to be entirely irrelevant.

A less misleading analogy than the Golden Straitjacket is to regard a nation as a relatively unprotected island in a large, sometimes turbulent, ocean. The nation's economy and financial system may be likened to the harbors through which all shipping into and out of the island pass. The practical question for the nation's government is whether the harbors can be modified to function as partially sheltered lagoons. The sea cannot be kept entirely out of the harbors; it would be foolish to pretend otherwise. When storms break out on the open ocean, the harbors and hence the entire island will inevitably be buffeted. But it is reasonable to build breakwaters around the harbors, to render them less unsafe when storms do occur. Breakwaters have limited effectiveness, especially in severe typhoons. But they are better than no protection at all.

---

32. Friedman (1999, p. 86). See also Friedman's challenge "Does Your Country Dare To Be Open?" (p. 179) and his praises of "the virtues of keeping your economy as open as possible" (p. 182).

As argued above, a nation open to the rest of the world may decide, voluntarily and wisely, to accept reductions in its formal sovereignty and in its de facto autonomy. The resulting benefits can decisively offset any costs from erosion of indigenous values and institutions and from erosion of the ability to sustain local economic conditions marginally different from conditions outside the nation.

A notable example is that the nation can strongly benefit from access to savings generated in the rest of the world. Borrowing the savings of foreigners can prove sensible when the nation has unexploited but potentially profitable investment opportunities. Just as for a region within a single economy, economic activity and well-being will fall well short of their potential levels if local investments must be restricted to the savings that the local economy is currently capable of generating. Yes, borrowing from the rest of the world constrains the nation. It often entails a reduction in de facto autonomy, a diminution in local control. Yet the nation is better off with the borrowed savings and some reduction in autonomy than it would be without the borrowed savings but undiminished autonomy.

Borrowing from abroad can be overdone, just as individual firms or individual households can imprudently borrow too much. Mishaps and instability in cross-border finance are all too possible. Even when a nation's own policies are sound, moreover, the national financial system can be whipsawed by turbulence originating abroad or the erratic behavior of foreign investors. A major objective of chapter 6 is to identify and analyze the relevant costs and benefits when a nation's financial system is significantly open to the rest of the world.

For the time being, the reader should keep an open mind about this difficult trade-off. Neither your nation nor others must resign themselves to being fitted out exclusively for Friedman's Golden Straitjacket. Neither should any nation yearn for a great wall that will insulate it from foreign influences. Think of breakwaters, but not walls and not straitjackets. That pragmatism is the appropriate frame of mind for digesting the analysis in what follows.

A further dimension of pragmatism is also needed. Estonia's circumstances are, again, very different from Japan's. China, Brazil, Swaziland—indeed, every one of the more than 180 nations in the world—have circumstances that are different, often unique. Nowhere is it written that each nation should build the same type of breakwaters or have a broadly similar posture about the trade-off between autonomy and openness. A venerable pragmatic aphorism suggests "different strokes for different folks." That thought, too, is a helpful guideline for the analysis that lies ahead.

Global Standards and a Level Playing Field

Increasingly large numbers of individuals are inclined to deemphasize their rootedness in particular nation states and to espouse, as complements or sometimes even substitutes, universal or nonnational values. These cosmopolitan individuals, as noted earlier, feel progressively freer to challenge the political sovereignty of the nations in which they are resident. Such individuals tend also to favor the *harmonization* of standards across nations, sometimes even the harmonization of governance institutions. At the least, they advocate *minimum standards* to be adhered to by all nations.

Issues about standards inevitably arise when the policies of several different nations are alleged to be competitively inequitable. The incidence of such allegations naturally tends to rise as cross-border spillovers increase. Nation A may permit companies to emit pollutants, whereas nation B imposes tight restrictions on emissions. Nation C may reduce its tax rates and prudential regulations on banking to low levels, hoping to induce banks to relocate their activities in C rather than elsewhere. Nation D may require commodities, whether produced at home or abroad, to meet certain design standards, justified for safety reasons. Foreign competitors may find it too expensive to meet these standards. In that event, the standards in D act very much like tariffs or quotas, effectively narrowing or even eliminating foreign competition for domestic producers.

Citing examples of this sort, producers or governments in individual nations often complain that business is not conducted on a level playing field. Typically, the complaining nation proposes that the other nations adjust their policies to moderate or remove the competitive inequities.

Arguments for creating a level playing field in the world economy are troublesome at best. International trade occurs precisely because of differences among nations in resource endowments, labor skills, and consumer tastes. Nations specialize in producing goods and services in which they are relatively most efficient. In a fundamental sense, cross-border transactions are valuable because the playing field is *not* level. David Ricardo, when first developing the theory of comparative advantage, focused on differences among nations attributable to climate or technology. But Ricardo could as easily have ascribed the productive differences to differing national standards or "social climates" as to physical or technological climates. Taking all "climatic" differences as given, the theory of comparative advantage argues that free trade among nations tends to maximize global welfare.

Taken to its logical extreme, the cliché of leveling the playing field implies that nations should become homogeneous in all major respects. But the recommendation for homogenization—for sweeping harmonization—is unrealistic and even pernicious. Suppose nation A decides that it is too poor to afford the costs of a squeaky clean environment and will thus permit some production of goods that pollute local air and water supplies. Or suppose it concludes that it cannot afford stringent protections for worker safety. Nation A will then argue that it is inappropriate for other nations to impute to nation A the value they themselves place on a clean environment and labor market standards (just as it would be inappropriate to impute the A valuations to the environments and labor markets of other nations).

A core component of the idea of political sovereignty is to permit national residents to order their lives and property in accord with their own preferences. Seen from that perspective, the notion of a level playing field is an unhelpful mantra, a rule of thumb that can mislead as often as it conveys a sound objective for equity across nations.

Which perspective about differences among nations is more compelling? Is nation A merely exercising its national preferences in setting national standards, appropriately exploiting its comparative advantage in goods that are dirty or dangerous to produce? Or does a legitimate cross-border problem exist that justifies pressure from other nations urging nation A to accept changes in its environmental and labor market policies (thus curbing its national sovereignty)?[33]

When national governments negotiate resolutions to such questions—trying to agree whether individual nations are legitimately exercising sovereign choices or, alternatively, engaging in behavior that is unfair or damaging to other nations—the dialogue is invariably contentious. Cooperative resolution of the differences, and efforts to agree on international standards, depend on the typically complex circumstances of the cross-border

---

33. An important component of the notion of political sovereignty is that institutions exist within a nation that legitimately map the preferences of individuals into national legislation and administrative priorities. "Legitimately" implies some form of democratic processes and institutions. If nation A is ruled by a dictator who permits other, wealthier nations to dump toxic wastes in the nation in exchange for personal kickback payments, for example, the preferences of nation A's residents for environmental standards are not being adequately represented. The observations in the text about cross-national differences cannot be applied in situations when the underlying preferences of a large majority of a nation's residents are egregiously distorted by the nation's political rulers.

spillovers and on the relative weights accorded to the interests of particular individuals and particular nations.

Prospering in an Intermediate, Multination World

To recapitulate, the awkward reality is that we live in a world economy and world polity that are hybrid along most key dimensions. Nation states are messy mixtures of market and government institutions. The peoples and policymakers of these nations typically value decentralized decisionmaking and the efficiencies of market-determined price signals. But they dislike market failures. Peoples and policymakers know that collective governance is sometimes necessary to prevent or mitigate market failures. But they are generally averse to the high degree of centralized decisionmaking in a planned, dirigiste economy. When they observe government failures, which they often do, they dislike them, if anything, more than they dislike market failures. The least inadequate approach seems to be a middle ground—a complex mixed economy, varying in its details from one nation to another given the idiosyncracies of history and culture.

The implications of increasing cross-border interdependence are equally messy and intermediate. As peoples and policymakers confront de facto declines in effective autonomy for purely national policies, they are driven to consider enhanced intergovernmental cooperation and stronger international institutions. But they are simultaneously reluctant to surrender national sovereignty, even though they are often confused about what sovereignty means in practice. Individual nations do in fact face a difficult trade-off between preserving autonomy and reaping the benefits of openness. The principle of subsidiarity argues both in principle and in practice for retaining most aspects of governmental decisionmaking at the level of the nation state. Yet an increasing number of problems cannot be resolved with independent actions at the level of national governments.

Individuals and responsive policymakers in their national governments often espouse worldwide, universal standards. Some focus on human rights and religious freedoms, others on the environment, others on child or prison labor, still others on health and safety. More will be said later about international standards for the supervision and regulation of financial institutions. If not fully harmonized standards across all nations, should not the globe at least require minimum standards in some or all of these areas?

No sooner is this question asked, however, than the mind should flood with recognition that full homogenization across nations—of standards or anything else—is probably neither feasible nor desirable. On almost any subject, it has been difficult, and will continue to be difficult, to reach international agreement even on minimum standards. Furthermore, individual nations have often adopted policies on standards and competition that, whatever the stated rationale, have had the protectionist effect of blatantly favoring their own residents at the expense of other nations' residents.

These untidy fundamentals of political economy are frustrating. But the generalizations here are a faithful reflection of how things actually stand as the world moves into the twenty-first century. It is better to acknowledge this messy intermediate status with open eyes than to pretend that the facts can be summarized with less complicated interpretations.

5 The Progressive Internationalization of Finance

Chapters 2 and 3 reviewed fundamental ideas about financial activity and its collective governance, but with the cross-border dimensions suppressed. Those fundamentals must now be adapted to the actual messy, intermediate world of heterogeneous nation states but increasingly integrated national economies described in chapter 4.

The adaptation starts by sketching some historical background and extending the discussion of geographical variations in financial activity to multiple nations and the cross-border capital flows that increasingly knit national financial systems together. The chapter then provides a brief empirical overview of the last five decades. It concludes by explaining how and why the cross-border dimensions of financial activity are today so much more important than in the past.

National Reservoirs in an Increasingly Integrating World

World War I, the global depression of the 1930s, and then World War II caused severe disruptions in world economic activity. At the end of World War II, cross-border transactions in goods and services were thus greatly hampered by frictions and obstacles. Financial transactions among nations were impeded even more. In numerous cases, exchange and capital controls prohibited cross-border financial activity altogether. Individual national economies were partially isolated from each other.

For most practical purposes, the financial system of each nation was a separate reservoir. Participants in international trade or finance at that time did not think in terms of a "world financial system." Nor would they have found it revealing to describe the conglomeration of national financial systems as a single global reservoir.

Within each national reservoir, savings flows were somewhat viscous. Savings and investment transactions in some sectors or subnational regions were significantly impeded by market imperfections. No single nation's financial system corresponded exactly to the textbook notion of a fully integrated capital market, with savings flowing like water rather than molasses.

Internal conditions within nations, however, were sufficiently flexible to encourage an eventual convergence of rates of returns on investment projects (adjusted for differential risk) throughout most parts of each nation's economy. At the very least, the mobility of funds within each national reservoir was many orders of magnitude greater than the mobility of funds from one national reservoir to another.

In recent decades the individual national reservoirs have become progressively better connected. Flows of money and capital across the borders of nation states are tantamount to a ladling of savings funds from one national reservoir to another. This ladling activity became more and more energetic with each passing decade. And, figuratively speaking, financial institutions installed more and more pipes, siphons, and pumping stations to facilitate the inter-reservoir transfers of funds. The levels of the savings fluid in most national reservoirs are today much less independent than they were at the end of World War II.[1]

The reasons that national reservoirs are growing more closely connected fall into two broad classes, as identified in general terms in chapter 4. First, at-the-border financial restrictions—the separation fences built by national governments' policies to inhibit cross-border financial transactions—were lowered or became more porous over time. For some nations, the separation fences were even wholly dismantled. Second, and even more important, the costs of ladling funds among national reservoirs were diminished

---

1. The quantitative degree and qualitative nature of the increased interconnectedness varies significantly from one nation to another, as I emphasize below.

by nonpolicy factors such as technological innovations in communications and transportation and by the increasing diffusion of economic and social knowledge across borders. Both sets of forces, interacting together, caused a shrinking in the effective economic and psychic distances among the national reservoirs.

Geographical Variations in World Financial Activity

Financial activity reconciles the differing needs and preferences of ultimate savers and ultimate investors. The reconciliation is in part geographical (chapter 2). When residents or owners of assets in one particular region have desired withdrawals from the financial reservoir that exceed that region's saving flows into the reservoir, the region can pull savings from other geographical parts of the reservoir. During the transitional period when the region has an excess demand for saving, it experiences a net savings inflow. An excess supply of savings in a particular region results in a net savings outflow.

In principle, these analytical points apply no less to geographical areas in the world economy than to particular regions within a single national economy. Savings can be transferred not only from one region within a nation to another, but across national borders from one national reservoir to another. The lending and borrowing transactions that traverse national borders are essentially similar in function to the lending and borrowing that occur among different regions within a single economy.

When reservoirs of different nations are highly interconnected, there need be no close relationship for any single nation between the aggregate decisions of its ultimate savers and the aggregate decisions of its ultimate investors. Savings and investment decisions can be independent not only for individuals within each nation, but for nations as a whole. A nation experiencing a net savings inflow (outflow) runs a current account deficit (surplus) in its balance of payments with the rest of the world.

In sharp contrast, the nearly complete separation of national financial reservoirs during the immediate years after World War II forced a fairly tight correspondence between each nation's national saving and its national investment. Only very limited scope existed for net capital flows and corresponding imbalances in current account transactions. The main exception was intergovernmental assistance from the United States to other nations under the Marshall Plan. Those government capital flows permitted the reconstructing economies to run sizable current account deficits in the transitional years following the war. But there was little scope for private economic agents to effect a net transfer of savings across borders. Even the cross-border shipments of goods and services—but especially the net ladling of savings from one national reservoir to another—were modest relative to the sizes of national outputs. Because the national reservoirs were nearly separate, the reconciliation between savings and investment necessarily proceeded independently, individual nation by individual nation, with very little scope for aggregate national investment to differ from aggregate national saving.

By the beginning of the twenty-first century, the linkages between aggregate investment and aggregate savings for many individual nations had been greatly loosened. The reconciliation between aggregate investment and aggregate savings for the world as a whole no longer proceeds, as it were, separate national reservoir by separate national reservoir. Rather, the worldwide reconciliation, and the linked reconciliations for each national economy, are significantly modified by sizable net ladlings of savings from one national reservoir to another.

An Empirical Overview of the Last Five Decades

Economic integration across national borders, especially the integration of nations' financial markets, has greatly increased in the last five decades. A few summary statistics will help to fix perceptions about this progressive internationalization of economic and financial activity.

Cross-Border Trade in Goods and Services

The curves charted in figures 5-1 and 5-2 illustrate the general trend that cross-border trade has been growing faster than domestic economic activity. Figure 5-1 plots the ratio of exports of goods and services to total output for an aggregation of all industrial nations. Figure 5-2 plots corresponding curves for the United States alone, showing the ratio of imports to GDP (gross domestic product) as well as the ratio of exports to GDP. All industrial nations and most developing nations have experienced this general trend of increasing trade openness.

Ratios of the aggregate value of trade in goods to the value of output were also quite high in the late 1800s. (The periods of lowest values in the twentieth century were the two world wars and the decade of the Great Depression.) Economic historians therefore debate among themselves whether the extent of trade openness in the late 1900s is higher than, or

Figure 5-1. *Ratio of Nominal Exports of Goods to Nominal GDP for All Industrial Nations, 1962–2001*[a]

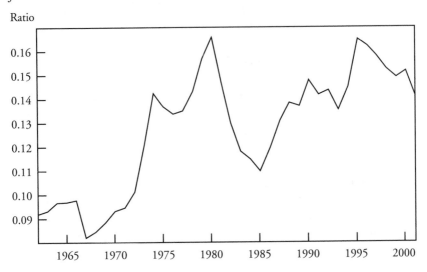

Source: IMF, *International Financial Statistics Yearbook,* various issues.

a. Industrial countries as defined by the IMF comprise the United States, Canada, Australia, New Zealand, Japan, the twelve European nations of the euro currency area, Denmark, Iceland, Norway, Sweden, Switzerland, and the United Kingdom. Exports of goods are f.o.b. The series for nominal output in the denominator of the ratio was calculated by the author from *IFS Yearbook* index series for real GDP and the GDP deflator of the industrial countries, benchmarked to a nominal value for 1995. The levels of the two underlying series are shown for selected years in table 5-1.

instead has just returned to, the levels at the beginning of the 1900s. Additional insight into the historical trends has been sought through study of the share of cross-border trade in the output of tradables production (defined as only manufacturing, mining, and agriculture, rather than all of domestic output), the growth of trade in services, and the increases in production and trade by multinational firms. On the basis of this further evidence, some analysts have argued that cross-border trade relative to output is qualitatively more intense and quantitatively more important than it was a century ago.[2]

2. Bordo, Eichengreen, and Irwin (1999) take this position; see also the comments on their paper by Jeffrey Frankel and Alan Taylor in the same volume. For additional commentary on the history, see, for example, Bordo, Eichengreen, and Kim (1988); Krasner (1999); and Sachs and Warner (1995).

Figure 5-2. *Ratio of Nominal Trade in Goods and Services to Nominal GDP, United States, 1945–2001*[a]

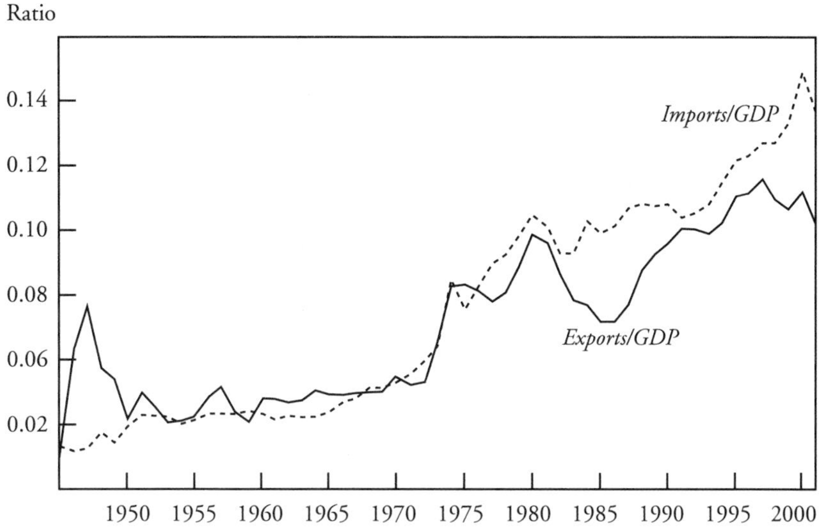

Ratio

Source: U.S. national income and product accounts, obtained from the *Survey of Current Business* and from the national accounts section of the website of the Bureau of Economic Analysis, U.S. Commerce Department.

a. The data for the nominal values of exports and imports pertain to both goods and services (national accounts definition); the denominator is nominal GDP.

Further research will undoubtedly refine our understanding of how the recent past compares with the more distant history. No matter how the historical comparison may be resolved, however, it is unambiguous that much of the second half of the twentieth century should be characterized as a *re-globalization* of economic and financial activity (in other words, not as the de novo creation of high interdependence, but rather as a return to levels observed many decades earlier).

Cross-Border Financial Activity

Financial interdependence in the world has been rising even faster than goods-market interdependence. Figure 5-3, with two curves for goods-market data and two for financial-market data, is one way of illustrating that striking fact. The curve with diamond markers is the nominal value of the aggregate gross domestic product of all industrial nations (the level of the output data series in the denominator of the ratio in figure 5-1). The

Figure 5-3. *Nominal Output and Exports of Industrial Nations, Cross-Border Banking, and International Debt Securities, 1964–2001*

Billions of U.S. current dollars, logarithmic scale

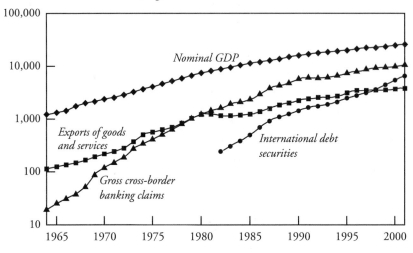

Source: See figure 5-1 for the definition of industrial nations and sources for their aggregate output and export data. The financial-market data underlying the curves are identified in table 5-1.

curve with squares is the nominal value of aggregate exports of goods for the industrial nations (the series in the numerator of the ratio in figure 5-1). The vertical axis of figure 5-3 has a logarithmic scale, making it visually possible to compare the rates of growth of the plotted series (the steeper the slope of a curve, the faster the rate of growth). The curve with triangles is one measure of aggregate financial activity, the most comprehensive measure historically available for the stock of cross-border banking assets. The fourth curve, shown with circles and available only from the early 1980s, plots data for the outstanding stock of international debt securities (bonds, notes, and money market instruments). The very much faster growth of cross-border finance than that of nominal output, and even of international trade, is immediately evident from the chart.[3]

Observations for selected years for the series plotted in figure 5-3 are shown in table 5-1, together with compound rates of growth for various subperiods and for the whole period between 1964 and 2001. Over the

3. See the notes for figure 5-1 and table 5-1 for the definition of industrial nations and for data sources. The data for international debt securities are not available for years prior to 1982.

twenty-five-year period between 1964 and 1989, the value of industrial nations' output grew at an annual average compound rate of 10.8 percent, the value of the exports of those nations grew at an annual average rate of 12.4 percent, but cross-border lending and borrowing through banks surged upward at a rate of some 25 percent a year. Over those two-and-one-half decades, cross-border banking thus grew twice as fast as trade and substantially more than twice as fast as the value of economic activity. In the more recent years between 1989 and 2001, cross-border trade has grown only slightly faster than output. Cross-border banking, however, has expanded at a rate one-and-a-half percentage points faster than cross-border trade. International debt securities have continued to grow some three times faster than cross-border trade.

Focusing on the levels of the series makes the comparisons even more dramatic. In the mid-1960s, as shown in table 5-1, the stock of cross-border banking claims was only one-fifth the size of the annual flow of the industrial nations' exports; by 2001 it was fully three times larger. For 1982, the first year for which stock estimates are available, international debt securities were 22 percent of the flow of industrial nations' exports; by 2001 the ratio had risen to 189 percent!

Table 5-1 also reports data on the volume of foreign exchange trading, another type of broad indicator that confirms the general trend. These data first became available for the United States (New York exchange market) in 1977. Triennial survey data are available for selected dates thereafter. Japanese (Tokyo) data were first collected in 1983, U.K. data for the London market in 1986, and data for an increasingly larger sample of national markets from 1989. The limited data for the period before 1989 show phenomenally high rates of growth. For example, the volume of trading in the United States between 1977 and 1986 grew at a compound annual rate of more than 26 percent. For Japan, the corresponding annual growth rate between 1983 and 1986 was 59 percent. Between 1986 and 1989 the annual growth rate for the combined volume of trading in the U.K., U.S., and Japanese markets was nearly 30 percent. For the nine years between 1989 and 1998, the growth for these three markets was still at the high rate of about 12 percent a year.[4]

---

4. The volume of foreign exchange activity in the London and New York markets actually declined between the 1998 and 2001 surveys (and had declined in the Tokyo market between 1995 and 1998). One contributing factor to this decline was the consolidation of eleven (later twelve) individual European currencies into the single currency for the European Union, the Euro. The weakness in foreign exchange activity in Japan (volume in 2001 was still below the volume in 1995) reflected the sluggish performance in Japanese economic and financial activity.

Table 5-1. *Summary Indicators for Aggregate Output, Cross-Border Goods Trade, and Cross-Border Finance, Selected Years, 1964–2001*[a]

Year	Industrial nations, nominal output	Industrial nations, nominal exports	Cross-border financial activity (BIS database)				Foreign exchange trading (survey data)			
			Net inter-national bank lending	Gross cross-border banking claims	Gross "inter-national" banking claims	Inter-national debt securities	United States only	Japan only	United Kingdom only	All reporting nations
Levels										
(U.S. $ billions)										
1964	1,201.5	115.8	11.9	19.9	23.9					
1973	3,356.3	405.1	175.0	291.6	350.0					
1978	6,103.4	873.1	555.0	893.4	1024.5					
1983	9,857.6	1,162.7	1,700.0	2,094.7	2,606.7	350.0	26.3	12.0		
1989	15,504.1	2,127.9	3,030.0	5,370.2	6,582.3	1,336.8	115.2	110.8	184.0	718.0
1995	21,028.1	3,469.4	4,755.0	8,072.7	9,495.3	2,704.0	244.4	161.3	463.8	1,572.0
2001	27,330.9	3,863.2		11,482.7	13,047.4	7,236.8	253.7	146.8	504.4	1,617.9

Compound growth rate (percent per year)

1964–73	12.09	14.92	34.77	34.74	34.77					
1973–78	12.70	16.60	25.97	25.10	23.96					
1978–83	10.06	5.90	25.09	18.58	20.54					
1983–89	7.84	10.60	10.11	16.99	16.69	25.03	27.91	44.84		
1989–95	5.21	8.49	7.80	7.03	6.30	12.46	13.36	6.46	16.66	13.95
1995–2001	4.47	1.81		6.05	5.44	17.83	0.62	–1.56	1.41	0.48
1964–89	10.77	12.35	24.79	25.09	25.21					
1989–2001	4.84	5.10	6.54	5.87		15.11	6.80	2.37	8.77	
1964–2001	8.81	9.94	18.74	18.58						7.00

Sources: IMF, *International Financial Statistics Yearbook*, various issues; Bank for International Settlements, *International Banking and Financial Market Developments*, recent and historical issues; Bank for International Settlements, triennial surveys for foreign exchange market activity.

a. When data are unavailable, cells in the table have been left blank. The series in the first two columns are nominal output series. See figure 5-1 for definition of industrial nations and method for calculating nominal output data. Specifically, the banking series includes all the cross-border assets of banks reporting to the BIS; the historical cross-border banking data have some discontinuities, and the figures for the 1960s and early 1970s are partly estimates by the author based on older BIS statistics. The BIS data for international debt securities are not available for years prior to 1982. Surveys of foreign exchange market activity are now coordinated every third year by the BIS. The data are for average daily turnover, net of so-called local market double counting (the so-called net-gross definition), in April of the survey year. The survey for April 1998 collected results for forty-three national exchange markets; data for April 2001 pertain to forty-eight national markets. Descriptive papers and statistical tables are available from the BIS website (www.bis.org).

Figure 5-4. *Actual and Hypothetical Growth in Cross-Border Bank Assets and International Debt Securities Relative to Nominal GDP of Industrial Nations, 1964–2001*

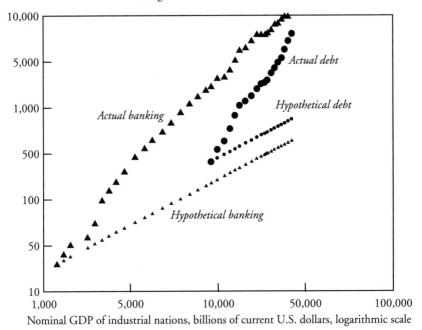

Cross-border bank assets or international debt securities,
billions of U.S. current dollars, logarithmic scale

Nominal GDP of industrial nations, billions of current U.S. dollars, logarithmic scale

Source: For underlying data, see figure 5-1 and table 5-1.

The scatter diagram in figure 5-4 provides a further perspective on the much faster growth rates for international financial aggregates than for output, and even for trade. Figure 5-4 uses the same series for the values of industrial-nation output, cross-border banking, and international debt securities charted in figure 5-3 and reported in table 5-1. But it compares the actual data points with points showing what the growth of the cross-border banking and the international debt securities series would have been if they had expanded each year in exact proportion to the growth of the value of output. As before, the cross-border banking series begins in 1964, the international debt series in 1982. Both the vertical and horizontal axes in the diagram use logarithmic scales. As the diagram strikingly shows, if cross-border banking assets had grown merely at the pace of output over the 1964–2001 period, they would have been on the order of only $453 billion in 2001—4 percent of their actual size of $11.5 trillion. If international debt securities had grown only at the pace of output over the 1982–97 period, their aggregate size would have reached only $776 billion in 2001, less than 11 percent of their actual size of $7.2 trillion.

Figure 5-5 uses data for capital flows in the U.S. balance of payments between 1961 and 2001 to illustrate an analogous point for the U.S. economy alone. The bars in the chart show, for capital movements except official reserve transactions, the gross outflows from and the gross inflows to the U.S. economy, with the flows deflated by the value of nominal U.S. gross domestic product. Over time, as the chart makes visually clear, capital flows relative to the size of the economy have substantially grown, albeit with some interesting ups and downs.[5]

The rapid growth in cross-border financial activity in the second half of the twentieth century was due especially to capital movements among (within) the industrial, relatively advanced nations. Yet in recent decades cross-border capital flows between the advanced financial nations and some developing nations—more generally, the degrees to which emerging-market developing nations have been able to access world capital markets—have also expanded substantially. The integration of developing nations into the world financial system has been very uneven. Many of the poorest developing nations are still relatively excluded. Even for the fastest growing and most stable emerging markets, the integration has proceeded in fits and starts. The so-called Tequila crises triggered by Mexico in 1995, the Asian and Russian crises of 1997–98, and the financial turbulence in Turkey, Argentina, Brazil, and Uruguay in 2001–02 significantly (albeit temporarily) dampened capital flows to emerging-market nations. But the powerful underlying trend toward cross-border financial interdependence was an important fact of life for those nations too.

The preceding overview emphasizes that the intensity and relative importance of cross-border financial activity have greatly increased in recent decades. But a long historical perspective cautions against exaggeration of the degree to which the recent past represents a qualitative departure from earlier times. Capital flows across borders from one local reservoir to another have a venerable history. Cross-border banking began in

5. For both gross inflows (the bars above the zero line) and gross outflows (below the zero line), the division of the total between direct investments and all other types of nonofficial capital is also shown.

Figure 5-5. *Gross Capital Flows in U.S. Balance of Payments as Percent of Nominal GDP, 1960–2001*

Percent of nominal GDP

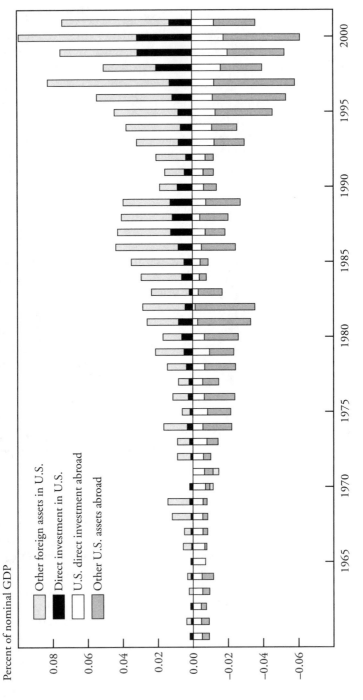

Source: Data from the balance-of-payments accounts for the United States, as published in the *Survey of Current Business* (for example, for June 2002). Earlier historical data are from the international section of the website of the Bureau of Economic Analysis, U.S. Commerce Department.

Europe in late medieval and early modern times, with financial families like the Fuggers and the Medici. Notable financial houses such as the Rothschilds and the Warburgs were prominent in international banking in the nineteenth century; the house of Morgan was one of many financial institutions deeply involved in international finance in the early twentieth century. As noted moreover, historians continue to argue about the degree to which globalization existed in the nineteenth century and to which the increasing financial interdependence of the second half of the twentieth century constitutes a re-globalization.[6]

Alternative Explanations for the Growing Linkages of National Reservoirs

Why did financial interdependence increase so rapidly? What caused national financial reservoirs to become much more closely interconnected in the second half of the 1900s? Alternative explanations fall under three broad headings, according to whether cross-border financial activity followed transactions in goods and services, led goods and services transactions, or responded to supervisory, regulatory, and tax incentives.

Finance Following Goods Transactions

The generally faster expansion of cross-border trade than of national incomes and outputs would by itself have given rise to a faster growth of cross-border financial activity than of domestic financial activity. To pay for cross-border shipments of goods and services, for example, a nation's residents needed to hold, borrow, or otherwise acquire cash balances denominated in foreign currencies (or foreign residents needed to acquire home-currency balances). Thus the transactions-balance requirements of trade alone would probably have induced a significant increase in cross-border assets and liabilities. In many instances, traders sought credit to finance trade transactions. Nonfinancial traders could have extended credit directly to each other, and to some degree they did so. At least as much as in domestic transactions, however, they resorted to financial institutions. Hence financial transactions such as bankers' acceptances and short-term

---

6. On early European finance, see De Roover (1948, 1963, 1974); for the Rothschilds, see Corti (1928) and Ferguson (1998, 2000). Chernow provides overviews of the Warburgs (1993) and the House of Morgan (1990). Bordo, Eichengreen, and Irwin (1999) and Zevin (1992) are more general historical retrospectives; see also Krasner (1999).

bank loans against trade collateral expanded with the growth in international trade.

When cross-border financial activity is merely the financing counterpart of trade transactions, the goods trade may be said to drive the financial activity associated with it. An imbalance in the current account of a nation's balance of payments associated with such transactions may be described as the causal result of the export and import transactions; the capital flows can be considered a passive accompaniment. The resulting net transfers of savings between nations are the by-product of the goods transactions and the incentives that drive those transactions.

The simplest cross-border relationships involve arm's-length transactions between a home resident and a foreign resident, each of whose business is primarily domestic in orientation. But as the nineteenth and twentieth centuries progressed, some nonfinancial firms developed a much deeper involvement in foreign business. Rather than merely engaging in limited export or import transactions with foreign residents, some firms oriented their business primarily to foreign residents. And to facilitate this more ambitious involvement, they established production facilities or sales and trading offices abroad.

Because some of their most important nonfinancial customers were establishing offices abroad, banks and other financial institutions themselves had incentives to set up physical offices abroad—branches or separately incorporated subsidiaries—to supplement the support they could give to customers from the home economy. Some of the lending and borrowing transactions with their customers were then booked on the balance sheets of the foreign offices.

As with the simple financing of international trade, here, too, financial transactions were driven by economic decisions about the production and selling of goods and services. The financial institutions setting up foreign offices followed their existing customers to retain, or to participate in the growth of, the customers' financial business. When financial institutions established offices within foreign economies, the production and selling activities being financed need not have been cross-border trade in goods and services. The goods activity and its counterpart financing may have been, wholly or in part, domestic within the host-nation economies.

Finance Leading Goods Transactions

Although the nonpolicy factors shrinking the effective economic distances among nations encouraged cross-border trade, those forces had an even more dramatic impact on cross-border financial transactions. New developments in communications technology were especially important. Innovations in electronic equipment—computers, switching devices, and telecommunications satellites—permitted the processing and transmission of information, the confirmation of transactions, and the making of payments for transactions in a progressively less costly manner. Sophisticated methods of using the new equipment, such as computer software for electronic funds transfer and accounting, and for trading securities over the Internet ("World Wide Web"), revolutionized the delivery of financial services. In the mid-1900s large sales or purchases of foreign exchange could be executed only during conventional business hours in the initiating party's time zone. Such transactions can now be carried out instantaneously twenty-four hours a day. Large financial institutions pass the management of their worldwide foreign-exchange and liquid-asset positions around the globe from one branch or subsidiary to another, staying continuously ahead of the setting sun.

Partly in response to such technological innovations, information and education about financial opportunities in foreign nations became much more readily and cheaply available. Those changes in turn helped to alter consumers' and producers' tastes. Cross-border assets and liabilities became much less a rarity than had been true in earlier decades.

The implications for financial activity were far-reaching. Economic agents became more sensitive to, and had improved capacities to take advantage of, incentives for arbitrage among the national financial reservoirs. Financial instruments denominated in different currencies and issued by borrowers in different nations became less imperfect substitutes in the portfolios of increasingly sophisticated investors. Accordingly, larger amounts of cross-border ladling of funds occurred. Much of this ladling, moreover, was not directly related to cross-border trade in goods and services or other real-sector transactions. Saving units could decide to take advantage of higher expected yields on financial assets in foreign reservoirs by purchasing foreign securities or making loans to foreigners rather than placing the funds somewhere in the home reservoir. Investing units could arrange loans from or issue securities in foreign reservoirs if they could thereby obtain more favorable borrowing terms than at home. Increasingly, decisions about the national location of the investment and borrowing of funds were divorced from decisions about the national location of production and consumption.

Although the economic distances between reservoirs were effectively shrinking for all types of economic agents, financial institutions—at first large commercial banks, but then virtually the entire range of financial institutions—were best equipped to exploit the enhanced arbitrage opportunities. They had more and higher-quality information about foreign financial systems. They were often better placed to introduce new communications technology. The relative costs of cross-border financial transactions thus fell most rapidly for banks and other financial institutions.

Ladlings of funds between reservoirs that were directly induced by newly profitable or newly perceived arbitrage opportunities may be described as leading rather than following goods transactions. The gross financial flows and the resulting net transfers of savings were, ex ante, independently initiated. The ensuing imbalance in current account and goods transactions was a passive by-product of the capital flows.

In addition to arbitraging among national reservoirs by initiating financial transactions from their home bases, some financial institutions, again on their own initiative, moved abroad to establish actual physical offices within foreign reservoirs. Such offices enabled them to conduct arbitraging and intermediation activities directly from foreign locations. For example, by establishing foreign branches or subsidiaries, banks with head offices in a home ("parent") nation were able to facilitate their collection of funds from and their lending of funds to the residents of foreign ("host") nations. Many of those host-nation residents may not have had any goods transactions with parent-nation residents. Such internationally oriented banks wanted not merely to service home customers with cross-border transactions or foreign facilities; they also wanted new foreign customers and wanted to become active borrowers and lenders in host-nation financial markets.

The last half-century of cross-border expansion by financial institutions controlled from head offices in the economically most powerful nations was merely another chapter in a story several centuries old. As in earlier history, foreign-owned establishments imported financial innovations and practices, thereby catalyzing an increased differentiation and sophistication of host-nation financial systems. Important examples of the cross-border transmission of new financial instruments included negotiable certificates of deposit, variable-rate and syndicated loans, commercial paper and note issuance facilities, financial futures contracts and options contracts, and the securitization of packaged loans. Foreign financial institutions were often the first to offer new services in host-nation jurisdictions. The foreign institutions were also, of course, more internationally oriented than indigenous institutions. At least in their initial years of operation in host nations, the foreign institutions had a higher proportion of their businesses denominated in foreign currencies and conducted with nonresidents. Similarly, they could not initially rely on a natural deposit base in host nations and therefore tended to be unusually active participants in host-nation wholesale money markets.

Supervisory, Regulatory, and Tax Explanations

From the perspective of private participants in financial systems, government-erected separation fences around their home reservoirs impose extra costs on cross-border financial transactions. For national reservoirs around which the fence is very high and effectively monitored, the cost of transferring funds in or out may be prohibitive. For given economic distances among reservoirs attributable to nonpolicy factors, government actions to lower separation fences cause a decline in the differential costs required to get across the fences, thereby enhancing incentives for the ladling of funds among national reservoirs. The partial dismantling of policy-erected barriers to cross-border capital flows is thus a third, conceptually distinct category of explanation for the rapid growth of international financial intermediation in the last half century.

Still other incentives caused by governmental policies were important. They resulted from the interaction between nonpolicy technological innovations and supervisory, regulatory, and tax restraints on financial transactions *within* national reservoirs. Such incentives would have been operative even if separation fences at national borders had not been altered.

These latter stimuli were important in nations having a domestic supervisory, regulatory, and tax environment that was more constraining than the environments in foreign nations. High reserve requirements against deposit liabilities, binding interest rate ceilings on deposits, high ratios of required capital to assets, unusually strict procedures for accounting, audits and examinations, and higher-than-average effective tax rates on domestic profits are examples of such constraints on banks and thrift intermediaries. Financial institutions in nations with tighter constraints had incentives to locate affiliated offices outside their home nation and to book transactions through those offices to take advantage of the less constrained operating environments abroad.

By locating offices abroad, a financial institution gained access to possibilities for financial activity in the wider world economy without the encumbrances of the home environment. To be sure, financial institutions with offices in foreign host locations still had to cope with the domestic operating environments in the host nations. Those environments often hampered their business with host-nation customers. And the institutions still had to cope with getting across the separation fences of third nations to conduct business with residents of those nations.

The incentives for getting outside the home regulatory environment were related to, but not the same as, the incentives for getting over the home nation's separation fence. The distinction is between continuously shuttling over the home separation fence (engaging in profitable cross-border transactions in and out of the home reservoir on an ongoing basis) versus jumping over the separation fence once and then staying outside of it.

Important variants of behavior of financial institutions for getting outside home-nation separation fences occurred as national supervisory authorities permitted financial institutions to establish "offshore" facilities—typically, segregated accounting units—for conducting transactions with foreign customers or transactions in foreign currencies. In effect, the financial institutions were permitted to carry out "offshore" transactions as though the facility were just outside the home separation fence, even though the facility was physically located within geographical borders of the home nation. Supervision, regulation, and taxation were altered to discriminate in favor of the offshore transactions. In contrast with the treatment of domestic deposits, for example, banks were only required to hold lower (or even zero) fractional reserve balances at the central bank against offshore deposits. In exchange for the ability to operate offshore facilities, the financial institutions typically agreed to limitations on transactions between the facilities and domestic residents (often including their own "onshore" offices), thereby posing less of a challenge to the integrity of the separation fence.

The Relative Importance of Different Explanations

The first and second categories of explanation above are *nonpolicy hypotheses* about the progressive interlinking of national financial reservoirs. The third category may be labeled *government-policy hypotheses*.

No one of the three categories of explanation can be ignored. In particular, none of the three can carry the whole burden of explanation alone. The technological nonpolicy factors were so powerful that they would have caused a progressive internationalization of financial activity even without changes in government separation fences and without the inducement of differing supervisory, regulatory, and tax environments. But government-policy changes were significant enough to have promoted a significant integration of national financial systems even if nonpolicy technological innovations had not created any shrinkage in the economic distances among reservoirs. Indeed, the interaction between nonpolicy innovations and changes in government policies was itself an important part of the history. Each set of evolutionary changes reinforced the effects of the other.

What relative weights should be assigned to the two categories of nonpolicy explanation? Did finance follow or independently lead goods transactions in the internationalization of economic activity? Whether international finance has been following or leading is an aspect of the subtle interrelationships between financial activity and the production, sales, and consumption of goods ("real-sector" activity). Financial activity with a cross-border dimension has grown much faster than either output or cross-border trade (table 5-1). Because cross-border goods transactions were growing faster than purely domestic goods transactions, cross-border financial activity would have grown faster than domestic financial activity merely because of the increasing openness of the real sectors of national economies. But because cross-border financial activity grew markedly faster than cross-border goods trade, one is tempted to infer that one can validly extend to the world aggregated as a whole the proposition that financial superstructure tends to expand relative to real-sector infrastructure in the earlier stages of economic development.

Many facts about relative growth rates are consistent with the presumption that cross-border finance has tended to lead more than to follow real-sector activity. Observers of foreign exchange, interbank-fund, and equities markets more often than not perceive financial transactions as independently initiated in response to cross-border and cross-currency arbitrage opportunities. Bankers and brokers speaking about the location decisions for their foreign branches and subsidiaries often portray their organizations as behaving in an anticipatory way, seeking new customers and profit opportunities in advance of the current service requirements of existing customers. The available evidence suggests that financial institutions themselves have often been the cutting edge of internationalization. Cross-border finance has certainly been much more than a passive veil draped over or molded by real-sector activity.

How Far Has Internationalization Progressed?

Are national financial reservoirs now so closely joined that one must speak of a single world reservoir with a more or less uniform level throughout? Is there little scope left for autonomous financial conditions within individual national economies?

Because the financial structure of the world economy underwent a sea change in the second half of the twentieth century, markedly shrinking the economic distances between nations' financial systems, the analogy of nearly autonomous national savings reservoirs is no longer appropriate. To a much greater extent than in the early years after World War II, the levels in national reservoirs tend to be pulled together toward a common level. The stronger interconnections between national financial systems are now evident even to informed laymen. They are a dominant fact of life for financial system participants and government policymakers.

Even so, financial activity in many parts of the world is still significantly segmented along national lines. Thus the conceit of a unified world financial system, implying a nearly uniform level throughout a single world reservoir, is likewise an inappropriate analogy for analyzing cross-border financial intermediation. For both financial and real-sector activity, national borders have economic influences that are large, pervasive, and durable.[7] Sweeping generalizations about financial globalization and the "globalization system," though recently attracting much attention, are a seriously misleading characterization of the actual world in which cross-border finance is conducted.

The actual situation is intermediate, conforming to neither of the polar cases. On the spectrum running from completely separated national reservoirs at one extreme to a fully unified world reservoir at the other, the major nations and currencies are probably some two-thirds to three-fourths of the way—but no further than that—toward the single world reservoir. The permanent salience of social networks and of geographical distance itself means that the world will never experience the polar case of a fully unified world reservoir in which national or regional centers of gravity are completely absent.

This untidy state of affairs is vexing for analysts and policymakers. It is yet another illustration of the messy intermediate state of the world emphasized in chapter 4. Analysts and policymakers must mentally simplify a complex reality when trying to understand events and reach conclusions. The easiest simplifications to apply are the extreme assumptions of the "nearly closed" paradigm (nearly separate reservoirs) or the assumptions of the "small and open" or "supranational" paradigms (both presuming a uni-

7. Helliwell (1998, chap. 4; 2000); Frankel (1992, 1994); Tesar and Werner (1994, 1998).

fied world reservoir). Yet the assumptions of each of those approaches conflict too greatly with the actual, intermediate facts. If theorists and empirical researchers hope to illuminate actual experience, they must struggle more directly with the analytical difficulties of intermediate interdependence. Similarly, if policymakers hope to avoid seriously overestimating or underestimating the autonomy of national economic policies, they too must abandon the polar assumptions as a basis for analysis.[8]

8. Bryant (1980b) discusses these traditional paradigms, as well as a preferred "intermediate interdependence" paradigm, for analyzing international economic events.

6

Analytical Issues in Cross-Border Finance: An Introduction

This chapter completes the adaptation of the fundamentals of finance in chapters 2 and 3 to a world of multiple, heterogeneous nations whose economies and financial systems are becoming progressively more integrated.

Potential Gains from Cross-Border Financial Intermediation

When the financial reservoirs of different nations are highly interconnected, the aggregate decisions of the ultimate savers in any single nation and the aggregate decisions of ultimate investors in that nation do not need to be closely linked. Savings and investment decisions can be independent not only for individuals within each nation, but for nations as a whole.

Loosening of the links between the aggregate saving and the aggregate investment of an individual nation substantially enhances the potential for the nation's economic well-being. Just as financial transactions within national reservoirs generate major benefits for individual economic agents, significant benefits may result from financial transactions between agents in different national reservoirs.

The potential benefits from cross-border financial transactions are a subset of the substantial gains to a nation's residents from all types of cross-border transactions. Because the basic argument is familiar and widely accepted when applied to trade in goods, both between regions within a nation and across national borders, I limit the summary here to the essential points and then draw out some less familiar implications for financial transactions.

If a nation's residents could not trade with foreigners, the pattern of national spending would have to match slavishly the goods produced at home. So long as relative prices differ at home and abroad, however, the nation's residents can unambiguously improve their consumption possibilities by exchanging goods with foreigners. Furthermore, such *exchange gains* can be augmented by *production gains*. Production gains result when the structure of production in a nation becomes specialized along the lines of *comparative advantage*. Resource and factor endowments are used more efficiently when production is specialized, permitting the nation to sell domestic production at favorable relative prices abroad, which in turn raises national consumption possibilities still further.

Traditional expositions of the gains from trade focus on goods transactions. But the argument applies with similar force to other cross-border transactions. For example, some nations tend to have a comparative advantage in the provision of financial services, perhaps because of intercountry differences in liquidity preferences or because of increasing returns to scale and external economies associated with the historical development of financial centers. As with goods, trade in financial services yields exchange gains and production gains. Changes in cross-border assets and liabilities are a necessary counterpart of goods and services transactions (see below). Benefits associated with cross-border financial transactions accrue to both the "importing" and the "exporting" nations.

Because of cross-border transactions, a nation's residents thus can enjoy higher standards of living—time paths for their consumption that are higher, better adapted to their particular preferences, and not rigidly tied to the peculiarities of their geographical circumstances—than would otherwise be possible. What is true for the individual nation is true for the world as a whole. Cross-border transactions among nations permit a more efficient allocation of world resources than could otherwise occur and thereby increase world consumption possibilities.

The potential gains from cross-border transactions can be very substantial. The gains may be proportionately larger for small nations and nations with relatively poor endowments of natural resources. The gains from some types of cross-border transactions are no doubt much more consequential than for others. But there is a strong presumption that most if not all nations can, and in practice do, enjoy sizable benefits.

Not that each resident in each nation invariably benefits. Practical observation and economic theory agree that particular individuals or particular factors of production can be harmed. For example, firms and workers who produce goods and services that are displaced by increases in competitively priced imports can experience at least temporary losses. Sectors of a nation's economy specializing in particular goods that are now becoming obsolete because of changes in consumer preferences or technological innovations can suffer losses as resources are allocated away from those sectors. Business and financial interests are the driving forces promoting cross-border transactions and are usually better placed politically to influence policies affecting such transactions. Individuals whose values or well-being are partly in conflict with business and financial interests may believe, sometimes justifiably, that their values or well-being are adversely affected, in relative if not absolute terms.

Nor can it be justifiably claimed that each nation, on balance, invariably benefits from all the cross-border transactions conducted by or with its residents. Because of externalities and market failures, not every movement toward liberalized cross-border transactions is invariably beneficial. Nor does every imposition of new restrictions unambiguously reduce welfare. Interpersonal comparisons of well-being are problematic, and aggregative comparisons between nations even more so. Assertions about the welfare of entire nations or the world as a whole are thus inescapably controversial.

These important caveats notwithstanding, there is widespread acceptance of the view that the gains from cross-border transactions are substantial. There is virtually no scholarly support for the argument that a typical nation can improve its standard of living by a wholesale movement toward autarky.

A nation cannot engage in cross-border transactions in goods and services without permitting a commensurate degree of openness for financial transactions. Goods and services can be exchanged with foreigners only if the corresponding financial payments and receipts can be readily consummated. For efficiency, lending and borrowing associated with the goods transactions and their settlement is also required. Properly construed, therefore, the fundamental points supporting the case for cross-border transactions constitute an argument for transactions on both the current and the capital accounts of the balance of payments. The "gains from trade" can also be labeled the "gains from cross-border finance."

Cross-border financial intermediation is the essential counterpart of another dimension of the gains from trade. Suppose a nation's residents were not able to engage in goods and financial transactions with the rest of the world. The time profile of the nation's aggregate consumption plus investment would then have to conform precisely to the time profile of aggregate national production. Similarly, aggregate national savings would have to be exactly equal to aggregate investment. An autarkic nation with bright investment prospects in which ex ante demand for investment spending exceeded national saving would have to accept a higher rate of inflation that restored a balance between saving and investment. Alternatively, the nation would have to ratchet its investment, production, and income downward or find some way to raise the aggregate saving rate. An autarkic nation with an ex ante excess supply of saving would be afflicted with an analogous lack of flexibility.

With cross-border financial intermediation, the otherwise rigid link between national savings and national investment can be severed. The resulting gains for the nation as a whole are analogous to the benefits that financial intermediation within a nation brings to individual households and firms. The intertemporal pattern of households' aggregate spending can be matched to national needs and preferences instead of having to conform with the intertemporal pattern of earnings. Just as individual firms can hedge against events that could alter the profitability of their operations, an entire nation can collectively hedge against the future by accumulating income-earning assets abroad. Just as adventurous individual producers willing to assume the basic risks of business enterprise can borrow funds in excess of their current cash flow, a nation with better than average investment prospects can assume greater than average risks by importing capital funds and real resources from the rest of the world, thereby raising future consumption possibilities for the nation as a whole. With individual nations able to alter the intertemporal profiles of their consumption, the world as a whole can attain an improved allocation of savings and investment, with nations with ex ante excess savings employing them in nations where the ex ante return to investment is higher.

Economic history contains numerous examples of nations for which savings inflows from abroad crucially supported economic growth. The United States in the nineteenth century, for example, made extensive use of savings from Europe. Argentina, Canada, Australia, and New Zealand had analogous experiences. In recent decades, many developing nations, in particular those that came to be labeled emerging-market economies, were at various times major importers of foreign capital. The prospects for growth in many developing nations depend in part on their capacities to constructively absorb savings from capital-rich nations.

Financial prices and valuations within national reservoirs respond promptly and sensitively to new information. The cross-border and cross-currency transactions that increasingly link the national reservoirs together respond at least as rapidly and sensitively. I emphasize later in the chapter that this sensitivity can be a major source of difficulty. Here, however, it is the favorable aspects of these information signals that are relevant. The prompt transmittal of information within and among the national financial reservoirs helps to generate the exchange and production gains from cross-border transactions. Similarly, cross-border capital flows facilitate the transfer of knowledge and expertise, particularly when some or all of the capital flows are direct investments. Such benefits would not be realized to the same extent in a world in which information was disseminated less fully and less promptly. The transmission of information among geographically separated nations accelerated enormously in the twentieth century. The information benefits from cross-border financial intermediation have almost surely increased correspondingly.[1]

A word of interim warning is needed to maintain perspective. The potential efficiency gains from cross-border transactions and financial openness are sizable. But other types of potential gains remain to be identified. And the potential risks and costs remain to be discussed. Much remains to be said before trying to draw up an overall balance sheet of benefits and costs. It would thus be premature to jump from the preceding summary of potential efficiency gains to a conclusion that, for every nation in all circumstances, unfettered cross-border financial transactions will always be beneficial. Nations differ enormously in their needs and circumstances. One individual nation's overall balance sheet of the net benefits (or net costs) from cross-border finance may differ sharply from those of other nations.

---

1. Readers wanting a more detailed and technical discussion of the benefits from, and issues raised by, savings-investment differences across nations may wish to consult Obstfeld and Rogoff (1995, 1996).

Additional Uncertainties in a Multination World

Uncertainty and risk are the essence of domestic financial activity. With cross-border finance in an intermediate, multination world, the uncertainties are multiplied. Risks are even more complex.

The most basic complications are political and social. Individual nations have distinctive histories. Differences in cultural, ethnic, and social norms lead to information networks, social capital, and political and economic institutions that differ widely across nations. In a multitude of ways, these differences add to the uncertainties and risks of financial transactions between nations.

Numerous other complications are economic and financial rather than political or social. Informational asymmetries and principal-agent problems become even more complex than for domestic financial activity. Risk evaluation is more difficult. Flows of financial funds across borders take many different forms, with significant differences in the issues that they raise. Cross-border financial contracts are still more complex and uncertain than within-nation contracts. Accounting standards, auditing standards, data collection and dissemination, and legal systems differ significantly across nations. National governments pursue dissimilar macroeconomic policies. Other collective-governance components of the utilities infrastructure for financial activity—notably, the prudential supervision and regulation of financial institutions—differ widely from one nation to another.

Each of these sources of incremental uncertainty is examined in the remaining sections of this chapter. Those sources are in turn integrally associated with another pervasive cause of uncertainty, namely, that nations have separate currencies, with each nation's domestic economic and financial transactions typically denominated largely in its own currency unit.

A multiplicity of currencies requires the existence of exchange rates, determining the price of each currency in terms of the others. Most of these exchange rates vary over time, in one fashion or another. To understand any of the analytical issues to which cross-border finance gives rise, therefore, one has to grapple with the uncertainties associated with exchange rates and exchange regimes.

Exchange Rates and Exchange Regimes

A cross-border contract between a resident of nation A and a resident of nation B must be denominated in the A currency, in the B currency, or in the currency of some third nation C. Whatever the currency denomination of the contract, substantial uncertainty is likely to exist about what the exchange rate will be at the future time when the contract is to be completed. One or both parties to the contract are thus inescapably exposed to potential losses due to changes in the exchange rate relative to expectations at the time the contract is written. Even for contracts made and simultaneously executed today, one or both parties are subject in the other aspects of their economic life to risks and uncertainties associated with possible future changes in the exchange rate.

In a special but quite limited set of cases where nations A and B participate in an irrevocable currency union, cross-border transactions between A and B can be relatively immune to exchange rate risks and uncertainties. Such A-B transactions are unlikely to be denominated in the currency of a third nation not participating in the A-B currency union. But the currency union must be credibly irrevocable, such as the currency arrangements existing among the individual states of the United States. The new European Monetary Union launched at the beginning of 1999 did not fully meet such criteria, because at that time there was still a small probability that the prospective currency union could unravel. In all cases except within an irrevocable currency union, future exchange rates among currencies are uncertain and may turn out to be different from those observed—and expected—today.

Individual nations can choose from a variety of possible exchange regimes. One polar choice is to permit private market participants complete flexibility in determining the nation's exchange rate with other currencies.[2] In that case of *untrammeled floating*, the nation's monetary authority refrains from any purchases or sales of foreign currencies intended to influence the market-determined exchange rates. Toward the opposite end of the spectrum of choices, the monetary authority can commit to an indefinite pegging of the national currency against some major foreign cur-

---

2. I speak loosely here, and later, about "the" exchange rate for a nation's currency (a single exchange rate, rather than the plural "exchange rates"). This simplification, usually not misleading, is a shorthand expression for the idea of a weighted-average measure of the nation's many bilateral exchange rates with each foreign currency of any significance in the nation's cross-border transactions. In empirical practice, a weighted-average measure is typically a much better gauge of the overall valuation of the nation's currency against all other currencies than the bilateral exchange rate with any single foreign currency. Although a few difficult issues are involved in choosing which weighted average is the preferred measure of "the" exchange rate for alternative empirical purposes, the general remarks I make about exchange regimes in the text can safely suppress these complications.

rency (or a weighted basket of foreign currencies), subject perhaps to very small day-to-day fluctuations within a very narrow band. These *minimum variability* options are described as a *currency-board* regime, or alternatively as an *infrequently adjusted peg,* depending on the degree of discretion permitted for conducting domestic monetary policy. A currency-board regime permits the nation to have its own separate currency unit. The authority administering the currency board, however, must fully back all issues of the national currency with foreign currency assets and must peg the nation's exchange rate by law, not merely by policy. Under an infrequently adjusted peg, the national monetary authority minimizes the variations in the exchange rate with discretionary policy, not by law. The degree of commitment to a pegged exchange rate is obviously greater under a currency board than with an infrequently adjusted peg.

The most extreme form of the minimum variability option is the polar case of *currency union,* in which the nation has no separate currency unit and no separate national monetary authority. The currency unit used for the denomination of all domestic contracts, and the currency notes that actually circulate in the nation, are identical to the currency used in one or more neighboring or trading partner nations.

A wide range of intermediate cases exists between the polar extremes. The most widely discussed regimes are labeled with terms such as *adjustable pegs, target (reference) zones, crawling pegs* or *crawling bands,* or *managed floats.* For our purposes here, it is not necessary to identify the details of these intermediate regimes. The intermediate cases all entail some degree of what may be labeled *managed pegging* or *managed floating.* Some of the managed-pegging or managed-floating regimes entail announcement of rules or guidelines for how a nation's monetary authority will presumptively conduct the management. Others leave discretion to a nation's monetary authority without announcement of management guidelines, thereby permitting or even encouraging uncertainty about how the discretion may be exercised.[3]

Scarcely any other question in international finance is more controversial than the choice a nation should make about its exchange regime. I return to this controversial topic in later chapters. For the moment, a noncontroversial point needs emphasis: future exchange rates for a currency are uncertain

---

3. When management of exchange regimes is based on rules or guidelines, the guidelines have sometimes been referred to as "BBC rules" (referring to bands, baskets, or crawls). For recent classifications and discussions of alternative exchange regimes, see among others Frankel (1999b), J. Williamson (2000), and Goldstein (2002).

regardless of the exchange regime currently being implemented by a nation's central bank or government. Exchange rate uncertainty is self-evident for cases where exchange rates for the currency are permitted to float relatively freely and are subject to market forces, private expectations, and all the factors that can change them. But even when a central bank or government intervenes in foreign exchange markets to peg the nation's currency, exchange rate uncertainty is also highly relevant. The intensity and longevity of the government's commitment can be in doubt. Even under a currency board, it is conceivable that the nation, faced with extreme circumstances, could abandon the regime by rewriting the legislation that established the currency board in the first place.[4] Analogous doubts exist about any of the managed-pegging or managed-floating regimes.

More generally, a nation's government can change its mind about which exchange regime is deemed appropriate. Pressures on the government, and circumstances themselves, can change. The government can change. No exchange regime—none—can reduce this uncertainty to a negligible level.

What about hedging through contingent contracts, or otherwise buying insurance, against possible changes in exchange rates? Is it not possible for lenders or borrowers entering into cross-border contracts to shift some of the exchange rate risk to other parties? To a limited degree, some shifting of risk is possible. Markets have been established in *forward exchange*, contracts that specify an agreed price for the purchase or sale of a currency at specific future dates. Many fancy types of currency swaps and so-called derivatives transactions have been devised. But all these measures shift exchange risk and uncertainty to someone else more willing and able to shoulder them, such as some financial institution or some resident of a foreign nation. They do not eliminate the risk and uncertainty. The longer the relevant time horizon, moreover, the more difficult it tends to be to persuade other counterparties to shoulder the risk and uncertainty about future exchange rates. Uncertainty is well known to increase nonlinearly as the time horizon is extended further and further into the future. Futures markets and their contracts for forward exchange are fairly readily available for several months ahead, more rarely available for several years ahead, and available not at all for a decade or two ahead.

---

4. Argentina's decision to abandon its currency-board arrangements in the midst of financial crisis in 2001 is a recent prominent example.

A subtle relationship exists between currency risk and default risk. A creditor in nation B with a claim on a borrower in nation A may have sufficient bargaining power to insist that the claim be denominated in the B currency, thereby avoiding the exchange risk himself. But the B-nation creditor avoids the exchange risk only by shifting it entirely onto the A-nation borrower. From the perspective of the creditor with the B-currency claim, exchange rate fluctuations may then merely lead to a substitution of default risk for exchange risk. A depreciation of the A currency could push the A-nation borrower into insolvency by raising the value of his debt service payments in the local A currency relative to his local-currency income stream.

Cross-Border Dimensions of Information Asymmetries and Risk Evaluation

Borrowers inevitably have superior information about their own activities relative to the information of those lending to them; lenders inevitably have limited capacities to monitor and adjust to changes in borrowers' circumstances and behavior. When a borrower and lender are residents of different nations, these information asymmetries and principal-agent issues are heightened. Geographical distances tend to be greater. Effective communication is often more costly or difficult. Cultural, social, and political differences between the nations add complexity to the lender's assessment of the creditworthiness of the borrower and of the future economic environment that will help to determine the ability of the borrower to service its debt. The thorny problems of adverse selection (hidden knowledge) and moral hazard (hidden actions), inescapable in domestic finance, thus loom still larger for cross-border finance.

Banks, other financial intermediaries, and specialized financial institutions (for example, securities rating agencies) have a comparative advantage in dealing with information asymmetries. Relative to individual lenders, they can more efficiently appraise the creditworthiness of borrowers and act as delegated monitors. Not surprisingly, such financial institutions play an especially vital role in cross-border finance.

Financial institutions from abroad may establish branches or subsidiaries within the borders of a home nation, collecting savings to be channeled abroad or to serve as conduits for importing foreign savings to lend to home borrowers. These multination branches and subsidiaries can mitigate the incremental information discrepancies associated with cross-border lending and borrowing. Appraisals of the creditworthiness of borrowers will often be less expensive when conducted by financial institutions resident in the borrower's own nation. Financial institutions with offices in a host nation can more readily carry out timely and perceptive analyses of economic conditions in that nation.

Even efficient financial institutions, however, cannot altogether overcome the incremental information asymmetries that are inherent in lending and borrowing across national borders. Worse still, individual financial institutions engaged in cross-border finance are exposed—in addition to the ways they can get into trouble in the domestic financial reservoir—to further opportunities for trouble. Poorly managed and hedged foreign exchange positions are a prominent example.

Participants in international financial transactions have strong incentives to design contracts that take into account cross-border and cross-currency complexities. Clauses in debt contracts can be written to try to provide greater protection to lenders against unwarranted default. Clever things can be done with collateral provisions. Contracts can sometimes cope with exchange rate risk through the purchase of forward exchange or futures, thus shifting the exchange risk to third parties. National governments have set up institutions such as government insurance agencies or export-financing banks that subsidize international transactions, thereby again shifting risks to other parties.

"Complete contracts" in which all contingencies faced by the contracting parties are foreseeable and spelled out, however, are even less possible for cross-border than for domestic financial relationships. It is even more complicated to foresee contingencies. A wider range of contingencies has to be considered. Monitoring is more complex. And legal enforcement of contracts is very much more difficult (see below).

Expected returns on financial instruments embody risk premiums that vary over time. The *credit-risk* component of the risk premium is a function of the perceived creditworthiness of the individual borrower, which in turn depends on expected changes in the borrower's circumstances and their effects on the willingness and ability of the borrower to repay. For cross-border borrowing, the credit-risk component of the risk premium is still more complex. In addition to the possibility that the individual borrower may default because of circumstances idiosyncratic to the borrower, general economic conditions in the borrower's nation may alter his willingness or ability to honor the borrowing contract. In effect, adverse circumstances within a nation or adverse shocks originating abroad may force the nation as a whole into a collective default on its external borrowing. Such possible circumstances are especially relevant if a cross-border lender denominates the contract in the lender's ("foreign") currency rather than in the borrower's ("domestic") currency. In effect, a cross-border lender must incorporate a "country premium" element into the credit-risk component of the overall risk premium.

For negotiable financial instruments traded in markets, the overall risk premium typically contains a *market-risk* element. For cross-border and cross-currency financial instruments, the element of exchange risk is an important additional category of market risk. Evaluation of the exchange-risk component on the overall risk premium for cross-border lending can be especially difficult. As stressed above, exchange rates and exchange regimes introduce incremental, highly consequential dimensions of risk and uncertainty into cross-border and cross-currency financial transactions. In a national economy significantly open to the rest of the world, exchange rate risk is indirectly pertinent even for purely domestic transactions. But the exchange-risk component of the overall risk premium is relevant, directly and powerfully, in cross-border finance.

The specialized knowledge lodged in financial intermediaries and securities rating agencies facilitates the evaluation and monitoring of risk premiums for cross-border financial activity. But even with such help, risk evaluation is much more difficult than for domestic finance.

Cross-Border Capital Flows

Not all cross-border capital flows are alike. Differences among types of financial assets and liabilities, important for domestic finance, can be still more important when financial relationships have cross-border and cross-currency dimensions.

Direct versus Securitized Lending

Chapter 2 distinguished between financial activity occurring through direct intermediation versus securitized intermediation. Direct intermediation exists when a financial intermediary (for example, a bank) is interposed as an asset-holding entity between ultimate savers and ultimate borrowers. The ultimate savers have a legal claim only on the intermediary (such as a deposit in the bank), whereas the intermediary holds the direct, legal claim on the ultimate borrower (such as a loan to a business enterprise).

With securitized intermediation, the ultimate borrowers issue debt-instrument or equity liabilities in the form of securities that are held by the ultimate savers themselves (for example, market-traded or privately placed bonds, or public offerings of new equity shares). Although financial intermediaries may well assist in the design, risk evaluation, and marketing of the securities, the ultimate borrowers have a legal obligation to the savers, not to the assisting intermediaries.

In cross-border finance, the chain of financial intermediation between ultimate savers and ultimate borrowers typically involves additional steps. Several different intermediaries are likely to be involved. After all, in addition to the maturity transformation and risk pooling that takes place in a domestic context, the cross-border element requires the savings to be ladled from one national reservoir to another. Yet basic analytical distinctions remain relevant. In particular, for cross-border finance it is often necessary to differentiate between liabilities of ultimate borrower-investors that are direct claims of financial intermediaries versus those that are negotiable securities not held by the intermediaries. The behavior and financial institutions involved in the portfolio trading of securities, for example, are often different from those involved in direct bank lending to borrowing enterprises.

Capital flows are, in principle, measured at the national border. Balance-of-payments data for individual nations typically distinguish between bank-reported assets and liabilities ("banking"), assets and liabilities reported by other financial institutions (loosely referred to as "portfolio flows"), and assets and liabilities reported by nonfinancial enterprises ("direct investments" and "other corporate capital flows"). The reporting institution is a domestic "resident" (in the legal sense of the term). The assets or liabilities are claims on or borrowings from entities that are foreign residents.

Several different intermediaries are likely to be involved in the whole chain of financial relationships linking ultimate savers in one national reservoir with ultimate borrowers in another. Hence the capital flows measured at the border of a home nation may often involve transactions merely between two financial intermediaries rather than between a foreign ultimate saver and a home-resident ultimate borrower (or home ultimate saver and foreign ultimate borrower). Examples of such cross-border capital flows dominated by intermediaries themselves include lending by foreign banks to home banks and purchases by foreign-based mutual funds from home brokers of domestically issued securities.

The securitization of liabilities of ultimate borrowers produces a pattern of risk sharing among savers, financial institutions, and the ultimate borrowers themselves different from the pattern of risk sharing associated with direct lending. The explicit maturity transformation resulting from a bank's intermediation—borrowing at shorter term from depositors and making loans at longer term to borrowers—entails extensive risk bearing by the bank itself. When arranging for securitized intermediation, the assisting financial institution shifts the risk to the purchasers and issuers of the securities (unless it holds some of the securities on its own balance sheet).

Direct borrowing and lending by commercial banks across borders thus typically marches to different drummers than the cross-border issuance and portfolio trading of securities. Mishaps and instabilities originating with bank lending generate different pressures and can have quite different outcomes than when mishaps and instabilities afflict securities trading. The prudential supervision and regulation of banking, in both its domestic and cross-border aspects, likewise entail different problems than the prudential oversight of securities trading.

The distinction between direct and securitized intermediation can be blurred in practice. This blurring is even more prevalent for cross-border than for domestic transactions. Numerous types of derivative securities with international dimensions, based on futures contracts and options contracts that prominently feature exchange rates, are now commonplace in international finance. Just as with derivative securities developed for domestic financial systems, moreover, the unbundling of risks permitted by international derivatives provides greater opportunities for individuals, enterprises, and financial institutions—resident in differing nations, exposed to very heterogeneous circumstances—to tailor their risk bearing to their own idiosyncratic needs and preferences. The benefits to particular economic agents and to individual nations from such unbundling can be substantial. For cross-border lending and borrowing at least as much as within domestic financial systems, however, extensive securitization can also cut as a double-edged sword. It increases the proportion of financial activity that can be significantly affected by large short-term variations in security prices, driven possibly by volatile expectations.

Direct Owner-Investors versus Portfolio Creditors

When analyzing cross-border capital flows, it can be analytically important to differentiate direct investment from other types of capital flows (banking, portfolio flows, and corporate flows that are not direct investment, such as accounts receivable and payable). Direct investments across national borders typically entail significant participation by foreign entities in the management and control of home-resident business enterprises (and, when they are the target of direct investment, home-resident financial institutions). Other types of cross-border capital flows are presumed not to involve such participation (or at least not nearly to the same extent).

The distinction at issue here is closely analogous to the distinction made in chapter 2 between the two classes of creditor-lenders to a borrowing enterprise, direct owner-investors and portfolio creditors. Direct owner-investors either own outright or exert effective power over a sizable fraction of the total equity claims on the borrowing enterprise. Thus, as a group, they are the key decisionmakers that control the enterprise. The direct owner-investors manage the enterprise themselves, or they appoint professional managers who act as agents on their behalf. Portfolio creditors of a borrowing enterprise typically are not involved in its management and control.

Portfolio flows and banking transactions across borders respond primarily to expected return and risk differentials across nations. Cross-border direct investments are undertaken by direct owner-investors whose equity claims and lending reflect a more extensive engagement in and commitment to the borrowing enterprises. To understand the motives underlying cross-border direct investment, analysis must contend not only with perceptions of expected return and risk differentials across nations, but also with the objectives and constraints stressed in the literature on industrial organization and management (modified, of course, by cross-border complications).

A foreign investor engaging in direct investment in a business enterprise located in a home nation holds an equity claim that crosses the home border. Equity claims differ in an essential way from debt instruments: the holders of equity claims, proportionately to the degree of their fractional ownership, assume all the risks and participate in all the gains accruing to the enterprise. The foreign investor engaging in a direct investment typically holds a substantial fraction of the total equity claims on the borrowing enterprise. Direct investments thus typically involve a much greater degree of influence over the activities of the borrowing enterprise than other types of capital flows. Direct investments tend to have a longer effective time horizon (the explicit or implicit maturity date of a direct investment contract is further in the future). Correspondingly, they are less reversible on short notice.

Portfolio creditors resident outside the home nation, those who are on the lending end of inward portfolio capital flows, are committed less firmly, if at all, to the home-resident borrowing enterprise. More readily than the foreigners engaging in inward direct investment, therefore, the portfolio creditors can escape from their financial contract—selling the security claim to someone else or reversing the loan credit—if the weather should turn from sunny to stormy conditions.

The differences between cross-border direct investments versus cross-border portfolio and banking flows reflect differing approaches to the fundamental tensions inherent in financial contracts. A home-nation borrower or issuer of equity claims inevitably faces the difficult trade-off that access to external funds requires surrendering some degree of influence or control to the creditors, the more so if the external funds are to have a long maturity and be immune to sudden withdrawal. If the creditors are outside the home nation so that the external funds are external not only to the borrowing enterprise but to the national financial reservoir itself, exchange rate risks inevitably complicate the financial contract, and the borrower's trade-off may be especially steep. Creditors face a corresponding, but reverse, trade-off: acquiring influence over a borrower or issuer of equity so as to enhance monitoring and reduce the risk of loss requires sacrificing some degree of liquidity. If the borrowers are located in the home nation and the creditor is a foreigner, exchange rate risks are highly relevant (whether borne directly by the creditor or the borrower), and the creditor's trade-off between influence and liquidity becomes still more difficult.

How large a proportion of the equity of a business or financial enterprise must an individual direct investor own before having effective control? That question has murky aspects even within a domestic economy. The murkiness is increased when cross-border and cross-currency dimensions are present. Hence there exists an arbitrariness in nations' balance-of-payments statistics about where the borderline should be drawn to differentiate direct investments from other types of capital flows.

For the purposes of collecting balance-of-payments data (capital flows being measured, again in principle, at the nation's border), statistical agencies differentiate direct investments from other capital flows by relying on a fixed cutoff for the percentage of equity ownership by foreign investors. The United States today, for example, uses a benchmark cutoff of 10 percent or more (the cutoff was 25 percent in the 1950s). Some efforts, only partially successful, have been made to standardize definitions of direct investment across nations. The use of an arbitrary cutoff for statistical purposes is probably inevitable. But it means that empirical data will not always closely match the underlying conceptual distinction. In some instances, a foreign investor may in practice have effective control with ownership of only a small fraction of the equity claims on an enterprise (for example, less than the cutoff of 10 percent). In situations toward the other extreme, a foreign investor may own a large fraction (say, 35–45 percent), yet still not exert effective control.[5]

Sticky Capital and Voice, Skittish Capital and Exit

Creditors can be arrayed along a spectrum according to the degree to which their financial claims represent, at the extremes, *sticky capital* or *skittish capital*. The behavior of capital that is relatively sticky is dominated by *voice*. Skittish capital is prone to exercise the option of *exit* (chapter 2). These distinctions, applicable purely within domestic financial reservoirs, are highly relevant for the analysis of capital flows among national reservoirs.

The distinctions between sticky and skittish, and voice and exit, are especially helpful for understanding differences between direct investments and other types of cross-border capital flows. Because cross-border direct investments involve ownership of a significant fraction of the equity claims on a business enterprise, they are the least skittish of international capital flows. The greater degree of stickiness reflects the factors just summarized. Relative to other types of capital flows, direct investments entail more influence over operating decisions, have a lengthier effective time horizon, but cannot be as readily reversed even if conditions confronting the enterprise should turn adverse. Correspondingly, direct investments are the most likely forms of cross-border capital flows to exercise the option of voice, remaining engaged to exert constructive influence rather than heading for the exit at the first sign of trouble.

---

5. Stekler and Stevens (1991). Measurement and accuracy issues plague the available empirical data for all types of cross-border capital flows. The issues are at least as severe for direct investments as for bank borrowing and lending, securities trading that is not direct investment, commercial paper, trade acceptances, and accounts receivable and payable. Despite the conceptual importance of distinguishing between direct owner-investors and portfolio creditors, therefore, analysis of actual data for capital flows should not treat the distinction between direct investment and other flows as the difference between day and night.

The initiators of banking and portfolio capital flows are less likely to perceive their cross-border extensions of credit as embodying stickiness. Their asset-liability relationships typically have shorter-term maturities and often have looser linkages to the goods and services sectors of the host economy. Such creditors can be preoccupied solely with their own expected returns over a short time horizon. They usually want to be able to reverse their lending on short notice if the fortunes of the borrower or prospects for the host economy are perceived to be less propitious than when their original lending commitments were made. The degree of their skittishness is itself subject to sudden, perhaps volatile, change. With even minor changes in information or expectations, the creditors' commitments may turn footloose. Avoiding efforts to remain engaged in their lending contracts and thereby exercising voice, skittish creditors will often disengage by using the easier option of exit.[6]

Direct investment is far from impervious to the turbulence that can buffet a host nation's financial reservoir. New direct investments by foreign creditors are eschewed in hard times and accelerated when prospects look rosy. The innate characteristics of most direct investments, however, reduce the scope for capital flight and capital surges. It is much more difficult to disengage from a direct investment, for example by selling a factory and its installed real capital, than it is to refuse to renew a maturing short-term bank loan or to offload bond or equity claims by selling them in markets where they are traded. Direct owner-investors are thus less inclined than portfolio creditors to exit during stormy weather rather than remaining to ride out the waves and exercise voice.

From the perspective of a host nation, inward direct investment is another illustration of how cross-border finance can be a two-edged sword. By encouraging relatively sticky direct investments rather than relying on potentially skittish banking and portfolio capital inflows (especially those that are merely short term), a nation can import savings from the rest of the world to nurture its own growth and development without maximum exposure to the potentially destabilizing behavior of fickle foreign investors with short-time horizons. Direct investments from abroad are more likely to exert voice, to show greater awareness of national needs and sensibilities than exhibited by portfolio creditors.

Yet the longer horizons, lesser volatility, and greater voice associated with direct investments can also cut the other way. The political challenges

6. For elaboration of the concepts of exit and voice, as noted in chapter 2, see Hirschman (1970).

associated with direct investments are more demanding. From the perspective of some home residents, greater voice exerted by foreigners may be unwelcome. Management and control by foreigners of major parts of the home nation's economy can be attacked by home citizens as undesirable. They may argue that the nation should have businesses and institutions that are organized, owned, and controlled locally. This preference for indigenous rather than foreign control presumes that local businesses will provide better services to national residents than nonlocal businesses, because indigenous decisionmakers are more likely than foreign decisionmakers to be attentive to local needs and problems. Extreme proponents of this nationalistic perspective may even argue that large-scale inward direct investment will undermine the cohesiveness and integrity of the social and political, and perhaps even the cultural, life of the nation.

Mishaps and Instability in Cross-Border Finance

Mishaps—mistakes and accidents—are inevitable in any financial system. When particular large investments go sour in an open national economy, international repercussions may be significant. The mishaps can be especially problematic if the investments have been financed with direct shifts of savings from one national reservoir to another, thus creating cross-border or cross-currency liabilities.

Because of the greater risks and uncertainties, the incidence of mishaps associated with cross-border financial activity may be greater than the incidence of purely domestic mishaps. (Empirical evidence to generalize about relative incidence is not readily available.) Beyond doubt, coping with the consequences of mishaps is more complex and difficult.

Accounting, Auditing, Data, and Legal Processes

Within a national reservoir, the occurrence of a mishap in domestic finance triggers remedial procedures. If the financial system is relatively advanced, acceptance of standardized accounting and audit procedures underpins the monitoring and enforcement of contracts and backstops the prudential oversight of financial institutions. Collection of data from individual financial institutions and dissemination of aggregated statistical data permit evaluation of trends and risks for the financial system as a whole. The legal system provides a foundation of laws and rules that facilitate the resolution of disputes about contracts and the handling of defaults and insolvencies.

For domestic finance, no national financial system meets the ideal accounting, auditing, data, and legal requirements for a robust utilities infrastructure. Even the advanced financial systems of North America, Europe, and Japan exhibit points of major weakness (think, for example, of the severe accounting problems with nonperforming loans in Japan in the 1990s or the accounting and auditing scandals in 2001–02 in the United States of corporations such as Enron, Tyco, WorldCom, and Adelphia). Nonetheless, in advanced financial systems the collective-governance underpinnings of legal, accounting, auditing, and data procedures are present and often relatively well developed.

For cross-border financial transactions, such underpinnings exist in only a rudimentary way, even in the advanced financial systems. In poorer developing nations with relatively unsophisticated financial systems, standards and institutions in these collective-governance areas are egregiously weak—weak for domestic finance, and weakest of all for cross-border financial transactions.

The application of accounting, auditing, data dissemination, and legal processes to cross-border financial transactions at the beginning of the twenty-first century is thus plagued by some awkward facts:

—An internationally standardized set of accounting and audit procedures does not yet exist.

—Data for cross-border, and even domestic, assets and liabilities for many nations' financial systems are often unavailable and, when available, may be unreliable.

—International law is much less well developed than nations' internal legal systems.

—No "world" legal system exists, nor any universally accepted method of resolving differences among national legal systems.

Differences across nations in the norms and standards for business and financial accounts can be large. The substantive content of accounts, not least for financial statements, varies from one nation to another. National practices are sometimes in direct conflict. Traditions differ about the amount and timing of disclosure and the degree of reliance to place on formal audits.

A single example illustrates the point. When a bank's loan becomes nonperforming in some nations, only the unpaid installment of the bad loan is considered past due in the reporting of the bank's condition. In other nations, however, the entire loan—current unpaid installment and all future installments—is classified as nonperforming if any installment payment is overdue. The latter accounting standard is obviously much more stringent than the former and more likely to signal future difficulties.[7]

Deficiencies in accounting practices and audit standards have been a significant underlying contributor to financial crises throughout past history. They are widely perceived to have been an important contributor to the financial crises in Asia in 1997–98. A Group of Twenty-Two report in the fall of 1998, for example, summarized the "damaging consequences" of accounting deficiencies:

> In many Asian countries, the absence of consolidated financial statements for related companies and, more generally, poor accounting practices hid serious financial weaknesses—the result of bad lending or investment decisions—in the corporate and banking sectors and contributed to the misallocation of resources that led up to the crisis. Faced with inadequate information about firms' financial performance, investors and creditors appeared to give issuers and borrowers the benefit of the doubt until the crisis broke and then to assume the worst after problems became apparent.[8]

Lawrence Summers, at the time deputy secretary of the U.S. Treasury, observed in a similar vein that

> If you were writing a history of the American capital markets, . . . the single most important innovation shaping that capital market was the idea of generally accepted accounting principles. We need that internationally. It is a minor, but not insignificant, triumph of the IMF that in Korea somebody who teaches a night school class in accounting told me that he normally has 22 students in his winter term, and this year he has 385. We need that at the corporate level in Korea. We need that at the national level.[9]

International efforts to design an agreed set of global accounting standards have been undertaken through the auspices of the International Accounting Standards Board (IASB, formerly the International Accounting Standards Committee, or IASC). Global standardization of auditing proce-

7. Group of Twenty-Two (1998, p. 8).

8. Group of Twenty-Two (1998, p. 5).

9. Quoted in Friedman (1999, pp. 147–48). Summers (1999) emphasizes the same general point.

dures has been discussed through the International Federation of Accountants (IFAC). International discussions about standards for securities firms have taken place under the aegis of the International Organization of Securities Commissions (IOSCO), and for the activities of insurance companies through the International Association of Insurance Supervisors (IAIS). Improvements in the collection, aggregation, and dissemination of financial data in recent years have been made by the IMF, the Bank for International Settlements, the World Bank, and the OECD. Chapter 10 further identifies the standards issues that these institutions confront and summarizes the progress on nascent international standards that has been made through these cooperative efforts. The institutions themselves are more fully described in the appendix.

Consider next the complications for legal system issues stemming from cross-border transactions. For several centuries, of course, problems have arisen in which a plaintiff and a defendant—individuals, firms, or organizations—are residents of different nations. Thus international law is an acknowledged subdiscipline of law. Numerous volumes concerned with one or another aspect of international law reside on the bookshelves of courts and some lawyers. Even so, there are few institutional mechanisms for formal arbitration procedures and for reconciling differences among national legal systems.

The International Court of Justice (ICJ) is, in principle, an exception. The ICJ, located in the Hague in the Netherlands, is the primary judicial organ of the United Nations. It was created in 1946 as the successor institution to the Permanent Court of International Justice (created under the League of Nations in 1922). The functions of the ICJ are twofold: "to settle in accordance with international law the legal disputes submitted to it by States, and to give advisory opinions on legal questions referred to it by duly authorized international organs and agencies."[10] Opinions differ widely about the authority that the ICJ has in fact, and should have, and how well it performs the functions assigned to it. As its mandate makes clear, however, one significant fact is beyond controversy: nongovernmental entities such as private businesses and financial institutions are not able themselves to initiate cases at the ICJ.

The relatively new dispute settlement mechanisms in the World Trade Organization can now help to reconcile trade policy features of national

---

10. General information about the International Court of Justice can be obtained from its website (www.icj-cij.org).

legal and regulatory systems.[11] The United Nations Commission on International Trade Law (UNCITRAL) and the International Bar Association have catalyzed international discussions about model standards for insolvency and bankruptcy (summarized in a later chapter). Every international institution has its own history of legal precedents and their status vis-à-vis national laws.[12]

Nonetheless, the overwhelming fact remains: the institutional mechanisms for reconciliation of differences among national legal systems are few in number and limited in scope. The Supreme Court and the subsidiary court systems in the United States have sufficient political authority to be accepted as a third branch of the U.S. government. The legal systems and their enforcement in many other nation states have an analogously strong political standing. None of the international legal institutions or procedures has a comparable political muscle for resolving cross-border legal issues.

Even for purely domestic finance, the best-practice treatment of contract defaults and of insolvencies requires a delicate balancing of the rights and obligations of debtors and creditors. The valid objectives of bankruptcy procedures are partly in conflict: the legal provisions must encourage adherence to the ex ante provisions of contracts, yet simultaneously try to prevent an uncoordinated "grab race" among creditors that produces a collective loss for all parties much larger than the losses that would otherwise occur through an orderly and cooperative bargaining process.

Given that bankruptcy procedures require a subtle balancing of competing objectives, differing national cultures and social norms have coped with the trade-offs in different ways. As observed by the Group of 30:

> The legal authorities available to deal with a financial insolvency vary greatly from country to country, often based on quite different social preferences, with different priority assigned to protection of creditors, borrowers, employees, and shareholders. Some are well tested and provide a fair and effective basis for working out competing claims with the national context; others much less so. In addition, virtually none were written with attention to the cross-border dimensions of an insolvency, offering no mechanism for dealing with matters out-

11. Jackson (1998a, 1998b); Ostry (1999); Petersmann (1998).
12. For example, for the IMF, see Gold (1984, 1990).

side of home jurisdiction or reconciliation of national differences. There is therefore substantial scope for conflict and miscalculation.[13]

In a situation of domestic insolvency when the national bankruptcy code is implemented, the issue of appropriate legal jurisdiction never arises. The creditors and debtor have no uncertainty about which system of national law applies. But for defaulted contracts and insolvencies with cross-border (and often cross-currency) dimensions, which legal procedures should apply, those of the debtor's nation or those of the lender's?

The design of a contract itself can resolve the most obvious aspect of the uncertainty by specifying in advance which nation's law applies as the "proper law of the contract." In real life, however, complex situations can arise where the differences among national legal jurisdictions become important. Suppose a firm in nation A borrows from a lender in nation B with a contract specifying that the law of B applies, but also borrows from a lender in C with a contract written to specify that the law of C applies. If the borrower in A becomes insolvent, an important feature of domestic bankruptcy law is absent: no court system has jurisdiction over the totality of the debtor's obligations, and hence no court is able to compel all dissident creditors to accept an orderly, generally agreed restructuring (or, in the extreme, liquidation) of the debtor's liabilities and assets.

Just as contracts cannot be "complete" in all their domestic dimensions, many types of cross-border legal contingencies cannot possibly be foreseen. The incremental uncertainties arising from the cross-border aspects of a contract turn out to be especially problematic. For domestic contracts, there at least exists a single, unambiguous legal jurisdiction for the resolution of disputes about the consequences of unforeseen contingencies. Dispute resolution for the inevitable, unforeseen contingencies of cross-border contracts—not to mention bankruptcy and liquidation resolutions in extreme difficulties—are troubled by a lack of clarity about whether multiple national legal jurisdictions are relevant and how differences between the jurisdictions are to be reconciled.

So-called sovereign borrowing, where the debtor is the government of a sovereign nation and incurs liabilities to creditors in different foreign nations (possibly denominated in several foreign currencies as well as the domestic currency), can be especially problematic. National governments

---

13. Group of Thirty (1998, p.4).

may default on debt contracts and have fairly often done so.[14] But there is no simple sense in which an entire nation can be insolvent or undergo bankruptcy proceedings (see below). Even skillful contract design, specifying which nations' laws apply to particular debt contracts of a particular nation's government, cannot eliminate the political and legal complications associated with sovereign debt defaults.

Financial Instability Exacerbated by Cross-Border Capital Flows

Within a nation's financial reservoir, mishaps inevitably cause waves and may generate storms. Storms can spread, becoming virulent because of herding behavior, contagion, and excessive volatility in asset prices. The fragility that is inherent in domestic financial activity can be powerfully exacerbated by international risks and uncertainties. The cross-border and cross-currency dimensions of financial intermediation amplify the consequences of distressed financial conditions. In particularly adverse circumstances, many national financial reservoirs can be simultaneously afflicted by volatile cross-border capital flows, disruptive fluctuations in exchange rates, and severe balance-of-payments crises.

From the perspective of any one nation whose economy is open to the rest of the world, the additional sources of potential instability can be classified into two groups. First, the home economy and financial reservoir may be buffeted by mishaps or disturbing events that originate abroad. Second, when mishaps or disturbances originate within the home nation, the consequences for the home reservoir and economy can be still more devastating because of the nation's openness.

Mishaps and disturbances originating outside the home nation can take many forms. They may originate in overseas goods markets. Production disruptions may result from wars or natural disasters (such as crop failures) or cartel-originated changes in supply (such as a cut in petroleum production by members of OPEC, the Organization of Petroleum Exporting Countries). Rapid implementation of a major technological innovation might lead to shifts in foreign production processes. Alternatively, the foreign mishaps or disturbances may originate within foreign financial reservoirs. A foreign bank or brokerage intermediary, for example, may become

---

14. "Default" by a government on its sovereign debt typically does not entail a permanent refusal or inability to service its debt. Rather, the government unilaterally imposes a standstill on servicing its debt, hoping the standstill will force its creditors to renegotiate the debt's terms and the timing of servicing payments.

insolvent. If it has extensive financial relationships with home-nation firms and financial institutions, the consequences may ripple through the home reservoir, affecting the perceived solvency of home financial institutions. Large and unexpected shifts in economic policies taken by foreign governments, for example, those that trigger inflationary booms or recessionary contractions, are still another type of external disturbances.

Whether the proximate cause is real-sector, financial, or policy driven, shocks occurring elsewhere in the world can have major effects on the home nation's exports, imports, capital flows, and terms of trade (export prices relative to import prices). Home production, consumption, and financial variables will be affected. Those changes can in turn cause sudden changes in expectations about asset prices and the solvency of individual firms. Were the home economy less open to the rest of the world, the foreign shocks could not cause such strong and pervasive effects.

Now consider the second class of mishaps and disturbances, those originating within the home nation itself. When the national economy and financial reservoir are significantly open to the rest of the world, the waves or storms generated by home mishaps are not bottled up at home. In principle, this lack of bottling up can have favorable as well as unfavorable aspects. In practice, the economy's openness on balance exacerbates the vulnerability of the home reservoir and economy. The incremental vulnerability stems from additional behavior options available to national citizens and to foreigners who are lending to or doing business in the nation.

Imagine that a major fraud is discovered in a large home firm, that the firm has borrowed extensively from several home banks, and that the announcement of the fraud generates grave doubts about the solvency of those (and perhaps other) home banks. As a second illustration, suppose that a contentious national election has just been held and that the incoming political leaders are suspected of planning to adopt an irresponsibly expansionary budget and to put pressure on the central bank to ease monetary policy. In such situations, one or another aspect of the home economic or financial situation unexpectedly goes sour, or at least the perceived risk of things going sour suddenly increases.

Unlike in the hypothetical case of the closed economy, both national citizens and foreigners can flee the situation. Risk-averse and skittish creditors, for example, can liquidate financial claims on home institutions and move the proceeds out of the home reservoir. Such exit options are especially open to portfolio creditors, both home and foreign residents, whose financial claims have a short maturity or are perceived as relatively liquid.

If participants in the home reservoir temporarily or even permanently abandon the home reservoir by exercising the option of exit rather than voice, the exiting behavior can greatly exacerbate the pressures as the nation adjusts to the triggering mishap. If the home currency is permitted to fluctuate in response to market pressures, it may depreciate sharply and disruptively. If instead the home nation follows an exchange regime where the exchange rate is pegged or heavily managed, official reserves may decline sharply and disruptively. Home interest rates may rise precipitously. Fears of further bankruptcies may be heightened.

Some adjustments to the internal mishap are appropriate, and in any case inevitable. Interest rates, for example, may have to rise somewhat (at least temporarily and possibly permanently). Some depreciation of the currency may need to occur. But the risks of overreaction, of informational cascades that lead to herding behavior, can be significantly increased by the availability of the exit options.

The exit options in such circumstances contrast starkly with behavior in which creditors do not pull their funds out of the home reservoir and instead remain to exercise voice. Voice behavior would try to smooth the adjustment to the mishap and improve the home situation. Direct owner-investors, both those who are domestic residents and foreign creditors who have made direct investments in the home economy, have the strongest incentives to exercise voice (because their ability to exit is more constrained).

In stormy weather, both exit and voice options are normatively controversial. The freedom of home residents and foreigners to pull their funds from the reservoir and disengage from the economy, it can be argued, helps to hold the government of the nation more politically accountable than it otherwise would be. The fear of capital flight can exert a strong discipline, forcing a government to behave better—for example, choosing sounder economic policies—than it might otherwise be tempted to behave. Some observers would argue normatively that individuals should have a basic right freely to invest their wealth wherever they see fit. Others would even go so far as to argue that individuals themselves should be free to leave their original nation and establish residence elsewhere.

An opposite normative perspective, however, can be and often is articulated. As seen from that perspective, the easy transfer of wealth from one nation to another is a negative rather than positive influence in the domestic political situation. Only foreign creditors and the wealthiest of home residents have effective access to the requisite information and established institutional connections that facilitate the exit option of capital flight. The critics of easy exit options also perceive a high correlation between large holdings of financial wealth outside the home nation and domestic corruption and tax evasion. Instead of viewing the freedom to shift financial wealth in and out of the nation as a constructive discipline on the national government, these critics view that freedom as reducing the incentives of residents and foreigners to participate actively in helping to achieve political resolution of the nation's problems. Because exit is too easy, voice and loyalty are not nurtured.

The difficult issue of whether the ready availability of exit options should be judged, on balance, good or bad for an individual nation will continue to surface in the subsequent analysis. The point to recognize here is that the availability of exit options from a nation's financial reservoir raises the probability that what might otherwise be small storms in that reservoir can be quickly magnified into larger ones.

Cross-Border Aspects of Herding Behavior

Because information asymmetries are significantly greater for cross-border than for domestic finance, assessments of risk premiums are more difficult. Informational cascades and herding behavior thus have an enhanced potential to generate instability in a multicurrency world with relatively well-connected financial reservoirs.

Modern communications technology, by reducing the relative costs of financial transactions, has significantly expanded the scope for herding behavior and contagion. Applicable to purely domestic finance, that generalization applies with special force to communications among national financial reservoirs. High-speed computers and telecommunications satellites, for example, now permit financial storms to propagate virtually instantaneously across national borders. In the nineteenth century, before the first transatlantic cable was laid, information could take as long as three weeks to travel between London and New York. The time delay fell to one day thereafter, and was down to less than a minute by 1914. Radio-telephone technology shortened the information lag further. Today, massive amounts of information are electronically transmitted in microseconds between different points on the globe.[15]

National stock and bond markets, foreign exchange markets, and international interbank borrowing and lending through eurocurrency markets are all highly sensitive to new information ("news"). With longer trading

15. Bordo, Eichengreen, and Irwin (1999, section 5).

hours in national markets (twenty-four-hour trading in some cases), differences in time zones have become much less significant than they once were. News reports originating in any part of the globe, and associated perceptions of the need for alterations in the risk premiums on particular assets, are immediately available everywhere on the globe. Sharp changes in confidence about particular financial assets are transmitted very quickly. Conditions in particular national reservoirs, never easily kept segregated, are now impossible to keep localized.

Thus the prompt flow of new information, which contributes to the efficiency benefits of cross-border finance, again has to be identified as a mixed blessing. Even more than in domestic finance, highly sensitive market valuations introduce an element of precariousness into cross-border saving and investment decisions. Especially in stormy weather associated with cross-border herding behavior, sudden sharp changes in asset prices and exchange rates can unhitch asset valuations from the long-term profit and risk calculations that ought to be the fundamental determinants of investment decisions. Excessive volatility in asset prices and exchange rates can in turn augment the damaging real-sector consequences of financial turbulence.

A nation's choice of exchange regime is controversial partly because the exchange rate for its currency is the single most influential price, of any kind, for its economy and financial reservoir. The adverse welfare consequences for a nation can be large if its exchange rate becomes misaligned with, or fluctuates excessively in relation to, variables that are its fundamental determinants over the long run.

What are the relevant fundamentals? Candidates include the relative (that is, home versus foreign) prices of goods, relative levels and rates of growth of employment and incomes, relative interest rates, and imbalances in national savings and domestic investment (which in turn are imbalances in the current account of the balance of payments). All theories for open economies postulate interrelations of these macroeconomic variables with the exchange value of a nation's currency.

When such variables are examined for their potential contributions to an empirical explanation for exchange rate variability, a presumptive puzzle is found. The variances of such variables tend to be an order of magnitude smaller than the variances of exchange rates. This fact is, to be sure, no more than suggestive. Careful assessment of whether the variability of exchange rates is "excessive" requires the specification of explicit analytical models of the fundamentals. Whether exchange rates are excessively volatile, or become misaligned for extended periods, is thus another of the difficult, highly controversial issues in international finance.

Just as the economics and finance professions have not yet generated an empirical consensus about the general issue of whether asset prices are excessively volatile and are sometimes unhitched from their fundamental determinants, no empirical consensus yet exists about the particular case of exchange rate variability. Given the very large short-run changes and medium-run swings in exchange rates that have been observed for most nations, however, there are, at the least, presumptive grounds for skepticism that fundamental determinants can completely account for exchange rate variations.

Cross-Border Contagion

The notion of contagion applied to financial activity rather than medical diseases has slippery nuances. Clarity requires a distinction between contagion effects traceable to shifts in financial and economic fundamentals on the one hand and so-called pure-contagion effects on the other. Pure contagion involves turbulence traceable not to alterations in fundamentals, but rather to sudden shifts in the interpretation of existing information.

Openness of a nation's economy can exacerbate both fundamentals contagion and pure contagion. Recent instances in which fundamentals contagion and pure contagion are both perceived to have been evident include the "Tequila crises" in the first half of 1995 in Latin America, which followed Mexico's devaluation in December 1994; the "Asian flu" crises in 1997–98, which followed Thailand's devaluation in July 1997; and the "flight to quality" and panic widening of risk spreads (even in domestic U.S. financial markets) caused by the August 1998 debt default and ruble devaluation in Russia. Fundamentals contagion, but less clearly pure contagion, was prominent in the financial crises experienced by Turkey in 2000–01 and Argentina in 2001–02.

Two types of fundamentals contagion have been differentiated, *monsoonal effects* and *spillovers*.[16] Monsoonal effects occur when a common external shock buffets a group of nations simultaneously. Many emerging-market nations, for example, might be subject together to major shifts in macroeconomic fundamentals originating in the rest of the world (such as sudden large changes in interest rates in the OECD nations, or sharp

16. Masson and Mussa (1995) and Masson (1999a, 1999b).

changes in oil prices triggered by production shifts in OPEC nations). Spillover effects result from direct financial or economic linkages among nations.

To make the distinction concrete, consider examples from the 1995–98 period, focusing on Asian nations. The easing of financial conditions in North America and Western Europe in 1995–96 was a monsoonal effect that simultaneously influenced all Asian emerging-market nations. As nominal interest rates fell in the largest financial reservoirs in the world, the Asian nations experienced a marked easing of the terms on which they could borrow externally. The easing of terms occurred not only because of declining external interest rates; Asian nations even found they had to pay lower risk premiums on their external borrowing as investors from North America and Europe sought higher yields on their investments than they could obtain at home. The monsoonal easing of financial conditions in non-Asian financial markets thus contributed significantly to the 1995–96 surge of capital inflows to Asian emerging-market nations.

The behavior of Japanese banks in 1997 provides a revealing example of direct spillover effects. Just before the Thai devaluation crisis, more than half of Thai external liabilities were to Japanese banks, many of them short term in maturity. Asian nations such as Indonesia, Malaysia, and South Korea also depended heavily on lending, including short-term loans, from Japanese commercial banks. When the Thai crisis materialized and undercut the profitability and capital of the Japanese banks (which had been in any case under strong pressure from internal Japanese conditions), the Japanese banks attempted to strengthen their positions by calling their loans, not merely in Thailand, but in other Asian nations as well. This behavior contributed to a regionwide liquidity crisis.[17]

The behavior of portfolio managers of OECD-nation mutual funds in the Asian crises also illustrates financial spillovers. As prices fell sharply in the Asian stock markets, causing large unrealized losses in the mutual funds' assets, the portfolio managers began to experience redemptions. To raise liquidity in anticipation of future redemptions, the managers needed to sell assets. A natural strategy to follow was to sell, not the assets whose prices had already collapsed (say, Thai stocks), but rather other assets where price declines had been less severe (say, stocks in Korea, Singapore, and Hong Kong). But of course as many portfolio managers followed this strat-

---

17. Kaminsky and Reinhart (2000).

egy, stock prices declined more sharply in the other Asian stock markets, thereby spreading the original disturbance to the other markets.

Linkages in goods trade among Asian nations provide even more straightforward illustrations of direct spillover effects. As the Thai baht depreciated against other currencies and the Thai financial reservoir became turbulent in 1997, incomes in Thailand came under downward pressure, and Thai imports began to fall sharply. Other Asian nations exporting to Thailand began to see spillover declines in their incomes, which in turn put downward pressure on their own imports from other nations in the region.

These examples of fundamentals contagion are merely different manifestations of the transmission of financial and economic pressures among interdependent national economies. Seen from one perspective, it is even misleading to affix the "contagion" label to such interdependencies. Monsoonal effects and direct spillovers are the essence of modern economic life, both within and among national economies.

Pure-contagion effects are less straightforward. Analysts try to understand pure contagion in financial activity by studying analytical models giving rise to multiple equilibriums or speculative bubbles, both involving self-fulfilling expectations. Subsequent to the Tequila, Asian flu, and Russian devaluation crises, numerous attempts have been made to study multiple-equilibrium models permitting expectational effects and herding behavior to generate cross-border or cross-currency contagion. Just as in the domestic context, however, the analysis in international finance of multiple-equilibrium models with self-fulfilling expectations has not yet generated a consensus view.[18]

Fundamentals Contagion or Pure Contagion?

Do pure-contagion effects significantly contribute to financial storms within national reservoirs and their propagation across borders? Or, instead, should one diagnose financial crises as primarily attributable to adverse fundamentals and fundamentals contagion?

Many analysts of crises emphasize the fundamentals. They argue, with cogency, that financial crises are never spontaneous but rather can invariably

---

18. Numerous papers dealing with the technical issues of modeling multiple equilibriums, many incorporating cross-border or exchange rate effects, or both, have recently been written or are now in preparation. For references additional to those given in chapter 2 and earlier in this chapter, see Masson (1999a, 1999b).

be traced to one or another triggering mishap or to various government policies deemed to be inappropriate. Within a national reservoir, market participants look least kindly on individual firms or financial institutions known to be experiencing difficulties. The analogous point is true for national economies. If market participants form a bearish view about a government's policies and the likely consequences for the nation's economy and currency, for example, there will seldom if ever be baseless grounds for some degree of pessimism. Even when the behavior of a private financial institution or the policy of some government agency seems appropriate ex ante (so that no clearcut "mistakes" are being made), the behavior or the policy may no longer be appropriate after unexpected changes in conditions have occurred. (The situation, in other words, is an "accident" in the sense defined in chapter 2.) With the wisdom of hindsight, fundamentals analysts also tend to fault private institutions or government policymakers for being insufficiently risk averse and prudent before the onset of a crisis. The fundamentals analysts argue, in effect, that financial activity is like a thermometer and that it is misleading to confuse an underlying fever and its causes with the thermometer that reflects and measures it.

In contrast, other analysts are prone to emphasize herding behavior and self-fulfilling expectations. They argue, with cogency, that changes in the fundamentals are sometimes insufficient to account for the virulent dispersion of contagion. Such analysts acknowledge that financial crises typically commence with some triggering mishap involving a change in fundamentals. They do not assert that bearish views about particular financial institutions or particular national economies tend to be baseless. Rather, they contend that investors and creditors tend to overreact in their pessimism or optimism (typified by the cliché that financial market participants move in only two gears, overdrive or reverse). For example, the spread of contagion in the Tequila, Asian flu, and Russian devaluation crises, these analysts assert, cannot be understood unless one appeals to informational cascades, herding behavior, and the pure-contagion effects attributable to self-fulfilling expectations.

Adjudicating a debate between diehard fundamentals analysts and extreme pure-contagion analysts is problematic. If both types of contagion are present in a crisis, they are intimately entangled. The diehards and extremists tend to respond to empirical and historical evidence as they would to the inkblots in a Rorschach test. For the fundamentalists, the inkblots typically suggest sensible private agent responses to unexpected disturbances or to faults in underlying government policies. For the contagion purists, the inkblots invariably look like herding-behavior blemishes.

There is no compelling reason to focus on one of the types of effects to the exclusion of the other. A diagnosis combining the two is often more illuminating. It is frequently true that before a crisis some weakness in fundamentals is present. Yet that weakness, in the absence of self-fulfilling shifts in expectations, may not be so serious as to make a crisis inevitable.

Fundamentals contagion is self-evidently consistent with so-called rational individual agents trying to protect themselves against financial loss. The pure contagion of herding behavior and self-fulfilling expectations should likewise be seen as consistent with rational attempts to minimize individual loss. On this dimension, there is no conceptual difference whatever between domestic and cross-border finance. An unchecked financial crisis spilling over national borders is a situation in which each nation's individuals, firms, and financial institutions can behave rationally and strategically, yet through herding behavior and contagion create an outcome highly adverse for the global financial system as a whole.

Waves and storms in financial reservoirs not only generate problems in their own right but can also lead to droughts or floods in investment in reproducible real capital goods. Such failures in the smooth reconciliation of savings and investment decisions undercut the most basic of all rationales for financial intermediation. Cross-border financial instability represents, of course, a similar undermining of the efficiency rationale for capital flows from one national financial reservoir to another. Seen from a cosmopolitan, global perspective, cross-border capital flows facilitate a worldwide reconciliation of the needs and preferences of ultimate savers and ultimate investors. But this potential for gains for both borrowing and lending nations cannot be realized if the capital flows themselves become important sources of financial and macroeconomic instability.

The bottom-line conclusion is that the world financial system—the conglomeration of all national financial reservoirs—is inherently fragile, inherently vulnerable to instability. This potential for instability cannot be attributed primarily to cross-border features of financial activity. The causes are deeply rooted in informational asymmetries, expectational and informational cascades, and adverse selection and moral hazard problems that pervade all aspects of financial behavior, domestic as well as cross-border. But there is no question that the cross-border features magnify and aggravate the potential instability.

Adjustment, Asset Financing, and Liability Financing for Payments Imbalances

One's natural inclination is to associate mishaps—mistakes and accidents as defined earlier—with the difficulties of particular individuals, firms, or financial institutions. For example, a bank may become insolvent because of inappropriate connected lending to insiders, imprudent speculation in foreign exchange, or outright fraud. Firms may fail because of poor judgments about market trends.

In a multination world with extensive economic integration across national borders, the concept of mishaps needs to be generalized further. Virtually the whole of a nation's financial reservoir and economy can be afflicted by a severe shock with pervasive effects—an *economywide accident,* so to speak. And if a nation's government adopts ill-conceived and badly implemented policies with widespread effects throughout the economy, the resulting situation is, in effect, an *economywide mistake.*

To put economywide accidents and mistakes in analytical context, one first needs an understanding of the balance-of-payments constraints faced by individual nations with open economies. This section digresses briefly to review the requisite concepts.

A nation with cross-border payments for its imports of goods, services, and transfers greater than cross-border receipts for its exports of goods, services, and transfers is said to have a deficit in the current account of its balance of payments. In conjunction with a current account deficit, the residents of the nation surrender financial claims on or incur financial liabilities to the rest of the world. By definition, given how balance-of-payments statistics are compiled, a current account deficit is identically matched with offsetting net capital flows—payments or receipts on capital account that alter the outstanding stocks of cross-border assets and liabilities.[19]

Some part of a deficit in current account transactions may be readily "financed" (in the sense of matched or paid for) by a voluntary net inflow of funds from private economic agents at home and abroad. This easy financing occurs, for example, to the extent that some capital flows are

---

19. A net transfer of wealth in the opposite direction, toward the residents of the home nation, occurs in periods when the nation has a surplus in the current account of its balance of payments (an excess of current account receipts over current account payments). For expositional simplicity, the text discusses only the case of a deficit in the current account or in the overall balance of payments. The analysis of surplus cases is essentially similar except that the signs of imbalances and their effects are reversed.

closely and voluntarily associated with current account transactions (for example, payments for purchases of goods or extensions of trade credit closely associated with such purchases). But many other types of capital flows do not constitute easy financing of a current account deficit. On the contrary: the incipient total net flow of voluntary private capital may be insufficient to finance an incipient current account imbalance, or may even move in the "wrong" direction (for example, if private economic agents on balance wish to withdraw funds from the nation at the same time as the current account is in deficit). In general, incipient current account deficits are *not* matched by incipient voluntary net inflows of private capital.[20]

To fix ideas, focus in what follows on a situation in which the home nation has an incipient current account deficit and incipient net private capital *outflows*. To better understand the constraints, consider first a hypothetical extreme case. Suppose the home government and all foreign governments were to eschew intervention in the exchange markets for the home currency. Suppose governments likewise refrained from capital account transactions except those directly associated with payments for or receipts from current account transactions. With such assumptions about government behavior, the hypothesized situation is one in which ex ante plans are plainly inconsistent. Such an outcome could not possibly occur in practice.

What would happen? Which features of the situation would have to give? The exchange rate for the home currency, home and foreign financial variables such as interest rates, and other home and foreign macroeconomic

---

20. The word "incipient" in these sentences has complex nuances but is analytically important. It indicates that the imbalances referred to are ex ante analytical concepts rather than statistical definitions of imbalance in ex post actual data. The remainder of this footnote explains the distinction. Ex post balance-of-payments accounts are prepared in accordance with the principles of double-entry book-keeping. Each transaction between a home resident and a foreign resident is, in principle, recorded twice, once as a credit and once as a debit. In a complete ex post balance of payments (including allowance for statistical discrepancies), credits are always exactly offset by equal debits. Thus a "deficit" in one category of ex post balance-of-payments transactions is exactly matched with a "surplus" in all other categories of ex post transactions. Ex post identities should not be confused with ex ante analytical concepts. Ex post balance-of-payments data are a record of what actually happened in a given historical period; ex post identities always hold true, by definition and construction. Ex ante concepts and theories are fundamentally different. They deal with why agents do what they do and analyze the consequences of that behavior. The ex ante plans of agents can be inconsistent. The text refers to a situation in which—at current and expected values of the exchange rate, interest rates, and other macroeconomic variables such as incomes and prices—the ex ante, incipient plans of agents about current account transactions and the ex ante, incipient plans of other agents about capital flows are mutually inconsistent.

variables would have to change sufficiently to ensure that net flows of private capital completely and exactly financed any current account imbalance of the home nation. One likely outcome is that the home currency would depreciate. The resulting capital flows in the home nation's balance of payments would be voluntary given the new values for the exchange rate, interest rates, and other macroeconomic variables. The changes in the exchange rate and other variables required to achieve such an outcome, however, could prove to be large or disruptive. Accordingly, the home government (and possibly also foreign governments) might be reluctant to allow unconstrained variability in the exchange rate and interest rates and the domestic consequences associated with such variability.

Now consider the same initial situation (an incipient current account deficit and an incipient net outflow of private capital), but assume that the home government is prepared to engage in exchange market intervention or other capital account transactions. Define the algebraic sum of the incipient current account deficit and the incipient net outflow of private capital as the incipient *overall imbalance*, that is, the net sum of planned transactions on current account and net private capital account. Now suppose that—at the existing exchange rate, interest rates, and other macroeconomic variables inside and outside the home nation—the home government is willing to undertake transactions for its own account that would completely offset the incipient overall imbalance. (This assumption about the government's behavior is, of course, the opposite extreme from that assumed in the first case.) To offset the incipient overall imbalance, the home government must draw down its own assets, increase its borrowings from foreigners, or take some combination of the two actions. For this hypothetical case, the home government would be using *official financing* to cover 100 percent of the incipient overall deficit in the nation's balance of payments. To the extent that the government draws down its official reserves (for example, through supporting the home currency in exchange markets) or draws down some other government assets, the actions are *asset financing*. If the government increases its borrowings from foreigners, the actions are *liability financing*.[21]

---

21. Sometimes a government may adopt special targeted measures to induce private economic agents in the home nation to reduce their external assets or increase their external liabilities as a substitute for the government taking asset-financing or liability-financing actions itself. To keep the exposition simple, I omit this complication from the text discussion.

The two extreme cases just described are analytical benchmarks. Real government behavior when reacting to incipient deficits in the overall balance of payments tends to fall in between the extreme cases. Asset financing, and often liability financing as well, are commonly observed, at least over shorter runs.

Yet 100 percent financing of a nation's incipient overall deficit is typically risky or impossible, especially over longer periods. Instead of relying solely on financing payments imbalances, therefore, governments and analysts are often preoccupied with adjustment of such imbalances.

The concept of *adjustment* has many nuances. The home government's policies influence cross-border transactions in a variety of ways. Some operate selectively on cross-border payments and receipts (such as tariffs on imports or at-the-border restrictions on capital flows). Other policies work indirectly (for example, budgetary and domestic monetary policies) but nevertheless exert pervasive effects on cross-border transactions. The government itself has cross-border transactions that can be altered. Changes in the exchange value of the home currency, whether brought about by market forces or government management, strongly influence cross-border transactions. The home government thus has considerable discretionary ability to try to "adjust" the magnitude of an incipient overall imbalance in cross-border payments.

The first extreme case above may be described as *all adjustment, no financing,* in contrast with the opposite extreme of *complete financing without policies to support adjustment.* In practice, the government confronts a difficult trade-off between financing and adjustment. Making choices about the mix of financing and adjustment requires judgments about, among other things, the likely persistence of the incipient imbalance. If an imbalance is expected to be small and temporary, asset financing or liability financing may seem attractive relative to changing the exchange rate or taking other policy actions aimed at facilitating adjustment. Conversely, if an imbalance is caused by large changes in the economic environment that are likely to persist, the wiser and safer course would typically be for the home government to rely primarily on policies that promote adjustment rather than resort to financing.

History is replete with examples of economic and financial crises triggered, wholly or in part, by preceding periods in which the exchange value of a nation's currency was maintained by official financing for too long at an overvalued or undervalued rate. Persisting ("permanent") changes in the domestic or external economic environment of an open economy very often necessitate, later if not sooner, an adjustment of the exchange rate. Excessive reliance on the financing options instead of policies to facilitate adjustment is a surefire way for the nation to get into trouble.[22]

With the financing options themselves, the government confronts a trade-off between asset financing and liability financing. Both types of financing, to be sure, involve opportunity costs that may be roughly similar along some economic dimensions. For example, with asset financing the interest earnings forgone on drawdowns of reserve assets may not be so very different from the additional interest that has to be paid on new external borrowings with liability financing. The differences between asset financing and liability financing, however, are more important than the similarities. The government can typically plan for asset financing of an overall deficit without becoming involved in consultations and joint decisionmaking with foreign governments or other foreigners. Decisions can be made entirely within the home government, for example, about the amounts and timing of drawdowns of reserve assets. Asset financing thus gives the home government maximum freedom for independent maneuver in selecting that position on the financing-adjustment trade-off judged to be in the nation's best interests. Asset financing is an available option, of course, only if the home nation owns a sufficiently large amount of readily usable external assets.

Liability financing of an overall deficit, in contrast, is more complex and politically more delicate. Liability financing inevitably involves consultations and joint decisionmaking with foreign creditors. Liability financing thus leaves the home government with less room for independent maneuver and tends to shift the nation to a different position on the financing-adjustment trade-off than would otherwise be observed with asset financing.

Foreign governments or foreign private financial institutions are likely to be willing to lend to a home nation in overall deficit, thereby enabling it to engage in liability financing, only if the debtor nation can offer satisfactory

---

22. The generalizations in the text omit several complications. Many forces outside the control of the home government influence the nation's cross-border transactions. For example, the policy actions of foreign governments also can have significant effects on the home nation's payments imbalance. Foreign economic variables might move fortuitously so as to mitigate—or adversely so as to magnify—the need for domestic adjustment or for adjustment in the exchange rate. It is thus no straightforward matter for a nation's government to adopt policies for adjustment of a net imbalance in the balance of payments, even when the government deliberately eschews financing and chooses to emphasize adjustment policies.

assurances of timely repayment. Such assurances typically include agreements to meet certain conditions—for example, specified adjustments in the home government's policies. The performance conditions and terms associated with the lending arrangements for a home government's liability financing are often referred to as *conditionality*.

Creditors always require assurances about the likely ability of debtors to repay loans at maturity. Some creditors may expect to roll over their loans to sound debtors at maturity, continuing to earn a profit indefinitely. At a minimum, however, all creditors expect borrowers to have the capacity to repay and to be willing to repay if the creditor does not wish to renew the loan. To raise the probability that borrowers will have the capacity to repay, creditors often refuse to make a loan without firm undertakings that borrowers will carry out specified actions or refrain from certain types of behavior.

For these basic reasons, conditionality attached to the home government's liability financing of overall deficits is not surprising in any way. Creditors in nations with overall surpluses, the potential acquirers of the prospective loan claims generated by the home government's liability financing, will naturally seek assurances about the future capacity of the home nation to repay the loans. They will be aware, moreover, that "repaying" may well require not only ceasing to run the overall deficit but thereafter running a sufficient overall surplus for a long enough period to restore a net external asset position for the home nation, something like the one that existed before the original borrowing. Inevitably, therefore, prospective lenders will be drawn into forming judgments about the sustainability and appropriateness of the home nation's economic policies. In effect, they will second-guess the home government's judgments, developing their own independent judgments of the preferred trade-off between financing and adjustment of the home nation's payments imbalance.

The basic interests of foreign creditors differ markedly from those of the borrowing nation. The difficult judgments about when an imbalance requires adjustment necessarily involve normative preferences. Prospective foreign creditors therefore tend to prefer a different point than the home nation on the financing-adjustment trade-off. The foreign creditors will probably urge the home government to take more prompt or more ambitious adjustment actions than the home government itself, if unconstrained, would choose.

Various adjustment actions taken in foreign surplus nations could help to reduce the home nation's payments imbalance. The home government typically views that set of alternatives favorably, especially when it believes that events or policies originating outside the home nation are the primary causes of its own unsustainable or inappropriate deficit. Not surprisingly, however, and no matter what the merits of the arguments may be, foreign creditors tend to be unenthusiastic about the notion that foreign governments rather than the home government should take policy actions to bring about adjustment of the home nation's deficit.

Unavoidably, then, plans for the liability financing of an overall deficit in cross-border transactions lead to potentially conflictual discussions with prospective foreign creditors. The option of liability financing becomes actually available only when the borrowing nation accepts constraints on its policies. In a nirvana where good fairies make wishes come true, nations wanting to finance a deficit by borrowing rather than drawing down assets would have automatic access to liability financing without any need to accept conditionality. So far, however, though the fact is regretted by many, good fairies have shunned international financial affairs.

With the preceding discussion of adjustment, asset financing, and liability financing as background, I now return to the issues of mishaps that can affect virtually the whole of a national financial reservoir and a national economy.

Exit versus Voice for an Entire National Economy

Economywide accidents often originate outside the nation. A single illustration can bring out many of the points that apply to all types of severe disturbances occurring abroad. Imagine, therefore, that a home nation unexpectedly suffers an adverse movement in its terms of trade. Suppose that the nation is a major exporter of agricultural commodities and is suddenly confronted with a sharp fall in the world market price of its primary exports.

The immediate effects of the shock would include a fall in export receipts and hence also domestic incomes. The current account in the balance of payments would move sharply in the direction of deficit. Something in the situation must give. If the home government is following some variant of an exchange regime pegging the exchange rate, the nation's reserves would be drawn down in the first instance (asset financing of the developing imbalance). If the exchange rate is permitted to float, the home currency might sharply depreciate. If the home government adopts expansionary fiscal or monetary policies to offset the contractionary forces from the external shock, the pressures on the exchange rate and the balance of payments would be heightened. The home government might decide to try to arrange liability financing to cushion the pressures, but the negotiations over conditionality would at the least be uncomfortable.

The shock inevitably causes some amount of contraction in domestic incomes and consumption, with the initial effects on the exporters and agricultural producers spreading to incomes and employment throughout the economy. If the currency depreciates sharply, the depreciation in turn may put severe financial pressure on a variety of national firms and financial institutions, especially those that may have borrowed in foreign currencies but that have most of their receipts denominated in the domestic currency. Associated increases in interest rates could increase the financial pressures further. The damaging effects on balance sheets could then add to the contractionary forces in the economy, spreading the adverse shock even more widely.

Throughout the financial reservoir and the economy, costly adjustments to the new situation have to be made. If asset financing or liability financing is part of the short-run response but the shock appears to be permanent, the only plausible choice may be to include some depreciation of the currency as part of the longer-run adjustment. All the available choices will be painful, whatever combination of adjustment and financing policies may be chosen by the home government. If the external shock is large, virtually the entire economy will feel some of the pain.

Economywide mistakes, in contrast to economywide accidents, tend to originate within the home economy or financial system. Most often, they arise from general government policies that are demonstrably faulty. A single illustration again suggests many of the relevant analytical points. Suppose that the policymakers deciding about the home government's budget embark on new tax and expenditure policies that in the circumstances are fiscally irresponsible (for example, a combination of major expenditure increases associated with tax cuts rather than tax increases when the economy is already operating near its productive capacity). Worse, suppose that the central bank adopts new monetary policies that imprudently accommodate, rather than offset, the irresponsible budget policies.

The notion of "demonstrably faulty" government policies—for example, the identification of particular fiscal or monetary policies as "irresponsible" or "imprudent"—is self-evidently contentious. One critic's "mistake" is often another person's favored policy. Professional analysts often disagree about the appropriateness of many specific policies.

I restrict the notion of economywide policy mistakes to instances in which a large majority of relatively disinterested analysts can agree, applying the least inadequate objective standards available, that the policies are markedly inferior to feasible alternatives. For the purposes of the illustration here, imagine that a commanding majority of home-nation professional analysts (excluding those supporting the policies inside the government) *and* virtually all foreign analysts believe that the newly announced macroeconomic policies are inappropriate.

The immediate consequences of the altered policies of the home government are likely to be financial. Many home residents and many of the economy's foreign creditors who are able to do so may adopt the exit option, reversing their lending to the nation and shifting their assets to a location abroad deemed to be safer. The foreigners who in the past made inward direct investments are also likely to become nervous; their ability to use the exit option is more limited, but even these investors will take advantage of any opportunities open to them to hedge their exposure to a deteriorating home economic situation. As creditors and investors attempt to exit from the nation's financial reservoir and economy, the currency may depreciate sharply (or, if the exchange regime is some form of pegging, official reserves may fall precipitously). The general state of financial confidence may deteriorate badly. The resulting turbulence may even deserve the label "crisis." The central bank may eventually be required to abandon its accommodating policy by sharply raising domestic rates of interest.

The skittishness of creditors exercising the option of exit has been colorfully captured in Thomas Friedman's analogy of "the Electronic Herd." Friedman describes global financial markets as "made up of millions of investors moving money around the world with the click of a mouse . . . and this herd gathers in key global financial centers, such as Wall Street, Hong Kong, London and Frankfurt, which I call 'the Supermarkets'." A group of "short-horn cattle" includes buyers and sellers of stocks, bond, and currencies who move their money around from place to place on a very short-term basis, thinking of expected returns on a daily or even hourly basis. The "long-horn cattle" have somewhat longer time horizons for their commitments when they invest in or lend to a country. The long-horn cattle, however, are also part of the Electronic Herd and "they now move in and out, like a herd, with surprising speed." Friedman writes of the Electronic Herd as being like a herd of wildebeests grazing over a wide area of Africa. When a wildebeest on the edge of the herd sees something move in the tall, thick brush next to where it's feeding, that wildebeest doesn't say to the wildebeest next to it, 'Gosh, I wonder if that's a lion moving around there in the brush.' No way. That wildebeest just starts a stampede, and these wildebeests don't stampede for a mere hundred yards. They stampede to the next country and crush everything in their path.[23]

The analogy of a stampede exaggerates the degree to which everything in the path of fleeing creditors gets crushed. But the dangers to an open economy from creditors' skittishness, from their potential to magnify a financial crisis, is very real. Not the least of the dangers are the damaging consequences, for both expectations and actual behavior, of deterioration in balance-sheet positions resulting from sudden depreciation of the currency and sharp falls in the domestic-currency prices of market-traded assets.

Although the immediate consequences of the economywide mistake in this example are financial, the adverse effects can spread quickly to the real sectors of the economy. In addition to the capital flows associated with creditors' attempts to flee the home economy, the incipient current account balance would move toward deficit. The home government would be acting in a way that reflects a poor understanding of the external constraints facing the nation. Nonetheless the nation would, as always, be tightly bound by the external constraints manifested through its balance of payments. The nation would, as always, confront the difficult trade-off between adjustment and financing of its incipient overall deficit and, to the extent that financing is chosen, the trade-off between asset financing and liability financing. The longer-run sustainability of the precrisis exchange rate would certainly be called into question.

The economywide mistake hypothesized here would be a prominent example of a general government failure in the sense defined in chapters 2 and 3. The government failure would have been a primary cause of the resulting distressed financial conditions. The financial turbulence, probably fueled by a combination of fundamentals contagion plus some pure contagion due to herding and flee-for-the-exits behavior, would in turn

---

23. Friedman (1999, pp. 11–13, 95–97, 145–46).

constitute a set of market failures superimposed on the triggering government failure.

Economywide accidents and especially economywide policy mistakes can generate problems for the financial system that are an order of magnitude more difficult than the problems resulting from smaller-scale mishaps. One way to grasp these additional difficulties is to focus on issues posed by defaults and insolvencies.

When an individual firm or financial institution defaults on debt obligations or otherwise is threatened with insolvency, it is typically forced into bankruptcy or arbitration procedures. Sometimes it must be liquidated altogether. Insolvency and bankruptcy are messy. Yet such problems are usually manageable in the domestic legal system provided that the entity's balance sheet contains few cross-border assets and liabilities.

When cross-border relationships are significant, the legal aspects are considerably more complex. The complexities can be magnified enormously, furthermore, in situations in which economywide mishaps lead to generalized conditions of financial distress. Both home and foreign portfolio creditors, who are even more skittish than in normal times about the claims they hold, would be trying to exit the home financial reservoir so as to relocate their assets abroad. The resulting increases in domestic interest rates and the depreciation of the home currency would put severe pressures on balance sheets and raise the specter of multiple defaults and insolvencies. Even the government itself may be in default, or threatened with default, on its own debt. The resulting crisis can be especially complex if mistaken government policies have significantly contributed to the generalized financial distress.

If the government itself defaults on its sovereign debt obligations, virtually all capital flows into and out of the nation would be affected. Numerous defaults by a nation's banks on their liabilities to foreigners can be similarly disruptive. Because default by the government on its debt often reduces the value of bank assets and because the government is often expected to intervene to avert widespread default of the nation's banks, a two-way reinforcement can occur between sovereign default and banking-system default. Outside the financial system, governments are less widely expected to provide implicit or explicit guarantees for loans to nonfinancial enterprises and individuals. Widespread defaults by nonfinancial entities, however, typically impair the solvency of the nation's banks. Those developments in turn raise expectations of the government having to intervene to protect the banking and the payments systems. These more complex distress and insolvency situations have been termed (albeit somewhat misleadingly; see below) episodes of "national default."[24]

An increment in creditor skittishness is a problem for borrowing enterprises and financial institutions regardless of the form in which the capital is held. If the creditors' claims are holdings of long-maturity bonds or equity shares traded in markets, the attempts to sell the claims will drive down their prices and shatter confidence. Buyers for the claims can only be created by sharp markdowns in price. For these cases where skittish capital takes the form of marketable bonds or equity shares, however, the underlying real capital investments—the machine tools and factory buildings whose purchase was permitted by the issuance of the bonds and equity shares—at least remain in place.

The consequences of creditor skittishness may be worst of all if the financial claims are in the form of nonmarketable shorter-maturity debt instruments, most notably short-term loans from banks and finance companies. If the creditors holding these claims can succeed in exiting the home financial system by refusing to renew their lending, the pressures on borrowing enterprises and financial institutions can be especially severe. In such circumstances, borrowers would somehow have to try to raise funds to repay the loans and may often be able to do so only by selling their real capital assets at firesale prices. Efforts to raise funds to pay off the loans from skittish lenders may well fail, throwing the borrowers into default.

A financial crisis affecting the nation as a whole, with the threatening possibility of widespread insolvencies, soon raises the question whether it may be desirable to mitigate the crisis by arranging for some sort of emergency lending from external sources. As the crisis develops, the home government may already have used asset financing (drawing down the reserves) to cover part of the outflows of funds from the home reservoir. Both the government and private financial participants are keenly aware, however, that asset financing has a definite limit: assets can be drawn down to zero, but not lower than that. When the scope for asset financing of the payments drain is exhausted, liability financing must be arranged beyond that point unless there is a willingness to permit unconstrained variability for financial variables, in particular for the exchange rate and interest rates. National residents themselves are likely to ask whether emergency lending from abroad is a preferred way of trying to resolve the crisis. Because of

24. Mussa and others (2000, p. 95).

spillover effects to other nations, foreigners affected by the crisis may also prefer to see the home nation arrange for incremental liability financing.

The home nation's government itself is the most likely recipient of emergency financial assistance. Foreign governments might extend emergency bilateral loans to the home government. Alternatively, the home government and an international institution such as the International Monetary Fund might negotiate an emergency stabilization package, in which the IMF lending is conditioned on agreed adjustments or reforms of home government policies. The home nation's commercial banks are another conceivable recipient for foreign emergency lending.

Chapters 8 and 9 focus in a more detailed way on economywide financial crises, including those for which spillovers are strong enough to render them dangerous for entire regions or even the global financial system as a whole. The analysis there discusses crisis management and evaluates the pros and cons of emergency lending to nations troubled by economywide mishaps, paying special attention to the role of the IMF. The issues already identified in a domestic context—moral hazard difficulties, possible "bailouts" of creditors, concerted lending to "bail in" creditors, collective action to manage workouts and debt restructurings—surface with still greater intricacy when the cross-border, multination complications are taken into account.

A final point, alluded to earlier, deserves emphasis in this first-pass discussion of economywide financial crises: it is inappropriate to apply mechanically the concepts of insolvency and bankruptcy to a nation as a whole. In distressed financial conditions, the distinction between illiquidity and insolvency is extremely difficult even for an individual firm or financial institution in a purely domestic context. The difficulties and ambiguities of the distinction become virtually insurmountable for nations as a whole.

An entire nation can certainly experience generalized mishaps, as I have just been stressing. Numerous individual firms and banks can default and become insolvent. A nation's government can default on its sovereign debt. When many insolvencies occur simultaneously and interact, it is tempting to label the situation as a "national default." But entire nations do not become insolvent or bankrupt in a meaningful sense. A nation, unlike a private firm or a financial institution in bankruptcy proceedings, cannot be liquidated and cease to exist. Further, it is extremely difficult (in practice impossible) to distinguish between the *ability* of a nation to service its debts to foreigners and its *willingness* to do so. From some perspectives and analytical calculations, a nation's resources may far exceed its external debts. Yet many of the nation's residents may find it economically or politically unacceptable to divert sufficient national resources away from domestic uses to permit full service of its external debts.

In bankruptcies of individual private entities, it is typically possible to identify a residual value for the enterprise or financial institution. If remaining assets can be sold, the liquidation value is fairly straightforward. If the firm or financial institution is to be reorganized (so that creditors are given new claims on the reorganized entity) and if the value of intangible assets must be estimated, some valuation difficulties ensue. But in almost all cases it is feasible to reach a consensus on reorganized value.

Not only is it politically impossible to liquidate a nation as a whole. An entire nation also cannot be reorganized in the sense typical of the court-approved and court-monitored bankruptcies of private firms within national financial systems. True, individual private firms and financial institutions within the nation can be reorganized (under the terms of national bankruptcy law). Foreign creditors and investors can be forced to accept equity or debt claims on the reorganized private entities. Negotiations can be undertaken to reschedule or restructure the nation's sovereign government debt. New elections or a coup d'etat can replace the political leaders responsible for a nation's government (an outcome that might meaningfully be described as a government reorganization).

But there is no meaningful sense in which foreign creditors interacting with the nation's government and citizens would be able to reach a consensus on the ("residual") present value of the nation's resources as a whole. Nor can foreign creditors unambiguously estimate the ability and willingness of the government to raise taxes or reduce spending over future years. Political uncertainties may prevent even the existing government itself from making a credible estimate of the future tax and spending policies it (or its successor government!) will follow. No more normatively contentious subject will be debated in the nation's postcrisis political life than the tax and spending policies of the government—and hence the relative merits of using the nation's resources for domestic objectives rather than for paying interest to foreign creditors.[25]

---

25. For nations with large external debts, and in particular when the national government has a substantial amount of its debt held by foreigners, it can be revealing to make calculations (under alternative analytical assumptions) about the relationships between the nation's export earnings and its ability to service the external debt. For example, it can be interesting to compare the rate of growth of

Some analysts have argued that the world community should establish a cooperative international mechanism for facilitating the rescheduling or restructuring of a nation's debts (especially its sovereign debt) after economywide mishaps and financial crises have resulted in a standstill of cross-border debt service. These ideas are discussed in chapter 10.

---

export earnings with the rate of interest paid on the external debt. Cohen (1985) illustrates these calculations. Despite the title of Cohen's paper ("How to Evaluate the Solvency of an Indebted Nation"), such calculations do not really permit a clear definition of solvency or insolvency for the nation as a whole. Guidotti and Kumar (1991) and Boughton (1994) also discuss these issues.

7   International Collective Governance

Many of the fundamental points in the book so far can be combined into a syllogism, boiled down into three sets of summary propositions:

A. Financial activity, when it functions smoothly, is enormously beneficial in promoting growth and efficient resource allocation. It permits the diversification and sharing of risk. It allows ultimate savers and ultimate investors to make independent localized decisions, yet renders the decisions consistent in the aggregate. Modern economic life would be impossible without financial institutions and financial intermediation.

B. Completely unconstrained financial activity may not be able to deliver the potential benefits. Informational asymmetries, adverse selection and moral hazard, informational cascades leading to herding behavior and contagion, and excessive volatility in asset prices cause financial activity to be inherently vulnerable to instability.

C. The way out of this dilemma is to establish and maintain collective-governance components of a utilities infrastructure for the financial system. The critical features of collective financial governance are well-designed and competently administered legal procedures for enforcing contracts and adjudicating disputes; high standards for accounting, auditing, and information disclosure; widespread availability of accurate data about financial and economic activity; skillful prudential oversight of private financial institutions; sound and predictable macroeconomic policies; and an effective but limited potential for crisis management and crisis lending.

The logic summarized in the A and B propositions is compelling for a single closed economy (chapter 2). The A and B propositions apply with at least equal force to a global system of integrated national financial reservoirs (chapter 6). The C conclusion is compelling for a single closed economy (chapter 3). Why not, then, apply the C conclusion to cross-border finance? If a well-functioning utilities infrastructure is a precondition for a domestic financial reservoir to operate smoothly, perhaps a financial utilities infrastructure on a world scale is needed for the smooth and stable operation of the conglomeration of all national financial reservoirs?

One's intuition wants to respond that the same logic does apply at the world level. And the economic aspects of the logic are, indeed, persuasive. Because national economies and financial systems are increasingly integrated, collective-action problems with cross-border dimensions—externalities, market failures, and public goods issues affecting many nations simultaneously—have become more numerous and conspicuous. As the twenty-first century progresses, such problems will continue to grow in importance relative to national domestic problems (chapter 4). Suppose that there could exist supranational analogues to the collective-governance functions carried out within domestic reservoirs by nations' central banks and supervisors of financial institutions. Then the global economy and financial system would be better able to evolve in a smooth and stable manner.

The political preconditions, however, do not exist in our messy intermediate world. The evolution of governance mechanisms capable of dealing with cross-border collective-action problems has lagged far behind the cross-border integration of markets. Neither cooperation among national governments nor the strengthening of international institutions has kept pace with the rapidly increasing interconnectedness among national economies. The logic of the A-B-C syllogism therefore cannot be fully applied to the global financial system. The global polity does not yet contain collective-governance institutions that can effectively carry out the functions of a supranational financial utilities infrastructure.

For the next several decades, political considerations are unlikely to permit a radical increase in international collective governance (chapter 4). National governments will retain the legal forms of de jure sovereignty. They will be reluctant to delegate greatly strengthened authority to existing or new international institutions. Sometimes that reluctance may be justified: a valid presumption exists for the constitutional principle of subsidiarity (decentralized decisionmaking in the absence of any compelling reason for centralization). At other times, reluctance will stem from a failure to differentiate de jure sovereignty from de facto autonomy. De facto autonomy has already been lost in large measure. Misunderstandings about national sovereignty may often prevent nations from acting collectively to foster their mutual interests. Whatever one's normative views about whether radical enhancements in international collective governance should be made, the dream of cosmopolitan visionaries to establish the beginnings of a federal world government stands no chance of fulfillment until, at the earliest, many decades into the future.

Notwithstanding the presumption of subsidiarity and despite the inevitable inertia, national governments increasingly will be forced to consider various sorts of international collective action. Pressures will grow for the strengthening of various forms of intergovernmental cooperation and for the strengthening of international institutions to serve as the locus of that cooperation. National governments will ask international institutions to carry out a wider range of functional responsibilities. However reluctantly, national governments will delegate increased operational authority to them.

These generalizations apply in particular to intergovernmental financial cooperation. Existing international financial institutions, after all, are nascent sources of capacity for the global financial utilities infrastructure that is eventually likely to evolve. The needed functions of such a financial utilities infrastructure amply qualify as reasons for encouraging, in the short and medium runs, enhanced intergovernmental financial cooperation and a lessened degree of decentralization for governmental financial decisionmaking.

The range of conceivable functions for intergovernmental financial cooperation is wider than is typically appreciated. Setting priorities among them requires, as a precondition, an understanding of the potential functions and the fundamental issues they raise. As background for the subsequent chapters on cross-border financial governance, this chapter accordingly addresses analytical issues at a general level about the functions and institutions of international collective governance.

Governance and Government in a Multination World

Collective governance is a synonym for collective action. But governance is not a synonym for government. Governance encompasses collective action channeled not only through government institutions but also through many groups and institutions that are not part of government at any level. Because societies have grown in complexity, nongovernmental collective actions have proliferated. Governance is thus less and less the exclusive preserve of governments.

Although the broad concept of governance and the narrower concept of government both entail purposive behavior underpinned by a presumptive sharing of goals, the concepts differ in significant ways. Governments typically are backed by greater formal authority. Nongovernmental groups often have weak powers to ensure compliance. Because the broader concept of governance embraces the activities of not only widely inclusive but also more limited groups, governance subsumes all of civil society. In contrast, government institutions derive their authority from, at least in principle, the entirety of individuals and groups in the territorial jurisdiction where their collective action is exercised.

The preceding generalizations are equally valid for collective actions within nation states and those that cross or transcend national borders. But of course governance issues become still more complex when international or global dimensions are present.[1] The actors involved in governance, their numbers and heterogeneity, render collective action on regional or world scales even more difficult than within a single nation's borders. The progressive integration of the world economy further complicates the traditional organization of collective action along the lines of geographical territory.

The social and technological forces underlying Daniel Bell's "eclipse of distance" have not progressed so far as to eliminate the significance of national borders. Quite the contrary: national borders are still critical fault lines shaping the world polity and world economy. Extreme ideas about "supraterritoriality" should be heavily discounted. Yet it is true that attitudes about territoriality are continuing to evolve.

The current state of flux in our messy, multination world means that an increasing proportion of collective governance must grapple with the polit-

---

1. Rosenau (1997); Rosenau and Czempiel, eds. (1992).

ical spaces within which domestic and foreign issues interact. James Rosenau labels these spaces the "domestic-foreign frontier"and argues that along this frontier a relative decline in the salience of *government* institutions in governance may occur:

> While the pervasiveness of the [domestic-foreign frontier] necessitates probing governance on a global scale, this does not require an exclusive focus on the agents and structures that are global in scope. On the contrary, the organizing perspective [in Rosenau's book] is that of governance *in* the world rather than governance *of* the world. The latter implies a central authority that is doing the governing, an implication that clearly has no basis in fact. The former suggests patterns of governance wherever they may be unfolding in the world as a consequence of wherever authority may be located—in communities, societies, nongovernmental organizations, international relationships, and along the Frontier. To assess global governance, in other words, is to trace the various ways in which the processes of governance are aggregated.[2]

Observations of this nature, from political and international relations theorists, reinforce the general point that governance is not the preserve of governments alone.

Although the nongovernmental dimensions of international collective governance are increasingly important, it is not feasible to factor them carefully into the analysis here. The objective of my book is, rather, to analyze those key aspects of international governance involving cooperation among national governments and the international institutions created by those governments. Apart from this chapter, my focus is narrowed still further to intergovernmental cooperation on financial and economic subjects.

Thus in subsequent chapters the reader will encounter few references to international NGOs (nongovernmental organizations), cross-border epistemic communities, and other international or transnational dimensions of civil society. Nor will it be possible to examine the ways that

---

2. Rosenau (1997, p. 10). In the same passage, Rosenau goes on to quote Marin and Mayntz (1993, p. 258): "Political governance in modern societies can no longer be conceived in terms of external governmental control of society but emerges from a plurality of governing actors."

such groups aspire to exert greater influence over the activities of national governments and quasi-governmental international institutions such as the WTO, the IMF, and the World Bank. The most that is feasible here is to acknowledge these civil society forces in our lateral vision and to keep constantly in mind the proposition that governance in its broader connotations is not a synonym for government.[3]

Alternative Forms and Venues for Intergovernmental Cooperation

Few governmental institutions exist above the level of nation states. The exceptions are a modest number of international or regional institutions established by treaties among member national governments. International collective governance, if manifested through government institutions, thus occurs primarily through *cooperation* among national governments. Such cooperation can take a variety of forms. In fact, cooperation is best used as an umbrella term for the entire spectrum of interactions among national governments.

Consultation, mutual recognition, various forms of *coordination,* and *explicit harmonization* are varieties of intergovernmental cooperation, each involving some element of management of the interactions among nations. Consultation alone involves only a small degree of cooperative management. Mutual recognition and coordination are more ambitious, and explicit harmonization still more so. At the opposite extreme of the spectrum, which entails no cooperation and may be labeled *unrestricted de jure sovereignty,* the decisions of national governments are completely decentralized and no attempt is made to manage cooperatively the increasing integration of national economies.[4]

---

3. The distinction between governance and government, and the interrelationships between governance and social order, are subtle. Rosenau and Czempiel (1992, p. 6) indicate that in some languages, such as German, there is not even a readily identifiable word that signifies the broader concept of "governance." Some authors, such as Strange (1996), dislike the distinction between governance and government but nonetheless put great emphasis on the diffusion of power away from governmental institutions toward corporate and other private, nongovernment institutions. References to the academic literature on civil society, including its application to the global polity, are given in chapter 4, footnote 2.

4. These distinctions, amplified below, are discussed in Bryant (1995) and in the preface to the entire series of books on *Integrating National Economies* published by Brookings in the years 1994–97, for example, Cooper (1994). Bryant (1987) contains an initial development.

Top-Level Cooperation: International Regime Environments

Intergovernmental cooperation can usefully be construed as a two-level process. During exceptional, intermittent episodes of negotiations at a "top level," typically characterized by intensive consultations and bargaining, national governments reach formal agreements or informal understandings defining the processes and institutions through which they will interact with one another. At the time they are reached, such intermittent agreements usually seem to the participating governments to be one-time decisions (although valid for the foreseeable future). Then during the lengthy periods between these top-level negotiations, governments interact through the agreed processes and institutions at a "lower level." At this lower level, each government makes ongoing decisions in a largely decentralized way, independently choosing settings for the policy instruments under its control.

The *regime environments* agreed to episodically at the top level can be interpreted as norms and traffic regulations (sometimes loosely called rules of the game) that govern continuing interactions at the lower level. Intergovernmental economic relations in the last one and a half centuries have conformed moderately well to this two-level characterization.[5] The regime environments negotiated at the top level are usually labeled simply as *regimes* in the literature on international relations.[6]

My notion of an international regime environment is associated exclusively with episodic, top-level decisions by national governments. The most widely used definition of a regime in the literature on international relations, one that captures well the main elements in my notion, is

> sets of implicit or explicit principles, norms, rules and decision-making procedures around which actors' expectations converge in a given area

---

5. Economic theorists, notably Hamada (1974, 1977), have applied the idea of two levels of cooperation in game-theoretic analyses of interdependence in macroeconomic policies. I used the distinction in Bryant (1987). The two-level characterization is implicit if not explicit in much of the literature on international relations among nation-states. For example, O. Young (1989a, 1989b, 1991) refers to the top-level negotiations as "institutional bargaining" for international society and perceives the national governments as trying to create "constitutional contracts" or "interlocking sets of rights and rules" that are expected to condition their subsequent interactions.

6. The use of the term *regime* in international relations differs from a second connotation of the term used widely by economists in analyzing macroeconomic or exchange rate policies for a single nation. Regime in that second sense refers to the week-to-week operating procedures used by an individual national central bank to implement its monetary or exchange rate policies or by the national fiscal authority to implement its fiscal policies.

of international relations. Principles are beliefs of fact, causation, and rectitude. Norms are standards of behavior defined in terms of rights and obligations. Rules are specific prescriptions or proscriptions for action. Decision-making procedures are prevailing practices for making and implementing collective choice."[7]

Some parts of the international relations literature define regime even more broadly, equating it comprehensively with any patterned regularity in the behavior of national governments (and even nonstate actors) interacting with one another. Other international relations authors prefer a more restricted definition, reserving the concept for explicit multilateral agreements among nation-states that regulate national actions within an issue area (in effect, only the rules, but not the principles and norms, in the preceding quotation).[8]

At least two dimensions are involved in identifying an international regime. The horizontal dimension in figure 7-1 refers to the incidence of agreements and treaties among national governments and the principles, norms, rules, and decisionmaking procedures around which expectations converge. The vertical dimension shows the numbers and strengths of nonnational institutions and the forums, processes, and decisionmaking procedures that may be associated with them. Such institutions are "international" or "supranational" in strict senses of those words.[9]

---

7. Krasner (1983b, p. 2). See also Keohane (1984, pp. 57–61).

8. Haggard and Simmons (1987) discuss differences among definitions of "regime" in international relations. The concept seems to have been introduced in Ruggie (1975). Keohane and Nye (1977), Keohane (1980), and E. Haas (1980) used it. Two issues of *International Organization* were devoted to the subject in 1982, with much of the material republished in the volume edited by Krasner (1983); see especially Krasner (1983a, 1983b); Ruggie (1983); Keohane (1983); E. Haas (1983); Stein (1983); and Strange (1983). For subsequent discussion, see Keohane (1984); O. Young (1986, 1989a, 1989b, 1991, 1999); and a special 1992 issue of *International Organization* devoted to multilateralism, which includes contributions by Ruggie (1992); Caporaso (1992); and Kahler (1992). Kahler's book (1995) for the Brookings Integrating National Economies series contains further references to the literature on international regimes and institutions. O. Young (1999) makes a distinction between the adjectives "international" and "transnational"; he wishes to reserve the label *international regimes* for institutional arrangements whose members are states and prefers the description *transnational regimes* for the increasingly important cross-border institutional arrangements whose members are nonstate actors.

9. For studying some aspects of international cooperation, one would need to make finer distinctions—in particular, in the vertical dimension a distinction between institutions with a regional, versus those with a global, domain.

A vertical movement in figure 7-1 from top to bottom involves a shift from complete decentralization of authority among nation states (top border) to international regimes in which there is more—but not complete (even at the bottom border)—centralization of authority through international or supranational institutions. A horizontal movement from left to right, for any given degree of decentralization, entails more cooperative activity through the establishment of agreed principles and norms and the acknowledgment of constraints (rules and decisionmaking procedures) that have prescriptive and proscriptive force for the "local" decisions of national governments.

The space in the extreme top left corner of the diagram is a hypothetical polar case: de jure sovereignty with an absence of international cooperation. For such an international regime, relations among national governments would be exclusively determined by the relative powers of the nation states. Interactions among governments would be noncooperative. Disputes might be settled largely by force or the threat of force. National sovereignty would be formally unrestricted in the legal sense.[10]

As one moves in the diagram away from the top left corner toward the lower right, the regimes still involve essentially decentralized national decisions, but they begin to have elements of international cooperation. With further, larger movements toward the lower right, transnational norms and non-national institutions become more salient, and some aspects of decisionmaking begin to have more centralized dimensions.

International regimes near the extreme lower right corner of the diagram are hypothetical, certainly in today's intermediate world polity and perhaps even throughout most of the twenty-first century. But such regimes can be imagined and can be used as benchmarks for analyzing other spaces in the diagram.[11] That extreme would entail mutual governance facilitated by strong federal, supranational institutions. When dealing with an extensive range of economic and social concerns, national governments might be restricted to "local" roles. Close political union would have evolved. Transnational norms would presumably be salient.

10. For smaller states, of course, de facto autonomy would be severely constrained. (Recall the discussion in chapter 4 of the complexities in the concept of sovereignty and the important distinction between de jure sovereignty and de facto autonomy.)

11. The spaces in the top right and lower left corners of figure 7-1 are presumably irrelevant, even in principle, because of the strong positive (but not perfect?) correlation of the horizontal and vertical sets of variables.

Figure 7-1. *Alternative International Regime Environments: Interactions among National Governments and International Institutions*

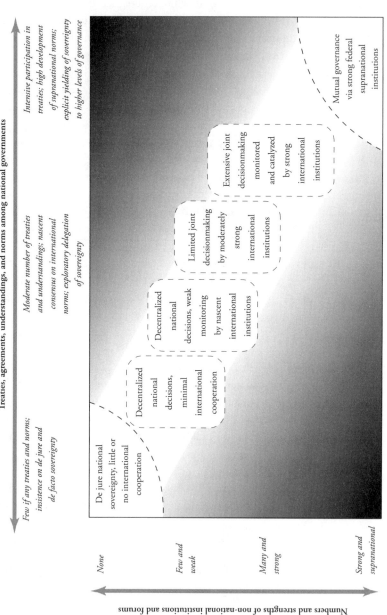

Treaties, agreements, understandings, and norms among national governments

Few if any treaties and norms; insistence on de jure and de facto sovereignty

Moderate number of treaties and understandings; nascent consensus on international norms; exploratory delegation of sovereignty

Intensive participation in treaties; high development of supranational norms; explicit yielding of sovereignty to higher levels of governance

De jure national sovereignty; little or no international cooperation

Decentralized national decisions, minimal international cooperation

Decentralized national decisions, weak monitoring by nascent international institutions

Limited joint decisionmaking by moderately strong international institutions

Extensive joint decisionmaking monitored and catalyzed by strong international institutions

Mutual governance via strong federal supranational institutions

Numbers and strengths of non-national institutions and forums

None

Few and weak

Many and strong

Strong and supranational

The locus of political authority would have shifted substantially away from national governments to the federal, supranational level (regionally, globally, or both).

Lower-Level Cooperation: Mutual Recognition and Coordination

Figure 7-2 extends the taxonomy in figure 7-1 to another dimension by considering the interplay between top-level episodic decisions and lower-level intermittent decisions. The vertical axis in figure 7-2 represents the degree of ongoing cooperation affecting lower-level decisions, with little or none at the top border and continuous, intensive amounts at the bottom. The horizontal axis, representing the diagonal that runs from the top left to the bottom right in figure 7-1, arrays the international regime environments established in the periodic top-level negotiations. Several concepts widely used in the literatures on international economics and international relations—in particular, mutual recognition and international coordination—can be associated with specific regions in figure 7-2.

Unrestricted de jure sovereignty, in the top left corner, is again a limiting polar case. It is useful as a benchmark in analyzing differing degrees of international cooperation in either or both dimensions. Moving toward the lower right, I identify two areas characterized by mutual recognition, one with infrequent consultations, and the other with more intensive interactions in the context of internationally monitored presumptive guidelines about which national policies are systemically appropriate. Regions still further along toward the lower right, with still more ongoing lower-level cooperation and still more structure in the regime environment, are identified as variants of coordination. To suggest the spectrum of possibilities, I distinguish three categories of coordination: internationally agreed presumptive guidelines, weak activist, and strong activist. The polar cases near the lower right corner may be labeled *federalist mutual governance* facilitated by continuous bargaining and joint decisionmaking.

Mutual recognition, a term widely used in discussions about European integration but also applicable in a worldwide context, can be defined narrowly or broadly. Defined narrowly, mutual recognition pertains only to a few dimensions of government activities such as regulatory policies, product standards, and certification procedures. Each member state of the European Union, for example, agrees to permit doctors licensed in other EU countries to practice in its country, even if licensing procedures differ in the other countries. Wine or liquor produced in any EU country can be

Figure 7-2. Interplay between Top-Level Intermittent Decisions and Lower-Level Ongoing Cooperation

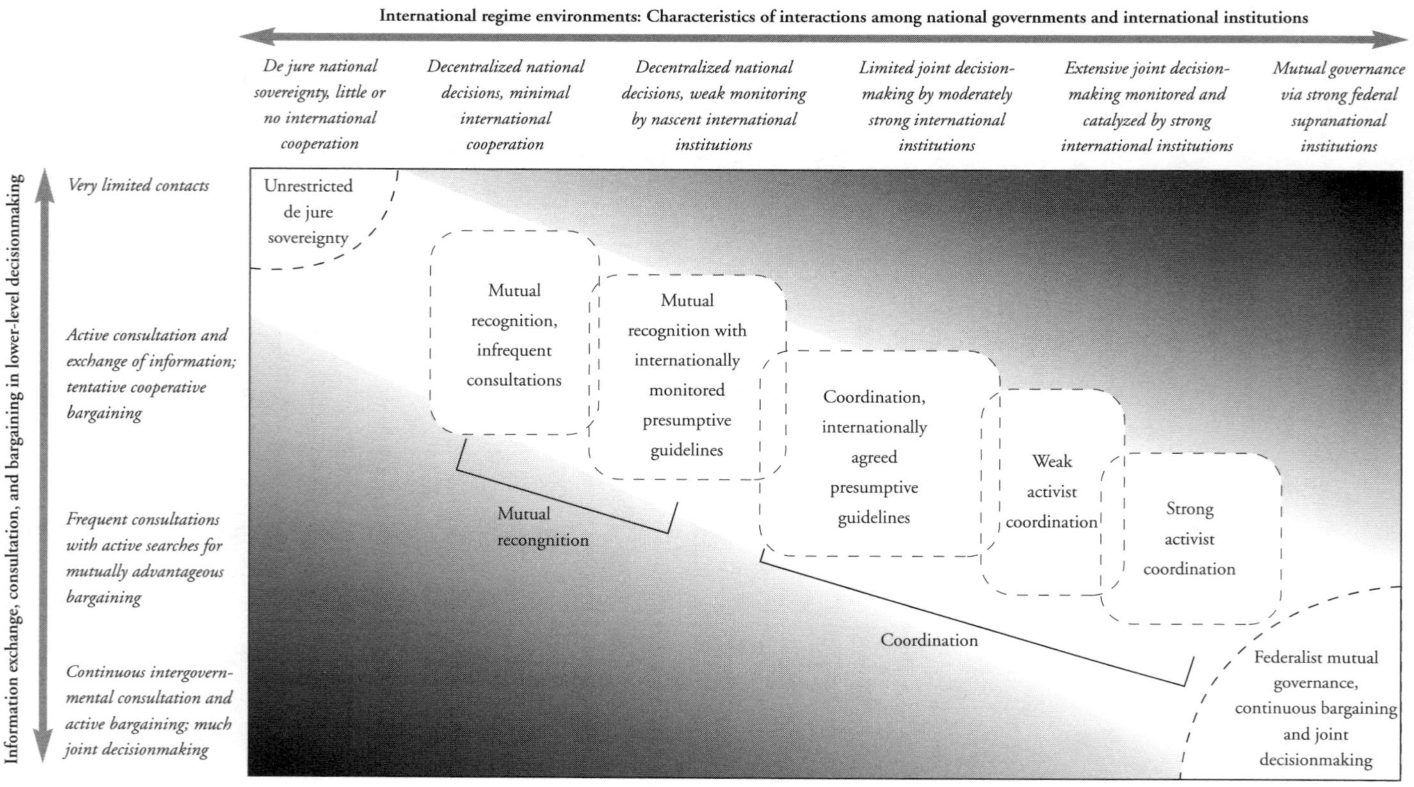

International regime environments: Characteristics of interactions among national governments and international institutions

De jure national sovereignty, little or no international cooperation

Decentralized national decisions, minimal international cooperation

Decentralized national decisions, weak monitoring by nascent international institutions

Limited joint decision-making by moderately strong international institutions

Extensive joint decision-making monitored and catalyzed by strong international institutions

Mutual governance via strong federal supranational institutions

Unrestricted de jure sovereignty

Mutual recognition, infrequent consultations

Mutual recognition with internationally monitored presumptive guidelines

Coordination, internationally agreed presumptive guidelines

Weak activist coordination

Strong activist coordination

Federalist mutual governance, continuous bargaining and joint decisionmaking

Mutual recongnition

Coordination

Very limited contacts

Active consultation and exchange of information; tentative cooperative bargaining

Frequent consultations with active searches for mutually advantageous bargaining

Continuous intergovernmental consultation and active bargaining; much joint decisionmaking

Information exchange, consultation, and bargaining in lower-level decisionmaking sold in all member countries despite differing production standards. And so on.[12]

A broader interpretation of mutual recognition, which I use in this book, assumes that national governments make decentralized, independent decisions about the whole range of their policies, yet to a limited degree acknowledge the interdependence of the separate national policies. Mutual recognition avoids extensive traffic regulations. Instead it relies primarily on competition among national policies and regulations—through private decisions and market forces—to guide transactions among nations. But mutual recognition also involves exchanges of information and consultations among governments and even nascent reliance on non-national forums or institutions.

For international regimes embodying more intergovernmental agreements and some collective monitoring of the agreements, and especially as intergovernmental consultations become more frequent and intensive, the term mutual recognition becomes less appropriate. Governments may operate under internationally agreed and monitored *presumptive guidelines* that constrain their ongoing policy decisions. In such a situation, the emphasis is not only on (mutually recognized) competition among the decentralized national decisions but also on some agreed norms and constraints that condition the national decisions. As collective monitoring of compliance with such guidelines becomes more important, one might begin to speak of this situation as monitored decentralization. An intergovernmental agreement about exchange rate arrangements, including some guidelines constraining official intervention in exchange markets, would be an example.

Areas in figure 7-2 still further toward the lower right begin to warrant the label international coordination. The coordination can vary from weak and hesitant to strong and activist, depending on the degree of cooperation built into the international regime as a result of the intermittent top-level decisions. The detailed nature of the coordination is shaped especially by the frequency and intensity of the ongoing consultations and bargaining.

12. Mutual recognition, narrowly interpreted, originates from the 1979 decision of the European Court of Justice in the now famous *Cassis de Dijon* case (requiring that cassis liqueur be sold freely and without border restrictions in Germany even though produced in France). Mutual recognition in the narrower European sense is discussed in Wallace (1994) and in several of the chapters in the volume edited by Sbragia (1992), including those by Peters and Shapiro (1992). Baldwin (2000) discusses trade policy issues raised by the mutual recognition approach of the European Union.

It is also significantly influenced by the effectiveness of whatever procedures, if any, are provided for collective monitoring and enforcement of agreed decisions.

Because the horizontal and vertical dimensions in figures 7-1 and 7-2 are continuums, no precise boundary exists between the domains of mutual recognition and coordination. Indeed, some might prefer to describe the concepts as partly overlapping. In my diagram, I characterize both the lower-right parts of the mutual recognition region and the upper-left parts of the coordination region as regimes using presumptive guidelines. Nothing of substance turns on whether presumptive-guideline regimes are labeled as mutual recognition, as a weaker form of coordination, or as a combination of the two.

The larger part of the domain of coordination lies further to the right, and especially further toward the lower border, relative to mutual recognition. Some significant information exchange and consultation must occur even when the mode of intergovernmental interaction is merely mutual recognition. Still more frequent and intensive consultations will typically occur, however, if the cooperation is sufficiently ambitious to achieve coordination.

What are the essential features of international coordination? To a greater degree than mutual recognition, coordination focuses on cross-border spillovers and the arbitrage pressures eroding the differences among national economies and policies. And coordination is more ambitious in promoting intergovernmental cooperation to deal with these spillovers and pressures. Coordination involves jointly designed, mutual adjustments of national policies—commitments about the time paths of policy instruments, not merely aspirations about the time paths for ultimate target variables. In clear-cut cases of coordination, bargaining occurs, and governments commit themselves to behave differently—to implement different rules or discretionary settings for policy instruments—than they would have behaved without the coordinating agreement.

Strong activist coordination differs from weak activist coordination mainly in the frequency and strength of consultations and bargaining. Strong activist coordination is characterized by fairly continuous rather than intermittent exchanges of information and consultations and by more frequent and intense bargaining about alternative outcomes. Strong activist coordination also tends to be associated with agreed procedures for a supranational monitoring of ongoing national policies and enforcement of cooperatively agreed decisions.

States of the world near the lower right corner of figure 7-2 are hypothetical. As emphasized earlier, for at least the next several decades they are merely a fantasy. Yet such world polities can be imagined and are useful as analytical benchmarks. In such circumstances, the economic and political integration of the world would be highly advanced, and international cooperation would be very greatly intensified. Nations could decide to create political institutions that would, for a wide range of concerns, reach centralized decisions for the entire integrated domain. In the extreme, for example, monetary policies for the entire integrated area might be harmonized, with a supranational central bank and, eventually, a single unified currency. The supranational institutions might have a central fiscal budget, which could become an increasingly important part of total governmental expenditures and revenues for the entire integrated area (supranational plus national plus within-nation local).[13]

If the world polity and economy were ever to move as far as the lower right corner of figure 7-2, the distinction between top-level and lower-level decisions made by national governments could become outmoded. In effect, in such extreme circumstances top-level decisions would be those made by federal supranational institutions, while lower-level decisions would be those that were still made by national governments (now "local" political authorities in the highly integrated area). The situation would have evolved well beyond domains of coordination into federalist mutual governance with its continuous bargaining and joint, centralized decisionmaking.

For brevity, I have spoken of "world" political and economic integration and the harmonization of national policies into world policies. At least for the early decades of the twenty-first century, such ideas will have relevance, if at all, only for multicountry *regions,* such as the European Union, rather than for the world as a whole.

Venues for Intergovernmental Cooperation

Because the existence of federal supranational government institutions is so unlikely in the foreseeable future, the possible venues for collective

---

13. Important differences between monetary and budgetary policies—not least their macroeconomic stabilization aspects—would arise in such a highly integrated world. *Explicit harmonization* has a relatively clearcut meaning for monetary policy, but much less so for the different layers of governmental revenues and expenditures. Fiscal policies (still plural, not singular) for such a world would require analysis of all the political and economic issues that have been discussed within federal nation-states under the heading of *fiscal federalism.*

actions taken by national governments fall into just two broad classes. National governments can interact through *consultative groups.* Or they can explicitly establish *international or regional organizations* through which their interactions and cooperation are institutionalized.

Consultative groups serve merely as forums for cooperative interactions. They have no powers of their own. Meetings of a consultative group tend not to have a single, specific geographical location but rather float over time from one locale to another (such as the capital cities of the participating governments).

In contrast, international or regional organizations are usually more than mere forums. If and when established, the organizations typically have specific delegated powers, albeit narrowly circumscribed in most cases. An international or regional organization is situated in one or more specific geographical locations. Most of its meetings occur at those locales.

For any given consultative group, typically a subset of national governments is involved. Many such groups are created by a limited cluster of governments so as deliberately to exclude other nations. Some groups have a functional orientation and therefore comprise only those nations for whom that function is especially important. Some groups are regional. Only a very few worldwide consultative groups have been formed (worldwide in the comprehensive sense that the governments of all, small as well as large, nations are included as participants). At the lower limit, the governments of only two nations may participate, rendering the group a purely bilateral channel for interaction.

International or regional organizations tend to be inclusive rather than exclusive. This tendency stems from the political awkwardness of excluding particular individual nations once a collective decision is taken to establish an explicit organization. If the organization's scope is regional, no nation in that region can be gracefully excluded from joining provided that it is actually able and willing to satisfy the criteria for membership. Similarly, if a subset of national governments decides to create a new international organization on a world scale, strong political pressures exist to make the membership potentially universal. In practice, an international organization may not be universal because some potential participating nations cannot or will not satisfy the general eligibility requirements.[14]

14. Eligibility requirements can also, of course, be deliberately designed to give the cosmetic appearance of generality yet still exclude particular individual nations.

Intergovernmental consideration of a new regime environment must necessarily be tentative and informal at the outset of discussions. Episodic, top-level intergovernmental cooperation is therefore most likely to occur within the venue of consultative groups. Exceptions to this generalization occur when negotiations focus on a change in regime that predominantly affects an international or regional organization already created in earlier times. In such a situation, the organization itself may provide the venue for the intergovernmental negotiations.

Intermittent, lower-level types of intergovernmental cooperation, especially if they proceed beyond minimalist mutual recognition to more ambitious forms of cooperation, often require some institutionalization to support the collective decisionmaking. Lower-level cooperation thus is often channeled through the venue of international or regional organizations. Indeed, the very existence of an international or regional organization presupposes prior top-level cooperation to establish an institution capable of sustaining an ongoing, lower-level cooperation.

The requirements for and availability of support resources are key differences between consultative groups and established organizations. The national governments participating in a consultative group typically do not allocate resources to the group itself. In fact, such groups operate with little or no collective administrative support. Often, for example, the group itself does not even have a supporting secretariat. (Each participating national government allocates staff and resources to backstop its own representatives; but typically there is no collective support for the group per se.) Thus, for consultative groups, issues about support resources either do not arise or are secondary.

In contrast, resource issues are a primary concern for international and regional organizations. Established organizations have permanent staffs that must be paid and are often given functions that require nonstaffing expenditures. National governments must therefore allocate resources to the organizations themselves. But how are the resource costs to be allocated among the member governments? This question is particularly acute for organizations whose activities require large operating resources. The size of an organization's budget must be periodically agreed, and then that total must be allocated among the member nations. Jockeying among individual governments is inevitable. Other things being equal, each government will try to shoulder a smaller share of the support burden itself, thereby pushing a larger share on other governments.

Issues of relative power in established organizations are of course highly correlated with issues of how to share the burden of support resources. The relative powers of individual nations are most manifest in decisionmaking procedures, and in particular in voting rights where decisionmaking entails formal votes. Consultative groups often require unanimity for positions taken cooperatively. Seldom do such groups operate by taking explicit votes. Issues of relative authority within a consultative group are thus typically suppressed rather than openly confronted. The issues of relative authority and voting power, just as the issue of resources, inevitably have to be confronted more directly for an established organization. If an international or regional organization has been given significant delegated powers, it will typically reach decisions through a weighted-voting procedure with the most powerful nations having relatively larger shares of the total votes. Conversely, if an international or regional organization is established to operate by unanimity or consensus, it is much less likely to have significant powers delegated to it.

The relative permanence of the venues is a further key difference between consultative groups and established organizations. New consultative groups can be easily created. Existing ones can be relatively easily disbanded. Because considerably more political effort and resources have to be expended to establish international or regional organizations, they are less likely to come into existence than consultative groups but more likely to be permanent once initial inertia has been overcome.

Because established organizations have staffs and resources, they can develop institutional cultures and acquire interests of their own. Particular individuals in the organizations may thus express views significantly different from the views of the member governments. Over time, even an organization as a whole can evolve to a point where it takes official positions somewhat inconsistent with those of its member governments and exerts a somewhat independent role in international discussions and negotiations. Such an evolution toward independence is most likely, of course, in areas where member governments significantly disagree among themselves.

Both types of venues for intergovernmental cooperation raise important political and governance issues beyond the scope of this overview. I will identify only one example, the political accountability of the venues. For both consultative groups and international or regional organizations, the main channel of accountability runs through the national governments themselves.

Because a consultative group is merely a channel for cooperative inter-actions, does not acquire delegated powers or resources of its own, and may even be transitory, accountability issues are much less pressing for those venues. Each national government is politically accountable for its participation in the intergovernmental group in much the same complex, controversial, and imperfect ways that the government is accountable for its domestic activities.

An international or regional organization, in contrast, poses additional accountability issues. The member national governments that established the organization in the first place are, to use the language of corporate gov-ernance, the shareholders. They appoint the management of the organiza-tion and exercise the votes shaping the organization's decisions. The orga-nization is thus, directly and powerfully, accountable to its member national governments. But just as the modern literature on corporate gov-ernance distinguishes between the shareowners of and (more broadly) stakeholders in a corporation, an international or regional organization can be perceived as having stakeholders in addition to its member national gov-ernments. The work force and suppliers of a private corporation are non-shareowning stakeholders. Some analysts have likewise perceived individ-ual national citizens and their nongovernmental, civil society associations as nonshareowning stakeholders in international and regional organiza-tions. These analysts have begun to argue that international and regional organizations should—somehow, to some degree—be accountable to "international civil society" as well as directly to national governments.

Predictions about the future evolution of intergovernmental venues are no less uncertain than other predictions. For at least the first few decades of the twenty-first century, multiple and heterogeneous venues for inter-governmental cooperation will continue to be observed. Both consultative groups and established organizations will be needed. Both will persist. This heterogeneity is yet another manifestation of the messy, intermediate sta-tus of the world polity.

As the century progresses, the balance between the two types of venue is likely to tilt gradually in favor of international and regional organizations. Relatively more lower-level intergovernmental cooperation, in increasingly complex forms, will be required. It may seem natural, and politically less contentious, to delegate larger amounts of the associated responsibilities to government-like organizations with explicit cross-border mandates.

Yet not all political forces will foster that evolution. Controversially but inevitably, consultative groups and established cross-border organizations will both be dominated by the largest, wealthiest, most powerful nations. The governments of those nations will continue to find it easier to nurture their collaborative efforts by meeting in smaller, exclusionary consultative groups rather than openly and more inclusively through established cross-border organizations.

In the cross-border organizations themselves, it is true, the most powerful nations will have the largest voting shares (and the largest fractional shares in the budgets). But only if the governments of the most powerful nations confidently perceive the cross-border organizations as, on balance, decisively advancing their own nations' interests will those governments shift the loci for intergovernmental cooperation toward established organizations.

Smaller, less wealthy, less powerful nations will inevitably chafe at their exclusion from important consultative groups. They will continue to try to raise their relative shares and amplify their voices (but perhaps hope to raise their budget contributions less than proportionately?) in the cross-border organizations. The probability of increasing the relative power of the world's populous but poorer nations in worldwide intergovernmental decisionmaking probably has the same order of magnitude as the probability of reducing skewness in the distribution across nations of the world's income and wealth. Many individuals, myself included, hope that that probability is not too low and will rise over time. Hopes are not the same thing, alas, as confident predictions.

Within-Nation Government and Nascent Cross-Border Governmental Functions

Having surveyed the possible types of intergovernmental cooperation and noted the venues through which they may be channeled, the exposition next needs to identify the functions to be carried out by intergovernmental collective action. What goals should intergovernmental cooperation seek to accomplish? What is feasible now? What may be desirable, and become feasible, in the future? An illuminating way to begin that discussion is to recall the varying functions—the types of collective actions and collective goods—that national and subnational governments are asked to supply in a purely domestic context.

A Sketch of the Domestic Functions of Government

Institutions and laws for collective governance must be initially designed and established before governmental activities can proceed. Forums for discussion, debate, and the shaping of collective decisions need to be created. A first, fundamental function for government is therefore *institution building, institution maintenance, and law making*. Some aspects of this function have an episodic or once-for-all nature, such as the initial writing of a constitution. Many others are ongoing, for example continuing meetings of legislative assemblies and the consideration of new legislation.

The creation and continuing support of *legal processes and institutions* are, in effect, a subcategory of institution building and institution maintenance. Legal processes and institutions are essential to the functioning of all aspects of society and the economy. Key features of this function are systems of courts and judges, which in turn provide for the interpretation of laws, the enforcement of contracts, and the adjudication of disputes.

Government exists at several layers, from the smallest local or municipal governments up through county, province, or state governments all the way to government institutions at the level of the entire nation. This multiplicity of layers gives rise to a further function, *the oversight and coordination of the lower layers of government*. Upper levels of government may be able, in effect, to tutor the lower layers on ways to improve political, economic, or social conditions within their individual jurisdictions. The upper levels may be able to help rectify government failures at the lower layers. For such oversight to be successful, of course, the upper layers must have better knowledge and information or be more competent or responsible. An argument against top-down oversight of the lower layers of government is that problems of government failure at the upper levels might be exacerbated by this oversight and coordination function. The principle of subsidiarity, which applies to all governmental functions, is especially relevant here.

Numerous functions of government entail some form of monitoring and, more ambitiously, enforcement on behalf of the community, province, or nation as a whole. *Surveillance* is a convenient umbrella term for functions that comprise not only monitoring but enforcement. In the remainder of the book, surveillance is used as a rough synonym for activities that include collective monitoring and also procedures (even if quite limited) for enforcing compliance with collective decisions.

The *provision of collective security* is a prominent example of surveillance. At the local level, police departments are established to inhibit collectively undesired activities. Criminals are detained and prosecuted. Streets are patrolled at night and kept safe for individual citizens. Traffic laws are enforced. At the national level, defense forces are created and maintained with the presumption that security for the nation as a whole is thereby enhanced.

Governmental surveillance is also involved in *crisis management and humanitarian assistance.* Governments institute measures to lower the probability that crises will occur. And they provide collective management and crisis assistance in the event that crises do occur. At the local level, for example, fire-fighting equipment is maintained by permanent or volunteer fire departments to enable quick responses to community fires. Regulations lowering the probability of fires are enforced. Zoning restrictions inhibit the construction of dwellings in flood plains. Contingent mechanisms are created to supply emergency services or mobilize humanitarian assistance for generalized disasters such as floods or earthquakes.

The domestic functions of government include numerous *other classes of surveillance activities* for fostering collective goals. Government institutions license or authorize individuals and private institutions for professions— for example, doctors or lawyers—where some form of collective certification can foster safety and efficiency or prevent abuse. Collective surveillance may be judged necessary for laws, regulations, or standards in such areas as zoning, construction, factory and mine safety, health care (such as inoculations against infectious diseases or authorization for the marketing of new drugs), and environmental protection (such as emission standards for cars, disposal of toxic wastes, and prevention of overfishing). In all such areas, the laws, regulations, and standards require monitoring to ensure adequate observance. Remedial enforcement procedures are also required for coping with instances of violation.

Still other government activities are best described as the *direct provision of utilities and other collective goods.* Individual localities and individual nations have differing preferences about whether goods with collective dimensions are best supplied by government or by private institutions. The creation and maintenance of infrastructure such as roads, ports, and airports are usually treated as a function of government. Provision of water, the disposal of sewage and trash, and postal services are also typically (but not invariably) regarded as government functions. Energy supplies such as electricity or gas are governmental in some nations, private in others.

Education and health care are among the most important goods in society where collective and private dimensions are subtly combined. Because of the private element, some localities and some nations prefer to minimize government involvement. Other localities and nations comfortably assign the primary responsibility for education and health functions to government institutions. No localities or nations have kept government provision or government standards and regulations entirely out of the areas of education and health care.

Still another function of government, potential or actual, can be identified as the *provision of research and the enhancement of the knowledge base of society*. Because basic research is quintessentially a public good, a social consensus has often supported government activity to carry out or subsidize this research.[15]

A final broad category of functions exercised by domestic government institutions can be summarized as collectively sponsored *measures to redistribute income or wealth*. Progressive tax systems or government social welfare programs may result in deliberate transfers from wealthier to poorer citizens. Transfers from middle-age working citizens to children or the elderly may result from government education programs or government social security and pension schemes. Many government expenditures or subsidies benefit some parts of the society more than others, thereby indirectly redistributing income.

Social critics at one extreme assert that governments are controlled by elites who implement policies that redistribute income and wealth strongly in their favor (or at least prevent policies that would foster a more equitable distribution). Critics at the opposite extreme argue that governments implement a variety of policies to confiscate income and wealth, unfairly transferring it from enterprising economic agents to others who have come to rely for their livelihood on excessive intervention by the welfare state. At best, a trade-off exists between the goals of political equality and economic efficiency.[16]

No governmental functions are more controversial than policies to redistribute income or wealth. None differ more across localities and nations. The true situation in a majority of jurisdictions is somewhere in between the extremes of "the dominant rich feather their own nest and get richer" and "the welfare state unfairly takes from the rich to give to the working poor and the lazy poor." In some fashion and to some at least minor degree, redistributive activities are in evidence at virtually all levels of government within most nations.

---

15. Public goods have one or both of two distinctive properties: if a public good is provided, all who value it tend to benefit whether or not they contribute to the cost of providing it (sometimes termed the "nonexcludability" property); and if a public good is provided to any individual, it is or can be provided at little or no additional cost to others (so-called "nonrivalry in consumption").

16. Okun (1975).

The primary concerns in this book are financial. To the preceding general list, the already discussed collective-governance functions especially pertinent to an individual nation's financial system need to be added:

—The *macroeconomic policies* of a national government critically influence the general climate within which a nation's financial system and the wider economy operate.

—Sound accounting, auditing, and data standards require collective monitoring and sometimes even enforcement. Monitoring and enforcement are the essence of the supervision and regulation of financial institutions. The domestic functions of government thus include the *establishment of standards for and prudential oversight of financial activity* as an important special case of collective surveillance.

—The exercise of *collective leadership in times of financial crisis* by a lender of last resort, including the possible provision of emergency assistance to temporarily illiquid and troubled financial institutions, is a specific example of the general government function of crisis management.

More controversially as a financial function, local or national governments may establish a *financial intermediary operated as a government (or quasi-government) institution*. The financial transactions of a government intermediary seek different matches among borrowers and lenders in the financial system than would otherwise prevail if financial activity were left entirely to private sector financial institutions.[17]

Nascent Governmental Functions That Transcend National Borders

Over a very long run, all the domestic functions of government might conceivably have supranational analogues. For the next few decades, many of those functions plainly cannot, and will not, be applicable above the level of individual nation states. Intergovernmental collective action in the current messy intermediate global polity should *not* aspire to adopt the entirety of within-nation functions of government as a template.

One can gain insight by comparing government functions performed domestically (collective goods supplied by government institutions within nations) with functions that might be usefully performed, now or eventually, on a supranational scale (international collective goods that could be supplied through intergovernmental cooperation). Looking for such analo-

---

17. Three possible motives for operating a government financial intermediary, all controversial, are identified in chapter 3.

gies can be revealing in two opposite ways. First, one can be jolted into a realization that certain governmental functions taken for granted in a within-nation context may have cross-border analogues that should be performed internationally. Second, one can be sensitized to differences that are more important than similarities, which then undermines facile presumptions that intergovernmental cooperation should aspire to emulate the domestic functions of government.

The domestic functions of government, grouped into nine broad categories, are shown in the rows of figure 7-3. The first column in figure 7-3 suggests whether a category of domestic functions of government has significant cross-border or supranational analogues at the beginning of the twenty-first century. A checkmark indicates that a domestic category has one or more such analogues that already can, unambiguously, be observed today. An asterisk indicates that analogues can be observed only to a lesser or uncertain degree. A tilde suggests that analogues exist, if at all, in merely a minor or trace fashion.

The remaining columns in figure 7-3 conjecture whether, and if so when, cross-border or supranational analogues to the various domestic functions might come into existence. The figure sketches a rough vision of the future evolution of international collective governance. The second column indicates whether, for the next decade, an analogue for some aspect of a domestic function will very likely be deemed important (a double dagger), may be seen as desirable (a dagger), or might possibly be sought (a question mark). The third column uses the same symbols as in the second column but with the time horizon extended to the medium run of two to five decades. The final column makes the point symbolically that the world might conceivably reach—but only over some very long run—a stage of economic and political integration such that all the domestic functions of government would have full supranational analogues.

Top-level intergovernmental cooperation aimed at regime design and maintenance, category A in figure 7-3, is already salient. It will undoubtedly have to be strengthened further. Consultative groups will continue to foster intergovernmental discussions and collective decisionmaking. New regional and international organizations will have to complement, or replace, existing organizations. Virtually by definition, regime design and maintenance is a precondition for the emergence of any governmental functions that cross or transcend national borders.

How soon might cross-border legal processes and regional or international legal institutions (category B) mature into weighty components of

Figure 7-3. *Within-Nation Functions of Government Compared with Nascent Governmental Functions That Transcend National Borders*[a]

Domestic function	Cross-border or supranational analogue			
	Already operative to some degree	May be needed now or during next decade	May be helpful over medium run (2–5 decades)	If ever, only when there will exist federalist mutual governance via supranational governmental institutions
A. Institution building, institution maintenance, and law making	✓	‡	‡	⊛
B. Legal processes and institutions	~	?	~	⊛⊛
C. Oversight of the lower layers of government	~	?	†	⊛
D. Provision of collective security	~	?	†	⊛⊛
E. Crisis management and humanitarian assistance	*	‡	‡	⊛
F. Other surveillance activities	✓	‡	‡	⊛
G. Direct provision of collective goods (utilities, education, health care, etc.)	~	?	~	⊛
H. Support of research	*	†	†	⊛⊛
I. Redistribution of income and wealth	*	?	†	⊛⊛

a. In the first column, ✓ indicates that a domestic category has one or more cross-border or supranational analogues that already can, unambiguously, be observed today; * indicates that such analogues can be observed only to a lesser or uncertain degree; ~ suggests that they exist, if at all, in merely a minor or trace fashion. For the future time horizons in the second and third columns, ‡ indicates that a cross-border or supranational analogue will very likely be deemed important; † indicates that such analogues may be seen as desirable; and ? indicates that they might possibly be sought. Conceivably, for the very longest time horizon in the fourth column every domestic function might have a cross-border or supranational analogue.

supranational governance? Extensive institutional progress and the development of so-called "hard law" rather than "soft law" is probably decades away. The International Court of Justice is at best a weak, nascent precursor of a genuinely supranational system of courts and judges. (The European Court of Justice, on the other hand, may be an example of a court that is gradually acquiring genuine supranational muscle on a regional scale.) Yet significant progress has occurred in certain legal areas.[18] Some close observers of the World Trade Organization perceive progress in the evolution of legal mechanisms for the settlement of trade disputes. International tribunals in issue areas such as the law of the sea, environmental protection, intellectual property rights, and human rights have been created. A nascent International Criminal Court is under development, amid considerable controversy (and, unfortunately, without support from the United States).[19] Limited progress in international cooperation about bankruptcy law has been made.[20]

Direct oversight by regional or world institutions of the national or subnational layers of government (category C) would imply a significant exercise of political authority by supranational governmental institutions. Such supranational exercise of political authority is not in the cards for a long time to come. To suggest that national governments should invite a supranational authority to "tutor" them on ways to improve political or social conditions within their own borders, for example, would be regarded by many as an egregious infringement of de facto national autonomy, not to mention de jure sovereignty. An essential presumption of direct supranational oversight, analogous to the counterpart domestic presumption, would be that some activities of nations and their governments should conform to cosmopolitan world (or regional) norms. If an individual nation

18. A special issue of the journal *International Organization* published in the summer of 2000 (vol. 54, no. 3) on "Legalization and World Politics" is a good introduction to the international dimensions of legal issues. See in particular the introductory essay and the articles by Abbot and Snidal (2000) and by Abbott and others (2000). The bibliography to the special issue contains numerous specialized references.

19. The process establishing the International Criminal Court began in July 1998. The court is intended as a permanent court for trying individuals accused of committing genocide, war crimes, and crimes against humanity. Complex issues about its jurisdiction and procedures, including the potential status of military personnel, have prevented the emergence of a consensus. Some 120 nations have supported the creation of the court. Countries *not* supporting its establishment include China, Israel, Iraq, and the United States.

20. Progress in the development of cross-border bankruptcy law is discussed in the companion study *Prudential Oversight and Standards for the World Financial System*. See also chapter 10 of this volume.

were to depart too far from such cosmopolitan norms, it might be argued, the nation should be pressured to conform. Refusal to comply might justify the world community in denying the recalcitrant nation some benefits of participating in the wider world community (for example, activities of international organizations valued by the nation).

The difficulty here is that national governments, let alone individual citizens, have very different notions of what cosmopolitan norms, if any, are appropriate on a world (or regional) scale. Even economic norms are highly contentious. Political, social, and cultural norms are still more so. Suppose the charter of an international organization were to prohibit membership by nations with dictatorial or authoritarian governments or with governments that otherwise violate the human or civil rights of their citizens. Could nation states acting through their governments reach practical agreement on the definition and implementation of the underlying human rights norms?

The situations of powerful nations and weaker nations are highly asymmetric. A powerful nation typically regards its own norms as beyond question. It may also, self-righteously, seek to impose its norms on other, weaker nations. When a powerful and a weak nation disagree, the weak nation is invariably the one that must fall in line. A few powerful nations might create a supranational organization with "cosmopolitan" norms agreed essentially among themselves. They might then charge that organization with "oversight" responsibilities to pressure weaker, smaller nations to conform to those norms.

The realistic situation about these matters in today's and tomorrow's world is complex. Asymmetric oversight may be feasible; it might become significant in some areas. But equitable supranational oversight, respecting the wishes of the weak as well as the strong, will probably not be practiced for the foreseeable future.

Figure 7-3 shows a question mark in the second column and a dagger in the third column for category C. Those conjectures may seem surprising given my pessimistic generalizations about the impossibility of reaching widespread agreement on world or regional norms. In part, my hunch about the evolution in this category reflects the likelihood that powerful nations will push for asymmetric "oversight." Even more, my hunch is based on probable increases in the demand for coordination of national decisions and for cooperative surveillance of the outcomes, not least among the most powerful nations themselves. Issues about coordination and surveillance, especially for national macroeconomic policies, will arise frequently in the subsequent analysis.[21]

The subject of collective security is outside the scope of this book. Yet I am temperamentally unable to pass down the rows of figure 7-3 without mentioning category D and without registering a hope that the cells in that row will not remain blank throughout all the first half of the twenty-first century. The provision of collective security is a thorny matter even within nations. At the cross-border and supranational level, the thicket of thorns is massive and, so far, all but impenetrable. During the decades of military rivalry between the Soviet-bloc nations and the alliance of Western nations led by the United States, collective security on a world scale was fragile. A major military conflict, perhaps even a nuclear war, seemed always a possibility. Even following the breakup of the Soviet bloc and the sharp decline in relative power of Russia in the 1990s, little genuine progress was made in intergovernmental cooperation to inhibit military violence.

No area of international governance and cooperation more urgently demands strengthened, effective cooperation. As the probability of a nuclear confrontation between major powers has diminished, recent years have brought an increased incidence of violence and human rights violations in local or regional conflicts. (Think only of the 1990s and the first two years of the new century: violent applications of military force, sometimes even approaching genocide, occurred in Rwanda and Burundi, Somalia, Angola, Sierra Leone, and the Congo in Africa; East Timor, Sri Lanka, Kashmir, and Afghanistan in Asia; Bosnia and Croatia, Kosovo, and Chechnya in Europe; Iraq, Israel and the West Bank and Gaza in the Middle East.) Yet no area of international governance seems less likely to witness the required strengthening in cooperation.

Imagine a heterogeneous local community in which every residential block maintains its own police force. Suppose the sole mandate of each local police is to provide security for, and to protect the narrowly defined interests of, the individuals living in the local block. Suppose none of the blocks is prepared to support a suprablock police force answerable to the

---

21. Differences between direct oversight of lower layers of government (category C) and various types of surveillance activities (category F) are a matter of degree. Both presuppose some form of cosmopolitan norms. Overt, explicit supranational oversight of national governments, however, is politically more contentious than cooperative development of surveillance oversight for circumscribed policy areas.

community as a whole and with authority to inhibit collectively undesired activities throughout the community, including those that spill from one block to another. Suppose each block's local policemen are reluctant to cooperate with the police forces of other blocks and are unwilling to participate in communitywide operations in which they would be subservient to suprablock commanders. And suppose that, when events originating in "foreign" blocks seriously threaten the interests of a local block, each local police force is authorized to override the inadequate security being provided in foreign blocks. One may safely conclude that a community composed of such blocks might experience inadequate communitywide security.

Is the analogy misleading? Nations are not simply like blocks in a heterogeneous local community. Only a small (but growing!) minority regards the entire world as a larger community with common goals that sometimes outrank national objectives and national differences. The analogy is inadequate in other ways as a guide for thinking about collective-security issues in international governance.

But the analogy is not essentially misleading. It points to an overwhelming but little acknowledged truth: on balance, it is strongly in the self-interests of individual nations, not least the largest and most powerful, to begin creating a supranational police force that is not strictly beholden to the armed forces of individual nations and that, in carefully defined circumstances, has some degree of authority over the national forces.

I regard the United States and its government, my own nation, as distressingly short-sighted in recognizing this truth and shamefully slow in exerting international leadership to this end. From the perspective of the United States, intergovernmental cooperation in military matters has been thought to require an organization in which U.S. influence is dominant, such as the North Atlantic Treaty Organization. Procedures and resources for peacekeeping forces under broader international sponsorship, such as the United Nations, have been weakly supported at best. The United States and other major nations typically insist on direct control of any units of their armed forces made available to UN peacekeeping efforts. For some circumstances, even today and certainly in future decades, the world's nations need to establish and maintain an international police force that will have more independence from particular national governments. Achieving greater legitimacy and effectiveness for international peacekeeping efforts almost certainly requires that greater independence.

Of course a federalist world government is impossible and undesirable in the short and medium runs. Of course a truly effective supranational police force to oversee collective world security cannot exist until those halcyon days of federalist mutual governance. But what about more support for a few small baby steps in the right direction, with the governments of the world's most powerful nations taking a more enlightened view of their own selfish interests?

Both national governments and international NGOs are already active in the area of crisis management and humanitarian assistance (category E in figure 7-3). Significant international cooperation in disaster relief, for example, has emerged in recent times of severe famines, floods, hurricanes, and earthquakes (Somalia, 1992–93; Kobe, Japan, 1995; Bangladesh, 1998; Central America, 1998; western Turkey, 1999; Mozambique and Madagascar, 2000). The need for emergency humanitarian assistance is often more quickly and widely recognized than other needs for international cooperation. This pattern seems likely to continue in the future.

For this book, the germane example of this category of nascent cross-border governmental functions is of course the case of financial turbulence and how cooperatively to manage it, especially if it should spill across national borders.

Just as within nations, many other types of surveillance (monitoring and enforcement) activities (category F) can in principle be envisaged at the cross-border or supranational level. As at the domestic level, the category covers a large, heterogeneous range of potential activities.

Some domestic government functions in this category do not now, and may never, have supranational analogues. The certification of doctors, and the setting and monitoring of safety standards for food products, for example, seem likely for the foreseeable future to be carried out at local or national levels rather than on a regional or world scale. Intergovernmental cooperation through mutual recognition rather than through coordination or explicit harmonization may well suffice. For monitoring and enforcement activities at all levels of governance, the principle of subsidiarity is a sound initial presumption.

Yet for an increasingly wide range of cases, the incidence of cross-border externalities and cross-border spillovers suggests a more ambitious form of intergovernmental cooperation. Notable instances already exist. Sentiment appears to be building within many nations to add others to the list. For this book, the key examples are the monitoring and enforcement of traffic regulations for cross-border transactions; the promotion of adjustment and catalyzing of coordination for exchange rates and macroeconomic policies; and the prudential oversight of financial standards and financial institutions.

As a further example, not analyzed in this book, consider the area of environmental protection. As awareness has risen of the long-run unsustainability of many activities using or abusing natural resources, opinions favoring stronger control have become more widespread. This trend has been manifest within individual nations about their own national policies affecting the environment. Issues about the use of the so-called global commons have also arisen more frequently and with greater urgency—for example, how to prevent excessive exploitation of ocean fisheries, how to manage mining of the sea bed and to share the resulting benefits, how to allocate the limited band for geostationary orbits for telecommunications satellites, and how to respond to the global environmental risks attributable to carbon-dioxide "greenhouse" effects and the depletion of the stratospheric ozone shield caused by releases into the atmosphere of chlorofluorocarbons. Proposals for various types of collective action are thus being advanced more insistently. Views underpinning proposed actions are increasingly based on cosmopolitan values that are deemed to justify significant constraints on the exercise of sovereign authority by individual nations.[22]

Environmental protection is therefore one of the specific areas for which substantially enhanced intergovernmental cooperation seems likely (hence the double daggers in row F of figure 7-3). Not that progress in that area has been or will be easy. The Montreal protocol restraining the use of chlorofluorocarbons, though highly significant, was less difficult to negotiate because of relatively favorable underlying conditions.[23] Cooperative progress on global warming is proving to be much harder and more contentious.[24]

The presence or absence of consensual knowledge about a common problem is an important determinant of whether cooperative action can be successfully mounted. The point certainly applies to environmental protection issues. But it is applicable to any problem that may require collective monitoring and enforcement. The likelihood of generating widespread

22. For illustrative references, see, for example, Morse (1977); Brown and others (1977); Miles (1977); O. Young (1989a, 1989b); Sooros (1982); Downing and Kates (1982); Cumberland, Hibbs, and Hoch (1982); P. Haas (1992a, 1992b); Lave (1982); Cline (1992); Cooper (1994); McKibbin and Wilcoxen (1997a, 1997b, 1999, 2000, 2002a, 2002b, 2002c); and McKibbin (2000).

23. Cooper (1994).

24. Cline (1992); Cooper (1994); McKibbin and Wilcoxen (1997b, 2000, 2002a, 2002b, 2002c); Frankel (1999a); and McKibbin (2000).

support for a cooperative international program to control the spread of a contagious disease depends on the degree of consensus among physicians about the causal mechanisms by which the disease is spread. Regardless of scientific or technical knowledge, groups or nations with latent mutual interests may fail to further those interests. But intergovernmental cooperative action is especially unlikely to occur without a large measure of agreement on the nature and magnitude of the cross-border interactions giving rise to the collective problem.[25]

The type of governmental function that within nations directly provides a wide range of collective goods such as utilities or education (category G) is unlikely, with perhaps a few exceptions, to be observed at a regional or world level for many decades to come. Within nations, many such collective goods are supplied below the national level by municipalities or provinces (in accordance, once again, with the principle of subsidiarity). Even if a sound case could be made for supplying them on a regional or world scale, the required governmental institutions will not soon come into existence.

The public goods aspects of education and health care illustrate the point. Virtually all of the governmental support for education and health occurs at national and subnational levels. The training and technical assistance programs of several international organizations such as the World Bank, the IMF, and the World Health Organization, together with limited educational initiatives such as the United Nations University system, are exceptions of relatively minor importance.

It might be argued that the Universal Postal Union or the International Telecommunication Union are exceptions where a collective good is supplied on a supranational scale. Intergovernmental efforts to cooperatively dispose of nuclear wastes might well be beneficial. Space exploration may be an area where physical infrastructure might be created on a supranational scale. Even in these cases, however, the relevant intergovernmental cooperation is more likely to take some form of coordination of national governments' activities instead of an international organization directly supplying a collective good. Most of the functions of the Universal Postal Union, for example, involve a coordination of the activities of the various national-level postal services rather than direct provision of postal services themselves.

25. This importance of knowledge, especially technical or scientific knowledge, was identified long ago by E. Haas (1980). Cooper (1989, 1994) has stressed it; see also Bryant (1995).

Figure 7-3 shows government support of research as a separate category of collective goods (row H). More generally, this function includes efforts to enhance the knowledge base of society. This government role is an exception to the earlier generalization that the public goods aspects of education are and should be handled at national or subnational levels. Intergovernmental cooperation over the next several decades could make a significant contribution to the world's knowledge base by encouraging basic research. A wide variety of cross-border and global issues might justify such support. The specific case of research on the functioning of the world economy and financial system is discussed in chapter 8.

The final class of governmental functions comprises measures intended to redistribute income and wealth (category I). For reasons already identified, redistributive policies are highly controversial even within nations. The notion that intergovernmental cooperation, probably channeled through regional or international organizations, should try to coax wealthier nations to bring about an improved distribution of world income and wealth (for example, transferring resources to poorer nations from the richer industrial nations of North America, Europe, and Japan) is no less controversial.

Awareness that this possible function for intergovernmental cooperation is controversial does not, understandably, deter numerous individuals, nongovernmental organizations, and even national governments from proposing it. Similarly, no shortage exists of individuals and organizations prepared to attack such proposals. In virtually every intergovernmental consultation or negotiation about cross-border governance issues in recent decades, a redistributive dimension has been present, often prominently. This pattern is sure to continue in future decades.

Intergovernmental Cooperation on Financial Issues: The Range of Conceivable Functions

With the preceding as background, the next chapter narrows the focus sharply and concentrates on intergovernmental cooperation about cross-border *financial* issues.

An unpruned catalogue of the conceivable functions for intergovernmental financial cooperation includes all of the following:[26]

---

26. The letter or letters in parentheses after each function indicate the relevant category or categories of general government function summarized in figure 7-3.

1. Designing and fostering support for international financial regime environments, including especially the establishment and maintenance of intergovernmental consultative groups and international financial organizations (A).
2. Collective surveillance functions, including
2a. Monitoring and enforcing traffic regulations for cross-border transactions (F);
2b. Promoting adjustment and catalyzing coordination for exchange rates and macroeconomic policies, domestic as well as external (F,C); and
2c. Providing prudential oversight of financial standards and financial activity (F).
3. Managing financial crises, possibly including the provision of emergency lending during crises (E).
4. Facilitating lending intermediation among national governments during noncrisis conditions (G, F).
5. Conducting research and disseminating information about the functioning of the world economy and financial system (H).
6. Advising individual national governments on the formulation and implementation of improved economic policies, thereby fostering economic growth and development and reducing poverty (G, I).
7. Encouraging a more equitable distribution of world income and wealth through the transfer of resources from wealthier to poorer nations (I).
8. Managing the reserve money base of the world financial system, providing a clearinghouse for the intergovernmental settlement of payments imbalances, and other possible functions eventually to be assigned to a world central bank (G).

Top-level intergovernmental cooperation about regime environments (the principles, norms, rules, institutions, and decisionmaking procedures through which national governments interact with each other) was discussed in general terms earlier in the chapter. Those earlier generalizations apply in particular to *financial* regimes and institutions.

Regime design and institution building is a fundamental underpinning for all types of intergovernmental financial cooperation. That function is invariably present, at least at the outset, for all the other conceivable functions.

Consultative groups might serve to a limited degree as the institutional channels for the other categories of financial governance functions. Because so many of those functions involve ongoing lower-level cooperation, however, many would have to occur largely or wholly under the aegis of international financial organizations rather than through consultative groups.

Much of international financial history during World War II and the years immediately thereafter is a story of attempted top-level cooperation to design or strengthen financial regimes and international organizations with cross-border financial responsibilities. The emphasis at that time on top-level cooperation can be readily explained: when regime and institutional foundations do not yet exist for extensive intergovernmental cooperation at lower levels, a large fraction of whatever cooperative activity occurs necessarily occurs at the upper, regime-design level. During the second half of the twentieth century, a growing proportion of cooperative activity took the form of operational, lower-level cooperation. The relative importance of ongoing, lower-level cooperation will continue to increase in the early decades of the twenty-first century.

Institutions Supporting Intergovernmental Financial Cooperation

A variety of existing institutions—intergovernmental consultative groups and explicitly established international organizations—support intergovernmental financial cooperation. The allocation of nascent collective-governance functions to particular institutions has a predictably complex history. Readers may find it helpful to view a bird's-eye cross-classification of the existing institutions and the key functional areas in which they are engaged. Accordingly, the rows in figure 7-4 are the broad categories of conceivable financial functions. The columns pertain to institutions that support intergovernmental financial cooperation at the beginning of the twenty-first century.[27]

---

27. I use the umbrella term *institutions* in a broad, generic sense to refer both to intergovernmental consultative groups and international organizations. *International organizations* refers to well-established international institutions such as the International Monetary Fund, the World Bank, the Bank for International Settlements, and the World Trade Organization. The existing literature sometimes refers to international financial organizations (with the loose acronym IFOs) and at other times to international financial institutions (with the acronym IFIs). That terminology fails to emphasize the role of intergovernmental consultative groups. Nothing of substance turns on the semantics, however, and the reader can for most purposes interpret international financial organizations and international financial institutions as synonyms.

When an international institution or group of institutions has been unambiguously active in a functional area, the relevant cell in figure 7-4 contains a checkmark. An asterisk suggests that the institution has been active to a lesser degree; a tilde, merely in a minor or trace fashion. A blank cell indicates no activity.[28]

Consider the first row (function 1) in figure 7-4. Each of the international financial institutions has been involved, at least to a limited extent, in the design, building, and maintenance of the regime environments undergirding the world financial system. The degree of explicit involvement has often been minor. Most international organizations, once established, have subsequently become engaged in regime design only if their own individual functions are being reevaluated or amended. Most international organizations become involved in regime support only in the limited sense of maintaining their own operations.

Whenever a major change in international institutions or regimes was being considered in the twentieth century, the primary venues for discussions or negotiations were intergovernmental consultative groups. The most influential example in recent decades has been the Group of Seven (G-7), composed of the representatives of the national governments of the seven largest industrial nations.

The Group of Ten (G-10), still in existence, was a precursor of the G-7. Government officials from developing nations have formed several consultative groups, in part intended as counterweights to the G-7 and G-10; these include the Group of Twenty Four (G-24) and the Group of Seventy Seven (G-77). The International Monetary and Financial Committee (IMFC), formerly called the Interim Committee, and the Development Committee are consultative groups comprised of finance ministers and central bank governors from the member-nation constituencies of the IMF and World Bank. Yet another consultative group known as the Group of Twenty (G-20), comprised of finance ministers and central bank governors from "systemically important countries," was established in 1999.

Ongoing responsibility for monitoring the traffic regulations for cross-border transactions (function 2a) has been allocated primarily according to whether the transactions are on current account or capital account. The

28. Knowledgeable observers of the international financial institutions might in a few instances hold views marginally different from mine about the details of their activities. By and large, however, the rough-and-ready overview judgments implicit in figure 7-4 are noncontroversial.

Figure 7-4. Functions of Institutions Supporting Intergovernmental Financial Cooperation at the Beginning of the Twenty-First Century[a]

	Consultative groups of major national governments	International Monetary Fund	Bank for International Settlements	Other international financial committees, organizations[b]	GATT and the World Trade Organization	Organization for Economic Cooperation and Development	World Bank and its affiliates	Regional development banks[c]
1. Regime design and support	✔	*	*	~	*	*	*	~
2a. Monitoring traffic regulations for cross-border transactions		✔	~		✔	~		
2b. Promoting adjustment and catalyzing coordination	*	*	✔	✔		*	~	
2c. Prudential oversight of financial standards and financial activity		~	✔	✔		~		
3. Managing financial crises	✔	✔	~					
4. Lending intermediation among national governments in noncrisis periods		✔					✔	✔
5. Conducting research and disseminating information		✔	✔			✔	✔	✔
6. Advising national governments on economic policies to promote growth and development		✔					✔	✔
7. Encouraging redistribution of income and wealth		~					✔	✔
8. Potential functions of a world central bank								

a. ✔ indicates the international institution or group of institutions has been unambiguously active in a functional area; * indicates activity merely in a minor or trace fashion. A blank cell indicates no activity.

b. Basel Committee on Banking Supervision, International Organization of Securities Commissions, International Association of Insurance Supervisors, Financial Stability Forum, Joint Forum on Financial Conglomerates, BIS-sponsored Committee on the Global Financial System, BIS-sponsored Committee on Payment and Settlements Systems, International Accounting Standards Board, International Federation of Accountants, International Organization of Supreme Audit Institutions, United Nations Commissions on International Trade Law, and Financial Action Task Force.

c. Inter-American Development Bank, Asian Development Bank, African Development Bank Group, and European Bank for Reconstruction and Development.

monitor for current account transactions was initially the General Agreement on Tariffs and Trade. More recently, and with somewhat more authority to resolve disputes, the monitor has been the World Trade Organization, the successor to GATT. The GATT and WTO are not international *financial* organizations. I nonetheless include them in figure 7-4 because of the importance of the function of monitoring traffic regulations and the marked interdependence of current account and capital account transactions. The IMF has been the monitor for capital account transactions. In a subsidiary way and to a limited degree, the Organization for Economic Cooperation and Development has also been involved in this functional area.

The world economy and financial system has so far had neither a strong adjustment referee nor a genuinely effective coordination catalyst (function 2b). Yet intergovernmental consultative groups have periodically been forced to confront issues of promoting adjustment or inducing coordination for nations' economic policies. General surveillance and monitoring of economic policies, to the extent international organizations have become engaged in this function, have been primarily the province of the IMF. The Bank for International Settlements has been a venue for surveillance discussions among national central banks. Especially in the 1960s and 1970s, the OECD contributed significantly to this function through its Economic Policy Committee (EPC) and the EPC's Working Party Three (WP-3). The World Bank can be interpreted as having modest responsibilities in this area for developing nations.

Cooperation about the prudential oversight of financial standards and financial activity has been carried out primarily through the BIS and a number of other specialized international financial committees and organizations (aggregated together in a separate column in figure 7-4). Responsibility for banking has fallen to the BIS and the Basel Committee for Banking Supervision (BCBS); for securities markets to the International Organization of Securities Commissions; and for insurance companies to the International Association of Insurance Supervisors. International cooperation in the areas of accounting and auditing takes place under the auspices of the International Accounting Standards Board and the International Federation of Accountants. Still other international committees and organizations that operate in this area include the Financial Action Task Force (FATF) and the United Nations Commission on International Trade Law.

Crisis management and emergency lending (function 3) have been carried out predominantly through small meetings of officials from the largest nations, for example through meetings of the G-7. The IMF has several times been an important venue for crisis management. To a lesser extent, especially when central banks have been instrumental, the Bank for International Settlements has been involved. Emergency lending to provide liability financing for payments imbalances in nations troubled by financial and economic crises has been organized mainly through the IMF. Bilateral lending has sometimes been undertaken from creditor national governments to crisis-afflicted national governments (an example is lending to Mexico in 1995 from the U.S. Exchange Stabilization Fund).

The IMF has been the dominant institution engaged in lending intermediation among national governments during noncrisis periods (function 4). In principle, the IMF may lend to any of its member nations, whether developed or developing, whether rich or poor. The World Bank and the regional development banks—the Inter-American Development Bank (IADB), the Asian Development Bank (ADB), the African Development Bank Group (AfDB), and the European Bank for Reconstruction and Development (EBRD)—are also deeply engaged in intergovernmental lending intermediation, but only to developing nations or so-called transition economies.

Several international organizations were engaged in conducting research and disseminating statistical and other information (function 5). The most focused of these efforts were lodged in the IMF, the OECD, and the World Bank. The regional development banks also devoted resources to research and information dissemination.

Advice to national governments about growth and development (function 6) and facilitation of the redistribution of income and wealth across nations (function 7), to the extent that they have been exercised at all, are mainly the responsibility of the World Bank and the regional development banks. In a significant evolutionary change, the IMF was also increasingly drawn into activities aimed at the promotion of growth and development, and even in a minor way at cross-nation redistribution, after the collapse of the Bretton Woods exchange rate arrangements in the mid-1970s.[29]

29. The exchange rate arrangements and other provisions of the original Articles of Agreement of the IMF are often referred to with a "Bretton Woods" label. Bretton Woods was the site in New Hampshire where the final negotiations for the IMF and World Bank took place in July 1944.

No international institution was engaged in management of the reserve money base of the world financial system or other potential activities for a world central bank (function 8).

Readers not already familiar with the international institutions identified in figure 7-4 will find considerable further detail about their origins and activities in the book's institutional appendix. The appendix gives disproportionate attention to the IMF because at the outset of the twenty-first century the IMF figures most prominently in the debates about the evolution of international collective governance for cross-border finance.

8 International Financial Architecture

When discussing world financial issues, policymakers and analysts spoke for decades of the international monetary system or the international financial system. In 1998, perhaps to suggest that there can be something new under the sun, policymakers began to use the term *architecture* instead of *system*. Since that time, policy statements, journalistic commentary, and academic studies have typically portrayed intergovernmental discussions as efforts to "reform the international financial architecture."[1]

Architectural terminology applied to international financial issues has problematic nuances. If discourse requires a broad analogy, the notion of a financial utilities infrastructure is often more appropriate.

Even so, it is quixotic to buck current fashion on matters of terminology. To conform with current fashion, this chapter is titled *international financial architecture*. The phrase *architectural reform* is used in the title and text of chapters 9 and 10.

Whatever the terminology, my perspective on matters architectural differs from the conventional wisdom. Before proposing architectural reform,

---

1. Robert E. Rubin, then secretary of the U.S. Treasury, first used the architectural analogy in a speech at the Brookings Institution in April 1998; see Rubin (1998, 1999). Official documents of the Group of Seven and the IMF often use the analogy. Council on Foreign Relations Independent Task Force (1999), Eichengreen (1999), and Kenen (2001) are examples of private sector or academic use.

Box 8-1. *Intergovernmental Cooperation on Financial Issues:*
The Range of Conceivable Functions (Elements of International
Financial Architecture)

1. Designing and fostering support for international financial regime environments, including especially the establishment and maintenance of intergovernmental consultative groups and international financial organizations.
2. Collective surveillance functions:
    2a. Monitoring and enforcing traffic regulations for cross-border transactions.
    2b. Promoting adjustment and catalyzing coordination for exchange rates and macroeconomic policies, domestic as well as external.
    2c. Providing prudential oversight of financial standards and financial activity.
3. Managing financial crises, possibly including the provision of emergency lending during crises.
4. Facilitating lending intermediation among national governments during non-crisis periods.
5. Conducting research and disseminating information about the functioning of the world economy and financial system.
6. Advising individual national governments on the formulation and implementation of improved economic policies, thereby to foster economic growth and development and to reduce poverty.
7. Encouraging a more equitable distribution of world income and wealth through the transfer of resources from wealthier to poorer nations.
8. Managing the reserve-money base of the world financial system, providing a clearinghouse for the intergovernmental settlement of payments imbalances, and other possible functions eventually to be assigned to a world central bank.

one should first have a clear sense of what the existing architecture is—and is not. A dependable architect does not suggest changes in a building without sound knowledge of the relevant engineering constraints and without good blueprints. Blueprints are needed not only for the proposed additions but for the existing structure.

All the conceivable functions for intergovernmental financial cooperation—for the international financial architecture—were identified toward the end of the preceding chapter. For convenient reference, they are listed in box 8-1. That entire range of functions is an overall, comprehensive blueprint for international financial architecture. Not all the functions identified in box 8-1, of course, could or should be actually exercised in the next few decades. The choice of priorities for the short and medium runs should nevertheless be informed by solid understanding of the blueprint as a whole.

This chapter provides an analytical survey of the overall blueprint. The primary emphasis is on issues that have so far been relatively neglected in the debates about architectural reform. I highlight the collective surveillance functions dealing with traffic regulations, adjustment promotion, and policy coordination (2a and 2b in box 8-1). Lending intermediation among national governments in noncrisis conditions (function 4) is much less understood than emergency financial assistance as part of crisis management. The survey here accordingly provides analytical background about that function needed for later chapters.

The groundwork for understanding the other key components of a potential utilities infrastructure for the world financial system—the prudential oversight of financial activity (surveillance function 2c) and the management of financial crises (function 3)—was laid in earlier chapters. The survey here builds on the earlier analyses and indicates how those important functions are made more difficult by cross-border and cross-currency transactions.

The chapter concludes by examining the remaining parts of the blueprint (functions 5 through 8). Though currently not regarded as important, those functions are likely to become salient over the longer run.

Monitoring and Enforcing Traffic Regulations

International regimes agreed in top-level negotiations serve in part as traffic regulations for ongoing, lower-level cooperation. Just as drivers of automobiles mutually consent to interpret red lights as a stop signal and to drive on the right side of the road (or in some countries the left), national governments consent to understandings such as those embodied in the Articles of Agreement of the IMF or the legal agreements for the WTO. These understandings ensure against the worst excesses of unconstrained noncooperative behavior—in effect, inhibiting each driver from choosing independently which side of the road on which to drive.

In the absence of agreed procedures for monitoring and enforcing what nations do, traffic regulations may not be rigorously observed. Such an outcome may be especially likely if the traffic regulations themselves have been deliberately left unclear (what lawyers call *soft law*). Therefore one function for intergovernmental cooperation, perhaps delegated to international organizations, is to play a role analogous to that of a traffic police-man. In effect, the monitoring institutions are asked to keep track of how nations behave, to identify breaches of the traffic regulations, and where necessary to provide interpretations of what is and is not permissible. The institutions may even be given limited enforcement powers, such as the authority to invoke sanctions, when they decide that the regulations have been breached. They might even be given limited authority to supplement or modify the traffic regulations.

If major revisions in existing regulations should be deemed appropriate, that is, if national governments temporarily revert to the bargaining of top-level cooperation, the monitoring organizations might be asked to partici-pate in, perhaps even help to administer, that negotiating process. Hence the international organizations might partly function as a designer, not merely as a monitor, of the traffic regulations.

Effective monitoring of traffic regulations for cross-border transactions among nations requires surveillance of all types of transactions. Inter-national financial organizations or financial consultative groups under-standably pay greater attention to cross-border financial transactions than to cross-border trade in goods and services and cross-border movements of people. Hence the financial monitors focus on traffic regulations governing exchange rates and exchange rate arrangements, cross-border flows of cap-ital, and the settlement of payments imbalances.

Because current account and capital account transactions are non-independent, a logical economic case can be made for conducting the sur-veillance of traffic regulations for trade in goods and services together with that for capital account and financial transactions. Politics, however, has overruled economic logic. A shared reluctance to give concentrated sur-veillance authority to a single international institution has produced a con-sensus for separation rather than integration.

Since World War II, the rough consensus has been that the General Agreement on Tariffs and and Trade, and more recently the World Trade Organization, should have dominant responsibility for monitoring and enforcing the traffic regulations for cross-border trade in goods and ser-vices. The same consensus has designated the IMF as the primary interna-tional organization for surveillance of capital flows and other cross-border financial transactions.

The Articles of Agreement of the IMF give limited responsibilities to the IMF as a traffic policeman for cross-border trade because of its respon-sibilities for overseeing payments for trade and other current account transactions. The Organization for Economic Cooperation and Development and the World Bank also have limited roles in the supranational surveillance of trade transactions. But the responsibilities of other international organizations for surveillance of trade transactions are definitely secondary to those of the WTO.

The collective-governance issues involved in surveillance of traffic regulations for cross-border trade have many similarities to the surveillance issues for macroeconomics and finance. Much could be said about how the WTO is evolving in its monitoring and enforcement of international agreements about trade and property rights. Trade issues, however, fall largely outside the scope of this book. To keep the analysis manageable, the book does not try to cover the GATT, the WTO, and the evolution of supranational surveillance for trade.[2]

Promoting Adjustment and Catalyzing Coordination for Exchange Rates and Macroeconomic Policies

Interactions among nations about financial and economic matters can extend beyond the monitoring of traffic regulations to more ambitious forms of cooperation (as chapter 7 explained). Most notably, consultative groups and international financial organizations may act to promote adjustment among national economies and to catalyze coordination among the decisions of national governments. Promoting adjustment and catalyzing coordination are in part an intensification of the monitoring function. Because of their more ambitious purpose, however, they are qualitatively different.[3]

Which types of national policies should receive the greatest attention in supranational surveillance? A first, superficially plausible reaction to this question would be to presume that surveillance should focus merely on cross-border transactions and on other external sector variables such as exchange rates and imbalances in national balances of payments. Those external-sector variables are jointly determined by—"belong to"—the economies of several nations together. The appeal of this first reaction rests on the pragmatic instinct that surveillance should not be asked to extend

---

2. For a recent set of papers providing background about the WTO, see the volume edited by Krueger (1998). Other background references about the WTO and GATT include Dam (1970); Hoekman and Kostecki (1995); Jackson (1997, 1998b); and Collins and Bosworth (1994).

3. In figure 7-3 in chapter 7, the coordination of national macroeconomic policies might be classified in category C and to some extent even in category G as well as in category F.

its reach unnecessarily into domestic matters and thereby raise fears about excessive infringements of national sovereignty.

When that initial reaction is examined, however, it turns out to be economically illogical. Given the marked increases in the integration of the world economy and financial system, individual national economies are more and more non-independent. They are like balls in a bowl. If one ball is moved, typically several others must move as well.

Views about the sustainability and appropriateness of an individual nation's external position invariably differ, especially between the home and foreign governments. Views about the global pattern of imbalances and exchange rates thus also differ. But, ex post, there can be only one global pattern. Every exchange rate is two-sided. One nation cannot usually run a balance-of-payments surplus unless one or more other nations incur deficits. These stark facts create a presumptive rationale for intergovernmental cooperation to develop a systemic perspective.

Systemic judgments about the sustainability and appropriateness of payments imbalances and exchange rates are notoriously difficult. Such judgments inevitably rest on normative as well as objective criteria. Yet consultative groups or international financial organizations can try to identify apparent ex ante inconsistencies in national policies and to foster mutually preferred methods of reconciliation.

More ambitiously still, the world as a whole might substantially benefit if an international financial organization were to act as an impartial referee for the adjustment of payments imbalances and as a forum and catalyst for the coordination of nations' economic policies. Monitoring and refereeing of national policies might be especially useful in the area of exchange rate arrangements. Such activities may be labeled the functions of *adjustment referee* and *coordination catalyst*.

One important difference between the more ambitious responsibilities of adjustment promotion and catalyzing cooperation (2b in box 8-1) versus the monitoring of traffic regulations (2a) is the wider scope of the former. Traffic regulations designed in intermittent, top-level negotiations are typically limited to rules about cross-border transactions and external-sector variables. But the progressively stronger non-independence of national economies means that supranational surveillance must monitor all national policies having important influences on foreign nations. Ongoing cooperation to promote adjustment and catalyze coordination thus in principle must focus not merely on compliance with cross-border traffic regulations, but also on the effects of all national policies, domestic as well as external. In particular, adjustment promotion and coordination must examine the consequences of the domestic budgetary decisions made by fiscal authorities and the domestic monetary policy decisions made by central banks.

The rationale for intergovernmental cooperation on macroeconomic and financial issues is straightforward and analytically sound. Decentralized national decisions that fail to take into account the cross-border spillovers from policy actions can produce outcomes that are inferior to more efficient outcomes attainable through informed collective action. Intergovernmental cooperation can help national governments avoid sequences of decentralized decisions that would produce mutually undesired outcomes.

Inferior outcomes from decentralized decisions are examples of situations in which negative externalities lead to market failures. If instead governments consult and bargain with one another cooperatively, they may be able to identify mutually beneficial adjustments of their policy instruments that offset the market failures and thereby permit their nations to reach higher levels of welfare. Because economic integration across national borders has generated a growing variety and intensity of collective-action problems with cross-border dimensions, the rationale for a systemic perspective and intergovernmental cooperation is even more compelling at the beginning of the twenty-first century than it was half a century earlier.

Efforts to cooperate are not invariably successful. Governmental intervention intended to remedy market failures can be counterproductive. In some circumstances, cooperative intergovernmental decisions can lead to government failures. Welfare can thereby be undermined rather than enhanced. Nonetheless, if intelligently pursued and not overly ambitious, cooperation among national governments can be plausibly expected to advance the common interests of their citizens.[4]

When governments agree to make some decisions cooperatively, they also want to ensure compliance with those decisions. The more ambitious the efforts at cooperation, the more likely is an associated emphasis on compliance. The basic rationale for intergovernmental cooperation thus also comes with a corresponding rationale for surveillance over national policies. Processes and institutions for surveillance—both monitoring and enforcement—facilitate compliance. In principle, surveillance should be exercised

---

4. Bryant (1995) has an extended exposition of the analytical arguments for and against cooperation in the area of national stabilization policies.

in noncrisis and crisis conditions alike. When exercised skillfully in noncrisis conditions, surveillance reduces the probability of crises occurring.

Lending Intermediation among National Governments: General Considerations

The possibility that a national government troubled by crisis conditions might borrow from other national governments is, though problematic and controversial, straightforward in concept. But national governments might also borrow from or lend to each other in times not troubled by financial crises. Furthermore, national governments might establish an international financial organization to act, in noncrisis as well as crisis circumstances, as a *lending intermediary to facilitate the liability financing of payments deficits*. National governments did of course establish just such an institution, the International Monetary Fund, in the middle of the twentieth century.

To fix ideas about this function for intergovernmental cooperation (4 in box 8-1), recall first some general observations that apply to crisis and noncrisis circumstances alike. An individual nation faces difficult choices about how to cope with external payments imbalances (chapter 6). When imbalances are likely to persist, the nation's government will, later if not sooner, be forced to focus more on adjustment than on financing. Changes in the nation's exchange rate may often be part of a required adjustment. Over a shorter run, however, the government can try to cushion some types of shocks through use of official financing as a supplement for adjustment. For temporary imbalances, official financing may even seem preferable to immediate adjustments in policies since those adjustments might subsequently have to be reversed. Financing that takes the form of asset financing, drawdowns of the government's external assets, can be better controlled by the home government. But asset financing may not be possible in some circumstances. If financing is to be used, it may thus have to be liability financing (increased borrowing from abroad by the home government).

When a nation's overall deficit is liability financed, one or more nations in overall surplus necessarily acquire the counterpart loan claims. Such borrowing could be handled entirely through bilateral lending arrangements between lenders in particular surplus nations and the deficit nation's government. (The foreign lenders might be governments, or they might be private financial institutions extending credit on commercial or quasi-commercial terms.) Rather than relying on bilateral arrangements, however, the government in the deficit nation might find it advantageous to have some or all of the liability financing of its deficit channeled through a multilateral international institution established to expedite such transactions.

If it is established, a multilateral lending intermediary does not alter the essential economic facts of liability financing: funds supplied by lenders resident in surplus nations will be loaned to the borrowing nation in deficit. And such lending, whether from private creditors or the governments of surplus nations, will inevitably be accompanied by performance conditions and lending terms that constrain the freedom of maneuver of the debtor nation.

Yet a multilateral intermediary may permit more flexibility in the lending from surplus to deficit nations than would otherwise be possible. When the foreign lenders to a deficit nation are governments rather than private creditors, additional dimensions of intergovernmental cooperation come into play. As a formal matter, moreover, the deficit nation's government incurs liabilities to the international intermediary rather than direct liabilities to the creditor governments in surplus nations. Similarly, surplus nations' governments hold claims on the intermediary rather than direct claims on the borrowing nation's government.

Numerous variants of a multilateral intermediary can be imagined. Alternative criteria could be devised for determining which nations will participate. The rights of participating nations to borrow when in deficit and their obligations to lend when in surplus could be specified in a variety of different ways. Numerous provisions could be agreed to govern the particulars of lending operations—for example, performance conditions to be satisfied by a deficit nation before it would be permitted to borrow.

Similarly, a multilateral intermediary could acquire the resources for its lending in different ways. One possibility would be to have participating national governments irrevocably transfer certain amounts of standard reserve assets to the intermediary at the outset of its operations. A second possibility would be to have participating national governments commit themselves on a contingency basis to make certain amounts of standard reserve assets available to the intermediary as and when needed for its lending operations. A third possibility, economically very similar to the second, would be to have each participating nation transfer to the intermediary a certain amount of funds in its own currency on the understanding that the intermediary can lend the participant's currency to liability-financing deficit nations when the participant itself is in a strong balance-of-payments or a strong reserve position. Under any of the three preceding possibilities, the amounts of resources made available by individual participating nations might be made proportional to "subscription quotas," the relative sizes of which in turn could be proportional to the relative economic sizes of the participants (as measured by, for example, populations, gross national products, exports). Still a fourth possibility would be to authorize the intermediary to borrow funds selectively, as and when needed for its lending operations, from individual nations having strong balance-of-payments or reserve positions. The borrowed funds could supplement those obtained from subscription quotas or, in another variant, could constitute the sole source of funds. In practice, today's IMF obtains the bulk of its resources by the third of these four methods, with smaller amounts coming from borrowed funds.

Differences among the possible variants of a multilateral intermediary could significantly determine the amounts and timing of its lending. The details of the obligations of participating national governments to lend to the intermediary when in balance-of-payments surplus or in a strong reserve position would obviously determine whether the intermediary could be generous or alternatively would have to be cautious in its decisions extending credit to the national governments of deficit nations. An intermediary obtaining resources through quota subscriptions would have greater assurances about its lending ability—and could correspondingly take bolder lending initiatives—than an intermediary that had to rely on intermittent selective borrowings.

Intergovernmental lending intermediation facilitates the liability financing of payments deficits. Such liability financing might at first blush seem to be conceptually separable from efforts to encourage adjustment of those same deficits. In practice, the financing of deficits through a multilateral intermediary cannot feasibly be divorced from the encouragement of policy actions to promote adjustment.

As in all arm's-length lending arrangements, a home government wishing to finance an overall deficit by borrowing will become involved in consultations and then negotiations with prospective creditors. Possible performance conditions, in some form, will invariably arise in those negotiations. In particular, any potential acquirer of the prospective loan claims will express a judgment about the appropriateness of financing the home nation's deficit. The prospective creditors will also seek assurances about the likelihood that, following any required adjustment actions, the inappropriate portion of the deficit will be eliminated (and, eventually, reversed). Prospective adjustment and the capacity of the borrowing nation to repay are—inescapably—preoccupations of the lenders in bilateral arrangements for liability financing between a deficit nation and creditors resident in surplus nations. Use of liability financing thus necessarily subjects the borrowing nation's government to "conditionality" imposed by foreign lenders (either private institutions or foreign governments). Even so, the ability to arrange liability financing may sometimes cause the borrowing government to accept, if not positively embrace, the creditors' imposition of conditionality.

There is no reason to expect creditors' preoccupations with conditionality to be less salient—indeed, they may be more important—if liability financing of a deficit is arranged through a multilateral lending intermediary. Nations in surplus or expecting to be in surplus will not support the intermediary's operations—after all, the lending is on their behalf—unless there is assurance that the loans are accompanied by appropriate performance conditions and suitable provisions regarding repayment. Invariably, therefore, a multilateral intermediary will be compelled to act as an adjustment promoter, not merely as an originator and curator of loan claims.

The interests of debtor and creditor nations diverge, which in turn is certain to lead to differing judgments about the sustainability of individual nations' balance-of-payments positions and the appropriateness or inappropriateness of particular values for exchange rates (chapter 6). A multilateral lending intermediary will thus unavoidably become enmeshed in reconciling the differences in normative judgments held by the national governments that are its lending and borrowing participants.

Why do governments of prospective surplus nations participate in multilateral organizations like the IMF rather than restricting liability financing of deficits to direct bilateral intergovernmental transactions? Indeed, why do governments themselves choose to act as lenders? Why not leave financing of payments deficits entirely to private capital flows?

The general answer to these questions is analogous to why a government, in a purely domestic context within a nation, might establish a government lending intermediary. National governments may believe that market imperfections in the world financial system, such as information asymmetries influencing private lenders' willingness to lend to nations in overall deficit, could inhibit the smooth flow of financial funds between surplus and deficit nations. By establishing an intergovernmental mechanism for the liability financing of payments deficits, governments might hope to offset such market failures and thereby enhance the efficiency of the world financial system. This motive for government involvement in cross-border financial intermediation is of course controversial, just as is direct government lending intermediation within a nation.

A particular motive underlying the participation by governments of prospective surplus nations is a belief that negotiations with a borrowing government in a deficit nation can be handled more efficiently if lending governments coordinate their judgments and decisions. For example, creditor governments may believe they can more easily negotiate appropriate performance conditions and repayment terms if the various potential creditors work together through a single intermediary. Similarly, lending governments may believe that pressures on deficit nations to adjust can be more effectively monitored if applied through a multilateral organization. The government of a surplus nation concerned about criticism of its own imbalance and its own policies might also perceive political advantages to participation in a multilateral lending process.

What may induce the governments of deficit nations to participate? A variety of motives can be relevant here, too. Deficit nations' governments may believe that their potential access to liability financing can be larger, more assured, or available on less costly terms than by relying on bilateral governmental arrangements or borrowing from private foreigners. They may hope that the involvement of surplus nations in a multilateral lending intermediary would expose individual surplus nations to pressures to adjust their surpluses. They may regard a multilateral lending intermediary as a means of partially mitigating the hegemony of a single large surplus nation or a dominant group of surplus nations.

If sufficiently farsighted, individual national governments may recognize that over a long period their nation may not be accurately characterized as primarily a surplus or primarily a deficit country. That perspective would be especially appropriate if payments imbalances in the world economy were on average adjusted reasonably promptly and smoothly. In such a world, deficits and surpluses would alternate or revolve over time. Neither deficits nor surpluses would be "permanent." Nor would exchange rates be persistently misaligned for long periods.[5]

Notice that the generalizations in the preceding paragraphs make no distinction between—in fact, they apply equally to—noncrisis conditions and times of financial crisis. Lending intermediation among governments, and in particular the lending activities of an international financial organization

---

5. The statements about deficits and surpluses in the text apply, of course, to overall payments imbalances. They do not apply to current account imbalances. See chapter 6 for definitions and discussion.

acting as a multilateral intermediary, may be initiated during times of crisis. If so, the lending may be regarded as emergency financial assistance and analyzed as part of the function of managing financial crises. If the lending occurs in noncrisis conditions, its purpose may better be described as *crisis prevention* rather than crisis management.

Lending Intermediation and Surveillance by the IMF

The preceding section emphasizes general analytical points about intergovernmental lending intermediation because those points are poorly understood and too seldom remembered in current discussions about the IMF. With that background, it is now appropriate to focus on the IMF itself, paying particular attention to rationales for noncrisis lending by the IMF and to the interrelationships between the IMF's lending and its surveillance of nations' economic policies.

IMF lending, especially in noncrisis circumstances, has become controversial in recent years. A basic question lurks beneath the surface of the controversies: should the IMF be in the business of lending intermediation at all? Some market enthusiasts, greatly impressed by the functioning of financial markets and the growth of cross-border finance, have argued that virtually all lending in the world—including specifically any borrowing by government entities—should be conducted by and for the account of private economic units. These persons emphasize that the private sectors of national economies are the overwhelming source of savings in the world financial system. From that correct observation, they go on to conclude that the only appropriate role for governments is to provide an infrastructure within which strong and sustainable private lending can flourish. They therefore argue that governments themselves should not lend. Some with stiff convictions on this matter even conclude that intergovernmental lending routed through international financial organizations such as the IMF should be prohibited.

Criticism of noncrisis lending intermediation by the IMF is readily understandable at one level. Within a nation with an advanced financial reservoir, one does not normally expect a government institution to act as a financial lender to private borrowers in noncrisis times. If such a government-run intermediary were to subsidize its domestic lending, for example by charging borrowing rates below market interest rates plus a market-related risk premium, its activities would be especially controversial. Analogously, noncrisis lending to a national government by the IMF can be criticized as "unfairly" competing with private lending. If the borrowing government has access on some kind of terms to private capital in foreign financial systems, the IMF lending can be criticized as "unwarrantedly cheap" financing to the nation at below-market cost.

But analysis must go beyond such observations. The untrammeled markets position that all lending, to all borrowers in all circumstances, should be conducted solely by private sector creditors is badly misguided. At a minimum, proponents of that extreme view fail to acknowledge that emergency lending in financial crises, either within nations or to the governments of entire nations troubled by crisis, cannot reasonably be left just to financial markets and private financial institutions.

Rationales for intergovernmental lending intermediation in noncrisis periods are less straightforward than emergency rationales. They engender still sharper differences of view. But such rationales certainly exist and apply unambiguously to the activities of the IMF.

The general argument for government involvement in lending activities is that borrowers in some circumstances may not have access to private credit and financial markets because of market imperfections and externalities. Government lending may then be able to induce matches among borrowers and lenders preferable to those that would otherwise prevail, offsetting the market failures. Government lending may be able to achieve social goals by reallocating financial resources. Government lending may aim at inducing a redistribution of income and wealth.

One rationale for IMF lending intermediation is a special case of the market imperfections and externalities argument. Information asymmetries and political factors strongly influence private lenders' willingness to lend to nations in overall deficit. A smooth flow of financial funds between surplus and deficit nations, as indicated above, may sometimes be undermined even when the borrowing nation has a sound case for the liability financing of its deficit. In such circumstances IMF lending intermediation can contribute to the efficiency and stability of the world financial system.

A further rationale merits even greater emphasis. IMF lending intermediation can support and reinforce the IMF's surveillance of nations' policies, exchange rates, and payments imbalances. Creditor nations may be better able to negotiate repayment terms and appropriate performance conditions for lending to deficit nations if they work together through a lending intermediary such as the IMF. At the same time, the access of debtor nations to liability financing for their deficits may be larger, more assured, or less expensive if they borrow from the IMF. The powers for adjustment promotion associated with the conditionality of its lending thus can facilitate the IMF's role as an adjustment referee for payments imbalances and exchange rate misalignments.

The IMF's powers for adjustment promotion accompanying its lending exert pressure on borrowing nations. Someone with a fondness for symmetry in surveillance might yearn for comparable adjustment pressures to be applied to surplus nations as well. But that yearning would not be realistic. The adjustment powers accompanying the lending, integrally derived from the IMF's imposition of conditionality, are inherently asymmetric. The IMF does not lend to the governments of surplus nations and has no directly comparable opportunity to exert pressure on them to adjust their surpluses. The IMF's lending function is thus a single-edged, not a double-edged, sword in its support of its surveillance function.

Because of the asymmetry that conditionality can constrain only deficit nations, IMF lending cannot be regarded as a necessary accompaniment to supranational surveillance. Surveillance would be lopsided and ineffective if it could be conducted only in association with IMF lending. The IMF's ability to impose conditionality in conjunction with its lending to deficit nations is thus a desirable, but not essential, handmaiden to surveillance.

To drive home the point that supranational surveillance is needed and that ways must be found to make it effective in the absence of IMF lending intermediation, one need think for only a few seconds about the situation of the wealthier industrial nations. From the inception of the IMF through the 1960s, industrial nation members often accounted for more than half of the total use of IMF credit. But after the collapse of the Bretton Woods exchange arrangements in the early 1970s, industrial nations were prepared to permit wider movements in the exchange rates among their currencies. They also typically had ready access to external financing from private commercial sources. Italy borrowed from the IMF in 1974–75; the United Kingdom did so in 1976–77. After that, however, major industrial nations never again borrowed from the IMF in the so-called credit tranches. A few smaller industrial nations borrowed from the IMF until 1982. Thereafter, for the rest of the century, the industrial nations were lenders but never borrowers in the IMF.[6]

6. Several industrial nations drew on their so-called reserve tranche positions (counted as the drawing down of a reserve asset rather than a borrowing of credit) in the 1980s. The last such drawing by industrial nations occurred in 1987. The appendix at the end of the book provides an overview of the original Bretton Woods concept of the IMF and the subsequent evolution of its lending activities.

Today's conventional wisdom is that the wealthier industrial nations will never again borrow from the IMF. That prediction is likely to be correct for the shorter run. The case for subjecting wealthier industrial nations to supranational surveillance is at least as strong as for smaller and developing nations. Thus the world community should want to nurture IMF procedures and mechanisms for surveillance that are applicable to all nations and that are *not* contingent on IMF lending intermediation.[7]

Although the IMF's lending does not by itself facilitate an even-handed, systemic approach to the adjustment of payments imbalances, it bears repeating that the IMF can adopt an even-handed, systemic approach in trying to promote adjustment for exchange rates and macroeconomic policies. The surveillance powers of an impartial adjustment referee can be applied symmetrically to surplus and deficit nations.

Recent controversies about the IMF have tended to focus on the lending-intermediation issues identified above. But some differences of view stem from broader disagreements about what the IMF's missions ought to be. The term *mandate* can conveniently refer to the variety of missions that are now or potentially could be assigned to the IMF. The functions in box 8-1 are the entire catalog. Applied to the IMF, how should the catalog be pruned? Some participants in debates about the IMF would like to narrow its existing mandate and correspondingly curtail its lending. Other participants, heterogeneous in their motives, argue for broadening the IMF's mandate and therefore also augmenting its lending powers. Chapters 9, 10, and 11 address those mandate questions as well as the surveillance and lending-intermediation issues surveyed in this chapter.

Prudential Oversight of Financial Activity

The establishment of financial standards and the supervision and regulation of financial intermediaries are essential in a purely domestic context. In an integrated world financial system, cross-border transactions and multiple national jurisdictions create severe additional difficulties for legal, accounting, auditing, and data systems. Cross-border transactions and multiple

---

7. The conventional wisdom that industrial nations will "never" again borrow from the IMF in their credit tranches is an extremely strong prediction. I am more agnostic about that prediction than most. I can at least imagine occasions in the distant future when exchange rate variability might be markedly less than it is today and when industrial nations might therefore again choose to borrow from the IMF for the liability financing of payments deficits.

jurisdictions likewise cause issues of prudential oversight—already complicated within nations—to become that much more complex and difficult.

Supervisory, regulatory, and tax environments differ greatly from one nation to another. Such disparities can generate competitive inequities (or at least the appearance of competitive inequities) among national financial systems. Financial institutions perceiving themselves as disadvantaged in one nation thus have incentives to relocate their borrowing and lending activities to nations with lower taxes and less stringent supervision and regulation.

As cross-border financial transactions grow in relative importance, disparities in national regulatory and tax environments become more difficult to maintain. Nations with the most stringent and pervasive prudential oversight accordingly feel pressured. Financial business in those nations that is primarily domestic in nature can sometimes be conducted through cross-border transactions, thereby enabling financial intermediaries and their customers to avoid domestic regulatory restrictions. Supervisory, regulatory, or tax issues that formerly were viewed as a domestic matter thus cannot now be coherently discussed without reference to cross-border flows of funds and the supervisory, regulatory, and tax environments in foreign nations.

The erosion of individual nations' regulatory environments associated with the internationalization of financial intermediation illustrates the general phenomenon of innovations in response to supervision and regulation. In a closed domestic context, financial institutions trying to avoid regulations or supervisory constraints could do so only by devising new financial instruments or discovering some other innovation that would allow them to escape the existing constraints. In an open economy, another and potentially more powerful alternative exists: a financial institution experiencing stringent regulation can decide to move the regulated activities outside the jurisdiction of the national regulators. Unless the home-nation regulators can induce their counterparts in other nations to adopt a posture as stringent as theirs, the financial institution may succeed in escaping the home regulations. Alternatively, the home-nation regulators may see that they cannot prevent the relocation of the institution's activities and may therefore decide to relax their regulations sufficiently to keep the activities at home.

Financial intermediation is more footloose than most other forms of economic activity. It can shift locations with less difficulty and without incurring prohibitively large costs. The innovations in electronic communications and data processing in recent decades have enhanced this differential mobility. Even more than for industry in general, therefore, the scope exists for an individual locality or nation to try to lure financial activity within its borders by imposing less stringent regulation, supervision, and taxation than that prevailing elsewhere. The governments of small nations aspiring to become "offshore financial centers" have been especially aware of this relocation possibility. The rapid expansion of financial activity in offshore financial centers has been partly attributable to the differential location incentives created by government policies.[8]

Cross-border and cross-currency transactions in open financial systems make life more demanding for the supervisors charged with prudential oversight. Individual private financial institutions are exposed to additional and more complex risks. Monitoring the institutions and evaluating the riskiness of their activities is correspondingly more difficult. For example, more data and more difficult judgments are involved when appraising an individual institution's assets and liabilities denominated in foreign currencies, and forming a view about the appropriateness of gross and net positions in particular foreign currencies. To form judgments about the riskiness and liquidity of the financial balance sheet of the nation as a whole is an order of magnitude still more difficult.

Cross-border and cross-currency finance permits individual financial institutions and the nation as a whole to enjoy substantial benefits. It permits, at least along some dimensions, a greater diversification of risks. Conceivably, individual institutions and the nation as a whole could experience a reduction rather than an increase in overall risks. The net consequences of cross-border and cross-currency financial intermediation for the safety and soundness of a nation's financial institutions are thus subtle and complex. The supervisors are often unable to make simple generalizations about the net consequences. At the least, however, the supervisory authorities of a single open economy concerned with the microprudential protection of depositors and investors and the macroprudential stability of the

---

8. The locations referred to as offshore financial centers include Anguilla, Antigua and Barbuda, Aruba, Belize, the British Virgin Islands, Cayman Islands, Costa Rica, the Bahamas, Barbados, Bermuda, the Netherlands Antilles, Panama, St. Kitts and Nevis, St. Lucia, St. Vincent and the Grenadines, and the Turks and Caicos in the Caribbean area; Bahrain, Lebanon, and the United Arab Emirates in the Middle East; Singapore, Hong Kong, the Philippines, Macau, Labuan (Malaysia), Mauritius, the Seychelles, Guam, Vanuatu (New Hebrides), Samoa, the Cook Islands, the Marshall Islands, Nauru, and Niue Island in Asia and Oceania; and Luxembourg, Andorra, Liechtenstein, Cyprus, the Channel Islands (Jersey and Guernsey), the Isle of Man, Malta, Gibraltar, and Monaco in Europe. The issues raised by offshore financial centers are discussed further in chapter 10.

national financial system have a much more intricate job than would their counterparts in a hypothetical closed economy.

Requirements for capital adequacy illustrate the general point. The supervisors would face complex issues in setting such requirements even in the absence of financial assets and liabilities that cross the nation's border and that are denominated in foreign currencies. But devising capital adequacy guidelines that reflect international complications requires still more subtle standards for the appropriate levels of a financial institution's net worth. Worse still, if different nations choose differing capital adequacy standards, competitive equity across nations becomes a further complication. Footloose financial institutions then have incentives to relocate their activities to jurisdictions with less stringent capital standards.

Supervisors are appointed and monitored by national governments. The private financial institutions being supervised and regulated are multinational in their activities. The potential scope for jurisdictional confusion is therefore substantial.

To illustrate the dilemmas, consider some thorny questions. Suppose a banking office located in nation A with a head office located in nation B gets into financial trouble. Which national supervisors should have primary responsibility for monitoring and evaluating the office's problems? And which national central bank should have responsibility for providing lender-of-last-resort support should such assistance be merited? (The answers to the preceding two questions might, but would not necessarily, identify the same nation.) Should the allocation of supervisory, or lender-of-last-resort, responsibilities differ according to the legal status of the banking office in nation A—for example, whether the office is a branch or a subsidiary of the parent bank in A? How should consortium banks— joint ventures located in A but owned by banks or investors not only in B but in several other nations as well—be treated? Should the allocation across nations of the prudential oversight of multinational securities and brokerage institutions be handled analogously to the cross-national allocation of responsibilities for banks? How worrisome is the risk that national central banks might behave too timidly in a generalized financial crisis, thereby exposing the world financial system as a whole to inadequate provision of lender-of-last-resort assistance? If coordination among national central banks about lender-of-last-resort assistance is required to ensure world financial stability, do the associated moral hazard dilemmas require a commensurate degree of intergovernmental coordination in the supervision and regulation of financial institutions?

Questions such as these would be thorny even if each national jurisdiction on its own were characterized by high standards for "domestic" prudential oversight. But the scope and stringency of supervision varies significantly across nations. Some jurisdictions may be unable or unwilling to implement high supervisory standards, which can mean that supervisory monitoring and enforcement in those jurisdictions is weak. Spillovers and externalities may then disturb jurisdictions with stronger prudential oversight. Private financial institutions seeking weaker oversight thus have opportunities to engage in regulatory arbitrage by locating some of their activities in the inadequately supervised locations. Such jurisdictions can then become weak links—to use an even more provocative term, loopholes—in the prudential oversight of an increasingly integrated world financial system. At worst, the weak-link jurisdictions might frustrate cooperative intergovernmental efforts to reduce the risks of global financial instability.

The preceding summary of issues only scratches the surface of the complex problems. But together with the analysis in earlier chapters, it underscores the assertion that another important subcategory of intergovernmental cooperation in providing for supranational surveillance entails the prudential oversight of financial activity and financial standards (2c in box 8-1).

Because financial standards and supervisory procedures differ so greatly across nations, intergovernmental cooperation in the first instance has to confront "design" issues. One such key issue is whether standards and prudential oversight at the world level should involve explicit harmonization of the differences across nations, or rather conformity to agreed minimum standards and procedures (chapter 4). Other prudential oversight issues directly involve monitoring or enforcement, such as how to encourage individual nations to conform to minimum or harmonized standards at the world level.

Intergovernmental cooperation on issues of prudential oversight and standards acquired a significant forward momentum in the late 1990s. That nascent cooperation, and the numerous unresolved issues, are summarized in chapter 10.

Managing Financial Crises

Because financial crises require the exercise of collective leadership, crisis management is a prominent potential function for intergovernmental financial governance (3 in box 8-1). Just as a national financial reservoir needs to be provided domestically with an offset to its propensity for crowd behavior and financial fragility, so may regional or the world financial systems benefit from procedures or institutions for promoting the collective interest in regional and world financial stability.

Cross-border finance differs significantly from financial transactions solely within a single nation's reservoir. The differences arise from the cross-border and cross-currency nature of assets and liabilities, their effects on the behavior of private sector institutions, and the potential complications thereby posed for collective governance. Storms originating in one national reservoir can spill across into other national reservoirs. Contagion and volatility in asset prices can be more widespread, and possibly have more virulent consequences. Entire national economies can come under suspicion or fall into explicit crisis (chapter 6).

The exercise of collective leadership in financial crises is thus much more complicated in a multination context than for a single economy. Because financial turbulence is not contained within individual national reservoirs, multiple national jurisdictions must be involved. No single national government can act unilaterally to assume primary responsibility for crisis management. The existing international institutions, furthermore, have relatively weak powers. In addition to all the other sources of cross-border complications, confusion thus arises about where leadership responsibility should be lodged and which venues should be used for its exercise.

Is collective governance for financial crises in a world of many nations somehow less necessary than within each nation's reservoir? If anything, the general case for leadership and possible emergency lending during a crisis is stronger at the global than at the national level. What is true is that the specifics are more complex and politically still more difficult.

Possible governmental actions in a multination world fall into three groups. Many measures will be undertaken within individual nations by national lenders of last resort acting independently. Cooperation among national governments can be catalyzed by delegating responsibilities to international organizations and giving those organizations the resources and powers necessary to act on behalf of national governments. Alternatively, intergovernmental cooperation can occur less formally through bilateral contacts or consultative groups, for example the Group of Seven.

Intergovernmental cooperation about politically delicate issues—crisis management is a prime example—tends often to occur through bilateral conversations or small consultative groups. To delegate primary responsibility for crisis management to one or more international financial organizations would entail giving them much greater powers than has so far been contemplated.

Should the management of financial crises be bundled together with the overall conduct of monetary policy and with responsibilities for prudential oversight of the financial system? Within individual nations the institutional answer to this question differs greatly from one jurisdiction to another (chapter 3). The nascent efforts at international governance for prudential oversight have been murky even about the allocation among different international organizations of prudential oversight responsibilities themselves (discussed in chapter 10). The question has scarcely been asked whether international dimensions of prudential oversight should ideally be cojoined with international aspects of crisis management and crisis lending. In practice, a limited consensus of sorts exists among the main national governments that the subjects of prudential oversight and lender-of-last resort activities should *not* be discussed together.

Although the functions of crisis management and crisis lending need not be performed together by the same institution within an individual nation, a presumption tends to exist that the two belong together. No such presumption exists for crises that spill across national borders. But, again, the question has scarcely been asked at a level above that of national governments. The diversity of institutional arrangements within nations can by itself create difficulties for cross-border cooperation among national lenders of last resort, whoever they may be. And for international organizations themselves, the boundaries between crisis management on the one hand and crisis lending on the other (if and when crisis lending is undertaken) are altogether unclear. International organizations such as the IMF, and to a lesser extent the Bank for International Settlements, have been asked at times to serve as an intermediary for actual crisis lending. Lending through international organizations has sometimes been the predominant form of crisis lending. On other occasions it has supplemented bilateral crisis lending by major governments themselves. Key decisions about crisis management, in contrast, have often been initially formulated in consultative groups or through bilateral contacts.

If international organizations are to be directly involved, which of the existing organizations should be responsible for exerting leadership and which organizations should extend the actual emergency loans? In the second half of the twentieth century, the IMF was most frequently pulled into discussions about cross-border financial crises and carried out the largest volume of crisis lending by any international organization. But the BIS was also significantly involved. The BIS itself participated in the network of central bank swap arrangements and served as a locus for consultations about, and coordination of, the national monetary policies of major central banks. Even the World Bank was pressed into providing emergency liquidity support during the Asian crises of 1997–98.

What should be the first priority response from national central banks to a burgeoning crisis with cross-border complications? The answer in logic is clear: as in the closed-economy analysis, the primary responsibility should be to make appropriate adaptations in overall monetary policy, thereby assuring sufficient liquefaction of national financial systems (and subsequent reversals once the crisis has passed). But in a multination world, the menu of problems to be considered when exercising this mandate is still more daunting than in a closed financial system.

Coordination among national lenders of last resort is the only feasible mechanism for achieving the requisite liquefaction. Neither the IMF nor the BIS nor any other international organization has the authority to create and extinguish reserve money. For the financial system of the world as a whole, it is not even clear which assets, if any, fully qualify as reserve money (discussed later in the chapter). Thus at the current time the world community, *acting through its existing international organizations*, has no ability to conduct the open-market operations that are the core feature of effective lender-of-last-resort assistance to a severely distressed financial system.

The possible need for emergency lending directly to individual private financial institutions is probably greater in an integrated world financial system than it would be in a single closed economy. The potential difficulties are at least as great. If such lending is required, the judgments and actions will fall mostly on the national lender of last resort in the jurisdiction in which the offices, especially the head office, of a troubled institution are located. The emergency lending may itself have to cross national borders. If the recipient of the lending is a multinational intermediary with establishments in several national jurisdictions, consultations among the central banks will be desirable. But actual sharing of the direct lending among the central banks would require delicate negotiations about the appropriate terms and proportionate shares.

The international financial organizations cannot extend emergency loans to private financial institutions. The IMF and the World Bank, for example, are legally empowered to lend only to national governments. As now envisaged by its member central banks, the BIS is not and should not be in the business of extending emergency loans to private financial institutions (as opposed to placing its short-term investments with private financial institutions in normal times). Whatever contingent need may exist for direct emergency lending to private financial institutions must be handled by the national lenders of last resort.

Similar remarks apply to efforts to "bail in" private lenders to troubled private debtors and to facilitate workouts for the liabilities of troubled private debtors. Acting within their own nations, the national lenders of last resort may find it desirable, though difficult, to try to arrange for concerted lending. A national lender of last resort has some scope for exercising leadership to encourage creditors and debtors in its jurisdiction to reach a cooperative agreement for rescheduling debts or for a more ambitious restructuring of the troubled debtor institution. When the balance sheet of a private sector debtor contains significant amounts of assets and liabilities in cross-border or cross-currency form, all the complex issues of cross-border bankruptcy and liquidation come into play. Cooperative consultations among the national lenders of last resort and national bankruptcy courts are then desirable. But the scope for actual international coordination of actions is limited. The international organizations as yet have no formal mandate and no effective powers to facilitate concerted lending or workouts for troubled private sector debtors. So far the most that they can contribute is to exert leadership behind the scenes and make public statements in support of the actions of the national authorities.

If a nation suffers an economywide accident or experiences an economywide mistake, thereby afflicting the entire nation with a financial crisis and the threat of national default, the national government itself is the most likely recipient of emergency financial assistance. Emergency lending to the government in such circumstances is a function where intergovernmental cooperation through bilateral contacts, consultative groups, or the international financial organizations becomes indispensable. Similar conclusions apply to the contingent needs to catalyze concerted cross-border lending by private sector lenders to the national government of the troubled economy or to facilitate a workout for the sovereign debt of the troubled government. There are of course no analogues for these functions within an individual nation's financial system. The possible need for these functions arises only because the world is a multination polity.

National governments wishing to arrange liability financing for balance-of-payments deficits and the governments whose nations run the counterpart surpluses have underlying rationales for sometimes engaging in lending intermediation among themselves, either bilaterally or through a lending intermediary such as the IMF. When the government of a troubled nation is the borrower during a financial crisis, and even more so if other national governments rather than private lenders are the crisis lenders, the issues of how to set the terms and conditions of emergency loans become especially difficult. Crisis conditions typically require speedy decisions. Protracted intergovernmental negotiations are often not feasible.

Trying to encourage concerted cross-border lending by private lenders to the governments of nations experiencing crises entails even more difficulties than efforts to bail in lenders within a national financial system. Exhortations to avoid bailouts and to encourage bailing in are murky guidelines even in a closed economy. The cross-border complications make such exhortations even harder to follow. Efforts to facilitate workouts for the sovereign debts of troubled governments are still more complex than analogous efforts to arrange workouts for private debtors.

Conclusions and recommendations about the difficult cross-border aspects of crisis management and crisis lending are presented in chapter 10.

Additional Roles for International Financial Governance

The features of international financial architecture reviewed above (functions 1 through 4 in the overall blueprint of box 8-1) are the collective-governance issues of dominant importance today. Chapters 9 and 10 concentrate on them and make recommendations for their future evolution.

Although they are secondary, the remaining functions 5 through 8 in the blueprint should be retained in one's lateral vision. With limited exceptions, they are not now prominent activities of international financial institutions. They are thus typically given short shrift in commentary about the international financial architecture. Yet as the world economy and financial system continue to become more integrated, these further dimensions of collective governance are likely to move closer to center stage.

Research and Information Dissemination

To facilitate cooperation in surveillance, consultative groups and international organizations need to collect, analyze, and disseminate a variety of statistical and other data about nations' cross-border and domestic transactions. The systemic analysis of such data and the dissemination of the resulting conclusions become still more important if consultative groups or international organizations extend their activities beyond the monitoring of traffic regulations to promoting adjustment and catalyzing coordination. In fact, an improved analytical understanding of interactions among national economies is a prerequisite for making progress on virtually every significant economic and financial issue, positive or normative, confronting national policymakers. Such an improved understanding is unquestionably required for more successful intergovernmental cooperation about exchange rates, payments imbalances, domestic macroeconomic policies, and the management of financial crises.[9]

In the twentieth century the governments of major nations took little direct interest in promoting an improvement in analytical understanding of the world economy and financial system. They did not push the staffs of international financial organizations to give this objective high priority. Such efforts as were made were sponsored by individual central banks, individual groups within international organizations, or research or academic institutions.

Even over a shorter run of the next decade, national governments ought to perceive that it would be beneficial to give higher priority to the need for basic research and information dissemination. Over the medium and long runs, this function for intergovernmental cooperation will almost surely have to be strengthened. One mechanism for promoting this function would be to give greater resources to staff groups at international organizations charged with the collective task of improving analytical knowledge about cross-border macroeconomic and financial interactions and diffusing that knowledge more widely.

Building more solid analytical foundations is the only reliable way to improve policy debate and render policy decisions more robust to error. Progress in model evaluation and model improvement, for example, is the ultimate answer to the problem of analytical models that compete and conflict with one another.[10]

Advising National Governments about Growth and Development in Conjunction with Lending Intermediation

Some nation states in today's world have reached considerably more complex stages of economic and financial development than others. Intensive use of recently invented technology is a salient feature of the more complex economies. Although critics debate whether the nations

9. The analytical basis for these conclusions is spelled out in Bryant (1995, chaps. 7 and 9).
10. Bryant (1995, chap. 7).

with modern technology and greater complexity merit the label *advanced,* most residents of the less-developed, poorer nations wish for growth and development that will catch them up to the wealthier nations.

When particular persons or private institutions in an individual nation, or the national government itself, perceive the nation lagging behind other nations, they may wish to request advice, training, or technical assistance from foreigners to promote growth and development at home. Private sector foreigners may be well placed to provide such advice and assistance. Inflows of private capital from abroad are often accompanied by it, particularly if they take the form of direct investment.

The focus of analysis here is *intergovernmental* cooperation. Intergovernmental advice and technical assistance for development promotion can, and often is, provided bilaterally, from one national government to another. But national governments have also established international organizations whose mandate includes the formulation and implementation of improved economic policies designed to foster growth and development.

Intergovernmental advice and technical assistance for development, whether bilateral from an individual foreign government or from regional or international organizations, are often extended in conjunction with official lending. A package of advice and technical assistance combined with intergovernmental lending is functionally similar to the composite functions associated with flows of private capital, particularly inward flows of direct investment. The cross-border transmission of knowledge and financial intermediation often go together. Both intergovernmental and private lending typically involve some form of conditionality, pressuring a borrower to adopt policies favored by the creditors.

Why would national governments establish and participate in an international organization that provides advice, training, and technical assistance? One set of reasons is associated with the close links between advice and actual lending. If an international organization has the resources to act as a lending intermediary, borrowing governments will have incentives to access such resources. The organization's advice to a borrowing government will be part and parcel of successful access. The staff of such an international organization might also be able to marshal knowledge and expertise that are not as readily available through other channels to the borrowing governments receiving the loans and associated advice. Recipient governments might find it politically more palatable to accept such help from a multilateral intergovernmental organization than from direct bilateral arrangements with other national governments. National governments participating in such an organization as donors of resources rather than as recipients of advice and resources might support the organization because of a presumption that the organization could pressure recipient governments to adopt "better" policies.

Contentious issues arise when intergovernmental cooperation assumes the function of providing advice and technical assistance for development. No normative consensus exists about the relative importance of goals for the different aspects of growth and development, even when analysis and advice are carefully tailored for the specifics of an individual nation's economy. Nor, for given goals, is there a professional consensus about the most effective policies to foster development.

Encouraging Redistribution of Income and Wealth in Conjunction with Lending Intermediation and Development Advice

Intergovernmental development advice could be offered independently of any intergovernmental lending intermediation. In practice, advice and lending are typically offered together. Similarly, development advice and lending could in principle be provided without any intention, explicit or implicit, to redistribute income and wealth. Yet, in practice, the camel's nose of redistribution is almost always inside the tent of intergovernmental lending intermediation.

Three types of collective-action arguments have been used to justify direct government involvement in financial activity within the financial systems of individual nations (chapter 3). One justification appeals to the correction of market failures. A second seeks to redirect financial resources to investments for which social returns are expected to exceed private returns. The third justification appeals straightforwardly to a goal of redistributing resources.

Any one or all of these arguments can be extended to the world financial system as a motive for governmental involvement in cross-border financial activity. Each of the three might justify lending operations of an international financial organization. The motive of correcting market failures applied to intergovernmental capital flows, as discussed already, is an explanation for why governments might choose to set up a multilateral lending intermediary for the liability financing of payments deficits. More generally, the correction-of-market-failure and higher-social-than-private-returns arguments can be applied to all flows of financial capital, private as well as governmental. Hence those arguments may be used to justify lending, carried out by international financial organizations, that seeks an allocation of saving and investment across nations somewhat modified from the allocation that would result from untrammeled private transactions. The third argument is again straightforwardly redistributive: in conjunction with its lending operations, an international financial organization could try to achieve a transfer of resources from richer to poorer nations (and perhaps also, within borrowing nations, a redistribution from richer to poorer citizens).

These various arguments used to justify lending intermediation by international financial organizations are at least as contentious at the world level as within an individual nation. The objective of encouraging a "better" distribution of income and wealth across nations is most controversial of all. Yet the maldistribution of the world's income and wealth attracts increasing attention and comment, as it should. The increasing backlash against globalization in many nations is closely related to dissatisfaction with its distributional consequences.

Those who want international organizations to encourage redistribution observe, in addition to their fundamental normative arguments, that it is not feasible for international organizations to be completely and genuinely "distribution-neutral" in their lending or in any other of their activities. Thus, according to the advocates of redistribution, the organizations should have an explicit mandate for the redistributive aspects of their operations.

The degree to which the preceding observation and its associated recommendation are valid depends, of course, on the particular international financial organization and its mandated functions.

The World Bank and regional development banks such as the Asian Development Bank, the African Development Bank, and the Inter-American Development Bank, are one type of intergovernmental lending intermediary. The formal mandates of those organizations emphasize—essentially give primacy to—the function of fostering economic growth and development. More recently, those organizations have also focused on the reduction of poverty. Implicitly if not explicitly, the development banks' mandates have a redistributive dimension.

The fact that the redistributive camel's nose is inside the tent can be most easily seen in the operations of a development bank if, rather than loans, an outright grant is extended. But even for loans made by development banks, the redistribution motive is likely to be important when a loan contains a large subsidy element (such as loan rates of interest far below market interest rates). The loans of the International Development Association, a lending window of the World Bank focused on the world's poorest nations, have a sizable grant component and are widely understood to be justified in part on redistributional grounds.[11]

For the development banks or any other organization giving primacy to the function of fostering growth and development, redistribution issues are unavoidable. Furthermore, even though in theory one can draw a line between explicit redistribution and the mere giving of advice and technical assistance, in practice the two functions get hopelessly entangled.

Consider the complex causal linkages between economic growth, poverty reduction, and explicit redistribution of income and wealth. Those linkages are hotly debated in development economics. Is the reduction of poverty a precondition, or at least an essential accompaniment, for sustainable economic growth? Alternatively, should a nation's strategy focus primarily on increasing growth for the aggregate economy as a whole, leaving poverty reduction for attention further down the road? Professional opinion seems to be moving in the direction of the former view, away from the latter, but no consensus yet exists. Even if poverty reduction is essential to growth, what are the most effective mechanisms for reducing poverty? Can a nation lift the incomes and wealths of its poorer citizens solely by augmenting their productivity, without resorting to explicit redistribution from the richer to the poorer? For entire nations, can income and wealth be lifted through improved productivity and growth performance, without resort to explicit redistribution from richer to poorer nations? Or might explicit redistribution be a necessary component of productivity-enhancing strategies, a sine qua non of poverty reduction?

These difficult questions are, to repeat, unavoidable for international organizations whose primary mandate is the promotion of growth and development. Now consider organizations whose primary responsibilities are *not* development promotion (that is, *not* functions 6 and 7 in box 8-1) but rather some combination of regime support, surveillance, crisis management, and the liability financing of payments deficits (1 through 5 in box 8-1). In particular, consider the International Monetary Fund.

The IMF is not (at least in its original design was not intended to be) an organization with primary responsibilities for advising national governments about growth and development or for fostering a redistribution of world income and wealth. Yet the IMF was definitely created as an

---

11. During 2001–02, a significant public debate began about whether lending by the World Bank and other international financial institutions should *primarily* or *exclusively* take the form of grants. The U.S. Treasury during this period supported the view that grants should be preferred to loans.

intergovernmental lending intermediary. In its lending intermediation function, the IMF was perceived as providing shorter-run liability financing for temporary payments imbalances—perhaps to prevent a financial crisis, perhaps to help manage such a crisis, but in any event only for *temporary* imbalances. Any development-advisory or redistributive roles for the IMF, if envisaged at all, were distinctly subsidiary. Evolution of the IMF since the early 1970s has significantly muddied the waters of its original mandate. (For further discussion, see the appendix at the end of the book.)

Assume for the moment that the IMF were formally assigned a mandate to pursue surveillance and crisis-management functions, to provide liability financing for overall payments deficits, *and* simultaneously to provide development advice and technical assistance. Suppose also an objective were to exist—implicit in a formal sense, but explicit in the minds of many poorer borrowing nations—to have the IMF's activities result de facto in a transfer of real resources from richer to poorer member nations. With such multiple objectives, the IMF would find it impossible to keep its various functions from blurring together.[12]

The conditionality and adjustment-promotion aspects of its lending-intermediary role inevitably require the IMF to monitor, and establish performance conditions for, the policies of nations that borrow from it. Those policies of a borrowing nation that have the most powerful impacts on its balance of payments will be especially salient in the IMF's conditionality and its monitoring. Yet no clear demarcation exists between national policies predominantly influencing the balance of payments and policies predominantly influencing long-run growth and development. Moreover, borrowing nations may often aspire to import capital to sustain a persisting current account deficit as well as possibly to borrow shorter-term funds to finance a temporary deficit in the overall balance of payments. Net use by a developing nation of savings from the rest of the world requires a current account deficit. From the perspective either of borrowing nations or the IMF, therefore, the functions of adjustment promotion and shorter-run liability financing of overall deficits are certain to become entangled with issues of longer-run development policies and

---

12. Such a combined mandate, partly formal and partly implicit, would not in fact be very different from the objectives that the IMF was actually pursuing at the outset of the twenty-first century (again, see the appendix for further discussion).

long-run development assistance. If longer-run development policies and long-run development assistance are in turn inseparably entangled with issues about the redistribution of incomes and wealth across nations, the camel's nose of redistribution will inevitably be, at least a little bit, inside the IMF's tent, not merely inside the tent at the World Bank and regional development banks.

Are a multiplicity of objectives for the IMF an appropriate mandate for that organization? *Should* the world community be asking the IMF, in addition to the development banks, to be deeply involved in the collective-governance functions of development promotion and resource redistribution? In any case, how should the mandate and functions of the IMF be differentiated from those of the World Bank and the regional development banks? Chapter 10 addresses those important questions.

Functions for an Evolving World Central Bank?

At the beginning of the twenty-first century, virtually no interest exists in intergovernmental cooperation for managing the reserve-money base of the world financial system or providing a clearinghouse for the intergovernmental settlement of payments imbalances (function 8 in box 8-1). The notion of a deliberate "world monetary policy" implemented by a world central bank can be imagined in the abstract, but of course is just a fantasy. The world aggregation of separate national monetary policies today does reflect periodic cross-border consultations among national central banks. But it very seldom benefits from explicit coordination.

Neither the IMF nor any other international institution has the capacity to create reserve money. This important fact features prominently in chapter 10's discussion of intergovernmental cooperation for managing cross-border crises in the world financial system.

Eventually, the world community will have to face issues of this type. Such issues will especially come to the fore if over time the number of separate national currencies declines, currency unions expand, and governments try to sharply reduce variability in exchange rates.

Within an individual nation, the central bank serves in part as a payments clearinghouse. Private financial institutions and other economic agents settle net imbalances in payments and receipts with each other when net debtors transfer claims on the central bank to net creditors. These claims are the central bank's reserve-money liabilities (currency and reserve deposits at the central bank). The payments mechanism within a nation typically combines hand-to-hand circulation of currency with clearing-house arrangements operated by the central bank for both currency and reserve deposits.

The central bank within a nation also functions in part as a lending intermediary. Some of the central bank's assets are loans to private financial institutions, made at the initiative of the private institutions. The terms and conditions associated with such loans (often referred to as made through the "discount window") vary widely from nation to nation. Typically, however, some or all of the loans help private financial institutions finance transitory shortfalls in liquid assets. The loans are accordingly temporary with short maturities. Such loans can typically be made in noncrisis periods as well as on an emergency basis during times of widespread financial crisis.

In addition to its functions within the nation as a payments clearing-house and lending intermediary, a national central bank also has an explicit ability secularly to expand or contract its total balance sheet, thereby creating or destroying reserve money. The central bank itself can take the initiative in implementing such transactions (for example, purchases or sales in the open market of already outstanding securities). The financial system within a nation is like an inverted pyramid balanced on a small apex, the balance sheet of the central bank. An incremental expansion or contraction of the central bank's balance sheet will stimulate an expansion or contraction of the pyramid as a whole, and hence ultimately exert significant influences on the pace of real economic activity and the general level of prices (chapter 2).

In a hypothetical closed economy that has no transactions with the rest of the world, one could regard part or all of the pyramid's apex, the central bank's liabilities, as *outside money*. In contrast, the liquid liabilities of private financial institutions to each other and to nonfinancial economic agents would be *inside money*. For the world financial system as a whole, it is helpful to make an analogous analytical distinction between outside reserve assets and inside reserve assets.[13] One also needs to distinguish between *reserve centers*, a small number of nations serving as a primary financial center, and all the remaining nations, referred to for analytical convenience as the *periphery*.

---

13. The distinction between outside money and inside money was developed for closed-economy monetary theory by Gurley and Shaw (1960).

Suppose periphery nations regard demand deposits denominated in the currency unit of some particular nation as a primary international means of payment. Suppose the periphery nations typically hold interest-earning liquid assets denominated in that currency unit as part of their standard reserve assets and are prepared to accumulate further amounts of such assets when running overall surpluses in their balances of payments. A nation whose currency unit is widely used in this way—a reserve center— will also be one of the economically largest and politically dominant countries. A reserve-center nation will have large amounts of *reserve liabilities* (the liability counterparts of the reserve-currency reserve assets held by periphery nations). The United States is the most important reserve center in today's world.[14]

Outside reserve assets are assets accepted for settlements among national governments that are not at the same time a liability of some governmental or private economic unit resident in a particular nation. Gold held by monetary authorities and special drawing rights (SDRs, an asset created through the Special Drawing Rights Department of the IMF) are the two important examples currently in existence.[15] In contrast, *inside reserve assets* are assets accepted for settlements among national governments that are, in addition to being a reserve asset for the holding country, a liability for some governmental or private economic unit in another nation.

Liquid assets denominated in a reserve currency held by the central banks or governments of periphery nations are inside, rather than outside, reserve assets since a reserve-center nation has a counterpart liability corresponding to the asset owned by the holding central bank or government. Reserve-currency assets held by periphery nations are quantitatively the most important type of inside reserves.

14. Historically, the use of a nation's currency as an international means of payment and store of value has accompanied use of the currency as an official reserve asset. A reserve-center nation therefore also tends to have large liquid liabilities to, and claims on, *private* foreign residents. The United Kingdom was the primary reserve center in the world in the second half of the 1800s and early 1900s. Before the introduction of the euro in the European Monetary Union, the deutsche mark served to some extent as a reserve currency, and Germany was a secondary reserve center. The euro is likely to be a reserve currency in the first several decades of the twenty-first century. Japan has also had a limited role as a reserve center.

15. SDRs in normal times are not a liability of any nation (and in a formal sense are not even a liability of the IMF). Liabilities would arise in connection with SDRs only if an IMF member nation terminated its participation in the SDR Department, if the SDR Department were liquidated, or if the IMF itself were liquidated.

If one can imagine a protracted political evolution that shifts the world close to mutual governance through strong supranational institutions (the lower right corner in figure 7-2), one can also imagine a world central financial institution eventually being given responsibilities to manage outside money for the world as a whole in a manner analogous to the role played within a nation by the national central bank. A possible fulcrum for such world management could be the quantity of outside reserve assets. In particular, an international organization acting in accord with the cooperative decisions of its member central banks and national governments could create or destroy outside reserve assets, thereby influencing the behavior of the world economy as a whole. The creation and destruction of outside reserve assets could also be an essential part of developing a genuine world lender-of-last-resort capacity for handling cross-border financial crises.

Will such a function for managing reserve money on a world scale be economically needed? For example, will a secular growth in outside reserve assets eventually be needed to sustain secular growth in the whole pyramid of the world financial system? Alternatively, could stable growth of the world financial pyramid be assured merely by expansion in inside reserve assets and other types of inside financial assets? If not for secular growth, is international cooperative management of the base of the world financial pyramid necessary or desirable for some other reason, for example to manage systemic turbulence in the world financial system?

Suppose for a moment that the international traffic regulations agreed by national governments might eventually come to include guidelines for significantly constraining the variability of exchange rates, including exchange rates among the world's most important currencies. For example, suppose nations were to accept obligations to maintain market exchange rates within fairly narrow margins around reference par values, with the reference values themselves changing only slowly. (Such arrangements would be target reference zones, one of the "managed-pegging" exchange regimes identified in chapter 6.) Suppose further that nations accepted guidelines to keep their goods and financial markets relatively open to the rest of the world and agreed not to impose incremental restrictions on cross-border transactions without prior consultation with and endorsement by an international organization.

Under such traffic regulations, each national government would pay close attention to the level of its reserve assets in relation to other national macroeconomic variables.[16] Transitory declines in reserve assets would be desirable from time to time to finance temporary deficits. But most if not all nations would seek to have their reserve assets grow secularly. Reserve-center nations would have to be concerned with their *net* external reserve position and would seek to have their holdings of outside reserve assets grow secularly, the more so the faster their reserve liabilities increased over time.

These macroeconomic preferences and behavior patterns would be translated into effective demands for reserve assets (including the composition of reserves between outside reserves and inside reserve claims on reserve centers). With no change or a decline in the world stock of outside reserves, individual nations would not be able to experience desired increases in reserve assets except to the extent that other nations experienced desired or undesired declines.[17] An incremental growth in the world stock of outside reserves, however, would make it possible for many more nations to achieve their ex ante preferences for reserve increases without forcing other nations to experience unwanted declines. Insufficient growth in world outside reserves would impart a contractionary bias to the world financial system and the world economy. Excessive expansion in world outside reserves would foster world inflation. Hence cooperative management of the change in world outside reserve assets might be able to mitigate the tendency of noncooperative national decisions about reserves to produce macroeconomic outcomes mutually agreed to be undesirable.

This line of reasoning is less intuitively plausible if one makes quite different assumptions about international traffic regulations. For example, the argument needs amendment for a world monetary environment with few if any binding constraints on exchange rate variability. The analytical issue is whether changes in the stock of world outside reserve assets continue to have significant impacts on world macroeconomic outcomes when many nations practice managed floating of their currencies. If the line of reasoning were still broadly valid even for a world with substantial variability in exchange rates, cooperative management of world outside reserves could

---

16. Each national government would also pay close attention to its potential access to foreign borrowing for the purpose of liability financing of prospective overall payments deficits. The line of reasoning in the text can be readily amended to take into account the interrelations between access to foreign borrowing on the one hand and the holding and use of reserve assets on the other.

17. The preferences of reserve-center countries would be expressed as desires for a gross increase in outside reserve assets related to any gross increase in reserve liabilities, which in turn would imply desired changes in net reserve positions.

contribute to better world macroeconomic outcomes than would otherwise be possible.[18]

In principle, a world central financial organization could facilitate still other collective efforts to manage the world financial system. Suppose, for example, that periphery nations were to develop a preference for holding a larger proportion of their international reserves in the form of outside, rather than inside, reserve assets. Suppose the reserve-center nations in whose currencies the inside reserves were denominated were prepared to cooperate in effectuating this shift in asset preferences. The international organization might then play a catalytic role in what has been termed the consolidation of reserves. In one possible approach, it could issue new amounts of outside reserve assets to the periphery nations, who in exchange would surrender inside reserve assets of equivalent value; the international organization could itself hold these inside reserve claims. To the extent that such consolidation occurred, the world financial system seen from the asset side would have experienced a "substitution" of outside for inside reserves. The reserve-center nations would continue to have and to service reserve liabilities (the counterpart of the claims of the international organization). Those liabilities, however, could differ in detailed characteristics and could have somewhat different behavioral consequences than the former inside reserve liabilities to individual national governments.

As with the other aspects of the potential management of world reserve money by an international organization, possibilities for the consolidation of reserve assets are not now even being given scholarly, much less governmental, attention. The world monetary system is unambiguously dominated by multiple reserve currencies. The U.S. dollar is the single most important, but periphery nations also hold significant amounts of European euros, Japanese yen, and a few other major currencies in their reserves. Gold has sunk to the bottom of the barrel as a reserve asset. SDRs are far out of favor. Practically speaking, the world thus has no effective outside reserve asset. This multiple-reserve-currency system of exclusively inside reserves is potentially unstable. But that potential lies below the horizon.

---

18. The preceding paragraphs presumed that changes in the balance sheet of a world central financial organization would take the form of changes in the stock of outside reserves. A full analysis would also need to consider changes in the organization's balance sheet associated with changes in inside assets. The lending operations of a multilateral intermediary generate inside loan claims held by the governments of surplus countries. Depending on how the inside loan claims are packaged, and hence regarded by the holding countries, the inside claims may even be regarded as reserve assets. This creation of inside claims can also have effects on world economic activity and inflation.

9 Priorities for Architectural Reform: Supranational Surveillance and IMF Lending

A collective-governance utilities infrastructure is essential if a nation's financial reservoir is to function efficiently and prove resilient when buffeted by storms. The world financial system does not yet have well-established utilities infrastructures at regional or worldwide levels. The highest priorities for short- and medium-run reform of the international financial architecture are to develop and strengthen the nascent international infrastructures that began to evolve in the last decades of the twentieth century.

Needed enhancements in the world utilities infrastructure fall into three groups. First, national governments and international organizations should upgrade the collective supranational surveillance of cross-border traffic regulations and of nations' macroeconomic, exchange rate, and balance-of-payments policies. Concurrently, they should streamline and strengthen intergovernmental lending intermediation for the liability financing of payments deficits in noncrisis periods. That group of architectural reforms encompasses, for shorthand reference, changes in *supranational surveillance and lending intermediation*.

A second group likewise entails enhanced collective surveillance. Governments and international organizations should foster further major improvements in the prudential oversight of financial activity and in the associated design and monitoring of financial standards. For short, the improvements are changes in *prudential financial oversight* (or simply *prudential oversight*).

The third priority group comprises enhancements in the cooperative management by governments and international organizations of financial turbulence—both domestic and cross-border. Needed procedures and capacities include the contingent provision of emergency lending during financial crises, the handling of moral hazard difficulties, and the involvement of private financial institutions in concerted lending. This group of improvements comprises, for short, reforms in *crisis management*.

All three types of reform—supranational surveillance and lending intermediation, prudential oversight, and crisis management—are vital. Chapter 8 summarized general analytical points about these functions for international collective governance. The task in this chapter and the next is to dig more deeply into the three reform areas and to highlight policy recommendations for making incremental progress.[1]

Linkages among the reform areas can be understood with an analogy from domestic collective governance. The cooperative management of financial crises is like the activities of firefighting departments in local governments charged with extinguishing unexpected blazes. Surveillance at a supranational level over the economic and financial policies of national governments is akin to the activities at a local level of police departments, traffic regulators, and municipal agencies charged with licensing, inspection, health, and safety standards. Supranational surveillance seeks to encourage compliance with international norms and intergovernmental agreements. It monitors cross-border traffic regulations. Surveillance is exercised in noncrisis and crisis conditions alike.

Police inhibit crime. Traffic regulators discourage traffic violations. A major purpose of supranational surveillance is to inhibit nations from deliberately or inadvertently pursuing policies likely to cause economic disruption for others. Put the other way round, collective surveillance aspires to encourage sound, preventive policies. The philosophy that underpins preventive policies is the catechism about hurricanes followed by sailing-ship captains: when asked what to do when finding yourself to the wind-

---

1. Reforms in supranational surveillance and lending intermediation fall under the functions 2a, 2b, and 4 in box 8-1. Reforms in prudential oversight fall under 2c, and in crisis management under 3. Self-evidently, progress in the three areas for reform emphasized in the text is not tantamount to denigrating the function of regime design and maintenance (1, box 8-1). Regime design and maintenance underpins all the other dimensions of international collective governance.

ward of an island in a hurricane, the appropriate answer is "you do NOT find yourself to the windward of an island in a hurricane!"

Recent policy concern with cross-border finance has been driven by the disruptions stemming from financial crises. Skillful crisis management is essential. It is thus one of the three areas on which the analysis concentrates. Sound economic management in noncrisis conditions, however, is even more critical. Choosing sound policies in normal times can substantially reduce the probability that crises will occur. Enhancements for the two types of collective surveillance of national policies thus should have the highest priority among all proposed changes. Intergovernmental lending intermediation to facilitate the adjustment of macroeconomic imbalances in national economies, most notably lending by the IMF, can beneficially reinforce such surveillance. More than anything else, in other words, architectural reform should emphasize the *prevention* of economic and financial crises. The primary preoccupation should be the encouragement of healthy growth and financial stability—*prosperity management* rather than crisis management.

Among the international financial institutions, the IMF and intergovernmental consultative groups loom most important in the analysis to follow. The reforms needed for crisis management and for supranational surveillance and lending intermediation presume central roles for the IMF and the national governments who are the dominant IMF shareholders. Reforms in prudential financial oversight, in contrast, involve numerous international organizations and consultative groups. One reason for differentiating prudential oversight from the macroeconomic dimensions of supranational surveillance and lending intermediation is its greater variety of institutions and the specialized complexity of their activities. The needed architectural reforms for supranational surveillance and lending intermediation are summarized in this chapter. Reforms for prudential financial oversight and crisis management are summarized in chapter 10.[2]

---

2. The reforms are not presented in specialized detail. Backstopping for the conclusions and recommendations is found instead in the companion volumes, comprising the series *Pragmatic Choices for International Financial Governance.* Policy issues and choices for supranational surveillance and lending intermediation are discussed in *Crisis Prevention and Prosperity Management for the World Economy.* The other two companion volumes, *Prudential Oversight and Standards for the World Financial System* and *Crisis Management for the World Financial System* supply specialized analyses of the policy alternatives in the other two reform areas. General readers requiring more supporting argument or more extensive background than can be found in chapters 8 through 10, and of course policy specialists who have doubts about the conclusions summarized, should consult the companion volumes.

Before proceeding, a final introductory remark about the terms *supranational* and *international* is appropriate. My approach to international financial governance seeks a middle ground between polar extremes. Hence even my use of adjectives to modify collective governance reflects the preference for being in the middle of the road. The governance optimists who favor sweeping institutionalist reform for the world in effect advocate genuine supranational collective governance. But with very few exceptions, genuine and strong supranational governance is not politically feasible. It is not, at least not yet, even desirable. I have therefore been consistent in making recommendations for international rather than supranational governance.

In contrast, I often speak of supranational surveillance rather than international surveillance. *Collective surveillance* is a subset of the potential functions for international collective governance. The surveillance dimensions of collective governance that can be envisaged today, furthermore, are weak precursors of more extensive and more muscular forms of collective governance. The surveillance activities of the IMF and other international financial institutions merit the adjective supranational. That use of language is appropriate because of the nature and content of collective surveillance, which by definition requires a perspective above the level of national governments. But supranational in the context of surveillance definitely does *not* presume that those who exercise surveillance have significant independent authority to influence national governments. Quite the contrary. Surveillance in practice so far has been, and even when strengthened with incremental reforms in the near future will be, only tentative and shaped by "soft" rather than "hard" guidelines. The real exercisers of supranational surveillance are the national governments themselves. They choose to act collectively not because they agree to bend to the will of an independent authority above them but because their mutual interests require such cooperation.[3]

---

3. The other context in which the book uses the adjective supranational is when referring to problems (for example, as in the phrase "cross-border and supranational problems that require collective action by national governments"). The literal meaning of supranational stems from the Latin *supra*, meaning "over" or "beyond" or "transcending." It would be misleading to speak of supranational governance in the sense of governance *over* national governments. Conversely, the nuances of supranational are appropriate when speaking of surveillance *over* national governments or problems that *transcend* the level of nation states.

Supranational Surveillance

The basic rationales for collective surveillance have already been summarized (chapters 7, 8). National governments cooperate because decentralized national decisions ignoring cross-border spillovers can produce outcomes inferior to those attainable through informed collective action. Yes, efforts to cooperate can sometimes lead to government failures and prove counterproductive. If intelligently pursued and not overly ambitious, however, intergovernmental cooperation can foster mutual interests. Cooperative decisions presume compliance. Processes and institutions for surveillance facilitate compliance.

The IMF: The Main Conduit for Macroeconomic Surveillance

A gradual strengthening of supranational collective surveillance of macroeconomic policies, exchange rates, and traffic regulations for cross-border financial transactions is the single most promising way for national governments and the world as a whole to foster prosperity management—to prevent crises and to promote a healthy evolution of the world economy. More than any other international institution, the IMF has authority for the collective surveillance of national policies. The IMF also has the greatest potential for fostering the gradual strengthening that is required. If the IMF's mandate is appropriately defined, its principal functions thus should be to serve as a traffic monitor, an adjustment referee, and a coordination catalyst endowed with supplementary lending powers.

The position advocated in this chapter, that surveillance of national policies should be at the core of the IMF's mandate, differs from today's conventional wisdom. It also differs, at least in emphasis, from the vision of the institution held by most of its founders at the end of World War II. The functions of collective surveillance were more implicit than explicit in the original IMF Articles of Agreement. Yet in subsequent decades national governments did support a gradual strengthening of the surveillance responsibilities of the IMF and other international financial institutions.[4]

The IMF's surveillance of nations' exchange rate arrangements, never strong, was weakened further by the 1971–73 collapse of the Bretton

---

4. The original Bretton Woods concept of the IMF and its subsequent historical evolution are summarized in the appendix at the end of the book.

Woods par value system. But the compromise amendment of the IMF's Articles of Agreement that went into force in 1978 preserved the principle that exchange rates are properly the subject of scrutiny by the IMF. (The revised version of Article IV states that "the Fund shall exercise firm surveillance over the exchange rate policies of members, and shall adopt specific principles for the guidance of all members with respect to those policies.")

The primary impetus for gradually strengthening the IMF's surveillance activities came not from its residual authority over exchange rate arrangements, but from the obligations of member nations, under other provisions of Article IV, to consult with the IMF about the entire range of their macroeconomic and external sector policies. Over time this consultations process has gradually acquired greater muscle and deeper analytical support. The IMF has also devoted increasing resources to assessments of the economic outlook and financial market developments for the world as a whole. The biannual reports on the *World Economic Outlook* and the annual report on *International Capital Markets*, for example, illustrate IMF efforts to develop a systemic perspective that can identify inconsistencies and problems in national policies and therefore signal the need for possible adjustments.

Supranational Surveillance by Other International Institutions

Supranational surveillance is also conducted by international institutions other than the IMF. The Bank for International Settlements with its associated committees is the key venue for surveillance discussions among the major central banks. BIS monthly meetings provide a forum in which the central banks come together to consult about issues of mutual interest and to develop their own systemic perspective. When crises have buffeted foreign exchange and national financial markets, BIS meetings have been influential in designing joint initiatives to be undertaken by the central banks. Current conventional wisdom holds that a nation's central bank should have a large measure of political independence from the remainder of the nation's governance structure. So long as that consensus prevails, the BIS is likely to remain an influential conduit for supranational surveillance of national monetary policies.

The Economic Policy Committee of the OECD and its working parties (especially Working Party Three) have served as an institutional channel for exchanges of projections and policy analyses among OECD member governments. In the 1960s and 1970s, and perhaps into the 1980s, these committees may have been more influential venues for nascent collective surveillance than either the IMF or the BIS. The OECD staff began at an earlier date than the IMF to prepare, and then to publish, an overview world "outlook" of aggregate demand and international trade, including an effort to judge the consistency of nations' projections. By the 1990s these OECD venues waned somewhat relative to the IMF and the BIS as a locus of surveillance activity for macroeconomics, exchange rates, and payments imbalances.

The annual economic summit meetings of heads of state and the periodic meetings of finance ministers of the Group of Seven nations are the most influential examples of intergovernmental consultative groups not tied directly to international financial organizations. The G-7, or a somewhat expanded variant of the G-7, is virtually certain to survive for some time and to be a dominant locus of efforts by the largest nations to reach cooperative decisions about international financial issues. Other consultative groups, such as the Group of Twenty ("systemically important" countries) and the Group of Twenty-Four (developing nations), have more uncertain futures as mechanisms for surveillance and intergovernmental cooperation.[5]

A Systemic Perspective: The Core of Effective Surveillance

If supranational surveillance could focus merely on cross-border transactions and on other external sector variables such as exchange rates and imbalances in national balances of payments, its scope would not extend into domestic matters and thereby raise fears about infringements of national sovereignty. Although such an approach would be less contentious politically, such a restricted scope would be economically illogical. Virtually all aspects of individual national economies are now non-independent. Hence effective surveillance must examine all national policies having significant influences on foreign nations, including the budgetary and tax policies of fiscal authorities and the monetary policies of central banks that are ostensibly "domestic."

More than anything else, therefore, skillful supranational surveillance needs to develop a *systemic perspective* that offsets the inevitable biases in the perspectives of individual national governments. A systemic perspective

---

5. Meetings of the IMF's International Monetary and Financial Committee have played a significant role, and may play an even more important role in the future, in reinforcing consultations taking place through the G-7 and the annual economic summits. The functions and compositions of the G-20, G-24, and other consultative groups are discussed further in the appendix.

seeks to identify ex ante inconsistencies in national policies and then to foster cooperative reconciliation procedures that would be mutually preferable to sequences of decentralized decisions. Ongoing international organizations are more likely than intergovernmental consultative groups to carefully formulate a systemic perspective. A coherent systemic perspective is a necessary (though not a sufficient) condition for an international organization to act effectively as an adjustment referee and coordination catalyst.

Hard Law versus Soft Law

Lawyers often debate the merits of so-called soft law and hard law. Where social consensus exists, it is argued, hard law is often to be preferred. In principle, supranational surveillance could be more effective if it could be underpinned by hard, rather than soft, guidelines. For example, the IMF's surveillance over macroeconomic policies and exchange rates is severely limited by the softness of the definition of nations' "good behavior" and their underlying obligations.

But a yearning for hard law should be tempered by pragmatism. When social consensus does not exist, hard law is frequently unreachable. For those not uncommon circumstances, society may often have to choose between no law or soft law—between no traffic regulations or fuzzy traffic regulations, between no guidelines at all or guidelines that enunciate principles but fail to facilitate clear monitoring and firm enforcement.

Prospects over the shorter run for clearer guidelines for supranational surveillance are not bright. Harder guidelines are certainly a worthy aspiration for the longer run. Without stronger analytical underpinnings and harder guidelines for surveillance, it will not be possible to have any institution act truly effectively as a traffic monitor, an adjustment referee, or a coordination catalyst. But soft, rather than hard, guidelines are the only feasible possibility for the time being.

Confidentiality and Transparency

Confidentiality is a delicate and controversial feature of surveillance consultations. Policy dialogues between a government and the IMF in an Article IV consultation, for example, may not be frank and meaningful without confidentiality. Effective surveillance requires extensive access to a government's data, analyses, and projections. But that information is often politically or market sensitive. Understandably, a nation's government prefers to decide itself what information and policy advice is, and is not, made available to a world public.

Transparency—dissemination of information about the procedures, conclusions, and differences of view involved in surveillance—is the opposite side of the coin of confidentiality. Disclosure of relevant, accurate information contributes to an efficient allocation of resources by ensuring that economic agents have sufficient information to identify risks and to distinguish the circumstances of one enterprise, or one nation, from those of others. Disclosure shapes market expectations and thereby often reinforces the effectiveness of sound government policies. The beneficial effects of information disclosure are no less important in enhancing the effectiveness of supranational surveillance.

The dilemma is that transparency and confidentiality must be traded off against each other. Because of the beneficial effects of transparency, confidentiality should be restricted to circumstances where the balance of benefits and costs argues strongly against information disclosure. To gain the benefits from confidentiality, transparency and full disclosure of information sometimes must be limited. The general dilemma, found in many parts of life, arises in an acute form for supranational surveillance of nations' economic policies.

The international financial organizations in the very early years of their existence were not notably forthcoming in their disclosure of information. The governments that had created them did not push for wide public dissemination of detailed information about their activities. To some observers outside of governments, the international organizations appeared as aloof and opaque, even secretive. But views within governments and the organizations themselves have gradually shifted about the appropriate balance between confidentiality and transparency. A drift toward more transparency—evident for the IMF, the BIS, the World Bank, and the OECD—was especially pronounced in the last years of the 1990s.

The expansion in information available about the international financial organizations and their nascent supranational surveillance seems not well known to many commentators about reform of the international financial architecture. Yet it is a striking fact that major improvements have been made in the transparency and accountability of international financial institutions. Considerable further progress is possible and highly desirable. But commentary should at least recognize the progress that has already been made.

The benefits of greater disclosure and transparency have on balance substantially outweighed the costs and risks. Most observers do not feel that confidentiality, where constructive and desirable, has been significantly undermined by the drift toward greater transparency. Instances have not come to light, for example, in which the release of IMF analysis of a nation's economy or disclosure of communications with a national government has created significant moral hazard. (In theory, extensive IMF disclosure could lead private foreign investors and private creditors of a nation to rely on the IMF to issue warnings and identify risks rather than undertake their own risk analysis.)

Surveillance over Exchange Rates and Exchange Regimes

The subject of exchange rate regimes and and exchange rate policies pervades popular discussions of reforming the international financial architecture. Many commentators regard the choice of an exchange regime as the single most important policy decision to be made by national governments. Some go even further to presume that if a nation makes the supposedly all-important choice of exchange regime correctly, then other national choices and other dimensions of architectural reform will pale into secondary significance.

That emphasis on exchange regimes is excessive and misguided. Chapter 11 summarizes the more balanced approach that an individual nation should take in choosing an exchange regime and integrating the regime into its overall macroeconomic policies. The appropriate stance for supranational surveillance of exchange regimes is a straightforward extension of that more balanced approach.

The IMF and other international forums for surveillance should eschew the extremist conclusions that afflict this subject. Effective surveillance should certainly avoid the widespread tendency to disproportionately stress the choice of exchange regime. Any conceivable exchange regime is subject to uncertainties and potential instabilities, especially if a nation's domestic policies are unsound or if foreign financial markets lose confidence in the nation. Good exchange rate policy is context dependent. No single exchange regime will work well for all nations in all circumstances at all times.

Nations can readily err by pegging their exchange rates or excessively constraining rate changes when future developments will probably dictate adjustment in the rates. But if domestic policies are unsound or if foreign financial markets lose confidence, floating exchange rates will not prevent trouble.

Recently fashionable conventional wisdom has asserted that intermediate exchange regimes are bound to be unstable and that the only regimes viable for an extended period are the extremes of a pure flex (untrammeled floating) or a hard fix (currency-board arrangements or participation in a currency union). But that view is not compelling. Just as for an individual nation, for the world financial system as a whole the manner and degree of exchange rate variability are not, in themselves, the financial policy issues of primary importance.

Surveillance and Coordination of National Policies

Coordination of nations' policies, especially if activist, is an ambitious form of intergovernmental cooperation. As intergovernmental cooperation evolves further, the governments of the larger nations should give more attention to possibilities for explicit coordination of their economic policies. Supranational surveillance will be increasingly asked to serve as a catalyst for that coordination.

Coordination entails the self-interested mutual adjustment of behavior. It is not a synonym for altruism or benevolence. Nor should coordination be confused with "harmonization." One would not normally expect, for example, that coordinated national monetary and fiscal policies would be harmonized. With coordination, national governments will not necessarily adjust policies in the same direction, with every government contracting or every government expanding. If confronted with different disturbances hitting their economies, sound policymaking and effective coordination typically require governments to do different things.

Some analysts believe that the risks and costs of possible government failures resulting from ambitious efforts at coordination could greatly outweigh the potential benefits. But that assessment is too pessimistic and not supported by empirical evidence. The potential benefits deserve at least as much emphasis as the potential risks. In selected circumstances and if wisely conducted, attempts at coordination by national governments can advance the common interests of their citizens.

Belief in subsidiarity as a principle for collective governance (chapter 4) supports a favorable bias toward coordination of national policies. Subsidiarity can act as a safeguard inhibiting national governments from trying to coordinate policies with excessive zeal. With subsidiarity as a guideline, governments will attempt coordination only when strong evidence is accumulated suggesting that cross-border spillover externalities are causing major difficulties and that a feasible adjustment of national policies seems likely to improve the outlook significantly. Analysts in the IMF and other international financial organizations who aspire to catalyze effective supranational surveillance should likewise be guided by the principle of subsidiarity.

Analytical Uncertainty and the Need for Research Supporting Surveillance

Analytical uncertainty, not the risk of government failure, is the primary reason to be skeptical about an explicit coordination of national macroeconomic policies. Coordination cannot be more successful—and international financial institutions cannot serve more effectively as a catalyst for such coordination—in the absence of enhanced analytical knowledge as a foundation for the process.

Not only are deficiencies in analytical knowledge an obstacle to policy coordination. They are the single greatest impediment to sound policymaking within national governments. They inhibit development of clearer guidelines for all the dimensions of supranational surveillance. Policymakers and their advisers have limited knowledge about the functioning of their own national economies. Their understanding of how national economies interact to generate regional and global economic outcomes is still more imperfect. Although perhaps slightly better, the analytical understanding at the international financial organizations of these interactions is still highly uncertain.

Weakness in analytical understanding tellingly reveals itself in *model uncertainty*—the prevalence of competing analytical models and no consensus about which of the models may be the least inadequate approximation of the actual relationships that will in reality determine actual outcomes. The competing claims of rival models and the other dimensions of analytical uncertainty would not vex policymaking and supranational surveillance so greatly if analysis could safely downplay uncertainty. But in any practical policymaking or surveillance situation, it is well known that analysis cannot safely downplay uncertainty.

The macroeconomic models that pose the greatest analytical difficulties and that are most uncertain are those attempting to study the interactions among multiple national economies. Such models are of course the frameworks required as an analytical foundation for supranational surveillance.

Because improvements in analytical understanding are a prerequisite for better policymaking and for enhanced surveillance, one might think that this fundamental point would be emphasized in discussions about reforming the international financial architecture. Surprisingly, it seldom receives attention. National governments, even those of major nations, have taken little direct interest in promoting an improvement in the analytical under-standing of macroeconomic and financial interactions among national economies. Nor have they put pressure on international institutions to make this objective a high priority for staff work.

Governmental support for improving the analytical foundations under-pinning supranational surveillance will probably remain anemic in the short run. But it should be strengthened over the medium and long runs. A key feature of such support would be the establishment of an interna-tional staff group charged with the collective task of improving analytical knowledge and diffusing that knowledge more widely. The IMF (or per-haps some combination of the IMF, the World Bank, BIS, and the OECD) is the most logical institutional locus for this staff support. Analytical foun-dations are not a sexy subject for policymakers or general publics. But over the longer run, building more solid analytical foundations is the only reli-able way to render policy decisions and supranational surveillance more robust to error.

By tradition and comparative advantage, society looks to the academic community for new knowledge to be created and analytical foundations to be rebuilt. For cross-border macroeconomic interactions, as in general, the academic community should play an important role in improving analyti-cal foundations. But policymakers cannot count solely on the academic community to make sufficient progress on its own.[6] To complement and supplement academic research, policymakers need to make adequate resources available for officially commissioned research in support of strengthened supranational surveillance.

Two types of research should be commissioned. One would focus on topics figuring prominently in discussions about current policy or policy in the immediate future. Analyses of controversial aspects of the current

---

6. Most academic researchers have only limited knowledge of the ways in which unresolved ana-lytical issues surface in policy discussions. Without sustained contact with the policy community, researchers are much less likely to condition their research in ways helpful to policymakers. Even more important, the structure of incentives and rewards for advancement in the academic community inhibit academics from giving priority attention to the analytical needs of policymakers. Fellow academics accord much higher praise, and give much greater weight in decisions about university appointments, to new theoretical wrinkles published in prestigious academic journals than to thoughtful efforts to refine empirical models by better application of existing analytical knowledge. Even the small group of academic economists who develop forecasting and simulation models usable for policy analysis are reluctant to devote their limited resources to model validation and model evaluation. Few academics hand out kudos to researchers who do the hard work of identifying the deficiencies in existing analyt-ical frameworks or who carefully try to remedy inadequacies in existing data sources.

economic outlook, for individual economies or the world system, would dominate the work. The second type would have a longer horizon. Projects would be chosen because of their potential importance as building blocks for improved analytical foundations, not because they could be expected to have an immediate payoff.

As an example of the longer-horizon type, analysts would be charged with careful evaluation of the strengths and weaknesses of alternative national operating regimes for domestic monetary and fiscal policies. Such research would also seek to develop alternative specifications of presumptive guidelines for the supranational surveillance of the regimes. The research would begin with quite simplified specifications of regimes and guidelines before more complex and realistic alternatives could be examined. Model evaluations and comparisons would inevitably be at the core of this work.[7]

As a second example, analysts would be charged with defining and estimating alternative concepts of equilibrium exchange rates and equilibrium interest rates (national and global). What normative and analytical assumptions have to be specified if policymakers wish to identify when a nation's exchange rate is "misaligned" or "overvalued" or "undervalued"? How can policymakers tell when a nation's real interest rate (or "the global" real interest rate) is too high or too low? Under what circumstances might a policymaker conclude that an exchange rate or an interest rate should be judged "excessively variable"?

Analysts have great difficulty in supplying nontautological answers to these questions. A carefully defined equilibrium rate must be characterized as a dynamic time path rather than a single value. Any specific calculation of an equilibrium path necessarily makes use of normative assumptions and therefore cannot be "neutral" about policymakers' goals. Moreover, estimates of equilibrium paths, for exchange rates or interest rates, are inescapably contingent on the particular theoretical or empirical model(s) in the context of which the estimates are made. Because estimates are both goal contingent and model contingent, a multiplicity of useful calculations of equilibrium paths may exist. Analysts and policymakers have only begun to clarify the relevant concepts and empirical procedures, despite their clear importance for national policy decisions and intergovernmental cooperation.

---

7. This research would constitute an intensification of the "rule analysis" discussed in Bryant (1995, chap. 4) and Bryant, Hooper, and Mann (1993).

Collection and publication of statistical data, for national economies and for the global economy, are an important collective good supplied by international institutions. Data collection and publication always require improvement and rethinking. Even within nations the quality and availability of data leave much to be desired. As regional economies and the world economy become still more integrated, the demand for reliable and consistently compiled data will increase further. International institutions should play a catalytic leadership role in meeting this need.

The primary impetus for enhanced analytical support for supranational surveillance must come from policymakers and their advisers. But in a modest way there exists an epistemic communitiy outside of governments and international organizations that also tries to advance theoretical and empirical knowledge about cross-border macroeconomic interactions. Farsighted policymakers have a clear interest in nurturing this epistemic community, encouraging it to play an active role in developing analytical knowledge, and applying that knowledge to supranational surveillance.

IMF Lending Intermediation

Intergovernmental lending carried out through an international organization functioning as an intermediary can facilitate the liability financing of nations' external payments deficits. Such financing is relevant not only in crises but also in noncrisis conditions. It can beneficially support and reinforce supranational surveillance for borrowing nations. Lending to encourage the adjustment of underlying macroeconomic imbalances while simultaneously smoothing the liability financing of payments deficits has been a primary function of the International Monetary Fund.

Rationales for IMF lending intermediation, especially in noncrisis circumstances, are more controversial than the rationales for collective surveillance. Criticisms of IMF lending, if anything, have intensified rather than waned in recent years. Many critics of the IMF have seemed to lose sight altogether of the original concept that brought the IMF into existence at the end of World War II. The harshest critics espouse the untrammeled markets position that all cross-border lending—including any borrowing by government entities—should be conducted by and for the account of private sector economic units. They thus question whether the IMF should be in the business of lending intermediation at all (chapter 8).

Yet IMF lending intermediation, if prudently conducted, can contribute importantly to the efficiency and stability of the world financial system.

Lending to encourage the adjustment of underlying macroeconomic imbalances while simultaneously smoothing the liability financing of payments deficits thus should continue to be a primary function of the International Monetary Fund.

The most persuasive rationale of all for IMF lending is that it can support and reinforce the IMF's surveillance activities. Creditor nations in surplus may be better able to negotiate repayment terms and appropriate performance conditions for lending to deficit nations if they work collectively through the IMF. Debtor nations may have greater, more assured, and less expensive access to liability financing for their deficits if they borrow from the IMF. The powers for adjustment promotion associated with the conditionality of IMF lending, though inherently asymmetric, undergird the IMF's role as an adjustment referee for payments imbalances and exchange rate misalignments. The recommendation from severe critics of the IMF to eliminate or drastically curtail its authority to lend to member nations with noncrisis payments difficulties has weak analytical foundations and merits outright rejection.

Practical Details of IMF Lending

Difficult issues, many of them specialized or technical, arise in connection with the IMF's various lending facilities. Critics of the IMF have argued, for example, that IMF lending facilities are excessively differentiated and complex and hence ought to be simplified. Significant revisions were in fact made in 2000 and 2001.

Controversy also surrounds the interest charges, repayment terms, and access conditions that accompany IMF lending. The contentious general issue is whether borrowing member governments make "excessive" use of IMF financial resources because the interest charges are too far below market interest rates and because there is excessive leniency in obligations to repay the borrowings.

The details of IMF lending have acquired heightened saliency as world capital markets and multinational private financial institutions have developed further and as some developing nations have obtained increased access to those institutions and markets. Interest charges, repayment terms, and access conditions were tightened somewhat in a delicate political compromise as part of the 2000 revision of IMF facilities. Proponents of those changes expected them to strengthen the incentives for borrowing IMF members to avoid overly prolonged and unduly large use of IMF resources.

As part of an effort to enhance the IMF's capacities for dealing with financial crises, IMF member nations created a new lending facility in 1999, the Contingent Credit Lines (CCL). Significant changes were subsequently made in the CCL's terms and procedures in 2000. The facility is intended to be a precautionary line of defense against crises and has provisions for prequalification of an IMF member nation that may need liquidity assistance in case a crisis actually strikes. The prequalification feature is attractive in principle yet also raises serious difficulties. No IMF member had asked to use the CCL facility as of December 2002. Thus no experience is yet available to help with its evaluation.[8]

The conditionality accompanying IMF lending has been contentious throughout the IMF's existence. It became even more so in the 1990s. Recent controversy stems from disagreements about which types of a nation's policies should be subject to performance conditions, how the conditions should be designed and decided, and how assertive the IMF should be in its efforts to monitor the conditions. Many of the disagreements stem from differences of view about the purposes for which the IMF should be lending. Much of the controversy about the appropriate scope of IMF conditionality, in other words, is entangled with fundamental debates about the IMF's mandate. Alternative visions of the IMF's mandate are discussed in chapter 10.

Resources for the IMF

What aggregate amount of financial resources should be available to the IMF to lend to member nations with balance-of-payments difficulties (in either crisis or noncrisis circumstances)? Given that the IMF lends funds contributed to it by member nations in proportion to their quotas, the aggregate size of lending resources is primarily a function of the aggregate total of IMF quotas.[9] The main presumptive guideline for IMF quotas is that the world community should want the total to grow secularly over time with growth in the world economy. Lending resources available to the

---

8. *Crisis Prevention and Prosperity Management for the World Economy* identifies the specialized and technical issues referred to in the text and discusses key points of controversy. The analysis there suggests an agnostic judgment on whether the prospective advantages of the revised Contingent Credit Lines will outweigh the difficulties.

9. In appropriate conditions the IMF can supplement its quota resources by borrowing under two contingent commitments known as the New Arrangements to Borrow (approved in 1998) and the General Arrangements to Borrow (created in 1962).

IMF probably need not grow as rapidly as cross-border capital flows and financial activity more generally. Perhaps IMF lending resources should not even increase as fast as cross-border trade. As a modest presumption, however, it seems plausible to expect that the aggregate of IMF resources for lending, adjusted for inflation, ought broadly to keep pace with the growth in the real (inflation-adjusted) value of world output.

That modest presumption was *not* met over the second half of the twentieth century. The ratio of total IMF quotas to nominal world gross domestic product fell significantly (continuously after the 1960s). If IMF quotas at the end of the century had been of the same size relative to world GDP as at the creation of the IMF, total quotas would have been substantially more than three times their actual size. Had total quotas been as large relative to aggregate world imports, they would have been some ten times larger than they actually were. These observations about total IMF quotas suggest, at a minimum, that the lending resources of the IMF in recent decades did not expand at an exorbitantly rapid pace. The opposite—inadequate expansion—is more likely to have been true.

As of the year 2002, no urgent need appears to exist for an immediate further increase in IMF quotas. By the time of the twelfth quinquennial review of quotas in 2003–04, however, consideration should be given to a substantial percentage increase over the quotas prevailing in 2000–02 (the result of the eleventh quinquennial review in 1998).

Assessment of IMF Lending and Adjustment Programs

Assessing the effects of an IMF lending program and its performance conditions is analytically difficult. Many efforts claiming to do so have been superficial and inappropriately designed. Some studies, for example, resort to simple comparisons of a nation's economic variables in two time periods, before adoption and after adoption of an IMF program. Such comparisons are definitely not satisfactory analytically and provide little insight about whether IMF conditionality in any given situation has on balance been constructive. The best studies trying to evaluate the success of IMF programs reach mixed conclusions but point to net favorable influences in a majority of cases.

The IMF's implementation of conditionality is far from perfect. It can doubtless be improved and simplified in several ways. Yet one should have empathy for the difficulty of the IMF's position. In the messy, intermediate world polity in which the IMF operates, guidelines for its performance conditions— indeed for all the dimensions of its surveillance—pull it in opposite directions. On the one hand IMF conditionality has to avoid being overly intrusive. It needs to be highly sensitive to the legal supremacy of a nation's government as the arbiter for that nation of political, social, and economic priorities. On the other hand, the IMF must be sensitive to the systemic interests of the world community as a whole. IMF conditionality and surveillance must avoid being overly lax and too flexible, thereby not even succeeding in facilitating a borrowing nation's self-identified own best interests. In practice the IMF seeks an appropriate compromise between its opposing guidelines for conditionality. Its efforts to do so have often been a constructive influence on nations experiencing economic and financial difficulties.

Keeping Sight of Basic Points about IMF Lending

The preceding overview of IMF lending omits most details and necessarily alludes to specialized issues. Even that much discussion may seem excessive. If you are a general reader not interested in the details of IMF operations, you can without qualms leave the specialized issues to others directly engaged.

For example, your instincts may or may not lead you to the conclusion that some of the IMF lending facilities ought to be further simplified and revised. You might or might not believe that the IMF's interest charges and repayment terms have been sufficiently tightened by the changes made in 2000. You might remain agnostic about the balance of pros and cons associated with the Contingent Credit Lines facility and its procedures for prequalifying borrowing members for emergency liquidity assistance. You may be hesitant to express judgments about the appropriate size of IMF lending resources and whether it would be helpful to revise the scope and design of the IMF's performance conditions.

No matter. Although those issues are significant and you should want the IMF and national governments to try to resolve them thoughtfully, taking due account of objective outside analysis, the issues are nonetheless second-order relative to more basic points about IMF lending. To help keep the basic points in mind, here is a synopsis.

Fundamental, valid rationales exist for asking the IMF to serve as a focal point for intergovernmental lending intermediation. As cross-border finance and world economic integration become still more important— and hence as the need for international financial governance grows apace—the need for skillful IMF lending will increase further. Two rationales stand out above all others. First, IMF lending, in both crisis and noncrisis circumstances, can play a helpful role as a handmaiden and backstop for the supranational surveillance of national economic policies. Second, for the foreseeable future, emergency crisis lending by the IMF coupled with IMF leadership for crisis management is the closest approximation the world community can have to collective governance for coping with financial turbulence that disrupts entire nations' economies and threatens to spill contagiously across national borders.

Notwithstanding the valid rationales for IMF lending and notwithstanding the IMF's compromise policies steering a middle course among conflicting guidelines, IMF lending does entail risks. Notably, some IMF member nations may seek excessive or overly prolonged borrowing. In a world in which savings generated in one nation can increasingly be readily transferred across borders to other nations, IMF noncrisis lending could unfairly compete with private lending to governments. If a borrowing government has reasonable and reliable access to private capital from foreign financial institutions and markets, lending from the IMF to that government could constitute the "unwarrantedly cheap" financing at below-market cost about which critics have complained.

IMF lending should be a backstop for occasions when external borrowing by a nation's government is warranted but private-sector finance is available only on unreasonably expensive terms—or is not available at all. Potential borrowing governments should certainly not be able to regard IMF lending merely as a low-cost substitute for private finance. Probably few borrowing governments do hold such an attitude. A "conditionality-adjusted" rate of interest for borrowing from the IMF is likely to be high, perhaps virtually as high as a private market interest rate (if private lenders are willing to lend at all). Even so, continual IMF vigilance is required to prevent governments of borrowing nations from perceiving IMF lending as a subsidized substitute for private capital inflows.

The world community should not even wish the IMF to be a major source of low-cost, below-market funds for "development finance" (investment programs to promote growth, reduce poverty, and achieve structural reforms). The world community *should* want to make large amounts of low-cost development finance available to poorer nations, especially those that do not have ready access to private capital markets. That goal is a valid objective for international collective governance. But the World Bank and regional development banks should be the primary international sources of that development finance, not the IMF. The more IMF lending is pulled into the support of growth, poverty reduction, and structural reform, the greater are the risks that the IMF's activities will be dissipated across too many functional areas and that the IMF's effectiveness will be compromised in its core areas of macroeconomics and finance. This important conclusion about the IMF's mandate is developed further in chapter 10.

Another major risk has to be avoided. Human nature and politics being what they are, the governments of some nations from time to time either will not or cannot maintain sound economic policies. Imagine that such nations were to succeed in borrowing from the IMF, either during noncrisis periods or because they fall into crisis (a crisis being likely sooner or later if the unsound policies continue). Those nations would be unlikely to repay their borrowings promptly, if at all. Greatly delayed payments would be a clear violation of IMF guidelines stipulating that IMF lending should be temporary. At worst, to use provocative language, the governments of those nations might attempt just to stay on "welfare" rather than pulling up their socks, reforming their policies, and "getting off the dole." Such outcomes would be undesirable, for the world community and ultimately for the individual nations themselves.

When making judgments about an "irresponsible" government, other IMF member nations and the IMF itself should exhibit caution and humility. National governments, just like ordinary mortals, are prone to apply a double standard. The government in any particular nation judges other nations' governments by their actions but judges itself by its motives. Unsound and irresponsible macroeconomic policies are some *other* nation's policy stance. When difficulties arise in adopting appropriate policies within one's own nation, delays and shortfalls are readily excused because of domestic political constraints. In principle, all governments should try to understand their counterparts' difficulties and not rush too quickly to judgment ("why beholdest thou the mote in thy brother's eye but considerest not the beam in thine own eye?"[10]). Nor should the IMF be pushed hard by the governments of big nations to be tough on the governments of small nations but, heaven forbid, not on themselves. Difficult cases, and judgments about complex trade-offs, will inevitably arise. Nevertheless, the basic principle is clear: applications to borrow from the IMF should typically be denied to member nations whose governments are pursuing policies that are unsound on the basis of objective criteria.

10. Matt. 7:3, *King James Bible*.

As with IMF surveillance, so it should be with IMF lending: what is needed is a balanced perspective. Allowing lending by the IMF to become either an easy substitute for improved national policies or borrowing from private lenders in world financial markets would be wrong. But severely constraining or eliminating IMF lending because of its risks would also be wrong. IMF lending is a collective good that, prudently supplied, can underpin the efficiency and stability of the world financial system.

10 Priorities for Architectural Reform: Prudential Financial Oversight, Crisis Management, and the Mandate for the IMF

This chapter identifies priority reforms for the international financial architecture in the areas of prudential oversight and crisis management and summarizes policy recommendations for achieving them. As in the preceding chapter, the International Monetary Fund is the international institution singled out most prominently. The chapter concludes with analysis of alternative views about the IMF's institutional mandate and recommendations for how it should be defined.

Prudential Oversight and Financial Standards

Before the revelations in 2001–02 of several scandals in accounting and auditing that affected private companies in the United States and elsewhere, prudential oversight and standards for financial activity had low visibility in public discussion. Individuals not working in the financial system had little knowledge about them. Particular issues were not perceived as overridingly important, sometimes even by financial specialists. Controversies among the experts seldom became heated enough to attract widespread attention.

How the issues in these areas are, or are not, resolved will have major implications for the health of the global financial system. Intergovernmental cooperation to nurture supranational surveillance over the first decade of this century is likely to make the most progress in these specialized areas.

The discussion that follows here concentrates on incremental collective governance for prudential financial oversight and the institutions that must carry out that governance. Chapter 11 highlights the policy choices confronting individual nations and the world community about traffic regulations and guidelines for cross-border financial transactions.

The Current Status of Intergovernmental Cooperation

Although principles for financial standards and prudential oversight at the world level have not been explicitly articulated in official documents or elsewhere, appropriate principles can be discerned.[1] Cooperation about the design of prudential oversight and standards, furthermore, has acquired a significant forward momentum. Numerous consultative groups and international financial organizations are involved, working on a variety of issues.

The Basel Committee on Banking Supervision, established following the occurrence in 1974 of banking crises with cross-national dimensions, has been active for several decades in discussing international aspects of the supervision and regulation of banks. Its significant efforts include a concordat on the supervision of banks' foreign establishments, international standards for measuring the capital adequacy of banks, and the development of Core Principles for Effective Banking Supervision intended to stimulate improvements in supervisory standards in all nations (whether or not participants in the BCBS itself).

Cross-border aspects of the supervision and regulation of securities markets are the primary responsibility of the International Organization of Securities Commissions. IOSCO has developed several guidance documents on the supervision and operations of securities and brokerage firms, including in 1998 the Objectives and Principles of Securities Regulation, a document analogous to the BCBS Core Principles. The International Association of Insurance Supervisors, the analogous international institution for insurance, has been developing principles and guidelines for the supervision of insurance firms and discussing mechanisms for their implementation. The Joint Forum on Financial Conglomerates is a collective venture of the BCBS, IOSCO, and IAIS to ensure that national regulators and the three international organizations focus on problems raised by the progres-

---

1. The world principles are summarized in chapter 11. The companion study *Prudential Oversight and Standards for the World Financial System* develops and explains them.

sive blurring of distinctions between the activities of banking, securities, and insurance firms.

The primary institutional venues for catalyzing cooperation among nations about accounting standards and auditing procedures are the International Accounting Standards Board (formerly the International Accounting Standards Committee before its reorganization and renaming in 2001) and the International Federation of Accountants. The IASB has developed more than forty documents setting out international accounting standards. The IFAC through its International Auditing Practices Committee has developed international standards on auditing and international audit practice statements. The BCBS, IOSCO, and IAIS have conducted exercises to evaluate all three sets of standards within, respectively, the banking, securities, and insurance areas.

The World Bank has been coordinating an effort to develop world principles and guidelines for dealing with insolvency and bankruptcy. Other organizations involved in this effort include the United Nations Commission on International Trade Law, the IMF, the International Bar Association, the regional development banks, the OECD, the International Association of Insolvency Practitioners, and the INSOL Lenders Group. With the drafting assistance of more than forty nations, UNCITRAL in 1997 developed a Model Law on Cross-Border Insolvency to deal with the international aspects of statutory insolvency procedures. The INSOL Lenders Group has sought to generate international cooperation for pre-statutory cross-border workouts. The International Bar Association has developed a model insolvency code to provide a prototype for nations in the process of reforming and updating their insolvency laws.

Responsibility for monitoring and strengthening payments and settlement systems, with special emphasis on the cross-border and multicurrency dimensions, is lodged with central bank representatives on the Committee on Payment and Settlements Systems at the BIS.

The OECD and the World Bank have taken the lead in catalyzing international discussions of corporate governance standards. The OECD Council in 1999 endorsed a set of standards and guidelines intended for international applicability, OECD Principles of Corporate Governance. Standards to ensure the integrity of financial markets, for example to prevent financial crime and money laundering and more recently to inhibit the financial activities of terrorist organizations, are the special responsibility of the Financial Action Task Force on Money Laundering (FATF). The FATF was formed at the 1989 G-7 meeting and was active throughout the

1990s. By 2000 the FATF had progressed a substantial distance toward developing a process of self assessments and "mutual evaluations" of jurisdictions' performances judged against the FATF international standards, known as The Forty Recommendations of the Financial Action Task Force.

The IMF, the World Bank, the BIS, the OECD, and a multiorganization Task Force on Finance Statistics (TFFS) are all involved in international efforts to raise standards for data collection and dissemination. Important initiatives include the establishment of a Special Data Dissemination Standard and the General Data Dissemination System, lodged at the IMF.

The IMF has developed documents setting out principles and a manual for good practices in the conduct of national fiscal policies. A corresponding set of principles and a draft manual for monetary and financial policies has been developed by the IMF in collaboration with the BIS and national central banks and supervisory authorities.

The Financial Stability Forum (FSF), established by the G-7, is a relatively recent, overarching institutional mechanism intended to enhance cooperation among the various national and international financial supervisory bodies and international financial institutions. The activities of the FSF in its initial years included the preparation of a draft Compendium of Standards to span all financial areas and the establishment of various working groups or task forces to study specific problems of general policy concern. Reports of these FSF subgroups focused on the activities of highly leveraged institutions in financial markets, the uses and activities of offshore financial centers, the implementation of international financial standards, recent experiences with deposit insurance schemes, and the evaluation of policy measures that might be taken in borrower and creditor nations to reduce the volatility of capital flows and to improve the assessment and management of the risks of excessive short-term external indebtedness. Those reports, and the endorsement of their recommendations by the full FSF, are an important indication of intergovernmental consensus on these sensitive problems. Although not as influential or as broad in its scope as the Financial Stability Forum, the BIS-sponsored Committee on the Global Financial System has also been an intergovernmental venue in which cooperative studies and policy recommendations have been developed.

This sketch of institutions and their activities indicates only a little of the substance of their ongoing efforts. But it gives a correct impression of the multiplicity of fronts along which intergovernmental cooperation has been evolving. The progress so far has been genuine and significant. It deserves more widespread attention and commendation than it typically receives.[2]

Unresolved Issues about Financial Standards

Despite the ongoing progress, numerous important issues remain unresolved. In no sense has the progress so far been sufficient to deal satisfactorily with all the key issues—not for banking, securities markets, and insurance, not for accounting and auditing, not for insolvency and bankruptcy, not for corporate governance or financial market integrity, not for data collection and dissemination, not for macroeconomic policies.

For one thing, international standards and norms are typically not legally binding on firms or financial institutions in individual nations. Each nation's government and the nation's private associations have to encourage their acceptance and use within the nation's borders. When the already existing regulations and laws of nations differ, however, the design and implementation of international standards and norms pose difficult challenges. This issue and the tensions surrounding it are general. Some form of this dilemma arises over the core principles of the BCBS for banking, of IOSCO for securities firms and markets, and of the IAIS for insurance. Analogous issues arise for insolvency and bankruptcy, for payments and settlements systems, for corporate governance, and for the collection and dissemination of financial statistics.

The most difficult obstacles inhibiting international agreement about standards and norms arise when national laws or practices are fundamentally inconsistent. In such situations the only possible resolution of the dilemma is for individual nations to alter national arrangements to conform to a single, internationally agreed arrangement. The preferred approach to the design of standards at a world level is usually to encourage *agreed minimum standards* combined with the presumption of *mutual recognition*. But the more difficult situations of direct conflicts among existing national laws cannot be resolved with that approach. Direct conflicts significantly affecting cross-border transactions will sooner or later have to be resolved by eliminating the inconsistencies through *explicit harmonization*.

The treatment of insolvency liquidations of multinational private enterprises is a noteworthy example of direct conflict. One approach to cross-border insolvencies, labeled "universalist" and followed in the law of the

---

2. Further information about the various institutions is given in the appendix. Details about their recent activities are provided in *Prudential Oversight and Standards for the World Financial System*.

United Kingdom, advocates a "single-entity" regime for liquidations. A second "territorial" approach, adopted in U.S. law, espouses "separate-entity" regimes for liquidating the multiple parts of a multinational enterprise. Under the universalist approach, the headquarters of an insolvent multinational enterprise is deemed to be located in a single "home" nation and the courts of that home nation have worldwide control of the liquidation proceedings. In case of conflicts, the insolvency laws and procedures of the home nation take precedence over those of other nations where other parts of the enterprise are located. In sharp contrast, the territorial approach presumes that each nation has insolvency jurisdiction for the portion of the multinational enterprise located within its borders. For that portion, the separate-entity regime applies the laws and procedures governing insolvencies in that nation. This conflict of laws is especially problematic for multinational banks and other financial institutions, especially for multinational banks whose foreign offices are mainly branches rather than separately incorporated subsidiaries.

A second type of tension arises when individual nations worry that newly agreed international standards will prove inferior to their national standards already in force. As an illustration, consider the stance of American accountants and U.S. government supervisors about the emerging standards of the International Accounting Standards Board. The United States, with the largest of all national incomes and the most extensive worldwide economic interests, ought to be taking the lead in encouraging adoption of the IASB core standards. Yet in the past Americans have dragged their feet. Their concern has been that the proposed world standards are less stringent in some respects than the Generally Accepted Accounting Principles (GAAP) of the U.S. Financial Accounting Standards Board that prevail in the United States. If American accounting firms and supervisors accept the IASB rules as a substitute for GAAP, it has been argued, the safety and soundness of the American financial system could be undermined to the extent that GAAP rules really are superior to the world rules. The controversy over world standards even spilled over into a tussle between the United States and key European countries about the governance structure of the IASB itself.

The United States should treat the IASB core accounting standards as a *minimum* and require U.S. institutions to supplement those standards with GAAP rules where it can be convincingly demonstrated that the GAAP standards are more stringent. At the least, however, both Americans and Europeans should endorse and encourage widespread adoption of the IASB core standards—even if some of the standards can be still further improved. Reluctance to apply the IASB standards or any other of the emerging international standards within the largest, wealthiest nations will surely have unfavorable repercussions on the postures of many developing nations as those nations decide how to respond to the pressure for strengthening accounting and auditing standards in their economies.

International Standards for Capital Adequacy

The design of world standards for minimum capital adequacy at banks and other financial institutions is an especially difficult and controversial topic. Supervisory requirements that an institution maintain adequate capital—a market-based, incentive-based regulation—gives managers and owners a strong incentive to be prudent. If the institution acts imprudently and goes bankrupt, the owners have a lot to lose. Conversely, if an institution's capital is allowed to fall below some low threshold, managers and owners will be tempted to take excessive risks rather than avoid them (chapter 3).

The Basel Committee on Banking Supervision first agreed on a version of international standards for banks' capital in 1988. Although the introduction of these formal minimum capital requirements in the G-10 nations (the nations represented on the BCBS) probably induced weakly capitalized banks to maintain higher capital ratios than would have otherwise prevailed, those standards were criticized on several grounds. The BCBS itself acknowledged the criticisms as serious. A new draft version of the standards, released in 1999, retained many features of the 1988 requirements (such as the general guideline that capital must be maintained at a minimum 8 percent or more of risk-weighted assets) but tried to address the detailed problems acknowledged to be weaknesses. During the following three years, amendments to the 1999 draft were actively considered, including significant revisions in January 2001 and further revisions in December 2001.

The process of reaching consensus on a new accord has proven to be protracted and difficult. All the major nations appear to have been guilty of special pleading on particular points and consequent foot dragging. Many European participants, for example, held out for a provision like the one in the 1988 accord that gives claims secured by commercial real estate a markedly lower risk weighting than other claims on corporate entities. (The lower a risk weighting on an asset, the smaller the amount of capital the bank is required to hold against it.) The lower risk weighting in the old accord deferred to views in Europe, especially in Germany, where exceptionally strong legal requirements apply to commercial mortgages and where loss experiences for that category of bank lending have been historically low. Credit rating agencies that provide external credit assessments of companies and financial institutions are much more active in North America than in Europe; American participants were accordingly more sympathetic to the use of external assessments by credit-rating agencies. A meeting of the BCBS in July 2002 reached agreement on some of the outstanding issues, but further progress has to be made to achieve a final document spelling out the new accord.

Continued progress in refining standards for minimum capital adequacy is a vital element of intergovernmental cooperation on prudential oversight issues. Over time, progressively more attention will also have to be paid to improvements not only in the standards themselves, but in the monitoring and assessment of banks' capital positions.

Monitoring and Enforcement of World Standards and Norms

Monitoring and enforcement of world financial standards and oversight norms will soon become at least as important as sound design. Without adequate monitoring and enforcement, even well-designed standards are of little worth.

As a practical matter, the bulk of monitoring and enforcement activity must take place within individual nations and be carried out by each nation's collective-governance infrastructure. Each national government needs to "own" the world minimum standards, that is, to take domestic political responsibility for explaining their importance to the nation's residents. Each needs to strengthen its own indigenous procedures for self assessment. Implementation can be encouraged from outside the nation by the world community, but it cannot be imposed or enforced from the outside.

Although self assessment must be the dominant focus for monitoring and enforcement, self asessment alone is unlikely to be sufficient. To ensure rigor, to foster consistent application of world standards across national jurisdictions, and above all to enhance credibility, national self assessments need to be complemented by external verification and probably even by external assessments. Thus the world community needs to nurture a beginning, tentative process of overview assessments by international financial organizations. The international overviews should concentrate initially on a straightforward description of a nation's existing standards and practices and the degree to which those are consistent with the standards and guidelines evolving at the world level.

A strategy along these lines is in fact evolving. The key organizations are the IMF, the World Bank, the BIS, and the BCBS. Others such as IOSCO and IAIS are also involved. The Financial Stability Forum provides integrating coordination. The key features of the strategy are experimental reports on the observance of standards and codes (known by the acronym ROSCs) and pilot efforts to prepare financial sector assessment programs (FSAPs). The pilot evaluation procedures used by the Financial Action Task Force in the specialized area of financial crime and money laundering are another illustration of this approach to external assessments of nations' compliance with world standards.

Another part of the evolving strategy is an increasing advocacy of the use of external assessments of a nation's financial standards and oversight procedures as an integral part of surveillance of the entire range of a nation's economic policies. The main practical issue so far is whether and to what extent the IMF should incorporate the evolving ROSCs and FSAPs into its annual Article IV consultations with member nations.[3] An analogous question is how the ROSCs and FSAPs should be used by the World Bank (and even the regional development banks) in decisions about lending programs to individual nations.

Views on these questions have recently converged on the position that the IMF should be using the ROSCs and FSAPs in its overall surveillance of a nation. Similarly, it appears to be uncontroversial that the World Bank should use the reports as an input into its lending decisions. No consensus exists, however, about which organization or organizations should have primary responsibility for actually conducting the various assessments incorporated in ROSCs and FSAPs. Although cooperation among the IMF, the World Bank, the BIS, BCBS, IOSCO, and IAIS appears to have intensified under the umbrella of the Financial Stability Forum, significantly more progress in this area is needed.

Nations That Fall below World Standards

Because many emerging-market and developing nations lag behind the more advanced industrial nations in maintaining a satisfactory utilities infrastructure for their financial systems, financial standards and prudential

---

3. The IMF's Article IV consultations are briefly discussed in chapter 9. For an extended discussion, see the companion study *Crisis Prevention and Prosperity Management for the World Economy*.

oversight often fall below the evolving minimum international standards. When assessing such situations, the world community should recognize that nations at different stages of economic and financial development have differing capabilities for remedying the shortfalls. Administrative skills and capacities for the tasks of collective governance are especially scarce in developing nations. Budgets may be especially constrained.

It would therefore be fruitless and unwise for the world community to ask for an across-the-board raising of national to world minimum standards over a short period of time. Other priorities will compete for the limited administrative and budgetary resources. Slowness in learning new behavior and the inevitable inertia that impedes institutional change will cause the process to be protracted. Today's industrial nations took decades to improve their own standards, norms, and procedures. (And those nations themselves need to strengthen their own standards and procedures still further.) The diversity in capacities among nations is a primary reason for supporting international minimum standards rather than harmonized standards to be applied uniformly across nations at all stages of financial development.

For nations that have recently experienced financial crises, international assessments of their financial systems need to be especially sensitive to downside risks in urging the nations to move rapidly. Financial crises reveal the need for improvements in standards and prudential oversight. But the periods immediately following a crisis may not be a propitious time for trying to make the improvements. It is at least conceivable that supervisors of a troubled financial system should exercise regulatory forbearance and permit insolvent or nearly insolvent institutions to continue operating for the time being. By mitigating the severity of a postcrisis credit crunch and postponing the liquidation of financial institutions, regulatory forbearance might avoid a spiraling and self-defeating contraction of credit that would undermine economic recovery.

Such forbearance, however, would also be highly risky. It would encourage the moral hazard risks that insolvent financial institutions may gamble for resurrection by extending still riskier credits. It could easily raise the eventual costs of recapitalizing and restoring the soundness of the financial system. Financial history is full of admonitory episodes in which regulatory forbearance was a primary contributor to outcomes that, seen with the wisdom of hindsight, were unwise and very expensive. Neither a nation's own nor the general world's interests will usually be well served by protracted regulatory forbearance.

For external assessments of nations' financial systems, as for so many other issues, the world community needs to espouse a balanced position. A case-by-case approach that is sensitive to the circumstances of an individual nation is far preferable to a mechanical application of "one size fits all." Yet the world community does need to send firm, clear signals about the desirability for nations gradually to raise their own standards up to international minimums. The course of least political resistance within a nation is often an easy resort to the argument that "we are different," that the international minimum standards suitable for other nations "cannot apply to us because of our unique culture, politics, and institutions." Some of the backlash among developing nations to the pressure to adopt international minimum standards is probably of this less thoughtful nature. Politically difficult though their adoption may be in the first instance, improved accounting and auditing standards, strengthened procedures for insolvency, better collection and dissemination of data, and more stringent supervision and regulation of financial institutions are fundamentally in the long-run interests of developing nations themselves.

A few smaller developing nations may find it convenient to pursue the "piggybacking option." Rather than strengthening their own financial standards and indigenous capacities for prudential oversight, they could choose to encourage foreign financial institutions to play a dominant role in their national financial system, thereby importing the standards and prudential oversight of the nations in which the foreign financial institutions have their head offices. The world community should be willing to accept a jurisdiction's choice of this option if the piggybacking is truly effective in producing sound prudential oversight. But nations should not be pressured to choose this option if their policymakers are hesitant to grant foreign financial institutions such a large role (provided they are prepared to raise their own indigenous capacities up to internationally agreed minimums).

Dealing with Renegade Jurisdictions

A few national jurisdictions in the world financial system act in effect as "renegades." They foster regulatory arbitrage and supervisory laxity as a way of promoting their attractiveness as a location for unfettered financial activity. Those jurisdictions deliberately have weak financial standards and prudential oversight. They intentionally restrict transparency in disclosure policies. They have exhibited a limited willingness to cooperate internationally (at least until very recently).

The main renegade jurisdictions are a subset of the so-called offshore financial centers. These centers are heterogeneous. Some are relatively well supervised and acknowledge that a cooperative strengthening of the infrastructures for national financial systems is essentially a global public good. They therefore share information with other nations and cooperate responsibly with international initiatives to establish world minimum standards and to strengthen national infrastructures. Some other centers, however, are content with their weak prudential oversight and resist suggestions for cooperative change. The need to judge which jurisdictions are acting irresponsibly and failing to cooperate with collective efforts to enhance stability of the world financial system is a particular example of the broader need for international monitoring and assessment of financial systems.

To the degree that renegade jurisdictions abet financial crime and money laundering, fail to discourage financial transactions associated with terrorist groups, maintain little or no taxation of capital themselves, or do not discourage tax evasion or improper tax avoidance, the governments of responsible nations have additional potentially valid arguments for maintaining some regulations and restraints on private financial transactions and for considering certain "breakwater" measures to inhibit cross-border transactions. Such motives do not stem from a wish to discriminate in favor of domestic versus foreign residents. Rather, if responsible jurisdictions decide to respond with prudential restraints or breakwater measures, the motive is to prevent illegal or damaging activity by (either) domestic or foreign residents.[4]

One of the suggested principles for world-level standards is that no governmental jurisdiction should be accorded the full benefits of participation in the world economic and financial system and its supporting international organizations if it persists in maintaining standards and prudential oversight for financial activity that are weak relative to world minimum standards. To implement this principle, the world community needs to devise means of discouraging opportunistic free-riding behavior by renegade jurisdictions. A mild but sometimes effective option is to cooperate in an international "name-and-shame" policy of identifying offending jurisdictions.

More drastic options would entail actual sanctions. One sanctions option, for example, would be to deny a free-riding jurisdiction the benefits and legitimacy of membership in international financial organizations.

---

4. "Breakwater" restraints on cross-border financial transactions are identified in chapter 11 and discussed in detail in *Prudential Oversight and Standards for the World Financial System*.

Supervisors in nations with strong standards and prudential oversight might cooperate in adopting various restrictions on the ability of private financial institutions resident in their nations to transact with institutions in a renegade jurisdiction. In extreme cases of continued nonadherence to world minimum standards and failure to cooperate internationally, national governments or the international financial organizations might restrict or even prohibit altogether financial transactions with counterparties or accounts resident in the free-riding jurisdiction.

The name-and-shame approach began to be used explicitly in 2000. A report by a working group of the Financial Stability Forum divided the off-shore financial centers into three groups on the basis of the quality of their supervision and their degree of international cooperation. Members of a first group were deemed to be cooperative with a high quality of supervision and largely adhering to international standards. Jurisdictions in a second group were characterized as having performance falling below international standards, with substantial room for improvement. The third, most problematic group were "jurisdictions generally seen as having a low quality of supervision, and/or being noncooperative with onshore supervisors, and with little or no attempt being made to adhere to international standards." In May 2000 a press release by the full Financial Stability Forum actually named the individual jurisdictions in each of the three groups.

Significantly, two other examples of the name-and-shame approach appeared in 2000. The Financial Action Task Force released a report on detrimental rules and practices that impede international cooperation to discourage money laundering. Out of twenty-nine jurisdictions reviewed, fifteen were categorized as "non-cooperative in the fight against money laundering." The OECD's Forum on Harmful Tax Practices released a report criticizing a variety of preferential tax regimes and identifying thirty-five jurisdictions as meeting the technical criteria for "tax havens" as defined in an earlier report.

In the months following the September 2001 terrorist attacks on the World Trade Center in New York and the Pentagon in Washington, the financial aspects of terrorism became of great concern and heightened the momentum of FATF activities. The U.S. government also showed enhanced interest in the efforts of the OECD Forum on Harmful Tax Practices to persuade tax havens to discourage the financing of terrorist networks through money laundering and tax evasion. By April 2002 a majority of the jurisdictions that had been listed in the forum's 2000 report had made adjustments in their tax regimes in negotiations with the members of the forum. But seven jurisdictions—Andorra, Liechtenstein, Monaco, the Marshall Islands, Nauru, Vanuatu, and Liberia—were identified as uncooperative tax havens and were warned that they could face sanctions within a year if they continued to refuse cooperation. The FATF list of jurisdictions not cooperating in the fight against money laundering contained eleven states as of October 2002 (down from nineteen states as of September 2001).[5]

Given the natural hesitation in international discussions to point fingers at specific nations, the FSF, FATF, and OECD activities in 2000–02 were remarkably assertive. Name-and-shame efforts, although controversial (particularly on tax issues), now appear to have considerable momentum and to indicate significant progress in beginning to deal with renegade jurisdictions. These recent constructive steps toward international collective governance were almost unimaginable a decade or two earlier. In a fit of optimism, I am tempted to imagine that in future decades the world community, acting collectively, might even turn the spotlight on some dubious and unneighborly practices within large wealthy nations that merit being named and shamed.

Standards and Resources for Data Collection and Dissemination

Collective-governance mechanisms for data collection and dissemination are a vital component of the utilities infrastructure for financial systems. Disclosure of reliable data by individual private institutions is essential for the sound management of credit risks. The aggregation of data for individual institutions into national statistics and the dissemination of those statistics is also essential. It is not sufficient that individual institutions in the financial system know their own and their counterparties' financial positions. Good risk management and decisionmaking requires aggregated information that permits institutions and individuals to evaluate their overall vulnerability to financial turbulence and hence to the risks of general repayment problems and volatility in asset prices. These data issues are especially difficult for developing nations, but no less important than for advanced financial systems.

---

5. The FATF noncooperative jurisdictions in October 2002 were the Cook Islands, Egypt, Grenada, Guatemala, Indonesia, Myanmar, Nauru, Nigeria, Philippines, St. Vincent and the Grenadines, and Ukraine.

The availability of adequate financial data lags far behind need. Many important gaps in available data, including some of central importance for assessing financial stability, have not been filled for many nations. New gaps arise as new financial institutions and new financial instruments become available that escape or distort existing reporting nets. Data deficiencies are an important obstacle blocking improved monitoring and assessment of nations' external vulnerability. The current cooperative initiatives to improve data, such as the Special Data Dissemination Standard and the General Data Dissemination System of the IMF, are a significant beginning, but only a beginning. Although some potential building blocks for regional and world financial data are assembled at the BIS, the IMF, the OECD, and the World Bank, policymakers have so far given only perfunctory thought to these data issues at the world systemic level.

Private institutions and governments alike often underestimate the importance of data collection and dissemination. Lip service is paid to the value of reliable and timely data. But at budget time, resources for the statistical agencies are among the most vulnerable to cuts or poaching for other purposes. The international financial organizations themselves fail to give data collection and dissemination sufficient priority. Better statistics are a collective good not only within nations but at the world level. More active leadership and more far-sighted perspectives on statistical issues from the international organizations of course require complementary leadership and farsightedness from national governments.

Management of Financial Crises

Financial crises with cross-border and cross-currency complications buffeted many nations in recent years, including Mexico and much of Latin America in 1994–95; Thailand, Indonesia, Malaysia, Korea, and other Asian nations in 1997–98; Russia in 1998; Brazil in 1998–99 and again in 2002; Turkey in 2000–01; Argentina and Uruguay in 2001–02. For several months after the Russian devaluation and default in 1998, national financial systems throughout the world were unsettled, not merely in emerging-market and developing nations but even in the United States, Europe, and Japan. Such episodes were a vivid reminder that severe financial distress can be highly disruptive and that timely cooperative efforts to manage it can help to minimize the disruption. If financial instability originating within a nation spreads across its borders and threatens wider systemic effects, in regional parts of the world financial system or in its entirety, the exercise of international collective governance to manage the financial turbulence becomes essential.

The following guidelines for architectural reform focus on the institutions and procedures for intergovernmental cooperation in crisis management. The summary here condenses key conclusions from the more extensive analysis in the companion volume *Crisis Management for the World Financial System*.

Which Institutions for Crisis Management?

The crisis management function within each individual nation should be explicitly lodged in a collective-governance institution (typically the central bank, but possibly in several such institutions jointly). The locus of this responsibility should ideally be transparent, understood, and accepted throughout each national financial system. For crisis management in the world financial system, political constraints do not yet permit a comparable degree of transparency, understanding, and acceptance. Consultative groups in which only a few of the wealthiest, largest nations are represented will inevitably play a key management role for the next few decades. Gradually with the passage of time, the IMF and perhaps also the BIS should progressively become more influential as loci for intergovernmental cooperation for crisis management.

Leadership for the resolution of financial crises in the short and medium runs will have to be undertaken primarily by national lenders of last resort. In the instances when distressed conditions remain largely localized within an individual nation, that central bank can and should act independently. When cross-border spillovers threaten to be large (an increasingly likely situation), consultations and coordination with lenders of last resort in other nations are essential. Although the IMF and the BIS will have to remain secondary to the national lenders of last resort, they should constructively try to catalyze those consultations and coordination.

The Overriding Priority: General Monetary Policies

Within a single nation's financial reservoir, the overriding priority during and after a crisis is to make appropriate adjustments in overall monetary policy through open-market operations, thereby ensuring sufficient but not excessive liquefaction of the national financial system. Exercise of this function requires the ability to create and extinguish national reserve money (chapter 8).

When crisis conditions buffet parts or all of the world financial system, it is no less important to make appropriate adjustments in overall national monetary policies through open-market operations. The complex objective is to try to ensure sufficient liquefaction of the world financial system (in regional parts or in its entirety) *and* an appropriate distribution of the liquidity among national financial systems.

The only feasible device for achieving this objective is a constructive coordination of overall national monetary policies, especially those of the largest and wealthiest nations. The required degree of coordination is, self-evidently, great. Whether the requisite coordination would be fully forthcoming in a hurricane-level international crisis is a question that has not yet been tested in practice. Fortunately, the need for consultations and potential coordination seems to be well understood within the major central banks. A suggestive example of the needed cooperation occurred in the minicrisis of mid-October 1987, when the stock markets in most major industrial nations fell precipitously.[6]

The general principles to be followed in a multination financial crisis are clear enough. National central banks should accommodate a general scramble for liquidity in domestic currencies by aggressively expanding their own balance sheets. In conditions of general financial distress, it will typically not be sufficient merely to prevent a contraction in reserve money liquidity; the amount of high-powered liquidity may actually need to be temporarily increased, differentially more in the nations and currencies where the demand for incremental liquidity is greatest. Net shifts by private sector institutions out of one particular currency into another that appear to be sparked by herding behavior and unwarranted contagion should be accommodated by opposite changes in the currency composition of the assets or liabilities of the central banks. After the conditions of financial distress have passed, of course the central banks must then reverse some or all

---

6. In the first few days of this stock market turbulence, stocks in most national markets lost some 15 to 25 percent of their precrisis valuations. Market participants became highly uncertain and concerned about the soundness of financial institutions. To restore confidence, central banks considered, and in several cases implemented, temporary expansions of liquidity in their national money markets. The deliberations within each central bank could have been troubled by a trade-off dilemma. Had an individual central bank chosen to act unilaterally, it could have achieved an easing of domestic financial conditions, but it might also have triggered a depreciation of the nation's currency. Because the central banks could agree simultaneously to inject temporary liquidity, however, the combined cooperative adjustments in monetary policies had still more favorable effects on market confidence and averted concerns that any one nation's currency might depreciate strongly against the other major currencies.

of their earlier accommodating transactions as private asset preferences return to normal.

It is reassuring to know that if national lenders of last resort can coordinate their actions, they have sufficient tools available permitting them to cope with the cross-border and cross-currency as well as the domestic dimensions of financial crises. Yet the *if* premise underlying that reassurance reveals how limited it may be. The availability of tools in principle is no guarantee that the tools can be successfully used in practice! Coordination of monetary policies even among just a few of the major nations is extremely difficult. Information about the size, direction, and currency denomination of private sector asset shifts is uncertain even in normal times. It is highly uncertain in periods of financial crisis.

Notwithstanding the great difficulties, coordination of overall monetary policies by national lenders of last resort would be indispensable in a contagious financial crisis spilling simultaneously across the borders of several nations. The need for this coordination has typically received much less attention than it merits in general discussions of the management of international financial crises.

Emergency Lending Directly to Private Financial Institutions

In some crises, the crisis management institutions of individual nations may be justified in lending directly to troubled private financial institutions (domiciled in or chartered by those nations). Exercise of this traditional lender-of-last-resort function within a nation is most likely to be warranted if distressed conditions are widespread and the crisis is creating systemic risk within the national financial system.

Such direct lending in crises with cross-border and cross-currency dimensions poses new complications. Because of the increasing importance of multinational private institutions, there is some risk of a lack of clarity about which national lender of last resort has primary responsibility for emergency lending to particular private entities. On these matters, too, there exists a need for international coordination. The national lenders of last resort should strive to think through the relevant issues in advance and to design contingent guidelines that will enable them to act quickly in the event of crises that require their coordination. Particular attention needs to be paid to situations in which distressed conditions spill widely over national borders and the crisis is creating, or threatening to create, severe systemic risk in the world financial system as a whole.

If it is judged necessary to lend directly to troubled private institutions, the national lenders of last resort should try to restrict their emergency loans to institutions likely to remain solvent, require the troubled borrower to post sound collateral, and charge a penalty interest rate. However, practical implementation of these guidelines—originally proposed by Bagehot (chapter 3)—is even more problematic in an integrated world financial system than within a relatively closed economy. In a crisis situation, the distinction between illiquidity and insolvency is especially murky. The value of collateral is uncertain. Even the concept of a penalty interest rate is shaky. The national lenders of last resort cannot escape making discretionary judgments that can, and will, be second-guessed with the wisdom of hindsight.

No international financial organization has authority to extend emergency liquidity assistance to a *private* financial institution. That status should remain unchanged for the short and medium runs.

Emergency Lending to National Governments

Emergency lending to an entire national economy troubled by financial crisis raises issues still more complicated than those of lending to individual private institutions. Yet such lending may be critically important in some crises. In such situations the feasible borrowing entity is the government of the troubled nation.

The lending entities are usually, directly or indirectly, the governments of key creditor nations.[7] Those creditor governments may extend direct bilateral loans. They may sometimes route their loans through the BIS. But the main institutional channel for intergovernmental crisis lending is the International Monetary Fund. Lending national governments and relevant international financial organizations together constitute an official creditor community.

The IMF's lending facilities that permit quick reaction in a crisis are its Supplemental Reserve Facility and its Contingent Credit Lines. The two facilities, established in 1997 and 1999, respectively, were reviewed and streamlined in September 2000. The prequalification features of the CCL facility pose untested difficulties. (As of December 2002 the CCL had never been used.) For the shorter run, the primary burden of IMF emergency lending is likely to fall on the Supplemental Reserve Facility.

---

7. In conceivable but atypical circumstances, a consortium of private financial institutions from creditor nations might agree to make emergency loans to the troubled nation's government.

When considering emergency crisis lending to entire national economies, the official creditor community cannot use the traditional Bagehot guideline of refusing loans to potential borrowers that are insolvent while granting loans to borrowers that are solvent but merely illiquid. Entire nations do not become insolvent. Typically, a nation's aggregate economic resources far exceed its external debts. Yet a nation troubled by crisis may be unwilling or politically unable to divert sufficient national resources away from domestic uses to permit full service of its external debts. Entire nations are not put through bankruptcy proceedings; they cannot be repossessed, reorganized, or liquidated. Nor should the world community be willing to have the entire population of a nation experience great distress just because its government has been badly managing national affairs.

Just as the official creditors cannot base their decisions on the distinction between illiquidity and insolvency when the recipient of emergency liquidity assistance is a troubled nation's government, they also cannot rely on the other two Bagehot guidelines (requiring sound collateral and charging a penalty interest rate). Instead, they must base their decisions on judgments about whether the policies of the potential recipient government are sound or unsound, responsible or irresponsible. Making such judgments about policies is extremely difficult but is a better analytical basis for decisions than judgments about supposed "national solvency."

Basic Options for Crisis Management

If a financial crisis evolves and if one or more troubled nations request emergency liquidity assistance, the official creditor community will be forced to choose one of three options for each national situation:

—extend liquidity assistance to mitigate the deterioration of confidence and possible herding behavior by market participants;

—decline to extend emergency liquidity assistance but offer instead to help facilitate an orderly, cooperative postcrisis workout; or

—stand aside altogether for the time being.

The official creditors' decisions should be based primarily on two criteria: whether the government of the troubled nation requesting temporary liquidity assistance is deemed to be pursuing sound or unsound policies; and whether the situation has a significantly high or only relatively low probability of contagion and systemic risk.

The essence of collective leadership in crisis management is to make judgments about the likely severity of systemic risk. Thus the official creditors cannot rely entirely on the test of whether the government of a prospective borrowing nation is pursuing sound or unsound policies. The key decisions of the official creditors are complicated by agonizing trade-offs. Refusing emergency liquidity assistance because the policies of a prospective borrowing government are unsound could raise the probability of contagion and instability elsewhere in the world financial system. Yet because concerns are great about the risks of systemic contagion, if assistance is granted to a nation pursuing questionable policies, then the official creditors' decision will augment the problems of moral hazard. If concerns about systemic risk lead to decisions to make emergency loans in situations where the borrowing government's policies have been questionable, it becomes even more important to try to achieve improvements in those policies. Thus the essence of collective leadership in crisis management is to impose conditionality that keeps pressure on governments to pursue responsible policies.

Bailouts and Moral Hazard

Within individual nations, collective decisions to establish a lender-of-last-resort institution, to charge it with crisis management, and to grant it contingent authority to carry out emergency lending during crises inevitably generate moral hazard. Emergency lending by the lender of last resort may be seen as a bailout of private lenders. Intergovernmental crisis lending in the world financial system likewise generates moral hazard and concerns about possible bailouts.

Those charged with crisis management and prudential oversight—national lenders of last resort, national prudential supervisors, consultative groups of creditor governments, and international financial organizations—should seek to mitigate this moral hazard. But they cannot, and should not try to, eliminate it completely. The only way to eliminate the moral hazard altogether would be to prohibit international collective action in financial crises. Such a prohibition would foster worse outcomes than tolerating some degree of moral hazard while designing measures to contain it within acceptable limits.

The fundamental point about moral hazard is no different in an international than in a domestic context. The appropriate perspective is the same attitude one should have about insurance. The pervasiveness of moral hazard difficulties cannot be accepted as a valid reason for failing to provide insurance. Rather, for many circumstances insurance should be supplied but combined with incentives that seek to limit moral hazard. At the same time, policy must vigilantly seek a balanced position that keeps moral hazard incentives within reasonable bounds.

Balanced assessments of international efforts to manage financial crises should not casually employ the moral hazard label when discussing official creditor efforts to mitigate such crises. Balanced assessments should not rush to describe *any* official creditor or IMF emergency lending as a bailout.

Transparency and Constructive Ambiguity

When articulating its policies in advance of crises, a national lender of last resort should seek transparency as one of its important objectives. Yet some degree of deliberate vagueness—*constructive ambiguity*—is also desirable. The goals of transparency and constructive ambiguity compete, requiring the lender of last resort to trade them off against one another.

Constructive ambiguity can help to contain moral hazard incentives that affect private behavior. Without some degree of ambiguity, private behavior in normal periods might fall well short of adequately taking risk into account and applying caution to financial transactions. Private decisionmakers who have not been cautious in normal times will of course strongly pressure a national lender of last resort to provide emergency assistance in crises. But a skillful lender of last resort will not wish in normal times to give unambiguous assurance to private institutions that it will provide them emergency assistance on stormy days independently of how prudently they have behaved when the sun has been shining.

Yet for the development and announcement of policies about the likely collective behavior of the official creditor community during international financial crises, some substantial degree of transparency is likewise a worthy objective. With the passage of time and accumulated experience, incremental improvements in transparency should be possible. In the current intermediate state of the world polity, however, a high degree of transparency is even less attainable than within a single nation. Some degree of constructive ambiguity is not only desirable but inevitable.

A posture of constructive ambiguity is a two-edged sword. Constructive ambiguity can help by ameliorating some types of moral hazard behavior. But by adding to general uncertainty, it can enhance the skittishness of private investors. International collective governance for crisis management cannot escape this dilemma.

Concerted Lending (Private Sector Involvement in Crisis Resolution)

If a national lender of last resort extends emergency loans to individual troubled private institutions, it should simultaneously try to arrange for concerted lending by private sector creditors of the same institutions. Such "bailing in" of private creditors, though often preferable, will not be possible or even appropriate in all crisis circumstances. Foreign private creditors with cross-border claims on a troubled nation of course should not be helped to make easy use of the exit option in crisis situations. But it is a disservice to pretend that bailing in is invariably feasible. Bailing in of private creditors should not be a rigid precondition for a national lender of last resort's own emergency loans.

Intergovernmental crisis lending in the world financial system raises still more complex bail-in issues. Concerted lending arrangements that bail in the foreign private creditors of a troubled nation in recent years have come to be labeled as *private sector involvement in crisis resolution.* Accompanying intergovernmental emergency lending with such concerted lending arrangements may often be desirable from the perspectives of the troubled nation's citizens and the world community as a whole. But few measures designed to mitigate moral hazard and to bail in foreign private creditors— in fact, only a very few—are feasible.

The few possibilities are each subject to problems. Concerted cross-border lending is typically less difficult to arrange for syndicated bank loans than for bond claims. The primary steps that could be taken to improve prospects for bailing in bondholders would be for governments to encourage the more widespread use of so-called collective-action clauses in bond contracts. Official encouragement for more use of these clauses has so far been relatively weak. It could and ought to be much stronger. The governments of the wealthy industrial nations—in particular the United States— should set examples for other nations by placing such clauses in the contractual documents for their own government debt (denominated in their own currency as well as in foreign currencies).[8]

---

8. Collective-action clauses in bond contracts, a highly specialized subject for international lawyers and bond dealers, are explained and analyzed in *Crisis Management for the World Financial System.* During 2002 the views of the United States and other large industrial nations about including collective-action clauses in most bond contracts appeared to converge somewhat, with the United States signaling more support than had been evident in earlier years.

No matter how much the official creditor community may encourage private sector involvement in the resolution of international financial crises, a bailing in of foreign private creditors will not be possible in all crisis circumstances. For most nations in most crises, the official creditor community will have to decide whether or not to extend temporary liquidity assistance *before* the prospects, if any, for bailing in foreign private creditors can be clarified. Even when prospects may be favorable for attempting some type of concerted lending, there can be little assurance that bailing-in measures will eventually prove effective—regardless of whether the official creditors decide to extend or refuse temporary liquidity assistance. Thus while the official creditor community should try to encourage constructive efforts for concerted cross-border lending, it should avoid the preoccupation with the subject that frequently characterized discussions of international financial crises at the beginning of the century.

Crisis Workouts, Debt Standstills, and Debt Reschedulings and Restructurings

Especially when troubled borrowers are denied temporary liquidity assistance, financial crises may require collective leadership in facilitating orderly postcrisis workouts. When organized cooperatively and efficiently, workouts achieve a least-cost resolution of the adverse situation created by the crisis and its causes. As part of its crisis management leadership within a nation's financial reservoir, a national lender of last resort should try to facilitate orderly, expedited workout arrangements for insolvent or marginally solvent private borrowers. This facilitation is typically possible only after the heat of a crisis is past.

The official creditor community, as part of collective leadership for the world financial system, should similarly be willing to facilitate orderly and prompt workout arrangements for a troubled nation. Such a workout may often have to deal with the sovereign debt of the national government. Sometimes it may involve large groups of insolvent or marginally solvent private borrowers in the nation. In the most severe postcrisis cases, the workout may entail a rescheduling or a restructuring of both sovereign and private debt. The official creditor community can play an influential role in the negotiations for a workout by pressuring the troubled nation's government to shift away from bad or questionable policies to policies that are credibly responsible. The official creditor community can also help to prevent a chaotic grab race among the nation's external creditors, where each creditor attempts to retrieve what fraction of its assets it can through uncoordinated and uncooperative behavior, including through legal actions that undermine the prospects for a prompt and orderly workout.

Financial crises that reach an advanced stage may force private borrowers in a troubled nation to default on their external debts. The government itself may declare a debt standstill, ceasing to service its sovereign debt. Debt standstills are contentious but may sometimes be unavoidable. They can have persistent, damaging effects on a nation's ability to restore normal financial contracts and capital inflows. Yet in the exigencies of a crisis, they can also provide a breathing space and catalyze workout negotiations with foreign creditors. If a standstill is to occur, the formal decision to declare it should be a unilateral decision of the troubled nation's government.

The official creditor community, usually the IMF, may decide to make incremental loans to a crisis-afflicted nation that has declared a debt standstill ("lending into arrears"). Such lending into arrears is a provision of funds after a standstill rather than a pre- or mid-crisis extension of temporary liquidity assistance.

Official lending into arrears is tantamount to an ex post international sanction of the nation's debt standstill. Such official "approval" will be controversial, but under some circumstances may be justified. Decisions about IMF lending into arrears should be discretionary decisions of the IMF's executive board. The IMF should not require a nation's government to impose a standstill for its external debts as a mandatory condition for the IMF's agreement to lend into a postcrisis workout situation.

Although efforts to bail in private creditors and ex post international endorsements of standstills through lending into arrears can be desirable, such measures can also have destabilizing effects on private expectations and therefore on private behavior. To the degree that private creditors expect concerted-lending initiatives and debt standstills to function as prominent tools for handling financial crises and subsequently required workouts, they may make a still earlier and still more aggressive rush for the exit in conditions when a nation's position is perceived to be deteriorating. Some potential private lenders to developing nations might be scared away altogether. Such enhanced skittishness could exacerbate crisis conditions and bring forward in time the difficult decisions that the official creditors must make about bailing in, standstills, workouts, and possible lending into arrears. Because of "time-consistency" and "unsustainable-incentive" problems, the official creditors should not specify progress on concerted lending as a necessary condition of IMF lending to a nation, either for emergency temporary liquidity assistance or for postcrisis lending into workout situations.

As with other crisis-management measures originating from the official creditor community, cooperative arrangements for postcrisis workouts have to strive for a balanced approach serving the interests of both troubled debtor nations and the wider world financial system as a whole. Care must be taken that incentives are not created for debtor nations that cause them to be too willing to engage in opportunistic defaults. At the same time, the norms and procedures for resolving crises must avoid the opposite risk that workouts prove too costly and are too long deferred because of insufficient collective cooperation.

Institutional mechanisms that might facilitate efforts by the official creditor community to catalyze orderly and prompt workout arrangements for troubled debtor nations received increasing study and debate in 2001–02. The IMF itself suggested several variants of new procedures for the postcrisis restructuring of sovereign debt, including some that would require an amendment of the IMF Articles of Agreement. The largest private financial institutions and several important governments, including that of the United States, at first opposed proposals for involving the official creditor community in postcrisis restructuring. By the September 2002 annual meetings of the IMF and World Bank, however, some additional governmental support for moderate initiatives in this direction was being expressed. Such initiatives, despite the controversy surrounding them, merit further careful development. Ultimately, the international community should implement a refined version of one of the variants.

A World Lender of Last Resort?

The phrase *lender of last resort* is inseparable, for historical and substantive reasons, from discussion of financial crises. For an individual nation's financial reservoir, one can meaningfully speak of the nation's lender of last resort (chapter 3).

Not surprisingly, lender-of-last-resort language has spilled over into discussions of international financial crises. It is essential to recognize, however, that the notion of a supranational or international lender of last resort is *not* compatible with today's institutions and political conditions. No one of the central banks or governments of the wealthiest creditor nations has the aspiration or the political will to be a genuine lender of last resort for the entire world financial system. None of the existing international financial organizations—not the IMF, not the BIS, not the World Bank—can shoulder the entire range of crisis functions that collective governance is (justifiably) expected to exercise within individual nations' financial reservoirs. The international organizations can lend only to national governments. Still more important, none of the international organizations has the authority, necessary for effective lender-of-last-resort operations, to incrementally create and extinguish reserve money of any kind (high-powered liquidity usable throughout the world financial system). Regrettable though it may seem, it is thus nonetheless an awkward truth that for at least the next several decades the world cannot have a genuine centralized lender-of-last-resort capability for financial crises. The only realistic alternative for the shorter run is a constructive coordination of overall national monetary policies, especially those of the largest wealthiest nations.

Hence I avoid the phrase *international* (or *supranational*) *lender of last resort* in this book. That phrase invokes expectations that cannot be fulfilled and thus are misleading for unwary readers. It *is* sensible to want international organizations to improve their nascent capabilities for crisis management and crisis lending. Strengthened intergovernmental cooperation in these areas is crucial. But a clear-eyed appreciation of institutional constraints must underpin practical recommendations.[9]

Specialization of International Collective Governance?

Chapter 8 summarized key functions for international collective governance in finance and macroeconomics (for the "international financial architecture") but said little about the different institutional venues through which the functions might be carried out. Chapter 9 and the earlier sections of this chapter have identified short- and medium-run priorities for architectural reform. The IMF is the institutional venue that has figured most prominently in that identification. But other international organizations and various consultative groups have also been identified.

Decisions about institutional venues are self-evidently important. The general issue is how to allocate the various functional responsibilities across different collective-governance venues and how to deal with overlaps or conflicts when they arise.

A wise evolution of international collective governance requires specialization of function among international organizations and consultative groups. If the mandates of institutions are unclear or overlapping and if

---

9. Many of the recommendations made here for summary guidelines for crisis management require more careful support than can be provided in this book. Readers seeking such details should consult the extended analysis in *Crisis Management for the World Financial System*.

mission creep occurs over time at some or all of the institutions, the result can be a confusing duplication of responsibilities, unclear lines of accountability, and a diminution in effectiveness.

Within nations, specialization of function is a hallmark of government. Municipal fire departments are charged with fighting fires and overseeing measures to prevent fires, but not with ensuring the safety of the local water supply or collecting tax revenue. If the police were asked to directly monitor and enforce every type of regulation in a society, they would have an impossible job. Even if they could carry out such extensive responsibilities, they might become too large and powerful. A nation's central bank sets general monetary policies and usually participates in the maintenance of the utilities infrastructure for the financial system. But the central bank is not asked to oversee public health policies, the distribution of welfare payments, or the operation of bankruptcy courts. Specialized inspectorates with detailed technical knowledge are assigned the responsibilities for ensuring safe working conditions, vetting new drugs, or monitoring air pollution. And so on.

Specialization of function in principle should be no less applicable for international levels of collective governance than for the various levels within nations. If anything, the arguments supporting specialization are stronger at levels above the nation state. This subject is primarily a matter of politics and public administration, not economics. Theorists of international relations will develop refinements to the arguments as international collective governance becomes still more important. Nonetheless, at least for the time being, specialization of function is an appropriate rough guideline for thinking about how to allocate functional responsibilities across collective-governance institutions. Ideally, each individual international institution should remain focused on only a few responsibilities. Asking any one institution to perform too wide a range of activities could thwart its effectiveness in exercising its primary responsibilities. Mission creep occurring at many institutions is likely to lead to confusion and costly duplication of effort.

What Mandate for the IMF?

Issues about the appropriate allocation of functional responsibilities across international institutions arise most insistently for the IMF. Setting clear priorities for architectural reform thus also requires clarity in defining the IMF's mandate.

The principle of functional specialization suggests that the IMF ought to concentrate on a core set of responsibilities uniquely assigned to it. Other international institutions should defer to the IMF in those areas of core competence. Correspondingly, the IMF should be discouraged from straying significantly outside its core areas into issues that are the primary responsibility of other institutions.

A half century ago, the architects of the IMF believed the logical core areas for the IMF's mandate would be cross-border finance and macroeconomics. Particular attention would be paid to payments imbalances, exchange rates, and cross-border barriers, which in turn would require an emphasis on macroeconomic policies. That vision of the IMF's core competence is, I believe, still broadly valid today. But many dispute that vision in some way. Some want the IMF's mission more narrowly defined. Others recommend a much broader mandate. To a significant extent, the IMF's mandate was de facto broadened in the final decades of the twentieth century (for details, see the appendix).

Narrow the Mandate to Crisis Vulnerability?

The influential voices suggesting a narrower mandate recommend that the IMF concentrate on crisis prevention and, should crises occur, on their amelioration. These voices accordingly want the IMF to focus on the external vulnerability of national economies and financial systems and the prevention of "modern capital account crises." The focus of IMF surveillance would shift toward crisis vulnerability. IMF lending would be confined closely to crisis or precrisis situations and hence would not be used for liability financing of noncrisis payments deficits.

Serious analytical difficulties arise when trying to distinguish crisis from noncrisis circumstances. Even if that distinction could be made reliably, it would be unwise for the IMF to narrow the focus of its surveillance to the point where noncrisis aspects of a nation's situation and policies receive markedly less attention than in the past. Techniques are being improved to analyze the external vulnerability of a nation's economy and financial system. Efforts to monitor and assess aggregated risk and liquidity exposures are an important component of a prudent overall strategy for managing a nation's financial openness.[10] But the operational murkiness of separating crisis and precrisis circumstances from noncrisis situations, not to mention

---

10. Measures for assessing risk and liquidity exposures are summarized in chapter 11 and considered in more detail in *Prudential Oversight and Standards for the World Financial System*.

the rapidity with which an economy can move from the noncrisis to the crisis side of the dividing line, argues strongly against emphasizing crisis vulnerability to the exclusion of other aspects of surveillance. The IMF should enhance its surveillance of vulnerability to capital account crises but should not weaken the other, noncrisis aspects of its surveillance that have been slowly developing stronger legs in recent years.

The difficulty of differentiating crisis from noncrisis circumstances would be a still more formidable obstacle if the IMF were to try to restrict its lending intermediation solely to situations of actual or threatened crisis. It is neither practical nor desirable to try to sharply separate crisis and precrisis lending from more general crisis prevention and nonemergency lending. Prosperity and stability in the world system require individual nations to pursue sound policies in good times and bad. Some national governments lag well behind others in adopting sound policies and helping to integrate their nations as responsible units in the world economy and financial system. If a nation has a payments imbalance that appears to justify IMF lending, if it wants to borrow from the IMF even though it cannot claim (and of course does not want to claim) that a crisis is threatening, and if the conditionality associated with IMF lending can significantly raise the probability that the nation will pursue improved policies, the IMF should preferably lend sooner rather than waiting until a crisis can be shown to be imminent. IMF lending can sometimes be helpful for a nation and the world financial system even in circumstances when current crisis vulnerability is judged to be very low because the conditionality associated with the lending can inhibit a nation from pursuing beggar-thy-neighbor adjustment policies (such as new trade restrictions). For such reasons the IMF's operational mandate should *not* be restricted to a narrow definition of crisis vulnerability.

Responsibilities for Prudential Financial Oversight

Pressures to broaden the IMF's original mandate come from several different directions. One source of pressures is identified above: the IMF has been increasingly urged to widen its surveillance activities to cover financial standards and prudential oversight of financial systems. At the time the IMF was created, those issue areas were not prominently discussed and were not envisaged as part of the core competence of the IMF. Very recently, a consensus has begun to form that prudential financial oversight should be included within the IMF's core competence. (However, recall that this emerging consensus, while endorsing *use* by the IMF of ROSCs and FSAPs in its overall surveillance, has not endorsed allocating the primary responsibility to the IMF for actual *conduct* of the assessments incorporated in ROSCs and FSAPs.)

Within an individual nation, it is controversial whether to have prudential financial oversight concentrated at a single government institution or dispersed across multiple government agencies. The analogous question for the world as a whole is whether it would be preferable to lodge the international dimensions of standard setting and prudential supervision in a single international institution or disperse them across several such institutions. Because the existing international dimensions are today allocated to a variety of international organizations, intergovernmental committees, and even some nongovernmental associations, that question is academic. But it is nonetheless sensible to step back and thoughtfully consider whether the existing allocation of functions to particular institutions will serve the world well as international governance becomes still more complex and important. The mechanisms for coordination among institutions also deserve thoughtful review. Coordination among institutions with somewhat different but partly overlapping functional responsibilities is even more important internationally than within a domestic context.

The Joint Forum on Financial Conglomerates in principle will cope with needs for coordination among the supervisory authorities for banking (BCBS), securities firms (IOSCO), and insurance companies (IAIS). The Financial Stability Forum is intended to address the broader coordination issues where the IMF and still more international financial institutions are involved. The BIS committees on the Global Financial System and on Payment and Settlement Systems can continue to play a helpful coordinating role among central banks. Ad hoc cooperation can be intensified among the IMF, the Financial Stability Forum, and the numerous other organizations with related responsibilities identified earlier (such as the IASB, IFAC, UNCITRAL, the OECD, and the FATF). But the most important longer-run issues about the allocation of prudential oversight responsibilities between the IMF and other international financial institutions remain to be faced.

Bank supervision and regulation is a revealing illustration. Although the IMF has increasingly been pulled into assessments of banking supervision, the major initiatives in international cooperation in this area have taken place through the BIS and the BCBS. On the basis of past history, and even judging by the current intensity of activity, banking supervision is more a core area for the BIS than for the IMF. Collection and dissemination of aggregated financial data is a second vital area where both the IMF and the BIS have major and partly overlapping responsibilities.

In recent decades, the BIS has been quintessentially an institution run primarily for, and controlled by, the world's major central banks. The central banks perceive the BIS as the primary locus for their cooperation and the BCBS as the forum through which their representatives and others discuss core principles and prudential oversight for banks. The thorny issues of capital adequacy, for example, are unambiguously seen as the responsibility of the BCBS.

But what of the longer run? Some observers can be expected to argue that the IMF should gradually assume a dominant role in the global aspects of standard setting, data dissemination, and prudential oversight for banking, with the BIS and the BCBS playing a declining and just supporting role.

Sorting out the relative responsibilities of the IMF and the BIS of course involves much more than the functions of standards, data dissemination, and prudential supervision. Still more difficult is the issue of whether the IMF's mandate should include primary responsibility for the surveillance of national monetary policies. Consensus exists that the IMF should appraise the monetary policy of an individual nation as an integral part of IMF surveillance during that nation's Article IV consultations. But the central banks of the largest nations tend to perceive the BIS rather than the IMF as the primary institutional conduit for cooperative consultations and supranational surveillance of their monetary policies. To the limited extent that the major central banks have had a need for direct cooperation on issues of crisis management and lender-of-last-resort emergency lending, the BIS has also been their preferred venue.

The most delicate and fundamental issue at stake in defining the relative responsibilities of the IMF and the BIS is the desirable degree of political independence for central banks. Because today's major central banks prize the BIS as their institution, they have not welcomed finance ministries inserting themselves into BIS activities. The IMF is often perceived as more beholden to finance ministries in national governments than to national central banks. Academic and public support for the political independence of central banks waxed strong in the last two decades of the twentieth century.

Some single international organization may eventually come to be perceived as the principal locus for collective financial governance on a global scale—as a global central bank for national central banks. Over a very long run, the world community might even choose to establish a world central bank with its own instruments of global monetary policy (chapter 8). From today's perspective, it is difficult to say whether the IMF or the BIS is the more likely embryo for such an institution. It is equally unclear whether the IMF, if perceived as the embryonic world central financial institution, will have to be given greater political independence from national governments. An alternative line of speculation about the longer-run future is that the IMF and the BIS will both survive as powerful global financial institutions.

For the shorter run, the Financial Stability Forum can serve as a main institutional mechanism for coordinating decisions of the IMF, the BIS, and the finance ministries, central banks, and supervisory agencies of the major national governments. At some point, however, the world community—in particular, the central banks of the major nations—will have to formulate a clearer vision for the BIS and a refined mandate for the IMF in the areas of monetary policies and crisis management as well as financial standards, data dissemination, and prudential oversight. If both the IMF and the BIS are to survive and prosper, moreover, a day will eventually dawn when, de facto if not transparently, difficult decisions will have to be made about how to divide or share functional responsibilities between the two institutions.

Broaden the Mandate beyond Finance and Macroeconomics?

Although the mandate issues just discussed are controversial, the most contentious and difficult issues about the IMF's mandate arise because of expansion of its mission—and proposed further expansions—beyond the core areas of cross-border finance and macroeconomics. Numerous but diverse critics of the IMF urge an ambitious, expanded agenda. Opponents of a broadened mandate are concerned that mission creep has already undermined the IMF's capacities for surveillance and lending intermediation in its core areas of finance and macroeconomics.

The current debates on these matters take place against a historical background in which the IMF's mandate was de facto broadened after the mid-1970s. For multiple and complex reasons, the IMF today is deeply involved in promoting growth, supporting structural adjustment, and reducing poverty in developing nations. In its lending activities, the IMF has become an intermediary extending longer-term loans to a subset of the world's nations tending to have a persistent demand for development finance, not merely a temporary need for the liability financing of an overall payments deficit. This emphasis on lending to developing nations is a substantial departure from the original vision framed at the middle of the twentieth century.

Expansion by the IMF into the areas of growth promotion, structural adjustment, and poverty reduction greatly blurred earlier notions of how responsibilities would be allocated between the IMF and the World Bank. The World Bank was originally charged with addressing longer-term and structural aspects of promoting economic growth and development. To the extent that either institution had an explicit mandate to focus on income distribution issues and promote poverty reduction, it was the World Bank, not the IMF.

Some enthusiasts for international governance would go still further in expanding the IMF's mission. They recommend that the IMF use international environmental standards as a component of its surveillance of national policies. Others, especially concerned with labor markets and working conditions for the world's poor, recommend that the IMF help to monitor and even enforce international labor standards.

Individuals and groups push the IMF to become engaged in a wider range of issue areas for essentially political reasons. The conditionality that accompanies IMF lending to a nation's government gives the IMF leverage over national policies. Other international organizations provide little direct financial assistance to national governments and therefore usually do not have comparable leverage. Legislators or interest groups, especially those based in creditor nations, may thus be encouraged to think that they can mobilize greater force for their own objectives if they can succeed in lobbying the IMF to incorporate performance conditions about their objectives into IMF programs. Political pressures on the IMF to engage in other issue areas can also originate within the borrowing nations themselves. Domestic residents with reform agendas, for example, may regard the negotiations between the borrowing government and the IMF as an opportunity to get their particular reforms adopted.

Yet these political pressures on the IMF, if yielded to, can undercut the IMF's ability to carry out the functions in its core areas of competence. The principle of specialization in function cautions against spreading staff resources too thinly. It suggests resisting the pressures to incorporate more and more performance conditions in lending programs when those conditions are not directly related to the financial and macroeconomic purposes that are the primary rationale for IMF lending. Looking backward at the last several decades, one can empathize with the pressures on the IMF to become more deeply engaged in growth promotion, structural adjustment, and poverty reduction. Yet that de facto expansion of the IMF's mandate did represent mission creep and was not in the best long-run interests of the developing nations, creditor nations, or the IMF itself.

Promoting growth and structural adjustment and facilitating reduction in poverty should be the priority responsibility of the World Bank and the regional development banks. (A nation's government itself has the ultimate responsibility within that nation.) Those objectives should *not* be a primary responsibility of the IMF. It is a corollary of this perspective that the division of labor between the IMF and the World Bank should be clarified. The two organizations should of course cooperate closely. Both have responsibilities for surveillance of policies within individual nations. The World Bank as well as the IMF must pay attention to the effects of World Bank lending on a nation's macroeconomic and exchange rate and balance-of-payments outcomes. The IMF as well as the World Bank must assess the effects of IMF surveillance and IMF lending on a nation's growth and on its longer-term structural and social policies. To insist that the two organizations cooperate closely, however, is not to argue that the two share identical mandates. The comparative advantage of the IMF is in cross-border finance and macroeconomics. The activities of the IMF should be shaped by that core competence. The comparative advantage of the World Bank is in growth promotion, poverty reduction, and structural economic reform.

Pragmatism has to recognize that a clearcut specialization of functions for the IMF and World Bank is not now possible. Thus regardless of the merits of functional specialization, the IMF's Poverty Reduction and Growth Facility is likely to stay in the IMF. Pragmatism also counsels against unnecessary challenges to political symbolism. The IMF on behalf of all its member nations should believe, and should say publicly, that economic growth and poverty reduction are vitally important goals for the world community. The IMF must be careful not to send inadvertent signals that can be misinterpreted as implying it is disinterested in the effects of its policies and actions on poverty and injustice. Nevertheless, it would augur better for an efficient evolution of international governance if over time the World Bank could be more clearly and unambiguously assigned the leadership role in growth promotion, poverty reduction, and structural reform. The IMF does not have to be charged with a leadership role in those areas just because men and women of good conscience agree that those goals are important.

The case for extending the IMF's mandate into areas such as the surveillance of international labor and environmental standards is even weaker than the case for IMF engagement in growth promotion and poverty reduction. Here again, the issue is not the inherent worthiness of international labor and environmental standards as goals of national public policy or goals for the world community. It is a worthy aspiration to design non-protectionist international labor standards and to encourage surveillance of them by some international organization. Soundly designed international standards to protect the environment—taking the form of world minimums rather than harmonized uniform standards at the highest levels prevailing in the wealthiest industrial nations—are likewise a worthy aspiration. Surveillance of labor and environmental standards by international organizations may well be a prominent feature of international governance later in the century.

Yet the relevant issue for the IMF is whether those responsibilities should be included in its mandate. The contention that the world community should encourage surveillance of international labor or environmental standards, valid in itself, does not constitute a persuasive argument that the IMF should be charged with such surveillance. It makes more sense to allocate those surveillance functions to international organizations or other forums with specialized competence in labor market or environmental issues. In short, the IMF should not be assigned a bloated agenda that includes every important world economic problem. The IMF can be more effective and the world served better if IMF energies are focused on its core competence in cross-border finance and macroeconomics.

A subtle related issue needs brief mention. If the IMF is not to become deeply engaged in functional areas such as structural reform and microeconomic policies, does that mean IMF lending packages should never include performance conditions pertaining to structural and microeconomic policies? Caution should certainly be used in applying IMF conditionality broadly, and in particular when structural and microeconomic policies are included in performance conditions. But weighty arguments sometimes argue for such inclusion. A nation's balance-of-payments problems and its susceptibility to crisis turbulence can often be traced to structural weaknesses in the economy or financial system. If the IMF's lending and conditionality were to ignore structural weaknesses entirely, its financial assistance might often have a poor chance of turning the nation's troubles around. Financial markets do not ignore structural weaknesses and deficiencies in microeconomic policies once they are brought to light. Indeed, financial herd behavior can put disproportionate emphasis on deficiencies in structural policies after some market participants call prominent attention to them. In some circumstances, therefore, the IMF has no effective choice but to take the structural issues into account in its lending decisions.

Tension will always exist between two guidelines: keeping the IMF focused on its core-competence mandate of macroeconomics and finance; and fostering IMF lending packages that deal appropriately with nations' heterogeneous balance-of-payments difficulties, which sometimes requires extension of performance conditions into the functional areas of structural and microeconomic policies. An approach that gives weight to both guidelines is the only sensible way for the IMF to proceed.

An important part of such an approach is for the World Bank to take the lead in framing recommendations about structural and microeconomic policies for nations that wish to borrow from any of the international financial organizations. (In some specialized areas, still other international organizations should have the leadership responsibilities.) The IMF, if and when appropriate, can then apply performance conditions derived from those recommendations as a component of its lending arrangements. The IMF need not have the lead responsibility in functional areas such as structural reforms and microeconomic policies. Its conditionality can be supportive of the other international organizations and consistent with their leadership. This intermediate course can keep the IMF's agenda from becoming bloated with detailed staff work outside its core competence but yet permit its conditionality to cover noncore policies when the circumstances of a nation make that inclusion desirable.

This summary, reflecting more detailed analyses in the three companion volumes, emphasizes issues about the IMF's mandate. It also comments briefly on the missions of the BIS and the World Bank. Where and how does the OECD fit into the evolution of international governance? Significantly, and unfortunately, that question cannot be answered clearly. The OECD's mandate and functional responsibilities are the least clearly defined of all the largest international organizations. Significant overlaps in function exist between parts of the OECD and the IMF and World Bank. For a few areas such as corporate-governance standards, tax-system competition, and tax havens, the OECD has a relatively clear mandate. But for supranational surveillance of economic policies and some other broad functions of international governance, major governments appear schizophrenic about how the OECD's responsibilities should be differentiated from those of other international organizations. Several European nations with transition economies and a few of the more important developing nations have now become members of the OECD, thereby broadening its geographical mandate still further from the original historical rationale focused on Europe. OECD staff have sought to develop expertise on newly topical subjects such as the problems of population aging and of economies making a transition from socialism to capitalism. The fact remains, however, that national governments have been slow to actively reconsider and reshape the OECD's responsibilities. As with the BIS, governments will not be able to indefinitely postpone some thorny decisions about the future of the OECD.

The IMF: Whose Institution?

The drift in IMF activities since the mid-1970s toward increased engagement in the growth, structural-reform, and poverty-reduction problems of developing nations has significantly influenced popular perceptions about the institution. In many quarters the IMF is now seen as an institution whose "clients" are exclusively the developing nations. That impression, though badly misinformed, nonetheless damages efforts to strengthen and improve the IMF.

The origins of the damaging impression have already been mentioned: none of the industrial nations has been a borrower of IMF credit resources since the early 1980s. Thus for several decades the only recipients of IMF lending have been the developing nations. That change in the composition of lending in turn gradually transformed the IMF's role as a lending intermediary. The impression that the only clients of the IMF are developing nations, however, pays exclusive attention to IMF lending. It completely ignores the other functions of the IMF, most notably the IMF's surveillance of the policies of member nations (industrial as well as developing, borrowers and nonborrowers alike).

To talk about "clients" in a balanced manner, one must obviously acknowledge the asymmetries among IMF member nations. The primary asymmetry stems from the differences in the sizes and wealths of nations, and hence in their relative political power. This asymmetry inevitably influences IMF surveillance and other IMF interactions with members. For example, the IMF consults assertively with smaller members and leans on them strongly to consider changes in policies if such changes should seem appropriate. In contrast, it is less assertive with its largest and most powerful members and is more hesitant to make recommendations for policy changes in their economies. A second dimension of asymmetry is also significant. The IMF has considerably more potential leverage with members who are currently borrowing (or contemplating the possibility of borrowing in the near future) than with nonborrowing members. That leverage stems from the conditionality associated with IMF lending. Given the absence of borrowing by industrial nations since the early 1980s, the IMF has influenced the economic policies of developing nation members to a much greater extent than those of industrial nations.

The asymmetries have unsurprising consequences. When IMF consultations bring to light differences between a member nation's government and the IMF, for example, the resolution of the differences reflects the asymmetries. When a small nation and the IMF disagree, the small nation usually bends and falls into line. If one of the largest nations and the IMF disagree, the IMF typically falls into line.

Asymmetry in the relative political power of nations is a fact of life. The wealthiest, most powerful nations have the largest IMF quotas. Since the large industrial nations are no longer borrowing from the IMF, on average those nations are much the most important creditor-lenders in the IMF's lending intermediation, accounting for a very high percentage of the total resources lent to developing nations borrowing from the IMF. Because the large, wealthy nations have the largest quotas, they also control the bulk of the voting power in the IMF. Hence they "call the shots" in important IMF decisions.

The inevitable asymmetries contribute to the impression that the only nations benefiting from the existence of the IMF are developing nations. The mistaken corollary of that mistaken impression is that the IMF exists because the large wealthy nations condescend to contribute their resources to it. The simple-minded version of this sloppy caricature is that the IMF is a charity run by the wealthy nations for the benefit of poor nations.

This mistaken caricature of the IMF would not merit mention here if those holding this view were lacking any influence in political discussions of cross-border financial problems. Unfortunately, the caricature is often encountered in the national legislatures of industrial nations. Some members of the Congress in the United States, for example, frequently invoke that characterization of the IMF. A version with its rough edges polished off even permeates the criticisms of the IMF in the March 2000 report to the U.S. Congress and Treasury Department of the International Financial Institution Advisory Commission (the so-called Meltzer Commission).

The frequently voiced caricature is fundamentally wrong because it fails to appreciate the significance of supranational surveillance and additional IMF functions other than IMF lending intermediation. Worst of all, it embodies a badly distorted understanding of the selfish interests of the major industrial nations. The wealthiest nations have the most to gain from a healthy stable evolution of the world economy. They have the most to lose if the world economy and financial system malfunction. The best hope for improved prosperity management—for the world as a whole, and not least for the largest and wealthiest nations—is to nurture a gradual strengthening of collective surveillance over national economic policies. That evolution requires increased and more thoughtful support of the IMF.

Consider, for example, the selfish interests of the United States. The United States has an even greater stake in an effective IMF than smaller, developing nations. Constructive supranational surveillance and crisis management over time are likely to bring gross benefits to U.S. citizens that are an order of magnitude larger than the gross benefits for most other nations. Informed citizens in the United States and other wealthy, powerful nations should regard the IMF as "*our* institution" serving *our* interests, not as an altruistic charity that drains *our* resources to benefit *other* poor nations in the rest of the world.

11

Single-Nation and Systemic Guidelines for Cross-Border Finance

Earlier chapters traverse a wide terrain, raising difficult issues. The topography is complex: numerous peaks and valleys, few paved roads, trails sometimes poorly marked. Those not already having a reliable map and who have not trekked in these territories before may miss landmarks and lose sight of the higher peaks. Readers may thus welcome help in trying to take stock of where the analysis has led them.

An ideal stocktaking suppresses details and emphasizes landmarks and the higher peaks. In effect, the author and intrepid readers together put their arms around the complexity and compress the whole into a manageable, integrated perspective. The stocktaking goal of singling out key points and differentiating them from the larger whole motivates the final three chapters in this book.

Chapters 8 through 10 examined international financial architecture and suggestions for its reform from the perspective of the world financial system as a whole. Policy choices were analyzed as collective choices for the world community, not as choices for a single nation.

Yet for practical purposes, policymakers and analysts typically approach the problems of cross-border finance and collective governance from the perspective of the individual nation. Most citizens of a nation, after all, have interests and identities associated primarily if not exclusively with that nation. Policymakers in the nation's government are politically accountable to home citizens. The initial sections of this chapter accordingly put the spotlight on issues of cross-border finance as they arise for key policymakers in a single nation. The analysis constitutes, in effect, a normative answer to the policy dilemma for individual nations identified in chapter 1: how to resolve the inevitable trade-off between national autonomy and openness to the global economy.

After the initial focus on the individual nation, the final sections of the chapter continue with normative analysis but revert to a cosmopolitan, global perspective. Adopting a cosmopolitan view is consistent with a realistic acknowledgment of the intermediate messiness of the world polity and the fact that the predominant political constituencies will continue to be nation states. The cosmopolitan perspective does imply, however, that the individuals whose views are relevant are policymakers and citizens of particular nations whose interests and identities are *not* primarily associated with their own nation. Instead, such individuals perceive themselves as seeking to encourage an appropriate functioning for the economy and financial system of entire regions or the world as a whole. Correspondingly, the archetypal policymakers whose perspective is emphasized in the latter parts of the chapter are top officials or staff members of international financial organizations.

Policy Choices for an Individual Nation

To give realism and nuance to what follows, the exposition abandons abstraction and adopts hypothetical specificity. You the reader are asked to sit in the chair of the minister of finance and economy for a particular nation. Your job is to weigh policy issues as they come across the minister's desk.

To sharpen consideration of alternatives, imagine that your government came to power following an election just a few weeks ago. Imagine further that you and your staff have been working hard since your appointment to prepare an economic and financial strategy for the nation. You are due to summarize the draft strategy in a presentation at tomorrow morning's cabinet meeting.

As you sweat over the draft strategy, you are acutely aware that your government is politically accountable to *home* citizens and residents. Home citizens, with perhaps few exceptions, are deeply rooted in the values, culture, and institutions of your nation. They typically judge outcomes by whether the home polity and economy do well or poorly. They tend not to have a cosmopolitan outlook and give little weight to the welfare of foreign nations. As minister, your decisions must be driven primarily by the interests of home constituencies. In short, your perspective is firmly and unabashedly national.

For which nation are you the minister of finance and economy? For the general discussion here, it is convenient to suppress your national identity. The goal is to summarize generalizations that will apply to most, in some cases all, nations. But as you sit in the minister's chair, do not presume that you are making choices for one of the very wealthiest and most powerful of the world's nations. Suppose, rather, that you have earned your cabinet job in, for example, an emerging-market or other developing nation.

Overall Economic and Financial Strategy and the Nation's Openness

Your government has numerous goals. For your job and your strategy, the economic and financial goals are paramount. You must nonetheless keep the noneconomic goals always in mind. In particular, you cannot be impervious to influences and trends that undermine indigenous values and institutions or threaten valuable features of home culture and home social life. To the extent feasible, you want the nation to be buffered against forces that merely homogenize home culture with trends in the rest of the world. Yet you know it is essential for the nation to engage in extensive transactions and communications with foreign nations. Management of the nation's openness to the rest of the world is thus a central preoccupation.

Even though your strategy presentation tomorrow will highlight economic and financial goals, the full list of such goals is a long one. They include

—avoidance of sharp fluctuations in output and employment (no recessionary busts or excessive booms);

—maintenance of reasonable price stability (no pronounced, persistent inflation or deflation in the prices of goods and services);

—continued robust growth and development of the economy;

—rapid adoption of technological innovations and new products originating abroad that will aid in raising home productivity and incomes;

—preservation of a stable, smoothly operating, and efficient financial reservoir;

—maintenance of accounting and audit procedures, financial standards, and legal processes and institutions to underpin the economy and financial system;

—reduction of poverty within the nation and encouragement of less inequality in the distribution of income and wealth;

—monitoring of the nation's external vulnerability and, to the extent feasible, shoring up of the nation's ability to adjust to adverse developments (originating either at home or abroad);

—avoidance of disruptive fluctuations in the nation's exchange rate and unsustainable trends in the nation's balance-of-payments and international investment positions; and

—establishment of a reputation for the nation as a responsible component of the regional and world economy (no perceptions by the rest of the world that the nation is a renegade jurisdiction).

You are a realist. You well know that these goals are complex and that they cannot all be achieved simultaneously. Trade-offs among them are inevitable. A major part of your task in coming months will be to help your fellow cabinet members better appreciate the difficult trade-offs that have to be made.

Many considerations constrain the choice of an overall strategy. The relative sizes of the nation's economy and population, its geography and endowment of natural resources, its existing patterns of cross-border trade and communication, and the sophistication of its technological capacities and institutions relative to those in the rest of the world, for example, are all crucial factors shaping the limited range of possible policy alternatives.

Given the limited range of choices available, management of the nation's openness requires a policy posture about the overarching trade-off between the degree of the nation's autonomy and the extent of its integration with the rest of the world. Nurturing the existing openness and possibly encouraging more of it could bring sizable benefits. But doing so would come with pressures for homogenization, would expose the nation's economy and financial system to stringent and sometimes fickle discipline from external influences, and could induce political and social backlashes. The more the nation lags behind in its stage of economic and financial development and the less robust are its governance infrastructures, the steeper the trade-off in trying to manage its openness.

In your presentation for your cabinet colleagues, you plan to summarize guidelines for general macroeconomic policies. You will suggest guidelines for the choice of exchange rate arrangements and how you propose to manage them. You will speak of the utilities infrastructure supporting the nation's financial reservoir, and, in particular, you will recommend policies for financial standards and the supervision and regulation of financial institutions. Because of the salience of the degree of openness of the national financial reservoir, you will suggest a general stance about financial breakwaters and how you propose to manage liquidity and external vulnerability exposures.[1]

Before you turn to the specifics of your proposed strategy, you would like to give your colleagues some general way of thinking about the variety of policy trade-offs that will shape their prospective decisions. You recall a textbook exposition encountered as a student earlier in your life and accordingly draft some remarks inspired by it.

To simplify, you consider asking your colleagues to concentrate on three financial objectives consistent with and derived from the longer list of basic goals already summarized. The nation would prefer to retain economic and financial independence from the rest of the world and in particular to have its central bank pursue an independent monetary policy. Designate that first objective as *financial autonomy*. The nation would like to avoid disorderly fluctuations in financial prices. In particular, because the external exchange value of the nation's currency is a financial price with pervasive effects throughout the economy and financial system, the nation seeks *exchange rate stability*. Third, the nation would prefer to enjoy the many benefits associated with *full financial integration with the rest of the world*.

The textbook exposition, you recall, labels these three objectives as an "impossible trinity." The insight stressed in the textbook is that the three objectives are mutually incompatible. Any two of the three may be attainable. Full financial integration with the rest of the world and exchange rate stability could be realized if the nation were to join a currency union and give up an independent monetary policy. Financial autonomy and exchange rate stability could be achieved if the nation were to erect barriers to prevent cross-border financial transactions. If the exchange rate were allowed to fluctuate freely, it might be possible to have financial autonomy and complete freedom for cross-border capital flows. But the three taken together are not mutually attainable. The more the nation strives to attain any two of the three, the more it must surrender aspirations to simultaneously achieve the third.

1. The presumption is that all of the nation's economic policies will be thoughtfully reviewed by the new government, not that the new government will necessarily implement fresh choices for all the policies. Some significant degree of continuity through time for government policies, including before and after elections, is likely to be beneficial for the nation's welfare.

You rightly regard this impossible-trinity insight as important. But staff members have warned you not to use the textbook catechism in your presentation unless you modify it substantially. They point out that the cabinet is not required to be purist about these objectives. For example, rather than striving for the whole loaf of financial autonomy and the whole loaf of full freedom for cross-border financial transactions, the nation could surrender some of both objectives, aiming at half a loaf of autonomy and half a loaf of financial integration with the rest of the world. More generally, rather than striving for full attainment of any two of the three objectives, the nation may be better off aiming at some mixture of all three.

You have therefore revised your draft presentation, with thanks to your staff for helping you avoid too simplified a view about trade-offs. You will now stress to your cabinet colleagues that they should not think in terms of purist choices. They need not suppose that they must wholly surrender their hopes for any of the three derived objectives (not to mention all of their more basic goals). You will, to be sure, still stress the difficult nature of the trade-offs, not allowing your colleagues to believe that all the nation's goals are mutually compatible. But you will urge them to be eclectic and pragmatic in seeking a *compromise combination* of the nation's goals.

You plan to stress two other general points in your presentation. First, once a coherent strategy and combination of goals has been decided, the government should articulate the strategy to both citizens and foreigners. When informed observers have an accurate grasp of the nation's strategy and the combination of goals that shape it, implementation of the strategy is much more likely. Second, you want your colleagues to understand that they must be prepared to adjust the strategy (and publicly explain the adjustments) if circumstances should substantially change the compromise combination of goals that best suits the nation's prospective needs.

Macroeconomic Policies

Several other ministers in the new cabinet are known to regard you as a risk-averse conservative on economic and financial matters. You expect them to stir restively when you emphasize the overriding priority to be given to sound macroeconomic policies. Notwithstanding their attitudes, in fact partly because of them, you plan to blow that tune on the trumpets at the outset.

Responsible monetary policy conducted by the central bank and prudent fiscal policies—the budget revenues and expenditures of the varying layers of government, and especially the balance between aggregate revenues and aggregate expenditures—shape the general climate within which all decisions are taken in the wider economy and financial system. Stable macroeconomic policies are no less a collective good, and even more vital, than many other collective goods supplied by government. When macroeconomic policies are unsound, those weaknesses seep into every area of the government's economic and financial strategy. Sooner or later, the weaknesses can undermine all other policies, even if the other policies are competently designed.

Hence you plan to warn your colleagues that they should never believe that special effort in their functional area of responsibility can be a valid substitute for sound macroeconomic policies. Temptation always exists to cut a corner here or there. When two ministries competing for new resources would prefer to avoid the hard choice of which should have priority, the cabinet must avoid the easy route of expanding resources for both departments, thereby undermining agreements about overall budget targets. The government must avoid supporting short-run hopes for boosts to investment by pressuring the central bank to postpone interest rate increases at times when the general macroeconomic situation requires a stabilizing tightening of financial conditions. And so on.

Establishing sound overall budget targets is difficult for any economy, no less so in your open economy aspiring to robust growth and development. For the objective of growth, the government as a whole should over time run a significant budget surplus, not a budget deficit. The government's economic behavior thereby *adds* government savings to domestic private savings generated for the economy, permitting higher investment for the economy as a whole. Budget deficits—government dissaving—reduce total national saving and thereby *subtract* from the ability of the economy to invest and grow. In an open economy such as yours, only limited scope exists for using the government's budget balance as a tool for shorter-run macroeconomic stabilization. And there will virtually never be justification for permitting the "cyclically adjusted" budget to slip into large and progressively increasing deficit.[2] Setting a target for surpluses in the overall budget also has an international justification: budget surpluses typically have favorable effects on the expectations of foreign private investors, encouraging them to bring foreign-generated savings into the

---

2. The cyclically adjusted budget balance refers to the difference between revenues and expenditures when both are adjusted to exclude shorter-run changes due to macroeconomic fluctuations beyond the government's control.

nation's financial reservoir and thereby raising still further the total savings available to finance domestic investment.

Never mind if your colleagues may grow tired of the mantra about sound macroeconomic policies. The mantra is right. If challenged, you can respond with an authoritative statement by the head of the U.S. central bank, Alan Greenspan: "We may be in a rapidly evolving international financial system with the bells and whistles of the so-called new economy. But the old-economy rules of prudence [about sound monetary and fiscal policies] are as formidable as ever. We violate them at our own peril."[3]

(Earlier chapters do not discuss the domestic aspects of macroeconomic policies in detail. Nor as minister do you review the specifics of those policy choices here. The omission of the specifics is because the book focuses on cross-border finance and international governance, not of course because the choices about macroeconomic policies are of secondary importance.)

Exchange Regime

International finance discussions, whether in policy circles, academic analyses, or newspapers, are interminably preoccupied with exchange rate regimes and exchange rate policies. Many commentators, and possibly even one of your fellow ministers, regard the choice of exchange regime as the single most important decision to be made by a nation's government. Some go still further to presume that other national choices pale into secondary significance if a nation makes the all-important choice of exchange regime correctly.

You and your staff understand, however, that the conventional views about exchange regimes and exchange rate policies are misguided. You want the cabinet to guard against the disproportionate emphasis that this subject commonly receives relative to other, still more important dimensions of the nation's economic and financial policies.

Any exchange regime is afflicted by a variety of uncertainties. Any exchange regime will reflect and exacerbate financial turbulence if your nation adopts seriously faulty macroeconomic policies and inadequate prudential oversight policies. No exchange regime can insulate the nation from unexpected adverse shocks, originating either at home or abroad. When national policies are unsound or adverse shocks are large, the financial system can readily fall into major trouble as the world capital markets lose

3. Greenspan (2000).

confidence in the nation. The nation can then suffer large disruptions to its economy—no matter what the exchange regime.

One of the easiest ways for a nation to get into bad financial trouble is to peg its exchange rate when developing circumstances will probably require changes in the rate. But a floating exchange rate will not prevent trouble if domestic policies are badly out of whack or if foreign financial markets lose confidence.

The more open your nation's financial reservoir is to the rest of the world and the fewer its frictions inhibiting cross-border transactions, the greater is its vulnerability to unsound national policies and unexpected adverse shocks. Complete freedom for cross-border financial transactions will certainly undermine any regime that pegs exchange rates. Yet complete freedom can also facilitate severe turbulence within an exchange regime that permits untrammeled flexibility in the exchange rate. Any conceivable exchange regime can be temporarily overwhelmed in stormy conditions, the more so if there are no cross-border or cross-currency breakwaters.

Although many analysts yearn for an "optimal" exchange regime, no such regime exists. Good exchange rate policy is highly dependent on the context in which it is implemented. For your individual nation, no single regime may be best in all times and all circumstances. There is certainly no single regime that is ideal for all nations in all circumstances at all times.

Conventional wisdom in recent years gravitated toward the view that the only viable options for a nation are the two extremes: either the pure flex of free floating, or the hard fix of irrevocable pegs through a currency board or actual currency union. That "corner-solution" view asserts that the middle ground of intermediate exchange regimes is bound to disappear in the short or medium runs. Yet that view does not rest on sound theoretical foundations or robust empirical evidence. And, again, no exchange rate regime—none—can insulate your nation from financial turbulence and economic disruption if its macroeconomic and prudential oversight policies are unsound.

The awkward truth is that the yearning for an ideal set of exchange rate arrangements is misguided. You thus must convince your cabinet colleagues that the manner and degree of exchange rate variability are not, in themselves, the financial policy issues of overriding importance for your nation. The cabinet should avoid a preoccupation with the choice of exchange regime and make its exchange regime decisions jointly with decisions about the rest of the government's macroeconomic and financial system policies. The highest priority should be placed on developing sound macroeconomic policies and ensuring high standards and competent prudential oversight for the nation's financial system.

Policies and Oversight for the Financial System

The general public has little knowledge about the collective-governance utilities infrastructure for the financial system. For many, the subject has not even swum into their ken. Some of your cabinet colleagues regard this subject as unsexy and relatively unimportant. You and your staff know otherwise.

The nation's financial reservoir cannot function well without adequate systems for accounting, auditing, and data collection and dissemination. Sound legal processes and institutions are fundamental. Workable procedures must exist for the monitoring and enforcement of contracts and for working out the consequences when particular contracts are not honored. Procedures for accounting and auditing underpin the enforcement of contracts. The collection, aggregation, and dissemination of data about the activities of financial institutions support the evaluation of risks and trends for individual financial institutions and for the financial system as a whole. The legal system provides laws and rules that facilitate the resolution of disputes about contracts and the handling of defaults and insolvencies. Prudential financial oversight—collective-governance supervision and regulation of financial institutions and financial markets—is a vital foundation for a smoothly functioning economy and financial system. Prudential oversight is essential for both macroprudential stability and for microprudential efficiency.

The utilities infrastructure in your nation's financial system has noteworthy weaknesses at the current time but appears not desperately in need of repair. Financial standards and prudential oversight are significantly below the world minimum standards evolving in international discussions. Yet in your judgment the infrastructure can be built upon and strengthened. Radical scrapping and rebuilding from new foundations appears, fortunately, to be unnecessary.

An important initial task for you is to persuade the cabinet that a strengthening of financial standards and prudential oversight is an important objective for the nation. The cabinet and then the wider public need to perceive this goal as a critical element of the overall strategy.

You frankly acknowledge that it is not feasible for your nation immediately to raise financial standards and prudential oversight to evolving world minimums. The human and budgetary resources available to the government do not permit such a rapid move. Slowness in acquiring the needed administrative capacities and in learning new behavior, and the inertia inevitably involved in changing government institutions, will make the improvement process protracted. Today's most advanced nations took decades, not merely years, to improve the standards, norms, and institutions in their own financial systems.

You had been thinking of suggesting another reason that the pace of reforms in the areas of financial standards and prudential oversight should not occur full speed ahead. The failures last year of two moderate-size banks and an important brokerage institution are still vivid memories for both national and foreign investors. Those failures revealed several shortcomings in the supervisory and regulatory structure. Worse, you surmise (though your staff is still trying to obtain reliable judgments from your bank, securities, and insurance regulators) that several prominent financial institutions are carrying large amounts of nonperforming loans on their balance sheets and have much weaker than desired capital positions. It may eventually prove necessary, you can imagine, for your supervisory authorities to close one or more of these institutions. Yet during the initial months of your government's incumbency, you yourself are not eager—and you can confidently predict that your cabinet colleagues will be even less willing—to have the financial news dominated by such supervisory actions.

But your staff has warned you that regulatory forbearance—the go-slow, act-later-rather-than-sooner treatment of the weak financial institutions you had been considering—could turn out to be dangerous and even bad politics. The financial history of other nations, you have been reminded, is littered with episodes of regulatory forbearance that in hindsight were shown to have been unwise and costly. If at its outset the new government condones and is perceived to condone excessive regulatory forbearance, the economic and political costs of dealing with the situation later on might be even greater. In principle, you believe that supervision and regulation of financial institutions should be conducted on sound principles without short-run political interference. On further reflection, therefore, you may not bring up the subject of the possibly weak financial institutions tomorrow morning. You will recommend a measured pace for reforms of financial standards and prudential oversight but not rest the case on regulatory forbearance.

You expect to be asked by another minister about the nation's policy toward financial institutions owned or partially owned by foreign investors. Because you believe the nation's existing capacities to operate a financial utilities infrastructure are worth preserving and strengthening, you do not sanction the piggybacking option of encouraging foreign institutions to play a dominant role in the financial reservoir as a substitute for strengthening the nation's own financial standards and its own indigenous apparatus for prudential oversight. You thus expect to recommend a halfway-house approach to your colleagues.

You can recite several arguments in favor of foreign involvement in the financial system. Foreign-owned institutions may improve the quality and range of available financial intermediation services, directly for their own customers and indirectly by serving as role models for domestically owned institutions. The foreign institutions may use better accounting and auditing procedures; they may disclose more and better-quality data about their operations; they may bring newer and more efficient technologies with them. Conceivably, they may help the national economy and financial system to better withstand local shocks. They might be less tempted to engage in connected lending, bribery, or other forms of corruption.

But you also want to remind your colleagues of arguments that cut the other way. In times of financial distress, foreign-controlled institutions might be *less* rather than more of a stabilizing force than domestic institutions. For example, they might be more prone than domestic institutions to use the exit option to flee the national reservoir. No guarantee exists that foreign-owned institutions will always be on their good behavior and import best practices from abroad. Foreign financial institutions may not be attentive to the particular needs of local borrowers; they may be less responsive to local culture and values; they are capable of sparking local resentment and political tension. More generally, an increasing relative role for foreign institutions may further undermine national autonomy.

You find the general arguments of limited help in formulating a policy about the penetration of foreign-owned institutions in the national economy. Your recommendation is for an eclectic stance: permit somewhat greater penetration by foreign institutions, but keep the policy under continuous watchful review.

You propose to remind your colleagues that investments in the national economy taking the form of sticky capital are preferable, other things equal, to skittish capital. Sticky capital is somewhat more likely to exercise "voice" in stormy weather. Skittish capital can precipitously decide to use the "exit" option. Inward direct investment from abroad, therefore, is usually more stable and more beneficial than bank loans from abroad or foreigners' lending in other short-term or skittish forms. You also feel obliged to emphasize, however, that financial activity without potentially skittish capital is impossible, either within nations or across national borders. All capital is skittish to some extent. The best the nation can do is to formulate policies that encourage sticky capital (especially inward foreign direct investment) and that establish prudent guidelines for avoiding excessive exposures to the most skittish forms of foreign capital. Some degree of skittishness is an inescapable aspect of borrowing savings from the rest of the world. The cabinet, and the public generally, should realize that policies to encourage sticky capital cannot alone ensure financial stability.

On these matters, in sum, you want the cabinet to acknowledge that the vigor and stability of financial and economic activity critically depend on sound financial standards and effective prudential oversight. You do not want to leave a misleading impression that good policies in this area can somehow be magic bullets that slay all financial difficulties. Even with further improvements in the nation's standards and oversight, you feel it likely that financial problems will now and again afflict the nation. You are recommending that the government should strengthen standards and prudential oversight. You want to proceed cautiously rather than abruptly. But you do want to proceed. Caution, you will remind the cabinet, is not procrastination.

Financial Breakwaters

The part of your overall strategy that you expect to be most controversial with the cabinet is your eclectic attitude about cross-border financial transactions. You hope your nuanced adaptation of the impossible-trinity insight will help lay the ground for a balanced discussion. But you also know that views within the cabinet differ greatly. One of your colleagues is known for privately espousing the view that the national financial system should be entirely open to the rest of the world. His perspective is essentially the Golden Straitjacket position of Thomas Friedman (chapter 4). In sharp contrast, another fellow minister has instincts similar to those who would build relatively high barriers at the border. The extreme version of his view is the Great Wall position.

Your hope is to win support for an intermediate approach to cross-border transactions, just as more generally you want the nation to seek a compromise combination of the nation's economic and financial goals rather than a purist pursuit of some subset. You plan to recommend a modest but carefully circumscribed use of *financial breakwaters*. But you know you are swimming upstream against the current of journalistic commentary and the professional opinions of many economists and policymakers in the outside world.[4]

To refresh your cabinet colleagues on the issues at stake, you plan to sketch a summary of the general arguments for and against unfettered capital flows. On the benefits side, you will begin with the basic point that capital flows in and out of the nation mean that the nation's residents can enjoy higher standards of living than would otherwise be possible (time paths of consumption that are higher, better adapted to national preferences, and not rigidly tied to the peculiarities of their geography). National investment decisions do not have to be inflexibly linked to national saving decisions. Financial prices and valuations within national reservoirs respond promptly to new information, which further enhances economic efficiency.

Another consideration on the benefits side of the ledger: freedom for financial transactions across borders permits residents to hold their assets as they wish, not only inside but outside the nation. If one holds the normative views that individuals should be free to receive information from anywhere in the world, to express their views openly, to travel freely not only at home but abroad, and to buy and sell not only home-produced but also foreign-produced goods and services, the freedom to invest one's wealth anywhere in the world is a logical concomitant to the other freedoms.

Next you plan to make a provocative argument. Relatively unfettered cross-border financial transactions exert discipline on our government, you plan to say. Cross-border capital flows help to hold us politically accountable. The ability of foreigners and our home residents to pull funds out of our financial system (the exit option) forces us to behave better—for example refraining from unsustainable economic policies—than we might otherwise behave. Furthermore, when we pursue policies perceived as exemplary, we will induce net capital inflows, thereby enhancing economic welfare in the nation. In effect, you will argue, participants in world financial markets vote continuously in an ongoing election about the soundness of our policies.

You plan to observe further that your government could erect nonporous barriers to cross-border financial transactions only with difficulty

---

4. Identification of alternative postures toward the openness of a nation's financial system, definition and analyses of financial breakwaters, and detailed discussion of the points summarized in the text of this section are included in the companion study *Prudential Oversight and Standards for the World Financial System*.

and at significant costs to the nation's residents. Administrative costs might be sizable. Such barriers would in some degree cause resource misallocations in the wider economy. Pressures would be severe to make administrative exceptions. Such exceptions would create enhanced opportunities for government failures, notably capture by special interests, or even outright corruption.

With some of your cabinet colleagues squirming in their chairs and imagining the strictures of the Golden Straitjacket, you will then shift to the other side of the balance sheet to emphasize the possible costs associated with unfettered cross-border and cross-currency financial transactions.

You will first acknowledge that financial openness to the rest of the world has adverse consequences for the autonomy of the nation's economic policies and the controllability of the national economy. The autonomy of the nation's economic policy is the effectiveness of its policy instruments in influencing national target variables. Increases in financial interdependence typically diminish this autonomy. Openness of the economy also means that policy actions taken abroad and nonpolicy disturbances originating abroad spill over into our nation. To an uncertain degree and, frequently, in an undesired direction, these externally generated forces can buffet our domestic economic targets. Increases in our financial openness thus typically diminish the degree of control we can exert over our national target variables, you will say. Our policy decisions become more difficult to make, and more uncertain in their consequences. In particular, we are less able to maintain financial conditions at home that diverge greatly from financial conditions elsewhere in the world.

Next on the costs side of the balance sheet, you will emphasize that unconstrained cross-border finance comes with enhanced risks of financial vulnerability. You will speak of the informational asymmetries, adverse selection, and moral hazard issues that are peculiarly difficult with cross-border capital flows. And you will summarize the potential fragilities associated with herding behavior and contagion, and possibly excessive volatility in asset prices. You earlier noted that the prompt and sensitive responses of financial markets to new information can be a blessing. But to be even-handed, you will also now acknowledge that this sensitivity is a double-edged sword, enhancing the risks of instability.

From the perspective of your nation, the risks of financial instability from cross-border finance are exacerbated by the exit options available to domestic residents and foreign creditors alike. Those exit options limit the policy choices open to the nation's government precisely because they give freedom to individuals, firms, and financial institutions to transfer assets out of the nation. You mentioned this point on the benefits side of the balance sheet, observing that this freedom can be construed as a constructive discipline on the government's decisions. But the benefits of shifting assets and liabilities freely out of or into the nation is again a double-edged sword, generating added risks for the nation as a whole even as it enhances the freedom of individual economic agents.

Foreign investors, enthusiastic this month about future prospects for the nation's economy and unconcerned about this month's government policies, may this month ladle funds into the domestic reservoir with great abandon. But next month or next year—perhaps with a valid trigger for their actions, perhaps not—fickle foreign investors may rush for the exits and cause severe disruption to the economy's evolution. Do unfettered capital flows exercise constructive discipline, or rather do they act like a whipsaw, destabilizing the nation's reservoir and economy? (If you get a question on this point from your fellow minister who wants to wear the Golden Straitjacket, you plan to remind him of a remark made by the minister of finance from a neighboring nation of comparable size who traveled through your capital two weeks ago. That official observed that large capital flows surging into his relatively small nation reminded him of elephants trampling in a pond, making it muddy. He acknowledged that capital flows surging into a large nation might be analogous to elephants moving into the forest, where they may get lost in the general environment and cause little commotion. But if your nation is more like a small pond, he warned, watch out!)

Your final point about the potential costs of unfettered capital flows across the nation's borders is a reminder about the existence of financial crime and money laundering as an undesirable element in the world's financial system. Your nation is not an offshore financial center. Nor has it been accused of widespread laxity in its prudential oversight or in its regulations inhibiting money laundering and tax evasion. But you remind your colleagues that no nation is impervious to criminal activities. Not even the most ardent proponents of unfettered capital flows would apply the "freedom" argument to assets and liabilities incurred through criminal activities.

You know that the cabinet will find it difficult to reach a consensus on this aspect of your overall strategy. Many of your colleagues are eager to borrow savings from the rest of the world to promote the nation's growth and development. They believe, with some justification, that your nation has not done well in encouraging and mobilizing the savings of national residents. They argue that economic activity and welfare would fall well short of their potential levels if national investment were largely restricted to the savings that the nation's economy is currently capable of generating on its own. With the assistance of foreign investors and creditors, the nation's enterprises could raise domestic investment well above the flow of national savings. These colleagues, and you largely agree with them, feel that the *gross* benefits of cross-border capital flows for your nation could be very substantial, probably even proportionately larger than gross benefits experienced by financially more advanced nations.

At the same time, other cabinet colleagues are wary of extreme financial openness. You yourself and your staff share some of that concern. The earlier parts of your presentation for tomorrow emphasize that the financial utilities infrastructure in your nation requires strengthening. Without a strong utilities infrastructure the nation is especially vulnerable to financial instability. You are prepared to welcome some amount of foreign direct investment in the economy. But borrowing from abroad could be overdone. And you recognize that large amounts of capital inflow may provoke political controversy. You suspect many foreign bankers and portfolio investors of fickleness and an inadequate appreciation of your economy's strengths as well as its weaknesses. Possible risks loom large. Under unexpectedly adverse future conditions, you fear, the economy could suffer very substantial *gross* costs from unfettered financial openness.

The fact that weighty considerations can be advanced on both sides of the question drive you toward your intermediate position on financial openness. You believe that the nation can decide, wisely, to accept some reductions in its formal sovereignty and in its de facto autonomy. The benefits resulting from borrowing the savings of foreigners to exploit profitable investment opportunities at home could more than offset the costs from erosion of indigenous values and institutions and from erosion of the ability to sustain local economic conditions marginally different from conditions outside the nation. At the same time, you aspire to maintain modest frictions interposed between the national financial system and the outside world. Hence you are an advocate of selected financial breakwaters, chosen so as not to pose major obstacles to cross-border financial transactions but still to provide modest, partial protection against some of the potential risks and costs.

Your policy stance about breakwaters requires avoidance of drastic new measures. You believe it is easier to get things wrong by erecting new and excessive barriers to cross-border transactions than by taking an excessively liberal view. In fact, the best choices for the nation may turn on the appropriate pace and sequencing for relaxation of existing breakwater measures.

Your draft presentation for tomorrow suggests several guidelines for shaping the decisions about financial breakwaters. You will stress the need to keep such measures in perspective; in particular, you will point out that the government should give substantially more attention to its overall financial standards and prudential oversight policies than to its breakwater measures per se. You will underscore the importance of not perceiving breakwater measures as substitutes for sound national macroeconomic policies, for a suitably chosen exchange regime, for maintenance of a strong international investment position, or for competent supervision and regulation of the financial system generally. You will emphasize that breakwater measures should be based, whenever feasible, on price-related market incentives rather than on direct administrative controls.

As a further guideline for decisions, you will argue that your nation should design its breakwaters to try to moderate unwanted capital inflows rather than stem unwanted capital outflows. If excessive inflows of capital can be moderated in boom times, the nation can better inhibit the emergence of major imbalances and risks. It may be helpful, for example, to adjust the height of a breakwater measure upward when capital inflows are exuberant, especially if foreign investors' perceptions are increasingly based on short-run herding rather than sound decisions about the medium- and long-run fundamentals of the economy. Such prevention can in turn lower the probability of subsequent disruptive outflows in times of possible adversity. An emphasis on inhibiting excessive inflows is more appropriate than waiting to act until a crisis hits, at which time both domestic and foreign residents may higgledy-piggledy be using the exit option to get their funds out of the nation.

As a final guideline, you will observe that breakwater measures intended to be transitory typically prove more viable than measures intended to be permanent. Transitory breakwaters can be more effective than permanent measures because financial breakwaters tend to be eroded over time. In your nation, as in most others, the financial reservoir is now more closely connected with the world financial system than was once true when communications and information technologies were more limited. New channels for cross-border financial transactions can be devised in response to breakwater measures aimed at existing channels. The government typically cannot add monitoring and administrative capacities to the supervisory and regulatory agencies as fast as financial markets can innovate. Realism cautions, therefore, that it is simply infeasible to control closely many types of cross-border capital flows.

Over the longer run, the government's scope for maintaining financial breakwaters will probably decline further. Progressively more emphasis will have to be placed on managing the risks associated with cross-border finance rather than on trying to limit them directly. (For nations at early stages of financial development, breakwaters may play a more prominent role in the development transition than they will subsequently play later on. Higher breakwaters can provide greater initial protection for the financial system. Later they can be gradually lowered as the financial system becomes more sophisticated and, in particular, as the utilities infrastructure is elaborated and strengthened.)

You expect the cabinet to ask whether it is acceptable to design financial breakwaters that discriminate in favor of domestic and against foreign residents. At that point, you yourself expect to be squirming in your chair. You believe it is legitimate for the nation to want to nurture its indigenous institutions and culture. Hence you sympathize with the desire to slow down an indiscriminate homogenization with the rest of the world. You know that cross-border arbitrage transactions can undermine indigenous values and standards, including even the nation's collective-governance mechanisms for tax collection and prudential oversight of financial activity. At the same time, you are keenly aware that government regulations explicitly discriminating between foreign and domestic residents carry great risks. Such measures can be abused by inept administration or regulatory capture, if not outright corruption. They can foster expectations about the nation abroad that lead foreigners to behave skittishly when lending their savings to the nation, if indeed they are willing to lend at all.

Your draft presentation for tomorrow, if truth be told, waffles on this issue. You are unwilling to argue that the government should never adopt laws or policies that discriminate against foreign residents. You are not willing to argue that financial breakwaters should always treat domestic and foreign residents alike. You have some sympathy, for example, for the legislation already passed by a previous government that requires foreign direct investors in key sectors of the economy to include some minimum degree of domestic ownership in resident enterprises. You would like the government to retain residual powers to limit foreign investment if it should threaten to seriously undermine widely accepted social values or eliminate local influences over communications media and cultural institutions. Even so, this qualified stance makes you nervous. You know it would be easy for the government to make mistakes with discriminatory measures. You are confident that such measures will be sharply scrutinized and criticized in the rest of the world. Letting the camel's nose into the tent a little way runs the risks of too much.

If pressed in tomorrow's discussions, you are prepared to offer specific illustrations of financial breakwaters that satisfy your guidelines. The example about which you feel most confident is a prudential restraint requiring individual banks and nonbank financial institutions to limit their open (net) position in foreign currencies to no more than a given, modest percentage of their total capital. That restraint is in fact not really a breakwater measure per se, but rather a component of the prudential oversight regime in which government supervisors require financial institutions to hold minimum capital in relation to their total balance sheets. A second example is the imposition of reserve requirements on the short-term liabilities of the domestic offices of financial institutions to depositors and investors in foreign jurisdictions. The rate of reserve requirement on these short-term foreign liabilities would be set higher than the rates of reserve requirements on liabilities to domestic residents. If pressed, your third example will be a proposal for imposing a withholding tax on flows of financial funds into the nation (a cross-border capital withholding tax).

At the end of your discussion of breakwaters tomorrow, you will try to bring your colleagues back to the broad issues about openness with which you began your presentation. The pragmatic policy stance you are recommending is an integral part of your overall strategy of choosing a compromise combination of the nation's goals. The nation should avoid the purist extremes of both the Great Wall and Golden Straitjacket positions. At least for the time being, it should maintain some financial breakwaters. But it should not attempt a virtual segregation of the home financial system nor of course erect overly ambitious breakwaters with costs much higher than any benefits. What is needed is a middle way best suited to the nation's current and prospective circumstances. As with the choice of exchange regime, good breakwater policy must be context dependent. No stance about breakwaters will be right for all circumstances and all times. As the nation's economy and financial system evolve, some adjustments and experimentation may be required.

Monitoring External Vulnerability and Managing Financial Crises

You would prefer to conclude your presentation tomorrow on an upbeat note rather than warn your cabinet colleagues of potential risks that may lie ahead. Yet the Ministry of Finance and Economy is responsible for pushing the government, through monitoring of risks and contingency planning, to prepare for financial dangers in advance of their possible emergence. You and your staff are convinced that careful monitoring can lower the probability of the dangers occurring and that advance planning can at least mitigate the adverse consequences if they should occur. You thus intend, uncomfortable though it is, to emphasize the vulnerability of the nation's economy and the need for the cabinet to prepare in advance for how to cope with unpleasant developments.

The evolving openness of the nation's economy and the financial system, as noted already, increasingly exposes the nation to external shocks and to exacerbation of the adverse consequences of shocks that originate domestically. Notwithstanding a commitment to sound macroeconomic policies and a cautious maintenance of limited financial breakwaters, the financial system and economy could drift toward an enhanced and hazardous external vulnerability. Broadly speaking, excessive levels of the nation's external vulnerability would result from excessive risk and liquidity exposures.

The recent crisis experience of a neighboring nation is an example. For two years before the crisis, that nation's banks incurred sharply higher short-term foreign-currency liabilities to foreign banks and onlent the funds to domestic enterprises in the form of medium-term loans denominated in domestic currency. After that nation experienced an unexpected collapse in the price of its main exported commodity and an unexpected recession, the nation's currency depreciated and numerous domestic enterprises became insolvent. The banks then suddenly found themselves holding large amounts of nonperforming loans and suffered large losses on their debts to foreign banks. Because of the currency mismatch in the banks' positions, several of the banks themselves were perceived as insolvent. The resulting blow to confidence caused both foreign and domestic participants in the financial system to rush to the exits to move funds abroad, causing a still sharper depreciation of the currency, still more enterprise insolvencies, still more nonperforming loans, and even larger losses for the banks on their foreign currency borrowings.

The retelling of that case, you hope, will help convince the cabinet that your government needs to upgrade its ability to assess the risk and liquidity exposures of the financial system and the economy as a whole. One of your specific suggestions is that, as an integral part of the strengthening of financial standards and prudential oversight advocated earlier, the supervisory agencies and your own ministry devote substantial additional human resources to such assessment. The analysts would be charged with, among other things, identifying and monitoring the various channels through which external shocks can adversely influence the economy and financial system and preparing probability estimates of the most important shocks and adverse effects. Excessive exposures to liquidity drains and to losses from exchange rate changes are two of the most important sources of vulnerability to be monitored. The nation as a whole, you will stress, should not develop an excessive reliance on short-term capital flows nor permit a highly risky buildup of other types of concentrations in external exposures. The new analysts would be charged with detecting significant shifts in vulnerability over time. Subject to higher-level guidance, the analysts would also be directed to develop contingency plans for managing, and ultimately correcting, increases in vulnerability judged to be excessive.

To be able to conduct risk monitoring and assessment, the analysts must pay close attention to a national balance sheet, the nation's international investment position, and the liquidity position of the entire economy. Similar monitoring will be needed for the balance sheets and liquidity exposures of key sectors, both in the real sectors of the economy and in the financial system. The government at the current time, you regret to point out, does not have accurate enough and timely enough data for most of the relevant assets and liabilities. Better data will be especially needed for cross-border assets and liabilities, for the liquidity and foreign currency positions of the banking system and of nonfinancial enterprises, and hence for the nation's overall liquidity and international investment positions. Your second specific suggestion, therefore, is that the supervisory and statistical agencies be given additional budget resources to improve these types of data and to qualify the nation as soon as possible as a full participant in the IMF's Special Data Dissemination Standard. Improved data are an absolutely essential requirement for assessment of external vulnerability.

The government should pay attention not only to aggregative measures of risk for the nation as a whole, but should also develop sound risk-management strategies for the government itself. The cabinet should aim for a high level of transparency about the government's own policies for management of risk and liquidity and about its regulatory policies governing risk and liquidity management in the private sector. The government should have in place a prudent operating strategy for managing its public debt. Not least, it should follow prudent guidelines for managing the nation's official external reserves and the government's own external liabilities.

Following your appointment, the initial efforts of the ministry staff to analyze the current status of external vulnerability concluded that the nation's external reserves were well below a level providing an adequate cushion against severe shocks. As part of your recommended contingency planning, you intend to suggest that the cabinet set a goal of gradually building up the reserves over the next two years. That plan will require more careful analysis of the prospective evolution of the balance of payments and the economy. Subject to that further study, incentives and policy adjustments will then have to be devised to make the plan for building up the reserves feasible. You expect several cabinet members to challenge your suggestion about the reserves by pointing out that the current outlook for the economy appears tranquil and that the nation has satisfactorily carried on for several years without a higher level of reserves. But you will go into the cabinet meeting with a riposte already prepared. You plan to remind your questioning colleagues of the fundamental rationale for insurance. Just as higher reserves are often not needed, a spare tire for your automobile is not needed either—unless you have a flat.[5]

Your proposal about building up the reserves, you feel obliged to acknowledge, does itself create a risk. The initial analysis by your staff also concluded that private financial institutions in the nation may be inadequately managing their risk and liquidity exposures. If your government compensates for the deficiencies in private sector risk management by choosing itself to build up the nation's international reserves, the private financial institutions may have even weaker incentives to manage their own exposures prudently. A delicate trade-off exists. On balance, because of the moral hazard complications, you do *not* recommend that the government adjust its own balance sheet to compensate explicitly for private sector deficiencies. You believe there is a case to be made for higher reserves apart from the private sector deficiencies. And you feel strongly that the government should intensify its monitoring and prudential oversight, leaning on private institutions to remedy their inadequate management of risk and liquidity.

Finally, you intend to mention the highly uncomfortable subject of crisis management. Needless to say, the entire cabinet of the newly elected government wishes fervently never to have to deal with financial crisis conditions. But ex ante contemplation of the possibility is another form of insurance.

---

5. Greenspan (1999) uses this metaphor.

You will remind the cabinet that guidelines for the management of possible crises need to be understood and accepted in advance, most especially by the government and the central bank. Your nation's central bank is endowed by legislative statute with a qualified degree of political independence (not as extreme as that for the European Central Bank, but nonetheless providing the central bank with considerable immunity from short-run political pressures). Day-to-day monetary policy decisions in the past have benefited from extensive behind-the-scenes consultations with your ministry. From the general public's perception, however, the decisions are taken essentially by the central bank on its own. In the customary shorthand language, the central bank enjoys instrument independence but not goal independence. Those institutional arrangements, you believe, are appropriate for your nation. You certainly do not want to unleash market uncertainties and rumors by seeming to question that degree of political independence.

All things considered, therefore, you suggest that the cabinet reconfirm the policy that leadership in the management of financial-crisis conditions is clearly lodged in the central bank. You also ask the cabinet to understand, and accept in advance, that the central bank must be able to move swiftly in the event that a financial crisis actually were to materialize. In such circumstances the central bank's first priority would be to make appropriate adjustments in overall monetary policy to try to ensure sufficient but not excessive liquefaction of the nation's financial system. Direct emergency lending to private financial institutions, even though that course of action can raise formidable difficulties, may also be required.

Because the nation's financial system is open to the rest of the world, central bank efforts to ensure liquidity could of course be severely undermined by actions of private agents, foreign as well as domestic, that drain financial assets out of the national financial reservoir. The central bank's decisions about supplying liquidity and about possible intervention in exchange markets would thus entail very problematic judgments, necessarily made speedily and under fire. If a full-fledged financial crisis were to develop, the government and central bank acting together would need to approach the world official-creditor community for large-scale emergency liquidity assistance, probably through the IMF. If that course of action proved necessary, the government would become embroiled in delicate negotiations about performance conditions associated with such assistance. Those negotiations would likewise have to be resolved under a very tight time deadline.

The risk monitoring and assessment you will recommend to the cabinet is intended to keep the nation out of crisis conditions and to protect it from having to seek emergency liquidity assistance from abroad. But the cabinet needs to know, in their bones so to speak, that such a situation could happen. With blockbuster shocks and bad luck, such financial turbulence could occur *even if the nation pursues sound policies and competently manages the economy's risk and liquidity exposures.* On this discouraging subject, you can offer the cabinet one significant piece of encouragement: if the government manages external vulnerability competently and follows prudent, first-class economic policies, the international institutional mechanisms for obtaining emergency liquidity assistance from the outside world—most notably the Supplemental Reserve Facility at the IMF—would probably be readily available without onerous performance conditions.

Capital Account and Prudential Oversight Policy Choices for the World Community

As foreshadowed at the beginning of the chapter, you the reader now need to shift mental gears. When you were imagining the choices facing the minister of finance and economy for an individual nation, you had a narrow normative focus. Your perspective had to be entirely national. For the remainder of the chapter, however, you are asked instead to adopt a more cosmopolitan outlook. Ideally, you should now suppress attitudes and preferences shaped by the interests and circumstances of particular nations, including your own. In effect, your perspective should become supranational.

Imagine yourself, therefore, sitting in the chair of the managing director of the International Monetary Fund. You are, in effect, the prototype highest-level international civil servant. Your constituency is the entire world community. Your task is to foster an improved functioning for the economy and financial system not merely of individual nations, but of the world as a whole. Your judgments about policies and welfare consequences should span many or all of your member nations rather than be shaped by the needs or preferences of any single nation or group of nations.

Yes, some of your member nations are much larger and more powerful than others. You would soon be out of your job if you acted without sensitivity to that asymmetry. Nevertheless, to the best of your abilities and those of your staff, you try to take an aggregative view and to shape your judgments to reflect (a subtle weighted average of) the interests and identities of all member nations and hence of all the world's residents.

Cross-Border Financial Transactions from a World Perspective

From the discussion of policy choices facing an individual nation, it is apparent that the benefits and costs of cross-border and cross-currency finance cannot be summarized simply. Striking a *net* balance, even for a single nation, requires a complex weighing of very heterogeneous benefits and costs. Not all types of capital flow are alike. In some nations, most flows of financial funds cross borders freely. In others, breakwaters (or even a separation fence) impede cross-border financial transactions. Individual nations differ greatly in many other ways as well. The policy stance about financial openness advocated for any individual nation should be shaped by the particular circumstances of that nation.

How much more difficult, then, to strike a net balance between the benefits and costs of liberalized cross-border capital flows from a world perspective. Similarly, how complex a problem it is to design traffic regulations and guidelines for cross-border financial transactions to be used by international financial organizations in their surveillance of national policies.

From your perspective as the managing director of the IMF, what themes and conclusions should you emphasize? You start by observing that most economists and policymakers have long presumed that border restrictions on trade in goods and services should be limited if not eliminated altogether. In the second half of the twentieth century, relatively free trade in goods and services prevailed in practice. In contrast, you observe, the corresponding presumption for unfettered cross-border flows of money and capital was less widely accepted and is even more controversial.

International opinions and national policies about the freedom for cross-border financial transactions have oscillated greatly since the late 1800s. Liberalized capital movements were favored in the gold standard era in the later decades of the nineteenth century and in the early 1900s. The financial turbulence of the years from World War I through World War II soured most economists and policymakers on the merits of free capital flows. In the 1940s the original Articles of Agreement of the newly created IMF sanctioned the view that freedom for cross-border financial transactions was undesirable. Then in the final decades of the century, the pendulum of opinion gradually swung back again toward an emphasis on the benefits from liberalized capital flows. Ironically, the apogee of the drift back toward liberalization was reached in 1997 just as financial crises were beginning to erupt in Asia. In the initial years of the twenty-first century, it appeared likely that the pendulum of opinion was once again reversing direction. Suspicions of complete freedom for capital flows were partially renewed.

From a supranational perspective, the points you wish to make about benefits and costs of cross-border financial transactions are qualitatively similar to arguments at a national level, albeit with different nuances. Your weightiest point on the benefits side is a reminder of the fundamental advantages of financial intermediation when extended to the world as a whole. If national investment decisions do not have to be inflexibly tied to national saving decisions, nations with excess savings can transfer funds to nations with excess opportunities for profitable investment. Both groups of nations can thereby benefit greatly. Thus not only individual nations but regions and the world as a whole can experience a more efficient allocation of resources and therefore higher consumption. From your Olympian vantage point as managing director at the IMF, it is easier for you than for ministers or central bank governors at the national level to perceive the substantial worldwide benefits of cross-border financial intermediation.

You also accord weight to the other types of benefits associated with unfettered capital flows. For example, the freedom for individuals to invest their wealth anywhere in the world can complement other valued freedoms. Unrestrained capital flows exert disciplinary pressures on governments, encouraging them to refrain from unsustainable policies and to be politically accountable.

Notwithstanding the benefits of cross-border financial intermediation, you identify noteworthy costs and risks from a world perspective. You are keenly aware of the weaknesses in some national jurisdictions of how financial standards and prudential oversight of financial institutions are implemented. You know that financial crime, money laundering, and tax evasion bedevil many individual nations, with deleterious effects for the world as a whole. Some of the offshore financial centers are guilty of contributing to these problems rather than cooperating in measures to reduce their incidence. The very existence of these problems undermines the case for complete freedom for cross-border financial transactions. Cross-border capital movements are beneficial *if* they efficiently transfer savings among national financial systems and *if* they efficiently allocate funds worldwide to investments where marginal returns are highest. But you doubt that any economist of good conscience would wish to defend lax prudential oversight, financial crime, money laundering, and tax evasion on grounds that they foster allocative efficiency.

Your perspective on the consequences of financial openness for national autonomy is of course different from that of national governments. You share the diagnosis that financial openness undermines autonomy for nations' economic policies and the controllability of national economies. You perceive numerous examples of financially open nations where policymakers find their decisions more uncertain and more difficult. But you conjecture that this evolution, judged from a supranational rather than a national perspective, is not wholly bad. The trend is forcing national governments to cooperate more extensively, and it has led to greater responsibilities for international institutions. For your own organization, the IMF, for example, you can perceive positive as well as negative consequences of the gradual erosion of national autonomy.

The weightiest points you want to make on the negative side about liberalized capital flows concern the possible implications for financial stability. Like policymakers at the national level, you are impressed with how financial activity is pervaded by informational asymmetries and moral hazard. You too perceive that herding behavior and contagion, and excessive volatility in asset prices, can sometimes aggravate the vulnerability of financial systems. But as the IMF's managing director, you necessarily must go further than national-level policymakers in worrying about these issues. You must have a concern for systemic stability. Cross-border financial activity, you observe, has the potential for generating financial instability on a regional or even worldwide scale. Exchange rates, both nominal and inflation-adjusted, can be excessively and disruptively volatile. Financial turbulence originating in one nation's economy or financial reservoir can, through contagion, cause storms—in occasional instances, even typhoons—elsewhere in the world financial system. In extreme circumstances, the consequences of such systemic turbulence could be highly adverse for many different nations.

As you ponder the benefits and costs of cross-border finance from the perspective of the IMF, the weight of the arguments fails to push down the pan conclusively on either the benefits or the costs side of the scales. You know that your executive board is sometimes restive with conclusions that take the form "on the one hand, on the other hand." It would be easier to run executive board meetings dealing with traffic regulations and guidelines for cross-border capital flows if somehow the arguments and evidence pointed straightforwardly in one direction rather than the other. Some of your most influential board members, representing nations with highly developed financial systems, have convinced themselves that the arguments and evidence do point primarily in one direction. They argue that unrestrained capital flows and liberalized financial markets are the proper policy for the twenty-first century. Numerous other board members, including a majority of those representing nations with less advanced financial systems, however, have deep reservations about that view.

You were asked to assume the responsibilities of managing director in part because of your ability to listen carefully and sympathetically to a wide variety of views. You are also skilled at forging compromise positions. Those abilities and skills will be tested as you and the IMF staff try to craft a balanced approach to the traffic regulations and guidelines for capital flows that the IMF will be asked to use in its future surveillance of national policies.

Traffic Regulations and Guidelines for Cross-Border Financial Transactions

By far the most controversial issue about international traffic regulations for capital flows is the stance that the world community should adopt about nations' use of financial breakwaters. You recall with discomfort the proposed amendment to Article VI of the IMF Agreement, circulated in 1997 just as the Asian financial crises were erupting, that would have encouraged an eventual worldwide freedom for cross-border capital flows. In today's changed environment, you and the staff are now suggesting a more nuanced approach.

The starting point for this approach is an acknowledgment that a prudent use of breakwater measures by individual nations can be a sensible part of an overall national strategy. Most nations, not least those whose financial systems are at early or middle stages of evolution relative to those in the largest industrial nations, will want to pursue a compromise combination of the goals of financial autonomy, exchange rate stability, and financial integration with the rest of the world. No one compromise, and especially not one of the extremes, is appropriate for all times and all circumstances. Without question, no single combination is ideal for all nations in all circumstances at all times.

Nations can easily make mistakes when maintaining financial breakwaters. Injudicious use can deny the implementing nations sizable benefits and have some adverse effects on other nations. Breakwaters tend to be eroded over time. Nevertheless, some types of breakwaters are viable. Prudently used, they can provide modest protection. Two examples are a cross-border capital withholding tax and reserve requirements on the short-term liabilities to foreign depositors and investors of the domestic offices of financial institutions. Some prudential restraints that influence cross-border financial transactions, though not breakwater measures per se, should be a permanent part of the structure of financial supervision and regulation. Upper limits on the net open foreign exchange positions of financial institutions are an example.

If the world community takes the preceding observations as a starting point, international traffic regulations for cross-border financial transactions should respect the diversity of nations' circumstances and needs. National discretion and experimentation are desirable. Precise traffic regulations recommending extensive or complete liberalization of capital flows are not desirable and not politically feasible. The appropriate traffic regulations and international guidelines for cross-border capital flows should be "soft law," similar in spirit to the existing soft guidelines of the IMF for surveillance over exchange regimes.

Some general principles about capital flows and capital account convertibility, you suggest, could state that

—nations' governments should give substantially higher priority to their overall financial standards and prudential oversight policies than to their breakwater measures per se;

—breakwater measures should not be used as substitutes for sound macroeconomic policies, for a well-chosen exchange regime, for maintenance of a strong international investment position, or for competent supervision and regulation of the financial system generally;

—breakwaters should rely where possible on market forces rather than on direct administrative controls and should be designed as much as possible to limit opportunities for regulatory capture or corruption;

—nations are typically better advised to design breakwaters to try to moderate unwanted capital inflows than to try to stem unwanted capital outflows; and

—breakwater measures designed as transitional may often prove more viable than measures intended to be permanent.

The IMF principles should also explicitly emphasize that surveillance of an individual nation would focus on its particular circumstances and the specifics of its particular policies.

IMF surveillance of capital flows based on such principles could not be "firm surveillance" in the sense of clear operational guidelines uniformly applicable across all nations. Just as with the other dimensions of supranational surveillance, soft rather than hard guidelines are the only feasible possibility for the short and medium runs.

Your suggested compromise approach to traffic regulations and guidelines would mean that the IMF's executive board would not need, at least for the shorter-run future, to reconsider a formal amendment of the IMF's Articles of Agreement to modernize the provisions governing capital flows. Yes, the existing language in Article VI is out of date and in some ways unbalanced. But neither the IMF itself nor individual governments are seriously constrained by that language. It would probably be impossible, furthermore, to secure agreement on a formal and precisely written revision of Article VI and the other articles concerned with cross-border capital flows.

International Assessment of National Financial Systems

The monitoring of cross-border traffic regulations is only one part of the surveillance responsibilities that the world community is increasingly asking the IMF and other international institutions to shoulder. The monitoring and assessment of domestic aspects of the prudential oversight of national financial systems are gradually becoming at least as important. In your balanced overview of financial policies seen from a supranational perspective, you try to heighten awareness of those nonborder aspects of financial surveillance.

A cooperative approach to the evolution of financial standards and prudential oversight at the world level can be summarized in ten general principles.[6]

1. Responsibility for improved standards and prudential oversight should begin and end at home within the individual nation.
2. Standards and oversight at the world level should take the form of core principles rather than detailed codes or fully specified regulations.
3. The preferred approach at the world level is an encouragement of *agreed minimum standards* combined with the presumption of *mutual recognition.*

6. These principles are propounded and analyzed in *Prudential Oversight and Standards for the World Financial System.*

4. When possible, world standards and oversight should rely on market incentives rather than direct restrictions.

5. World standards and oversight should highlight disclosure and transparency.

6. Improvements are especially needed in emerging-market and developing nations, but the advanced industrial nations need to make improvements too.

7. Monitoring and enforcement of world standards and oversight will soon become at least as important as sound design.

8. The primary mechanisms for monitoring and enforcement of a nation's standards and oversight should be implemented internally within the nation (*self assessment*), but evaluation from outside the nation (*external assessment*) should be used as a supplement.

9. The authorities of individual nations, cooperating with international financial organizations, should prioritize specific goals and resource needs and embody the resulting strategy in an action plan to implement the goals.

10. No governmental jurisdiction should be accorded the full benefits of participation in the world economic and financial system and its supporting international organizations if it persists in maintaining standards and prudential oversight for financial activity that are weak relative to world minimum standards.

These principles, like the guidelines for financial breakwaters, are soft rather than hard. But they are shaped by pragmatism and thus constitute a feasible foundation for a near-term strengthening of surveillance of individual national financial systems and the world financial system as a whole.

From your perspective at the IMF, you identify four types of problems associated with implementing these principles and with conducting surveillance of national financial systems. First, standards based on international principles such as those above typically cannot be legally binding within individual nations. Their acceptance and use within nations has to be enforced by each nation's government and the nation's private associations. Many difficulties can arise in persuading individual nations actually to implement the necessary steps.

Second, financial standards and prudential oversight in many emerging-market and developing nations fall below the minimum international standards currently being designed by the world community. Those nations accordingly face challenging choices about the rapidity with which they should try to move their national standards up to the international minimums. The international financial organizations also face difficult choices in deciding how much pressure to put on those nations to reach the minimums quickly.

Third, there exists a growing need to supplement a nation's self assessment of its financial standards and prudential oversight with external assessment from outside organizations or experts. Together with other international organizations, the IMF has been increasingly asked to assume this outside evaluation role. You have even been experimenting with making the assessment of a nation's financial system an integral part of the IMF's annual process of Article IV consultations. But this trend in opinions about the conduct of supranational surveillance raises delicate questions about the allocation of responsibilities across international financial organizations.

Fourth, you are concerned about the problem alluded to earlier that a few national jurisdictions in the world financial system, primarily offshore financial centers, are characterized by weak financial standards and prudential oversight, inadequate transparency in disclosure policies, and limited willingness to cooperate internationally. At worst, some are renegade jurisdictions fostering regulatory arbitrage and supervisory laxity as a way of promoting their attractiveness as a location for unfettered financial activity. Your view is that jurisdictions acting in this way are opportunistic free riders in the world financial system and should be somehow chastened.

Assessing Risk and Liquidity Exposures

Given the faster expansion of cross-border finance relative to domestic finance and the consequently increasing probabilities that nations can experience so-called modern capital account crises, individual nations' governments need to be increasingly sensitive to the external vulnerability of their economies and financial systems. You are convinced that international financial organizations, as part of their surveillance activities, should give the assessment of economies' external vulnerability a higher priority than it has had in the past.

For the international organizations' surveillance to be more effective, you have come to believe, the staffs need to improve their analytical methods for monitoring and assessing vulnerability. Efforts to do so were put in motion during 1999–2002 in several of the international organizations. One feature of that work is a renewed emphasis on principles for the prudent management of a nation's external liabilities and of its government's debt. Some of the new work tries to develop improved early warning systems, including formal statistical models for estimating the probability of possible crises. Other parts seek, for example, to devise systems for high frequency monitoring of foreign exchange transactions.

If the staffs of the IMF, the BIS committees, and the World Bank can make further progress in improving techniques for analyzing vulnerability, it will then also be possible for the international organizations to provide better technical assistance to national governments trying to upgrade their own capacities for monitoring and assessing the risk and liquidity exposures of their economies.

Data requirements for such monitoring and assessment are demanding. Analysts need reliable and timely information about the liquidity and foreign currency exposures of individual sectors within a national economy and hence, by aggregation, for the balance sheet and international investment position of the entire financial system and economy. From the perspective of supranational surveillance, such data need to be skillfully aggregated across nations and regions.

As the top executive of the international organization most centrally involved, you know that better data, at all levels of the world financial system, are essential. But you also know that, although virtually everyone genuflects before the altar of improved statistics, few are willing to exert the leadership or undertake the legwork to ensure that good progress is actually made.

Different Nations at Different Stages of Financial and Economic Development

As part of your approach to traffic regulations and guidelines that could constitute a soft-law basis for IMF surveillance of financial activity, you called attention to the diversity in nations' circumstances and institutions. You perceive the differences among nations as a critical motivation for your nuanced, compromise approach to IMF surveillance of financial policies.

The specialization and sophistication of a financial system tend to increase over time pari passu with other aspects of economic development. In early stages, the financial infrastructure expands even faster than the real infrastructure. At more advanced stages, the financial and real sectors of the economy grow together proportionally. Financial development leads to an increasing diversity in the types of financial institutions and in the instruments in which they specialize. The relative share of direct intermediation through the banking system usually declines. The share of financial markets and indirect intermediation tends to increase.

The least advanced of the developing nations in today's world thus have financial reservoirs that are considerably less specialized, and in varying degrees less sophisticated, than those of the industrialized nations. Securities markets, for example, are absent or in their infancy. A large share of financial activity flows through the banking systems in those nations.

The so-called emerging-market nations are in an intermediate position. Their financial systems have manifested a growing specialization and sophistication relative to earlier decades. But they are not yet as advanced as those in North America, Western Europe, and Japan. Among other things, banks still account for a relatively high share of financial intermediation in emerging-market nations.

The fact that financial intermediation is less advanced in emerging-market and other developing nations has important implications for supranational surveillance of nations' financial systems. Accounting and audit standards tend to be less well developed, and often are less strongly enforced. The laws governing defaults and insolvencies are less complete. Bankruptcy and arbitration procedures are less fully worked out. Standards and procedures for prudential oversight of financial institutions are similarly less well developed, less stringent, and often less assertively monitored.[7]

Mistakes or accidents are more likely in the financial reservoirs and economies of developing nations. The weaker are accounting and audit standards and the less effective is prudential oversight, the greater the likelihood of individual mistakes or accidents. In any case, economywide accidents, and economywide mistakes in macroeconomic policies, are more probable. At the very least, the consequences of inappropriate economywide policies can be more damaging. Developing nations are more vulnerable and can be more badly damaged because their economies are smaller, and many are more open, than the economies of industrial nations. Herding behavior and contagion tend to be more virulent and cause greater difficulties. The chances of contagion getting started, and spreading, tend to be higher. The risks of general financial instability are thus higher.

---

7. Generalizations of this sort about developing nations should be made and interpreted cautiously, not only because of large differences among those nations, but also because of ambiguity in what constitutes best-practice world standards. Societies differ, for example, in the social conventions and legal requirements that govern the public disclosure of information. Those differences may not be attributable solely to different stages of financial development. Nor should standards in the so-called advanced nations be deemed unambiguously superior. The differences may also reflect fundamentally different cultural attitudes. For further discussion, see *Prudential Oversight and Standards for the World Financial System.*

Financial markets reevaluating the prices of securities react especially rapidly and thus can spread contagion quickly. Financial intermediaries catch contagion less rapidly. But if and when they do, the consequences for their balance sheets tend to be even more disruptive. Because banks and other intermediaries tend to be relatively more important in the financial systems of emerging-market and other developing nations, that structural feature of those nations contributes to their greater potential vulnerability.

To speak loosely but essentially correctly, much of the saving imported from abroad into the financial reservoirs of developing nations is skittish capital or can quickly become so. Portfolio investors and creditors from the financial reservoirs in the industrial nations—the dominant actors in world capital markets—can be very unforgiving about problems in the developing nations when their funds are invested there. Many such foreign investors may be potential members of a herd, prepared to exercise their disciplining exit option on slight provocation, especially if through informational cascades they observe other investors heading for the exit. As in the familiar cliche, such investors know only the two gears of overdrive and reverse. (Direct investors, though far from immune to such pressures, have more limited scope to indulge in herding behavior.)

The propensity of foreign investors to be skittish does not change the fundamental point that an individual nation can gain greatly from cross-border finance by intertemporally smoothing the path of its consumption over time. A prudent nation will try to hedge against the future through a net accumulation of income-earning assets abroad during good times. During difficult times it can then hope to be a net borrower from abroad, thereby preventing consumption levels from falling proportionately with temporarily diminished incomes. That strategy is undoubtedly correct in principle. But unforgiving foreign investors in a developing nation may limit the scope for it to operate in practice.

These observations about developing nations should not leave the impression that differences among financial reservoirs and utilities infrastructures are small within the advanced industrial nations. On the contrary. Differences are pronounced, for example, between continental European and Anglo-Saxon norms and procedures for corporate governance, which in turn lead to differences among banking systems. The so-called main bank system in Japan operates quite differently from banking in North America. Notable differences remain among Japan, Europe, and North America in the detailed norms, procedures, and institutions for prudential oversight.

It would also be seriously misleading to imply that all is well in the reservoirs of industrial nations and that it is the backwardness of developing nations that poses the primary risks of turbulence in the global financial system. Many commentators residing in the larger industrial nations perceive their nations as unambiguously the first team in finance, the "varsity." They describe emerging-market nations as a weak "junior varsity" and dismiss the other developing nations as merely amateur sandlot teams. Seen from this self-satisfied perspective, the enemy is weak private institutions and weak governance in the developing nations. But in the words of the American cartoon character Pogo: we have met the enemy, and the enemy is us, too! The industrial nations themselves have experienced numerous financial crises in recent decades. Their earlier financial history is replete with financial panics and inadequate prudential oversight of financial institutions. They too have deficiencies in financial standards and prudential oversight that need to be remedied.

These observations about diversity among the IMF's member nations require an eclectic, differentiated approach to the IMF's surveillance responsibilities. An individual nation's balance sheet of the net benefits, or net costs, from cross-border finance can differ greatly from the judgments made by other nations. The perceived balance between benefits and costs may vary over time even for that one nation.

When the IMF staff makes a presentation to the executive board summarizing the Article IV consultations with a member nation, the analysis of the financial system thus ought to depend sensitively on whether the member is a Brazil or a Honduras, a Nigeria or a Burkina Faso, an India, China, Malaysia, Mauritius, or a Vanuatu. The Article IV consultations for North American and European members, no less than for developing nations, should assess weaknesses in deposit insurance schemes and in the monitoring of banks' capital adequacy. The staff's evaluations of risks to financial stability in international capital markets need to pay close attention to the differences between London, Frankfurt, Tokyo, and New York. And so on. For supranational surveillance and other aspects of financial policy choices, the world community needs a common-sense approach that combines an effort to encourage all nations to achieve world minimum standards with an appropriate appreciation of the venerable maxim "different strokes for different folks."

12

A Perspective on Financial Activity and Financial Turbulence

W hat should the average citizen believe, it was asked in chapter 1, about the increasingly pervasive linkages among national financial markets? Is cross-border financial interdependence helpful, promoting economic prosperity? Or is it hazardous, placing prosperity at risk? The overview of main themes and conclusions about cross-border finance in this chapter, a continuation of the stocktaking begun in chapter 11, provides a balanced verdict about such questions of financial "globalization." The points summarized here undergird the analysis throughout the book.

Benefits of Financial Intermediation

Savings generated in an economy, that portion of current-period incomes of households and other economic agents that is not consumed, are like a pervasive fluid. The financial system acts like a reservoir for these funds. Savers place funds in the reservoir while businesses and others whose current-period spending exceeds their income draw funds out, borrowing to finance their excess spending.

Financial activity, the placement of savings in the reservoir and the withdrawal of savings to finance investment, is fundamentally beneficial. Financial intermediation and financial markets are vital underpinnings without which modern economies could not function and prosper.

Without financial activity, the behavior of economic actors would be severely restricted; no actor could invest more in real capital assets than its current saving because there would be no way to finance the excess expenditures. Financial activity permits individuals and enterprises to implement intertemporal patterns of spending that differ from the time profiles of their incomes. Saving and investment decisions can be taken independently. The economywide aggregate flows of investment and saving, and hence the growth of economic activity, can be substantially greater and more efficient.

Such generalizations would apply even to an economy completely closed to the rest of the world. But they apply with still greater force to actual open economies with extensive cross-border trade and financial activity. When the financial reservoirs of different nations are highly interconnected, the aggregate decisions of the ultimate savers in any single nation and the aggregate decisions of ultimate investors in that nation do not need to be closely linked. Net transfers of savings from one nation to another permit savings and investment decisions to be independent not only for individuals within each nation, but for nations as a whole. Loosening of the links between aggregate saving and aggregate investment for individual nations substantially enhances the potential for each nation's economic well-being and for prosperity for the world as a whole. Just as financial transactions within national reservoirs generate major benefits for individual economic agents, significant benefits may result from financial transactions between agents in different national reservoirs.

Financial Turbulence

Even in a well-functioning financial system, particular investments in real capital turn out to be disappointments. Some financial transactions go sour. Conditions change. Poor judgments are made. Mishaps—both mistakes and accidents—are inevitable when uncertainty and risk are rife, when asymmetric-information and principal-agent complexities abound, and when economic actors are fallible human beings.

When particular investments or financial transactions go sour in a national economy open to the rest of the world, repercussions of the mishaps get transmitted abroad. Accidents, and even more so mistakes, can be especially problematic when investments have been financed with direct shifts of savings from one national reservoir to another, thereby creating cross-border or cross-currency liabilities. Because of the greater risks and uncertainties and the differences between national cultures, coping with the consequences of mishaps associated with cross-border financial activity is especially complex and difficult.

Within national financial reservoirs, mistakes and accidents inevitably cause waves. They may even generate storms. Storms can spread and become virulent because of herding behavior, contagion, and excessive volatility in asset prices. Thus financial activity not only reflects, but can even sometimes itself cause, financial turbulence. Financial turbulence is counterproductive. It can disrupt basic nonfinancial activities and hence severely damage economic welfare. Financial systems are inherently fragile, inherently vulnerable to instability.

The fragility intrinsic in domestic financial activity can be powerfully exacerbated by cross-border risks and uncertainties. The cross-border and cross-currency dimensions of financial intermediation often amplify the consequences of distressed financial conditions. In adverse circumstances, many national financial reservoirs can be simultaneously afflicted by volatile cross-border capital flows, disruptive fluctuations in exchange rates, and severe balance-of-payments crises. Episodes of stormy weather can even lead to an occasional hurricane-level crisis.

The potential for instability in financial activity cannot be attributed primarily to cross-border finance. The causes are deeply rooted in the information asymmetries, the expectational and informational cascades, and the adverse selection and moral hazard problems that pervade all aspects of financial behavior, domestic as well as cross-border. Yet the cross-border features unquestionably magnify the potential for instability.

Weighing Benefits and Hazards

Because both the benefits and the hazards of financial activity are so consequential, overall judgments are difficult to make. The average citizen finds the subject especially difficult because policymakers and financial specialists espouse contradictory and sometimes extreme views.

Appropriate judgments must always be context dependent. Above all, a balanced perspective is essential. The fragility and hazards should not be exaggerated. The benefits should not be deemphasized. But neither should one be impervious to the risks and potential damage.

If analogies are helpful to you, think about cross-border finance in much the same complex way you perceive automobiles or electricity. The automobile comes with risks and dangers such as road congestion in urban areas, pollution of the environment, and increased loss of life in accidents. Yet a preoccupation with the risks and dangers is neither practical nor persuasive. No sensible person emphasizes the social costs of the automobile to the exclusion of its benefits. The automobile is simultaneously a good and a bad. Similarly, when used with appropriate caution and safeguards, electricity is immensely beneficial. But accidents can happen. Electricity can go awry, sparking fires that do lots of damage.

In an analogous way, modern financial activity comes with serious risks and problems. Yet a practical person will have little interest in comparing financial activity as it actually exists with a hypothetical nirvana in which financial activity is risk free and problem free. The relevant practical perspective is to ask whether some feasible alternative processes exist that could channel funds from ultimate savers to ultimate investors, within nations and among nations, in ways that would be obviously superior. Merely to ask that question is to begin to perceive the impracticality of creating feasible alternative processes that would be immune to financial turbulence.

Recent technological innovations, particularly in communications and electronics, have heightened the complexity of financial activity and made it still less likely that turbulence can be suppressed altogether. Computers, high-speed electronic communication, and Internet software have generated irreversible changes in the ways that financial activity is conducted. Just as a bell cannot be unrung, it is not possible to turn the clock back on these innovations. An important part of the increased mobility of financial funds in the world, both within nations and across national borders, is attributable to these technological developments. Major aspects of the rapid, price-sensitive movement of savings and financial funds around the world are thus also essentially irreversible. Policymakers and market participants have no other effective choice but to learn how best to adapt to this reality.

Collective Governance for Financial Systems

Within national financial reservoirs, we try to prevent financial instability—and to mitigate its consequences when it nonetheless does arise—by establishing utilities infrastructures. Those collective-governance infrastructures set standards, provide supervision and prudential oversight for financial institutions, maintain a macroeconomic climate conducive to healthy financial activity, and establish contingency measures for coping with financial crises if they should occur.

If such a utilities infrastructure is required for a domestic financial reservoir to operate smoothly, it was asked in chapter 1, why is not an analogous collective-governance infrastructure required for the stable operation of the conglomeration of national financial systems? The economic logic behind that question does apply at world and regional levels. Except for a few rudiments and nascent beginnings, however, the evolving world financial system does not yet have utilities infrastructures at a level above nation states (regional or worldwide). The analysis in this book argues that a further development and strengthening of the nascent international infrastructures is a top priority for intergovernmental financial cooperation in the initial decades of the twenty-first century.

But one must be realistic about how much can be expected from supervision and prudential oversight exercised through utilities infrastructures. There is no perfect design for a utilities infrastructure, either domestically within a single nation or at supranational levels. Collective governance, no matter how well designed and implemented, cannot guarantee that financial turbulence will be avoided altogether. Hurricanes and floods may sometimes occur despite the best collective efforts to prevent them and to limit their potential damage. Thus the appropriate aspirations for utilities infrastructures—at the world level as well as nationally—are to reduce the probability of mismanagement, crime, and crisis in the financial system and to foster cooperative and prompt resolution of such episodes when unfortunately they do occur.

Striking a Balance

How should you as a concerned citizen strike a balance? What summary verdict should you adopt about financial globalization, about capital flows and cross-border finance at the outset of the twenty-first century? To put the issue provocatively, echoing the colorful language favored by journalists, are the increasingly large and rapid movements of trillions of dollars across national borders beneficial, promoting greatly enhanced prosperity for the world? Or are these flows an enormous pool of footloose money that provokes financial turbulence, disrupts national economies, and severely damages welfare? For your own nation, and for the world community as a whole, what is the right policy vision?

The beginning of wisdom in addressing the conundrum of financial activity and financial turbulence is to resist either of the extreme views. Cross-border finance is not unambiguously beneficial. Nor has it on balance severely harmed welfare for particular nations and the world as a whole. The uncomfortable but correct answer to the conundrum is that cross-border finance is both helpful and hazardous. Critics of financial globalization are justified in concluding that sinners' ways sometimes prosper in the realm of cross-border finance. Yet, with equal validity, men and women of good conscience can believe that cross-border financial activity is—and should be—a prominent feature of economic life.

Financial capital will flow across national borders in ever larger amounts in future decades. It is thus certain that both the benefits and the risks of cross-border finance will increase further. What is also certain is that collective governance of cross-border finance, now in its infancy, will need to be substantially strengthened. Toward that end, policymakers and citizens alike should support pragmatic efforts to enhance international cooperation and to nurture the nascent components of utilities infrastructures for the world financial system.

Eschew Polar Views

Polarized positions about cross-border finance that emphasize only the benefits or only the hazards are simpler to state. They often command the greatest public attention. It thus may seem tempting to adopt one or the other extreme view. But that temptation should be resisted. Polar positions do not stand up to careful scrutiny.

As with the automobile, electricity, and numerous other features of modern life, hazards in cross-border finance have to be accepted. Benefits have to be sought while risks are minimized. When the blessings and blemishes of cross-border finance are weighed against each other, it is not true that the scales tilt unambiguously to one side or the other.

One polar position, held by a large group of financiers and analysts, is that the net benefits of liberalized capital flows are overwhelmingly positive—essentially for all nations. Seen by these advocates of untrammeled markets, cross-border finance is so efficient and beneficial that it is a mistake to interpose any government policy impediments at all. Advocates of this polar perspective, cousins of Dr. Pangloss (semi-Panglossians), believe that unfettered capital markets will be nearly all for the best in this nearly best of all possible worlds.

The opposite polar position, held by a surprisingly large group of critics of globalization, argues that cross-border finance is unbridled and invariably unstable. Advocates of this view believe that the costs of untrammeled capital flows far exceed any benefits. They perceive market failures as pervasive internationally as well as domestically. They yearn for comprehensive governmental policies that can reverse the "out-of-control" situation. Those sympathetic to this polar position thus often support recommendations for sweeping institutionalist reforms that would delegate greatly enhanced authority to international institutions. They sometimes also slide into recommendations that individual nations should erect very high breakwaters, if not a Great Wall, around national financial systems.

Neither of the polar positions is based on compelling analysis. Nor is either one politically realistic. Market failures and financial turbulence, as observed in chapter 1, put great pressure on governments to "do something." The untrammeled-markets advice to "Don't do something! Just stand there!" invariably buckles under crisis-generated political pressure (usually, appropriately so). The sweeping institutionalist reform view errs in the opposite direction by badly misjudging the relevant political constraints.

The general debate about international capital flows and financial globalization is likely to heat up further in coming decades. As this happens, policymakers and the informed public should be deeply suspicious of the extreme views. Reality—the true situation we actually confront in today's world—is actually more encouraging than either of the polar views suggests. But reality and a middle way are undeniably more complicated to describe in simple sound bites.

A Middle Way: Steadfast Eclecticism

When defending a middle way, you can draw comfort from the knowledge that you are, in essence, on familiar ground, participating in a debate that is several centuries old. Thoughtful analysts have always recognized a tension between market efficiency and market failure. The decentralized decisionmaking embodied in market supplies and demands can accomplish allocative feats of marvelous complexity. But markets can also malfunction. Decentralized noncooperative decisionmaking in some circumstances produces outcomes decidedly inferior to those attainable through collective action. Institutions of collective governance can supply, or induce private economic agents to supply, collective goods that would not be provided at all, or would be provided inadequately, in the absence of the collective decisionmaking. Yet institutions of collective governance can malfunction too. Soundly managed nations, and sensible evolutions of the world polity and economy, thus require safeguards against both market failures and government failures.

The analysis in this book emphasizes the superiority of an eclectic, middle-way approach to cross-border finance. That perspective is essentially the same mainstream stance that makes sense in resolving all the manifold tensions between market efficiency and market failure.[1] The view that cross-border finance is entirely out of control is second cousin to the traditional extreme criticism of capitalist society that sees Adam Smith's allocative virtues as a small island in a sea of market imperfections. The semi-Panglossian perspective is a nephew of the conviction that potential sources of market failure are a few fleas on the thick hide of an ox, requiring only a flick of the tail to be brushed away.

In cross-border finance, as in the broader debate, the judicious response to extreme views is a steadfast eclecticism. After all, economic analysis both supports a presumptive belief in the efficiency of market allocations and provides the tools for an incisive critique.

Imagine yourself cornered by the vice president of a London merchant bank or a writer for the *Wall Street Journal* editorial page. Suppose they argue vociferously that government regulations in all nations, but especially in emerging-market developing economies, are stifling and much too extensive. Suppose they try to persuade you that the G-7 nations and the IMF should insist on worldwide standards for open, liberalized, unregulated financial markets. When you are subjected to such talk, your mind should promptly overflow with thoughts of the bank executives and mutual fund managers who behaved like sheep in choosing their asset portfolios in Latin America in the early 1980s and in Asia in 1995–97, and who again behaved like sheep in running for the exits when euphoria was transformed into uncertainty. You should think of the drug-smuggling proceeds laundered through renegade offshore financial centers. You should recall stock prices and exchange rates fluctuating sharply in response to false rumors started by market participants to make exploitive trades. Remember the competition in laxity among governments trying to attract financial institutions to their jurisdictions by reducing taxation and the stringency of supervision. Remember the anxieties in the Turkish and Argentine financial systems in

---

1. In the following sentences, I shamelessly adapt several metaphors and phrases from the introductory paragraphs of Robert Solow's 1979 presidential address to the American Economic Association (Solow, 1980, p. 2). If Solow were less skillful in crafting the right phrase, we other economists would succumb less often to plagiarism.

2000–01. Recall the Russian default and devaluation, the near failure of the Long-term Capital Management hedge fund, and the resulting worldwide panic in 1998—not to mention the collapse of the Albanian pyramid schemes and then the entire Albanian financial system in 1997, the U.S. savings-and-loan institutions debacle of the 1980s, and the failures of Herstatt and Franklin National banks in 1974, of the Credit-Anstalt in 1931, and the South Sea Company in London in 1720.

Conversely, however, suppose you are being lectured by a dirigiste official of an emerging-market ministry of finance or the lead spokesperson for an anti-globalization nongovernmental organization. Suppose those critics assert that mutual funds and hedge funds are legions without commanders roaming the financial markets of the world, recklessly harming financial stability and economic growth. Suppose they try to persuade you that nations should rebuild the separation fences around their financial systems and that international financial organizations such as the IMF should have their responsibilities reduced rather than strengthened. In the presence of those views, your mind should fill with thoughts of the rigidities and loss of innovative investment caused by anachronistic government regulations. You should remember the beneficial discipline of interbank and inter-country competition, the merits of decentralizing lending decisions to the locations where information about credit risk is most reliable, and the potential for improved resource allocation and faster growth resulting from savings being channeled to investment projects yielding the highest returns. As a vivid concrete example, contemplate for a moment the financial system in the Soviet Union in the second half of the 1900s and the wasteful investments that were fostered by that system. As an antidote for the assertion that international financial organizations have too much authority, remind yourself of the manifold ways in which decentralized national decisions are not adequately coping with world-level problems and for which, hence, a strengthening, not a diminution, of intergovernmental cooperation is required.

A middle-way vision should acknowledge that cross-border finance is essential to healthy economic growth and development in the world. Collective governance can help to moderate, though not eliminate, the instabilities that are inherent in international financial intermediation. The nations of the world need thoughtful international norms and strengthened international institutions to try to facilitate this moderation.

When trying to work out improved eclectic policies for our messy intermediate world, it is quixotic and harmful to make recommendations that assume much more political integration and supranational decision-making than is currently feasible. It is an even bigger disservice to enlightened public policy to argue that markets would sort things out efficiently if governments would just stand aside and let the markets "get the prices right."

The eclectic's position is unsatisfyingly bland. But there continues to be deep wisdom in the aphorism that the middle of the road is preferable to the ditch on either side. Indeed, if asked to recommend an epigraph for the facade of either a single nation's central bank or an international organization such as the IMF, a fine choice would be the advice given by Phoebus to the impetuous Phaeton: *medio tutissimus ibis* (you will go most safely by the middle way).[2] That dictum is not an infallible guide to sound policy. But it will very often prevent those holding the reins from committing egregious errors.

2. Ovid, *Metamorphoses*, Book II.

13

The Evolution of International Financial Governance

This final chapter highlights conclusions about international governance. The stocktaking goal, as in chapters 11 and 12, is to identify landmarks and higher peaks—to compress the complexity of the subject into a manageable, integrated perspective. An underlying objective is to sketch a coherent interim vision of how the world polity and financial system might evolve for the first several decades of the twenty-first century.

The chapter begins with a review of the main themes and broad principles about collective governance that shape the entire book. It emphasizes points about the reform of international financial architecture with special salience for the political evolution of collective governance. Then two questions are asked: Can adequate political support be mobilized for the strengthening of international governance? Do substantial risks exist that international organizations will manifest governance failures? The chapter comments on the views of activists who aspire to reverse the trend toward financial and economic globalization. The stocktaking ends with a restatement of the maxim—pragmatic incrementalism—that should shape the evolution of international financial governance.

Collective Governance: Main Themes and Broad Principles

The world polity will be a messy, intermediate hybrid for many decades. Economic interdependence, especially the cross-border integration of financial reservoirs, will continue to increase. Yet national borders will continue to have immense economic significance.

Nations are dissimilar. They have diverse social and cultural norms. Private institutions and groups are organized differently. The types and jurisdictions of institutions for collective governance are different. Such cross-nation differences are a fundamental reason why national borders still have great significance despite the increasing pressures for cross-border integration and homogenization.

Not only borders, but even distance itself matters. Geographical proximity fosters interactions and networking. Geographical distance inhibits networking and reduces interactions—trade and financial transactions, but more generally interactions of all sorts. The greater the geographical distance between individuals, groups, or nations, the greater are the costs of transactions and interactions. The relevant costs include not only transportation expenses, but also a wide range of cultural, social, and networking expenses (pecuniary and nonpecuniary).

Some commentators, recognizing the power of recent innovations in communications and technology, have written cavalierly of the "eclipse of distance" or the waning of territoriality. Such phrases are seriously misleading exaggerations.

It is a basic characteristic of market capitalism that market extremes can lead to market failures. It is a basic characteristic of politics that government extremes and rigidities can lead to government failures. Virtually every nation therefore has some combination of decentralized markets and government infrastructures. The particular combinations of decentralized markets and government infrastructures—the specifics of each nation's "mixed economy"—differ widely. Those cross-nation differences are another reason why national borders continue to have great significance.

Collective-action problems with international dimensions will continue to grow in importance relative to the domestic problems of collective governance. As this trend persists, national governments will retain the legal forms of de jure sovereignty. They will continue to be reluctant to designate authority to international institutions. The illusion of sovereignty may often prevent nations from acting collectively to foster their mutual interests.

Even so, there exists a stark reality: in large measure, de facto autonomy has already been lost. National governments will thus face increasing pressures to interact more intensively across a wider range of issues, and hence to engage in various sorts of international collective action. The constitutional precept of subsidiarity—the presumption that decentralized allocations and exercises of political authority are to be preferred in the absence of compelling reasons for centralization—argues for proceeding cautiously. But governments will not be altogether able to resist the forces propelling them toward more collective action.

The international collective governance analyzed in this book will continue to evolve along two lines. The first will be enhanced cooperation and decisionmaking by interacting national governments. The second will be a delegation of greater authority by national governments to international institutions to enable those institutions to carry out a wider range of functional responsibilities.

International institutions are an outcome of "top-level" cooperation among governments as they periodically negotiate to design international regime environments. Ongoing "lower-level" cooperation and functions are also increasingly gravitating toward international institutions. The lower-level functions are a key means of implementing and maintaining the regimes designed in top-level negotiations.

The nongovernmental dimensions of international collective governance are increasing in relative importance. And governance is not the exclusive preserve of government institutions. To keep the scope of this book manageable, however, the international aspects of nongovernmental collective governance are excluded. The focus is on cooperation among national governments and the international institutions created by those governments.

International collective governance will continue to be characterized by stops and starts—by steps forward, second thoughts, and sometimes even reversals. Major steps forward may be galvanized only by crisis situations. Nonetheless, the evolution of international collective governance is likely to be the single most prominent feature of world politics for at least the next half century.

No less at the regional and the world level than within nations, economic life requires an appropriate mix of market decentralization and collective governance. Market failures and government failures are inevitable at regional and global levels, no less than within nations. Collective governance at levels above the nation state has not kept pace with the rapidly increasing interconnectedness of nations. But ultimately, as within nations, regions and the world as a whole will need to work out appropriate combinations of market decentralization and collective governance.

That eclectic view is not accepted by many. Numerous enthusiasts for globalization and cross-border finance prefer to emphasize markets to the exclusion of collective governance. Those enthusiasts favor untrammeled markets. They advocate Golden Straitjackets. They perceive governance failures everywhere, perhaps especially within international institutions. They are, in the language of the preceding chapter, semi-Panglossians, arguing that if only financial and economic markets could be allowed to function without impediments, then all would be for the best in this nearly best of all possible worlds.

The market enthusiasts at one pole are counterbalanced by governance optimists at the other polar extreme. Those observers perceive market failures as ubiquitous. They have faith that wise interventions by collective-governance institutions can offset the shortcomings of markets. The governance optimists tend to favor sweeping reform of existing international institutions or the bold creation of new institutions.

The approach to international collective governance advocated in this book, like its perspective on cross-border finance, steers well away from both of the polar positions. The governance optimists who favor sweeping institutionalist reform envisage a world with genuine supranational collective governance. But with very few exceptions, genuine and strong supranational governance is not politically feasible. The analysis here envisages progressively stronger international, but not supranational, governance.

Conclusions in earlier chapters about reforming the international financial architecture speak of supranational surveillance rather than international surveillance. But the use of the adjective *supranational* in conjunction with surveillance is consistent with the emphasis on international rather than supranational governance. Collective surveillance comprises a wide range of activities: monitoring traffic regulations for cross-border transactions, urging compliance with them when limited international mechanisms for encouraging compliance can be agreed, promoting adjustment and catalyzing coordination for exchange rates and macroeconomic policies, and providing prudential oversight of financial standards and financial activity. Yet collective surveillance is only a subset of the potential functions for international collective governance.

The surveillance activities of the IMF and other international financial institutions merit the adjective *supranational* because of the nature and content of surveillance. By definition, surveillance presupposes a per-spective above the level of national governments. But the surveillance dimensions of collective governance that can be envisaged today are weak precursors of more extensive and more muscular forms of collective governance. Those who exercise surveillance do not have significant independent authority to influence national governments. Surveillance in practice so far has been, and even when strengthened with incremental reforms in the near future will be, only tentative and shaped by "soft" rather than "hard" guidelines. The real exercisers of supranational surveillance are the national governments themselves. They act collectively not because they are subject to an independent authority above them but because their mutual interests require such cooperation.

Politically Salient Dimensions of Architectural Reform

Unlike financial systems within nations, the world financial system has only nascent rudiments of a collective-governance utilities infrastructure. Alternatively stated, the international financial architecture is a weak, incomplete structure in need of much strengthening and further construction.

The highest priorities for intergovernmental financial cooperation and international financial organizations over short and medium runs—for near-term "architectural reform"—are the development and strengthening of key components of the nascent international infrastructures for the world financial system. Chapters 9 and 10 summarized priorities for architectural reform in three key areas: supranational surveillance and lending intermediation, prudential oversight, and crisis management. Chapter 11 summarized policy choices in those areas of architectural reform as they appear to individual nations and then as they confront the world community as a whole.

The policy observations in the following paragraphs do not summarize the summaries already given in chapters 9, 10, and 11. Instead, a few conclusions are selectively highlighted that have special political salience for the evolution of international financial governance. These political conclusions warrant renewed emphasis as part of a final stocktaking.

Measures to strengthen the collective supranational surveillance of national policies are by far the most effective incremental steps that national governments and the world as a whole can adopt to prevent the emergence of crises and to foster a healthy evolution of the world economy. Neither official nor journalistic discussions of architectural reform have sufficiently focused on the issues of collective surveillance, despite their great importance. Excessive attention has been paid to financial crises and measures to deal with them. Prosperity management through collective surveillance of national policies can ultimately have much greater effects on economic welfare than skillful crisis management.

The core of effective supranational surveillance is the development of a systemic analytical perspective that offsets biases inherent in the perspectives of individual nations and their governments. A coherent systemic perspective identifies ex ante inconsistencies in national policies and fosters procedures for cooperative reconciliation of the inconsistencies that will be mutually preferable to sequences of decentralized, uncooperative decisions.

IMF lending intermediation, if prudently conducted, can contribute importantly to the efficiency and stability of the world financial system. Lending to encourage the adjustment of underlying macroeconomic imbalances while simultaneously smoothing the liability financing of payments deficits was a central objective of the IMF when the organization was first created. Far too much of the popular discussion about IMF lending fails to appreciate the underlying systemic rationale for that activity. Although IMF lending entails risks, will sometimes fail to achieve its intended objectives, and will invariably be controversial, it nonetheless is a helpful support to the broader activity of collective surveillance. Effective IMF lending in noncrisis as well as crisis conditions serves the interests of all IMF member nations. It should continue to be a primary IMF function.

The politics of architectural reform require commonsense attention to differences in the circumstances and needs of individual nations ("different strokes for different folks"). The appropriate political strategy for the world as a whole is to work toward the design and enforcement of worldwide minimum standards while encouraging national jurisdictions to compete cooperatively with each other in developing indigenous, national standards that improve on the world minimums. This strategy of combining world-defined minimum standards with diversity in the details of national systems is pragmatic and has a much higher chance of political success than efforts to standardize or harmonize all details across nations.

The political aspects of managing cross-border financial crises, for reasons given in preceding chapters, are complex and extremely sensitive. The beginning of political wisdom is to understand that the notion of a supranational or international lender of last resort is not compatible with today's institutions and political conditions. The awkward truth—the essential political observation about the management of international financial turbulence—is that for the next several decades the world cannot have a genuine centralized lender-of-last-resort capability for financial crises.

The only realistic alternative available to national governments in the shorter run is to foster a constructive coordination of general monetary policies by the central banks of the largest wealthiest nations. No conceivable actions of the existing international financial organizations can effectively substitute for this coordination among the major central banks.

Lending in precrisis and crisis conditions by the IMF can play a useful, supplementary role in facilitating resolution of financial crises. Moral hazard risks associated with IMF lending are inevitable. Concerns about potential bailouts of private lenders to troubled nations will always be present. Constructive measures to mitigate moral hazard and to dampen the exit incentives and opportunities for private lenders should be adopted by the official creditor community and the IMF whenever such measures are feasible. Yet the larger picture must always be kept in sight. Moral hazard and the risks of private sector bailouts have so mesmerized some academics and journalists that they have lost sight of the need for international collective action and the larger trade-offs that inescapably arise in international financial crises.

Just as the world financial system cannot have a supranational lender of last resort, it is also politically infeasible in the shorter run to establish a detailed, supranational mechanism for managing orderly workouts of crises when they do occur. Centralized world procedures for handling the debt rescheduling and restructuring problems of troubled nations—for example, a world bankruptcy court, or an explicit sovereign debt restructuring mechanism—are still beyond what is politically attainable. But it is equally wrong to pretend that purely market-driven resolutions of the debt problems of troubled nations will reliably lead to satisfactory outcomes for the creditors of those nations and the nations themselves. As in virtually all the aspects of architectural reform, the world community must find an interim political balance. An incremental strengthening of collective-action procedures for facilitating orderly workouts from cross-border crises is possible and ought to be cooperatively undertaken by national governments. IMF member nations, particularly the largest and wealthiest, are as yet unprepared to delegate greatly enhanced authority in this area to the IMF. But the IMF will gradually and progressively have to serve as a focal point for the needed intergovernmental cooperation.

The IMF has recently experienced strong pressures from all parts of the political spectrum, with contrary recommendations about what its mandate should be. Some influential voices want to restrict the IMF's mandate narrowly to a focus on crisis vulnerability. At the other extreme, IMF critics want the mandate extended well beyond the core areas of cross-border finance and macroeconomics. Many want the IMF still more deeply involved in promoting growth, supporting structural adjustment, and reducing poverty in developing nations. Some would even urge that the IMF play a major role in the surveillance of international labor and environmental standards.

It would be unwise for the IMF to so narrow the focus of its surveillance that it pays less attention than in the past to the noncrisis aspects of member nations' situations and policies. The IMF should enhance its surveillance of vulnerability to capital account crises. But it should not weaken the other, noncrisis aspects of its surveillance that seek to prevent altogether the macroeconomic conditions that may sow the seeds for eventual financial crises.

A very broad mandate for the IMF would likewise be a political mistake. The evolution of international financial governance making most political sense is to eschew assigning the IMF a bloated agenda that includes every important world economic problem. The IMF can be more effective and the world served better if IMF energies are focused on its core competence in cross-border finance and macroeconomics.

Misperceptions abound about the IMF. One of the most serious, prevalent in the largest and wealthiest nations, is that the IMF is an institution whose beneficiaries are exclusively the developing nations. Conversely, many individuals in developing nations perceive the IMF as unfairly enforcing, throughout the world, the preferences and economic policies of the large, wealthy nations. Both types of misperceptions badly damage political support for strengthening and improving the IMF.

Governments and citizens of the wealthiest nations should recognize—and act on the recognition—that the IMF is an institution advancing their own essential interests. The wealthiest nations have the most to gain from a healthy, stable evolution of the world economy. They have the most to lose if the world economy and financial system malfunction. The best hope for improved prosperity management for the world as a whole, and not least for the largest and wealthiest nations, is to nurture a gradual strengthening of collective surveillance over national economic policies. That evolution requires increased and more thoughtful support of the IMF.

Political Support for International Governance

Is there sufficient political support for an upgrading of international financial governance? Most notably, do the largest and most powerful nations genuinely espouse the gradual strengthening of effective supranational surveillance? Are they clearly committed to the design and implementation of improved prudential oversight of financial systems for all nations? Are they adequately sensitive to the needs for improved cooperative management of financial crises? Are the major nations, knowing their interests are most at stake, willing to put real muscle into thoughtful support for a more effective IMF?

If one judges merely from the rhetoric of national governments, one can answer these questions with an unambiguous yes. To illustrate, here are some passages taken from the April 2000 joint statement of the G-7 finance ministers and central bank governors:

> We underscored the central role of the IMF in advancing macroeconomic stability as an important precondition for sustainable global growth and emphasized the need for the IMF to continue to evolve to meet the challenges of the future. . . .
>
> Preventing crises and supporting the establishment of a solid foundation for sustainable growth are at the core of the IMF's work. Surveillance of economic and financial conditions and policies in member countries and the implementation of internationally agreed codes and standards are the primary tools for accomplishing those aims. . . .
>
> Strong surveillance must be at the center of the IMF's efforts to strengthen the world economy and the architecture of the international financial system.[1]

As a second illustration, Lawrence H. Summers, the secretary of the U.S. Treasury in February 2000, observed in testimony before the U.S. Senate:

---

1. The quotations are from paragraph 9 of the main communique and Annex I on IMF Reform (Statement of April 15, 2000).

We are committed to a deeper set of reforms going forward, particularly at the IMF. But as we work to reform these institutions it is important to recognize the crucial respects in which they defend, protect and enhance America's interests. . . . That is why our support for the [international financial institutions] and the strong policies that they promote is so important. Quite simply, they are one of the most effective—and cost-effective—investments we can make in the forward defense of America's core interests. . . . These institutions help promote a more stable world. They can help to promote vital humanitarian objectives. And, let there be no doubt, they promote changes that are central to our nation's economic and commercial future.[2]

Numerous other recent examples of such rhetorical support, from each of the major nations, could be given.

To keep perspective, however, you should realize that the rhetoric has almost always been supportive. Consider the following language from a Joint Statement on Monetary Undertakings issued in conjunction with the G-7 communique more than twenty years ago at the June 1982 economic summit:

[The nations represented at the summit] attach major importance to the role of the IMF as a monetary authority, . . . will give it our full support in its efforts to foster stability, . . . [and] are ready to strengthen our cooperation with the IMF in its work of surveillance, and to develop this on a multilateral basis. . . .[3]

Or here is a quotation from a September 1984 speech of the then U.S. secretary of the Treasury:

The United States is prepared to move ahead decisively to strengthen international surveillance. We believe that such measures as increased public awareness of Article IV consultations with member countries, and a greater use of ad hoc consultations between the Managing Director and Finance Ministers, could be very useful. We

2. Statement before the Senate Committee on Foreign Relations, U.S. Treasury press release, February 29, 2000.

3. Quoted in the *IMF Survey* for June 21, 1982, p. 189.

hope others will support proposals such as these for a stronger IMF surveillance role.[4]

As these quotations suggest, the political rhetoric about supranational surveillance, about the IMF, and about reform of the international financial architecture has by and large been supportive. Nor is it a small thing to get the political rhetoric right. Unless the rhetoric points the way appropriately, there is virtually no chance of actually moving forward.

Yet appropriate rhetoric is not sufficient to generate genuine progress. In practice, sad to say, the supportive political words often have not been followed up with deeds. Progress in deeds between the mid-1980s and the end of the century, for example, did not live up to such 1980s promises as those just quoted. Actual progress has been sluggish. Often it has taken new crisis conditions to galvanize cooperative action.

Actual progress is sluggish because of the tensions between economic arguments for moving forward and the political feasibility of actually doing so. One important obstacle to progress, emphasized in earlier chapters, is the insufficient analytical understanding of interactions among national economies. Such analytical uncertainty impedes stronger political support for international governance. It merits emphasis again that farsighted governments, understanding the significance of analytical uncertainty as an impediment to progress, should devote more resources to trying to improve analytical knowledge.

Yet analytical uncertainty is only part of the explanation for tensions between economic arguments and political feasibility. Actual deeds fall short of rhetorical words for another reason: the continuing prevalence of concern that steps toward stronger international governance will entail an inappropriate sacrifice of national sovereignty.

Many concerns about losses of national sovereignty exhibit an insufficient awareness of the distinction between de jure sovereignty and de facto autonomy. One frequently encounters confused arguments that participation in international treaties and international institutions will cause an illegitimate intrusion of foreign interests into domestic affairs. Fears are expressed that international commitments will inappropriately trump core national interests and national values. In the United States, those with these fears sometimes claim that smaller nations who support stronger

---

4. Speech delivered by U.S. Treasury secretary Donald Regan at the 1984 annual meetings of the IMF and World Bank, September 24, 1984.

international collective governance are motivated primarily by yearnings to constrain the power and abrogate the sovereignty of the United States.

Sovereignty is a slippery concept. In broader connotations, sovereignty presumes that nations have, within their geographical territory, indigenous political and authority structures that should be free from interference by outside actors. Speaking loosely, sovereignty presumes a norm of nonintervention in domestic affairs.

Throughout history, sovereignty has been abrogated by violations of the norm of nonintervention. But clear thinking requires a distinction between externally imposed interventions that disregard a nation's sovereignty and that are harmful to the welfare of its residents and reductions in national sovereignty that are welcomed within nations and that enhance the welfare of their residents. Reductions in sovereignty for nations suffering coercion or the imposition of force are understandably viewed by those nations as adverse. But when a nation's government enters voluntarily into welfare-enhancing arrangements that in some way supercede sovereignty, the departures from the status quo are not well described as "violations" or "intrusions." The sovereignty-reducing arrangements are invited. They represent voluntary accords. A nation's political leaders cannot be plausibly faulted if they override formal sovereignty by willingly entering into beneficial arrangements for shared international governance. Nor are the cooperative international arrangements a commitment that somehow trumps national interests. Quite the contrary: the international collective governance advances national interests.

Thinking clearly about sovereignty also requires a recognition that the de facto autonomy of a nation's policies declines because of increasing cross-border economic integration. A farsighted national government, aware of the gradually diminishing autonomy of its policies, will not only eschew an excessive preoccupation with loss of its formal sovereignty. It will actively seek voluntary, cooperative agreements with other nations' governments, directly or through international institutions, that can enhance the nation's welfare in the face of the diminishing autonomy of its policies.

National governments are likely to continue to insist on retaining the formal principles and norms of de jure sovereignty. Never mind. Formalities are the last thing to change in political life. But it will become progressively more important that national political leaders better understand, and publicly acknowledge that they understand, the continuing trends causing gradual erosion of the de facto autonomy of their national policies.

Farsighted political leaders also need to do a better job of educating their citizens about the complexities of sovereignty and autonomy. Rhetoric about "losing sovereignty" will surely persist outside as well as within national governments. The rhetoric will be especially strident from individuals and groups that want to slow, or even to try to reverse, the increasing economic integration across national borders. Yet confusion about sovereignty among the wider public should not be allowed to undermine constructive steps to strengthen international governance. Farsighted leaders should emphasize that a nation does not need to jettison its local and national commitments to participate in collective-governance initiatives at regional or world levels. Individuals and groups already have and can further develop multiple loyalties. *Local governance, national governance, and international governance need to be seen as complements, not substitutes.*

The political vision and skills needed to encourage a nurturing of international governance are not, it must be admitted, in excess supply. Worse still, national political leaders are prone to apply a double standard when asked to lead. A propensity exists to exhort others to virtuous, courageous behavior but to be relatively forgiving of one's own hesitancy. The double standard likewise manifests itself in the policies of national governments. Thus just as superstition is defined as some *other* person's religion, protectionism gets defined as some *other* nation's trade policies. Stubborn shortsighted resistance to constructive supranational surveillance is some *other* nation's policy stance, whereas foot dragging by your own nation is warranted because of severely binding domestic political constraints. When *other* nations and the IMF push your nation to accept a new international agreement, they are insensitively infringing your nation's sovereignty. When your nation's government twists the arms of foreign governments to secure international cooperation, that pressure on other nations is merely a reasonable assertion of your own nation's vital interests.

Such biased and self-serving national attitudes, unfortunately common, are a major obstacle to the evolution of international governance. Governments of the largest, most powerful nations in particular should resist those attitudes and instead try to espouse a more self-reflective and enlightened perspective. Again, it is the United States and other powerful nations that have the greatest stake in a healthy, prosperous world economy and financial system.

If the most powerful conceive their interests narrowly and if they manifest indifference to the interests of the less powerful, they will not induce the cooperation needed to create a stable, hospitable world. Self-restraint in choosing unilateral action and encouragement of collective-governance initiatives are not weaknesses. They are the wise use of great power.

Governance Failures for International Organizations?

Market failures and governance failures alike are prevalent features of modern economic life. Just as institutions for implementing collective action at the national and subnational levels are subject to possible governance failure, so, too, are international organizations. Thus it must be asked whether the risks from governance failures at international organizations are sizable.

A few commentators argue that national governments delegate excessive powers to international organizations, and in particular to international financial organizations such as the IMF and World Bank. Their concern is that the leaders and staffs of the organizations—international "bureaucrats" to use their pejorative term—are not sufficiently accountable through democratic processes to justify the authority that they wield. If an organization starts to use its powers inappropriately, suggest these commentators, there may not be adequate checks and balances in place to restrain the inappropriate behavior.

Claims that international organizations exhibit an "accountability deficit" or "representation failure" rest on three sorts of arguments. One is that the heads and key staff members of the international organizations are not chosen through direct elections. Within nations with democratic procedures, leaders tend to be directly elected. Those leaders may or may not behave in accordance with the aggregated, general interests of the nation as a whole; they can be captured by special interests. But at least the leaders selected through democratic elections are the focal points for forging consensus decisions and resolving conflicts among special interests. Because the leaders of international organizations are selected by national governments, by definition an extra link exists in the accountability chain. Whether this extra link merits terms such as representation failure or accountability deficit is debatable. But the existence of the extra link is a fact.

A second set of arguments emphasizes that national governments are not the only stakeholders in international organizations. To use the language of corporate governance, the member national governments are the shareholders of an international organization. Their top-level cooperation negotiated its charter and established it in the first place. The national governments appoint the management of the organization, and they exercise the votes shaping its decisions. The international organization is thus, directly and powerfully, accountable to its member national governments. But just as the modern literature on corporate governance distinguishes between the shareowners of and (more broadly) stakeholders in a corporation, an international organization can be perceived as having stakeholders in addition to its member national governments. The work force and suppliers of a private corporation are nonshareowning stakeholders. Some analysts have likewise perceived individual national citizens and their nongovernmental, civil-society associations as nonshareowning stakeholders in international organizations. These analysts have begun to argue that international organizations should—somehow, to some degree—be accountable to "international civil society" as well as directly to national governments.

The third set of arguments starts from the observation that international organizations can, given their established staffs and budget resources, develop institutional cultures and acquire vested interests of their own. An international organization might therefore take positions inconsistent with those of its member governments and try to exert an independent role in international discussions. In theoretical literature, such issues are referred to as principal-agent problems. Depending on the substance of the differing positions taken by national governments (the principals) and the international organization (the agent) and depending on the normative perspective used to shape judgments, the partial independence of the international organization could be judged as either beneficial or adverse. But in any case the agent's stance differs from the principals' stance and from a stance that might hypothetically have evolved if the organization were somehow more directly and democratically accountable to all its stakeholders.[5]

These issues about accountability will grow in significance over time. As international organizations acquire more delegated authority, efforts will increase to create new mechanisms for making them more democratically accountable and to devise new types of checks and balances to inhibit inappropriate behavior. Analysts of international law, international politics, and international civil society are increasingly addressing these issues.[6]

Although concerns about accountability merit serious attention, I am not persuaded that they are already so worrisome as to warrant being called

5. Principal-agent and accountability problems at international organizations are discussed by, among others, Stiglitz (1998, 1999).

6. Analogous issues about accountability on a regional scale are acquiring greater salience within Europe, and for similar reasons. Many citizens of European nations have become increasingly concerned in recent years that European Union institutions are not sufficiently accountable through demo-

governance failures. Consider as an illustration the processes by which individuals are selected to head the main international organizations. Those processes are messy and imperfect. But the weaknesses in the selection processes are not attributable to a delegation of excessive powers to the organizations or a tendency of the organizations to flout the intent of national governments. Quite the reverse is true.

The selection of heads for the IMF and the World Bank has long been subject to an unfortunate informal convention. European governments have acquiesced in the U.S. government choosing an American to be the World Bank president, and the U.S. government has acquiesced in European governments selecting a European to be the managing director of the IMF. This convention may have been an acceptable political compromise in the early years of the two organizations. It makes no logical sense and cannot even be defended as an acceptable political compromise at the beginning of the twenty-first century. The tradition was not challenged until 2000, when someone had to be chosen to succeed Michel Camdessus as the IMF's managing director. The process that eventually selected Horst Kohler, a German candidate, as the new head of the IMF was protracted and contentious. As of the end of 2002, no agreement had yet been reached on an improved procedure for appointing heads of the IMF and the World Bank.

An equally messy process occurred in 1999, when member governments of the World Trade Organization selected a new director-general. Analogous difficulties were manifest at the regional level in the spring of 1998, when European Union governments were jostling to select the initial head of the European Central Bank.

Sensible and equitable procedures for selecting the leadership of international and regional organizations are a prerequisite for nurturing their legitimacy. Given that the organizations are still in relative infancy, it is unsurprising that the existing procedures are somewhat ad hoc and highly politicized. But improving the current unsatisfactory procedures should be a near-term priority. For selection of the heads of both the IMF and World Bank, improved procedures at the least should aim to choose the best qualified and most able candidate regardless of nationality.

---

cratic processes. Some observers feel it is important that the European Parliament acquire more authority and interact with the European Commission and EU-level executive institutions (such as the Council for Economic and Financial Affairs, known as the ECOFIN Council) in ways more similar to the interactions within European nations between parliaments and executive authorities.

Improvements in leadership selection are likely to be contingent on generating more of a political consensus about the appropriate allocation of voting powers among the organizations' member governments. In the IMF, for example, improved procedures for selecting the managing director are entangled with disagreements among member nations about an appropriate redistribution of quotas (in particular, on the relative weights to be given to European versus non-European nations).

Many smaller nations, and especially developing nations large and small alike, are concerned that a handful of the wealthiest nations exert a disproportionate influence on the decisions of the international financial organizations. Resentment exists that the G-7 governments virtually dominate decisions. Some activist critics go so far as to assert that the IMF and the World Bank are effectively controlled by the United States alone. From the perspective of smaller and developing nations, the governance structure of the IMF is inadequately attuned to their interests. "Representation failure" may not be too strong a term to describe their perceptions of the existing situation.

An extreme variant of this concern asserts that international organizations are not merely dominated by a handful of the wealthiest nations but essentially serve the interests only of powerful elites within those nations. Corporate executives in nonfinancial and financial enterprises, government officials, and professional cadres are the elites most often alleged to have captured control of major national governments and hence also the international organizations that are primarily beholden to those governments.[7]

How should one assess "disproportionate" influence? What criteria can be used to appraise whether governance is "adequately" attuned to the interests of particular individuals, groups, or nations? To what degree do elites control governance within nations, and hence perhaps have "excessive" power in international organizations? Neither political theorists nor practical politicians have consensus answers to those thorny questions. Self-evidently, I cannot provide consensus answers here.

At every layer of governance—for both government and nongovernmental organizations, within nations and at regional and world levels—some realistic acknowledgment of asymmetric power is inevitable. For international organizations, it is thus inevitable that the largest and wealthiest nations will have "disproportionate" influence reflecting their disproportionate relative power. At the same time, some sort of balance has to be

7. See, for example, Strange (1996).

struck, one way or another, between acknowledging the greater relative power of large wealthy nations and giving smaller industrial nations and the numerous developing nations an "adequate" voice and influence.

The dilemma is well illustrated by the conundrum of how to determine the relative shares of member nations in the aggregate total of IMF quotas (and hence their relative voting power and influence in the IMF's decisionmaking). All nations can probably agree on a loose presumption that IMF quotas should reflect a member nation's "relative position in the world economy." That presumption, however, is so vague that it lends itself to a wide variety of interpretations. Objective measures of relative status point in very different directions. The presumption is almost meaningless because no consensus can be found about which objective yardsticks should be used to give it specificity.

In practice, IMF quotas have depended much more on variables such as relative incomes and trade volumes than on population. To take the most dramatic example, at the end of 2001 the People's Republic of China and India had, respectively, about 3.0 percent and slightly under 2.0 percent of total IMF quotas; their respective shares of world population were 21.1 percent and 16.7 percent. In short, the sometimes enunciated democratic ideal of "one person one vote" has virtually no applicability to the determination of relative quota shares in the IMF or to weighted voting schemes in other international organizations.

From several perspectives, the much greater weights on relative incomes than on population can be justified. For example, a member's quota in the IMF should undoubtedly give more weight to the member's ability to contribute financial resources to the organization than to the member's possible need to use IMF resources.

Nonetheless, in much of the world the suspicion lingers that too much emphasis is placed on relative incomes and trade volumes as yardsticks for measuring "relative position in the world economy." If somewhat greater weight were given to a yardstick such as population, the poorer nations of the world would acquire more voice and decisionmaking influence.

The aggregate share in IMF quotas of developing nations did increase significantly in the last four decades of the twentieth century. From a range of only 23–24 percent of the total before the 1960s, it rose to some 36 percent by 1984 and to nearly 38 percent by the end of the 1990s. Over the next several decades, the shares of developing nations in IMF quotas will need to rise still further, with Asian developing nations probably experiencing a disproportionately large increase in relative share. The biggest diminutions in quota shares are likely to have to come out of industrial Europe. The U.S. share, and probably that of Canada, will also have to decline.[8]

Among the charges of governance failure leveled at international organizations, the one that deserves to be taken most seriously is the claim that less wealthy and less powerful member nations are given inadequate voice. For the most part, the G-7 nations have met among themselves, reached tentative decisions, and only then reached out to other nations to generate support for their decisions. In the era when Arthur Burns was chairman of the Federal Reserve, disgruntled outsiders were known to complain about his power and magisterial style. Burns's concept of macroeconomic policies, they observed, was that the Federal Reserve, and Arthur Burns in particular, should make and explain the policies, after which the administration, the Congress, and the public should gratefully accept them. Somewhat analogously, the G-7 nations have tried to forge a consensus on difficult international issues and have then presumed that the rest of the world should gratefully accept their decisions. Not surprisingly, and with justification, this posture has left outsider nations restive. Strong pressures to modify consultative processes are already observable, such as through G-20 meetings and sessions with government officials from developing nations and smaller industrial nations held prior to G-7 summit meetings.[9] Greater legitimacy for international financial governance will over time require further and bolder steps to widen the decisionmaking process.

Just as informed outside scrutiny of any institution of collective governance can limit abuses or inappropriate behavior, improved transparency and disclosure at international organizations can help to mitigate the issues of accountability and representation identified here. Greater disclosure of information may also play a marginally helpful role in countering a disproportionate influence of the major nations.

As an example, consider the inevitable asymmetry in the IMF's supranational surveillance. Large and powerful nations experience less pressure from surveillance of their policies than nations that are small and borrowing from the international financial organizations. At its very best, supranational surveillance can never be completely evenhanded. The powerful

8. The companion volume *Crisis Prevention and Prosperity Management for the World Economy* contains an extended discussion of IMF quotas.

9. For discussion of the G-20 and other groupings of government officials from developing nations, see the appendix.

will always, alas, be better able to get away with questionable behavior than the meek. But extensive disclosure of information and analysis by the IMF can foster better accountability even for the largest wealthiest nations. A strategy of "name and shame" may be the most potent recourse available to the meek. Wisely used by international organizations on behalf of the wider world community, it can certainly enhance the impact of surveillance over powerful member nations.

The powerful themselves should also be more self-reflective on the subject of transparency and disclosure. Several of the G-7 nations have been in the vanguard encouraging the international organizations to be more transparent about their activities. Partly in response, the international organizations have in fact greatly increased their disclosure and dissemination of information. Yet the G-7 nations have been better at preaching the virtues of transparency than at practicing transparency themselves. The G-7 summit and finance ministers meetings, for example, release communiques that are carefully negotiated and worded. But most preparatory background documents and analyses are not released.

The asymmetry in perceptions identified earlier can also be observed about disclosure policies. The largest, most powerful nations tend to see poor transparency as some *other* nation's or organization's approach to information disclosure and dissemination, not their own. More generally, the largest nations feel comfortable putting pressure on smaller nations to improve *their* policies, but tend to cut themselves substantial slack when questions are raised about the soundness of their own policies.

The comments above about risks from possible governance failures at international organizations should not be taken out of perspective. Yes, smaller and developing nations may not have adequate voice. But some significant voice is much better than no voice. Over time the relative aggregated influence of less powerful nations will probably increase. It is an underappreciated truth, furthermore, that the international organizations, in particular the World Bank and the IMF, are the institutional channels through which the interests of developing nations are most assertively emphasized to the world's economic and political elites.

It is especially important that discussions about accountability at the international financial organizations be kept in perspective. It would be a wild and hopelessly misleading exaggeration to assert, for example, that the IMF is not politically accountable. The international organizations are directly and tightly accountable to national governments. When international organizations fail in their exercise of collective governance, the explanation is virtually always that the governments of the major nations, typically elected and accountable to their own citizens, have failed to demand and support more appropriate policies. International organizations are not independent entities with unconstrained powers. Far from it.

Rather, as noted at the outset in chapter 1, international organizations are new and fragile seedlings in the gardens of collective governance. The seedlings are graft cuttings, merely ancillary extensions of the governments who planted them. The fragile saplings will one day, it is hoped, grow into mature trees. When that day comes, substantial pruning may well be required. In the meantime, gardeners should not confuse saplings with deep-rooted trees and should be at least as concerned with judicious applications of fertilizer as with wielding the pruning shears.

Halt Globalization or Shape Globalization?

Activists critical of globalization trends and international institutions are numerous, are becoming increasingly vocal, and now receive extensive publicity. Most activists have perspectives different from mine and prefer different methods of expressing their views. But in essence we share a deep interest in the same problems.

Activists criticizing globalization are heterogeneous in background, values, and the sophistication of their analytical understanding. It would be unfair and misleading to group them all together. Toward one extreme, some critics are unalterably opposed to globalization as a matter of principle or ideology. They can see only threats but no opportunities stemming from cross-border economic and financial integration. They wish to halt the process and if possible turn the clock back. Such advocates of "de-globalization" have many affinities with earlier social movements labeled isolationist.

Toward the other end of the spectrum of views, one finds activists not opposed to globalization in principle. Some of those even recognize that the probability is nearly zero of halting or reversing the general trends causing globalization. But those activists, too, chafe at the inequities and instabilities they believe are caused by some aspects of globalization and free market capitalism. They are not blind to some opportunities created by cross-border economic integration. Yet they keenly perceive downside costs and risks. They want to remedy the problems and make globalization more humane and equitable.

The activists whose views deserve the most attention are those who carefully identify genuine problems and recommend realistic steps for shaping globalization to mitigate the problems. I sympathize even with those who cannot express more than a vague dissatisfaction but are open to constructive proposals to redress identified problems. (Parenthetically, note that concerns are more likely to be sympathetically heard if expressed with civility as well as firmness. Street demonstrations as a method of expressing one's view can sometimes usefully nudge public opinion. Yet street demonstrations can also be disrupted by individuals or groups who assign a low priority to courtesy and the avoidance of violence.)

Consider the wide range of activists' criticisms directed at the IMF. One should warmly endorse constructive recommendations from those who want the IMF to do a better job in its core areas of cross-border finance and macroeconomics. One can readily sympathize with thoughtful proposals for the IMF to be still more transparent in the way it discloses and disseminates information. Proposals to give developing nations a greater voice in intergovernmental consultations and IMF decisions, including adjustments in the relative sizes of their IMF quotas, deserve a serious hearing.

One can empathize with those who want to see the IMF and World Bank facilitate larger amounts of debt relief for developing nations or who wish to see the IMF more heavily engaged in poverty reduction. I personally share the view that the distribution of income and wealth in the world—both within individual nations and across nations—is far more unequal than can conceivably be justified on grounds of economic efficiency, let alone moral decency. Yet critics who want to push the IMF into still greater involvement in structural reform and poverty reduction in developing nations are ill advised. Such critics could better advance their objectives by turning up the heat on national governments to push the World Bank and the regional development banks rather than the IMF in that direction. Nonetheless, such critics merit attention when they express thoughtful views along those lines.

I would go still further. One should empathize with those who want nations and the world community to design and implement improved world minimum standards for safeguarding the interests of labor and for protecting the environment. Yes, it is a strategic mistake for activists to try to push the IMF into a major involvement in the functional areas of labor markets and the environment. Even so, the impetus underlying many activists' views about these issue areas is constructive (with the important exception of those whose motives are essentially protectionist).

More generally, activist critics of globalization are often correct in espousing a "leveling up" of world standards and regulations to adequate minimums rather than having governments pursue a competition in laxity that leads, inadvertently if not deliberately, to a "leveling down" of standards and regulations toward a low, least common denominator.

In short, the views of activist critics should be listened to with respect provided that their purpose is to shape globalization, making it more just and more humane. Any criticism of the IMF and other international institutions merits a hearing if the underlying purpose is to make the institutions function more effectively. And not merely a hearing. National governments and the international institutions themselves should give a measured response to constructive criticisms made in a responsible manner.

In contrast, one should not empathize with the ideological isolationists who want to halt or reverse globalization. They are throwing sand against the wind, getting further blinded as the wind blows it back again. There is no valid basis for railing at the IMF and other international organizations, portraying their activities as on balance harmful for the world. It is utter nonsense to urge that the IMF be abolished. Such views are based on no understanding of the growing need for nurturing international collective governance. They are so far removed from sound analysis and common sense that they simply have to be ignored.

Many activists concerned about globalization would be more effective if they could learn to be more pragmatic. They should be more clear-headed, for example, about the fact that political power is distributed unequally in the world, within their own nations and even more so in the world polity at large. One should hope over time to shift that distribution of power to make it less asymmetric. But the existing asymmetry is a fact of life. It does little good to rail flamboyantly against it. Energy is better spent in thinking through incremental ways to change it.

Similarly, several dimensions of the secular trend toward increased globalization cannot be halted, much less reversed. Even if they could be reversed, in several cases it would not be desirable to do so. Rather than taking an unqualified "anti-globalization" position, indiscriminately attacking globalization in all its dimensions, critics should acknowledge its benefits, identify its downside consequences, and support the strengthening of the international governance mechanisms that are the best hope of making it work better. (Similarly, those recognizing that globalization brings benefits should avoid an unqualified "pro-globalization" position and pay close attention to adverse consequences for particular individuals or particular nations.)

Activists no less than we other reformers would do well to shape their actions in the light of the traditional prayer attributed to Saint Francis of Assisi: Give us the courage to change the things that ought to be and can be changed, the serenity to accept the things that cannot be changed, and the wisdom to distinguish the one from the other.

Don't Ask Too Much Too Soon, But Don't Be Too Timid Either!

This concluding chapter sketches an evolution for international financial governance for the short and medium runs. The evolution, in effect an interim vision for the world economy and financial system, is characterized by pragmatic incrementalism.

Some of you reading this book may want to peer through a dark glass into the distant future. You may be inclined to frame a vision of international governance and institutional evolution for the very long run. If we were to try to discern that evolution, what might we glimpse (darkly)?

We would surely observe that the political economy of the messy, intermediate world had become messier still. But we would doubtless also observe intergovernmental cooperation and international governance on a scale beyond anything imaginable for the shorter run. International institutions would be much more numerous and specialized. And they would have much stronger delegated powers. More extensive coordination of national economic policies, and even in some appropriate cases their explicit harmonization, might be politically feasible. Many of our grandchildren's grandchildren might have a diminished sense of national territoriality and hence be seriously debating the possible creation of worldwide federalist supranational institutions (governmental and nongovernmental). Speaking loosely, the center of gravity of many functions of collective governance would have drifted much further above the level of nation states to the level of regions or the world as a whole.

Financial systems would be markedly changed. The crystal ball is much too murky to reveal the multiple innovations in communications and financial technology that are likely. We can vaguely discern that the number of separate national currencies and separate exchange rates still in existence might be much smaller. The idea of a few common currencies for large regions—conceivably, eventually even a single common currency for the entire world—might be seriously debated by policymakers as well as academics. Coordination of national monetary policies might evolve toward regional monetary policies, or even a world monetary policy, as national financial systems became very much more integrated than they are today. For many nations, aspirations for an independent national monetary policy and financial breakwaters at the nation's borders might seem an anachronism. Fascinating institutional issues about monetary and financial matters, one can predict, would gain salience. Our grandchildren's grandchildren, for example, might well be discussing the possible evolution of a world central bank and the political independence of that bank from supranational federalist institutions and from national governments.

What of the International Monetary Fund in that distant future? The governance structure of the IMF would probably have changed. One can even imagine that the IMF Council, a latent institutional mechanism already provided for in the Articles of Agreement, would have been activated. Perhaps the IMF Council would have formally replaced the International Monetary and Finance Committee and would have been gradually assuming in a more formal way the high-level consultative and proto-decisionmaking functions now exercised in the G-7. Perhaps our grandchildren's grandchildren would be perceiving the IMF as the evolving world central bank. But then again, how do we interpret that hazy outline of the office tower of the Bank for International Settlements lurking in the background of the crystal ball?

The glass seems darkest of all if we try to discern fiscal policies—tax collections and expenditures for governance institutions—in that far distant time. It is a safe prediction that fiscal policies would be even more complex and multilayered than in the world at the beginning of the twenty-first century. One would still observe national governments deciding upon and implementing national budgets. We would surely not be speaking of the explicit harmonization of national (and local) budgetary policies but rather of their coordination. Many layers of the fiscal policies would still be subject to the presumption in favor of subsidiarity, accommodating diversity in preferences, and tying governance and the provision of public goods to different political jurisdictions in which the differing preferences were manifested. But of course analysis and debate would also be focused on the budgets of the regional and supranational institutions and their interdependence with lower-level fiscal policies and with regional or world monetary policies.

Such glimpses into the longer-run future are tantalizing. They are the perfect subject of conversation for a long leisurely winter's evening in front of a roaring log fire. Merely to allude to those possibilities, however, is to underscore the fact that they can arise only in the distant rather than the near future.

This book, therefore, has not indulged in speculation in detail about what lies ahead that far down the road. It has seemed prudent and more productive to focus on improvements in international governance that are needed and might be accomplished during the next several decades.

Over that time frame, the only feasible approach is pragmatic incrementalism. Collective governance seldom changes by quantum jumps. It typically cumulates in a series of continuing, small steps (some of which may even be retrograde). National governments are likely to be willing over the next several decades to yield only small incremental amounts of authority to international institutions. Thus it is preferable for each individual institution to stay focused on a few core responsibilities with the highest near-term priority.

Pragmatic incrementalism seeks to foster substantial forward progress through time. But it accepts the likelihood that progress will have to be gradual and cumulative. To avoid possibilities for contentious defeats and disruptive disappointments, it does not unrealistically urge intergovernmental cooperation and international institutions to perform miracles. The first half of its motto is: Don't ask too much, too soon.

Substantial and genuine progress has been made in recent years toward strengthening international financial governance. That observation is one major conclusion to take away from this book. But another, less encouraging observation is a complement to that conclusion: progress has lagged behind the rapid pace at which collective-governance problems with cross-border dimensions have been evolving.

If the governments of the largest nations had been more determined and farsighted, progress could have been still more substantial. Yes, one side of pragmatic incrementalism demands caution and gradual progress. But the other side requires decisions that are often expeditious and even ambitious, not protracted and fainthearted. The complete motto of pragmatic incrementalism reads: *Don't ask too much, too soon. But don't be too timid either!*

Caesar Augustus commended a maxim to his Roman military commanders that is apposite for the entire process of nurturing international financial governance. His counsel, essentially a recommendation for pragmatic incrementalism, was *festina lente* ("without haste, but without rest").

Festina lente means proceeding cautiously rather than precipitously. But it does mean, unambiguously, to proceed. Caution should not slip into procrastination.

Before the mid-1990s, consultations among the major governments about strengthening international financial governance were proceeding sluggishly. Governments, and hence the international institutions too, were not seized by *festina lente*. But then the Tequila crises of 1995 caught the governments' attention and forced them to think more deeply about issues of financial stability. Concern and cooperation subsided somewhat in 1996 and the first half of 1997. The Asian financial crises and the credit-spread turbulence that followed the Russian devaluation in 1998 created a renewed sense of urgency and spurred much of the progress in the following two years. Turkey in 2000 and Argentina in 2001–02 were, though more localized than earlier crises, additional reminders that international financial governance needed to make further progress.

The past record suggests that turbulence may be required to galvanize progress. As this book went to press, the world economy had recovered from the period of severe weakness associated with the terrorist attacks of September 2001. Although economic uncertainties continued to trouble many parts of the world and shadows of military conflict in the Middle East and the Korean peninsula darkened prospects further, a majority of forecasters thought aggregate world economic activity would nonetheless continue to exhibit modest growth. The world financial system, moreover, was showing fewer obvious manifestations of fragility. There thus seemed again some risk that the major governments would forget Augustus's maxim.

A slowing in the pace of cooperative efforts to strengthen international governance would be most unfortunate. Pragmatic incrementalism is the preferred approach. But the increments should keep accumulating, even without the stimulus of further turbulence. Major governments ought to move forward at a brisk pace rather than on tiptoe.

In May 1945 John Maynard Keynes, a key British architect in the Bretton Woods negotiations, wrote a letter to Edward Bernstein in the U.S. Treasury, a key architect on the American side. The letter was penned in the midst of their governments' efforts to persuade the British and U.S. legislatures to approve the establishment of the IMF and the World Bank. Keynes told Bernstein of a communication he had just received from the economist A.C. Pigou, the literary executor for Alfred Marshall, the most eminent British economist early in the twentieth century. "Pigou has just called my attention," wrote Keynes, "to a passage in Marshall's Evidence before the [1887] Gold and Silver Commission - Question 10,005, more than fifty years ago (have we yet asked more than 10,000 questions about Bretton Woods?)." Keynes copied the 1887 passage from Marshall:

> I think that there is a real, though very slow-moving, tendency for national interests to overrule provincial interests, and international interests to overrule national, and I think the time will come at which it will be thought as unreasonable for any country to regulate its currency without reference to other countries as it would be to have signalling codes at sea which took no account of the signalling codes at sea of other countries.

Keynes then said to Bernstein: "So once more we may hope the old man has been right, with not much more of a time-lag than it is reasonable to expect, at least in international affairs."[10]

This exchange from more than half a century ago, referring back to views expressed at a time more than an entire century in the past, reminds us poignantly that the issues of international governance are scarcely new under the sun. The exchange is a salutary reminder that delays and slow learning are a part of the venerable history of international affairs. Even so, this glance back at history through the eyes of outstanding economists is also an essentially encouraging reminder. The slow-moving tendency for a strengthening of international governance is real and powerful. One can plausibly anticipate that incremental progress will continue. One can optimistically hope that such progress will be brisk and that pragmatic leaders will wisely steer it into the most constructive channels.

---

10. Keynes (1980, vol. 26 of *Collected Writings*, p. 195). President Franklin Roosevelt, in his opening remarks to the 1944 Bretton Woods conference, voiced an analogous thought using the metaphor of health: "Economic diseases are highly communicable. It follows, therefore, that the economic health of every country is a proper matter of concern to all its neighbors, near and distant." (Kapur, Lewis, and Webb, 1997, vol. 1, p. 65).

Appendix
The IMF and Other International
Financial Institutions

Chapters 7 and 8 describe potential functions for intergovernmental financial cooperation. The final section of chapter 7 identifies the institutions supporting intergovernmental financial cooperation at the beginning of the twenty-first century. Such international financial institutions—understood to comprise both intergovernmental consultative groups and formal international organizations—are the venues that must serve as the loci for future efforts to strengthen international financial governance.

This appendix supplies background sketches of the international financial institutions for readers that may not already be familiar with them. Figure 7-4, it will be recalled, provides a bird's-eye cross-classification of the existing institutions and the key functional areas in which they are engaged. It may be helpful to refer to the final pages of chapter 7, particularly figure 7-4, when reading this appendix.

The appendix gives a necessary minimum of institutional description to anchor the analysis in the book's chapters. Considerably more attention is given to background description and history of the International Monetary Fund than of other international organizations because the IMF is the focal point of debates about the evolution of international collective governance for cross-border finance. Readers wishing more detailed information about individual institutions are given suggestions for further reading in the footnotes.

Consultative Groups Formed by National Governments

A flurry of top-level intergovernmental negotiations among the largest industrial nations, especially the United States and the United Kingdom, occurred during and immediately following World War II. The negotiations successfully created the IMF and the World Bank as international financial organizations. The major governments were unable to agree on a comparably ambitious international organization for trade, but the less ambitious General Agreement on Tariffs and Trade was negotiated. After the postwar crises of 1947, the Marshall Plan for U.S. assistance to Europe and the institutions associated with that initiative contributed to the rebuilding of Europe.

That postwar period was in several respects a high-water mark for intergovernmental economic and financial cooperation. It was also a period in which political and economic power was unusually asymmetric. The critical consultative groups designing the international institutions created after the war were essentially bilateral committees of government officials from the United States and the United Kingdom. With few exceptions, officials from other national governments were involved in the negotiations only after key issues had been resolved between the Americans and the British.[1]

The most influential venues for intergovernmental consultations in the 1950s continued to be bilateral between the United States and other large nations. On some European issues, multilateral consultations within Europe occurred through the organization that gave birth to the Organization for Economic Cooperation and Development (see below). The United States did not permit the IMF to be an effective central forum for intergovernmental cooperation in the 1950s.

In 1962 the largest industrial nations established the General Arrangements to Borrow (GAB), a contingent mechanism permitting the IMF to buttress its resources by borrowing funds from them in defined emergency circumstances. The GAB participant nations subsequently constituted themselves as a consultative group, known as the Group of Ten, for continuing discussions on economic and financial matters. The G-10,

---

1. For overviews of the top-level negotiations during World War II and in the immediate postwar period, see Gardner (1969) and Skidelsky (2001). When theorists of international relations write about a hegemonic power inducing "hegemonic stability," they frequently have in mind the dominant position of the United States in the early postwar years.

which has eleven member nations (Switzerland was added to the ten original GAB nations), is chronologically the first of the multiple intergovernmental consultative groups bearing numerical labels and fostering numerological confusion. Though less influential than in the 1960s and early 1970s, the G-10 continued to meet throughout the rest of the century.

The member nations of the G-10 are Belgium, Canada, France, Germany, Italy, Japan, the Netherlands, Sweden, Switzerland, the United Kingdom, and the United States. The finance ministers and central bank governors of the G-10 usually meet twice a year in connection with the spring and autumn meetings of the IMF and World Bank. The G-10 central bank governors normally meet monthly at the Bank for International Settlements. The G-10 deputies (second-level officials from member nations' finance ministries and central banks) meet as needed, usually between two and four times a year. Ad hoc committees and working parties of the G-10 are set up as needed.

The General Arrangements to Borrow were expanded to include Saudi Arabia in 1983. A second borrowing option for the IMF, known as the New Arrangements to Borrow (NAB), was negotiated among twenty-five IMF member nations in 1996 and became operational in November 1998. The G-10, however, has remained the same original ten nations plus Switzerland.

During the 1960s, an increasingly integrated world economy and linked financial markets were experiencing greater cross-border pressures. Intergovernmental tensions about economic matters were growing. European governments, led by France, began to challenge the dominance of U.S. views on international monetary issues. The breakdown of the Bretton Woods exchange rate arrangements in 1971–73 and the first major increase by members of the Organization of Petroleum-Exporting Countries in their oil prices in 1973–74 severely strained the international institutions and the political impulses to cooperation. In response to these turbulent events, a sustained effort was made to reconfigure the international regime environment—to "reform the international monetary system"—through the negotiations of the so-called Committee of Twenty (see further discussion below). But in the end, only a minimalist rewriting of the IMF Articles of Agreement proved possible.[2]

---

2. Solomon (1982) provides a perspective on the Bretton Woods era as a whole. On the crises of the 1970s and the Committee of Twenty negotiations, see, for example, Solomon (1982),

Beginning in 1975 the heads of the governments of several major nations began to get together annually at "summit" meetings to discuss economic and political issues. The six nations at the initial summit, held in 1975 at Rambouillet, France, were France, Germany, Italy, Japan, the United Kingdom, and the United States. Canada participated in the 1976 and subsequent summit meetings. The summits attended by the heads of these seven governments, preceded by preparatory sessions conducted by lower-level officials known as "sherpas" and, later on, by meetings of finance ministers and central bank governors and their deputies, have together become known as the Group of Seven meetings.[3]

Since its inception in the 1970s, the G-7 has become the single most influential consultative group through which major governments discuss economic and financial issues and consider intergovernmental cooperative actions. The G-7 finance ministers and central bank governors now meet at least twice a year before the spring and autumn meetings of the IMF and World Bank. From time to time the G-7 leaders have also created task forces or working groups to focus intensively on issues of particular concern. The G-7 is an exclusive and powerful club that now frames many of the most important decisions about intergovernmental financial cooperation. Excluded nations are understandably uncomfortable with the central importance of G-7 discussions and decisions.

The G-7 began to involve the Soviet Union, subsequently Russia, in a "post-summit dialogue" at the 1991 summit. By the late 1990s Russia was a participant in the political and even some of the economic and financial discussions held at the summits. At the 1998 summit in Birmingham, England, Russia participated fully, and the expanded consultative group began to be referred to as the Group of Eight, or G-8. The G-7, however, continued to function alongside the formal summit meetings.

The nature and degree of Russia's future participation was unclear at the beginning of the century. At the 2000 summit meeting held in Japan,

---

J. Williamson (1977), International Monetary Fund (1974), and Fischer (1988). Horsefield and others (1969), De Vries (1976, 1985), and Boughton (2001) provide more detail, including essential documents.

3. U.S. Treasury secretary George Schultz convened a meeting of finance ministers from France, Germany, Japan, the United Kingdom, and the United States in 1973; these five nations have subsequently been referred to as the Group of Five. Italy was included in the first summit meeting of heads of state in 1975. The G-7 label originated after Canada joined the summit meeting held in Puerto Rico in 1976. Putnam and Bayne (1987) is a good source for the history of the early years of the summit process.

communiques were issued on behalf of both the G-7 (finance ministers) and the G-8 (heads of governments); key economic issues were discussed in the G-7, indicating a continued reluctance to involve Russia fully.[4]

The International Monetary and Financial Committee, formerly called the Interim Committee, and the Development Committee are umbrella groups dating from the years of the Committee of Twenty negotiations in the 1970s. Each voting constituency in the IMF and the World Bank sends representatives to the meetings of these two committees, held at the time of the autumn and spring meetings of the IMF and World Bank. Thus every IMF and World Bank member nation is in a formal sense represented in the meetings of the IMFC and the Development Committee. The two committees have functioned primarily as talk sessions at which finance ministers and central bank governors make policy speeches or signal policy intentions. They have not been effective as decisionmaking groups. These committees have formally endorsed collective decisions, but typically only after intensive informal consultations in much smaller groups (in particular the G-7) have prepared the decisions.[5]

Developing nations have formed several consultative groups, in part intended as counterweights to the G-7. These include the Group of Twenty-Four and the Group of Seventy-Seven, composed of government officials from developing nations. These groups typically have met and issued communiques at about the same time that G-7 meetings are held (prior to meetings of the IMFC and the Development Committee). Still another venue for developing nations has been the Summit Level Group for South-South Consultation and Cooperation, known as the Group of Fifteen, or G-15. The G-15, which by 2002 had nineteen member nations from Asia, Latin America, and Africa, was established in September 1989 at the Ninth Non-Aligned Summit in Belgrade; it is described as "complementary to the efforts of the larger South-South cooperation fora" like the G-77.

---

4. Talbott (2002) discusses the major international security issues raised by Russia's political evolution in the 1990s and, in passing, describes the pressures to include Russia in G-7 summit meetings.

5. The Interim Committee began meeting in October 1974 as a successor to the Committee of Twenty. The Interim Committee was reconstituted and renamed the International Monetary and Financial Committee in 1999. In the 1970s it was intended that the committee would meet only in an "interim period" before a comprehensive reform of the Fund's Articles could be "finally agreed and fully implemented." By the 1990s, however, the so-called interim period still had an indefinite duration and the label of "Interim" had become an embarrassing anachronism. The IMF Articles of Agreement as amended in the 1970s provide for the possibility of eventual activation of an IMF Council, which unlike the IMFC would be a true decisionmaking body.

In response to the Asian financial crises of 1997–98, finance ministers and central bank governors from twenty-two "systemically significant" nations met in April 1998 "to examine issues related to the stability of the international financial system and the effective functioning of global financial markets." This consultative Group of Twenty-Two, sometimes referred to as the Willard Group (after the Willard Hotel in Washington, D.C., where some of the meetings were held), was an initiative of the United States and several other major nations to widen planning discussions of international financial reform beyond the G-7 venue. In addition to the G-7, the members of the Group of Twenty-Two were Argentina, Australia, Brazil, China, Hong Kong, India, Indonesia, Malaysia, Mexico, Poland, Russia, Singapore, South Africa, South Korea, and Thailand. Three working groups were appointed at the April 1998 meeting of the Group of Twenty-Two, charged with focusing on transparency and accountability, strengthening financial systems, and international financial crises. The influential reports of the working groups were presented and discussed at a further meeting in October 1998.[6]

In September 1999 the G-7 finance ministers announced the creation of yet another consultative group of finance ministers and central bank governors, to be known as the Group of Twenty. The G-20 fulfilled a commitment made by the G-7 leaders at the June 1999 summit in Cologne, Germany, "to establish an informal mechanism for dialogue among systemically important countries within the framework of the Bretton Woods institutional system." In several respects, including its composition, the G-20 is a successor to the Group of Twenty-Two (the latter did not continue after its 1998 meetings).

The members of the G-20 include the seven members of the G-7 plus Argentina, Australia, Brazil, China, India, Indonesia, Mexico, Russia, Saudi Arabia, South Africa, South Korea, Turkey, and the European Union. The managing director of the IMF and the president of the World Bank, as well as the chairpersons of the International Monetary and Financial Committee and Development Committee, participate fully in the G-20 discussions. The G-20 met for the first time in December 1999,

6. The phrases quoted in the text were used by the Group of Twenty-Two in its news releases and reports. The heads of the BIS, IMF, OECD, and the World Bank as well as the chair of the Interim Committee attended the meetings of the Group of Twenty-Two as observers. President Bill Clinton launched the initiative for establishment of the Group of Twenty-Two at the November 1997 meeting of national leaders of APEC (Asia-Pacific Economic Cooperation Forum) member countries.

for a second time in October 2000, and has subsequently held meetings annually in November of 2001 and 2002.[7]

The International Monetary Fund

The Articles of Agreement for the IMF that emerged from the wartime consultations between the American and British governments and then from the July 1944 conference at Bretton Woods, New Hampshire, envisaged an institution with pathbreaking but limited responsibilities. The original Articles represented a complex compromise between American and British concepts (associated, respectively, with the team at the U.S. Treasury led by Harry Dexter White and the U.K. Treasury team led by John Maynard Keynes). Because of American political dominance, most of the key decisions reflected the postwar creditor position and more conservative financial views of the United States rather than the British preferences for a bolder plan supportive of nations with large postwar debts.[8]

Only two of the conceivable functional roles for financial cooperation identified in chapter 7 were prominently and explicitly emphasized in the original Articles. Three of the other functional roles were, arguably, consistent with the original design and included implicitly if not explicitly.

The evolution of the IMF in the final three decades of the twentieth century witnessed several major changes and a further expansion of functions. A summary of the original concept and the subsequent evolution helps to clarify the choices for the future of the IMF that are highlighted in chapters 9 to 13.

Original Concept at Bretton Woods

The designers of the original IMF presumed, first, that the institution would monitor new traffic regulations to govern economic, and especially financial, relations in the postwar world (function 2a in figure 7-4). The exchange rate arrangements spelled out in the original version of Article IV were to be a key element in the new rules of the road. Each member country would have a par value for its currency, established with the concurrence

---

7. Finance Minister Paul Martin of Canada was chosen as the initial chairperson of the G-20 for its first two years. The chairperson in 2002 was Jaswant Singh, the finance minister of India. The G-20 dating from 1999 should not be confused with the Committee of Twenty that was active during the 1970s in the discussions of possible reforms of the international monetary system.

8. Gardner (1969) and Skidelsky (2001).

of the IMF. In principle, the par value would not be changed without the concurrence of the IMF (although only the member, not the IMF itself, would have the power to propose a change in par value). Market exchange rates between currencies would be maintained within narrow margins around the cross rates determined by the par values. Most of the original designers regarded the lack of cooperative understandings about exchange rates as a contributing cause of the unsatisfactory performance of the world economy in the 1920s and 1930s. The new Article IV understandings were accordingly perceived as the linchpin of a more stable world financial environment.[9]

Other critical elements of the new traffic regulations discussed at Bretton Woods dealt with nations' restrictions on international transactions. Nations were not to intensify, and if possible were to reduce, their restrictions on trade in goods and services. To this end, the IMF was given explicit powers to approve or disapprove member nations' exchange practices and their practices with respect to payments and transfers for trade and other current account transactions.

At the time of the Bretton Woods conference in July 1944, efforts were still under way to establish a new International Trade Organization (ITO). The ITO, not the IMF, was intended as the primary locus of traffic regulations governing trade and other current account transactions. The efforts to negotiate the details of the ITO and to get them approved by national legislatures ultimately failed. The General Agreement on Tariffs and Trade, originally intended as a temporary agreement to precede the ITO, lived on as an organization embodying a diluted version of the earlier ambitions.

Although not considered the primary locus of traffic regulations about current account transactions themselves, the IMF was to be responsible for the regulations on payments for such transactions. As shown by early controversy in the IMF's history, the subjects of restrictions on trade and restrictions on payments for trade were strongly interlocked, which in turn made it difficult to separate the IMF's role from that of the GATT.

---

9. For an influential example of the widely accepted analysis that the 1920s and 1930s were a period of relative anarchy in international monetary affairs, see Nurkse and others (1944). Southard (1979, p. 2) argues that "the power to approve or disapprove par values was conceptually the most important provision in the [original] Articles; this was the first time that states had agreed to such an invasion of sovereignty."

Nonetheless, the original intent was to have the IMF help to prevent the intensification of restrictions on current account transactions.[10]

Restrictions on capital account transactions were perceived very differently. Capital account restrictions were acceptable and even encouraged in the original IMF Articles. For example, Article VI authorized member nations to "exercise such controls as are necessary to regulate international capital movements" (provided the controls were not designed to restrict payments for current transactions). Article VI also prohibited the use of the Fund's resources "to meet a large or sustained outflow of capital" and even authorized the IMF to "request a member to exercise controls to prevent such use."

The second major role envisaged for the IMF by its architects was to assist member nations in liability financing of their payments deficits (function 4 in figure 7-4). For this lending-intermediary role, the IMF would obtain its resources by quota subscriptions, payable partly in reserve assets and partly in member nations' own currencies. Nations running deficits would be able to borrow from the IMF the currencies of nations running surpluses (who of course would acquire a counterpart claim on the IMF).[11]

The financing provided by the IMF to deficit nations was explicitly intended to be temporary and short term. Borrowing nations were not to have indefinite access to the IMF's resources. It was presumed, moreover, that balance-of-payments deficits and surpluses would alternate over time across member nations. Hence all members were regarded as potential borrowers from the IMF at one time or another. Similarly, no nation or group of nations was to be a persistent net lender through the IMF.

The original Articles were unclear about the degree to which conditionality would be associated with IMF lending to deficit nations. Hence it was also unclear how active the IMF should be as an adjustment referee.

---

10. For the early history, see Gardner (1969) and Horsefield and others (1969). On the respective responsibilities of the Fund and the GATT, see Horsefield and others (1969, vol. II, pp. 332–46).

11. Each IMF member nation at the outset transferred to the Fund an amount of reserve assets (originally, gold) equivalent to 25 percent of its quota. Countries for which 25 percent of the quota exceeded 10 percent of net official holdings of gold and U.S. dollars were permitted to transfer the smaller amount as their reserve asset payment. The remaining portion of the quota was subscribed in the member's own currency. In addition to the currencies obtained from the three-fourths payment of quotas in national currencies, the IMF could obtain further amounts of currencies to lend by selling some of the noncurrency (gold) reserve assets transferred to it.

The fuzziness reflected unresolved differences of view. The United Kingdom and a number of other nations argued that a borrowing nation should have virtually automatic access to the IMF's resources and that the timing of its repayment should be contingent on the reversal of the payments imbalance giving rise to the loan. In contrast, the United States argued that IMF lending should be accompanied by performance conditions and that repayment should occur on a prespecified schedule. Because these key aspects of the IMF's role as a lending intermediary were not agreed in the wartime negotiations and in the original Articles, they had to be thrashed out in the early years of actual operation.[12]

The term *surveillance* is not used in the original IMF Articles. Nor is there a strong emphasis on promoting adjustment and catalyzing coordination (function 2b in figure 7-4). But in at least minor ways, the original concept for the IMF did imply a nascent role for collective, supranational surveillance. For example, Article I stated, as a purpose of the IMF, the promotion of cooperation "through a permanent institution which provides the machinery for consultation and collaboration on international monetary problems." The IMF was given powers to require member nations to provide certain types of information.[13] It was also given authority to require nations with exchange restrictions to engage in annual consultations with the IMF, an authority that was later strengthened and extended (see below).[14]

The original concept for the IMF was consistent in minor ways with two other potential functions in figure 7-4. Although the Articles of

12. In a formal accounting sense, the IMF as currently constituted does not make "loans" to "borrowing" deficit nations. IMF transactions with a deficit nation that "draws" on the Fund are formally "sales" of the currencies of nations in surplus or in a strong reserve position (in exchange for the deficit nation's currency). When a deficit nation repays the Fund, it "repurchases" its own currency. Similarly, in a formal accounting sense, a surplus nation whose currency is "drawn" by a deficit nation does not "lend" to the IMF. Nonetheless, the essential economic aspects of IMF transactions are accurately described by the language of lending, borrowing, and intermediation through the Fund. I use this language rather than the IMF's accounting language because the former is analytically clearer. The drafters of the original Articles avoided the language of debt and lending because the IMF's "loans" were to differ in significant ways from traditional commercial loans. The original drafters also seem to have wanted to obfuscate the reality that a deficit nation drawing on IMF resources would be obtaining a temporary loan from other nations' governments through the intermediation of the IMF.

13. For example, Article VIII, section 5(c) specified (and still specifies) that the IMF "shall act as a centre for the collection and exchange of information on monetary and financial problems, thus facilitating the preparation of studies designed to assist members in developing policies which further the purposes of the Fund."

14. The original authority is in Article XIV, section 4.

Agreement did not emphasize or clarify such a possibility, the IMF could use its lending facilities to help national governments manage financial crises (function 3). And the IMF was given authority to collect and disseminate information from members and, if only implicitly, authority for its staff to conduct research (function 5).

In essence, therefore, the original IMF was designed as a traffic monitor and a lending intermediary. With less clarity, the IMF also had nascent or implicit responsibilities for acting as an adjustment referee, a coordination catalyst, a crisis manager, and a producer of information and research.

Subsequent Evolution

The system of infrequently adjusted par values embodied in Article IV of the original Articles of Agreement was sustained during the IMF's first two decades. But it came under increasing strain as the 1960s drew to a close. In the event, even after traumatic changes in par values in 1971 and February 1973 (including a widening of the margins around par values in 1971), the Bretton Woods exchange rate arrangements proved unsustainable. The major nations abandoned efforts to establish and maintain par values after several weeks of exchange crisis in February–March 1973. The exchange rate arrangements that emerged were characterized by managed floating among the currencies of the major industrial nations and an assortment of pegging regimes for the currencies of developing nations. Strains on the adjustable par-value system ultimately became intolerable because the system embodied excessive inertia against changes in exchange rates among the major currencies.[15]

The breakdown of the par-value system cast a major shadow over the IMF's function as a monitor for traffic regulations. Following the U.S. suspension of gold convertibility for the dollar and the realignment of exchange rates agreed at the Smithsonian Institution in 1971, efforts were launched under the auspices of the Committee of Twenty to devise new cooperative presumptions for national policies and the IMF itself. These efforts, a return to "top-level" international negotiations, were intensified

---

15. The magnitude of payments imbalances among the major nations increased in the latter half of the 1960s and early 1970s. The situation became especially difficult when the United States, the dominant reserve-center country, progressively slipped into serious imbalance. Exchange rate changes as a means for bringing about adjustment of these payments imbalances were either forgone altogether or used only as a last resort. The burden of adjustment was thus thrown excessively on other types of policies. In particular, the par-value system proved to be extremely sluggish in permitting changes in the exchange rates of other major currencies against the dominant reserve currency.

after the onset of generalized floating in March 1973. The hope at the time was to develop revised, comprehensive traffic regulations for the world financial system.[16]

Unfortunately, the efforts of the Committee of Twenty proved largely unsuccessful. What little of the effort could be salvaged was incorporated into a Second Amendment of the Articles of Agreement, negotiated in 1975–76 and made effective in April 1978. The Second Amendment represented a legal "fix-up" for the exchange rate arrangements that had been in force, de facto but not de jure, since March 1973.[17] (Chapters 9 and 11 analyze exchange rate arrangements and IMF surveillance of them in future decades.)

The IMF's monitoring of traffic regulations governing restrictions on payments for current account transactions was less stormy than its experience with exchange arrangements. The actual outcome of the monitoring, however, fell short of the optimistic hopes expressed at Bretton Woods. The Articles of Agreement envisaged that all member nations would eventually adhere to the provisions of Article VIII, which includes the prohibition that "no member shall, without the approval of the Fund, impose restrictions on the making of payments and transfers for current international transactions."[18] It was recognized at Bretton Woods that many coun-

---

16. To many participants in the Committee of Twenty negotiations, including myself, this goal seemed attainable. The main features of a conceivable agreement included an effective and more symmetrical adjustment process, especially a better functioning of the exchange rate mechanism; the introduction of some form of convertibility of reserve currency balances into outside reserve assets, and hence a more symmetrical set of obligations for all nations for the asset settlement of payments deficits; better international management of the global stocks of reserve assets, with the role of gold and reserve currencies being reduced and special drawing rights gradually becoming the principal reserve asset; and measures of some sort to promote the net flow of real resources to developing countries. This set of principles seemed to represent a possible compromise among the positions of key groups of IMF member nations. The new exchange rate arrangements envisaged in the agreement were to be characterized by more frequently adjustable but relatively stable par values, with floating rates recognized as providing a useful technique in particular situations. The key phrases in this summary are taken from the June 14, 1974, "Outline of Reform," produced by the Committee of Twenty. See IMF (1974).

17. Without a formal change in the Articles, most nations would have been in continuing violation of an international treaty. For discussions of the Committee of Twenty negotiations and why they were unsuccessful, see Solomon (1982, pp. 235–97) and Williamson (1977). The first amendment to the IMF's Articles of Agreement, providing for the creation and allocation of special drawing rights, was adopted in 1968–69.

18. Full adherence to Article VIII entails avoiding restrictions on current payments and transfers (section 2), avoiding discriminatory currency practices (section 3), and assuring the convertibility for current account transactions of foreign, officially held balances of the national currency (section 4). Under Article I (iv), one of the stated purposes of the IMF is "the elimination of foreign exchange restrictions which hamper the growth of world trade."

tries could not or would not adhere to Article VIII during a postwar transitional period. Article XIV therefore authorized such countries to avail themselves of current account restrictions during a transitional period, subject to consultation with the IMF. The arrangements in Article XIV, however, proved durable rather than transitory. By the spring of 1984, only about two-fifths of the IMF's 146 member nations had accepted the obligations of Article VIII. The remainder considered themselves to be operating under the "transitional" arrangements of Article XIV. Nevertheless, gradually more and more member nations reduced their restrictions on trade in goods and services. By September 2000, a much smaller fraction of the IMF's member nations—only 33 out of the total 182—were still formally under the transitional arrangements of Article XIV.[19]

Prevailing attitudes about the traffic regulations for capital account transactions embodied in the original IMF Articles of Agreement evolved considerably in the decades following Bretton Woods. The initial consensus, as noted above, was that many types of cross-border capital flows were undesirable and that restrictions were not only permitted but helpful. Thereafter, views gradually changed in many nations. By the end of the century, the separation fences inhibiting cross-border capital flows were much lower and more permeable than they had been fifty-five years before.

The IMF's original mandate at Bretton Woods contained provisions for nascent supranational surveillance extending beyond the mere monitoring of traffic regulations (see above). Governments of the major nations, however, did not encourage the IMF to act in the broader roles of adjustment referee or coordination catalyst. More precisely, governments of the largest nations were prepared to have the IMF lean strongly on smaller member nations but did not welcome the surveillance spotlight turned on their own policies.

The most significant of the broader efforts timidly undertaken was associated with the process that came to be known as the "annual consultations." The original Articles empowered the IMF to conduct annual consultations only with member nations availing themselves of Article XIV. The purpose of the consultations was to evaluate the member's restrictions on payments and transfers for current account transactions during the presumptively short transitional period prior to the member's shift to Article VIII status. Such consultations began in 1952, amid some controversy about their scope and the appropriate procedures. By the late 1950s, IMF

---

19. Article XIV does not give a member authority to introduce new restrictions, but merely to retain existing restrictions.

staff missions to Article XIV countries had become relatively uncontroversial and had even evolved into a procedure for discussion of a wide range of the country's economic policies, not merely its Article XIV restrictions.

Members whose currencies were convertible under Article VIII were not obligated to participate in annual consultations. After the switch of many member nations from Article XIV to Article VIII status at the end of 1958, however, the IMF's executive board decided in 1959 that there would be "great merit" in arranging periodic consultations with all members. The largest members supported this decision only on the understanding that consultations for Article VIII members would be voluntary, rather than mandatory, and would not be completed (in contrast to Article XIV consultations) by an executive board "decision" containing recommendations for policy action.[20]

Some proponents of increasing the catalytic influence of the IMF wanted to rescind the 1959 understanding, thereby permitting consultations with Article VIII members to result in executive board decisions. But those efforts did not succeed and were abandoned when the Second Amendment was being drafted in the 1970s. Instead, a new provision applying to all member nations was inserted into Article IV governing exchange rate arrangements. Thereafter, this provision in Article IV became the legal basis for annual consultations with members.[21]

If the IMF as an institution were to act as an adjustment referee and coordination catalyst, its staff would need to develop analytical capacities for supporting those roles. In particular, analysis would have to be able to identify payments imbalances, exchange rates, and domestic macroeconomic policies judged to be unsustainable or internationally inappropriate. Although the major national governments were lukewarm in their support

---

20. The early history of the consultations process is discussed by Southard (1979, pp. 11–15); Brau (1981, pp. 13–16); Horsefield and others (1969, vol. I, pp. 310–21, 408–12; vol. II, pp. 229–48); and De Vries (1976, vol. I, pp. 569–90).

21. Article IV in the amended Articles, agreed to in 1976, resulted as a compromise between very different U.S. and European (especially French) proposals. Section 3 of the amended Article IV requires that the IMF "shall oversee the international monetary system in order to ensure its effective operation, and shall oversee the compliance of each member with its obligations under Section I of this Article." To fulfill that function, the IMF "shall exercise firm surveillance over the exchange rate policies of members, and shall adopt specific principles for the guidance of all members with respect to those policies." Additionally, Article IV requires that "each member shall provide the Fund with the information necessary for such surveillance, and, when requested by the Fund, shall consult with it on the member's exchange rate policies." For discussion, see Gold (1984, vol. II, "Strengthening the Soft International Law of Exchange Arrangements"). This 1976 use of *surveillance* in the amended Article IV is the first explicit mention of the term in the IMF's Articles of Agreement.

of this broader concept of surveillance, the IMF staff conducted research and took administrative steps to lay the required foundation gradually.

Beginning in 1969, for example, the staff initiated an internal forecasting and diagnostic exercise that projected macroeconomic indicators for the largest industrial economies. By 1973 the exercise was adjusting the projection for each national economy in the light of the projections for other economies, thereby seeking to make all the forecasts compatible and mutually consistent. Each round of the exercise produced a document known as the *World Economic Outlook* (*WEO*). The *WEO* gradually came to play a significant role in executive board discussions and in the meetings of the Interim Committee. The exercise also became gradually more public. In 1978 the IMF's managing director gave a summary of the *WEO* to the press. Actual publication of an annual *WEO* began in 1980 (though initially without much of the forecasting detail). Beginning in 1984 the *WEO* was published biannually.[22]

A second example is a survey exercise for world financial and capital markets begun in the 1970s. The staff work analyzes recent developments and prospects and identifies key policy issues. Beginning in 1980 the IMF published an annual report on this work, typically titled *International Capital Markets*. A quarterly publication on *Emerging Market Financing* was instituted in 2000. By 2002 the IMF was publishing a quarterly report on *Global Financial Stability* that replaced and amplified the previous *International Capital Markets* and *Emerging Market Financing* reports.[23]

To back up its diagnostic and survey analyses to underpin collective surveillance, the IMF staff also conducted extensive research studies. By the 1980s that research included the construction and use of multiregion macroeconomic models and efforts to identify alternative estimates of equilibrium exchange rates.

Before the 1980s, the IMF was little involved in international discussions about the prudential oversight of financial standards and financial institutions (function 2c in figure 7-4). Intergovernmental cooperation took place primarily through the Bank for International Settlements. Beginning with the IMF's 1982–86 lending to nations caught up in debt-servicing crises, however, the IMF staff began to be pulled into those

---

22. The history of the *WEO* exercise is reviewed in Boughton (1997).

23. The *Global Financial Stability* report focuses on current conditions in global financial markets, highlighting issues of financial imbalances and structural or systemic issues relevant to international financial stability. It also seeks to draw out the financial ramifications of macroeconomic imbalances highlighted by the IMF's *World Economic Outlook*.

financial surveillance discussions. The pressure for IMF involvement intensified after the Tequila crises of 1995 and the Asian-flu crises of 1997–98.[24]

Intergovernmental lending intermediation (function 4) got a slow start in the earliest years of IMF operations because of the controversy about whether conditionality should be associated with the lending. That controversy was in essence a debate about whether the IMF should divorce its lending for liability financing of a member's deficit from simultaneously applied performance conditions that would pressure the borrowing member to adjust the deficit. Even in the relatively cooperative environment of the 1940s and 1950s, it was highly unlikely that the proponents of automaticity could have won that debate. A divorce between liability financing of deficits and measures to adjust the deficits implies inherently implausible behavior by the surplus nations that accumulate—in this case indirectly through the IMF—the loan claims on deficit nations (see discussion in chapter 8).

By the end of the 1950s, there was no longer a major controversy about conditionality for IMF lending. At least the principle of specifying performance conditions to promote adjustment had been generally accepted. The form of IMF lending known as a "standby arrangement" had been invented, under which a member could be assured of borrowing a specified amount of IMF resources, in specified installments over a defined period, to support an agreed adjustment program. The presumption had also been established that conditionality would become more stringent as a member borrowed larger amounts of IMF resources.

Throughout subsequent decades, however, many aspects of the specification of conditionality and lending terms remained controversial. Strong differences of view persist to this day.[25]

During the 1960s, 1970s, and 1980s, new types of shocks buffeted the world economy. Prominent among these were the collapse of the Bretton Woods exchange rate arrangements in 1971–73 and very large increases in the relative price of oil, first in 1973–74 and then again in 1979–80. The

---

24. For a more detailed account of the historical development of surveillance activities at the IMF, see James (1995) and the references cited in his article.

25. For discussions of the conditionality of IMF lending, see Horsefield and others (1969, vols. I and II); Southard (1979); Gold (1979); Dell (1981); Guitian (1981); J. Williamson (1983); Polak (1991); and Schadler and others (1993, 1995).

shocks caused confusion about and raised novel challenges for the IMF's lending-intermediation function.

Four main types of evolutionary change can be identified in IMF lending, occurring in part as a response to the new shocks. Appraised with the benefit of hindsight, the changes taken together can be seen to have caused a major transformation.

The first change was the establishment of a succession of new lending facilities—in effect, special windows to provide financing of a particular sort or for a particular purpose. For example, the Compensatory Financing Facility, designed to assist member nations suffering from a shortfall in export proceeds of primary commodities, was created in 1963 and extended further in 1966, 1975, 1979, and 1981. A Buffer Stock Financing Facility was established in 1969 to assist members in balance-of-payments need in financing their contributions to international buffer stocks. A First Oil Facility was created in 1974, a second in 1975. An Extended Fund Facility was adopted in 1974.[26] The Trust Fund, administered by the IMF to extend balance-of-payments financing on concessional terms to the IMF's poorest members, was established in 1976–78. A Supplementary Financing Facility, agreed in 1977 and put into operation in 1979, permitted borrowing countries to draw in excess of the limits applicable to regular drawings. As a successor to the Supplemental Financing Facility, a Policy on Enlarged Access was adopted in March 1981 and revised in March 1983, enabling the IMF to continue its assistance to members facing payments imbalances that were large in relation to their quotas and which needed resources in larger amounts than available under ordinary drawings. The Enhanced Structural Adjustment Facility and its predecessor, the Structural Adjustment Facility, were established in the 1980s; the two facilities provided "concessional" financing (interest rates and other charges less than for ordinary IMF lending) for balance-of-payments difficulties confronting low-income developing nations.[27]

26. The Extended Fund Facility was designed for use by members with an economy "suffering serious payments imbalance relating to structural maladjustments in production and trade and where prices and cost distortions have been widespread" or an economy "characterized by slow growth and an inherently weak balance of payments position which prevents pursuit of an active development policy."

27. Detailed discussions may be found in the IMF's official histories: Horsefield and others (1969); De Vries (1976, 1985, 1987); and Boughton (2001). The earliest IMF special facility, the General

This proliferation of special facilities and policies increased, by a substantial proportion of its quota, the potential use of IMF resources by an individual member nation. The original Articles permitted a member to borrow a cumulative amount of up to 125 percent of its quota.[28] By the mid-1980s, an individual member with a serious balance-of-payments problem and a strong adjustment program could conceivably have borrowed a cumulative amount of up to 500 percent of its quota under the ordinary and extended facilities plus an additional 105 percent of quota under the Compensatory Financing Facility plus still another 45 percent of quota under the Buffer Stock Facility.[29] Although these increases in access limits appear large, they seem less striking when they are compared with the absolute size of IMF quotas in relation to members' international transactions. Over the decades of the IMF's existence, the value of IMF quotas failed to keep pace with the value of output, let alone world trade, and hence probably also with the size of payments deficits justifying liability financing. Whereas Fund quotas were roughly equal to 3.75 percent of world output and as much as 50–60 percent of world imports in the late 1940s, they had fallen to only 1.2 percent of output and 5.7 percent of imports by the late 1990s.[30]

The second evolutionary change in IMF lending operations was an increase in the average maturity of IMF loans. After 1974, for example, the

---

Arrangements to Borrow, was established in 1962. The GAB was a contingency mechanism for providing supplementary resources to the IMF, if needed, to support borrowings by the larger industrial countries. The GAB was revised and enlarged in 1983 to increase the lines of credit available to the IMF and to permit the IMF, under certain circumstances, to lend GAB resources to member nations that are not GAB participants. The second borrowing option for the IMF, the New Arrangements to Borrow, became operational in 1998.

28. The figure of 125 percent is the sum of the original 25 percent "gold tranche" corresponding to the member's original subscription of its quota in reserve assets, plus four "credit tranches" that together sum to 100 percent of quota.

29. After the adoption of the Policy on Enlarged Access, complex provisions were introduced defining the limits on a member's access to the Fund's ordinary and extended facilities. Separate limits were specified for annual, three-year, and cumulative access. The limits varied with individual circumstances, depending on "the seriousness of the member's balance of payments needs and the strength of its adjustment efforts." The Fund stressed that the access limits "should not be regarded as targets." In "exceptional circumstances," the executive board even had the flexibility to approve standby or extended arrangements that exceeded the limits. Access limits were subsequently reduced by a modest amount. By the end of the 1990s, access limits and lending facilities were again under active review.

30. For further discussion, see the companion volume *Crisis Prevention and Prosperity Management for the World Economy.*

Extended Fund Facility allowed borrowings for periods of up to four years with repayments within four to ten years (much longer than the previously normal one year with repayment expected within three to five years). Repayments of drawings under the Supplementary Financing Facility and the Policy on Enlarged Access could take as long as three and one half to seven years.

A third set of significant changes was a larger reliance by the IMF on borrowed resources rather than on ordinary resources from quota subscriptions. The Oil Facilities and the Supplementary Financing Facility in the 1970s were financed by borrowing agreements with the largest member countries and Switzerland. A medium-term borrowing agreement with the Saudi Arabian Monetary Agency helped to make the Policy on Enlarged Access operative in 1981.[31] This increased reliance by the Fund on borrowed resources rather than quota subscriptions necessitated a change in the terms of the Fund's own lending. The member nations in surplus or with strong reserve positions that extended the loans to the IMF wished the IMF to pay them a market-related rate of interest. In turn, deficit members making use of the IMF's borrowed, rather than ordinary, resources were required to pay a market-related rate of interest. The result of these developments was a significant reduction, on average, in the gap between commercial interest rates and the interest rates charged by the Fund to deficit members.

The fourth and most important evolutionary change in IMF lending was an increasing concentration of loans to developing nations. The main borrowing members in the 1970s were developing nations that did not have ready access to the international private capital markets. After the global recession of 1981–82 and a generalized perception of a developing nation debt crisis in the 1980s, larger developing nations also relied heavily on borrowings from the IMF. In contrast, industrial nation members borrowed less from the IMF in the 1970s. After the collapse of the Bretton Woods exchange arrangements, industrial nations were prepared to permit wider movements in the exchange rates among their currencies; they also typically had ready access to external financing from private commercial sources. From the inception of the IMF through the 1960s, industrial nation members had often accounted for more than half of the total use of IMF credit. Italy borrowed from the IMF in 1974–75. The United

---

31. Sizable borrowings were also made in the 1960s, under the General Arrangements to Borrow.

Kingdom did so in 1976–77. Except for those large loans, however, the proportion of total use of IMF credit by industrial nation members fell dramatically in the 1970s. After the Italian and U.K. loans in the mid-1970s, major industrial nations never again borrowed from the IMF in the so-called credit tranches. A few smaller industrial nations borrowed from the IMF until 1982. Thereafter, for the rest of the century, the industrial nations were creditors but never borrowers in the IMF.[32]

The combined net effect of these evolutionary changes in IMF lending was to greatly alter the IMF's role as an intergovernmental lending intermediary facilitating the financing of payments deficits. The original concept at Bretton Woods envisaged a warehouse offering stored currencies merely for temporary, short-term rental to a revolving clientele of all member nations. By the 1980s the IMF had drifted substantially away from that original vision. In practice the IMF had become an intergovernmental financial intermediary extending longer-term loans to a subset of the world's nations tending to have a persistent demand for development finance—a continuing current account deficit—not merely a temporary need for the liability financing of an overall deficit. (These distinctions are reviewed in chapter 6.)

No single explanation can account for the transformation of the IMF's role as a lending intermediary for the liability financing of payments deficits. One important factor was a consensus perception by national governments that the turbulence and structural changes occurring in the world economy necessitated changes in the type and maturity of official balance-of-payments financing. Another part of the explanation can be attributed to the relatively sluggish growth in IMF quotas. As the ordinary resources available to the IMF from quota subscriptions failed to keep pace with growth in the world economy, pressures mounted to stretch existing policies and to adopt new, specialized facilities. The slow growth in quotas was an especially important reason for the IMF's greater reliance on borrowed resources.

Yet another significant factor was an increasingly prevalent view that the IMF should give more weight in its operations to development and humanitarian objectives. That change in view occurred—to at least a mod-

---

32. Several industrial nations drew on their so-called reserve tranche positions (counted as the drawing down of a reserve asset rather than a borrowing of credit) in the 1980s. The last such drawing by industrial nations occurred in 1987.

est degree, willingly or reluctantly—within the governments of most or all developed nations. The governments of the developing nations themselves, numerically a large majority of IMF members, strongly urged a move in that direction. In response, the IMF gradually paid greater attention to the special problems of developing nations and gave increased consideration to policies having the effect of favoring poorer nations. In effect, the member nations of the IMF and the IMF itself became progressively more involved in trying to promote growth and development and even, to some extent, in trying to facilitate a redistribution of income and wealth from richer to poorer nations (functions 6 and 7 in figure 7-4).

The emphasis in IMF lending on developing nations after the early 1970s combined with the cessation of borrowing by industrial nations caused a subtle but profound shift in the IMF's effective center of gravity. Perceptions of the basic purposes of the IMF changed even more. Many private individuals and enterprises and even some government officials began to perceive the IMF as an international organization concerned with lending only to developing nations. Some perceptions went even further, characterizing developing nations as the exclusive "clients" of the IMF not only for balance-of-payments financing but also for the entire range of IMF activities.

In reaction to those evolving perceptions of the IMF, numerous others came to believe that intergovernmental lending intermediation by the IMF had less helpful, perhaps even harmful, effects on the world economy. According to those other views, nations with balance-of-payments deficits, including their governments, should rely for liability financing only on borrowing from private financial institutions or from private lenders operating in world capital markets.

Several contentious issues are identified in the preceding historical overview: what guidelines the IMF should espouse as part of its surveillance of traffic regulations for cross-border financial transactions, how the IMF should conduct its annual Article IV consultations with members, how it should exercise surveillance over exchange rate arrangements, whether and how the IMF should be an intergovernmental lending intermediary, whether IMF lending intermediation should be restricted to crisis situations or also be conducted in noncrisis conditions, whether the IMF should be integrally involved in surveillance of financial standards and the prudential oversight of financial systems, whether the IMF should have a broad mandate to promote development and redistribution, whether developing nations should be perceived as the only clients of the IMF. All of these issues are addressed in chapters 8 through 13.

The Bank for International Settlements and Related Committees

Earlier History

The Bank for International Settlements, located in Basel, Switzerland, is the oldest international financial organization identified in this book. The BIS was created in January 1930 at the conference in The Hague that reorganized German World War I reparations under the Young Plan. The BIS was charged with performing the functions of trustee for execution of the reparation payments and also with promoting cooperation among central banks and providing facilities for cross-border financial transactions.

That combination of responsibilities proved to be controversial and crippling. German reparations payments were linked to the debts of Allied European countries to the United States. Congressional opposition prevented the Federal Reserve System from joining the BIS because membership was deemed to conflict with the official position of the U.S. government on German reparations and Allied war debts. As a partial substitute, the BIS encouraged participation by a group of American commercial banks led by J. P. Morgan and the First National Bank of New York. But the BIS could marshal only relatively small amounts of financial resources and was not able to play an influential role in intergovernmental financial consultations during the turbulent 1930s. It was not until the 1970s that the Federal Reserve System was able to win U.S. congressional and executive branch permission formally to join the BIS.

In the years following World War II, the BIS began to assume more important functions for European monetary and financial cooperation. For example, it provided services to European central banks and governments in connection with the European Payments Union (1950–58) and the forerunner arrangements in 1947–50 for multilateral payments agreements. From 1964 through 1993 the BIS hosted the secretariat for the Committee of Governors of the Central Banks of the European Economic Community and the European Monetary Cooperation Fund, the key European bodies for supporting monetary cooperation in the European Community.[33]

---

33. For the earlier history of the BIS, see among others Eichengreen (1992), Clarke (1967), and Triffin (1957).

The Bank for International Settlements as a Venue for Regular Central Bank Consultations and Cooperation

In recent decades, the BIS has increasingly served as the venue in which the major central banks periodically come together to consult about issues of mutual interest. Meetings of the central bank governors are held monthly at the BIS offices in Basel. Governors are typically accompanied by a key staff member. The Basel offices are also the most frequent venue for meetings of various committees sponsored by the BIS, including the Basel Committee on Banking Supervision, the Committee on the Global Financial System, and the Committee on Payments and Settlements Systems.

The monthly meetings of the governors and the informal conversations carried out in conjunction with those gatherings are a central mechanism for cooperation among the major central banks. The regular meetings serve as an ongoing forum for confidential consultations and discussions. The relationships nurtured in the regular meetings can then be brought into play between meetings if and when bilateral or multilateral conversations are required (by telephone or in person). In practice, BIS meetings can be seen as a peer-group exercise for central banks in mutual surveillance. In addition, at certain times when crises have affected money or foreign exchange markets, the BIS has been a focal point for designing joint initiatives to be undertaken by the central banks.

By tradition and design, finance ministers or other government officials are not participants in the BIS meetings. The central banks prize the venue as their own forum. The BIS itself is now perceived, inside and outside of the central banks, as a manifestation of the political independence of central banks.

The BIS holds an annual general meeting at which some 45 shareholding central banks have rights of voting and representation. More than 120 central banks and international financial institutions use the BIS as a banking institution. The effective control of the BIS, however, is vested in its board of directors. The board at the end of 1999 comprised the heads of (only) the G-10 central banks, that is, of Belgium, Canada, France, Germany, Italy, Japan, the Netherlands, Sweden, Switzerland, the United Kingdom, and the United States. Although the G-10 central banks reached out somewhat to include some non-G-10 central banks in various BIS activities, the institution is still unambiguously run by and for the central banks of the major industrial nations. The staff of the BIS is headed by a general manager appointed by the board of directors.

Basel Committee on Banking Supervision

Two prominent banks, the Bankhaus Herstatt in Germany and the Franklin National Bank in New York, failed during 1974. Each bank had significant foreign exchange transactions and other cross-border business. The financial traumas associated with the failures convinced the major central banks and bank supervisory agencies that more systematic consultations and cooperation were required. Accordingly, in December 1974 the governors of the central banks and supervisory agencies of the G-10 nations established a new institutional mechanism, the Basel Committee on Banking Supervision. This committee was to operate under the auspices of, and to be served by a secretariat located at, the Bank for International Settlements. The BCBS is not a part of the BIS, however, and as a formal matter it reports to the G-10 central bank governors.

In the ensuing years the BCBS has become the most influential forum for catalyzing intergovernmental consultations and cooperation among banking supervisory authorities. The BCBS has provided a forum for intergovernmental discussions of supervisory problems associated with individual banks. It has coordinated the sharing and monitoring of bank supervisory responsibilities among national authorities. And it has served as a primary locus of efforts to enhance financial standards and prudential oversight for banks, especially the cross-border aspects of banking.

Representatives to the BCBS are senior officials from bank supervisory authorities and central banks of the member nations of the BIS. In recent years the BCBS with increasing frequency has consulted banking supervisory authorities from nations not members of the BIS and begun to involve them in some of its activities.[34]

Committee on the Global Financial System

In addition to the Basel Committee on Bank Supervision, several other international committees meet periodically under the auspices of the BIS to foster cooperation among central banks. Among these is the Committee on the Global Financial System (CGFS).

The origins of the CGFS date back to informal meetings in the 1960s of staff representatives of the G-10 central banks, in a group known as the BIS Eurocurrency Standing Committee. The G-10 central bank governors gave

---

34. Documents of the BCBS and other information about its activities are available at the BIS web site (www.bis.org/publ).

this committee a formal mandate in 1971 to monitor international banking markets more closely (the mandate was made public in 1980). The Euro-currency Standing Committee focused initially on the soundness and sta-bility of the eurocurrency markets. But it subsequently discussed a wide range of financial stability issues, including the policy implications of inter-national debt problems, the evolution of financial market structures, and the macroeconomic and prudential implications of financial derivatives. A number of reports were published under the committee's sponsorship. The committee also had responsibility for developing and overseeing improve-ments and innovations in the various sets of BIS statistics on international banking, financial derivatives, and foreign exchange market activity.

The G-10 central bank governors decided in February 1999 to clarify the mandate of this committee and to rechristen it the Committee on the Global Financial System. The CGFS is now charged with acting as a cen-tral bank forum for "the monitoring and examination of broad issues relat-ing to financial markets and systems with a view to elaborating appropri-ate policy recommendations to support the central banks in the fulfillment of their responsibilities for monetary and financial stability." The tasks of the CGFS fall into three categories: systematic short-term monitoring of global financial system conditions; in-depth longer-term analysis of the functioning of financial markets; and the articulation of policy recom-mendations aimed at improving market functioning and promoting sta-bility. The CGFS now meets quarterly.

Committee on Payments and Settlements Systems

The Committee on Payments and Settlements Systems (CPSS) is an-other committee operating under the auspices of the Bank for Interna-tional Settlements. Its mandate is to monitor and improve the safety and efficiency of payments and settlements systems with special emphasis on the cross-border and multicurrency dimensions. Before the establishment of the CPSS, the BIS sponsored other committees and ad hoc groups of central bankers charged with focusing on payments and settlements sys-tems (for example, a working group of Experts on Payments Systems and a Committee on Interbank Netting Schemes).

Formal representatives to the CPSS come from the central banks of the G-10 nations. In recent years, sometimes informally and sometimes explic-itly, the CPSS has increasingly involved central banks from non-G-10 nations and other international financial organizations in its activities. For example, representatives from the central banks of emerging-market economies and from the IMF and World Bank have recently been participating in a task force charged with developing core principles for the design and operation of payment systems.

Other Financial Groups and Organizations

In addition to the institutions already described, several other specialized financial groups or organizations have been venues for intergovernmental cooperation about financial matters. The activities of these specialized institutions are discussed in chapters 10 through 13.

International Organization of Securities Commissions

As cross-border securities transactions grew rapidly, it was recognized as early as the 1970s that an institutional mechanism was needed to promote cooperation and information exchanges among the national authorities with responsibility for securities markets. The result was the establishment of the International Organization of Securities Commissions, comprised of national regulatory agencies who have day-to-day responsibility for the supervision and regulation of securities markets and the administration of securities laws.

IOSCO has some 172 member agencies (as of 2002, after the 2001 annual conference), coming from approximately 100 different national jurisdictions. Members are classified into three groups: ordinary, associate, and affiliate. Ordinary members, 102 in 2002, are typically the primary securities supervisory body in a nation (for example, the Securities and Exchange Commission in the United States, the Commission des Operations de Bourse in France). Affiliate members are self-regulatory organizations such as stock exchanges or clearing corporations (for example, the New York Stock Exchange and the Chicago Board of Trade in the United States) and international organizations (for example, the IMF and the World Bank).[35]

Formal powers in IOSCO are vested in a president's committee, composed of all the ordinary and associate members. In practice, however, IOSCO operates primarily through an executive committee and two specialized working committees (a technical committee and an emerging-markets committee). Only ordinary members have a formal vote in

---

35. If there is no governmental regulatory body in a nation, a self-regulatory body such as a stock exchange from that nation is eligible for ordinary membership in IOSCO.

IOSCO decisions. Conferences are held annually. IOSCO is served by a general secretariat, headed by its secetary general, based in Montreal, Canada. Its income comes in part from annual fees charged to members.

Decisions and recommendations resulting from IOSCO deliberations are only advisory, not binding, on its members. An IOSCO recommendation can become legally binding within an individual nation only after being incorporated into legislation, regulations, or rulings adopted at the national level.[36]

International Association of Insurance Supervisors

Nascent international cooperation for the supervision and regulation of insurance companies has been encouraged through the International Association of Insurance Supervisors, the IAIS, established in 1992–94. The members of the IAIS are insurance supervisors from more than 100 national jurisdictions.[37] The activities of the IAIS include the setting of global insurance supervisory standards, helping to improve cross-sector financial supervision, and assisting in the implementation and monitoring of insurance supervisory standards.

The IAIS is headed by its executive committee whose members represent different geographical regions. The committee convenes and conducts a general meeting at an annual conference where main directions for the association are charted. The annual conferences are occasions at which insurance professionals from around the world (insurers, actuaries, insurance brokers, and insurance agents) meet and exchange views with the insurance supervisors. The executive committee has the powers to "take all decisions necessary to achieve the objectives of the IAIS in accordance with the decisions made at the General Meeting." The executive committee is supported by three main committees: a technical committee, an emerging-markets committee and a budget committee. Various subcommittees report to the main committees.

Since January 1998, the secretariat supporting the IAIS has been hosted by the Bank for International Settlements in Basel. The secretariat operates independently of the BIS but benefits from BIS support in certain technical and administrative areas. The proximity to the BCBS and

---

36. The IOSCO website is www.iosco.org.

37. For example, the member for the United States is the National Association of Insurance Commissioners (NAIC), and the member for the United Kingdom is the U.K. Financial Supervisory Agency. A jurisdiction may have more than one member; for example, both the Japanese Financial Supervisory Agency and the Japanese Ministry of Finance are members for Japan.

other secretariats lodged at the BIS facilitates cooperation and exchanges of information between the IAIS and the other organizations focusing on issues of financial stability.[38]

As with IOSCO, IAIS cooperative decisions are only advisory, not binding, on members. An IAIS standard or ruling cannot become legally operative in a nation until it is incorporated into legislation, standards, or rulings adopted within that nation.

International Accounting Standards Board and International Federation of Accountants

Cooperative efforts to design an agreed set of global accounting standards have been undertaken through the auspices of the International Accounting Standards Committee (IASC) and more recently through its successor, the International Accounting Standards Board. The IASC, a private sector body, was established in 1973. Its members as of the spring of 2000 were 143 professional accountancy bodies from 104 countries. (For example, the 3 member organizations based in the United States are the Institute of Management Accountants, the National Association of State Boards of Accountancy, and the American Institute of Certified Public Accountants.)[39] In the spring of 2001 the IASC was restructured; an IASC Foundation was established to act as the parent entity for a new International Accounting Standards Board, which assumed the responsibilities for setting accounting standards previously lodged with the IASC.[40]

The goal of the IASB is to "achieve uniformity in the accounting principles that are used by businesses and other organisations for financial reporting around the world." To this end, the IASB develops and formally adopts a series of international accounting standards, known by their acronym as IASs.

---

38. Further information about the IAIS can be obtained from its web site (www.iaisweb.org).

39. The total of 143 in spring 2000 included 134 member organizations, 5 associate members, and 4 affiliate members. Information about the IASC/IASB can be found on its web site (www.iasc.org.uk). On the origins and history of the IASC, see Cairns (1998).

40. The 2001 restructuring was based on the recommendations of a report, *Recommendations on Shaping IASC for the Future.* The new structure has the following main features: the IASC Foundation, incorporated in the state of Delaware in the United States, is an independent organization having two main bodies, the Trustees and the IASB, as well as a Standards Advisory Council and the International Financial Reporting Interpretations Committee. The IASC Foundation Trustees appoint the IASB members, exercise oversight, and raise the funds needed. The IASB, based in London, has sole responsibility for setting accounting standards.

International efforts to standardize auditing procedures have been undertaken through the International Federation of Accountants. The members of the federation are essentially the same 143 professional accountancy organizations belonging to the IASB; full membership in IFAC automatically includes membership in the IASB. Membership in the two organizations is open to accountancy bodies "recognized by law or general consensus within their countries as substantial national organizations in good standing."

IFAC has activities in six areas: auditing and related services, education, ethics, financial and management accounting, information technology, and public sector accounting. The International Auditing Practices Committee of IFAC takes into account the differing forms and contents of national practices and, based on knowledge of the differences, develops international standards for the auditing of financial statements and other information, known as ISAs. The International Auditing Practices Committee also develops international audit practice statements, referred to as IAPSs, "to provide practical assistance to auditors in implementing the ISAs or to promote good practice." The ISAs are intended for widespread international acceptance. IAPSs are not intended to have the authority of standards.[41]

The International Organization of Supreme Audit Institutions (INTOSAI) is still another international organization in the area of accounting and auditing. This organization links together national institutions whose responsibilities are to audit government agencies and to promote sound financial management and accountability within governments. It was founded in 1953 and adopted a set of auditing guidelines in 1977.[42]

National governments have not themselves created or sponsored international organizations with responsibilities for designing, implementing, and monitoring standards for accounting or auditing. Hence the IASB and IFAC are the primary institutional mechanisms for catalyzing cooperation among nations about accounting standards and auditing procedures.

Membership in the IASB does not require that member organizations or their nations adopt its international accounting standards. Similarly, the standards developed by IFAC and its International Auditing Practices Committee do not themselves have legal force. Whether a nation in fact adopts an IAS or an ISA depends on the decisions of its self-regulatory organizations

---

41. Information about IFAC is available on its website (www.ifac.org).

42. The guidelines are contained in the *Lima Declaration of Guidelines on Auditing Precepts.* Information about INTOSAI may be found on its website (www.intosai.org).

and perhaps also on decisions of the national government. Member organizations, however, are expected to use their best efforts to see that IFAC and IASB standards are used as a basis for developing their own nations' standards and practices. IFAC is said to encourage its members to undertake self-review of their nations' auditing practices to evaluate how they compare with IFAC's international auditing standards.

United Nations Commission on International Trade Law and Other Insolvency Associations

The United Nations Commission on International Trade Law is the core legal body of the United Nations system in the field of international trade law. It was established in 1966 by the UN General Assembly, with a mandate to "further the progressive harmonization and unification of the law of international trade."

The commission is composed of thirty-six member states elected by the General Assembly, with membership structured so as to be representative of the world's various geographic regions and its principal economic and legal systems. UNCITRAL carries out its work through working groups and at annual sessions.

The commission has produced a variety of legal documents during the last several decades. Examples include conventions or model laws on arbitration rules (1976); the carriage of goods by sea (the "Hamburg Rules" of 1978); contracts for the international sale of goods (1980); international commercial arbitration (1985); international credit transfers (1992); the procurement of goods, construction, and services by governments (1994); and electronic commerce (1996).

UNCITRAL is relevant to this book because its work on the legal aspects of insolvency and bankruptcy, including the drafting of a model law dealing with cross-border corporate insolvencies, is important for financial standards and the prudential oversight of financial systems. The Insolvency and Creditors Rights Committee of the International Bar Association, the International Association of Insolvency Practitioners, and the INSOL Lenders Group of INSOL International have also made contributions in this area. INSOL International is a worldwide federation of national associations of accountants and lawyers specializing in insolvency.[43]

---

43. Information about UNCITRAL can be found at its website (www.uncitral.org). The INSOL Lenders Group was formed in 1994; its contributions are summarized in Brierley and Vlieghe (1999).

Financial Action Task Force on Money Laundering

The Financial Action Task Force on Money Laundering, known by the acronym FATF, was created at the Paris 1989 G-7 summit meeting. Its initial mandate was to examine measures to combat money laundering.

The FATF has twenty-nine member countries (including territories) and two regional organizations. The major financial center nations of Europe, North America, and Asia are all represented in the FATF.[44] The FATF works cooperatively with a range of other international organizations, bodies and groups that are involved in combating money laundering (for example, Interpol, IOSCO, IMF, World Bank, the United Nations Office for Drug Control and Crime Prevention, and the World Customs Union).

The executive leadership of the FATF is a rotating, one-year position held by a high-level government official appointed from among the members of the task force. A small specialized secretariat supports the task force and its president. The secretariat is lodged at the OECD in Paris (although the FATF itself is an independent international body and is not a part of the OECD). The main guidelines resulting from FATF activities are summarized in the 40 FATF Recommendations on Money Laundering.[45]

The activities of the FATF have resulted in the establishment in several nations of financial intelligence units (known by the acronym FIUs). The objectives of FIUs include the protection of financial institutions from criminal abuse and the assurance of adherence to laws against financial crime. The Financial Crimes Enforcement Network (FinCEN) of the U.S. Treasury serves as the FIU for the United States.[46] The United Kingdom, France, Belgium, the Netherlands, Argentina, and Australia are other nations that have established FIUs.[47]

---

44. The member countries and governments of the FATF are Argentina, Australia, Austria, Belgium, Brazil, Canada, Denmark, Finland, France, Germany, Greece, Hong Kong, Iceland, Ireland, Italy, Japan, Luxembourg, Mexico, the Netherlands, New Zealand, Norway, Portugal, Singapore, Spain, Sweden, Switzerland, Turkey, the United Kingdom, and the United States. Argentina, Brazil, and Mexico were observer members prior to June 2000. The regional organizations are the European Commission and the Gulf Cooperation Council.

45. The FATF website is www.oecd.org/fatf.

46. The FinCEN website is www.ustreas.org/fincen.

47. The evolution of FIUs has led to the creation of an organization of nations that have implemented such units, known as the Egmont Group (after the Palais d'Egmont in Brussels where the initial meeting, hosted by the United States and Belgium, was held in June 1995.)

Following the September 2001 terrorist violence in New York and Washington, the mission of the FATF was expanded beyond money laundering to include worldwide efforts to combat the financing of terrorism. An October 2001 plenary meeting agreed to Special Recommendations for new international standards to combat terrorist financing and announced a plan of action to implement these standards. It was also agreed that the FATF would intensify its oversight work regarding corporate vehicles, correspondent banking, identification of beneficial owners of accounts, and regulation of nonbank financial institutions and would take the 2001 Special Recommendations into account when revising its 40 Recommendations on Money Laundering.[48]

Joint Forum on Financial Conglomerates

By the 1990s the national supervisors of banks, securities firms, and insurance companies were witnessing the growing emergence of financial conglomerates and a progressive blurring of distinctions between the activities of firms in these different financial sectors. They therefore also saw an increasing need for more explicit cooperation among the international organizations serving as separate venues for consultations about supervisory methods and approaches.

The recognition of this need led in early 1996 to the creation of the Joint Forum on Financial Conglomerates. The Joint Forum operates under the collective auspices of the three parent organizations of supervisors, BCBS, IOSCO, and IAIS. Its mandate is to catalyze a more formal cooperation among the bank, securities, and insurance supervisory authorities from the largest nations. (A less formal Tripartite Group from the three types of supervisory agencies had met before 1996 and had prepared a report released in July 1995.)

---

48. The 2001 Special Recommendations committed the FATF members to take immediate steps to ratify and implement relevant United Nations instruments; criminalize the financing of terrorism, terrorist acts, and terrorist organizations; freeze and confiscate terrorist assets; report suspicious transactions linked to terrorism; provide the widest possible range of assistance to other countries' law enforcement and regulatory authorities for terrorist financing investigations; impose anti–money laundering requirements on alternative remittance systems; strengthen customer identification measures in international and domestic wire transfers; and ensure that entities, in particular nonprofit organizations, cannot be misused to finance terrorism. All countries in the world were invited to participate in implementing these recommendations on the same terms as FATF members. The plan of action included intentions to implement the Special Recommendations by June 2002 and the initiation by June 2002 of a process to identify and take countermeasures against jurisdictions that lack appropriate measures to combat terrorist financing.

Thirteen nations are represented in the Joint Forum: the G-7 nations plus Australia, Belgium, the Netherlands, Spain, Sweden, and Switzerland. An equal number of senior-level bank, securities, and insurance supervisors participates from each national constituency. A representative from the European Union Commission attends in an observer capacity.

Financial Stability Forum

The growing need for more explicit and extensive coordination among international financial organizations went beyond the immediate needs of the supervisory agencies making up the Joint Forum on Financial Conglomerates. Amid the uncertainty and financial turbulence following the Russian default and devaluation and the collapse of the Long Term Capital Management hedge fund, the G-7 finance ministers and central bank governors discussed the broader need for coordination at their October 1998 meeting. Hans Tietmeyer (at that time president of the Deutsche Bundesbank) was then commissioned to prepare a report with recommendations for "new structures that may be required for enhancing cooperation among the various national and international supervisory bodies and international financial institutions." The G-7 nations adopted the recommendations in Tietmeyer's report in February 1999 and formally established the Financial Stability Forum. The initial meeting of the FSF was convened in April 1999.[49]

The members of the FSF are national authorities from individual nations (one each from the finance ministry, central bank, and main supervisory agency in the largest nations); representatives from the IMF, the World Bank, the BIS, and the OECD; representatives of the primary international regulatory and supervisory groupings, namely the BCBS, IOSCO, and IAIS; and representatives from the two BIS-sponsored committees of central bank experts, the Committee on the Global Financial System and the Committee on Payments and Settlements Systems. The national authorities represented at the first meeting of the FSF were restricted to the G-7 nations. In June 1999 the membership was broadened to include other "significant financial centres," interpreted as Hong Kong, Singapore, Australia, and the Netherlands. The FSF has a small secretariat based at the BIS.[50]

49. For the February 1999 report to the G-7, see Tietmeyer (1999).

50. The first chairman of the FSF, for a term of three years beginning in 1999, was Andrew Crockett, who was also general manager of the Bank for International Settlements.

The FSF is designed to be an institutional mechanism for "enhancing cooperation . . . so as to promote stability in the international financial system." It brings together, usually twice a year, "national authorities responsible for financial stability in significant international financial centres, international financial institutions, sector-specific international groupings of regulators and supervisors, and committees of central bank experts." Its stated objectives are "to assess vulnerabilities affecting the international financial system, to identify and oversee action needed to address these vulnerabilities, and to improve coordination and information exchange among the various authorities responsible for financial stability." When developing its priorities and programs for action, the FSF is to "work through its members."[51]

GATT and the World Trade Organization

In the years immediately following World War II and the establishment of the IMF and the World Bank, postwar leaders also tried to create an international organization for dealing with cross-border trade in goods. It was to be known as the International Trade Organization (ITO). Meetings were held in Geneva and Havana during 1947–48 to discuss a charter for the ITO. The Geneva conference also focused on negotiations for an agreement for multilateral tariff reductions.

As noted earlier, plans for the ITO never came to fruition, in large part because the U.S. Congress was unwilling to approve the draft charter. The agreement covering general principles and obligations for tariff reduction, however, was approved by the negotiating parties. Thus the General Agreement on Tariffs and Trade came into force on January 1, 1948.

Over subsequent decades the GATT facilitated eight rounds of negotiations for multilateral tariff reductions. Each round tried to reduce tariffs using the GATT principles of reciprocity, nondiscrimination, and national treatment. Prominent among these negotiations were the Kennedy Round held in 1962–67, the Tokyo Round in 1973–79, and the Uruguay Round

---

51. The stated criteria for selecting issues for FSF consideration are "to give impetus to work on issues that cut across the mandates and expertise of Forum members; to coordinate work among Forum members; to evaluate the completeness of and fill gaps in the body of work among Forum members; to endorse work by Forum members that would benefit from such endorsement; and to monitor, where appropriate, implementation and any follow-up in areas where policy recommendations have been issued." The quotations are from the FSF's website (www.fsforum.org).

of 1986–94. More than 120 nations participated in the Uruguay Round, which covered a wide range of trade and related issues.

During the final years of the Uruguay Round, harking back to the hopes that had been held for the ITO half a century earlier, the negotiators discussed a new organization. The negotiations were ultimately successful, and the World Trade Organization began formal life at the beginning of 1995. The WTO embodies the principles and much of the language found in the GATT. But it also goes further, specifying dispute settlement procedures and thus remedying the lack of enforcement powers in the GATT.

Some 23 nations were participants in the original Geneva conference in 1948. As with the IMF and other international organizations, additional nations became parties. By January 2002 there were 144 members of the WTO. Some 30 additional nations were at various stages in the process of applying to become members. The WTO, based in Geneva, Switzerland, has a secretariat with about 550 staff members. The secretariat provides technical support to the various councils, committees, and ministerial conferences of the WTO; in addition, it analyzes world trade, advises applicant governments, and provides legal support to the Dispute Settlement Body.

Over time the GATT and WTO acquired greater legitimacy. One indication of this evolution is the increasing willingness of members to bring trade disputes to the WTO Dispute Settlement Body. Under the nonbinding GATT dispute settlement procedures, only about 300 disputes were processed during the GATT's entire forty-seven years. Between the WTO's inception in 1995 and July 2002, 262 cases were brought under the WTO dispute settlement processes.

In addition to its more binding dispute settlement procedures, the WTO deals with an increasingly wide range of issues including trade in services, intellectual property rights, and antidumping procedures. The WTO has been under increasing pressure to deal with the trade dimensions of labor market and environmental issues. The WTO issues periodic reviews of the trade policies of its members.[52]

The Organization for Economic Cooperation and Development

The Organization for Economic Cooperation and Development began life in 1948 as the Organization for European Economic Cooperation

---

52. For history and background on the WTO and GATT, see Dam (1970); Hoekman and Kostecki (1995); Jackson (1997, 1998b); Krueger (1998); and Collins and Bosworth (1994).

(OEEC). The OEEC in its first years was primarily a forum for coordinating the rebuilding of Europe's economies following the Second World War. It was envisaged in part as a European complement to the U.S. Economic Cooperation Agency and played a significant role in coordinating the distribution of U.S. Marshall Plan aid to Europe.

Through the OEEC, the European Payments Union (EPU) was created in 1950. The EPU was in part a response to American demands that recipients of Marshall Plan aid move toward restoring an environment of multilateral payments and currency convertibility among European nations. The EPU, working through the BIS, acted as a central clearinghouse for OEEC member nations.[53]

As the functions of rebuilding European economies and coordinating the distribution of American aid waned, the OEEC gradually evolved into a forum for discussing and catalyzing European economic integration. In 1961, moreover, the membership of the institution was expanded to include non-European nations (originally the United States and Canada and then, three years later, Japan). The change in name from OEEC to OECD occurred together with the expansion in membership to non-European nations.

Given the changing economic conditions within Europe and the inclusion of non-European members, the OECD gradually adapted and expanded its institutional mission. The OECD increasingly became a forum for all its members and an international locus for intergovernmental dialogue and policy discussion. It also sought to become a center for the monitoring of national policies and for research about them.

Issues related to the monitoring and coordination of macroeconomic policies dominated the agenda of the OECD during the 1960s and 1970s. The OECD's Economic Policy Committee (EPC) and especially its Working Party 3 (WP-3) were central venues for these activities. The WP-3 had been originally established in 1949 by the OEEC Council as a group of productivity experts. Its role expanded, however, as it became a more general roundtable forum allowing member nations to debate and examine macroeconomic issues of global importance. Meetings of the EPC and its WP-3, benefiting from analytical support of the OECD staff, proved to be influential channels for mutual surveillance and policy coordination. The *Economic Outlook*, first published in 1967 and appearing twice a year, is a

---

53. Triffin (1957) gives the history of the EPU and analyzes the issues underlying its creation and operation.

prominent OECD publication focusing on macroeconomic and surveillance issues.

As OECD membership expanded and economic conditions changed, the OECD's monitoring and analytical agenda was further broadened beyond macroeconomic issues. The OECD now addresses issues as diverse as technology, agriculture, trade, development assistance, capital flows, taxation, intellectual property, and governance. As of 2002 the OECD had twenty-three European members (including the eighteen original members of the OEEC) and seven non-European members.[54] The European Union as a separate entity also participates in some of the OECD's work. The OECD is served by a secretariat, based in Paris, with a staff of some 1,850 persons. The secretariat is headed by a secretary general who is ultimately responsible to a ministerial council. Member nations of the OECD accounted for more than two-thirds of the world's output at the beginning of the century.[55]

The World Bank

The World Bank—strictly speaking, the International Bank for Reconstruction and Development, or IBRD—was created simultaneously with the IMF in the 1944 Bretton Woods negotiations. It began operations in 1946 as the first multilateral development bank. By 2000 the term World Bank was used to refer to the entire World Bank Group, comprising the original IBRD institution and four subsequently established affiliate organizations. The affiliates are the International Finance Corporation (IFC, created in 1956), the International Development Association (IDA, 1960), the International Centre for Settlement of Investment Disputes (1966), and the Multilateral Investment Guarantee Agency (MIGA, 1998).

The original membership of the World Bank numbered 44 nations. As with the IMF, membership expanded sharply during the second half of the 1900s. As of 2002 the World Bank had 184 member nations. Though its original mandate focused on postwar project-based reconstruction, the

---

54. The twenty-three European members of the OECD are Austria, Belgium, Czech Republic, Denmark, Finland, France, Germany, Greece, Hungary, Iceland, Ireland, Italy, Luxembourg, Netherlands, Norway, Poland, Portugal, Slovak Republic, Spain, Sweden, Switzerland, Turkey, and the United Kingdom. The seven non-European members are Canada and the United States (founding members in 1961), Japan (1964), Australia (1971), New Zealand (1973), Mexico (1994), and Korea (1996).

55. Further details about the OECD as an international institution may be found in Sullivan (1997), an OECD overview publication.

World Bank now has a much broader mission focused on development broadly defined. The geographic focus of the World Bank also changed dramatically during its history. Europe accounted for more than 80 percent of the IBRD's commitments during its first three years. Beginning in the 1950s, a growing share of outlays went to Asia, Africa, and Latin America. Even following the collapse of the Soviet Union and the resulting increase in scope for World Bank activity in Eastern and Central Europe, Europe's share in World Bank outlays in the early 1990s was only 16 percent. The Asian share had risen to 37 percent.

The governance structure of the IBRD, negotiated in 1944, reflected the relative political power of the largest and most powerful postwar nations. Thus with the World Bank, as with the IMF, effective control was given to the most powerful members with votes allocated in proportion to the size of capital subscriptions. Also, as with the IMF, nation states were designated as the formal "shareholders" and "clients" of the Bank.

The administrative head of the World Bank is a president, appointed collectively by member governments. (In the first decades of the World Bank, as discussed in chapter 13, an informal political convention existed under which European governments acquiesced in the U.S. government choosing an American to be the World Bank president and the U.S. government acquiesced in European governments selecting a European to be the managing director of the IMF.) The World Bank president has broad powers to staff the upper echelons of Bank management and reports to a board of executive directors organized into constituencies. Five large nations appoint their own executive director (United States, United Kingdom, Germany, France, Japan); the remaining nineteen executive directors are elected by nineteen groupings of member nations. Major policy decisions are made by administrative management in conjunction with the executive board.[56] The role of the Bank's executive board has emphasized oversight rather than management; in practice, the executive directors largely respond to proposals and actions of the Bank's management. The World Bank group as a whole has a staff of more than 10,000 individuals, some 8,000 based at the headquarters in Washington and the remaining staff spread among more than 100 country offices.

Funding for the IBRD was originally to be dependent upon private financial markets; the intent was to have the IBRD act as a guarantor for

---

56. The World Bank's board of governors, composed of appointees from each member nation, is formally superior to the board of executive directors.

loans originating with private lenders. Private markets resisted this approach, however, and the Bank instead adopted the role of direct lender, borrowing itself a large part of its loan funds from the private markets. Because the IBRD has a large endowment of paid-in capital, experiences a substantial flow of retained net income, and offers guarantees from member governments on its borrowing, it enjoys a high credit rating in private financial markets. Funding for World Bank group affiliates comes from diversified sources, including directly from member governments.

The majority of the organization's early and subsequent work has been carried out through the original IBRD. The newer affiliate groups have waxed and waned in relative importance in the periods since their formation.

The International Development Association (IDA) is the most important and politically salient of the affiliates. It was created in 1960 to serve the development needs of the poorest nations; its establishment reflected the change in the World Bank's mission from "reconstruction and development" to solely development. Unlike the IBRD, which borrows from private markets using its government-supported AAA credit rating, IDA is directly funded by member governments.

The funding structure of IDA means that the IBRD's credit rating and borrowing in capital markets tend to be isolated from the World Bank Group's efforts to aid the very poorest nations, loans to which carry a higher risk of default. IDA's establishment permitted a large increase in the number of client nations and the volume and variety of funded projects. Direct funding of IDA also increased the involvement of member nations (in particular the United States) in the management of the entire World Bank. An IDA "replenishment" exercise occurs every three or four years. Large funders of the IDA, principally the G-7 nations, have successfully used the various IDA replenishments to leverage their influences on the activities of IDA and the World Bank group as a whole.

Although the creation of IDA increased the lending options available to the World Bank, IDA lending by no means replaced the lending functions of the IBRD. Broadly speaking, the main forms of lending by the World Bank Group today are long-term market-rate loans provided by the IBRD and very-long-term, below-market-rates loans or credits provided by the IDA. Other activities such as the financing of private companies, dispute resolution, and provision of foreign investment guarantees are carried out by the other World Bank affiliates.

In addition to its roles in designing and supporting development projects and promoting structural adjustment in the economies of developing nations, the World Bank Group has evolved into a center for research on development issues and a locus of development policy advice and technical assistance. Over time these support roles have grown in relative importance. Increasingly, the Bank is also seen has a clearinghouse and leadership organization for global economic issues.[57]

As originally envisioned at the Bretton Woods conference, the IMF and the World Bank were expected to complement each other in advancing the postwar goals of financial stability, open trade, and productive cross-border capital flows. As both institutions experienced changes in the global economy and hence in their missions and clienteles, they also on occasion differed in their views on the appropriate policy actions member nations should follow. Issues about the comparative advantages of the IMF and World Bank and their respective missions are discussed in chapters 9, 10, and 13.

The last IMF loan to an industrialized country occurred in 1982. The last World Bank loan to an industrialized country occurred in August of 1948, only about two years after the Bank opened its doors. The Bank's transition from a bank of reconstruction with western industrialized countries as clients to a development bank focused on nonindustrialized nations was precipitated by the Marshall Plan supplanting the Bank as the instrument for U.S. financial assistance for European reconstruction. The early shift in the geographic focus of the Bank also required it to alter its mission. Although the current mission statement "to fight poverty" might seem an obvious choice for the World Bank, this was not always the clear aim. Similarly, the Bank has over time increased its direct involvement in the policies of member countries. Whereas loans in the early years of the Bank's history would be accompanied with oversight and technical expertise, loans made today (in particular the concessional aid supplied by IDA) are often contingent upon borrowing governments making significant policy adjustments.[58]

Regional Development Banks

Regionally focused multilateral development banks were established beginning in the 1960s. Four such institutions exist today: the African Develop-

---

57. An example of this role is the Bank's Multi-Country HIV/Aids Program, which provides both funding and technical support to various HIV/AIDS projects around the world.

58. For a recent history and overview of the World Bank group, see Kapur, Lewis, and Webb (1997).

ment Bank, the Asian Development Bank, the European Bank for Reconstruction and Development, and the Inter-American Development Bank.

The Inter-American Development Bank is the oldest of these four. Modeled on the World Bank and established in 1959, the IADB enjoys a high credit rating and finances much of its activities through borrowing in private capital markets. The IADB is an independent organization with its own separate management and financing. In fact, the IADB was founded in part to address the concerns of Latin American nations, who felt that the IBRD was overlooking lending in the social and agricultural sectors. The IADB has forty-six member nations. Its headquarters are in Washington, D.C.; there are twenty-eight field offices. In fiscal 2001 its lending was a bit less than half of the amount lent by the World Bank in the same year.

Like the World Bank, the IADB is engaged in a variety of activities in addition to lending, including technical assistance and research. Unlike the World Bank, the IADB and the other regional multilateral development banks were founded with development as their primary objective.

The Asian Development Bank, established in 1964, originally focused its activities on the smaller nations of Asia. Lending to India and China was restricted. Now the ADB lends throughout the Asia-Pacific region, with loans to China and India accounting for nearly half the total. The most influential donor nation in the ADB is Japan. Membership totals sixty-one nations, with seventeen member nations from outside of the region. The ADB has some 2,000 employees spread among its twenty-two regional offices. Its headquarters are in Manila.

The African Development Bank, also founded in 1964, is based in Abidjan, Côte d'Ivoire. With fifty-three regional and twenty-four nonregional members, the AfDB is the largest of the regional multilateral development banks by membership. Its loan and grant disbursements, however, are smaller than those of the IADB and ADB. Like the other regional development banks, the AfDB is involved in a variety of activities beyond lending and functions as an active center of technical expertise, research, and regional coordination.

The European Bank for Reconstruction and Development (EBRD), the youngest of the multilateral development banks, was launched in 1991 and is based in London. The EBRD was established in response to the collapse of the Soviet Union and the end of communism in Central and Eastern Europe. It was explicitly intended to serve as a vehicle for the promotion of democracy and the market economy. The EBRD has been more involved in private sector lending and investment than the other multilateral development banks and as a rule has sought partners in financing its activities.

The shareholder owners of the EBRD are sixty national governments, primarily from European nations. Two intergovernmental entities, the European Union and the European Investment Bank, are also shareholders of the EBRD. The lending activities of the EBRD are small relative to those of the World Bank. Nonetheless, the EBRD has been able to exert significant influence through its reliance on cofinancing and its concentration on specific policy goals.

References

Abbott, Kenneth W., and Duncan Snidal. 2000. "Hard and Soft Law in International Governance." *International Organization* 54 (Summer, *Legalization and World Politics*): 421–56.

Abbott, Kenneth W., and others. 2000. "The Concept of Legalization." *International Organization* 54 (Summer, *Legalization and World Politics*): 401–20.

Agenor, P. R., and others, eds. 1999. *The Asian Financial Crisis: Causes, Contagion and Consequences.* Cambridge University Press.

Akerlof, George A. 1970. "The Market for Lemons: Quality Uncertainty and the Market Mechanism." *Quarterly Journal of Economics* 89: 488–500.

Allen, Franklin, and Douglas Gale. 2000a. "Bubbles and Crises." *Economic Journal* 110 (January): 236–55.

———. 2000b. "Financial Contagion." *Journal of Political Economy* 108 (February): 1–33.

Almond, Gabriel A., and Sidney Verba, eds. 1963. *The Civic Culture: Political Attitudes and Democracy in Five Nations.* Princeton University Press.

Appleton, Arthur E. 1999. "Shrimp/Turtle: Untangling the Nets." *Journal of International Economic Law* 2 (3): 477–96.

Avery, Christopher, and Peter Zemsky. 1998. "Multidimensional Uncertainty and Herd Behavior in Financial Markets." *American Economic Review* 88 (September): 724–48.

Bagehot, Walter. 1873. *Lombard Street: A Description of the Money Market.* London: Kegan, Paul & Co. Reprint, John Murray, 1924.

Baker, Raymond W., and Jennifer Noordin. 1999. "A 150-to-1 Ratio Is Far Too Lopsided for Comfort." *International Herald Tribune*, editorial, February 5, 1999, p. 5.

Baldwin, Richard E. 2000. "Regulatory Protectionism, Developing Nations, and a Two-Tier World Trade System." In *Brookings Trade Forum: 2000*, edited by Susan M. Collins and Dani Rodrik, 237–94. Brookings.

Banerjee, Abhijit. 1992. "A Simple Model of Herd Behavior." *Quarterly Journal of Economics* 107 (3): 797–817.

Bank for International Settlements. 1992. *Recent Developments in International Interbank Relations.* (The "Promisel Report," prepared by a Working Group of the central banks of the Group of Ten.) Basel.

Barry, Brian, and Russell Hardin, eds. 1982. *Rational Man and Irrational Society?: An Introduction and Sourcebook.* Beverly Hills, Calif.: Sage Publications.

Bator, Francis M. 1958. "The Anatomy of Market Failure." *Quarterly Journal of Economics* 72 (August): 351–79.

Baumol, William J., and Wallace E. Oates. 1975. *The Theory of Environmental Policy: Externalities, Public Outlays and the Quality of Life.* Prentice-Hall.

Begg, David, and others. 1993. *Making Sense of Subsidiarity: How Much Centralization for Europe?* CEPR Annual Report on *Monitoring European Integration* No. 4. London: Centre for Economic Policy Research, November.

Bell, Daniel. 1999. *The Coming of Post-Industrial Society.* Basic Books.

Ben-Porath, Yoram. 1980. "The F-Connection: Families, Friends, and Firms and the Organization of Exchange." *Population and Development Review* 6: 1–30.

Berle, Adolf A., and Gardiner C. Means. 1932. *The Modern Corporation and Private Property.* Macmillan and Commerce Clearing House.

Bernanke, Ben S., and Mark Gertler. 1995. "Inside the Black Box: The Credit Channel of Monetary Policy Transmission." *Journal of Economic Perspectives* 9 (Fall): 27–48.

Bhalla, Surjit S. 2002. "Imagine There's No Country: Poverty, Inequality and Growth in the Era of Globalization." Draft manuscript, Oxus Research & Investments, New Delhi.

Bikhchandani, Sushil, and Sunil Sharma. 2001. "Herd Behavior in Financial Markets." *IMF Staff Papers* 47 (September): 279–310.

Bikhchandani, Sushil, David Hirshleifer, and Ivo Welch. 1992. "A Theory of Fads, Fashion, Custom, and Cultural Change as Informational Cascades." *Journal of Political Economy* 100 (October): 992–1026.

———. 1998. "Learning from the Behavior of Others: Conformity, Fads, and Informational Cascades." *Journal of Economic Perspectives* 12 (3): 151–70.

Blair, Margaret M. 1995. *Ownership and Control: Rethinking Corporate Governance for the Twenty-First Century.* Brookings.

Blair, Margaret M., and Lynn A. Stout. 1999. "A Team Production Theory of Corporate Law." *Virginia Law Review* 85 (March): 247–328.

Blanchard, Olivier J., and Mark W. Watson. 1982. "Bubbles, Rational Expectations, and Financial Markets." In *Crises in the Economic and Financial Structure,* edited by Paul Wachtel. Lexington, Mass.: Lexington Books.

Bordo, Michael D., Barry Eichengreen, and Douglas A. Irwin. 1999. "Is Globalization Today Really Different from Globalization a Hundred Years Ago?" In *Brookings Trade Forum: 1999,* edited by Susan Collins and Robert Z. Lawrence, 1–50. Brookings.

Bordo, Michael D., Barry Eichengreen, and Jongwoo Kim. 1988. "Was There Really an Earlier Period of International Financial Integration Comparable to Today?" NBER Working Paper 6738. National Bureau of Economic Research, Cambridge, Mass. September.

Boughton, James M. 1994. *The IMF and the Latin American Debt Crisis: Seven Common Criticisms.* IMF Papers on Policy Analysis and Assessment PPAA/94/23. International Monetary Fund, Washington. October.

————. 1997. "Modeling the World Economic Outlook at the IMF: A Historical Review." IMF Working Paper WP/97/48. International Monetary Fund, Washington.

————. 2001. *Silent Revolution: The International Monetary Fund, 1979–89.* Washington: International Monetary Fund.

Brainard, William C., John B. Shoven, and Laurence Weiss. 1980. "The Financial Valuation of the Return to Capital." *Brookings Papers on Economic Activity, 2: 1980,* 453–502.

Brau, Eduard. 1981. "The Consultations Process of the Fund." *Finance and Development* 18 (December): 13–16.

Brecher, Jeremy, and Tim Costello. 1994. *Global Village or Global Pillage: Economic Reconstruction from the Bottom Up.* Boston, Mass.: South End Press.

Brierley, Peter, and Gertjan Vlieghe. 1999. "Corporate Workouts, the London Approach and Financial Stability." *Financial Stability Review* (Bank of England) (November): 168–83.

Brock, William A., and Steven N. Durlauf. 1995. "Discrete Choice with Social Interactions I: Theory." NBER Working Paper 5291. National Bureau of Economic Research, Cambridge, Mass. October.

————. 2002. "A Multinomial-Choice Model of Neighborhood Effects." *American Economic Review* 92 (May): 298–303.

Brown, Seyom, and others. 1977. *Regimes for the Ocean, Outer Space, and Weather.* Brookings.

Bryant, Ralph C. 1980a. *Financial Interdependence and Variability in Exchange Rates.* Brookings.

————. 1980b. *Money and Monetary Policy in Interdependent Nations.* Brookings.

————. 1983. *Controlling Money: The Federal Reserve and Its Critics.* Brookings.

————. 1987. "Intergovernmental Coordination of Economic Policies: An Interim Stocktaking." In *International Monetary Cooperation: Essays in Honor of Henry C. Wallich.* Princeton Essay in International Finance 169. Princeton University, International Finance Section.

———. 1995. *International Coordination of National Stabilization Policies.* Integrating National Economies series. Brookings.

Bryant, Ralph C., Peter Hooper, and Catherine L. Mann. 1993. *Evaluating Policy Regimes: New Research in Empirical Macroeconomics.* Brookings.

Bulow, Jeremy, and Paul Klemperer. 1994. "Rational Frenzies and Crashes." *Journal of Political Economy* 102 (February): 1–23.

Burtless, Gary. 2002. "Is the Global Gap between Rich and Poor Getting Wider?" Draft presentation, Brookings. June.

Burtless, Gary, and others. 1998. *Globaphobia: Confronting Fears about Open Trade.* Brookings, Progressive Policy Institute, and Twentieth Century Fund.

Cairns, David. 1998. "IASC—25 Years of Evolution, Teamwork, and Improvement." *Insight* (Quarterly newsletter of the International Accounting Standards Committee). June.

Caplin, Andrew, and John Leahy. 1994. "Business as Usual, Market Crashes, and Wisdom After the Fact." *American Economic Review* 84 (June): 548–65.

Caporaso, James A. 1992. "International Relations Theory and Multilateralism: The Search for Foundations." *International Organization* 46 (Summer): 599–632.

Chernow, Ron. 1990. *The House of Morgan: An American Banking Dynasty and the Rise of Modern Finance.* Simon & Schuster.

———. 1993. *The Warburgs: The Twentieth-Century Odyssey of a Remarkable Jewish Family.* Random House.

Chua, Amy. 2003. *World on Fire: How Exporting Free Market Democracy Breeds Ethnic Hatred and Global Instability.* Doubleday.

Clark, Robert Charles. 1976. "The Soundness of Financial Intermediaries." *Yale Law Journal* 86 (November): 3–102.

Clarke, Stephen V. O. 1967. *Central Bank Cooperation: 1924-31.* New York: Federal Reserve Bank of New York.

Cline, William R. 1992. *The Economics of Global Warming.* Washington: Institute for International Economics.

Coase, Ronald H. 1960. "The Problem of Social Cost." *Journal of Law and Economics* 3 (October): 1–44.

Cohen, Daniel. 1985. "How to Evaluate the Solvency of an Indebted Nation." *Economic Policy* 1 (November): 139–56.

Cohen, Jean L., and Andrew Arato. 1992. *Civil Society and Political Theory.* MIT Press.

Collins, Susan M., and Barry P. Bosworth. 1994. *The New GATT.* Brookings.

Cooper, Richard N. 1974. "Worldwide or Regional Integration: Is There an Optimal Size of the Integrated Area?" *Economic Notes*, vol. 3, Siena, Monte dei Paschi di Siena. Reprinted in Richard N. Cooper, *Economic Policy in an Interdependent World*, MIT Press, 1986, pp. 123–36.

———. 1986. *Economic Policy in an Interdependent World.* MIT Press.

————. 1989. "International Cooperation in Public Health as a Prologue to Macroeconomic Cooperation." In *Can Nations Agree? Issues in International Economic Cooperation*, edited by Richard N. Cooper and others. Brookings.

————. 1994. *Environment and Resource Policies for the World Economy.* Integrating National Economies series. Brookings.

Corti, Egon Ceasar. 1928. *The Rise of the House of Rothschild*, translated by Brian and Beatrix Lunn. New York: Cosmopolitan Book Corporation.

Council on Foreign Relations Independent Task Force; Carla A. Hills and Peter G. Peterson, Co-Chairs; Morris Goldstein, Project Director. 1999. *Safeguarding Prosperity in a Global Financial System: The Future International Financial Architecture.* Washington: Institute for International Economics for the Council on Foreign Relations.

Cumberland, John H., James R. Hibbs, and Irving Hoch, eds. 1982. *The Economics of Managing Chlorofluorocarbons: Stratospheric Ozone and Climate Issues.* Washington: Resources for the Future, Inc.

Cutler, A. Claire, Virginia Haufler, and Tony Porter, eds. 1999. *Private Authority in International Affairs.* State University of New York Press.

Dam, Kenneth W. 1970. *The GATT: Law and the International Economic Organization.* University of Chicago Press.

De Bondt, Werner F. M., and Richard Thaler. 1985. "Does the Stock Market Overreact?" *Journal of Finance* 40 (July): 793–805.

De Roover, Raymond A. 1948. *Money, Banking and Credit in Medieval Bruges.* Cambridge: Medieval Academy of America.

————. 1963. *The Rise and Decline of the Medici Bank, 1397–1494.* Harvard University Press. (Also W. W. Norton, 1966.)

————. 1974. *Business, Banking, and Economic Thought in Late Medieval and Early Modern Europe.* University of Chicago Press.

De Vries, Margaret Garritsen. 1976. *The International Monetary Fund, 1966–1971: The System Under Stress.* 2 vols. Washington: International Monetary Fund.

————. 1985. *The International Monetary Fund 1972–1978: Cooperation on Trial.* Washington: International Monetary Fund.

————. 1987. *Balance of Payments Adjustment, 1945 to 1986: The IMF Experience.* Washington: International Monetary Fund.

Dell, Sidney. 1981. *On Being Grandmotherly: The Evolution of IMF Conditionality.* Princeton Essay in International Finance 144. Princeton University, International Finance Section. October.

DeLong, J. Bradford, and others. 1990a. "Noise Trader Risk in Financial Markets." *Journal of Political Economy* 98 (4): 703–38.

————. 1990b. "Positive Feedback Investment Strategies and Destabilizing Rational Speculation." *Journal of Finance* 45 (2): 379–95.

Diamond, Douglas W. 1984. "Financial Intermediation and Delegated Monitoring." *Review of Economic Studies* 51 (3): 393–414.

———. 1991. "Monitoring and Reputation: The Choice between Bank Loans and Directly Placed Debt." *Journal of Political Economy* 99 (August): 689–721.

Diamond, Douglas W., and Philip H. Dybvig. 1983. "Bank Runs, Deposit Insurance, and Liquidity." *Journal of Political Economy* 91 (June): 401–19.

Downing, Thomas E., and Robert W. Kates. 1982. "The International Response to the Threat of Chlorofluorocarbons to Atmospheric Ozone." *American Economic Review* 72 (May): 267–72.

Durlauf, Steven N., and H. Peyton Young, eds. 2001. *Social Dynamics.* MIT Press.

Edwards, Franklin R. 1999. "Hedge Funds and the Collapse of Long-Term Capital Management." *Journal of Economic Perspectives* 13 (Spring): 189–210.

Eichengreen, Barry. 1992. *Golden Fetters: The Gold Standard and the Great Depression, 1919–1939.* Oxford University Press.

———. 1999. *Toward a New International Financial Architecture: A Practical Post-Asia Agenda.* Washington: Institute for International Economics.

FDIC (Federal Deposit Insurance Corporation). 1997. *History of the Eighties, Lessons for the Future.* Vol. 1: *An Examination of the Banking Crises of the 1980s and Early 1990s.* Vol. 2: *Symposium Proceedings.* Washington.

Ferguson, Niall. 1998. *The House of Rothschild: Money's Prophets: 1798–1848,* vol. 1. Penguin Books.

———. 2000. *The House of Rothschild: The World's Banker, 1849–1999,* vol. 2. Penguin Books.

Fischer, Stanley. 1988. "International Macroeconomic Policy Coordination." In *International Economic Cooperation,* edited by Martin Feldstein, 11–43. University of Chicago Press.

———. 1999. "On the Need for an International Lender of Last Resort." *Journal of Economic Perspectives* 13 (Fall): 85–104. Longer version published as Princeton Essay in International Economics 220. Princeton University, International Economics Section. November 2000.

Flavin, Marjorie A. 1983. "Excess Volatility in the Financial Markets: A Reassessment of the Empirical Evidence." *Journal of Political Economy* 91 (December): 929–56.

Flood, Robert P., and Peter M. Garber. 1982. "Bubbles, Runs, and Gold Monetization." In *Crises in the Economic and Financial Structure,* edited by Paul Wachtel. Lexington, Mass.: Lexington Books.

Frankel, Jeffrey A. 1992. "Measuring International Capital Mobility: A Review." *American Economic Review* 82: 197–202.

———. 1999a. "Greenhouse Gas Emissions." Brookings Policy Brief 52. Brookings. June.

———. 1999b. "No Single Currency Regime is Right for All Countries or at All Times." Princeton Essays in International Finance 215. Princeton University, International Finance Section. August.

————, ed. 1994. *The Internationalization of Equity Markets*. University of Chicago Press.

Friedman, Thomas L. 1999. *The Lexus and the Olive Tree*. Farrar, Straus & Giroux.

Gardner, Richard N. 1969. *Sterling-Dollar Diplomacy: The Origins and the Prospects of Our International Economic Order*. Expanded edition. McGraw Hill (original edition published in 1956).

Gold, Joseph. 1979. *Conditionality*. Fund Pamphlet Series 31. Washington: International Monetary Fund.

————. 1984. *Legal and Institutional Aspects of the International Monetary System: Selected Essays*. 2 vols. Washington: International Monetary Fund.

————. 1990. *Legal Effects of Fluctuating Exchange Rates*. Washington: International Monetary Fund.

Goldsmith, Raymond W. 1955. *A Study of Saving in the United States*. Princeton University Press.

————. 1958. *Financial Intermediaries in the American Economy Since 1900*. Princeton University Press.

————. 1966. *The Determinants of Financial Structure*. Paris: Organization for Economic Cooperation and Development, Development Centre.

————. 1969. *Financial Structure and Development*. Yale University Press.

————. 1985. *Comparative National Balance Sheets: A Study of Twenty Countries, 1688–1978*. University of Chicago Press.

Goldstein, Morris. 2002. *Managed Floating Plus*. Washington: Institute for International Economics.

Goodhart, Charles A. E., and Dirk Schoenmaker. 1993. "Institutional Separation between Supervisory and Monetary Agencies." In *Prudential Regulation, Supervision and Monetary Policy*, edited by Frank Bruni. Centro di Economia Monetaria e Finanziaria "Paolo Baffi," Universita Commerciale Luigi Bocconi. Reprinted as chapter 16 in Goodhart, *The Central Bank and the Financial System*, MIT Press, 1995.

————. 1995. "Should the Functions of Monetary Policy and Bank Supervision Be Separated?" *Oxford Economic Papers* 47 (4): 539–60.

Gray, John. 1999. *False Dawn: The Delusions of Global Capitalism*. New York: Granta.

Greenspan, Alan. 1999. "Lessons from the Global Crises." 1999. Remarks before the World Bank Group and International Monetary Fund, Program of Seminars, September 27, 1999. [Available from Federal Reserve Board website, www.bog.frb.fed.us/boarddocs/speeches.]

————. 2000. "Global Challenges." 2000. Remarks at the Financial Crisis Conference, Council on Foreign Relations, New York, July 12, 2000. [Available from Federal Reserve Board website, www.bog.frb.fed.us/boarddocs/speeches.]

Greenwald, Bruce C., and Joseph E. Stiglitz. 1986. "Externalities in Economics with Imperfect Information and Incomplete Markets." *Quarterly Journal of Economics* 101 (May): 229–64.

Greider, William. 1997. *One World, Ready or Not: The Manic Logic of Global Capitalism.* Simon & Schuster.

Group of Thirty. 1998. *International Insolvencies in the Financial Sector: A Study Group Report.* Washington: Group of Thirty.

Group of Twenty-Two (Willard Group). 1998. *Report of the Working Group on Transparency and Accountability.* (Available on internet web sites for IMF, BIS, and U.S. Treasury.)

Guidotti, Pablo E., and Manmohan S. Kumar. 1991. "Domestic Public Debt of Externally Indebted Countries." IMF Occasional Paper 80. International Monetary Fund, Washington. March.

Guitian, Manuel. 1981. *Fund Conditionality: Evolution of Principles and Practices.* Fund Pamphlet Series 38. Washington: International Monetary Fund.

Gurley, John G., and Edward S. Shaw. 1956. "Financial Intermediaries and the Saving-Investment Process." *Journal of Finance* 11 (May): 257–76.

———. 1957. "The Growth of Debt and Money in the United States." *Review of Economics and Statistics* 39 (August): 250–62.

———. 1960. *Money in a Theory of Finance.* Brookings.

Haas, Ernst B. 1980. "Why Collaborate? Issue-Linkage and International Regimes." *World Politics* 32 (April): 357–405.

———. 1983. "Words Can Hurt You: Or Who Said What to Whom about Regimes." In *International Regimes*, edited by Stephen D. Krasner, 23–60. Cornell University Press.

Haas, Peter M. 1992a. "Banning Chlorofluorocarbons: Epistemic Community Efforts to Protect Stratospheric Ozone." *International Organization* 46 (Winter, *Knowledge, Power, and International Policy Coordination*): 187–224.

———. 1992b. "Introduction: Epistemic Communities and International Policy Coordination." *International Organization* 46 (Winter, *Knowledge, Power, and International Policy Coordination*): 1–35.

Haggard, Stephan, and Beth A. Simmons. 1987. "Theories of International Regimes." *International Organization* 41 (Summer): 491–517.

Hamada, Koichi. 1974. "Alternative Exchange Rate Systems and the Interdependence of Monetary Policies." In *National Monetary Policies and the International Financial System*, edited by Robert Aliber. University of Chicago Press.

———. 1977. "On the Political Economy of Monetary Integration: A Public Economics Approach." In *The Political Economy of Monetary Reform*, edited by Robert Z. Aliber. Macmillan.

Hann, C., and E. Dunn, eds. 1996. *Civil Society: Challenging Western Models.* London: Routledge.

Hart, Oliver. 1995. *Firms, Contracts, and Financial Structure.* Oxford University Press.

Held, David, and others. 1999. *Global Transformation: Politics, Economics, and Culture.* Stanford University Press.

Helliwell, John F. 1998. *How Much Do National Borders Matter?* Integrating National Economies series. Brookings.

———. 2000. "Globalization: Myths, Facts, and Consequences." Benefactors Lecture, 2000. C.D. Howe Institute, Toronto.

Hirsch, Fred. 1976. *Social Limits to Growth.* Harvard University Press.

———. 1977. "The Bagehot Problem." *Manchester School* 45 (September): 241–257.

Hirschman, Albert O. 1970. *Exit, Voice, and Loyalty: Responses to Decline in Firms, Organizations, and States.* Harvard University Press.

Hoekman, Bernard, and Michel Kostecki. 1995. *The Political Economy of the World Trading System: From GATT to WTO.* Oxford University Press.

Horsefield, J. Keith, and others. 1969. *The International Monetary Fund, 1945–1965.* 3 vols. Washington: International Monetary Fund.

Hull, John C. 1997. *Introduction to Futures and Options Markets.* 3d ed. Prentice-Hall.

———. 2002. *Options, Futures, and Other Derivatives.* 5th ed. Prentice-Hall.

International Monetary Fund. 1974. *International Monetary Reform: Documents of the Committee of Twenty.* Washington.

Jackson, John H. 1997. *The World Trading System: Law and Policy of International Economic Relations.* 2d ed. MIT Press.

———. 1998a. "Global Economics and International Economic Law." *Journal of International Economic Law* 1 (March) 1–23.

———. 1998b. *The World Trade Organization: Constitution and Jurisprudence.* Chatham House Papers. London: Royal Institute of International Affairs.

James, Harold. 1995. "The Historical Development of the Principle of Surveillance." *IMF Staff Papers* 42 (December): 762–91.

Jordan, Jerry L. 1999. "Financial Crises and Market Regulation." *Economic Commentary* (Federal Reserve Bank of Cleveland). October.

Kahler, Miles. 1992. "Multilateralism with Small and Large Numbers." *International Organization* 46 (Summer): 681–708.

———. 1995. *International Institutions and the Political Economy of Integration.* Integrating National Economies series. Brookings.

Kahn, Alfred E. 1966. "The Tyranny of Small Decisions: Market Failures, Imperfections, and the Limits of Economics." *Kyklos* 19: 23–47.

Kaminsky, Graciela L., and Carmen M. Reinhart. 2000. "On Crises, Contagion, and Confusion." *Journal of International Economics* 51: 149–68.

Kapur, Devesh, John P. Lewis, and Richard Webb. 1997. *The World Bank: Its First Half Century.* Vol. 1: *History;* Vol. 2, *Perspectives.* Brookings.

Kaul, Inge, Isabelle Grunberg, and Marc A. Stern, eds. 1999. *Global Public Goods: International Cooperation in the 21st Century.* Oxford University Press.

Keck, Margaret E., and Kathryn Sikkink. 1998. *Activists without Borders: Advocacy Networks in International Politics.* Cornell University Press.

Kenen, Peter B. 2001. *The International Financial Architecture: What's New? What's Missing?* Washington: Institute for International Economics.

Keohane, Robert O. 1980. "The Theory of Hegemonic Stability and Changes in International Regimes, 1967–1977." In *Change in the International System,* edited by Ole R. Holsti, Randolph M. Siverson, and Alexander L. George, 131–62. Boulder, Colo.: Westview Press.

———. 1983. "The Demand for International Regimes." In *International Regimes,* edited by Stephen D. Krasner, 141–71. Cornell University Press.

———. 1984. *After Hegemony: Cooperation and Discord in the World Political Economy.* Princeton University Press.

Keohane, Robert O., and Joseph S. Nye Jr. 1977. *Power and Interdependence: World Politics in Transition.* Little, Brown.

———. 2000. *Power and Interdependence: World Politics in Transition.* 3d ed. Longman.

Keynes, John Maynard. 1936. *The General Theory of Employment, Interest and Money.* Macmillan.

———. 1980. *The Collected Writings of John Maynard Keynes.* Vol. 26: *Activities 1941–1946: Shaping the Post-War World: Bretton Woods and Reparations,* edited by Donald Moggridge. Macmillan.

Kindleberger, Charles P. 1978. *Manias, Panics, and Crashes: A History of Financial Crises.* Basic Books.

Kindleberger, Charles P., and Jean-Pierre Laffargue, eds. 1982. *Financial Crises: Theory, History, and Policy.* Cambridge University Press.

Knack, Stephen, and Philip Keefer. 1997. "Does Social Capital Have an Economic Payoff? A Country Investigation." *Quarterly Journal of Economics* 112 (4): 1251–88.

Krasner, Stephen D. 1983a. "Regimes and the Limits of Realism: Regimes as Autonomous Variables." In *International Regimes,* edited by Stephen D. Krasner, 355–68. Cornell University Press.

———. 1983b. "Structural Causes and Regime Consequences." In *International Regimes,* edited by Stephen D. Krasner, 1–22. Cornell University Press.

———. 1999. *Sovereignty: Organized Hypocrisy.* Princeton University Press.

Kreps, David M. 1990. *A Course in Microeconomic Theory.* Princeton University Press.

Kristof, Nicholas D., with Edward Wyatt, David E. Sanger, and Sheryl WuDunn. 1999. "Global Contagion: A Narrative." Series of four front-page articles. *New York Times,* February 15, 16, 17, and 18, p. A-1.

Krueger, Anne O., ed., with the assistance of Chonira Aturupane. 1998. *The WTO as an International Organization.* University of Chicago Press.

Lakonishok, Josef, Andrei Shleifer, and Robert Vishny. 1992. "The Impact of Institutional Trading on Stock Prices." *Journal of Financial Economics* 32: 23–43.

Lave, Lester B. 1982. "Mitigating Strategies for Carbon Dioxide Problems." *American Economic Review* 72 (May): 257–61.

Lee, In Ho. 1998. "Market Crashes and Informational Avalanches." *Review of Economic Studies* 65 (October): 741–59.

Leland, H., and D. Pyle. 1977. "Informational Asymmetries, Financial Structure, and Financial Intermediation." *Journal of Finance* 32 (2): 371–87.

LeRoy, Stephen F., and Richard D. Porter. 1981. "The Present Value Relation: Tests Based on Variance Bounds." *Econometrica* 49 (May): 555–74.

Lintner, J. H. 1965. "The Evaluation of Risk Assets and the Selection of Risky Investments in Stock Portfolios and Capital Budgets." *Review of Economics and Statistics* 47 (February): 13–37.

Lipschutz, Ronnie D. 1996. *Global Civil Society and Global Environmental Governance.* State University of New York Press.

MacKay, Charles. 1841. *Extraordinary Popular Delusions and the Madness of Crowds.* Boston, Mass.: L. C. Page & Co., reprinted 1932.

Marin, B., and R. Mayntz. 1993. "Policy Networks." In *Modern Governance: New Government-Society Interactions*, edited by Jan Kooiman. London: Sage Publications.

Markowitz, Harry. 1952. "Portfolio Selection." *Journal of Finance* 7 (March): 77–91.

———. 1959. *Portfolio Selection.* Wiley & Sons.

Masson, Paul R. 1999a. "Contagion: Macroeconomic Models with Multiple Equilibria." *Journal of International Money and Finance* 18 (4): 587–602.

———. 1999b. "Contagion: Monsoonal Effects, Spillovers, and Jumps between Multiple Equilibria." In *The Asian Financial Crisis: Causes, Contagion and Consequences,* edited by P. R. Agenor and others, 265–80. Cambridge University Press.

———. 1999c. "Multiple Equilibria, Contagion, and the Emerging Market Crises." IMF Working Paper 99/164. International Monetary Fund, Washington. December.

Masson, Paul R., and Michael Mussa. 1995. *The Role of the IMF: Financing and Its Interactions with Adjustment and Surveillance.* Pamphlet Series 50. International Monetary Fund, Washington.

McGuire, Martin. 1974. "Group Segregation and Optimal Jurisdictions." *Journal of Political Economy* 82 (January): 112–32.

McKibbin, Warwick J. 2000. "Moving Beyond Kyoto." Brookings Policy Brief 66. Brookings. October.

McKibbin, Warwick J., and Peter J. Wilcoxen. 1997a. "A Better Way to Slow Global Climate Change." Brookings Policy Brief 17. Brookings. June.

———. 1997b. "Salvaging the Kyoto Climate Change Negotiations." Brookings Policy Brief. Brookings. November.

———. 1999. "Permit Trading Under the Kyoto Protocol and Beyond." Brookings Discussion Paper in International Economics 150. Brookings. May.

———. 2000. "The Next Step for Climate Change Policy." Background Paper 1. Brookings. February.

———. 2002a. "Climate Change After Kyoto: A Blueprint for a Realistic Approach." *Brookings Review* 20 (Spring): 7–10.

———. 2002b. "The Role of Economics in Climate Change Policy." *Journal of Economic Perspectives* 16 (Spring): 107–30.

———. 2002c. *Climate Change Policy After Kyoto: Blueprint for a Realistic Approach.* Brookings.

Meltzer, Allan H. 1986. "Financial Failures and Financial Policies." In *Deregulating Financial Services: Public Policy in Flux,* edited by G. G. Kaufman and R. C. Kormendi. Cambridge, Mass.: Ballinger.

Milanovic, Branko. 2002. "Worlds Apart: Inter-National and World Inequality 1950–2000." Draft manuscript, World Bank, Washington.

Miles, Edward, ed. 1977. "Restructuring Ocean Regimes: Implications of the Third United Nations Conference on the Law of the Sea." *International Organization* 31 (Spring, Special Issue).

Modigliani, Franco, and Richard A. Cohn. 1979. "Inflation, Rational Valuation, and the Market." *Financial Analysts Journal* 35 (March–April): 24–44.

Møller, J. Ørstrøm. 1995. *The Future European Model: Economic Internationalization and Cultural Decentralization.* Westport, Conn.: Praeger.

Morse, Edward L. 1977. "Managing International Commons." *Journal of International Affairs* 31 (Spring–Summer): 1–21.

Mussa, Michael, and others. 2000. "Moderating Fluctuations in Capital Flows to Emerging Market Economies." In *Reforming the International Monetary and Financial System,* edited by Peter B. Kenen and Alexander K. Swoboda. Washington: International Monetary Fund.

Nurkse, Ragnar, and others. 1944. *International Currency Experience: Lessons of the Inter-War Period.* Report of the League of Nations Economic, Financial and Transit Department. League of Nations.

O'Brien, Robert, and others. 2000. *Contesting Global Governance: Multilateral Economic Institutions and Global Social Movements.* Cambridge University Press.

Oates, Wallace E. 1972. *Fiscal Federalism.* Harcourt Brace Jovanovich.

———, ed. 1977. *The Political Economy of Fiscal Federalism.* Lexington, Mass.: Lexington Books.

Obstfeld, Maurice. 1998. "The Global Capital Market: Benefactor or Menace?" *Journal of Economic Perspectives* 12 (Fall): 9–30.

Obstfeld, Maurice, and Kenneth Rogoff. 1995. "The Intertemporal Approach to the Current Account." In *Handbook of International Economics,* vol. 3, edited by Gene M. Grossman and Kenneth Rogoff. Amsterdam: North Holland.

———. 1996. *Foundations of International Macroeconomics.* MIT Press.

Ohmae, Kenichi. 1995. *The End of the Nation State: The Rise of Regional Economies.* Free Press.

Okun, Arthur M. 1975. *Equity and Efficiency: The Big Tradeoff.* Brookings.

————. 1981. *Prices and Quantities: A Macroeconomic Analysis.* Brookings.

Olson, Mancur. 1969. "The Principle of 'Fiscal Equivalence': The Division of Responsibilities among Different Levels of Government." *American Economic Review* 59 (May, *Papers and Proceedings, 1968*): 479–87.

————. 1971. *The Logic of Collective Action: Public Goods and the Theory of Groups,* 2d ed. Harvard University Press.

Orszag, Peter R., and Joseph E. Stiglitz. 2002. "Optimal Fire Departments: Evaluating Public Policy in the Face of Externalities." Discussion paper. Brookings. January.

Ostry, Sylvia. 1999. "The Future of the World Trade Organization." In *Brookings Trade Forum: 1999,* edited by Susan Collins and Robert Z. Lawrence, 167–90. Brookings.

Peters, B. Guy. 1992. "Bureaucratic Politics and the Institutions of the European Community." In *Euro-Politics: Institutions and Policymaking in the 'New' European Community,* edited by Alberta M. Sbragia, 75–122. Brookings.

Petersmann, Ernst-Ulrich. 1998. "From the Hobbesian International Law of Coexistence to Modern Integration Law: The WTO Dispute Settlement System." *Journal of International Economic Law* 1 (June): 175–98.

Peterson, Paul E. 1995. *The Price of Federalism.* Brookings.

Platteau, Jean-Philippe. 1994. "Behind the Market Stage Where Real Societies Exist, Parts I and II." *Journal of Development Studies* 30: 533–77, 753–817.

Polak, Jacques J. 1991. "The Changing Nature of IMF Conditionality." Princeton Essays in International Finance 184. Princeton University, International Finance Section. September.

Putnam, Robert D. 1993. *Making Democracy Work: Civic Traditions in Modern Italy.* Princeton University Press.

————. 1995. "Tuning In, Tuning Out: The Strange Disappearance of Social Capital in America." (Inaugural Ithiel de Sola Pool Lecture at the American Political Science Association.) *PS: Political Science and Politics* 28 (December): 664–83. Abridged version published in *The American Prospect* (October 1995).

————. 2000. "Social Capital: Measurement and Consequences." In *The Contribution of Human and Social Capital to Sustained Economic Growth and Well-Being,* edited by John F. Helliwell. Ottawa: Human Resources Development, Canada.

Putnam, Robert D., and Nicholas Bayne. 1987. *Hanging Together: Cooperation and Conflict in the Seven-Power Summits.* Rev. ed. Harvard University Press.

Rogoff, Kenneth. 2002. "An Open Letter to Joseph Stiglitz, Author of *Globalization and Its Discontents.*" International Monetary Fund, Washington. July 2.

Rosenau, James N. 1997. *Along the Domestic-Foreign Frontier: Exploring Governance in a Turbulent World.* Cambridge University Press.

Rosenau, James N., and Ernst-Otto Czempiel, eds. 1992. *Governance without Government: Order and Change in World Politics.* Cambridge University Press.

Rubin, Robert E. 1998. "Strengthening the Architecture of the International Financial System." Remarks delivered at the Brookings Institution, April 14, 1998. U.S. Treasury, Washington.

———. 1999. "Reform of the International Financial Architecture." Remarks delivered at the Johns Hopkins School for Advanced International Studies, April 21, 1999. U.S. Treasury, Washington.

Rubinfeld, Daniel L. 1987. "The Economics of the Local Public Sector." In *Handbook of Public Economics,* vol. II, edited by Alan J. Auerbach and Martin Feldstein. Amsterdam: North-Holland.

Ruggie, John Gerard. 1975. "International Responses to Technology: Concepts and Trends." *International Organization* 29 (Summer): 557–83.

———. 1983. "International Regimes, Transactions, and Change: Embedded Liberalism in the Postwar Economic Order." In *International Regimes,* edited by Stephen D. Krasner, 195–232. Cornell University Press.

———. 1992. "Multilateralism: The Anatomy of an Institution." *International Organization* 46 (Summer): 561–98.

Sachs, Jeffrey D. 1995. "Do We Need an International Lender of Last Resort?" Frank D. Graham Memorial Lecture, Princeton University, April 20, 1995.

Sachs, Jeffrey D., and Andrew Warner. 1995. "Economic Reform and the Process of Global Integration." *Brookings Papers on Economic Activity, 1: 1995,* 1–118.

Salant, Stephen W., and Dale W. Henderson. 1978. "Market Anticipations of Government Policies and the Price of Gold." *Journal of Political Economy* 86 (August): 627–48.

Sbragia, Alberta M., ed. 1992. *Euro-Politics: Institutions and Policymaking in the 'New' European Community.* Brookings.

Schadler, Susan M., and others. 1993. *Economic Adjustment in Low-Income Countries: Experience under the Enhanced Structural Adjustment Facility.* IMF Occasional Paper 106. International Monetary Fund, Washington. September.

———. 1995. *IMF Conditionality: Experience under Stand-By and Extended Arrangements. Part I: Key Issues and Findings. Part II: Background Papers.* IMF Occasional Paper 128. International Monetary Fund, Washington.

Scharfstein, David S., and Jeremy C. Stein. 1990. "Herd Behavior and Investment." *American Economic Review* 80: 465–79.

Schelling, Thomas C. 1974. "On the Ecology of Micromotives." In *The Corporate Society,* edited by Robin Marris. Macmillan.

———. 1978. *Micromotives and Macrobehavior.* W.W. Norton.

Scholte, Jan Aart. 1997a. "Global Capitalism and the State." *International Affairs* 73 (July): 427–52.

———. 1997b. "The Globalization of World Politics." In *The Globalization of World Politics: An Introduction to International Relations*, edited by John Baylis and Steve Smith, 13–30. Oxford University Press.

———. 1999. "Civil Society and a Democratization of the International Monetary Fund." In *Poverty in World Politics: Whose Global Era?*, edited by P. Yeros and S. Owen. Macmillan.

———. 2000a. "Global Civil Society: Changing the World?" In *The Political Economy of Globalisation*, edited by Ngaire Woods, 173–201. Macmillan.

———. 2000b. *Globalisation: A Critical Introduction.* London: Palgrave Macmillan.

———. 2002. "Civil Society and the Governance of Global Finance." In *Civil Society and Global Finance*, edited by Jan Aart Scholte and Albrecht Schnabel. Routledge.

Scholte, Jan Aart, and Albrecht Schnabel, eds. 2002. *Civil Society and Global Finance.* Routledge.

Sebenius, James K. 1992. "Challenging Conventional Explanations of International Cooperation: Negotiation Analysis and the Case of Epistemic Communities." *International Organization* 46 (Winter): 323–66.

Seligman, Adam B. 1992. *The Idea of Civil Society.* Free Press.

Sharpe, William F. 1964. "Capital Asset Prices: A Series of Market Equilibrium under Conditions of Risk." *Journal of Finance* 19 (September): 425–42.

Shiller, Robert J. 1979. "The Volatility of Long-Term Interest Rates and Expectations Models of the Term Structure." *Journal of Political Economy* 87 (December): 1190–1219.

———. 1981. "Do Stock Prices Move Too Much to be Justified by Subsequent Changes in Dividends?" *American Economic Review* 71 (June): 421–36.

———. 1984. "Stock Prices and Social Dynamics." *Brookings Papers on Economic Activity,* 2:1984, 457–98.

———. 1989. *Market Volatility.* MIT Press.

Skidelsky, Robert. 2001. *John Maynard Keynes. Volume Three: Fighting for Freedom, 1937–1946.* Viking.

Smith, Jackie, Charles Chatfield, and Ron Pagnucco. 1997. *Transnational Social Movements and Global Politics: Solidarity Beyond the State.* Syracuse University Press.

Solomon, Robert. 1982. *The International Monetary System, 1945–1981.* Harper & Row.

Solow, Robert M. 1980. "On Theories of Unemployment." *American Economic Review* 70 (March): 1–11.

Sooros, Marvin S. 1982. "The Commons in the Sky: The Radio Spectrum and the Geosynchronous Orbit as Issues in Global Policy." *International Organization* 36 (Summer): 665–77.

Southard, Frank A., Jr. 1979. *The Evolution of the International Monetary Fund.* Princeton Essay in International Finance 135. Princeton University, International Finance Section. December.

Spero, Joan Edelman. 1980. *The Failure of the Franklin National Bank: Challenge to the International Banking System.* Columbia University Press for the Council on Foreign Relations.

Stein, Arthur A. 1983. "Coordination and Collaboration: Regimes in an Anarchic World." In *International Regimes,* edited by Stephen D. Krasner, 115–40. Cornell University Press.

Stekler, Lois E., and Guy V. G. Stevens. 1991. "The Adequacy of U.S. Direct Investment Data." In *International Economic Transactions: Issues in Measurement and Empirical Research,* edited by Peter Hooper and J. David Richardson. University of Chicago Press for the National Bureau of Economic Research.

Stewart, Taimoon. 1998. "The United States Embargo on Shrimp Imports: Legal and Economic Considerations." *Environment and Development Economics* 3 (May): 197–219.

Stiglitz, Joseph E. 1975. "Information and Economic Analysis." In *Current Economic Problems,* edited by Michael Parkin and A. R. Nobay, 27–52. Cambridge University Press.

———. 1985. "Information and Economic Analysis: A Perspective." *Economic Journal* 95 (*Conference Papers*): 21–41.

———. 1994. "The Role of the State in Financial Markets." In *Proceedings of the Annual World Bank Conference on Development Economics 1993,* edited by Michael Bruno and Boris Pleskovic. Washington: World Bank.

———. 1998. "The Private Uses of Public Interests: Incentives and Institutions." *Journal of Economic Perspectives* 12 (Spring): 3–22.

———. 1999. "The World Bank at the Millennium." *Economic Journal* 109 (November): F577–F597.

———. 2000. "The Insider: What I Learned at the World Economic Crisis." *The New Republic* (April 17 and 24): 56–60.

———. 2002. *Globalization and Its Discontents.* W.W. Norton.

Stiglitz, Joseph E., and Andrew Weiss. 1981. "Credit Rationing in Markets with Imperfect Information." *American Economic Review* 71 (June): 393–410.

———. 1990. "Banks as Social Accountants and Screening Devices and the General Theory of Credit Rationing." In *Essays in Monetary Economics in Honor of Sir John Hicks,* edited by Anthony Courakis and Charles Goodhart. Oxford University Press.

Strange, Susan. 1983. "*Cave! Hic Dragones.*" In *International Regimes,* edited by Stephen D. Krasner, 337–54. Cornell University Press.

———. 1996. *The Retreat of the State: The Diffusion of Power in the World Economy.* Cambridge University Press.

Sullivan, Scott. 1997. *From War to Wealth: Fifty Years of Innovation.* Paris: Organization for Economic Cooperation and Development.

Summers, Lawrence H. 1999. "The Right Kind of IMF for a Stable Global Financial System." Remarks at the London School of Business, London, England. December 14, 1999.

Talbott, Strobe. 2002. *The Russia Hand: A Memoir of Presidential Diplomacy.* Random House.

Tesar, Linda L., and Ingrid M. Werner. 1994. "International Equity Transactions and U.S. Portfolio Choice." In *The Internationalization of Equity Markets,* edited by Jeffrey A. Frankel, 185–227. University of Chicago Press.

———. 1998. "The Internationalization of Securities Markets since the 1987 Crash." In *Brookings-Wharton Papers on Financial Services 1998,* edited by Robert E. Litan and Anthony M. Santomero, 283–349. Brookings.

Thornton, Henry. 1802. *An Enquiry into the Nature and Effects of the Paper Credit of Great Britain,* edited by F. A. Hayek. Fairfield, Conn.: Augustus M. Kelley Publishers. Reprint 1978.

Tietmeyer, Hans. 1999. "International Cooperation and Coordination in the Area of Financial Market Supervision and Surveillance." Deutsche Bundesbank, Frankfurt. February. Available from the web site of Financial Stability Forum (www.fsforum.org).

Tirole, Jean. 1992. *The Theory of Industrial Organization.* MIT Press.

———. 1999. "Incomplete Contracts: Where Do We Stand?" *Econometrica* 67 (July): 741–82.

———. 2001. "Corporate Governance." *Econometrica* 69 (January): 1–36.

Tobin, James. 1958. "Liquidity Preference as Behavior Towards Risk." *Review of Economic Studies* 25 (2): 65–86. Reprinted in *Risk Aversion and Portfolio Choice,* edited by Donald D. Hester and James Tobin. Wiley & Sons, 1967.

———. 1981. "Money and Finance in the Macro-Economic Process." Nobel Prize Lecture. Published in *Nobel Lectures in Economic Sciences 1981–1990,* edited by Karl-Göran Mäler. Stockholm: Nobel Foundation.

———. 1984. "On the Efficiency of the Financial System." *Lloyds Bank Review* 153 (July): 1–15.

Tobin, James, and William C. Brainard. 1963. "Financial Intermediaries and the Effectiveness of Monetary Controls." *American Economic Review* 53 (May): 383–400.

———. 1977. "Asset Markets and the Cost of Capital." In *Economic Progress, Private Values, and Public Policy: Essays in Honor of William Fellner,* edited by Bela Balassa and Richard Nelson. Amsterdam: North-Holland.

Toussaint, Eric. 1999. *Your Money or Your Life!: The Tyranny of Global Finance,* translated by Raghu Krishnan with Vicki Briault Manus. Pluto/Mkuki na Nyota. Distributed by Stylus Publishing, Sterling, Va.

Triffin, Robert. 1957. *Europe and the Money Muddle: From Bilateralism to Near-Convertibility, 1947–1956.* Yale University Press.

Wallace, William. 1994. *Regional Integration: The West European Experience.* Integrating National Economies series. Brookings.

Wapner, Paul. 1995. "Politics Beyond the State: Environmental Activism and World Civic Politics." *World Politics* 47 (3): 311–40.

———. 1996. *Environmental Activism and World Civic Politics.* State University of New York Press.

Warkentin, Craig, and Karen Mingst. 2000. "International Institutions, the State, and Global Civil Society in the Age of the World Wide Web." *Global Governance* 6 (April–June): 237–57.

White, Michelle J. 2002. "Sovereigns in Distress: Do They Need Bankruptcy?" *Brookings Papers on Economic Activity, 2002:1,* 287–320.

Williamson, John. 1977. *The Failure of World Monetary Reform, 1971–74.* New York University Press.

———. 2000. "Exchange Rate Regimes for Emerging Markets: Reviving the Intermediate Option." Policy Analyses in International Economics 60. Institute for International Economics, Washington. September.

———, ed. 1983. *IMF Conditionality.* Washington: Institute for International Economics and MIT Press.

Williamson, Oliver E. 1989. "Transaction Cost Economics." In *Handbook of Industrial Organization,* vol. 1, edited by Richard Schmalensee and Robert D. Willig, 136–184. Elsevier.

World Bank. 2002. *Globalization, Growth, and Poverty: Building an Inclusive World Economy.* Oxford University Press and World Bank.

Young, H. Peyton. 1996. "The Economics of Convention." *Journal of Economic Perspectives* 10 (Spring): 105–22.

———. 1998. *Individual Strategy and Social Structure: An Evolutionary Theory of Institutions.* Princeton University Press.

———. 1999. "Diffusion in Social Networks." Center for Social and Economic Dynamics Working Paper 2. Brookings. May.

Young, Oran R. 1986. "International Regimes: Toward a New Theory of Institutions." *World Politics* 39 (October): 104–122.

———. 1989a. "The Politics of International Regime Formation: Managing Natural Resources and the Environment." *International Organization* 43 (Summer): 349–75.

———. 1989b. *International Cooperation: Building Regimes for Natural Resources and the Environment.* Cornell University Press.

———. 1991. "Political Leadership and Regime Formation: On the Development of Institutions in International Society." *International Organization* 45 (Summer): 281–308.

————. 1999. *Governance in World Affairs.* Cornell University Press.

Zevin, Robert. 1992. "Are World Financial Markets More Open? If So, Why and With What Effects?" In *Financial Openness and National Autonomy: Opportunities and Constraints,* edited by Tariq Banuri and Juliet B. Schor. Oxford University Press.

Author Index

Index

Accounting and auditing: in cross-border finance, 172–78; importance of, 49–50, 66, 72, 75; international issues, 159, 241, 446–48; monitoring and enforcement, 226; offshore facilities, 150; oversight and standards, 303, 305. *See also* Monitoring, oversight, and supervision

ADB. *See* Asian Development Bank

AfDB. *See* African Development Bank

Africa, 102, 231. *See also* individual countries

African Development Bank (AfDB), 242, 272, 458–59

Albania, 388

Andorra, 316

Arbitration, 50, 175, 198

Argentina, 158, 387–88, 424. *See also* Financial turbulence and instability— specific instances

Asia, 101, 174, 184–85, 387, 407. *See also* Financial turbulence and instability— specific instances

Asian Development Bank (ADB), 242, 272, 458–59

Australia, 158, 424, 451

Autonomy: cooperative agreements and, 122–23; de facto autonomy, 117; definition of, 114; economic goals and, 115; intergovernmental cooperation and, 130; loss of, 392, 401; national policies and, 122; openness and integration, 12, 124–28, 346, 357, 370, 371; sovereignty and, 205, 400; supranational oversight and, 229–30. *See also* Nations and nation states; Sovereignty

Bagehot, Walter, 83, 321

Bailouts and bailins. *See* Financial institutions

Balance of payments: capital flows and, 166, 427; collection of data, 169–70; financial crisis, 178; imbalances in, 429n15; IMF and, 427; international effects, 249; national current accounts, 134, 146, 188–202, 427; official financing and, 251, 252–53; surveillance of, 247

Bangladesh, 101, 233

Bank for International Settlements (BIS): central banks and, 286, 334, 335, 441; consultative groups and, 421; coordination